Challenging Depression

Challenging Depression
The Go-To Guide for Clinicians and Patients

Mark Zetin, MD

Cara T. Hoepner, RN, MS, CNS, NP

Jennifer Kurth, DO

W. W. Norton & Company
New York • London

For information about permission to reproduce selections from this book, write to
Permissions, W. W. Norton & Company, Inc., 500 Fifth Avenue, New York, NY 10110

For information about special discounts for bulk purchases, please contact W. W. Norton
Special Sales at specialsales@wwnorton.com or 800-233-4830

Manufacturing by Quad Graphics, Fairfield
Book design by Paradigm Graphics
Production manager: Leeann Graham

Library of Congress Cataloging-in-Publication Data

Zetin, Mark.
  Challenging depression : the go-to guide for clinicians and patients / Mark Zetin, Cara
T. Hoepner, Jennifer Kurth.
       p. cm.
  "A Norton Professional Book."
  Includes bibliographical references and index.
  ISBN 978-0-393-70610-9 (pbk.)
  1. Depression, Mental--Handbooks, manuals, etc. I. Hoepner, Cara T. II. Kurth, Jennifer.
III. Title.
  RC537.Z476 2010
  616.85'2706--dc22

                                    2009037834

ISBN: 978-0-393-70610-9 (pbk.)

W. W. Norton & Company, Inc., 500 Fifth Avenue, New York, N.Y. 10110
                      www.wwnorton.com
W. W. Norton & Company Ltd., Castle House, 75/76 Wells Street, London W1T 3QT

1 2 3 4 5 6 7 8 9 0

This book is dedicated to the many patients whose stories enrich our readers' learning experience, and to the teachers who have inspired us to become clinicians devoted to treating them.

Contents

Preface

We have written this book both for clinicians and patients. Many individuals suffering from depression have tried an antidepressant and have been disappointed. Antidepressants are lifesaving drugs for many people, but unfortunately they don't work for about a third of people who take them (Janicak et al., 2006). If you're reading this book, it may be because your antidepressant didn't work or had unacceptable side effects. Or perhaps you or a loved one has been recently diagnosed with depression and you want to learn all you can about the illness. You might be working with a doctor who doesn't seem to know what to do next or has not presented you with a clear strategy for managing your problem beyond the first or second medicine. We assume that you have acknowledged that you have a problem with depression, and you need all the help you can get. You have thought about different treatment approaches, including medicines, psychotherapy, alternative or natural approaches, and you've gotten to the point where you wonder what to do next.

Clinicians treating depressed patients will also benefit from this book. We have included technical details about treatment for patients who have not responded as well as was hoped when they started medication and psychotherapy. Our theme is "What's next?" in pursuing very thorough evaluation and optimal treatment and outcome.

We have attempted to provide an overview of depression in this book. We will explain what is known of the causes of depression. We will tell you how depression is diagnosed and about treatment approaches that involve medications, psychotherapy, electric or magnetic brain stimulation, and alternative and complementary approaches. Most important, we hope to teach patients how to best work with their clinicians and clinicians how to best help their patients.

Many patients find themselves in the unfortunate situation of receiving more and more drugs. They become more and more passive and more and more demoralized when they fail to get well. We will attempt to help patients change this by discussing how to develop an internal locus of control (the feeling that you are in control of your actions, environment, and circumstances—a sense that what you do makes a difference and can truly help in your recovery).

We will give many case examples throughout this book. The names have been changed, and some identifying data have been altered to make the people less easily identified, but all are real patients in our practice. Each has something to teach us.

About the Authors

Mark Zetin, MD, completed medical school at the University of California, Irvine, in 1975. He then went into internship and residency at the University of Colorado and University of California, San Diego. In 1979, he joined the full-time faculty of the University of California, Irvine, where he directed an inpatient adult psychiatric unit for 15 years. During this time, he taught medical students and residents the basics of psychiatry. He focused his research and treatment efforts on the diagnosis and pharmacological therapy of mood and anxiety disorders, especially treatment-resistant cases. In 1994, he left his professorship to develop his private practice, where he continues to focus on mood and anxiety disorders. Dr. Zetin has been involved as a member of the voluntary faculty of the University of California, Irvine, where he taught residents about the use of psychotherapeutic drugs from 1994 through 2008. He has taught courses in psychopharmacology for psychologists and marriage family therapists at California Graduate Institute, Alliant University, and Chapman University. He also lectures for various pharmaceutical companies, educating other psychiatrists and primary care doctors on the use of antidepressants.

Cara Hoepner, MS, RN, CNS, NP, completed nurse practitioner training at the University of California, San Francisco, where she focused on community-based treatment of underserved populations. She currently provides psychiatric urgent care to a largely homeless population in San Francisco. Her clinical interests include mood and anxiety disorders, as well as their intersection with the areas of substance abuse and traumatology. These interests are reflected in the numerous articles she has coauthored with Dr. Zetin on antidepressant research. Ms. Hoepner sits on the board of directors of San Francisco's National Alliance on Mental Illness (NAMI) affiliate and is the director of their speakers bureau, In Our Own Voice, which creates a public forum for people living with mental illness and their lived experiences.

Jennifer Kurth, DO, is a child, adolescent, and adult psychiatrist in Chicago. Currently, Dr. Kurth is the psychiatry residency director at Loyola University Medical Center. In addition to this, she is an assistant professor in the Department of Psychiatry and Behavioral Neurosciences at Loyola Stritch School of Medicine. Her clinical interests are primarily ADHD, autism, and mood disorders. Through Northwestern University, Dr. Kurth completed her child and adolescent psychiatry fellowship at Children's Memorial Hospital in Chicago. Her general psychiatry training was completed at the University of California, Irvine, Medical Center in Orange, California. Dr. Kurth is board certified in adult psychiatry, with subspecialty certification in child and adolescent psychiatry.

Disclosures

Dr. Zetin has received lecture honoraria for speaking about antidepressants including Serzone, Wellbutrin, Effexor, Prozac, Zoloft, Paxil, Celexa, Lexapro, Cymbalta, Pristiq, and Emsam. He has also received honoraria for speaking about antipsychotics such as Zyprexa, Abilify, Geodon, and Seroquel, and sleeping pills including Sonata, Ambien CR, and Lunesta. He has also spoken for the manufacturer of Lamictal. He has received research support for participation in the Cyberonics Vagus Nerve Stimulator registry trial.

Ms. Hoepner and Dr. Kurth have no potential financial conflicts to declare.

Dr. Zetin gratefully acknowledges the opportunity to provide treatment to all of the adult patients described in this book. Dr. Kurth similarly acknowledges the privilege of treating the children and adolescents. We are grateful to the many friends and patients who have read drafts of this book and provided editorial suggestions.

Challenging Depression

1

Knowing the Enemy:
The Faces of Depression

The depressed person looks different to his family, coworkers, and doctor. Each sees the loss of vitality, enthusiasm, and optimism in a different way. For the patient, depression may feel painful, frightening, or numb, his mind creating delusions that argue stubbornly for his distorted thoughts and feelings. He may feel impossibly empty and slow of mind. He may feel lonely among friends, or fear death, poverty, and loneliness in the cradle of a safe harbor. If depression persists long enough, his fears and delusions may become self-fulfilling. He may miss the life he once found enjoyable, or he might no longer recognize it, his recollection disfigured by the shadow of depression. Worst of all, he may no longer want to live it. Recognizing the common symptoms of depression and overcoming its stigma are the first steps toward getting help.

The diagnosis of depression is based primarily on a clinical interview. Laboratory and medical tests are often performed along with the clinical interview, but their use is primarily to help exclude physical causes of depression. We believe it is fair to say that there is no specific diagnostic biologic test for depression at this time. Often, researchers have developed tests they hoped would be diagnostic for depression, only to find that they lacked sufficient sensitivity and specificity, or ability to be precise and easily interpreted, to be widely useful.

Many patients seeking treatment ask about a test to diagnose depression. A few years ago, the dexamethasone suppression test was used for this, and we would get telephone calls from people asking for the test as a way to justify seeking treatment. They were sometimes disappointed when they were told that the test was not as helpful as a careful interview. The same can be said of the thyrotropin-releasing hormone thyroid-stimulating hormone test (for thyroid function), PET and SPECT functional brain-imaging scans, genetic markers, and many other elaborations of medical technology that attempt to connect mental function or illness with specific brain or gene dysfunction. These biological markers of illness are fascinating to researchers, but their practical application in helping to accurately determine which patients need which forms of therapy is still limited. Somehow, the presence of a biological marker demonstrating that there is something physically wrong has great appeal to people with depression. A picture of the brain or a measurement from a blood test seems to be such objective proof of illness that self-blame, guilt, and sense of failure are relieved.

There may be less stigma attached to an illness with a medical-biological marker, and we applaud researchers who continue to look for the biological basis of depression and improvements in its treatment, for they will shape the future of our field. Our book, however, is devoted to the elaboration of treatments that are available now and that have proven cost-effective benefit.

Stigma

We will deal with stigma at many points throughout this book. Many of our patients tell us it is a key issue for them, as the media often portrays mental illness in a less than favorable light, and there are long-standing societal fears of those who live with mental illness. Are the "mentally ill" frightening or unpredictable? Or perhaps the topic hits a bit too close to home? Suffering in silence and feeling stigmatized by others greatly contributes to lack of well-being, as well as to suicidal feelings.

A general lack of understanding may also exist among those who form the depressed person's support network. Family members or friends may say, "Pull out of it," or ask, "You seem fine now—why are you still taking medications?" We believe strongly in the biopsychosocial model: Psychiatric illness has a biological component (genetics, hormones, and neurotransmitters) and a psychological component (often related to childhood experiences), and occurs in the social context of the person's current life setting. All aspects must be addressed. As with diabetes or coronary artery disease, both medications and lifestyle changes are required for optimal outcome. Would anyone tell a diabetic, "Just lose weight and you won't need insulin"? Would anyone tell the person who has suffered a heart attack, "Just exercise and your heart will be fine without the blood pressure and cholesterol-lowering medications"? We believe it is equally absurd to tell the person who has suffered from several potentially life-threatening episodes of depression or mania to simply pray, exercise, and eat well in the hope that there will not be catastrophic recurrences of the mood disorder. Certainly these things help, but they alone are not sufficient to alter the course of the illness.

Another equally important issue is self-stigma, which may occur largely in response to one's social environment but also is due to feeling that mental illness is akin to a weakness or lack of normality. These people may feel that taking psychiatric medications represents dependence or a crutch.

Related to this issue is the question: "Aren't some medicines addictive?" Here it is important to make a clear distinction both between dependence and addiction, and between which medications may cause or encourage dependence or addiction. *Dependence* is a physiologic process wherein a person requires dose escalation to maintain effectiveness of medication, and where the patient may experience very uncomfortable withdrawal symptoms if the medication is discontinued rapidly. *Addiction* is a term used for the abuse of a medication (taking it for reasons other than those prescribed) to produce a high. I sometimes joke with patients that I never hear stories about Prozac or lithium being stolen by a roommate, accidentally dropped down the sink, or eaten by a dog; I've often heard such things about addictive stimulants like Ritalin or pain medications such as Vicodin. Patients who are addicted to medications tend to have multiple doctors prescribing the same type of medication, get it from many pharmacies or on the street, use far more than what is prescribed, and use the drug in a way that disrupts rather than facilitates normal life functioning.

Medications used in psychiatry that may cause dependence include the benzodiazepines (such as Ativan, Xanax, and Klonopin) when taken chronically (as opposed to as needed). Older benzodiazepine sleep medications may cause dependence, though this is controversial.

Opiate medications for pain relief and muscle relaxants such as Soma and Flexeril may also produce dependence. It is very important to note that other classes of medications, including the antidepressants and antipsychotics, do not produce dependence and are very rarely abused, with few exceptions.

Even after they've heard the clinical definition of dependence, patients may still feel uneasy about "needing" an antidepressant or other drug. This concern can be addressed by likening the situation to that of needing eyeglasses: If I require glasses to see the world clearly, is that addiction? The answer is clearly no; the glasses allow me to do what other healthy people can do naturally and easily—for example, read a book or a street sign. Will I need them forever and find the world very fuzzy without them? Of course! You could say I am dependent upon them. Antidepressants and mood stabilizers allow people to feel normal, as they personally define this. They may cause a slight physiologic dependence, but they have no abuse potential or value on the street.

Finally there is the issue of acute versus chronic illness. An acute symptom or illness is only treated as long as there are symptoms and perhaps for a brief time afterward. We are all familiar with taking an aspirin for a headache, an antibiotic for a few days for a respiratory or urinary tract infection, or a pain medication for a few days after a minor operation or dental procedure. Similarly, we are all aware of transient sadness when we have lost a loved one through ending a relationship or through death. These situations involve unpleasant emotions that are natural and time-limited. Major depression and bipolar illness, on the other hand, fit much more closely with the concept of chronic, recurrent, lifetime illness that is managed but doesn't just go away. In that sense, mood disorders are like diabetes, high blood pressure, or high cholesterol. There may be long periods without symptoms, but the disease will predictably take its toll eventually if it is not well managed in a forward-looking, preventive way. For some, the concept of a chronic, lifelong mental illness produces stigma, as there may be a tendency to identify with one's illness. In an effort to convince oneself that "there is nothing wrong with me," long-term management with medications or psychotherapy is often avoided.

How Does Depression Present in Different Contexts?

Depression has many faces, as it takes its toll on thinking, feeling, behavior, physical well-being, socializing, creativity, work productivity, and close relationships. It is truly a disease that affects the whole person. Just as in the fable of the blind men describing the elephant—wherein each describes a different part, from a different perspective, depending on which part he was touching—there are many ways that depression is seen in different contexts.

To an epidemiologic researcher, depression presents as a very common illness, affecting approximately 13% of the United States adult population at some point in their lives (Hasin, Goodwin, Stinson, & Grant, 2005), often with many recurrences spaced over the individual's lifetime. Depression is a major cause of disability: Major depression is the second leading cause of disability-adjusted life years in industrialized nations among persons age 5 and older. For women throughout the world, it is the leading cause (Costa & Silva, 2005). Depression may affect any social, demographic, racial, or ethnic group, but it clearly affects more reproductive-age women than men for reasons that generate a great deal of speculation.

The patient coming in to see a primary care physician may present with multiple physical symptoms, nine on average (Kroenke, Arrington, & Mangelsdorff, 1990). The symptoms occur among many different organ systems, and around 60% may not be adequately explained despite a careful medical workup (Kroenke et al., 1990). Often the symptoms include vague pain in areas such as the lower back, abdomen, or pelvis, or even headaches. Indeed, 50% of those presenting to primary care providers with depression complain of pain (Kroenke et al., 1994). Chronic pain and depression fuel each other, with each making the other worse.

Sometimes patients will have irritable bowel or chronic fatigue symptoms. This can put the physician in a difficult position, as he realizes that the patient won't be satisfied without a comprehensive medical workup including blood tests, X-rays, and perhaps sophisticated CT or MRI scans. The doctor must satisfy himself that medical causes of depression have been sought and ruled out. Yet he often knows that the more unexplained physical symptoms an individual has, the more likely it is that the underlying cause is a psychiatric rather than physical problem. The most common of the psychiatric diagnoses is depression. But most doctors don't tell the patient that depression may be causing the symptoms, especially without performing a wide range of diagnostic tests, because they find that it's a hard sell to convince the patient to try antidepressant medications.

The primary care doctor knows that depression is one of the most common illnesses he will treat, that most antidepressants are prescribed by primary care doctors, and that he must carefully look for depression among patients who present with somatic as well as psychosocial complaints. He also knows that depression is a risk factor for many medical illnesses, including diabetes and coronary artery disease, and he must evaluate the depressed patient for these as well as for any history of mania, alcoholism, and suicide attempts (Kirmayer, Robbins, Dworkind, & Yaffe, 1993).

The depressed patient may present to the psychotherapist in a very different way. Often, at the time of presentation for psychotherapy, the patient says there are major problems in relationships with significant others or in getting along at work. In some cases, the stressor that leads to therapy may be a life transition that is difficult to handle. Often the crisis is the loss of a significant relationship or a job. In trying to understand the meaning and importance of the current stressors, the therapist and patient will often work together to retell and understand the life story of the individual. Childhood traumas, abuse, neglect, or loss of a parent are common contributing factors to adult vulnerability to stress and depression. Sometimes the loss triggers the depression; this is the obvious, understandable cause-and-effect relationship. But sometimes the depression has made the person very difficult to live or work with, causing the frustrated employer or significant other to end the job or relationship.

The depressed patient coming to the psychiatrist may present with more intense physiological symptoms of depression and request medication. Often the person has been referred by the family doctor or the psychotherapist. Patients who present directly to a psychiatrist, requesting medicine, often say that biologic functions are not normal.

The patient may have problems with eating or sleeping (either too little or too much), feel unable to cope with life's stressors, or feel continually tearful, anxious, or overwhelmed. We sometimes hear the thinking of the depressed person described as "brain fog" and the feelings and behaviors described as "out of control." Sometimes the person with depression will simply say that although life is good, nothing is enjoyable, fun, worthwhile, or interesting. Even sex has become a chore. People often say that they have been treated with antidepressants in the past or that they have a family history of depression. Perhaps the person's mother was chronically depressed or a grandfather committed suicide. This individual often knows or fears, deep down, that there is a genetic component to the illness.

Case Example: Familial Depression

Betty was a very cute, smart, articulate 16-year-old who was brought for treatment by her father. She came to see me because both of her parents, who were in a long-standing divorce battle, and her therapist had said she might need medication for depression. Her initial comment was that she was reluctant and scared to take medicine that might "pollute" her body or change her behavior. She acknowledged that her depression had been going on for about 2 years and had worsened over time without any seasonal or menstrual variation or identified life stressor. Her main symptoms were a loss of interest in things she had previously enjoyed, such as school, as well as chronic stomach pain. Betty described herself as stubborn, self-reliant, and prone to keeping things inside. She denied feeling stressed by her parents' financial disputes and spent time with both of them. She sometimes felt like her mother's caretaker and had a sense of role reversal because of her mother's depression. She met all of the diagnostic criteria for major depression except one: She had never been suicidal.

Betty's story is interesting because I had met her parents on separate occasions. Her mother had come to see me 2 years earlier and told me of a history of depression since age 27 with subsequent chronic back pain. She was a physician whose career had suffered from her chronic depression and inability to organize and remember tasks and get along with people. She was stressed by financial demands from her soon-to-be ex-husband and tension with her daughter. Betty's father had come to see me 4 years earlier, at age 50, for depression that began at age 26. He was unemployed. Both parents had a history of requiring long-term antidepressant medications and psychotherapy to cope with their illness and life challenges.

Betty was in therapy to discuss life issues, but she reluctantly agreed to try a low dose of the antidepressant Prozac (fluoxetine) when I explained that it had been tested in adolescents and found safe and effective, especially in combination with psychotherapy (see Chapter 13). She didn't like hearing that depression was a genetic illness. Genetic illnesses sometimes show anticipation (earlier age of onset and more severe course) as they pass from one generation to the other, so treating Betty's depression early and vigorously would be important in our attempt to prevent a lifetime of frequent depressive episodes.

The depressed person may present to the bartender, the hairdresser, or the best friend with questions about the meaning of life. "What's the point of going on? Everything is a hassle. Life isn't worth it. Life is unfair. I can't handle what's happening to me. Is this all there is to life?" "Maybe my wife and kids would be better off without me" is a common thought, though the wife and kids would almost always prefer to have their relative healthy and present rather than receive the life insurance payment.

The depressed person may present at work in a very different way. Frequent absences are a major clue to depression or other psychiatric illness, and mental health conditions are the second leading cause—next to musculoskeletal conditions—of workplace absenteeism, resulting in a 50% increase in missed workdays (NMHA, 2006). Even moderate levels of depression or anxiety affect work performance and productivity (NMHA, 2006). An interesting concept is "presenteeism," or showing up but not doing much work and just watching the clock until it is time to go home. Careless mistakes, lack of attention, and inability to get the job done in a timely and accurate way are common symptoms. Productivity decreases, as do motivation and drive. Coworkers sense that the individual is grouchy, irritable, and doesn't seem to take pride in his work as he once did. He stays to himself and doesn't joke with others or go to lunch or after-work social activities with them anymore.

The depressed person may present to the pastor or rabbi with new doubts of God's existence, concerns about the lack of God's response to prayers, or questions about why God allows bad things to happen to good people.

The depressed person is different at home, too. The partner may recognize that the person isn't interested in doing things that used to be enjoyable, or that he drinks too much or has become more irritable and just wants to be left alone. The person simply does not seem like his old self. A loss of enthusiasm, a loss of enjoyment, and a sense of burnout are common symptoms. The loss of sexual drive may appear to be rejection, when it's actually a symptom of not enjoying *anything*, including sex. The significant other is the person who is most aware of the depressed individual's history of past depressions, past episodes of mania or hypo-mania, history of excessive drinking or drug use (perhaps as "self-medicating"), or past episodes of excessive gambling, shopping, or sexual behavior. This background information is invaluable in making an accu-rate diagnosis of depression, and it is extremely helpful to have the partner accompany the depressed person to his first psychiatric appoint-ment to give another, perhaps more objective, version of the history. Often, the partner's reaction to depression is to recognize it as an illness, to want to help, to be supportive, and to be nurturing, kind, and caring. When this approach doesn't work after a while, especially if the depressed individual refuses to seek professional help or drinks heavily, the partner becomes burned out. The sense of futility, feeling unable to be of any real help and unable to get a response out of the depressed individual, can lead to anger or withdrawal, which can in turn lead to separation or divorce in extreme cases. The significant other's reaction to mania is quite different. Here the person is seen as willfully, angrily, loudly, or selfishly spending money, having affairs, making demands, and getting his own way. The reaction is often an angry separation or divorce, rather than sympathetic understanding of the manic symptoms as being just as much a part of the illness as the depressive symptoms are.

2

Diagnosing the Enemy: Why Careful Differential Diagnosis Is Important

A clinician diagnoses depression based on the patient's symptoms, laboratory exam, past medical and psychiatric history, and family history. Differentiating major depression from normal sadness or life misery, bipolar disorder, and effects of substance abuse or medical problems requires skill and judgment on the part of the clinician and honesty on the part of the patient. Subtypes of depression and comorbid medical or psychiatric illnesses may influence treatment choices. In this chapter we give you several contexts in which to place depression and explain what it may look like in each case. We discuss the psychiatric and medical comorbidities that influence depression and its diagnosis and treatment. Finally, we present the diagnostic criteria by which depression is diagnosed. Case studies and some discussion of medication selection provide a well-rounded clinical picture of the diagnostic process, which can sometimes seem a rather technical exercise.

How Is Depression Diagnosed?

Depression is diagnosed after a careful clinical interview that focuses on the long-term course of illness and the details of current and past symptoms, on medical and family history, and on factors associated with stage of life.

We think of depression as primary or secondary; familial or nonfamilial; unipolar or bipolar; episodic or chronic; single episode or recurrent; atypical, melancholic, or with psychotic features; and triggered by life stressors or occurring in the context of a satisfying life. Sometimes it has childhood onset; other times it first appears in old age. We think of depression as an illness that may occur by itself or may be comorbid (that is, occurring with other psychiatric or medical problems). These may seem like very fine distinctions, but they are quite important in treatment planning. Our senior author, Dr. Zetin, is involved in teaching family practice physicians about the diagnosis and treatment of depression. There is a joke that the family practice doctor (who, in the United States, treats 80% of depressed adults) can diagnose and treat depression in a 10- or 15-minute appointment. The psychiatrist, on the other hand, will take an hour to make the same diagnosis. Dr. Zetin jokingly asks primary care doctors whether he is very slow or inefficient in understanding patients, or is doing an evaluation that is far more detailed and comprehensive than theirs. Hopefully the latter is the case!

Primary Versus Secondary Depression

The primary versus secondary distinction was used in the past for what our diagnostic rulebook, the *Diagnostic and Statistical Manual of Mental Disorders*, Fourth Edition, Text Revision (*DSM-IV-TR*), now refers to as major affective disorders (primary) or mood disorders that are due to a general medical condition or are substance induced (secondary mood disorders). The idea is simple: In a primary mood disorder, there is no other medical condition or substance abuse that came first and caused or triggered the depression. Also, the depression is not due to a drug being used to treat a medical problem. Secondary depression, on the other hand, follows in the wake of a medical condition, substance abuse, or other psychiatric disorder. Comorbidity (two disorders present in the same person) and causality (disorder A caused or evolved into disorder B) are difficult to tease out in many situations. Sometimes the patient presents with a medical or substance abuse problem before the onset of the depression and this is causal; other times it is coincidental. Sometimes the depression is the initial symptom presentation of the medical illness, while at other times the depression is a risk factor leading to the development of the medical illness. The terms "secondary depression" or "depression due to" or "substance induced" really suggest that we know which came first, and which condition caused the other. Generally there is evidence from the clinical history, physical exam, and lab tests that shows a relationship in time (and presumably in cause) between a medical problem (for example, cancer or hypothyroidism) or substance use disorder (for example, alcohol or opiate abuse) and the subsequent development of a mood disorder. Sometimes this distinction is just not clear. If causality cannot be determined, the conditions are considered comorbid. It is also true, however, that no matter which illness occurred first, once depression and substance abuse or medical illness coexist, the causal relationship becomes bidirectional: depression shares physiologic processes with any inflammatory illness, and the psychological effects of depression or disease worsen coping ability and self-care.

Primary depression is often recurrent, with many episodes occurring throughout a person's lifetime. It often runs in families. It may begin in childhood, adolescence, or adulthood, at times of change in a woman's reproductive life (menarche, postpartum, or perimenopause), or in old age.

Secondary depression can be due to substances such as a prescription medication or any substance of abuse. When the cause of the depression is treatment, this is known as iatrogenic depression. We have recently come to realize that there is a widespread epidemic of hepatitis C in the United States. Causes include transfusions before routine virus testing was implemented, sharing needles, and sexual contact. Hepatitis C is often treated with interferon, which is known to induce severe depression in some individuals. Some physicians are reluctant to begin interferon therapy in people who have had severe depression for this reason. It appears that the selective serotonin reuptake inhibitor (SSRI) antidepressants may be of some benefit for interferon-induced depression and may even prevent it (Raison et al., 2005; Schaefer et al., 2005). Another class of prescription medications that is known to cause depression in some individuals is the blood pressure medicines that are active in the brain (i.e., are centrally acting). These medicines work by affecting the brain centers that control the autonomic nervous system (nerves that control involuntary muscle, such as the heart). Propranolol and other beta-adrenergic blockers are included in this group, as well as older drugs like reserpine and alpha-methyldopa. Often there are very good alternative medications that are just as effective for controlling blood pressure, without the risk of causing depression. Some medications used to fight cancer are also known to cause depression. Again, the drug may be essential and lifesaving, and treatment of the ensuing depression might be required. Steroidal anti-inflammatory or immunosuppressant drugs (like prednisone), estrogens, opiate pain medications, Reglan (metoclopramide, a drug used to promote gastric emptying), and many others may also present risk of depression, as may many herbal preparations. The main clue to substance-induced depression is that the first episode of depression (or recurrence of depression after a long stable period) develops within a month or two of starting a new medicine.

Substances of abuse trigger another form of secondary depression or may be a manifestation of self-treatment. The most common substance abuse in our society is alcoholism. There are many other street drugs that can also bring on depression, including ecstasy, cocaine, methamphetamine, barbiturates, and opiates. In a very large epidemiologic study, among those suffering from major depressive disorder sometime in their lifetime, 40.3% had an alcohol use disorder, 17.2% had a drug use disorder, and 30% had nicotine dependence (Hasin et al., 2005). Among those with bipolar illness, 42% suffer from alcohol abuse or dependence, and around 60% from all forms of substance abuse (McElroy, 2001). Although many people consider marijuana benign, daily use may lead to a tremendous lack of motivation and drive. It is sad but true that most recreational drugs taken for the brief pleasure they may give also extract a huge price in the depression that follows. Substance abuse must be stopped before antidepressant medications have a reasonable chance of being helpful. On the other hand, adequate treatment of depression is essential in helping substance abusers to remain clean and sober.

Medical problems associated with depression are numerous: Any major medical illness that is debilitating, painful, or alters body chemistry in profound ways may cause depression. Often the initial symptoms of fatigue, weakness, loss of appetite, loss of energy, and a sense of tiredness are the general clues to a medical problem leading into a depression. The person will often say that she feels sick rather than sad or depressed. Common medical problems that are known to cause depression include endocrine disorders such as thyroid disease, diabetes, and Addison's or Cushing's disease (which involve the deficiency or excess of adrenal cortical steroid hormones such as cortisol); infections, including human immunodeficiency virus (HIV); hepatitis C; tuberculosis; and cancer of the pancreas, lung, brain, or other areas. Heart disease and depression commonly travel together and share some of the same causes, most notably inflammation. As many as 27% of patients with coronary heart disease have major depression, compared with just 10% of the general population, and a substantially larger number of cardiac patients have at least a few depressive symptoms (Rudisch & Nemeroff, 2003). Many neurological disorders, including seizures, and central nervous system degenerative disorders like Huntington's disease, Parkinson's disease, Alzheimer's disease, and multiple sclerosis can contribute to depression. Strokes are another common cause, with depression occurring in 19.3% of hospitalized patients and 23.3% of outpatient samples (Verkerk, Pop, Van Son, & Van Heck, 2003). As many as 94% of people with irritable bowel syndrome live with depression or anxiety (Whitehead, Palsson, & Jones, 2002). Unfortunately, having a primary care doctor is not protective against the possibility of having a medical illness, diagnosed or not, as the cause of psychiatric symptoms.

The connection between depression and physical illness was once viewed as a one-way street. An individual who developed cancer, had a heart attack, or had a chronic infection was understood as having a depression that was a reaction to their pain and disability. About 10–25% of cancer patients meet major depression criteria (Carr, Goudas, & D, 2002). We now realize that inflammatory cytokines released by the immune system to fight physical disease may be the connection between physical illness and developing depression (Dunn, Swiergiel, & de Beaurepaire, 2005; Elenkov, Iezzoni, Daly, Harris, & Chrousos, 2005). Of greater interest, we are realizing that depression substantially worsens the course of the medical illnesses both by adversely affecting physiological processes of disease and by substantially interfering with rehabilitation and effective self-care during recovery from major medical problems and during maintenance of complicated illnesses requiring lifestyle changes, such as diabetes. For these reasons, people who have a heart attack are three times as likely to die in the following months if they have depression (Rudisch & Nemeroff, 2003). The work of Frasure-Smith has shown that depression is an extremely important modifiable risk factor for development of coronary artery disease and a prognostic factor for long-term survival after its development (Frasure-Smith & Lesperance, 2003, 2006a, 2006b, 2006c, 2008; Frasure-Smith et al., 2000, 2007; Frasure-Smith,

Lesperance, & Julien, 2004; Frasure-Smith, Lesperance, Juneau, Talajic, & Bourassa, 1999). We have seen that antidepressants can prolong life after heart attack or stroke.

Case Example: Interferon-Induced Depression

Kate was a 63-year-old married woman who complained of depression and had been diagnosed as having hepatitis C. The depression had been present intermittently throughout her life. She was a candidate for interferon to treat the hepatitis C, and this treatment had been delayed repeatedly because of fear that she might become more depressed. Her recent psychiatrist had changed her antidepressant medication from Effexor to Lexapro. She was taking a high dose of the minor tranquilizer Ativan for chronic anxiety.

Kate had felt terrible while taking the antidepressant Effexor, saying that she felt like there was a "war in her head, body, and chest." She also felt exhausted, had vivid dreams, slept poorly, was easily startled, and could not relax. Her husband, who had retired, was reportedly "bossing her around" and telling her how to do household chores that she had always done quite well on her own. He commented on her fatigue, indecisiveness, and compulsive perfectionistic traits. She wanted to socialize, make new friends, get involved with her church, and work on decorating her home, but she often felt exhausted and lacked motivation. Her family history was positive: Her son, brother, and sister had all been on antidepressants, and other relatives had alcoholism.

Kate suffered recurrent major depression, now with a worsening induced by her interferon treatment, generalized anxiety disorder, hepatitis C, and hypertension. I advised her that her fatigue could be part of the depression or the medical problems, that tranquilizers might worsen this, and that because of the sedating side effects (as well as possible depressogenic effects with chronic use), tapering her Ativan would be advisable. I asked her to add Provigil to the Lexapro to control the fatigue. Low-dose lithium was added to potentiate the antidepressant. Lexapro, lithium, Provigil, and a very low dose of Ativan allowed her to tolerate the treatment for her hepatitis C. Over the course of 6 months, while she was receiving the interferon, marital therapy sessions were combined with medication management, and Kate was encouraged to vent her frustration about the family's having two different homes in retirement, her sense of not yet having an established community of friends in the local home, and her feeling that what she wanted to do in decorating the house might not be a priority for her husband. Over time, her husband's calm, supportive, attentive approach to her wishes was reassuring, and the medications allowed her to complete the course of interferon with the excellent result of no detectable hepatitis virus and normal liver enzymes. Her view of her husband as the mean, controlling ogre and herself as the powerless, long-suffering, angry victim emerged during treatment and led to ongoing efforts toward greater assertiveness.

This case is a good example of the importance of carefully considering and dealing with all potential contributors to depression. In this case, the biological familial depression, the interferon treatment, and the marital conflict were all addressed during treatment.

Comorbidity

Comorbidity means the presence of two or more illnesses in the same person. We just examined depression as being secondary to, or contributing to, a medical illness; with comorbidity, we see them as co-occuring disorders. People are complicated, and their illnesses often don't fit into simple categories. In some cases the illnesses may be truly independent of each other (occurring strictly by coincidence); other times the first might share a common underlying environmental, physiologic, or genetic causative factor. Perhaps the first illness is a milder, early form of the second illness, into which it evolves over time. It is possible that comorbidity is a result of our diagnostic system trying to split hairs among disorders that are part of a larger spectrum of mood, anxiety, and substance use disorders, many of which share clinical features.

Comorbid depression may occur in the context of another psychiatric illness or a major medical illness. The comorbid condition may be another psychiatric disorder (such as an anxiety disorder), a substance abuse disorder, or a medical problem. If depression occurs with another psychiatric problem, such as obsessive-compulsive disorder, panic disorder, or social anxiety disorder, it is very possible that this comorbidity will aid in selection of the best pharmacologic treatment. Some drugs can treat both depression and the other psychiatric problem. Other times two separate drugs are needed. For example, some individuals with schizophrenia (hallucinations, delusional beliefs, and disorganized thinking with inability to function socially) have periods of profound depression during the long-term course of their illness. Such individuals require treatment of the schizophrenia with an antipsychotic and often require an additional medication for the treatment of depression. When depression occurs in the context of a major medical problem, it is important not only to examine medications for the medical problem that may be contributing to the depression, but also to select a treatment that will not interfere with the primary medical condition. An example would be diabetes: Some antidepressants make it far more difficult to control appetite, weight, and blood sugar. Another example might be the individual who develops depression following a stroke. There are certain antidepressants that have been demonstrated effective for treatment of the depression that accompanies stroke. It would be quite important to avoid an antidepressant that risks raising blood pressure or causing a seizure in this context. If an individual develops depression after a heart attack, the old tricyclic antidepressants are contraindicated in the first month or longer, because they may have antiarrhythmic effects (which actually increase mortality), cause low blood pressure on standing up suddenly (postural hypotension), and can raise the heart rate. Conversely, the newer SSRI antidepressants may actually have an effect (decreasing the stickiness of platelets that form blood clots) that helps to prevent recurrence of heart attacks.

Familial Versus Nonfamilial (Sporadic) Depression

The familial versus nonfamilial dimension of depression is also interesting. Sometimes an individual with depression has relatives who have bipolar affective disorder, recurrent major depression, or alcoholism, or who have committed suicide. Sometimes a relative with undiagnosed depression just stayed in his or her room for a few months at a time. A bipolar relative might have made millions of dollars as a successful businessman when high and gone bankrupt or committed suicide when depressed. What runs in the family is very important in understanding and treating an individual who is suffering from depression. Often the first homework assignment for a patient presenting for depression treatment is to find out the details of the family history. What is most important is whether any relatives have had a truly excellent response to any psychiatric medications, as these medications may also work well for the patient. A strong family history of alcoholism may be a clue to a patient whose depression is due to drinking far more than "a few drinks on social occasions." Familial alcoholism may be a clue to bipolar illness, adding to any other evidence on that diagnosis. A family history of suicide is a risk factor for others in the family to do the same, perhaps because it is learned as an acceptable way of coping with psychic pain or perhaps because it is a marker of particularly severe depressive suffering. Science has also now demonstrated a genetic basis for suicidality.

Recurrent Major Depression (Unipolar) Versus Bipolar Affective Disorder (Manic-Depressive Illness)

Another aspect of the course of depression is whether it alternates with some periods of hypomania or mania. Episodes of mania are usually dramatic and obvious to everyone around. They are characterized as being very different from the person's usual normal self because of the extreme amount of energy, enthusiasm, hard work, pressured speech, and lack of sleep. Often there is a comparable lack of common sense and good judgment. Some individuals never get to the full-blown manic stage, but experience hypomania instead, which may manifest as irritability, but for others seems ideal. A person in a hypomanic period is often viewed as pleasant, productive, energetic, and social—the way that the person wishes to be at all times. In an individual who has been energetic, creative, and successful throughout life, it may be difficult to distinguish times of normal mood and energy from hypomanic periods. Fieve (1980, 2006) described the often colorful, creative, charming, and successful lives of some individuals with bipolar illness and how they often pay the price when depression comes along between the high periods.

The terms *unipolar* and *bipolar* have been applied to depression. Individuals who have had recurrent unipolar major depression suffer from only depressive episodes long-term. Those who have bipolar affective disorder, or manic-depressive illness, have a history of hypomanic or manic episodes in the past. It is very important to ask about these, because in the midst of depression no one spontaneously volunteers, "You should have seen me last month. I was high as a kite, spending money like it was going out of style, loads of energy, tremendous sex drive, partying, and having a great time. I didn't waste time sleeping more than 3 or 4 hours a night." Even subtler is the history of periods when "I felt like I wish I could feel all the time—confident, creative, energetic, social, and really productive—but it only lasted for a few days. I thought I was really out of my depression and doing great." These are the important clues that bipolar features are part of the long-term picture. Insight is often lost during a hypomanic or manic period, so patients seldom seek treatment during high periods and are most likely to be brought in by families or police when the mania becomes so out of control that threats, fights, irritability, or paranoia make the illness obvious.

In addition to diagnostic criteria, pay close attention to symptoms and history that provide clues to bipolarity, including depression with atypical features (oversleeping, lethargy, weight gain) and agitated, angry, irritable depressions in which overactivity, distractibility, and racing thoughts figure prominently (Akiskal, Benazzi, Perugi, & Rihmer, 2005; Benazzi, 2003a, 2003b, 2004; Benazzi & Akiskal, 2005; Benazzi, Koukopoulos, & Akiskal, 2004). Psychotic and postpartum depression are also clues. The depression may have a seasonal pattern, often with mood episodes peaking in the fall or spring. Depression responding to sleep deprivation therapy is often bipolar, and a switch to mania with drug initiation or withdrawal points to bipolar illness. Bipolar depression may respond acutely to antidepressant therapy, within 1 to 2 weeks rather than the usual 6 to 9 weeks. Conversely, episodes may go on for 3 months or longer without response to therapy, and resistance to three antidepressant trials is also a sign. If they do respond, these individuals may experience tachyphylaxis (when a once-effective medication stops working). Bipolar depressive episodes tend to be more severe and more protracted than those of unipolar depression. There may be a bipolar family history in first- or second-degree relatives, or of alcoholism, and the onset of depression is likely before age 25. A history of eating disorders or attention-deficit-hyperactivity disorder (ADHD) in adolescence or childhood is common in bipolar disorder. Four or more episodes of major depression are predictive of bipolar depression, as is cyclicity, even if there is no apparent hypomania. When not depressed, these patients may have mood and energy that run a bit higher than average ("hyperthymic temperament").

The Mood Disorder Questionnaire (MDQ) is a very simple self-administered screening evaluation for history of manic or hypomanic periods (Hirschfeld, 2002, 2007; Hirschfeld, Calabrese, et al., 2003; Hirschfeld, Cass, Holt, & Carlson, 2005; Hirschfeld, Holzer, et al., 2003; Hirschfeld & Vornik, 2004; Hirschfeld et al., 2000). If the severity and impairment criterion (the third item on the questionnaire) is eliminated (allowing for mild episodes), the sensitivity for bipolar II disorder is increased. Another screening test for bipolar illness is the Bipolar Spectrum Diagnostic Scale. Both tests are available online (www.dbsalliance.org/pdfs/MDQ.pdf and www.measurecme.org/educenter.php). If you or your significant other has any suspicion of bipolar illness, or if a close relative has had this diagnosis, these tests are very worth taking and bringing to your doctor.

Though the *DSM-IV* requires a 4-day duration for hypomanic episode diagnosis, many others have argued that 1 to 3 days is enough to make the diagnosis and makes it easier to discriminate bipolar from recurrent unipolar major depressive disorder and remind clinicians that underdiagnosis of the bipolar spectrum can lead to underuse of mood stabilizers and to overuse of antidepressants (Akiskal, 1996; Akiskal & Benazzi, 2003; Angst, 1998; Benazzi, 2001, 2003a, 2003b, 2005; Hirschfeld, 2000; Miller, Klugman, Berv, Rosenquist, & Ghaemi, 2004). Akiskal and Benazzi have suggested that the criterion be lowered to 2 days (Akiskal & Benazzi, 2003; Benazzi, 2001, 2005). Of 111 depression-remitted outpatients in one study, where patients were interviewed for history of hypomania and hypomanic symptoms on a modified checklist (hypomania was defined as an episode of increased goal-directed activity plus at least two hypomanic symptoms), 61.2% met criteria for hypomania. In those originally diagnosed with unipolar major depression, 39.5% had a history of hypomania, with an average of four symptoms (Benazzi, 2003b).

An important clue to the diagnosis of bipolar illness is the presence of cyclicity in the long-term longitudinal course of a mood disorder. Though bipolar depression shares some of the putative theories of causation with unipolar depression, various physiologic processes that happen inside neurons—especially those involving protein kinase C (PKC) and cyclic adenosine monophosphate (cAMP) divide the two. These processes are related to regulation of the intracellular activity of calcium, as mediated by overstimulation of the cell by the neurotransmitter glutamate. Overactivity of these substances results in what is known as excitotoxicity, which may cause mood cycling as well as damage to neurons and even death of the cells. Mood stabilizers such as lithium and anticonvulsants that act at sodium-gated ion channels may help to control this. Sometimes bipolar II disorder can look like unipolar depression if the more irritable or mild hypomanic episodes are missed. It may look simply like frequent episodes of depression. There are also unipolar depressed patients who experience their episodes very frequently. Though these patients meet *DSM-IV* diagnostic criteria for unipolar major depressive disorder, their cyclic depression may respond well to mood stabilizers.

Case Example: A New Diagnosis of Bipolar Affective Disorder

Dan presented at age 48, accompanied by his wife, telling me that he had a history of several brief depressions beginning about 5 years earlier, but the current one had been going on longer than any of the others and by now had lasted several weeks. Just prior to the recent depression, Dan had moved his small business to a larger building, was spending beyond reasonable expectations, and was making business decisions based more on hope than on actual income; both he and his wife agreed that he had an unusually high mood at that point. Two years earlier, Dan had a similar high period during which he bought his wife a new car as a Christmas present. Although it seemed affordable at the time, they had both agreed in advance that major purchases would be discussed before either of them spent such a large sum of money. Dan said that during both episodes of feeling high, he was trying to be spiritual, holy, righteous, and the best possible boss at work and husband at home, and he acknowledged that during those times, he felt really good and was impulsive and generous, had increased self-esteem, decreased sleep, talked more than usual, had rapid thoughts, and increased work productivity. Taking into consideration the fact that Dan's high periods did not cause significant functional impairment, lead to hospitalization, or involve psychotic symptoms, I diagnosed him as having bipolar II affective disorder (manic-depressive illness with mild episodes of high periods), currently in a depressive episode. Because of the severity of his depression, I gave Dan Symbyax (the antidepressant Prozac combined with the antipsychotic Zyprexa), and within a week he was starting to feel better. Zyprexa is an antipsychotic initially developed for the treatment of schizophrenia and mania but subsequently found to have antidepressant and mood-stabilizing properties.

Dan had recovered quite nicely after a month of treatment, with the exception of occasional insomnia, and we began discussing long-term preventive treatment options, which are often different from those used in the acute stage of illness. In this case, we chose to taper the Symbyax because of its metabolic risks (elevation of cholesterol and blood sugar). Dan was agreeable to starting Lamictal and tapering off the Symbyax. He did quite well on this for many months. Then he had a brief high period that was readily controlled with Zyprexa, as well as a recurrence of depression about a year later for which Symbyax was again added to the Lamictal. At that point, we discussed the fact that he had had breakthrough episodes while on Lamictal as a long-term mood-stabilizing medication, and therefore it would be optimal to try to prevent these breakthrough episodes by adding a second mood stabilizer. He was agreeable to adding lithium to Lamictal for long-term maintenance and did well on this combination for years, although regular blood tests showed that he eventually developed hypothyroidism, perhaps as a result of the lithium treatment. This might have happened anyway, because his blood tests showed an antibody attacking his thyroid (Hashimoto's thyroiditis, an autoimmune disorder). His hypothyroidism was readily treated with oral thyroxine.

Interesting issues emerged during Dan's treatment. He had enjoyed riding motorcycles since his high school years and had told his wife before they were married that he wanted to buy one. When this came up as an issue after his diagnosis of bipolar disorder, his wife viewed this as indicative of mania, an expensive and risky indulgence. He viewed it as one of his most enjoyable hobbies and a part of his identity. On another occasion Dan was upset when his wife cancelled Thanksgiving dinner plans with his parents because she wanted to do Christmas preparations. He yelled loudly at her in a way that was unusual for him, and she accused him of being manic. Both times he was insightful and sought my feedback. Was he being appropriately assertive and expressing important feelings and wishes, or was he becoming manic? I told him that I sincerely hoped he and his wife would discuss this in their ongoing marital therapy. These displays of emotion could only be labeled as a presentation of mania if they were accompanied by more classic symptoms such as decreased sleep, increased energy, fast speech, and impulsivity. People with bipolar illness have issues, feelings, values, and priorities, and expressing these in an assertive, outspoken way is not necessarily illness behavior. A key component of therapy is differentiating behavior borne of manic grandiosity and lack of judgment from behavior inspired by long-held values, goals, and beliefs. Making a lifestyle commitment to consult a trusted friend or relative, significant other, or therapist before making major or potentially life-altering decisions can help to slow down the process and decrease the chance of following through on potentially harmful decisions.

Time Course

Another dimension of depression is the time course. In order to understand the time course, clinicians can ask the patient if the depression occurs in episodes during discrete periods of time. An episode may come on over a few days or weeks, may last for a few days, a few months, or up to a year or two, and may suddenly lift or very gradually resolve. The *DSM-IV* criteria for a major depressive episode require duration of at least 2 weeks. The natural history of untreated depressive episodes is that most episodes resolve, even without treatment, by about 6 to 24 months. Unfortunately, some individuals have a very chronic depression that becomes almost normal to them. Dysthymia is less severe than major depression. The onset of this chronic baseline, long-term depression is often hard to determine. It may have started in young adulthood, adolescence, childhood, or even "as far back as I can remember," as some of our clients have said. Looking back, many people will say they had depression for many years before they sought psychotherapy or medication treatment. Sometimes being mildly depressed seems normal to the individual. Occasionally, the very chronically depressed person is amazed at how much an effective antidepressant medication helps. The response is almost miraculous and the individual will often say that she regrets not starting antidepressant medication many years earlier. The only reason people like this don't start medication sooner is that they are unaware of what "normal" feels like. Usually a very chronic depression justifies a fairly long trial of antidepressant medication to determine if it will be beneficial; a 2-month commitment to trying a new medication is reasonable if the medication does not cause many side effects. Though many people feel significant improvement in their depression after 6 to 8 weeks on a full therapeutic dose, others take as many as 12 weeks to respond, sometimes at a higher-than-average dose.

What happens between episodes of worsening depression? The natural history of the mood disorder may be that there is complete recovery to the individual's fully normal state. This may involve no residual (or leftover) symptoms such as sleep, anxiety, or energy problems, with full return to normal family, work, and social functioning. Clearly this state of complete wellness (remission) is the ideal goal of treatment. Sometimes there are severe episodes of depression lasting a few months every 1 to 5 years, with brief, milder periods of depression occurring under stress, when physically ill, or premenstrually. In other cases, there are a few residual symptoms and the person will say that she is feeling much better but still experiences some insomnia, fatigue, irritability, or other reminders that the depression is not fully gone (response without remission). This calls for further, more aggressive treatment, because "subsyndromal depression" or residual symptoms predict higher risk of relapse, recurrence, impairment in life functioning, suicide risk, and poorer outcome of some major medical illnesses.

Spontaneous Versus Triggered Episodes

A depressive episode may be either spontaneous or triggered by environmental events. The old "endogenous (from within) versus reactive (to external stressors)" distinction has been dropped from the current diagnostic system because it was neither necessary nor reliable. The concept remains that some episodes of depression occur without any apparent reason, warning, or cause. Other episodes of depression occur only under periods of great loss or stress. The difference between the spontaneous episodes and those that are precipitated by life events is relatively unimportant because both types of depression generally have the same symptoms and treatment response. Often the person whose depression is triggered by severe adverse life events will want and benefit from psychotherapy to help gain perspective and strategies to cope with those events. The individual whose episode came without an apparent trigger will feel less need for psychotherapy and may simply request medication. In the long-term course of depression, it is common to hear that early episodes were clearly related to major life events, such as relationship failures or job loss, and that later episodes seem to "come out of the blue." With repeated episodes, the brain trains itself to be vulnerable to the depressive state. The episodes may become more frequent or severe, or less treatment-responsive, as their number increases.

Sometimes the trigger for depressive episodes is the shortened period of daylight in the fall and winter, and patients will report craving bright light because it helps them to feel better. Moving to, or vacationing in, a sunnier area may greatly decrease the intensity of seasonal affective disorder (SAD). Bright artificial light from a light box may also help during the dark seasons.

DSM-IV Diagnosis

Now that the coverage of such topics as familial depression, polarity, depressive subtypes, medical illness, and stage-of-life issues have provided a broad, general context in which to situate depression, we are going to discuss some technical details as to what constitutes its diagnosis. Psychiatric diagnoses are interesting in that they describe discrete, neatly-packaged illnesses that are then assigned labels, which in turn are applied to individual people. We urge our patients not to overidentify with their illnesses or labels. One is not "bipolar," for instance; she simply lives with bipolar illness. So how are diagnoses useful? They facilitate communication between clinicians. Diagnoses can communicate in a single term what a few hundred words might otherwise be required to describe. For the sake of discussion, diagnoses can create a hub to which all the detail about a unique individual can then be attached. They are also very useful to the researcher, as consistent definitions of phenomena are required for scientific work. Further, they steer the clinician toward appropriate medications. Though drugs are ultimately chosen for an individual symptom profile, a diagnosis gives the doctor a place from which to start.

The Diagnostic Manual

The universally agreed-upon rulebook for making psychiatric diagnoses is the *DSM-IV-TR*, which is published by the American Psychiatric Association with input from other mental health professionals of all disciplines. The *DSM-IV* system is used throughout the United States and is widely referenced in other countries, which more commonly use the *International Statistical Classification of Diseases and Related Health Problems* (*ICD-9*). The development of the diagnostic system involved repeated series of meetings by experts, who tried to distill the most essential features of each diagnosis and put them into a very clear operational form. The attempt was made to have diagnostic criteria that are as simple, descriptive, and as free from theoretical bias (assumptions about cause) as possible. After the original diagnostic criteria were developed, they were sent to clinicians for a field trial to determine reliability. This process has been repeated through the drafts of *DSM-III*, *DSM-III-R*, and *DSM-IV*. The *DSM-IV-TR* is a text revision of the associated features, but not the diagnostic criteria, of the major psychiatric disorders found in *DSM-IV*. We certainly expect a *DSM-V* in the future; the final word on how it will suggest that psychiatric diagnoses be made is not yet in. It is very likely that future diagnostic systems will include the use of some genetic, brain-imaging, and biological markers of illness as these are discovered and correlated with characteristic symptoms, long-term course of illness, or drug responsiveness.

Diagnosis of Depression

The *DSM-IV* divides depression into major depressive episodes (as they present in major depressive disorder and in bipolar affective disorder), dysthymia, and depressive episodes that are due to medical conditions or substance use disorders. It also includes categories of adjustment disorder with depressed mood and normal bereavement.

MAJOR DEPRESSIVE EPISODES

The diagnostic criteria for a major depressive episode require a change from previous functioning during which there is either depressed mood most of the day nearly every day or markedly decreased interest or pleasure in all or almost all activities, again, nearly every day. In addition to one or both of these criteria, the individual must show three or four of the following, to total five criteria: changes in weight or appetite, which may be either increased or decreased; changes in sleep, which may be either insomnia or sleeping too much (hypersomnia); changes in motor (physical) activity, such as pacing and hand wringing (described as agitation), or slowness in thinking and moving (described as retardation); fatigue or loss of energy; feelings of worthlessness or excessive or inappropriate guilt; difficulties with thinking, concentrating, or making decisions; and recurrent thoughts of death. An individual must have a minimum of five of these symptoms for a 2-week period to qualify as having a major depressive episode. In addition to these criteria, there are specifiers: If the individual has only one such episode in his lifetime, this is considered major depression single episode. If an individual has two or more episodes, this is considered recurrent major depression. Subtypes are also specified: psychotic, atypical, melancholic, seasonal, and catatonic. The episode further must not be due to a general medical condition or its treatment, to a substance of abuse, to bereavement, or to another psychiatric illness, for instance bipolar affective disorder.

DYSTHYMIA

Dysthymic disorder is described as a much more chronic condition, and the diagnostic criteria require that an individual have depressed mood for most of the day, more days than not, for at least 2 years. In children or adolescents, the mood may be irritable rather than depressed, and the duration must be at least a year. In addition, the person must have at least two or more of the following additional symptoms: There must be poor appetite or overeating, insomnia or hypersomnia, low energy or fatigue, low self-esteem, poor concentration or difficulty making decisions, or feelings of hopelessness. These symptoms must have never been absent for more than 2 months in the last 2 years. Symptoms are either fewer or less intense or severe than those experienced in major depression. Though patients may experience major depression superimposed on dysthymia (double depression), a diagnosis of dysthymia requires that there was no major depressive episode present during the first 1 or 2 years of the disorder. If there was a major depressive episode, and there was a partial remission, that would be the diagnosis rather than dysthymia. This diagnosis is not made in an individual who has experienced episodes of mania or hypomania.

Diagnosis of Bipolar Illness: Mania, Hypomania, and Mixed Episodes

A manic episode is defined as a distinct period of abnormally and persistently elevated, expansive, or irritable mood for at least a week or requiring hospitalization. In addition, an individual who is euphoric must have at least three additional symptoms, and the person who has irritable mood must have at least four additional symptoms from the following list: inflated self-esteem or grandiosity, decreased need for sleep, being more talkative or experiencing a pressure to keep talking, flight of ideas or racing thoughts, distractibility, increased goal-directed activity, and excessive pleasurable activity with a high potential for painful consequences. During mania, the mood disturbance causes marked impairment in the individual's occupational or social functioning, requires hospitalization to prevent harm to self or others, or involves psychotic features such as hallucinations or delusions.

A mixed episode is diagnosed when an individual meets the criteria for both a manic episode and a major depressive episode concurrently (the 2-week duration required for major depressive episode does not apply in this case).

A hypomanic episode is similar to a manic episode, but it is milder and may be shorter. The diagnostic criteria involve elevated, expansive, or irritable mood, which lasts for at least 4 days and is clearly different from the usual normal mood. During that time the individual must have three additional symptoms if displaying elevated mood and four additional symptoms if experiencing irritable mood. These symptoms, as in the diagnosis for full-blown mania, include inflated self-esteem or grandiosity, decreased sleep, being more talkative or experiencing pressure to keep talking, flight of ideas or racing thoughts, distractibility, increased goal-directed activity, or excessive pleasurable activity with high potential for painful consequences. This must be a distinctly different state of functioning and mood than the person's normal self, which is observable by other people, but not severe enough to cause marked impairment in social or occupational functioning, require hospitalization, or involve psychotic features. Some argue that a hypomanic episode should be diagnosed with mood changes as short as 1 or 2 days, and with fewer criteria required, but the *DSM-IV* requires 4 days.

Although we would never argue that drug response should form the basis of a diagnosis, a surprising drug response can suggest consideration of a new diagnosis. For example, if a depressed patient gets better within days of starting an antidepressant and returns to the next appointment reporting that she feels better than she has in years, has great energy, and experiences not much need for sleep, she might be experiencing a mild drug-induced hypomania and truly be a bipolar patient who has not yet been diagnosed. Similarly, an individual with ADHD who gets much more irritable and agitated and develops insomnia after being given a stimulant such as Ritalin may have an underlying genetic predisposition for bipolar affective disorder that has not yet been diagnosed. Other medications used for medical illness that may trigger irritability, agitation, or hypomania include corticosteroids (in the acute phase of treatment), both taken by mouth and inhaled (in treatment of asthma), Synthroid at high doses, and others. In such cases, a careful diagnostic interview with family members present can determine if there is a family history or past personal history of spontaneously occurring hypomanic or manic episodes that were not revealed at the start of treatment. There is a divergence of expert opinion and the *DSM-IV* in such cases, with many mood disorder experts considering this very suggestive of bipolar affective disorder and the *DSM-IV* considering them substance-induced mood disorders.

Although many experts disagree, a hypomanic or manic episode that is induced by an antidepressant during the treatment of depression is considered a substance-induced mood disorder and is not diagnostic for bipolar affective disorder. Mood disorder experts sometimes diagnose the individual whose hypomanic or manic episodes occur only in response to antidepressant treatment as having bipolar III disorder.

Putting It Together

There are various combinations of the sets of criteria we have just outlined. For example, an individual who has full-blown manic episodes as well as major depressive episodes is described as having bipolar I disorder (though major depressive episodes are not required to make the diagnosis of bipolar I disorder). An individual with a history of hypomanic episodes and major depressive episodes is described as having bipolar II disorder. One who experiences numerous periods of hypomanic symptoms that do not meet criteria for mania and periods of depressive symptoms that do not meet symptom or duration criteria for major depression would be diagnosed with cyclothymic disorder, which, like dysthymia, is a long-term, chronic, cyclic disorder by nature. An individual who has recurrent major depressive episodes, superimposed upon dysthymia, is said to have double depression. All of these definitions assume that the episodes are not caused by substance abuse or a major medical problem.

Some specifiers of major depressive episodes are quite important in describing course of illness and guiding selection of symptom-specific optimal treatments. Some specifiers regard severity, chronicity, and remission; others indicate psychotic symptoms, catatonic symptoms, atypical symptoms, melancholic features, and postpartum onset. Those describing the course of recurrent depression include with full interepisode recovery, without full interepisode recovery, and with a seasonal pattern. Rapid cycling is a specifier applied to individuals with bipolar illness who suffer four or more episodes within a year. Full recovery between episodes is always the goal of treatment, as this state implies significantly lower risk for recurrence and functional impairment than partial recovery. Often full recovery comes gradually and may require the skillful blending of medications and psychotherapy.

MAJOR DEPRESSION WITH PSYCHOTIC FEATURES

Major depression with psychotic features involves the criteria for a major depressive episode that were described earlier, plus the presence of delusions or hallucinations. A person could, for instance, be diagnosed with a melancholic subtype of depression, with psychotic features. Delusions are firmly held, fixed beliefs—neither subject to dispute or disproof by reason or evidence, nor shared within a culture—that influence an individual's thinking and behavior. Delusions may be either mood-congruent or mood-incongruent, depending on the connection of their content to the themes of depression, decay, evil, punishment, or other negative thoughts. An example of mood-congruent psychotic features would be an individual who believes very strongly that the current episode of depression is being caused by God punishing her for something minor that she did many years ago, such as thinking about having an extramarital affair that never actually happened. Another example of a mood-congruent psychotic feature would be an individual who is certain that cancer is rotting away her insides during a depressive episode and who sticks to this belief even after a major medical workup demonstrates that she is physically healthy. A mood-incongruent delusion is a belief that doesn't fit with the overall theme of depression and decay. For example, an individual in a depressive episode might believe that the FBI is following her, that some outside source is controlling her thoughts, or that some other individual is putting the thoughts into her head. Hallucinations are subjective sensory experiences when there is no stimulus present. They may involve any sensory modality, but in most psychiatric disorders they typically involve voices. A person may be aware that the voices are coming from his or her own mind, or completely convinced that they are coming from an outside source. In either case, this is a psychotic symptom. Mood-congruent hallucinations might involve voices saying, "You're an evil person and deserve to suffer." Mood-incongruent hallucinations might involve comments like, "Jesus doesn't want you to have money or material possessions."

Individuals with psychotic features are particularly ill and may require a combination of an antidepressant and antipsychotic. Psychotic features of major depression often respond quite well to electroconvulsive therapy.

Case Example: Depression With Psychotic Symptoms

Debbie was a 27-year-old corporate executive, working as a planning analyst. She had recently been hospitalized for depression and had a long-standing history of obsessive-compulsive disorder (OCD), worrying about her weight, working out extensively, taking long showers, washing her hands repeatedly, and taking up to an hour a day to read the Bible. These symptoms had begun 8 years earlier. Her depression had begun 6 months ago, when she was given a work assignment that she could not complete successfully and was then reassigned at her job. She was angry, disappointed, and depressed, and she was hospitalized when she developed voices telling her to leave her marriage and her home. She thought that people were "talking to her spiritually" and that people were against her. She had intense dreams with religious themes. Past treatment with Paxil and Risperdal had helped her, and the voices were quieting down. The OCD would come and go, as it had long term. Debbie met diagnostic criteria for major depression single episode with psychotic features, as well as OCD.

By about a month later, the combination of Risperdal plus an SSRI antidepressant (Celexa) allowed Debbie to feel ready to return to work. She and her husband were appreciating marital therapy, and she was being given challenging new assignments at her job. She was able to taper off the Risperdal and continue Celexa. She had significant fatigue, for which Wellbutrin was added to the Celexa. She then tapered the Celexa and did well on Wellbutrin alone for control of depressive symptoms (Wellbutrin does not treat OCD, which was quite mild at the time), though because of anxiety in social situations, she chose to resume a low dose of the Celexa.

Over 5 years into treatment, Debbie continued to do well on Wellbutrin, with use of low-dose Risperdal on the rare occasions when she started to feel suspicion, paranoia, and other uncomfortable thoughts creeping back into her life. She had been promoted at work, her marriage was going well, and she felt that she understood how to use and adjust her psychiatric medications when needed. However, after she developed a pituitary tumor, we switched her from Risperdal (because both Risperdal and pituitary tumors can raise prolactin levels) to Abilify, which worked as well for her in controlling psychotic symptoms.

Several years later, Debbie had another brief psychotic episode, requiring hospitalization. Lifestyle and religious values had come between her and her husband, leading to a friendly divorce. The psychotic episode occurred during the week of its finalization. We responded by increasing her Abilify dose, which worked well. Almost 10 years into the time of our working together, Debbie began to experience "spiritual warfare." She and a new potential boyfriend from another state had met a couple of times and shared the same very strong religious values and life goals. Debbie found herself trying hard to slow down the intense emotions of a person falling in love but feeling it's going too fast. Her mother told her to go back to the hospital. I told her to talk to a pastor who shared her beliefs, pushed up her medication to cut the overwhelming intensity of feelings, and acknowledged that her sense of urgency, neediness, and wanting male attention and affection were all normal parts of being a single young woman—they did not necessarily mean she was about to have another psychotic episode.

CATATONIC DEPRESSION

Major depression with catatonic features involves profound changes in motor activity and movement. A person may be immobile or take on very unusual or abnormal positions and maintain them for long periods of time. The person may be in a stupor in which she does not respond to verbal commands. There may be excessive purposeless motor activity that is not in response to anything in the environment. There may be negativism or resistance, unusual involuntary movements or strange postures, strange repetitive movements or mannerisms, grimacing, or repetition of sounds or movements that others have made. Catatonia may occur as part of a major depressive episode, part of a manic episode, or (rarely) as part of a neurologic syndrome. Intravenous Ativan (lorazepam) or Amytal may help temporarily (and helps to clarify the diagnosis), and electroconvulsive therapy (ECT) may help to resolve the episode.

ATYPICAL DEPRESSION

Atypical features of a major depressive episode involve mood reactivity, so that the mood brightens when something nice happens, as well as two or more of the symptoms on the following list: significant increase in appetite or weight, oversleeping, a sense of heavy leaden feelings in the arms and legs (called leaden paralysis) that makes movement seem very effortful, and a long-term pattern of rejection sensitivity so that the ending of a relationship will often trigger depressions. Atypical features predict better response to some antidepressants than others. Monoamine oxidase (MAO) inhibitors or perhaps SSRI antidepressants work better than tricyclic antidepressants in this subtype (Henkel et al., 2006). Many people with bipolar depression or with seasonal affective disorder present with this subtype.

MELANCHOLIC DEPRESSION

Melancholic features of a major depressive episode involve a loss of pleasure in all or almost all activities, or a loss of reactivity to usually pleasurable stimuli. The person can't be cheered up if something nice happens. In addition, the patient must demonstrate at least three of the following symptoms: the mood is distinctly different from the feeling that would be experienced after the loss of a loved one; the depression is worse in the morning than in the evening (known as diurnal variation); and there is early morning awakening of 2 or more hours before the usual time, severe psychomotor retardation or agitation, loss of appetite or weight, and excessive or inappropriate guilt. Though not required for diagnosis, fear and intense anxiety often figure prominently in melancholic depression, as do problems with cognition. There may be sensitivity to light and to sound (photophobia and phonophobia). The person with melancholic depression typically scores quite high on any instrument designed to measure severity. Melancholic features strongly predict the need for biologic treatment rather than psychological interventions.

This sense that the person can't be cheered up is a key concept for friends and family. The support network may say, "Let's go out to dinner and a movie," intending to provide a momentary distraction and enjoyment, but the depressed person may feel that there is no relief in sight and no chance of really enjoying the fine food and funny movie. This can be very frustrating for others, who are totally stymied. It may be helpful to simply ask the depressed person if anything might help; perhaps assistance with some basic tasks like house cleaning or grocery shopping would mean much more to the person than the dinner and movie.

POSTPARTUM DEPRESSION

Around 10–15% of new mothers suffer from postpartum depression (Nielsen Forman, Videbech, Hedegaard, Dalby Salvig, & Secher, 2000). Risk factors include lack of social support, perceived social isolation during pregnancy, previous episode of postpartum depression, being single or separated, marital disharmony, depressive symptoms during late pregnancy, history of emotional problems, admission that a pregnancy was unwanted or unplanned, and prolonged infant health problems (Braverman & Roux, 1978; Nielsen Forman et al., 2000).

The diagnosis of postpartum depression requires that the major depressive episode begin within 4 weeks of childbirth. Postpartum depression is known to be highly recurrent and may sometimes be an indication of bipolar affective disorder. Postpartum blues, which occur in as many as 80% of new mothers, are normal phenomena of tiredness, letdown, and stress in response to having a baby. They often resolve fairly quickly and without treatment. Postpartum depression, on the other hand, usually requires some assistance for care of the new child and some treatment to resolve the depression with either medications or psychotherapy. Time is of the essence, as the depression interferes with mother-infant bonding. Postpartum depression can be very severe and even involve psychotic features that may endanger both mother and child.

Case Example: Postpartum Depression

Karen was a 37-year-old married teacher living with her 5-year-old child but separated from her husband. She was frustrated and depressed and had long-term episodic depression, as well as a family history of depression. She felt that the responsibilities of her job, her child, her new house, and the stress of marital separation were all hard to handle, and she wanted a medicine to help her think clearly, be more positive, energetic, and optimistic, and to concentrate better. Karen responded quite nicely to Prozac and Norpramin (desipramine), and she and her husband reconciled after a year of living apart. She became pregnant while on Prozac and Norpramin and went off of those medications through the pregnancy. She called me a month after the birth of her baby.

When she came for her appointment, Karen said that her baby, a healthy child, was 6 weeks old but not yet sleeping through the night. Karen was feeling like she was "in a tunnel"—nothing was interesting, nothing was fun for her, and she was feeling detached and disconnected from her husband, children, and everyday life. She felt worse in the morning and better in the evening.

Karen was afraid for the baby's safety. She stated she would never hurt the baby, but she was afraid she might "zone out" and be unresponsive to the baby's needs. She had asked her mother to come to her home and help her, yet she felt guilty asking for help. Her sisters told her to "snap out of it." She felt detached and unreal when she went shopping. She felt like she and her husband were "like ships passing in the night" because he had been working long hours at a new job. Doing the housework and taking care of the two kids felt overwhelming, and even when she was able to get some sleep she still awoke feeling tired. She said it was hard to interact with and bond to the baby.

The Prozac and Norpramin that had worked well for Karen in the past were quickly resumed. Two weeks after starting the medications, she was beginning to feel better, and she was able to send her mother home and to appreciate her husband's emotional support.

Every therapist treating a pregnant woman with a history of depression or bipolar disorder should be aware of the risk of depression within the first month or two postpartum, and provide frequent monitoring and aggressive treatment including cognitive-behavioral therapy (CBT), medications, arrangements for help with child care, or even hospitalization if the mother has psychotic features that present a risk to her own or the baby's safety.

SEASONAL AFFECTIVE DISORDER

Depression with seasonal pattern, also known as seasonal depression, may occur in either either bipolar affective disorder or recurrent major depressive disorder. SAD means that there has been a regular relationship in time between the onset of depressive episodes and the season over many years. In addition, there is usually a remission from the depression or switch into hypomania or mania that occurs at a specific time of year.

The diagnosis requires that this seasonal pattern has occurred for at least 2 years with no nonseasonal major depressive episodes during that time. In addition, the seasonal depressions must have outnumbered the nonseasonal depressions long-term. Often individuals with SAD crave bright light, dread gloomy dark days, and feel better if they vacation in a sunny climate during the winter or move to sunnier areas of the country where their symptoms are milder. Rarely, so-called reverse SAD occurs, where the person feels worse in the warm, sunny summer months. There is also a pattern among those with bipolar illness where mania comes in the fall and depression in the spring.

In California, we sometimes see people who had very significant SAD while living in other states. They often say that after moving from Chicago or Seattle to Southern California they notice their mood variations with the seasons are much milder or sometimes even fully gone.

RAPID CYCLING

Rapid cycling is another specifier of long-term course and can be applied to either bipolar II (where it is more common) or bipolar I disorder. This involves at least four episodes during a 12-month period, each of which meet the criteria for major depression, mania, hypomania, or mixed episodes. Historically, rapid cycling may lead to less lithium responsiveness in bipolar affective disorder and to better anticonvulsant mood stabilizer response, although it generally does not respond well to either. A study by Joseph Calabrese and colleagues (Calabrese, Shelton, & Rapport, et al. 2005) indicates that relapse into a mood episode among patients taking lithium was 56%, whereas Depakote failed to protect 50% of patients—a marginal difference. Rapid-cycling bipolar disorder is a reason to avoid or minimize antidepressant use in favor of mood stabilizers.

Other Contexts for Depression

DEPRESSION SECONDARY TO MEDICAL OR
SUBSTANCE ABUSE ISSUES

Depression may occur in the context of medical illness, substance abuse, or stressful life events including losses of health, job, or a loved one. Sometimes depression occurs in the context of a chronically miserable life situation. Each of these presents its own challenges in diagnosis and treatment. Earlier, we examined the distinction between primary and secondary depression, as well as that between uncomplicated depression and comorbidity. Here we look at the diagnostic process that helps to make these distinctions.

Diagnostic criteria involve prominent and persistent mood disturbance, with depressed mood and loss of interest or pleasure, or with elevated, expansive, or irritable mood. There must be evidence from the patient's history or from physical or laboratory findings that the mood change is a direct result of a general medical condition. It cannot occur only during an episode of delirium, which involves clouded consciousness and highly variable mental status over time. An episode may involve depressive features, manic features, or mixed features. Common examples include depression within the context of cancer of the pancreas or other organs, hypothyroidism, and chronic infections (e.g., HIV or hepatitis).

A substance-induced mood disorder involves a mood disturbance with depressed mood and decreased interest or pleasure in all or almost all activities, or with elevated, expansive, or irritable mood. There must be evidence from the patient's history or from physical or laboratory findings that the symptoms developed during or within a month of the time of substance intoxication or withdrawal. Such an episode may follow street drug or alcohol abuse, or prescription drug use. The substances known to cause mood disorders include alcohol, amphetamines, cocaine, hallucinogens, inhalants, opioids, PCP, sedative hypnotics, and others. High-dose steroids (e.g., prednisone for treatment of asthma or lupus) may cause depression or mania. The episodes may involve depressive features, manic features, or mixed features. The onset may occur during intoxication or during withdrawal from the substance use. Antidepressants themselves may cause mania, either during initiation or withdrawal.

This may seem like a very fine point, but a person who has depression due to a general medical condition or substance abuse has a different history, and perhaps treatment, than a person who has had recurrent mood problems and then subsequently developed a medical or substance-abuse problem. For example, a person who experiences her first episode of depression during detoxification and rehabilitation from serious cocaine and alcohol abuse has a very good chance of seeing the depression lift on its own after a month or two of sobriety. It is debatable whether the use of antidepressant medication would really be necessary or helpful. On the other hand, a person who has had numerous severe depressions without any substance abuse and later in life becomes an alcoholic is extremely likely to need an antidepressant or mood stabilizer long-term to prevent falling back into depression once she has achieved sobriety. Similarly, the person with depression that developed as a result of hypothyroidism may respond nicely to thyroid replacement and not need an antidepressant, whereas the person who became hypothyroid due to lithium used to treat long-term bipolar affective disorder will require both the mood stabilizer and thyroid replacement medication to maintain mood in the normal state.

Case Example: Manny

When substance abuse is an issue—regardless of whether it caused or followed the depression—helping the patient to achieve sobriety is essential for recovery. In some cases this may mean taking a firm stance against the substance abuse while also providing a treatment program. There is a point at which individual weekly psychotherapy and medications will just not work due to drug or alcohol abuse, and at this point the therapist does the patient a huge service by demanding that an inpatient or residential program is necessary for effective progress to be made in treating the depression.

Manny was a 60-year-old financial consultant who recently had been discharged from a psychiatric hospital where his depression, anxiety, and alcohol and tranquilizer abuse had been treated briefly. Manny had been previously hospitalized four times for depression, and it was only quite recently that minor tranquilizers, like Klonopin, as well as alcohol had been really problematic for him. He had been on numerous SSRI antidepressants and Depakote, and he was going through a stormy third divorce. The initial diagnostic impression was recurrent major depression, generalized anxiety disorder, and benzodiazepine dependence with possible abuse, as well as possible alcohol abuse. It was not until Manny had gone through multiple hospitalizations over the next 6 months that he was able to maintain a prolonged period of sobriety. At that point, his extremely difficult-to-treat depression and anxiety were very nicely resolved while taking Effexor 300 mg daily. Over the next 3 years he continued on Effexor 300 to 450 mg daily and was able to completely eliminate his use of Valium. He also realized that his chronic use of alcohol and minor tranquilizers had caused him to experience a very severe depression, and that the follow-up 12-step meetings and complete sobriety that had been so strongly recommended earlier were really important to his long-term recovery.

I treated Manny uneventfully for over 5 years as he dealt with retirement, the challenges of parenting a young daughter part-time, and trying to provide guidance to his 33-year-old daughter. Suddenly I got an emergency call from his older daughter, saying that Manny was hospitalized with acute onset of confusion, being very "out of it," and unable to take care of himself. On my recommendation he was transferred from a medical unit to the University of California Los Angeles Neuropsychiatric Institute. After his 6-day hospitalization he came to see me and told me that he had been having back problems and had been given hydrocodone and Valium by a friend. Realizing that he was hooked he went to a private detox outpatient clinic, where he was seen for only 15 minutes, given a package of pills, and sent home to "do it himself" without structure or monitoring. When he took the medications, he became delirious. Once again, he had learned the painful lesson that dabbling with abusable substances and trying to be his own doctor would not work for him.

BEREAVEMENT AND ADJUSTMENT DISORDERS

Another form of depression is bereavement. The *DSM-IV* categorizes this as a so-called V code, meaning that it is a condition that may present for professional attention but is not attributable to a mental disorder. A grieving person may "just need to talk to someone" and this isn't necessarily abnormal or considered an illness. No one can pinpoint an intensity or duration of grieving that is normal, because it varies so greatly among cultures and different personality styles.

Often, in response to the loss of a loved one, a person may have some symptoms that are similar to those of a major depressive episode, such as difficulties with sleeping or eating. Usually the individual will recognize this and the family and the clergyperson will counsel the individual that the symptoms are normal after a major loss. Short-term use of medications such as sleeping pills may provide much-needed relief.

Generally, one should consider a diagnosis of major depressive episode, rather than uncomplicated normal bereavement, when certain features are present. These may include guilt, thoughts about death, preoccupations with being worthless, profound psychomotor slowing, functional impairment in daily living, or hallucinations other than those of hearing or seeing the individual who has died. Often the persistence of symptoms or worsening of them beyond a period of about 2 months following the loss is very suggestive of a major depressive episode.

A data-based study compared bereavement-related depression to major depression related to other stressful life events and concluded that "the similarities between bereavement-related depression and depression related to other stressful life events substantially outweighs their differences." The authors challenged the DSM-IV exclusion of bereavement from the diagnosis of major depression (Kendler, Myers, & Zisook, 2008). A review summarized Freud's (1917) paper *Mourning and Melancholia*, drawing parallels between the psychological processes observed psychoanalytically and current neurobiological findings in depression (Carhart-Harris, Mayberg, Malizia, & Nutt, 2008).

Adjustment disorder with depressed mood is still another form of depression. An adjustment disorder involves emotional or behavioral symptoms that have developed in response to an identifiable stressor, usually within 3 months of the occurrence of the stressor, with marked distress in excess of what would be normal and expected, or with significant impairment in social or occupational functioning. This is differentiated from major depressive episodes and normal bereavement. Normally, an adjustment disorder resolves within 6 months after the stressor has been resolved. This is the diagnostic category that would most often describe an individual who has just suffered a loss of a relationship, a job, or some other disappointment or failure in life but does not meet the full criteria for a major depressive episode.

SITUATIONAL DEPRESSION

Dr. Michael Gitlin, director of the UCLA Mood Disorder Clinic, once said that "antidepressants are not anti-misery drugs." Some people live in a relationship characterized by fear and abuse. That situation is not conducive to getting well. One of the classic animal models of depression is learned helplessness: the sense that, no matter what one does, success will not follow, or punishment cannot be avoided. One's efforts, actions, and decisions make no real difference. Such individuals often view themselves as being victims of circumstance and controlled by others.

Miserable life circumstances do not equate with a diagnosis of any form of depression, though the two may coexist. In order to restore well-being, the situation must be changed or eliminated. Sometimes antidepressants can help an individual build up the courage to leave a difficult situation. Unlike the counsel of well-meaning but perhaps biased friends and family, psychotherapy can help to sort out the pros and cons of staying in a difficult relationship or job, rally the support system, and aid the patient in making healthy decisions. Sometimes escape from a miserable situation will relieve the necessity of an antidepressant. Psychoanalysts talk of repetition compulsions: An example would be the woman who repeatedly marries abusive alcoholic men, each time hoping that love will change the man, and each time hoping to rework the childhood issue of having a similarly alcoholic and abusive father. The goal of psychotherapy with such an individual is to recognize the pattern, acknowledge its roots in attempting to repair early life traumas, and learn from past mistakes that attempts to change others to meet one's needs are futile. Making good choices requires acknowledging and learning from bad choices! It is very important to distinguish a miserable life situation from a diagnosis of depression, because the treatment implications are so drastically different. Misery implies a need to make a careful, thoughtful decision and take action; a pill won't solve it!

Case Example: Marital Misery

Tina was a 35-year-old woman who seemed to have it made. She was an attorney, working as an assistant to a federal trial judge. She had been married for almost 5 years to a man her family liked. What they didn't know was that shortly after Tina and her husband had gotten married, his medical problems had worsened, and the couple had stopped having sexual relations. On several occasions, Tina saw her husband looking at naked women on the computer. When she confronted him about it, he said that he had wanted to assess his sexual performance in a situation in which he didn't feel pressure (by masturbating to pictures rather than attempting sexual relations with her).

Tina had been taught growing up that sex was something a woman was supposed to do to satisfy her husband, and she had never fully enjoyed it. She was also hurt by the lack of affection in her marriage, and said that she and her husband were not even very good as roommates anymore. She felt that she was constantly nagging him and that his response was to avoid her.

Tina had a history of an abnormal Pap smear and reported that a brief sexual trauma had occurred several years earlier. She had been taking Paxil for her recurrent major depression, as well as for generalized anxiety and social anxiety. She was suffering from inhibited sexual desire, but it was unclear whether this was due to the medication, the influence of the sexual trauma, or the difficulties in her marriage. Tina had some relief of her depression and anxiety symptoms while taking Effexor XR at 225 mg and BuSpar at 60 mg daily. After being briefly tempted to have a fling with a coworker, she finally acknowledged that her marriage was not working, and she did the responsible thing in seeking marital therapy.

After six sessions of marital therapy, Tina reported that she and her husband were better friends and roommates, but that there was absolutely no progress on intimacy as a couple. She met a new male friend and felt incredible guilt for having kissed him. The new man in her life was single, available, and talking about thoughts of marrying her. She realized that her husband had not changed and was unlikely to do so; he just wanted to keep her around for companionship. After coming to this realization, Tina decided that a month-long trial separation would help her to sort out her feelings. She told her husband, and his response was to listen, stare, and then fall asleep. She realized how unable to process feelings he had been. Over the next few weeks, he would hug her and occasionally cry. This made her feel guilty about moving out, but she did so anyway. Shortly after moving to a hotel and beginning to date the other man, she felt a sense of happiness and physical and emotional attraction to her new partner. She was enjoying her sexuality, felt compatible with the new man, and was optimistic about finding the fulfillment and happiness that she had missed out on during her marriage.

Three years into treatment, Tina got married to her boyfriend, and a year later they had their first baby. Tina's depression had not returned, and although regular life challenges continued to arise, she dealt with them well and appeared happier than I had ever seen her before.

Comorbidities

Medical and psychiatric comorbidities, as noted earlier, are relevant to diagnosis. Depression often does not travel alone, and comorbidities can complicate the diagnostic process as well as treatment. Here we discuss several discrete disorders that are often comorbid to depression. We also introduce the process of antidepressant selection in this context, so you can begin to see the relationship between diagnosis and treatment. Selection of medication for unipolar and bipolar depression is discussed in great detail later on.

Pain

Depression is commonly comorbid with chronic pain, occurring in as many as 50% of chronic pain patients (Ruoff, 1996). Furthermore, most subjects with major depressive disorder (61.6%) report having either a chronic, painful physical condition or a nonpainful medical condition (Obayon, 2004). Some chronic pain may be considered as a variant of depressive illness: Pain involving the head, face, and musculoskeletal system is common in depression (Gupta, 1986). Common forms of pain that are often seen along with depression include migraine headaches, tension headaches, chronic back pain, chronic abdominal pain, chronic pelvic pain, and other forms of pain that do not have a demonstrable anatomic cause. Fibromyalgia is another form of chronic pain that may be very debilitating. It is interesting that migraine and irritable bowel syndrome, as well as major depression, appear to share a similar neurotransmitter problem in the serotonin system. It is equally interesting that descending spinal pathways involving norepinephrine and serotonin are the modulators of pain sensitivity. Perhaps this is why antidepressants are often helpful for individuals with chronic pain. Triptans (such as Imitrex), the most widely used acute migraine-abortive medicines, also affect the serotonin system.

Anxiety

Anxiety disorders accompany depression in more than 50% of patients. Common anxiety disorders include OCD (present in 6.3% of depressed patients), with its intrusive, recurrent, repulsive thoughts and anxiety-reducing repetitive rituals; panic disorder (21.6%), with its sudden terrifying attacks of rapid heartbeat and shortness of breath; social phobia (27%), with tremendous fear of being watched and showing embarrassment by signs of anxiety; post-traumatic stress disorder (18.8%), with its vivid reexperiencing of a traumatic event; and generalized anxiety disorder (10.6%), with its chronic uncontrollable worry (Fava et al., 2000). In those living with bipolar illness, anxiety disorders affect approximately 42% of patients (McElroy, 2001). Each of these anxiety disorders is more common in individuals who have depression and vice versa. People who have anxiety disorders are more likely than the general population to have depression. Often, the symptoms of both the depression and the anxiety disorder can be treated with a single medication in the SSRI (e.g., Prozac, Zoloft, Paxil, Celexa, Lexapro, Luvox) or SNRI (e.g., Effexor, Pristiq, Cymbalta) families.

Substance Abuse

Major depression may occur in the context of substance abuse or dependence. In a very large epidemiologic study, among those suffering from major depressive disorder sometime in their lifetime, 40.3% had an alcohol use disorder, 17.2% had a drug use disorder, and 30.0% had nicotine dependence (Hasin et al., 2005). Among those with bipolar illness, 42% suffered from alcohol abuse or dependence, and around 60% from all forms of substance abuse (McElroy, 2001). In the case of alcoholism, the substance abuse often precedes the development of depression in men, whereas women often have depression first and then develop alcoholism.

In either case, it is essential that the substance abuse be treated along with the depression. Drinking a pint of vodka nightly while taking an antidepressant is a waste of a patient's time and money, because no antidepressant has a chance of working adequately in the context of ongoing substance abuse. One of our patients once said that he had learned in A.A. that there is no problem that alcohol cannot worsen. We concur.

Case Example: Major Depression With Drug Abuse

Damian was a 21-year-old single man who had moved away from home 5 years earlier but came back to live with his family after dropping out of college. He worked in his father's small business. His history included some psychotherapy after he had stayed out all night on one occasion during 11th grade. Two months after starting at a private liberal arts college, Damian declared that he was a "suicidal alcoholic" and was started on Prozac. He then wrecked a car and was arrested for drunk driving.

When Damian moved back into his parents' home, there were many requirements. He had to see a psychiatrist, abstain from using alcohol and street drugs, be home by 11 P.M. on weekdays, go to work daily, go to church with the family on Sundays, and go to A.A. once a week. He could only smoke cigarettes outside the house. He acknowledged a need to be accountable to someone for his behavior.

Family history revealed that Damian's mother was anxious and tearful. One of his sisters had been diagnosed as schizophrenic and was doing reasonably well on a typical antipsychotic medication. Another sibling was a "straight arrow" accountant who was working in the father's business, and still another was going to college and dealing with issues of being gay in the context of a family religious system that felt that this was wrong. The father had a history of some drinking bouts but had stopped those several years earlier.

Damian reported that his depression had begun in about 10th grade, at a time when he was not abusing substances. He said that he had felt very suicidal on at least a couple of different occasions, one of which involved going to drug houses, where he expected to get into a fight and be killed. My diagnostic impressions were major depression, which appeared stable on Prozac, and alcohol abuse. Damian was willing to take Antabuse (which produces a severe negative reaction in conjunction with alcohol) in front of his parents as a way of committing to sobriety. He was taking Prozac with occasional Wellbutrin, going to A.A., and going to church, and he was seen in regular psychotherapy sessions with his family.

The family reported numerous crises related to Damian's past alcohol and drug use. His mother, who did well on a very low dose of Prozac, acknowledged substantial problems with depression and difficulty coping with her children's mental problems, especially in light of her own alcoholic family background.

Four months into treatment, there was a setback when Damian did not come home for a couple of nights. When he returned, he slept through the day, did not show up for work, and said that he did not care about things. The family rules were reemphasized, along with a statement that the expectation was that he would live with the family for a year to become stable. An urgent session was held when he complained of feelings of anger, irritation, loss of interest, anxiety, self-destructive thoughts, and fear that he might get violent and hurt himself or others, along with a strong urge to use marijuana. Because of the anger, lithium was added and Wellbutrin was stopped. A few months later, Damian stopped the lithium on his own because he felt mentally cloudy on it. He continued the Prozac. Six months into treatment, the family reported that he had been somewhat disruptive, leaving church during the middle of a service, and he had relapsed into drinking at Christmas to avoid being around the family for their Christmas gathering. However, he was continuing to go to church most of the time and feeling some benefit from that, as well as from A.A. He acknowledged that he carried a lot of anger inside but did not really know where it was coming from.

Nine months into therapy, Damian got drunk and totaled his truck in a single-vehicle accident. He acknowledged that he was not actually working the A.A. steps and did not have a sponsor, and he agreed to go back on daily Antabuse, which he had discontinued several months earlier.

About a year into treatment, there was an urgent appointment during which Damian acknowledged abusing drugs. He had quit his job and said that he had been using marijuana and speed (amphetamine) throughout much of the last year. At that point I said that urgent admission to a residential substance abuse program was essential, because the family's ongoing effort to provide a supportive religious home environment with very clear rules and accountability were not working. Damian was abusing drugs despite the best support his family could give him. He was admitted to a sober living program, where he acknowledged cocaine abuse as well. When he walked in the door, he tested positive for marijuana, cocaine, and amphetamine. While in the sober living home for a few weeks, Damian became paranoid and pulled a knife on another client, so I suggested the use of a low-dose antipsychotic medication. Two months into the program, he went out, got drunk, was picked up by the police, and temporarily refused to go back to the rehabilitation program. By the end of 90 days in the rehabilitation program, he had only been sober for 3 weeks, so an extended program was arranged. Six months into the rehabilitation program, Damian was truly embracing the values of sobriety. He acknowledged that he had only gone 2 months at a time clean and sober while participating, and that his occasional abuse of stimulants was what had fueled his angry outbursts.

Eight months after his entry into the substance abuse program, Damian was coming home to the family again with clear-cut expectations on curfew, work, and ongoing program participation. The next 4 years saw continuing progress. Damian went from working on the manufacturing floor of his father's business to an executive position and mastered more and more aspects of running the business. He married his girlfriend with the parents' blessings and maintained his sobriety. He found that the benefits of sobriety, the 12-step program, church, marriage, and a loving, supportive family far outweighed the thrills he experienced as a rebellious teenager. He continued his low-dose Prozac and occasional Wellbutrin and, with ongoing sobriety, reported that these provided very good mood stability and that he had only very brief, mild, and easily managed depressive days. With his substance abuse in stable remission, Damian knew that there would be ongoing work ahead of him for his own emotional and spiritual growth. He saw this as very worth the long-term effort and commitment.

Nicotine

Major depression and nicotine dependence often co-occur in the same person. Nicotine dependence increases the risk of depression (John, Meyer, Rumpf, & Hapke, 2004), and sometimes quitting smoking will also trigger a depressive episode.

One of the fortunate accidental discoveries of antidepressant research was the discovery that people who smoke tended to lose their craving for nicotine when given the antidepressant Wellbutrin (also known as Zyban or bupropion). Subsequent studies have shown that nondepressed individuals also find it easier to stop smoking when taking Wellbutrin. The mechanism of action in this case appears to be increasing dopamine tone in the brain's reward center, the nucleus accumbens (Jorenby et al., 1999; McAfee & France, 1998; Pasternak, 1998). An important consideration with many drugs from various classes is that smoking induces certain liver enzymes and can lower the blood levels of some psychiatric drugs. Stopping smoking may lead to higher drug levels, so that the psychiatric drugs have more effects and side effects unless the dose is adjusted.

Eating Disorders

Major depression may occur in the context of an eating disorder. This will also influence the selection of an antidepressant. Some antidepressants, such as Elavil, Sinequan, Surmontil, and Remeron, tend to make people very hungry and increase their weight; these, of course, should be avoided in obese individuals. Other antidepressants, such as high-dose Prozac, may help to control bulimia or binge eating. Some anticonvulsants, such as Topamax and Zonegran, may also be helpful in curbing both appetite and impulsivity. Wellbutrin is contraindicated in individuals who have an eating disorder that involves purging because of a very significant risk of grand mal seizures in these patients, who may have an imbalance of electrolytes. This medication can be helpful, however, in decreasing appetite in depressed patients who are overweight.

Diagnosis and Prompt Treatment Are Important!

Psychotherapists have long argued with psychopharmacologists that depressive symptoms motivate introspection, self-awareness, struggle, growth, and change. Psychopharmacologists have argued that relief of human suffering through the use of medications is worthwhile and sometimes even life-saving. Fortunately, the psychotherapists and psychopharmacologists are gradually declaring a truce in this turf war, recognizing that collaboration and use of all appropriate treatment modalities allows the best treatment of both mind and brain.

Consequences of Untreated Depression

Depression that does not receive proper diagnosis and effective treatment creates many risks for the sufferer. Social limitations include strain on relationships and social isolation, and there may be ongoing limitations in workplace attendance and productivity. Persistently depressed workers are seven times less productive on the job, and the impact of depression on function at work is substantially higher than its association with missed days.

Depression that persists is also well known to worsen the course of medical illnesses, including heart attack, stroke, cancer, diabetes, acquired immunodeficiency syndrome (AIDS), and many other diseases. There will be a greater cost of medical treatment and a sustained risk of substance abuse or suicide. Depression is a leading cause of disability and suicide and should be very carefully evaluated and aggressively treated.

The newest generation of brain-imaging studies has demonstrated that a key memory-forming area of the brain, the hippocampus, is damaged by prolonged periods of untreated severe depression and actually shrinks in response (Czeh & Lucassen, 2007). Antidepressants, lithium, and the anticonvulsant Depakote appear to be protective and have been shown to cause the brain to synthesize growth factors for these neurons. In other words, it now appears that depression causes brain damage and treatment reverses this. Even more alarming is a Danish study demonstrating that the lifetime number of hospitalizations for major depression or mania that a person has experienced is correlated with the risk of being diagnosed as having dementia (Kessing & Andersen, 2004). These findings have been replicated by other study groups.

Finally, if a person does not get treatment to the point of achieving complete remission, there is a greater ongoing risk of relapse and recurrence, and the recurrent episode may be more difficult to treat.

Goals of Diagnosis and Treatment

A decade or two ago, response was the goal of treatment. In antidepressant drug trials, response has for many years been operationalized as a 50% reduction in symptoms as measured on a depression rating scale. Most new drug studies that have been performed for premarketing research to get Food and Drug Administration (FDA) approval have demonstrated about a 60–65% response rate for the drug and 25–30% for the placebo. The difference between the response rates of antidepressant and placebo is known as an "effect size," and any drug that can demonstrate a decent effect size in two randomized, double-blind controlled studies—without unacceptably dangerous side effects—will win the government's approval for sale in the United States. Although these trials also report their rates of remission (reduction of symptoms to a very low level on a depression rating scale), typically achieved by 35% of subjects, response is what has brought drugs to market.

As a result of Judd's work while at the National Institute of Mental Health, we know much more about the long-term natural history of depression, and both clinical psychiatrists and the pharmaceutical industry have raised the bar for what we consider good outcome of depression treatment (Judd & Akiskal, 2000; Judd et al., 1998a, 1998b).

The definition of a good outcome in current clinical practice is a return to the patient's previous level of functioning at work and at home, so that the person feels well and "normal," as she defines this, and is able to enjoy life. The current emphasis, therefore, is on attempting to use the most aggressive possible treatment to obtain complete remission of depression. Even a few residual symptoms—mild anxiety, sleep difficulty, or mild fatigue, for instance—can greatly increase the chances of relapse or recurrence. The advantages of achieving true remission are better long-term course, better functioning, less likelihood of developing treatment-resistant depression, less chance of a relapse or recurrence, better social adjustment, and improved general medical health.

3

Understanding the Enemy: Theories of What Causes Depression

Theories of what causes depression abound. Is it genes, neurotransmitter deficiency, inability to turn off stress hormones, abrupt changes in sex hormones, or early life deprivation and trauma with later presence of heightened fear, anxiety, and cognitive distortions? Different explanations appeal to different patients and clinicians, and often influence the type of treatment sought. For example, an individual who believes that there is a neurotransmitter imbalance in depression is most likely to see a physician for an antidepressant medication. The person who believes that he must get to the root cause of the depression by exploring the influence of early childhood events on current adult life will most likely seek a psychotherapist. The person who believes that depression is caused by lack of religious faith or by sin will probably talk to a clergyman. No one can say that one approach is better than another, and often these approaches work well together. It is not unusual for a psychopharmacologist to refer the patient for psychotherapy or pastoral counseling. The referrals often go in both directions.

Theories of what causes depression can basically be divided into two categories: biological and psychological.

Biological Theories

The biological theories of depression focus on genetics, neurotransmitters, and stress hormone responses.

Genes

"We used to think our fate was in the stars. Now we know, in large measure, our fate is in our genes." This quotation is from James Watson, codiscoverer of the DNA double helix as the basis of genetic transmission (Jaroff, 1989, p. 67).

The genetic risk of depression is substantial, and many depressed patients can readily identify parents or grandparents who suffered with long-term depression. In fact, the heritability of liability to major depression is almost 40% (Sullivan, Neale, & Kendler, 2000). Sometimes older relatives were hospitalized or received shock treatment (electroconvulsive treatment, or ECT), sometimes they died of suicide, and often they suffered chronically without receiving adequate treatment.

The genetic link between recurrent unipolar major depression and bipolar affective disorder is important, and often a person who has unipolar depression will have a bipolar relative or vice versa. We frequently ask the patient to find out the close relatives' best medication so this may be tried. We often hear that the patient hopes to lead a better life than his depressed mother or father, who turned to alcohol or tranquilizers as a means of coping or spent weeks or months in bed incapacitated by severe depression. One of the major hopes of biological psychiatry is that a gene chip will someday allow identification of individuals with depression and rational subtyping that will predict medication response or medication intolerance. Current studies are evaluating the genetic contribution to variations in drug metabolism, response, and side effects, including the risk of drug-induced mania (Garriock et al., 2006; Nnadi, Goldberg, & Malhotra, 2005a, 2005b).

There is often an interaction between genes and environment. Genes predispose for the risk of adult depression. Developmental issues may include childhood abuse, neglect, or early parental loss, followed by adult stressors such as loss of a relationship, medical problems, or substance abuse. The interaction of many of these factors typically precipitates a depressive episode in a genetically susceptible individual (Kendler, Kuhn, Vittum, Prescott, & Riley, 2005; Wilhelm et al., 2006).

Caspi has made a fascinating discovery about the genetics of depression, namely that the genetically determined form of the serotonin transporter is related to the risk of developing depression in response to adverse life circumstances. Maltreatment or abuse between ages 3 and 11 leads to depression at ages 18 to 26 years in a third to two-thirds of people, depending on their genetics. In a sense this is a genetic mediator of vulnerability to depression. Individuals with one form of the gene are at higher risk for developing adult depression if exposed to childhood adversity, whereas those with other forms of the gene are at low risk (Caspi et al., 2003). This finding has been independently replicated (Kendler et al., 2005).

Shelton (2007) has suggested that the pathophysiology of depression associated with early life adversity is different from that which does not have traumatic antecedents; trauma-related depression is more likely to involve the hypothalamic-pituitary-adrenal axis than depression not associated with trauma. He pointed out that adverse events cause negative mood states in normal people and that depression represents a dysregulation of normal responses. Based on Caspi's work, Shelton suggested that there is an interaction of "gene dose" and "stress dose" (both childhood and adulthood) that contributes to depression vulnerability. Heightened stress reactivity may have multiple different mechanisms in some individuals, both biological (via the hypothalamus-pituitary-adrenal pathways and via serotonin gene variations) and psychological (through maladaptive responses to stressors).

The presence of the short allele of the serotonin transporter gene along with maltreatment represents a high risk for childhood depression, but the presence of a positive support system can help to moderate this effect (Kaufman et al., 2004). Another gene-by-environment interaction has been demonstrated by examining adults with or without child abuse, looking at the corticotrophin-releasing hormone receptor gene, showing that the relationship between child abuse and developing adult major depression was moderated by this genetic factor (Bradley et al., 2008).

Neurotransmitters

Before discussing neurotransmitter theories, it is important to describe a few simple concepts about how the brain works. The brain consists of neurons and glial cells. The neurons have traditionally been considered the thinking, communicating, active cells. The glia have been considered to be the supportive, nurturing, insulating cells, though the role of glial cells now appears to be greater than originally thought. Glia supply glucose to neurons, protect neurons by stabilizing glutamate, modulate neurotransmitters, and facilitate neuronal repair and survival by synthe-sizing and releasing neurotrophic factors. Reduction of glial cell density and number occurs in frontal and limbic areas in depression (Rajkowska & Miguel-Hidalgo, 2007).

A neurotransmitter is a chemical messenger that is made within the neuron and released at the synaptic cleft (a space at the junction where two neurons communicate) to provide communication from one neuron to the next. In other words, a neurotransmitter is a chemical messenger, going across the gap from one cell to another. This neurotransmission can happen locally or can involve different areas of the brain, which are specialized for different functions and which contain neurons that produce specific neurotransmitters. To transmit these neurotransmitters from one part of the brain to another, the long tails on neurons, called axons—bundled and insulated with "white matter" (glia)—form tracts (in the rest of the body, these would be called nerves).

There are probably hundreds of different neurotransmitters within the human brain. For the monoamine transmitters such as norepinephrine and serotonin, it appears that levels of the chemicals within the synapse can be influenced by many factors. The synthesis of the neurotransmitter is influenced by the availability of amino acids that are used as building blocks, including 1-tryptophan and 1-tyrosine. The rate of release of the transmitter can be influenced by drugs and by incoming messages from other neurons. When the neurotransmitter is released, it diffuses across the synaptic gap from one neuron to another. When it arrives at the second neuron, it binds to a very specific receptor site that activates that neuron to do something. After carrying its message, the neurotransmitter is typically sucked back up into the original neuron that released it. A reuptake pump (transporter) performs this energy-requiring process. The most widely used antidepressants work here as selective serotonin reup-take inhibitors (SSRIs), selective norepinephrine reuptake inhibitors (NRIs), or selective serotonin and norepinephrine reuptake inhibitors (SNRIs). When the neurotransmitter molecule returns into the cell that released it, the neurotransmitter may either be degraded (broken down) or repackaged and reused to send future chemical messages.

The drugs that treat depression use various mechanisms to increase levels of neurotransmitters in the synapse by blocking their reuptake or breakdown. This finding led to the theory that deficiencies in neurotransmitter levels might cause depression. Although it is based on circumstantial evidence, there is tremendous support for the neurotransmitter deficiency theory of why individuals become depressed and why they get better on antidepressant medications. Neurotransmitter theories of depression have focused primarily on norepinephrine and serotonin and occasionally on dopamine. The earliest neurotransmitter theory of the cause of depression postulated that there is a deficiency of norepinephrine or serotonin in individuals who became depressed. The catecholamine hypothesis stated that a deficiency of norepinephrine or its effects was a cause of depression (Prange, 1964; Schildkraut, 1965). Serotonin alterations were found to permit instability of catecholamine systems, leading to both manic and depressive episodes (Masoliver et al., 2006). This theory followed quite nicely from the discovery that iproniazid, a drug used to treat tuberculosis patients, actually improved depression. That drug turned out to be a nonselective monoamine oxidase (MAO) enzyme inhibitor and was found in laboratory animals to block the breakdown of norepinephrine and serotonin (Janicak et al., 2006). The earliest tricyclic antidepressants were discovered as failed drugs that did not help the psychosis of schizophrenics but did help their mood (Janicak et al., 2006). These drugs blocked reuptake of serotonin and norepinephrine into neurons that had released them, so there was more of the neurotransmitter in the synapse. The blood-pressure-lowering medicines reserpine and alpha-methyldopa, which were used many years ago, sometimes caused depression at the same time that they were lowering blood pressure (Janicak et al., 2006). These drugs depleted norepinephrine and serotonin or caused the neurons to create an inactive lookalike instead of the normal neurotransmitter. It was realized that all of the early antidepressants, which included tricyclic antidepressants and MAO inhibitors, either blocked the releasing neurons from taking the neurotransmitter back up into them or blocked the degradation of the neurotransmitters. This is their effect in the test tube, but what do they do in ill humans?

Dr. Delgado posed this question in a very clever way. He asked patients who had recovered from depression with long-term use of a medication to risk a temporary reversal of their benefit. This allowed him to test how the drugs were working to help the depression. He did two key experiments. He asked patients who had responded to an NRI to temporarily take a drug that would block norepinephrine synthesis, and showed that this caused a brief worsening of their depression. He took a different group of patients, who had responded to an SSRI, and asked them to take a mixture of amino acids that would compete with tryptophan for transport into the brain. This starved the brain of the necessary precursor of serotonin. These patients, too, experienced a brief worsening of their depression. Each of these lines of evidence supports the theory that depression is a result of insufficient amounts of norepinephrine or serotonin in the brain (Delgado, 2000, 2004; Delgado et al., 1990, 1993, 1994, 1999; Delgado, Moreno, Onate, & Gelenberg, 2002).

Further support for the serotonin deficiency theory comes from findings of low serotonin metabolite (5-HIAA) in the cerebrospinal fluid of depressed and suicidal patients, the increased density of serotonin type 2 (5-HT2) receptors on blood platelets and in autopsy brain tissue of depressed patients, and the fact that serotonin reuptake inhibitors are effective antidepressants. There are approximately 14 serotonin receptors in the brain, and only a few of these appear to be relevant to antidepressant effects. The newest imaging studies (such as positron emission tomography) show decreased numbers of serotonin neurons and transporters in depressed persons' brains (Parsey et al., 2006).

The norepinephrine deficiency theory, or catecholamine hypothesis, is supported by findings in depressed individuals of decreased norepinephrine metabolite (MHPG) in urine, plasma, and cerebrospinal fluid, and increased binding sites (indicating less neurotransmitter being available) among lymphocyte beta-adrenoreceptors. The venous blood returning from the brain of patients with treatment-refractory depression has low levels of norepinephrine and dopamine metabolite (HVA), but not 5-HIAA, compared to healthy persons (Lambert, Johansson, Agren, & Friberg, 2000).

Similarly, the dopamine theory of depression is supported by the high comorbidity of Parkinson's disease (a movement disorder with death of dopamine cells leading to tremor and slow, stiff movements) and depression. There is a change in dopamine transporter binding potential in depression (Meyer et al., 2001), and a dopamine agonist used in treating Parkinson's disease, Mirapex (pramipexole), is helpful in treatment-resistant bipolar depression (Goldberg, Burdick, & Endick, 2004; Zarate, Payne, Singh, et al., 2004). Deprenyl (selegiline), a MAO inhibitor, is useful for treatment of both Parkinson's and major depression (Frampton & Plosker, 2007c).

Some antidepressants, including Wellbutrin (bupropion), act on dopamine neurotransmission, and MAO inhibitors prevent the breakdown of dopamine. Psychostimulants such as Ritalin (methylphenidate) and amphetamine may be used to augment antidepressant treatment. Antipsychotics also affect dopamine transmission. They were originally developed for the treatment of schizophrenia and mania but are also used in the treatment of some depressed patients.

Treatment-resistant unipolar major depression may respond to the addition of Abilify (aripiprazole), which is a dopamine modulator, to an SSRI or SNRI antidepressant (Berman et al., 2007; Marcus et al., 2008). The studies demonstrating this enrolled patients who had failed to respond to prior antidepressant trials, gave them an additional trial on an SSRI or Effexor for 8 weeks, and then gave the nonresponders 6 weeks of Abilify or placebo added to their antidepressant. The remission rate on Abilify was 25%, which is better than that seen in the stage 3 treatment (of people who had failed two antidepressant trials) in the very large STAR*D study (Fava, Rush, et al., 2006; Nierenberg, Fava, et al., 2006).

The neurotransmitter theories have some major weaknesses. The first is that reuptake inhibition or blocking degradation of the neurotransmitters is an immediate effect of antidepressants, yet depression does not immediately improve when antidepressant drugs are started (rather, it takes about 2 to 6 weeks to begin to lift). This would imply that correcting a deficiency of the neurotransmitter at the synapse is not enough to treat depression and that some resulting change in the brain is required in addition. The next problem with these theories is that they are very much based on what the drug does in vitro (in the test tube) and this might not correlate closely with what is actually wrong in vivo (in the brain of a sick human). To say that a drug increases levels of serotonin or norepinephrine in a rat brain preparation does not necessarily mean that people who get better while taking the drug had a serotonin or norepinephrine deficiency in the first place. Unfortunately, we cannot readily measure levels of norepinephrine or serotonin in living people. The majority of byproducts of norepinephrine or serotonin that can be measured in the blood or urine are produced outside of the brain. The more direct measurement of these neurotransmitters would require samples of spinal fluid, and very few patients would ever volunteer for a spinal tap to obtain this.

Early antidepressants would often affect many neurotransmitters beyond norepinephrine and serotonin, and these extra effects led to undesirable side effects. Shortly after the discovery of the tricyclic anti-depressants, scientists began looking for more selective and specific drugs. The result of this was the development of drugs that had a much more specific effect on blocking the reuptake of norepinephrine or sero-tonin. The norepinephrine drugs included Norpramin, Ludiomil, and a drug that is not available in United States known as Edronax. The sero-tonin drugs included Prozac, Zoloft, Paxil, Celexa, Lexapro, and Luvox. The puzzling thing was that it was very difficult to predict which patient with pure depression would respond to norepinephrine drugs or to sero-tonin drugs. Twenty years ago, many research careers were built upon looking at norepinephrine metabolites (urinary MHPG), serotonin metabolites (cerebrospinal fluid 5-HIAA), amphetamine challenge studies, and subsequent response to various tricyclic antidepressants such as Tofranil (imipramine) or Elavil (amitriptyline), with little lasting impact on the treatment of depression because these were not robust predictors of who would preferentially respond to which drug. Psychopharmacologists' lives became more interesting when it was shown that drugs that affected both neurotransmitters (such as Anafranil, Effexor, and Cymbalta) appeared to have slightly higher remission rates than those that affect only one neurotransmitter. Dopamine may also be implicated in depression, and its levels may be increased by Wellbutrin and the MAO inhibitor antidepressants.

There are two more important theories of depression that go beyond the neurotransmitter deficiency postulate and offer a better fit with the fact that antidepressants usually take several weeks to show benefit. The theories basically posit that slow changes in the brain with chronic anti-depressant exposure involve neurotransmitter receptors and what they do when they see the neurotransmitter that they are designed to recognize.

It may be that neurotransmitter deficiency leads to changes in the number and sensitivity of receptors on the surface of neurons, and that medication intended to relieve this deficiency is only effective after the receptors have adapted to the new levels of neurotransmitter availability over a period of several weeks. Further, the binding of a neurotransmitter to its receptor may have an immediate effect (change in voltage across the membrane) but also may have a "downstream" or secondary cascade effect of turning genes on or off in the nucleus of the cell. It is likely that this story involves "neurotrophic factors" that control cell growth and survival. Indeed, antidepressants (Stahl, 2008), lithium, and Depakote (divalproex, a mood stabilizer) all cause neurons to express brain-derived neurotrophic factor (BDNF) (Hammonds, Shim, Feng, & Calabrese, 2007; Yasuda, Liang, Marinova, Yahyavij, & Chuang, 2009).

It appears that protein kinases, cyclic AMP response element-binding protein (CREB), BDNF, and glucocorticoid receptors may be altered in depression (Shelton, 2007). Antidepressants affect cytokines (part of the inflammatory response) and gene regulation in complex ways. The link between depression and increased risk of cardiovascular disease may be related to elevated c-reactive protein (CRP), a marker of underlying low-grade inflammation, in depression. This relation is much stronger in men and those with recent or recurrent depression (Ford & Erlinger, 2004). Low-dose aspirin and statins (cholesterol-lowering drugs) may help to decrease cardiovascular risk, and these are worth considering in any depressed individual who has elevated CRP, cholesterol, or other cardiovascular risks such as smoking, high blood pressure, and family history of heart disease.

Stress, Thyroid, and Sex Hormones

Another interesting theory involves stress hormone abnormalities. Cortisol, a steroid, is a stress hormone made by the adrenal glands (located just above the kidneys) in response to the pituitary (master gland at the base of the brain) releasing adrenocorticotropic hormone (ACTH). High levels of cortisol may contribute to insulin antagonism and the development of type 2 diabetes, dyslipidemia, obesity, and immune system suppression. The adrenal catecholamine release that is part of this stress response may lead to myocardial ischemia, decreased heart rate variability, and arrhythmias, as well as platelet activation and inflammation that could contribute to atherosclerosis and hypertension.

Many years ago it was discovered in research centers that patients with severe depression had unusually high levels of cortisol in their blood and 24-hour urine samples (Mossner et al., 2007). These high cortisol levels also occurred in individuals who were undergoing extremely stressful medical or psychological events. The difference between these individuals and the patients with depression, however, was that the depressed patients failed to turn off their cortisol production when they were given a potent synthetic cortisol analog. This was the basis of the dexamethasone suppression test (DST; Sher, 2006). In this test, the person was given 1 mg of dexamethasone at 11 P.M. The next day, cortisol levels were measured in the blood in the morning, afternoon, and evening. If a person had failed to turn off (suppress) their cortisol production, this was considered a biological marker of depression. This test was widely publicized and often patients would call psychiatrists to ask for a DST to determine if they had depression. Some were disappointed to hear that the test could be ordered but was not as helpful as a careful clinical interview. Over time, the test was done on patients who were medically ill, losing weight through strenuous dieting, and abusing drugs, and it was discovered that the test was not sensitive and specific enough to be widely used as a diagnostic test for depression because many of these conditions could cause false positive or false negative results.

It now appears that high cortisol levels may be a direct cause of damage to the hippocampus in chronically untreated major depression. Sheline has shown that total duration of untreated depression is correlated with shrinkage of the hippocampus (Sheline, Gado, & Kraemer, 2003). The high cortisol level may also be the cause of hippocampal damage in patients with post-traumatic stress disorder. There is great interest in using drugs that block the signals within the brain that stimulate the adrenal glands to make cortisol. There are also drugs that directly interfere with cortisol production in the adrenal glands. These drugs may be useful in treating psychotic or other forms of severe depression, but they are not yet marketed for this purpose (Gallagher et al., 2008). Experimental animal models of depression suggest that antidepressants (Haynes, Barber, & Mitchell, 2004), lithium (Angelucci, Aloe, Jimenez-Vasquez, & Mathe, 2003), electroconvulsive therapy (Holtzmann, Polosan, Baro, & Bougerol, 2007), and exercise (Vaynman, Ying, & Gomez-Pinilla, 2003), in addition to causing expression of BDNF, help to reverse the loss of hippocampal neurons caused by depression.

The thyroid axis may be of particular relevance to the pathophysiology of mood disorders (Bauer & Whybrow, 2001), not only because it serves as a dependent variable that is studied as a function of mood (as most neuroendocrine systems have been), but also because it has been studied as an independent variable of some impact. The mechanism for these effects has been the subject of much speculation. Various models posit that the brain is functionally hypothyroid due to changes in hormone synthesis, transport, or metabolism, or due to increased demand; alternatively, other models propose that the brain has an excess of a thyroid-related substance, which is diminished by administration of exogenous thyroid hormone (Bauer & Whybrow, 1990, 2001; Joffe, Singer, & Levitt, 1993).

Gender differences in the activity of neurotransmitters and their interaction with estrogen may also be at play. The hormonal approach to understanding depression in women focuses, however, on the fact that, from the start of menstruation (menarche) through the age of menopause, women tend to have much higher rates of initial episodes of major depression than men of the same age. This largely implicates the sex steroids (Frank, Novick, & Masalehdan, 2003). Clinical depression affects two to three times as many women as men—one out of every eight women during her lifetime. Women also experience higher rates of seasonal affective disorder and dysthymia than men, as well as bipolar II disorder, where depression occurs far more frequently than hypomania (Frank et al., 2003; Nonacs, 2004). In addition to higher prevalence of depression, certain symptoms are more prominent in women, including anxious mood, physical or painful symptoms, and atypical symptoms such as overeating and oversleeping. Anxiety and eating disorder comorbidities are also more common in women (Nonacs, 2004).

Among women of childbearing age, 20–40% experience premenstrual mood and behavioral changes. Between 2% and 10% of women experience premenstrual dysphoric disorder (PMDD), a severely impairing form of premenstrual syndrome (Frank et al., 2003). The highest risk period in a woman's life for having a severe depression or being psychiatrically hospitalized is the first couple of months after delivering a baby, when hormone levels shift abruptly. As many as 80% experience the postpartum blues, a brief period of mood symptoms that is considered normal following childbirth. The related hormonal and biological changes associated with pregnancy or giving birth may give way to clinical depression. Over 10% of pregnant women and around 15% of postpartum women experience depression, and there is a three-fold risk of depression during or following a pregnancy among women with a history of mood disorders. A woman who has experienced a postpartum depression carries a 70% liability of depression with a subsequent delivery (Frank et al., 2003).

As they begin to approach the menopausal years, women often have irregular menstrual periods and worsening or new onset of depression (Frank et al., 2003). Estrogen addition to a partially effective SSRI antidepressant in women with perimenopausal symptoms may improve response (Morgan, Cook, Rapkin, & Leuchter, 2005). There appears to be no gender difference in response to dual-action antidepressants such as Effexor (venlafaxine). Menstruating women are more likely to respond to SSRI than to tricyclic antidepressants, whereas postmenopausal women respond equally to both classes of drugs.

All of these factors imply that hormonal fluctuations are a major factor in triggering depression in women, and in antidepressant response. Unfortunately, one can't interpret these findings too broadly because women are socialized differently in our society, are more often the victims of physical or sexual abuse (according to Frank et al., 2003, three of five women with depressive illnesses have been abuse victims), often receive lower pay and recognition than men in similar jobs, and suffer many other forms of discrimination. In men, the decline of testosterone with normal aging is very gradual, and sometimes testosterone replacement therapy, given to a man with low testosterone levels, can be a valuable addition to antidepressant treatment.

Psychological Theories

Early psychoanalytic theories hypothesized that depression was a result of internalized anger due to unconscious conflicts. Increasing insight into the origins of these conflicts, based on understanding early development and transference issues (feelings and expectations from the past projected onto the therapist) was the means of treatment, which was often unstructured and not time-limited. Because treatment was intensive (often four to five times a week) and prolonged over years, very few people could afford it and insurance companies often refused to pay for it. The modern approach to psychodynamically oriented psychotherapy still makes the assumptions that symptoms have meaning to the individual, that very early relationships with caregivers shape how we perceive important others in adult life (such as authorities and loved ones), and that insights into unconscious conflicts and transference projections can help to achieve a much clearer understanding of how we deal with the people and problems in our lives now.

Behavior therapy was based upon the theory that depressed individuals lack specific skills to engage in rewarding activities, and lacking positive reinforcement from relationships and activities was a central issue. Cognitive-behavioral therapy initially focused on rigid rules with "shoulds" and "musts" and a sense that failure to act in accordance with these unreasonable demands would result in catastrophic outcomes. Aaron Beck expanded the theory to state that specific patterns of thinking in response to environmental stimuli involved automatic thoughts, which are derived from intermediate beliefs, which are assumptions about the self, the world, and the future. He stated that schemas were underlying cognitive structures that organize information, attention, and memory. The therapist could assist the patient to observe, discover, explore, and use logic and hypothesis testing to change automatic thoughts, intermediate beliefs, and cognitive schemas (Beck, Rush, Shaw, & Emery, 1979). Beck's approach has revolutionized psychotherapy over the last several decades, making it a more focused, structured, and time-limited collaborative endeavor than the previous tradition of long-term exploratory psychoanalytic therapy.

Interpersonal therapy focuses on problems in interpersonal relationships with origins in early development. Relationship patterns can be explored, with skills training, education, and role-playing to enhance the individual's ability to cope with grief, disputes, role transitions, and interpersonal deficits.

Both cognitive-behavioral therapy and interpersonal therapy are focused, goal-oriented, present-oriented, and time-limited, with active therapist involvement and homework assignments.

Unfortunately, we can't really say why a person becomes depressed at a particular time in his life. The complex interaction of genes, childhood development (and possibly trauma or neglect), learned coping styles, support systems (or lack of them), ongoing stressors, and factors involving hormones and neurotransmitters are far too complex to allow any "one size fits all" theory of depression's cause. At best, a good clinician tries to formulate what biopsychosocial factors are operating in a given individual to trigger or perpetuate the presenting episode of depression. These factors are then used to synthesize a rational treatment plan, which often includes both psychological and biological interventions.

4

What Is "Me" and What Is "Illness"? Personality Versus Mood Disorder

Personality traits are formed in childhood and are persistent, pervasive ways of viewing and relating to the self and the world. Maladaptive eccentricities, emotional displays, and fearfulness can get in the way of getting along with others, and may be more common in people with depression. Psychotherapy can help to increase self-awareness and change old patterns.

Much of personality is formed in early childhood through interactions with parents, teachers, clergy, and other caretakers, who have a profound influence on a child's sense of security and being a good, lovable, worthwhile person who is capable of meeting life's challenges and getting needs met. Personality evolves through a lifetime of experiences with learning mastery of new situations. A healthy personality involves a sense of being worthy of love, capable of learning new things, and mastering life's challenges in work and relationships, able to relax and play, and able to experience close, loving relationships and a sense of trust with family and friends. One also feels able to adapt to life's changes and challenges. Unfortunately, not all of us receive this kind of parenting or develop these attitudes and skills as we grow up. Some children are told that they are incompetent, unlovable, unworthy, a failure, stupid, or ugly, and they grow up feeling dependent, victimized, angry, hostile, or aloof from the rest of the world. They may feel different from the rest of the human race, unable to connect with people, and unable to experience a sense of enjoyment and pleasure from relationships and work.

We sometimes meet people who come in and say that they don't know what it feels like to be "normal." They've had very chronic depression or unhappiness throughout most of their lives. Often they are skeptical about whether an antidepressant medication or psychotherapy can do them any good. They may be pleasantly surprised if they do get relief with treatment from some of their long-standing suffering. The question often comes up, "To what extent is being unhappy a part of who I am, and to what extent is it a symptom of illness?" Is stigma interfering with seeking treatment, or is there a realistic self-appraisal that long-standing unhappiness is unlikely to change? Though artificial constructs such as carefully circumscribed diagnoses cannot easily tease out where the illness ends and the person begins, people with long-standing, maladaptive, pervasive ways of viewing themselves and the world are often diagnosed as having personality disorder. Their place in the overall diagnostic picture is described in this chapter.

Personality as Described in *DSM-IV*

The *DSM-IV* divides psychiatric diagnosis into five separate, semi-independent axes. Axis I is the acute psychiatric disorder. Examples of Axis I diagnoses are major depression, dysthymic disorder, bipolar affective disorder, alcohol abuse, or panic disorder. These disorders usually have a relatively clear-cut onset, cause distressing symptoms or impairment in everyday functioning, and are obvious to the person who suffers from them. They are usually the main focus of pharmacologic treatment and the initial focus of psychotherapy. Axis II diagnoses involve personality. Axis II is used to list predominant maladaptive personality features or psychological defense mechanisms, which may or may not meet full criteria for a personality disorder diagnosis. It is also where mental retardation is coded. The other axes of the *DSM-IV* include Axis III, which is where medical problems are coded, Axis IV, where psychosocial life stressors are listed, and Axis V, where the global assessment of functioning in terms of current functional ability is coded.

Whereas illnesses coded on Axis I comprise clusters of symptoms, Axis II personality disorders are defined by characteristics or traits. People living with personality disorders do experience symptoms associated with disorders classified on Axis I. Although this overlap may confuse or complicate diagnosis, the diagnostician knows that personality disorders are essentially defined as enduring patterns of inner experience and behavior that differ from the expectations of the culture. As a more or less stable and ongoing pattern is required for diagnosis, personality disorders are only diagnosed in persons 18 years and older. These patterns may appear as cognitive problems related to the perception of oneself, other people, and events. They may involve problems with the range of intensity and appropriateness of emotional responses and affect. There may be problems in interpersonal functioning or impulse control. In order to be diagnosed with a personality disorder, the individual must have a long-standing, inflexible, pervasive pattern of maladaptive functioning that occurs repeatedly across a wide range of personal and social or occupational areas and causes impairment or distress. These stable, long-standing patterns often date back to adolescence or early adulthood. Personality disorders are grouped into three clusters: odd or eccentric (cluster A); dramatic, emotional, or erratic (cluster B); and anxious or fearful (cluster C).

On a more informal basis, personality disorders are often considered problems that bother those around the patient more than the patient herself. The patient will often say that people don't understand, are mean, are unfair, and that situations are constantly stacked against her. People who have a personality disorder very seldom say that their personality characteristics bother them, yet they may be quite aware that they don't get along in the world as well as other people do. They are aware that relationships don't work out, that they are passed up for promotions, that they have few friends, or that they are more needy, arrogant, or dramatic than other people. They may complain that there are many frustrations in jobs and close relationships, with repeated and unexpected disappointments or rejections. Getting fired or having a relationship end often prompts the response of "I did nothing wrong, and I didn't deserve it." Life seems unfair.

Often the simplest clue to diagnosing a personality style or disorder is to simply ask the patient, "How would you describe your personality most of your adult life? How would others who know you well describe you?" Another key question is, "Are there any themes or patterns of problems that keep recurring in your romantic or work relationships?"

The greatest mistake we see among clinicians is either to ignore personality issues completely—with a sense that "there's nothing that can be done about personality disorders so why bother to diagnose them?"—or to assume that a personality disorder diagnosis can't be made until the characteristic interaction styles emerge in the long-term relationship with the therapist. In either case, the therapist's failure to get the history of past relationship problems and patterns, and experiences with previous therapists, leaves the treatment open to unnecessary surprises. An extreme example would be the avoidant or schizoid individual who needs a great deal of emotional reassurance and warmth to prevent a lack of connection with the therapist, leading to a rapid termination of therapy due to the sense that the therapeutic relationship has nothing helpful to offer. At the other extreme would be the borderline personality disorder patient whose lack of clear boundaries necessitates consistent and firm limit-setting in the therapeutic relationship to prevent dramatic "overconnection" with intense dependency and demands for frequent extra time from the therapist to handle life's many crises.

DSM-IV Personality Disorders

The cluster A personality disorders include paranoid, schizoid, and schizotypal. The paranoid personality disorder displays long-standing distrust and suspiciousness and looks at others as having evil motives. People with paranoid personality demonstrate four or more characteristics including suspecting others of trying to exploit, harm, or deceive them; questioning loyalty and trustworthiness; reluctance to confide in others because the information may be used against them; seeing threatening meaning in others' comments; bearing grudges; overreading attacks on their character or reputation; and being suspicious of sexual partners' loyalty. When such an individual presents for treatment, it is often at the request of others, because the individual involved believes that her perception of the situation is accurate. She truly believes that people cannot be trusted and will repeatedly try to betray her or take advantage of her. Such a person lives a very lonely and isolated life, because she is always on guard for harm from others. Such individuals are very reluctant to take antipsychotic medications, and there is very little proof that they are effective. They are equally reluctant to become engaged in psychotherapy because the same mistrust of friends and lovers carries through to mistrust of the therapist.

People with schizoid personality disorder are extremely detached from social relationships and have a restricted range of emotions. They have four or more of the following symptoms: not wanting or enjoying close relationships; choosing solitary activities; having little interest in sexual experiences with another person; taking little pleasure in activities; lacking close friends; appearing indifferent to praise or criticism; and appearing cold and detached. Again, there is little evidence that medications are of any benefit to such people, and psychotherapy can be difficult because of the person's lack of desire to relate to other people.

People with schizotypal personality disorder have social and interpersonal problems, discomfort, difficulty in close relationships, and odd or eccentric behavior. They may have ideas that others are talking about them, odd beliefs or magical thinking, unusual perceptions, odd thinking and speech, suspiciousness, constricted affect, peculiar behavior or appearance, lack of close friends, and social anxiety that does not resolve with repeated contact. Some genetic studies have suggested that schizotypal personality disorder may be genetically linked to schizophrenia, and occasionally such an individual will demonstrate benefit from a low dose of antipsychotic medication.

The cluster B personality disorders include antisocial, histrionic, narcissistic, and borderline personality disorders. Antisocial personality disorder is characterized by a pervasive pattern of disregard for, and violation of, the rights of others with at least three additional criteria including unlawful behavior, deceitfulness, impulsivity, irritability or aggressiveness, disregard for the safety of self or others, irresponsibility at work or in financial obligations, and lack of remorse for hurting other people. The antisocial person is unlikely to benefit from medications or from psychotherapy but may demonstrate some ability to learn when brought into therapy by others who have been harmed by the person's behavior or who threaten to leave her because of it. Sometimes treatment is court-ordered as a condition of probation for criminal charges.

The person with histrionic personality disorder is excessively emotional and attention-seeking and demonstrates at least five of the following criteria: She (most often it is a woman) is uncomfortable when not the center of attention, seems seductive or provocative, shows shifting or shallow emotions, uses physical appearance to draw attention to herself, is impressionistic and lacking in detail when speaking, is self-dramatizing or theatrical, is suggestible, and often considers relationships to be more intimate than they actually are. Again, there is no medication treatment that is proven effective for such individuals, but in this case psychotherapy may be quite helpful because the person is very interpersonally related and has difficulty understanding others' reactions to her behavior.

People with narcissistic personality disorder demonstrate a need for admiration and a lack of empathy for others. There are at least five other characteristics present: The narcissist has a grandiose sense of her own importance; is preoccupied with fantasies of her own success, power, brilliance, beauty, or love; feels very special and unique; requires admiration; has a sense of entitlement; exploits others; lacks empathy; envies others; and is arrogant and haughty.

Perhaps the most important cluster B personality disorder is borderline personality disorder (BPD). This is the person who is most likely to seek both psychotherapy and medications to deal with chronic misery. BPD is characterized by unstable relationships and affect, with impulsivity, an unclear sense of self, and resulting lack of boundaries. The person living with BPD has five or more of the following characteristics: frantic efforts to avoid real or imagined abandonment; unstable intense relationships that may include idealization and devaluation (he's wonderful early on, then he's worthless later); unstable sense of self and identity; impulsivity in multiple areas; repeated suicidal behavior, gestures or threats; repeated episodes of self-harm (such as cutting or burning); extremely reactive mood with intense depression, irritability, or anxiety that is short-lived; chronic feelings of emptiness; intense anger; and stress-related paranoia or dissociation. This diagnosis is extremely important because it is often made in individuals who have chronic depression. Sometimes it is made when the therapist becomes very frustrated and angry at the patient due to numerous middle-of-the-night lengthy crisis telephone calls. Sometimes it is made when the therapist feels overwhelmed by the patient's intense neediness and anger. Often the emergency room psychiatrist makes it when the patient shows up with repeated wrist cutting or drug overdoses in response to romantic rejections. The diagnosis, which can be highly stigmatizing—to the point of affecting the patient's access to some social services—should be made only after a very detailed long-term history of difficult relationships has been obtained. This personality disorder may actually show benefit from symptom-specific treatment with antidepressants, mood stabilizers, and antipsychotic medications targeting the four domains of anxiety, depression, impulsivity and irritability, and thought disorder. In addition, long-term psychotherapy dealing with changing cognitions and behaviors and coping with feelings that arise in the course of close relationships and other stressful situations is essential for optimal response.

Case Example: Rachel

Rachel came to see me at age 35. She told me she'd been treated by a series of psychiatric residents at a teaching hospital who rotated each year and now she wanted someone stable. She had never been married, had no children, and was on long-term disability. She had suffered from chronic depression for 16 years, had recently refused ECT when it was recommended, and had a sister chronically institutionalized with schizophrenia. She lived with her mother, who had chronic medical problems. She had issues of low self-esteem, body image distortion, and childhood incest and molestation, and she had worked on these for about 20 years with a psychotherapist who was treating her at no charge. She would isolate herself, act hostile toward others, and alienate them. She reported a history of multiple medication failures on antidepressants of every type, mood stabilizers, major and minor tranquilizers, and stimulants. She had mild high periods, panic attacks that were stress-related, worries about her weight and appearance, and a history of bulimia and anorexia. She described herself as moody with low self-esteem, but intelligent, sometimes hostile, and snappy. In addition to meeting the diagnostic criteria for bipolar affective disorder, panic disorder, and bulimia and anorexia, Rachel met most of the criteria for BPD. She had made frantic efforts to avoid abandonment, but she rejected other people first. She had extremely unstable relationships with idealization and devaluation. She had a lack of stable sense of who she was. She was impulsive in areas of sex, driving, and binge eating. She had repeatedly self-mutilated but indicated that when she talked about suicide it was really a plea for other people to do something. She had affective instability, feelings of emptiness, intense anger and hostility, and temper problems, as well as transient paranoia and dissociation.

Over 12 years of working with me, Rachel repeatedly felt depressed, hopeless, suicidal, frustrated with not getting better, and unwilling to go into a hospital except when very severely depressed. She repeatedly showed up late for appointments or not at all, and yet always wanted much more time than we had scheduled and often stayed in the office talking to the secretary and waiting to ask a few more questions when I had finished up with my next patient. As is common for clinicians treating BPD patients, I felt that I had tried my very best to use all of my skills and yet nothing really helped, nothing was ever enough for her needs. She had persistent overwhelming anxiety, insomnia, depression, suicidal feelings, and conveyed tremendous neediness.

Finally, Rachel went into an intensive day treatment program and connected with a therapist there who was very caring but also very confrontational. He told Rachel that her life was truly frustrating and miserable and acknowledged that she had no joy and felt no purpose for living. She was self-loathing and self-abusive and burned people out. He told her that she had to take some responsibility for really changing in many ways.

After working with Rachel for about 8 months, this new therapist completed his rotation at the day treatment program and offered to work with her in his private practice if she would get a part-time job and pay for treatment. Once again, Rachel felt overwhelmed and said that this was an impossible demand, so therapy with him ended. She felt fragmented, regressed, emotionless, and abandoned by the therapist.

In the end, Rachel truly needed a team effort for any reasonable chance of successful treatment: a pharmacologist for medicines; a confrontive, directive therapist to deal with her childhood trauma issues and their impact on her adult life, as well as support from that therapist (and family) to keep her alive while doing all this hard work; and a series of support groups to enable some social connections with people dealing with similar mood and molestation issues. No one therapist could possibly do it all.

The cluster C personality disorders include avoidant, dependent, and obsessive-compulsive. The avoidant personality is characterized by social inhibition and feelings of inadequacy and being oversensitive to others. Four or more features are required for the diagnosis: avoiding work that requires contact with people; being unwilling to get involved with people without reassurance of being liked; remaining restrained in close relationships because of fear of shame or ridicule; being preoccupied with criticism or rejection from others; being inhibited because of feelings of inadequacy; viewing oneself as inept, unappealing, or inferior; and being reluctant to take personal risks or try new things out of fear that they may be embarrassing.

The dependent personality disorder individual needs to be taken care of, even to the point of being submissive and clingy. She has at least five of the following features: difficulty making everyday decisions without advice and reassurance; a need for others to assume responsibility for most areas of life; difficulty expressing disagreement due to fear of loss of others' support or approval; difficulty initiating projects and doing things because of lack of self-confidence; extreme attempts to obtain nurturance and support from others; feeling uncomfortable or helpless when alone, with a sense of being unable to take care of herself; urgently seeking a new relationship when an old caretaking relationship ends; and preoccupation with fear of being left to take care of herself.

Obsessive-compulsive personality disorder (OCPD) describes an individual who is preoccupied with orderliness, perfectionism, and control, at the expense of flexibility, openness, and efficiency, with at least four of the following features: preoccupation with details, rules, lists, and order, to the extent that the major point of activities is lost; perfectionism; "workaholic" behavior; being overly conscientious and scrupulous around moral and ethical issues; hoarding objects that are worn out or that lack personal value or meaning; being reluctant to delegate tasks or work unless others do things exactly her way; miserliness; and rigidity or stubbornness. Usually the person with OCPD believes that there is nothing wrong with her and that her personality traits are a key part of being successful in life. This is very different from OCD, in which there are intrusive, repulsive, unwanted thoughts, images, or impulses that are embarrassing because they seem foreign to the person's values. OCD is usually associated with compulsive, time-consuming, repetitive rituals that are very distressing.

Why Diagnose Personality Disorders?

As many as 64% of depressed outpatients meet criteria for at least one personality disorder (Fava et al., 2002), and this comorbidity doubles the risk of a poor outcome for the person's depression treatment (Newton-Howes, Tyrer, & Johnson, 2006). On the bright side, many of the behaviors and attitudes stemming from personality disorders are improved with successful pharmacotherapy, so when the depression lifts, patients may also find they meet fewer criteria for the personality disorder diagnosis. This is particularly the case with avoidant, dependent, passive-aggressive, paranoid, and narcissistic personality disorder diagnoses (Fava et al., 2002).

Drugs may help some of the mood, anxiety, and anger symptoms of the individual with a personality disorder, but they are not enough to achieve optimal response. Psychotherapy may help the individual living with a personality disorder challenge deeply held long-standing beliefs and to change long-term behavior patterns.

The reason for describing the personality disorders in such detail is not to imply that they cannot be helped. The goal is to promote recognition of these patterns of thinking, behaving, and feeling so that when they become problematic and cause suffering, they can be recognized and appropriate psychotherapy can begin. These discrete, consistent, widely accepted heuristics of clustered traits are also necessary for research into epidemiology and new treatment modalities. Although some psychotherapists may be skeptical about changing long-standing personality patterns, those involved in doing long-term psychoanalytic psychotherapy believe that long-term approaches in which the personality style is portrayed through development of transference reactions to the therapist may allow the patient to take a very close look at the assumptions and beliefs brought into a relationship based on childhood experiences. By reexperiencing these with the therapist, patients may become consciously aware of the patterns, which can then be changed. The cognitive-behavioral psychotherapist would ask the patient to try to look carefully inside herself whenever experiencing intense feelings in a relationship and try to identify the underlying thoughts and assumptions that are being triggered. The therapist would then ask the individual to look at alternative explanations and test their validity in hopes of facilitating long-term change.

No one should have to go through life assuming that she is any less entitled to the pursuit of health and happiness in satisfying relationships and career than anyone else. People who view themselves as unable to achieve these things because life is unfair or because they lack the self-confidence and social skills to aggressively pursue their major goals may benefit tremendously from psychotherapy.

5

Staying Alive: Dealing With Suicidal Thoughts and Impulses

The ultimate "complication" of severe depression is suicide. Prevention involves preparing for tough times by building a solid support system of family, friends, and treating clinicians, and being willing to reach out and ask for help in times of need. Depression causes "tunnel vision" that blocks effective problem-solving. Hospitalization is sometimes a necessary protection against self-harm.

Suicide is the 11th most common cause of death in the general population, and the third most in young adults. According to the Centers for Disease Control (CDC), it took the lives of 30,622 persons in the United States in 2001 alone. Long-term follow-up studies have shown that individuals who have been hospitalized for depression may have a risk as high as 10–15% for ultimately dying by suicide (Carroll-Ghosh, Victor, & Bourgeois, 2003). Some estimates are that these individuals have about a 1% annual risk of dying by suicide (Carroll-Ghosh et al., 2003). We believe everything possible should be done to prevent this tragic outcome.

Why Suicide?

There are many theories about why an individual would get to the desperate point of taking his own life, and why some view death by suicide as a solution to life problems. Unfortunately, the solution is permanent, and the problems are almost always temporary. Some explain suicide with a theory often used to explain depression: They view suicide as anger that is truly directed toward someone else but has been turned inward. Sometimes a person may so upset an individual that the only way to show others how badly he feels is to threaten suicide. The classic example was the rejected mistress in the movie *Fatal Attrac-*

tion, who cut her wrist to show her distress. The solution of suicide is really only one of many choices about life's dilemmas, but depression often puts on blinders that block out the healthier choices. The situation may seem terribly painful when a depressed person feels anxious and agitated, can't get to sleep, and experiences physical pain as well as emotional suffering. All of these may seem inescapable because there is no apparent way out. The key issue is to recognize that depression interferes with healthy, rational problem-solving.

People who have a more objective understanding of the situation, such as therapists, family members, or pastors, may see many options other than suicide. Some of the options may be tough. They may involve acknowledging a mistake in judgment or behavior, admitting a failure or flaw, entering a chemical dependency program, or making a major life change such as leaving a stressful job or abusive relationship. But all of these options are far better than death. Certainly they are far better than the other possible outcomes of a suicide attempt, which may include hospitalization or long-term disability. We have seen some people whose failed suicide attempt resulted in paralysis or permanent brain damage, leaving them totally disabled and dependent upon others for the remainder of their lives.

Risk Factors

> *I feel certain that I'm going mad again. I feel we can't go through another of those terrible times. And I shan't recover this time. I begin to hear voices.*
>
> Suicide note—Virginia Woolf, author, d. March 28, 1941

We know many of the risk factors that increase the chances of suicide. To remember the greatest risk factors where suicide is concerned, some clinicians use the mnemonic SAD PERSONS: Sex, Age, Depression (especially with global insomnia, severe anhedonia, severe anxiety, agitation, and panic attacks), Previous attempt, Ethanol (alcohol) use, Rational thought loss, Social supports lacking, Organized plan, No spouse, and Sickness.

A feeling of hopelessness, that things cannot get better, is a key psychological indicator. Psychotic symptoms, such as hallucinations of voices telling the person he would be better off dead or commanding him to hurt himself, are danger signals. Delusions, such as a healthy person believing he has a terrible painful terminal illness, are very dangerous. Those diagnosed with BPD may frequently attempt suicide. The bipolar mixed state with both profoundly depressed mood and highly agitated, anxious, and restless feelings is a high-risk state. Being both depressed and anxious, especially with panic attacks, also represents a high-risk state. In these cases, medication to decrease both the intensely painful arousal and the depression is critically important.

Certain demographic factors also place an individual at greater risk of suicide. It has long been known that elderly, single, unemployed, socially isolated males are at higher risk for suicide. Older men, in fact, have the highest suicide rates of anyone; young men (ages 19–25) have the fastest-rising incidence. Although three times as many women as men report a history of attempted suicide, men are three to seven times more likely to succeed. Old age presents a general risk for those who have little money, growing health problems, a lack of social support, and are thinking existentially about what the future holds. There is particular concern for individuals with alcohol or drug abuse, as well as those with life-threatening or disabling illnesses. People with Huntington's chorea have seen other family members with the same illness die after a prolonged, disabling downhill course of uncontrollable movements and dementia, and therefore they are at very high risk of suicide. Likewise, people who have lost friends to AIDS, or to metastatic cancer, and now have a similar illness themselves may be at very high risk as they see their own bodies failing them. Individuals who are socially isolated and lack a network of family and friends, as well as structure to their everyday activities, are at greater risk because of a lack of connection to the world or perceived purpose for living.

Psychological factors may also play a role in suicide. The person who experiences humiliating discipline or a loss of face followed by feelings of worthlessness, shame, or disgrace may be at risk of suicide. Examples would be a teenager who has been kicked out of school for cheating or selling drugs or who has suffered denigration by peers, a businessman facing jail for fraud, or a church-going family man whose adultery is about to be revealed. Sometimes a loss of a major relationship, especially if there is an active rejection by the significant other, will trigger a sense of hopelessness and a desire to die rather than suffer through a prolonged and painful grieving period. Sometimes a loss of status such as losing a high-paying job to which an individual has devoted many years can precipitate suicidal feelings. The loss may be a result of company down-sizing, voluntary retirement, or being fired. In one sense, the reason doesn't really matter because the loss of the daily routine and income, contact with friends, and sense of being important and valued damages the person's sense of identity and value as a human, which are tied in with the job. It is important to note that jobs aren't always the same thing as employment: A woman who has spent over 20 years as a wife and mother raising children may face the same loss of her role and identity when the last child moves out and her husband asks for a divorce; suddenly the meaning and purpose of her life have been taken away.

Everyone thinks about death at times. Teenagers may be more preoc-cupied with it than most adults. The elderly are often confronted with it when they lose a partner or friend. Most of us don't think about taking our own life, and if the thought were to pass through our mind, we would quickly reject it. The depressed person may not reject suicidal thoughts so easily, because death looks like a better option than continued suffering. This is why thoughts about suicide are so dangerous in the context of depression.

Coping With Suicidal Ideas

The person experiencing suicidal ideas needs encouragement and support from people who care. He may need the external structure of family, friends, or hospital staff watching carefully to prevent him from acting on his self-destructive impulses.

Shoring Up Supports

When suicidal thoughts begin going through a person's mind, the first and most important thing is to rally the support system. This means telling family and friends, telling the psychiatrist and psychotherapist, telling the members of a support group or a 12-step meeting, telling the pastor, and staying very active and connected with other people. Sometimes it means having a family member or friend stay with the person during the high-risk time. It always means getting the potential means of suicide, such as drugs or guns, out of the house. If these measures aren't enough, going to a hospital can provide temporary relief and safety.

Anyone coping with suicidal thoughts should have a support system in place. Some of the best options include individual or family therapy at least once a week during crisis times, a support group with at least a few names and phone numbers of people willing to be called in case of a crisis, a spiritual or religious group (for example, Bible study or meditation group), and a few close friends with whom tough times can be shared.

Clinicians seeing clients who suffer from depression must remain on high alert. Burns (1999) found that clinicians evaluating depressed patients often miss patients' suicidality. It is an unfortunate fact that most people who are considering suicide do not report it to their clinicians, and most of these same patients are not asked about it (Li, 2007). More than half of people who kill themselves visit a physician in the 6 months before they die, and almost a third of them in the week before the suicide (Li, 2007). Not all patients with suicidal feelings will put a support system in place, especially those with serious plans who are considering lethal means. It is important to regularly (at each visit) evaluate depressed patients for suicidality. Recognize also that suicidality is for many a signal of poor problem-solving skills. The treating clinician may choose to downplay suicidality while emphasizing problem-solving and emotional tolerance. Therapy can address the three *I*s: interminable, intolerable, and inescapable.

Hospitalization

Hospitalization may be voluntary or involuntary. It is important for patients to realize that if they call their therapist, best friend, or crisis hotline and say that they are considering suicide, the person hearing this will probably feel that the highest priority is keeping the patient alive. Sometimes that means sending a psychiatric emergency team or police officer to evaluate the person for emergency involuntary hospitalization.

Although this may seem like an extreme response, there is a very good chance that it will allow for a cooling-down period in which healthier coping approaches to the acute crisis can be developed. Most people who are involuntarily hospitalized feel grateful later that people cared enough to do something about their safety.

Psychiatric hospitals used to be called asylums because they were places that the person could go to get away from the demands of life for a few weeks or even months. As recently as 20 years ago, this was still true, especially at private sanitariums. Now, unfortunately, managed care and insurance exert very strong pressure on hospitals and doctors to discharge patients as quickly as possible. With short-term hospitalizations often averaging less than a week, patients frequently leave the hospital almost as depressed as when entering, because psychiatric medications very seldom improve depression within that period of time. Hopefully, the impact of the immediate crisis has lessened, and there is a good aftercare plan in place. The main use for hospitalization now may be providing a protective and safe environment during a very agitated and suicidal time, allowing for a comprehensive medical workup to evaluate the possible impact of physical illness, achieving detoxification from abusable drugs, affording an opportunity to eliminate nonessential prescription drugs that might be contributing to depression, and allowing the time to obtain multiple specialist consultations quickly. The short time spent in the hospital may be much more of an intensive evaluation period than a respite from the demands of life. It also provides what some patients cannot receive at home: safety monitoring, a regulated daily schedule, encouragement in performing one's activities of daily living (bathing, grooming, etc.), help with avoiding social isolation, and a warm meal at regular intervals.

Treatment in the hospital may be very different from outpatient care. Often group therapies far outnumber individual therapy sessions, if the latter are offered at all. Some hospitals offer occupational therapy, exercise class, or art therapy. In these sessions, some people benefit and others have a very hard time opening up with strangers, especially if they seem "sicker" or are from a different socioeconomic or cultural group. It is very important at the start of a hospitalization to try to clarify the probable duration and reasonable goals of the admission with the attending physician.

Many hospitals now offer partial hospitalization, or day treatment programs, in which a patient goes to the hospital for 4 to 6 hours a day, 3 to 5 days a week, for treatment that involves individual and group psychotherapies, medication management, educational classes on coping with illness, and some social and recreational activities. Because the patient is living at home, such programs are far less costly than inpatient treatment and often provide a very useful bridge between weekly outpatient therapy sessions and 24-hour-a-day inpatient treatment. Partial hospital programs may have programs such as those specializing in dual diagnosis (a psychiatric diagnosis plus substance abuse) or in depressed persons with eating disorders. Day treatment programs are a very good option for people who are having trouble coping yet want to avoid going into an inpatient hospital program.

Antidepressants and Suicide

The recent FDA "black box" warnings that antidepressants may increase suicidality in children and adolescents or young adults up to age 24 years may scare some clinicians and some patients to the point that they will not take (or allow their child to take) medication that is desperately needed. A controversial but tragic implication of the black box warning has been a growing reluctance on the part of nonpsychiatric physicians to diagnose and treat depression in children and adolescents, with increased rates of death by suicide since the warning came out in the United States (Gibbons, Brown, Hur, Marcus, Bhaumik, Erkens, et al., 2007; Libby et al., 2007; Valuck et al., 2007; Valuck, Libby, Sills, Giese, & Allen, 2004). In fact, a major study covering over 65,000 patients treated on antidepressants showed that it is the month before starting treatment that is the time of highest risk of suicide attempt, and patients beginning psychotherapy or antidepressants show a suicide risk that is high in the first month, with decreases in risk over time of treatment (Simon & Savarino, 2007). An increased risk of suicide after starting antidepressant medication was seen only with the older antidepressants, and not after starting treatment with those newer drugs that were the subject of the FDA warning (Simon, Savarino, Operskalski, & Wang, 2006).

One key point is that the studies that came to the attention of the FDA showed an increase, compared to placebo, of suicidal thoughts or gestures—not death by suicide. Suicidal ideation is common, but suicide is not: 10 million people have suicidal ideation each year, but only 30,000 (0.3%) commit suicide. There are an estimated 8 to 25 attempted suicides for each suicide death (Li, 2007). The black box warning has been amended accordingly to indicate that depression itself is associated with suicide risk and that patients over age 65 show a decrease in suicidal ideation upon starting antidepressants.

Interestingly, an analysis of over 23,000 patients treated in placebo-controlled trials through 2001 showed no difference in rates of suicide deaths or attempts at suicide between antidepressant-treated and placebo-treated groups (Khan, Khan, Leventhal, & Brown, 2001). A meta-analysis that synthesized results from 27 placebo-controlled studies of antidepressant use in persons under age 19 suffering from major depression, OCD, or other anxiety disorders concluded that anti-depressants are efficacious and that benefits are much greater than the risks regardless of diagnosis (Bridge et al., 2007). Data from the United States, Japan, Sweden, Nordic countries, Israel, England, Ireland, the Netherlands, and Australia have shown consistent, long-term statistical correlations: The greater the number of new-generation antidepressant prescriptions dispensed per person per year in each country, the lower the rate of death by suicide (Barak & Aizenberg, 2006; Bridge et al., 2007; Carlsten, Waern, Ekedahl, & Ranstam, 2001; Gibbons, Brown, Hur, Marcus, Bhaumik, Erkens, et al., 2007; Gibbons, Brown, Hur, Marcus, Bhaumik, & Mann, 2007; Gibbons, Hur, Bhaumik, & Mann, 2005, 2006; Grunebaum, Ellis, Li, Oquendo, & Mann, 2004; Henriksson & Isacsson, 2006; Isacsson, Boethius, & Bergman, 1992; Isacsson & Rich, 2005; Kelly, Ansari, Rafferty, & Stevenson, 2003; Millane, Suchard, Wong, & Licinio, 2006; Morgan, Griffiths, & Majeed, 2004; Nakagawa et al., 2007; Reseland, Bray, & Gunnell, 2006).

Clearly, untreated depression is a killer. Antidepressants save lives, and the black box warning should serve as a reminder to monitor depressed patients carefully at the start of treatment. The first few weeks of antidepressant treatment may be associated with multiple side effects before the onset of benefit, and often initial agitation, anxiety, or insomnia can worsen suicidal ideation. If these occur, call the doctor immediately! They can be managed.

Suicide Prevention

We believe that any individual who sometimes gets to the point of thinking about suicide should act preventively. Eliminating the possible means of suicide is the first step. Getting rid of guns, poisons, weapons, and old prescription drugs is an initial safety measure. Making a clear and binding agreement (no-suicide contract) with the doctor, the psychotherapist, family members, the 12-step sponsor, and the clergyman and reaching out and calling for help when feeling desperate are important steps. Finally, recognizing the impact of suicide on those who are left behind is critically important. Children who have a parent that committed suicide grow up feeling abandoned and believing that they were unworthy of being raised by the parent; they also may feel that the suicide gives them "permission" to commit suicide themselves if things get too tough in the future. Even when the surviving family member denies it, there is always some element of guilt, self-blame, or lingering sense that "if only I had done . . . he might not have died."

Outpatient Treatment for Suicide Prevention

It is important to recognize that medications may help alleviate suicidal thoughts and feelings. The most clear-cut evidence is that lithium decreases risk of suicidality in both bipolar affective disorder and recurrent major depression (Cipriani, Pretty, Hawton, & Geddes, 2005; Guzzetta, Tondo, Centorrino, & Baldessarini, 2007). Clozapine shows similar benefit for schizophrenic individuals. The Treatment of Adolescent Depression Study (TADS) has shown that the addition of cognitive-behavioral therapy to fluoxetine confers protection (March et al., 2007).

Regarding overdose, the tricyclic antidepressants and MAO inhibitors are potentially dangerous drugs, as a month's supply or less can cause death if taken at once. The SSRIs and other new-generation antidepressants are far safer in overdose.

We all experience impulses at times, whether they are pleasurable and affectionate or aggressive and harmful, and it is the ability to decide whether to act on them that makes us moral human beings. Disinhibition is the state of losing our thoughtful rational judgment and acting on impulses. There is a concern that benzodiazepine minor tranquilizers such as Xanax, Klonopin, Valium, and others may disinhibit impulsive, aggressive behavior and might worsen the risk of self-harm or an impulsive suicide attempt much like alcohol might. Alcohol is especially dangerous because of the combination of worsening depression and removing inhibitions against acting on feelings; benzodiazepines are also central nervous system depressants, and they, too, can worsen depression if taken chronically. For these reasons, most psychiatrists recommend very limited or no alcohol use and very limited as-needed (PRN) use of minor tranquilizers during severe depressive episodes.

Like all clinicians who have been in practice for several years, we have had the painful experience of treating people who have taken or attempted to take their own lives. We tell some of their stories here to show what can lead to this tragic outcome, with the hope that readers might learn from them.

Case Example: Jane

Jane was a 42-year-old single woman who had worked in advertising and marketing most of her life. She presented with a lifelong history of depression that had recently led her to go on disability and move in with her parents. Shortly before presenting for treatment, Jane had made an overdose attempt by taking sleeping pills and putting a plastic bag over her head, and she was immediately hospitalized.

Jane's mother had been treated for depression and had made four suicide attempts but was now stable. One brother had died of AIDS and four brothers required treatment for mood disorders. Jane had experienced her first depressive episode at age 17, and over the last 5 years her depression had never been fully gone. My initial diagnosis for her was recurrent major depression superimposed on a more chronic dysthymic disorder.

When Jane failed to respond to Prozac 80 mg daily, Wellbutrin was added to her regimen, and, shortly thereafter, the family called me saying that she had had a seizure. They refused to take her for medical evaluation, and she did well after stopping the Wellbutrin (which can lower the seizure threshold in some people). Later, three individual trials of augmentation included Lamictal, lithium, and amphetamine added to her Prozac. She did moderately well over the next 5 years while taking a high dose of Prozac, modest doses of amphetamine, and lithium, but she was never able to move away from the dependent situation of living with her parents.

Jane's parents allowed her to take over a large portion of their home in order to be actively involved in creating arts and crafts. She helped her mother to a great extent as her father began to develop dementia. She reported that her suicidal ideation had been gone for quite a while and felt that her mother was appreciating her help in taking care of her father. One night, however, Jane and her mother got into an argument. Things quickly escalated and Jane ended up hitting her mother. Her mother responded by telling Jane that she had to move out. After the fight, Jane quietly did her chores, went upstairs to her bedroom, and was found dead the next morning with a plastic bag over her head.

As the mother told me of this sad outcome, she pointed out that Jane had never allowed the mother or other family members to be involved in her treatment, and she acknowledged how much stress she had felt trying to look out for both Jane and her father. In a sense, this death was a catastrophic reaction to a situational stressor. The family would have provided more support and another place to live, but Jane was unable to actively problem-solve after the blowup with her mother. Her depression, anger, and response to her mother's demand to move out blinded her to the healthy problem-solving skills that she had been able to demonstrate most of her life.

Case Example: Dillon

Dillon was a brilliant, single 35-year-old. He had an enviable career as a biological chemical researcher, having been chosen as a research fellow at one of the nation's most prestigious research institutes. Several months after beginning the fellowship, Dillon developed severe panic attacks that did not respond to Xanax but did respond to antidepressants, although he had the very unusual experience of becoming depressed while taking them and began to have suicidal ideation.

In his position as a researcher, Dillon had access to morphine and amphetamine, which he began stealing shortly after his panic attacks had begun. He had been injecting himself with morphine twice a day and with amphetamine about twice a week for a month when he got caught. Instead of being arrested, Dillon was referred to a drug abuse treatment program. Just as he was about to start that program, he made his first life-threatening suicide attempt by overdosing with an intravenous injection of morphine and the animal anesthetic ketamine, as well as injecting his abdomen with a paralyzing agent. When he failed to show up for admission to the treatment program, his counselor called his home and work and sent the police to his apartment, where he was found still breathing but severely toxic. Shortly thereafter he was referred to me.

Dillon's research career had been extremely successful and productive, but his social life was quite limited. He had grown up feeling that he was very smart but an unpopular misfit who did not fit in socially. He had done very little socializing through high school, college, and graduate school. At the time of my initial evaluation, he appeared to have a mixed picture, with panic disorder, polysubstance abuse, and depression due to this abuse. He reluctantly agreed to attend 12-step support groups to deal with the substance abuse issues, and he began regular psychotherapy sessions. Over the next 14 months he did well, got along nicely with his parents (with whom he was staying during his recovery), reported his depression clearing well on low-dose Paxil, and was able to write up his research results for publication and look for a new job. He eventually moved away and restarted his research career. Four years after my initial evaluation, Dillon reported that his life was moving forward.

Dillon's potentially lethal suicide attempt was clearly precipitated by drug-induced depression and the immediate crisis of having been caught stealing drugs from the lab. When these crises were resolved and the substance abuse ended, he was able to continue with his challenging career.

Case Example: Bonnie

Bonnie was a 44-year-old, slender, blonde woman who was very soft-spoken and had a history of depression as far back as her college years. She had an excellent relationship with her previous psychiatrist, who had provided outpatient maintenance ECT in his office before he retired. She had been tried on numerous medications, including Prozac, Sinequan, Klonopin, and Valium, but none of them significantly improved her recurrent major depression.

Over the course of the 5 years that I treated her, Bonnie had some good times and established a very satisfying relationship that involved living with a man who was 30 years her senior but very supportive, energetic, and helpful. She sometimes came to the hospital for a course of ECT when she felt the depression was getting overwhelming. She also worked with her gynecologist on hormone replacement therapy and saw me for medication management. She was on lithium, Prozac, and Sinequan for many years and used Xanax when she felt anxious and Ritalin when the depression became so overwhelming that she could not get out of bed.

Bonnie also had very supportive relationships with her boyfriend, mother, and sister, but her sister felt that I had often overmedicated her and strongly pushed her to change doctors. About a year after Bonnie had discontinued treatment with me, I got a phone call from her father saying that she had killed herself. Her mother came in and told me that Bonnie had wanted to return to my care, but her sister had taken her to another local hospital after it was discovered that she had been using too much Xanax, and the staff there treated her as a substance abuser, withdrawing her from the medication quickly. Though substance use programs often encourage quick withdrawal, tapering Xanax comfortably can take as long as 6 months. Shortly after leaving the hospital detoxification program, her sister took her to a new doctor, who restarted her previous medicines, but when Bonnie failed to feel better in a few days, she committed suicide. The mother said that she expected her daughter to someday kill herself, because she had spent so much of her life depressed despite ongoing treatment. Both the mother and the father thanked me for my attempts to help their daughter and acknowledged that the suicide was a risk they were both quite aware of.

Lessons From Suicide

What can we learn from these cases? Jane clearly shows us that a problem with the primary support system (mother), in the context of ongoing depression, can trigger suicide. Would I have done anything differently with her? Her mother suggested that having the family involved with her treatment would have been helpful, yet the patient would not allow this. In retrospect, having more contact with other family members besides the parents might have helped Jane to weather the storm of the fight with her mother. Perhaps visiting her siblings more regularly and going to a support group and church would have allowed her to call someone and stay with a friend or relative during the cooling-off period after the fight with her mother. Bonnie's case shows us the hazard of the psychiatrist and family being at odds over the patient's treatment.

Dillon's experience clearly shows us an important lesson: Drug abuse can only worsen depression and must stop as part of depression recovery. Loss of face, and dealing with the embarrassment of being sent to a drug rehabilitation program and 12-step meetings, was too much for him to handle. Yet it was ultimately being pushed to do so by his therapist and me that led to his recovery. There is no mistake, failure, or error in judgment that is worth a self-imposed death sentence! Certainly Dillon's supervisor felt that treatment rather than jail was appropriate, yet Dillon's harsh sense of having done wrong led to the suicide attempt.

Bonnie's ultimate death by suicide was expected by her family because her depression was so chronic and treatment-resistant, yet it was apparently triggered by treatment disruption when her sister forced her into a program that took away a medication they felt she overused, and that I felt eased some of her pain. Clearly, major changes in treatment direction are worthy of a family meeting with the treating doctor and a second-opinion consultation with another doctor before they are imposed upon the patient. With the wisdom that comes only when looking back in time, I can see that the focus of treatment was perhaps too much on medications to decrease depressive symptoms and too little on shoring up the family and social support network to help cope with the rough times.

Case Example: Surviving!

Lori first came to see me when she was 65 years old. She was a devout Catholic who attended mass daily and had raised eight children. She was living with her husband, who was semiretired. She worried and obsessed over many issues and had a long-standing fear of mental illness because her mother had suffered from manic depression and multiple suicide attempts. Some of Lori's own children had substance-abuse issues, and one had required ECT for depression. Moe, her son, had a history of substance abuse and serving time in jail. Lori had a history that was consistent with long-term, chronic mild anxiety and depression, and I diagnosed generalized anxiety disorder as well as dysthymia. She also told me that she felt very uncomfortable—"high-strung and nervous"— in groups of people. Attending mass was difficult for her and it was hard for her to socialize with friends. She reported chronic difficulties with getting a full night of sleep.

Over time, we tried numerous antidepressants, including Serzone, Wellbutrin, Paxil, Lexapro, and the anxiolytic BuSpar. She did best on BuSpar long-term, and she came in about once a month for regular psychotherapy sessions over the 9 years that I worked with her.

As she was telling her life story during psychotherapy sessions, Lori began talking about her earlier course of depression. She spoke of having become extremely depressed more than 30 years earlier, at a point in life when she had five children, her husband had moved to another state to start a new job, and she was in charge of the children and selling the family home. She felt that the "top of my head was red-hot." She had a hard time focusing, and even moving her body felt like a huge effort. She felt that she needed rest but was unable to relax. She attempted to work off her tension by doing numerous things at home and for the children until she was exhausted.

Lori said that she considered herself strong, invincible, and able to handle many things at once. She kept telling herself that she was going to be stronger and tougher in dealing with depression than her mother had been, but she felt trapped and experienced no emotion—no sadness, no love—everything was rote behavior. She was able to perform her duties of feeding her family and cleaning the house, but she felt that she was without God and could not even pray during the worst times. She was 31 years old and felt that she would go on this way for the rest of her life. She felt she understood why her mother had tried to cut her wrists in a suicide attempt, commenting, "Of course I wanted to kill myself. How could I live like this for another 50 years?" Lori would drive her car and think about how much she wanted to swerve into an oncoming truck and end it all. Her strong religious faith told her that this was not an option, however, and having order and consistency in her home environment gave her some sense of external stability. Then one day she woke up, and the depression was gone. She couldn't believe it. Although she still had moments of anxiety and depression, she felt that her kids were a major distraction. She began to get more connected with her children and her church.

As Lori was talking about this, I realized that she was trying to teach me a very important lesson as a therapist. She was telling me very clearly that having a sense of purpose and duty, a sense of obligation to raising her children, and a strong religious faith kept her doing what she had to do to survive until the depression resolved. Looking back on it, she wished that she had sought psychiatric treatment and acknowledged that this was a severe depression, but she also felt that she was much stronger as a person for having gotten through it with her sense of purpose in raising her children and her religion to help her.

6

Finding Treatment and Paying for It: Dealing With the Health Care System and Insurance

Deciding whether to seek psychotherapy or pharmacotherapy (or both), finding the best possible clinician, and making it accessible and affordable are key elements of treatment.

It has been said that Americans want a lot from the health care system. We want treatment to be immediately available when we feel a need for it—a waiting list or rationing of care seems unacceptable. We want our treatment to involve high-technology diagnostic tests, the newest and best medications, and therapies delivered by the most highly skilled practitioners. And, of course, we want it all at very little personal cost. We'd like employers to provide insurance or a government plan to provide this high standard of health care to everyone who needs it. Unfortunately, we haven't reached this ideal: One in five American families has at least one member who lacks health insurance coverage, a situation that can place the entire family at risk healthwise and financially (NMHA, 2006).

This chapter is geared toward patients. It addresses the realities of finding and paying for care, offering practical ideas on dealing with insurance, access to medicines and psychotherapy, and low-fee resources in the community.

Which Type of Treatment Is Right for Me?

There's no such thing as a general template or recipe for treating everyone with depression. Although the extensive research literature can guide and inform well-read clinicians, it does not specifically tell them what will be best for an individual patient. Treatment of depression is based on careful assessment of an individual, filtered through clinical experience. There is an essential period of trial and error, both in terms of choosing the best medication and in terms of understanding which psychotherapeutic approaches will be most helpful for the individual.

When approaching treatment, it is very important to put together a list of both the major, most bothersome and disabling symptoms, and the more subtle or milder symptoms. This helps to both determine the targets of treatment and distinguish drug side effects from preexisting symptoms that were present before the medication was started. It is often desirable to treat depression with the simplest possible regimen, which may mean psychotherapy or a single drug, but often the complexity of the person suffering from depression requires a multi-modal approach. Sometimes substance abuse treatment, family therapy, individual therapy, and a rational combination of medications may be necessary to get the very best possible outcome for an individual. While a comprehensive and integrated course of treatment is the goal, our general approach is to start one thing at a time. That way, benefits or side effects can be evaluated for each component of treatment. Substance abuse and major medical illnesses always have first priority, followed by psychological or medication treatments for the depression.

Often the first decision is whether to seek medication treatment, psychotherapy, or both. Usually the combination is best. Although there isn't an absolute dividing line between who should be treated first with medicines and who should be treated first with psychotherapy, we have some general guidelines that may be of use. For people who are having symptoms of depression despite being happy with life, satisfied with their major relationships, and generally enjoying their work—especially when the person's life in general has been good since childhood—antidepressants would probably be the first-choice treatment modality. For people who present with any form of bizarre delusions or hallucinations, antipsychotic medications should be a priority. Also, the person whose depression seems to come out of the blue with no apparent stressor or trigger and who has highly recurrent depression, which may run in the family, will often recognize that medicines are the first requirement.

Conversely, people who present with a history of childhood trauma, abuse, or neglect, and who now as adults are dealing with relationship problems at home, at work, and with friends, may do best with psychotherapy. Seeking understanding and making behavioral changes may be the best initial treatment approach. This is especially true if the person is able to take care of basic life functioning and does not have many biologic symptoms.

Most often, drugs and psychotherapy are used together and affect different areas of life. Generally, drugs change biology, and psychotherapy changes thoughts and feelings, but medications often are necessary to "take the edge off" before a person can really make use of psychotherapy; people also find that relief of acute symptoms in and of itself produces changes in many behaviors. Likewise, research demonstrates that psychotherapy has an effect on physiology, although it works a bit more slowly. Some modalities may produce more rapid effects than others. Also, remember that psychotherapy tends to have some lasting effect in preventing future episodes, whereas drugs provide benefit only as long as they're taken. Early studies that compared cognitive-behavioral therapy and the antidepressant Tofranil (imipramine) showed that both were comparably effective in nonhospitalized individuals with mild to moderate depression and no history of psychosis or mania, but that anti-depressants worked a little faster (Elkin et al., 1989, 1995; Evans et al., 1992; Hollon et al., 1992; Klein, 1990; Kovacs, Rush, Beck, & Hollon, 1981; Ogles, Lambert, & Sawyer, 1995; Rush, Kovacs, Beck, Weissenburger, & Hollon, 1981). For the most severely depressed individuals, imipramine was more effective than cognitive-behavioral therapy.

A major study of adults with chronic depression that compared the antidepressant Serzone (nefazodone) with cognitive-behavioral analysis (CBASP, discussed in Chapter 8), a variant of cognitive-behavioral therapy modified for chronic depression, showed much higher response rates for the combination approach than for either the drug or psychotherapy alone. In addition, people who did not respond to one of these approaches during a 12-week experimental period of random assignment often responded when switched over to the other approach (Keller et al., 2000; Thase et al., 2002). A history of childhood adversity (physical or sexual abuse, neglect, or early parental loss) predicted the need for psychotherapy as part of successful treatment of the adult with chronic depression (Nemeroff et al., 2003).

These two approaches are often considered "top-down" and "bottom-up" treatments. Psychotherapy changes thinking and behaviors, which originate in the cerebral cortex (the outermost, more evolved layers of the brain), and these in turn modify lower brain centers involved in drives and feelings. Medication affects lower-level brain functions that control eating, sleeping, sex, and the ability to experience pleasure; when these improve, they project new signals to other parts of the brain, and these higher-level brain areas are more able to problem-solve in adaptive and resourceful ways.

The Treatment Provider

Choosing a clinician for psychotherapy or medication management involves many factors. Does the patient prefer a particular approach to psychotherapy? Does the patient prefer to receive medications from his or her family doctor or from a specialist? If both medications and therapy are desired, can one clinician provide both? Is insurance or cost an issue? Expertise, experience, affordability, and availability are important factors; the emotional "fit" or bonding experienced in the initial interaction may be an especially important guide.

Choosing a Psychotherapist

For psychotherapy, an individual clinician trained in either cognitive-behavioral therapy or interpersonal therapy is often the best treatment option because both of these involve highly structured approaches, a short-term, time-limited focus, homework assignments, and active engagement by the therapist. Also, both are proven highly effective. Not every psychotherapist is highly trained in these treatment approaches and many claim to have an eclectic approach, which often means the techniques are mixed and matched in whatever combination appears best to the therapist at the moment.

When long-term intensive exploratory psychotherapy is desired to deal with developmental (family-of-origin) or personality issues, and immediate symptom suppression is not the urgent goal, a psychodynamic psychotherapist or psychoanalyst may have the special skills needed for the job.

It is important to select a therapist who is highly trained, licensed by the state, and adheres to a set of ethical standards of clinical practice.

Anyone can call herself a "life coach" and charge for time and advice, but the specialized education, examinations, and apprenticeship (clinical supervised treatment hours) required of the degreed professional are significant steps in ensuring that a therapist has appropriate training. Most psychotherapists have a postgraduate degree such as master of arts (MA) in marriage and family counseling (MFCC, MFT), master of social work (DSW, MSW, LCSW, CCSW, LICSW), doctor of philosophy (PhD), doctor of psychology (PsyD), doctor of educational psychology (EdD), master of science in nursing (MSN, APRN) with specialist certification in psychiatry (PMHN, PMHNP, CNS), or MD with board certification in psychiatry.

No matter the license, you want your therapist to be experienced. Among the most common errors made by therapists of limited training and experience are those involving differential diagnosis. Nutritional deficits, sleep deprivation or a sleep disorder, neurologic damage, attention deficit, OCD, chronic pain disorders, and any other number of problems can mimic depression. Very often what looks like depression may primarily be driven by different conditions. An experienced therapist is more likely to pick this up and to have resources at the ready for consultation and further evaluation.

Choosing a Medication Management Provider

When psychiatric medication is appropriate, the primary question is whether to ask your primary care doctor to prescribe it or to seek treatment with a psychiatrist or psychiatric nurse practitioner whose practice focuses on the use of psychiatric medicines. Over the last decade, primary care physicians, including family doctors, internists, pediatricians, gynecologists, and others, have become increasingly comfortable prescribing antidepressant medications. Generally, the doctor will have one or two favorite medications and will ask the patient to try these. If the response is good, there's no need to go on to see a specialist. If the drugs cause problematic side effects or fail to give enough benefit for depression, a consultation with a psychiatrist is worthwhile. The key decision should basically be determined by whether there is adequate response to and tolerability of the medication prescribed by the primary care physician within the first month or two of treatment. Depression complicated by substance abuse, medical problems, suicidal impulses, psychotic features, a history of full-blown manic episodes, or failure to respond to multiple previous drugs is usually a very good reason to go directly to a psychiatrist rather than the primary care physician.

Among patients receiving antidepressant medication in the United States, those treated by psychiatrists rather than general medical practitioners were more likely to be males who had significant distress, with serious mood or anxiety symptoms, and to meet DSM-IV criteria for mood or anxiety disorders. They were more likely to receive higher doses of medications and to continue taking them for 90 days or longer. Those treated by nonpsychiatric physicians were often less ill and more likely to stop medication before 30 days (Mojtabai & Olfson, 2008).

Choosing Experts

As is the case in any profession, not all psychiatrists are equally competent or interested in psychopharmacology, and not all psychotherapists are equally competent and interested in the specific psychotherapies that work best for treating depression. Even though insurance companies refer to clinicians as "providers" and view them as interchangeable, this isn't really the case. If you want to find the very best professionals in your community, we have a few suggestions.

First, if you live near a medical school, ask for the name and phone number of the chairman of the psychiatry or psychology department. You can ask this person for a referral to a faculty member who has special expertise in what you need. In this case, be careful to consider only clinicians who spend a significant amount of their time seeing patients. Many faculty are more research-oriented.

Another approach is to contact a national support group and find out where its local meetings are. Groups such as the Depression and Bipolar Support Alliance (DBSA) and National Alliance on Mental Illness (NAMI) have chapters throughout the United States. At the meetings, you can ask others who have had similar problems for the names of the best psychiatrists and psychologists in the area.

Another approach is to call several local primary care physicians and ask for their usual favorite referrals for individuals requiring a psychiatrist or psychologist. Still another approach is to call a few local psychologists and ask who they recommend for medication management of their patients. You can also call the local psychiatric hospital and ask to speak to the nursing director or medical staff office. Ask the people there who they would recommend; many outpatient psychiatrists have admitting privileges at hospitals and are well-known to them. If finding a clinician of your own faith is important, it's worth talking to your pastor, priest, or rabbi, because he or she may be aware of psychiatrists and psychologists who share the same religious beliefs. You might want to try several of these approaches and look for the same names showing up repeatedly. It's true that this is a lot of work, but it can be a good way of determining who is considered by patients and professionals to be the best treating clinician.

Clinicians in private practice who are technically competent, compassionate, and kind often develop successful practices that might have a waiting list for new patients to come in for evaluation and treatment. Clinicians who are inconsiderate of their patients' feelings, disrespectful of referral sources, and don't keep up with the field of psychiatry or psychotherapy may also have busy practices, but the patients who have seen them will warn you to stay away, so it's important to get all of the information you can and to choose your treating clinicians carefully. If you are in the midst of a severe depression and this search process seems too complicated, perhaps a family member or close friend could be of some real assistance in making a series of information-gathering phone calls.

Once you have narrowed your search to a small number of psychiatrists or psychologists, it's worth calling the clinicians' offices to ask about important details including hours, fees, insurance billing, and whether they will meet you for a get-acquainted meeting without charge. How long is their waiting list for a new patient evaluation? How long is that evaluation? An adequate initial interview takes between an hour and an hour-and-a-half. Can you reach this clinician easily by phone, does she accept e-mail, and how can you reach the clinician when the office is closed? How does the clinician arrange for coverage when she is out of town? Does the clinician have hospital admission privileges, and at which hospitals? You should ask if the clinician is proficient in your native language, and, if not, whether she will make use of an interpreter.

If you are curious about how long a doctor has been in practice and whether she is board certified in psychiatry, the American Medical Association (AMA) offers this information in the Doctor Finder feature on its Web site. A visit to the licensing board's Web site can tell you whether the clinician has a record of formal disciplinary action or malpractice suits. Licensing boards can also be helpful where sourcing professionals in your area is concerned. Contact information for such boards is different in each state. In California, registered psychologists are licensed by the Board of Psychology; psychiatrists by the Medical Board of California; nurses by the Board of Registered Nursing; and marriage and family therapists, clinical social workers, and educational psychologists by the Board of Behavioral Sciences.

It is worth asking whether the clinician has a university teaching or research appointment, is involved in teaching or supervising interns and residents, has been publishing articles within the subspecialty field for which you need treatment, or has any books published. Scholarly work involving teaching and publishing implies efforts to keep current within the field and to maintain the self-discipline and study to be an expert. Of course, the downside of consulting an expert is that such a person might spend a great deal of time in research or travel and lecturing and be less readily available to see patients. How long might you wait for a routine or urgent/emergency appointment with this person, and does the person keep evening or weekend hours? These are all issues that must be addressed before the first appointment.

Is This Doctor or Therapist Right for Me?

During the first few appointments with the pharmacologist or therapist, it is important to evaluate your experience. Is there a sense of therapeutic alliance? Do you trust her to try hard to work with you and aggressively pursue your goals of treatment? Does she offer hope? Does she offer many different treatment options in case the first or second doesn't work? Does she have what you need in terms of expertise with medications, psychotherapy, medical problems, inpatient hospital work, electroconvulsive therapy, marital problems, substance abuse, or other kinds of issues that might be important to you? No one can have all the answers or know all the approaches. If the doctor or therapist does not have expertise in one of these, is she willing to refer to, or collaborate with, someone else? It's important to ask how much of the clinician's practice is spent in treating patients with problems like yours. Is it important that you and the doctor share religious values, or that she be recovering in a 12-step program? Is it important that she share your view of alternative therapies such as herbal remedies, meditation, or vitamins and supplements? Does the doctor invite your spouse or significant other to come into the sessions when you want your partner invited? Will the doctor offer to do both medications and psychotherapy or welcome and accept your ongoing psychotherapy with someone else?

Another area of evaluation of your clinician is her attitude toward your learning about the illness and its treatment. Some doctors want to be the absolute authority on treatment selection and recommendations, whereas others welcome the patient's ideas and questions. Some highly recommend support groups, reading books or articles, and Web sites for patient education whereas others feel that the doctor should be the ultimate source of information about treating the illness. Does your doctor's attitude match yours on most of these issues? In either case, at a minimum, the clinician needs to provide full information on any tests and interventions you will undergo or participate in. The clinician must also ensure that you understand and agree with her decisions. This is known as informed consent.

Obviously our bias is toward very well-informed patients who use every possible source of information in understanding how to control their illness. That's why we wrote this book! We believe that the patients who have the best chance of becoming and staying well are the ones who take responsibility for this on their own, utilizing a variety of professionals as specialized consultants and employing a well-rounded blend of modalities, techniques, lifestyle choices, and sources of information in their active pursuit of wellness. Sometimes the patient doesn't want to learn too much or put much effort into this kind of education, however, and wants the doctor to take charge and determine all the treatment options. Some profoundly depressed clients who have trouble with energy, cognition, planning, and making and following through on decisions will greatly appreciate a clinician with a take-charge approach. Different styles of physician and patient will often work well together, but it is important to at least recognize if there is a major difference in approaches and expectations.

One Clinician or Two?

There has been a quiet but long-standing debate within the mental health field as to whether a psychiatrist should do only pharmacologic therapy and collaborate with a psychotherapist who does the counseling. The alternative approach is that the psychiatrist does it all and sees every patient for whom she prescribes medicines for very regular sessions of therapy. It is perfectly appropriate to ask the psychiatrist if she does talk therapy or strictly medication management. Some psychiatrists are far more comfortable with one approach than the other. This is a major issue, because of both economics and expertise. Because of the economics of supply and demand, psychiatrists often charge significantly more per hour than other psychotherapists do. Also, psychiatrists, especially older ones, are much more likely to be trained in psychodynamic approaches than in cognitive-behavioral therapy, interpersonal therapy, or family therapy, whereas psychologists and clinical social workers may be better qualified to provide psychological treatment. Older psychiatrists are much more likely to want to do the psychotherapy along with medication management, whereas younger psychiatrists are more likely to focus their work on pharmacotherapy. This partially stems from the fact that current residency programs may contain very little content on psychotherapy, unless they specialize in it. Many psychiatrists who practice psychotherapy have pursued advanced training.

The issue of collaborative or split treatment is important in that some psychiatrists and psychologists work very well together, whereas others find that their approaches overlap, with the psychiatrist often stepping into the role of psychotherapist and the psychotherapist often suggesting medication changes. This can leave the patient feeling in the middle and wondering why the psychiatrist and psychologist are not talking to each other. If this should happen, it is quite reasonable to ask that the psychiatrist and psychologist confer with each other and coordinate treatment efforts. This can be done on an informal, as-needed telephone basis, or with exchange of treatment notes. When coordinated care is being given, it is quite important to ensure that there are no secrets between the care providers and the patient; the psychologist and psychiatrist must be given the patient's permission to openly exchange information if they are to work effectively together. Ideally, the psychiatrist and psychotherapist would communicate regularly, but in actual practice this often doesn't happen unless one sees a problem that the other should be made aware of, or if they share an office. A patient request that they exchange progress notes or call one another every month or two could be a helpful reminder.

Money

Concerns and questions about money make many people hesitant to pursue mental health treatment, yet we're sure you are already acquainted with the potential costs of remaining depressed. The risks of missed time from work, compromised physical health, strained relationships, death by suicide, and simply the agony of living with depression are all good reasons to pursue the best treatment you are able to arrange. The real question is not whether you can afford treatment for your depression, but how. In this section we hope to put you on the road to educating yourself regarding treatment options, the ins and outs of insurance coverage, and more.

The basic question is how to pay for treatment. Basing our rough estimates on current fees in Southern California in 2009, we believe that the total cost of treatment for about a year for a major depressive episode is probably a few thousand dollars if hospitalization is not required. We estimate that a comprehensive laboratory screening costs about $200 to $300. A psychiatrist to manage medications probably would spend 5 to 10 hours at a cost of $200 to $400 per hour for a total of $1,000 to $4,000. A psychotherapist providing counseling for between 10 and 30 sessions in a year would probably charge about $80 to $150 per hour, totaling from $800 to $4,500. If these professionals accept your insurance, you might expect copayments of anywhere from

$10 to $40 per visit for medication management and psychotherapy visits. Generic medication is often inexpensive, costing under a dollar per day, but if a combination of brand-name drugs is used, the cost of medication could easily be $2,000 to $4,000 in a year. Thus, the total cost for treating a depressive episode in the first year could be anywhere from $3,000 to about $12,000. Is this a lot of money? It depends on one's perspective. Would you spend this much money to repair your car or the roof on your house, or to buy a new computer, stereo, or television? The cost of missing work for a few weeks, or for a few days in a psychiatric hospital, could be far greater. The cost of eating lunch out every workday or buying a pack or two of cigarettes and a cup of latte daily could easily be comparable to this. The cost of an appendectomy would almost certainly be far greater than the cost of treating depression for a year. The risk of death by suicide certainly justifies obtaining the best possible treatment. Yet the question of how to pay for treatment is important to most people.

If you have no insurance, state and federally subsidized community mental health clinics are available in most cities and provide treatment on a sliding scale, with reduced fees for individuals of limited income. Often, university programs that train psychologists and psychiatrists have clinical internship and residency programs that also provide treatment on a sliding-fee scale.

If you belong to a health maintenance organization (HMO), the first step is to see your primary care provider. Ask if she is comfortable prescribing psychiatric medications and willing to give a referral to a psychiatrist if there are problems or if you have some of the complications described earlier. At the same time, it may be worth asking for a referral to a psychologist, clinical social worker, or other therapist for psychotherapy.

If you have insurance with a preferred provider list, the first thing to do is to call the insurance company for a list of providers who are geographically in your area and who specialize in treatment of depression.

Making Treatment Affordable

When you interview psychiatrists and therapists, don't be hesitant to raise payment issues. A therapist should talk to you about what can be accomplished in the number of sessions allotted and tell you the out-of-pocket cost for appointments and sessions. To make therapy more affordable, some therapists have a sliding-fee schedule or can arrange less frequent visits if appropriate. If your time together must be limited by finances, you and your therapist may agree to focus on a narrower problem area than you might if there were no constraints.

As an alternate to working with a psychotherapist in private practice, there are lower-cost alternatives: Some employers have an employee assistance program (EAP) in addition to or instead of mental health insurance, which allows employees to see a specified counselor for a limited number of sessions. If your employer has an EAP, you might investigate what services are offered and their limitations. Ask your insurance company if it covers counseling beyond the limited coverage you may have through your EAP.

Assistance in affording medication also exists for people who do not have insurance and who have a limited income. "Patient assistance programs" are offered by most drug companies for many of the brand name medications they manufacture. Your doctor may be familiar with these. If she is not, the Internet has many resources. NeedyMeds.com is an excellent nonprofit Web site that helps clients locate programs they qualify for. The service lists programs by both drug name and by manufacturer, gives a nice, concise summary of what you need to do to qualify, and facilitates your application. This is a much less time-consuming process than calling a manufacturer directly. Once you locate an assistance program, your doctor will fill out some simple paperwork and you will have to provide financial statements demonstrating limited income and financial resources. These are submitted to the drug company and you can pick up your prescription soon after. Your doctor will periodically renew the prescription for you.

Over time, patient assistance programs do take some management on the part of the provider. For clinicians who would like a company to manage and coordinate these services for a small fee, two services are Avenues to Medicine (www.ave2meds.com) and Health Med Assist (www.needymeds.com/sponsors/hma/hmainfopage.html). Mental Health Today's repository of assistance programs (www.mental-health-today.com/helpmeds.htm), which includes many educational materials on paying for treatment, lists links to patient assistance program resources, health care plans, and federal, state, and local government programs. There is even a source that will allow you to access medications not available in the United States (like reboxetine, a selective norepinephrine reuptake inhibitor). There is also information on military benefits and special resources for seniors.

Many large pharmacy chains offer very low-cost prescriptions for generic drugs. Often a generic medication like fluoxetine (Prozac) can be purchased for $4 for a 30-day supply or $10 for a 90-day supply. The store may consider this a "loss leader" to bring in customers who will shop while their prescription is being filled. We consider it a bargain opportunity if you and your doctor consider a generic drug to be appropriate for your treatment.

Low-Cost Alternatives for Treatment in Your Community

Often, university programs that train psychiatrists have clinical residency programs that also provide treatment on a sliding fee scale. Just as psychiatrists complete residency after completing medical school, therapists who have completed their formal academic training enter a period of supervised internship for a specified number of hours before they become licensed. One setting in which they do this is at a community counseling center, where clients may see therapists-in-training for very reasonable or sliding-scale fees. Though these therapists are relatively inexperienced, you may find one with whom you can build a therapeutic relationship—the caveat is that most therapists rotate to another clinical assignment or graduate and seek more lucrative work elsewhere after their 6- to 9-month internship with the center is complete, and they may or may not have the ability to offer you the same hourly rate at their new place of employment.

If you qualify for various government programs such as General Assistance, Medicare, and Medicaid, a call to your local Department of Public Health will begin your search for community mental health programs, which are delivered free of charge. Many of them also deliver services to people who are financially destitute or homeless, regardless of their eligibility for government insurance programs. Those with Medicare will qualify for services at many universities and some private practice offices. State and local insurance is further discussed later in this chapter.

Pastoral counseling is another option. Your church or synagogue can put you in touch with a pastoral counseling program. Certified pastoral counselors, who are ministers in a recognized religious body, have advanced degrees in pastoral counseling, as well as professional counseling experience. Pastoral counseling is often provided on a sliding-scale fee basis.

Another option is to join a self-help or support group. Such groups give people a chance to learn about, talk about, and work on their common problems, such as alcoholism, substance abuse, depression, family issues, and relationships. They are generally free and can be found in virtually every community in America. Many people find them to be effective, though they are run by peers and not by trained professionals, and as such they are not the equivalent of group therapy. Further discussion of self-help groups can be found in Chapter 8.

Insurance

There are several different forms of insurance available in the United States; each falls into the category of private insurance or public assistance. Private insurance plans may be purchased individually or may be offered by a person's employer. One type of plan is a standard indemnity policy, often called a PPO (preferred provider organization), which gives people freedom to visit any health care provider of their choice and pay for a set portion of the cost, with greater coverage if they choose a provider in the company's network. The other common plan is a managed care plan, or HMO. Under this plan, medically necessary care is provided in the most cost-effective, or least expensive, way available. Plan members must choose only from health care providers in the managed care plan's network and must receive referrals from a "gateway provider" (their primary care doctor) in order to see specialists such as psychiatrists. Generally, a copayment is charged to the patient, but sometimes all care received from providers within the plan is covered.

Those who are not insured by a private plan may qualify for any of several forms of public assistance. Medicare is America's primary federal health insurance program for people who are 65 or older and for those who have been legally disabled for more than 2 years. It provides basic protection for the cost of health care. Two programs exist to help people with low incomes receive benefits: the Qualified Medicare Beneficiary (QMB) and the Specified Low-Income Medicare Beneficiary (SLMB) programs. Medicaid, a state-provided insurance, pays for some health care costs for America's poorest and most vulnerable people. More information about Medicaid and eligibility requirements is available at local welfare and medical assistance offices. Note that some private-practice clinicians will not accept Medicare or Medicaid patients because the payment is less than their usual fees. Finally, General Assistance (GA) provides limited medical care to those who do not qualify for other cash programs administered by their state's Department of Human Services.

Because the provisions and limitations of insurance coverage differ by state (for public programs), by insurer, and by individual plan, each person reading this book may have slightly different conditions to navigate. Perhaps we can best help you by giving information about mental health parity and by suggesting questions you might ask your insurer.

The Mental Health Parity Act, passed in 1996, mandates that employers who employ more than 50 workers and offer group health insurance must also offer coverage for mental illness equal to the lifetime and annual caps set for physical ailments. It does not, however, force group health plans to offer mental health coverage if they don't already do so, nor does it apply to companies for which parity provisions would push insurance costs up more than 1%. Further, insurers may still charge higher copayments and deductibles and have lower treatment limits for mental health benefits (only lifetime and annual limits are stipulated), and the number of inpatient days and outpatient treatments don't have to equal coverage for physical medical needs. The act also applies to self-insured health plans exempt from state laws under the Employee Retirement Income Security Act (ERISA), as well as to fully insured state-regulated group health plans—but only to those policies that offer mental health benefits in the first place. Fortunately, many states have enacted legislation that goes above and beyond the federal Mental Health Parity Act. Each state is different in both the coverage it requires and in how it defines mental illness. In California, for instance, only "severe mental illnesses" are provided for, including schizophrenia, bipolar disorder, major depressive disorder, schizoaffective disorder, panic disorder, obsessive-compulsive disorder, autism, anorexia nervosa, and bulimia nervosa. Substance abuse and chemical dependency treatments are not covered. Some states are less generous, and others, like Connecticut, apply parity laws to all disorders covered in *DSM-IV*, including substance abuse. Full mental health parity like that in Connecticut would increase insurance premiums in other states by only 0.9 to 1.0% (NMHA, 2006). What this means to you is that, depending on the state you reside in, if you have a very difficult case of dysthymia, along with generalized anxiety disorder and attention-deficit-hyperactivity disorder, you may not qualify for coverage equal to that offered to a person with heart disease or diabetes.

In any case, the time to figure out if you have adequate insurance is before you actually require it. It is important to investigate your options thoroughly so you can make a plan for treatment that is comprehensive, flexible, and affordable over its full course. Find out from your insurance company what, if any, limitations exist to coverage for your diagnosis and the type of treatment you desire.

DEDUCTIBLES AND COPAYS

Some insurance plans have a deductible (an out-of-pocket expense before your insurance begins to pay your bills) for health benefits. Be sure to ask exactly how much your deductible is and which visits (to an MD or therapist), procedures, laboratory services, treatments, medications, and devices will count toward meeting it. In rare cases, there is a separate deductible for psychotherapy: You may have to pay for the first four sessions, for example, in order to pay off the deductible.

Many insurance plans contribute to your expenses by percentage; this is called a copay. In a PPO, the insured may pay 20% of a medical visit to an in-network provider, and perhaps 30–40% to a practitioner outside the network. If you carry a parity diagnosis, you may find that copays on visits to a psychiatrist are the same as those to your general practitioner, and that there are no limits to the number of visits. If your diagnosis does not qualify for parity in your state, you may find your benefits to be limited. If you see a psychiatrist for psychotherapy, the same will probably apply (because she is a medical doctor and can submit appropriate treatment codes for billing). Otherwise, nonmedical care for mental health is unfortunately not covered as well as medical services: If you see a psychologist or other therapist, your copay may be more (perhaps 50% of the hourly fee), the insurer may offer only a small offset (such as $25) per visit, and there may be limitations to the number of visits, an increased copay after a number of visits, or a cap on total expenditure for psychotherapy.

Practitioners within your insurance company's network will bill your insurance company, which will then send you a statement detailing the copay you must then pay the provider. If your doctor or therapist does not accept your insurance, you will pay them directly (perhaps monthly or at the conclusion of each session), you will submit a statement to your insurer, and you will then be reimbursed for the amount of the visit minus your copay. Ask your insurer about the details of this process and how long it takes.

YOUR CHOICE OF DOCTOR OR THERAPIST
Ask if you have a choice regarding whom you see: With some plans, clients may see any provider they choose, though those affiliated with the insurer have lower copay amounts. Other plans—HMOs, for instance—require that you see a practitioner within their network. If you have insurance with a preferred provider list (doctors and therapists within the insurer's network) the first thing to do is to call the insurance company for a list of providers who are geographically in your area and who specialize in treatment of depression.

Ask also if you can go directly to a psychiatrist or if you must be first referred by your primary care practitioner or some other gatekeeper. What happens if you don't have a primary care physician? In the case of psychotherapy, insurers require that a referral be made by an MD, physician's assistant (PA), or nurse practitioner for you to be eligible for coverage.

If you have your choice of psychotherapists, ask whether certain degrees or licenses, such as a PhD-prepared psychologist, marriage and family counselor or therapist, or licensed clinical social worker is required.

Will second opinion consultations be covered if ordered by your psychiatrist? If you yourself are not satisfied with your psychiatrist's or therapist's diagnosis or treatment plan, can you see another to obtain consultation? These are also important questions to ask.

AVAILABLE TREATMENT OPTIONS

Find out what inpatient treatments you are covered for in case these become necessary. If you're interested in a drug detoxification program, or in other assistance for a chemical addiction or dependency, is this covered? On an inpatient basis as well?

Group therapy may be a productive and cost-effective way for you to obtain treatment—is it covered by your plan? If you are having marital or other relationship problems, can you receive treatment to help relieve some pressure or stress resulting from that strained relationship? If therapy is required for your child, will that be covered? Does your insurance provide for family therapy?

Your psychiatrist or therapist may wish to order psychological testing, which is administered by a licensed clinical psychologist—is testing covered?

TREATMENT DECISIONS

Who determines the treatment decisions, your insurance company or your therapist/psychiatrist? Will the mental health practitioner be able to petition for additional or uncovered services if she feels they are necessary?

How comprehensive is the insurer's formulary (list of approved drugs)? Are you covered only for generic drugs or particular medications even if your doctor insists on specific brand-name prescriptions? Will you be able to get the medicines your doctor feels are best for you without paying large copayments out of pocket? If so, is there a yearly cap on the price (typically totaled by average wholesale price) of brand medications that you take? Or of all medications altogether? If so, is a smaller fraction of the average wholesale price of each drug tallied when using generic drugs, or when using certain pharmacies, such as a specific mail-order pharmacy? Additionally, what is the difference between your copay per medication for generic versus brand?

This may seem overly complicated, but for people who take several medications, or for medications that are expensive, planning at this level is smart. You work hard with your doctor to find just the right medication combination for you—make sure you will be able to afford your drug therapy throughout the year by planning ahead and keeping tabs on the total accrued toward your cap on drug expenditures, if you have one. If you take medications for other health conditions, take these into account as well, and perhaps strategize by switching to less expensive or generic medications if you and your doctor believe effectiveness and tolerability would be equivalent.

NOTES TO THE WISE
Insurers require a diagnosis from the psychiatrist or therapist, or completion of a detailed form asking details about your intake session (and perhaps others) and the issues you discuss, before they will pay toward your bill. Sometimes employers have access to this information, either in formal or informal ways. Ask your insurance company about this, and expect to be told who has access to that diagnosis or form. Insurance companies may demand very sensitive information about you; your doctor or therapist will be able to limit this by the manner in which she keeps her records (insurance companies request only certain chart notes).

Eligibility for insurance is not to be taken lightly. If you are currently employed but plan to become self-employed in the future, for instance, you may need to apply for private health insurance at some point, and applicants have been turned down or quoted exorbitant premiums for having nothing more than a prescription for an antidepressant on their record. One of our patients, a woman who took a single antidepressant for a total of 6 months, currently pays $200 monthly for "disaster insurance" (very high deductible and few benefits); others have been quoted $1,500 per month for a PPO plan or turned down altogether. Such policies unfortunately cause individuals to forego treatment out of fear of having it on their record, or to pay for it out of pocket. If you personally pay for insurance that you qualified for before you received your diagnosis, treat it like gold and don't ever let it lapse.

Getting treatment requires time, money, and effort. There is time involved in finding the best therapist and pharmacologist, going to regular appointments, doing homework assignments, going to support groups, and waiting for medications to start helping. There is often a copay fee for professional visits and medications. Getting well involves some work: self-observation, lifestyle changes, and challenging old ways of thinking and behaving. The time, money, and effort are essential investments on the road to recovery.

7

Facilitating Collaboration Between Patient and Clinician

We would all like to think that doctors are all-knowing, omniscient, and omnipotent. But the doctor only knows what the patient can tell him, and what he can see of the patient's behavior during the appointment. Psychiatrists who act like private detectives, spending long hours outside the office investigating the patient's past traumas, exist only in movies. The reality is that the doctor will probably have only about 45 minutes to an hour to spend during an initial interview with a new patient. A great deal of that time is spent gathering information about symptoms, past treatments, social and family history, and assessing mental status. Unfortunately, most doctors seeing a new patient do not have the benefit of substantial background information prior to the appointment.

Because the initial evaluation is so brief, it is important that patients do everything possible to make it productive. It is a good idea for you to put together a file of past medical, psychiatric, psychological, hospital, and pharmacy records for that first visit. List major and minor symptoms, document prior similar episodes and treatment responses, and find out what helped relatives with similar problems. This chapter also deals with what to expect during follow-up visits with your new clinician. Like the last chapter, this chapter is geared toward patients, but therapists will benefit from reading it as well.

The First Visit: Items to Bring to Your New Clinician

Past records, a medication list, a life chart, a family history, and a list of symptoms are several of the items that can be very helpful to your clinician on your first visit. You can bring these items with you or mail them ahead of time. You may choose to organize these items in an outline similar to that used by psychiatrists and therapists for their documentation. Two templates for a Psychiatric History are included at the end of this chapter: one offers the clinician a thorough outline for documentation of the clinical interview in a standard format, while the other provides questions patients can answer to provide some of this information for their new clinicians.

Past Records

If psychological testing has ever been performed, a copy of the psychologist's report will summarize psychological, emotional, and cognitive functioning as well as suggest the diagnostic impression based on the testing. If a person is currently seeing a psychotherapist, a brief summary of the psychotherapy issues, diagnostic impressions, and treatment approaches, as well as the reasons for the referral to a psychiatrist, can be extremely useful. Psychotherapists don't automatically send this information; the patient needs to specifically request it.

If there has ever been a psychiatric hospitalization, the admission and discharge summaries can be very informative. These are the dictated reports at the time of admission and discharge that every hospital requires of attending physicians. This is not the aftercare instruction sheet that is given to the patient the day of discharge; it must be specifically requested from the Medical Records Department, in writing. The full chart, which may contain nursing notes and perhaps lab values, is seldom necessary or informative.

If there are past psychiatrists or primary care physicians who have provided treatment, it can be extremely helpful to request a copy of the records or a brief summary of the treatments that were given and the responses. We have found that treating clinicians often write notes that are too brief or illegible to be of much use, so a treatment summary referral letter—that can be as short as one or two pages—is often invaluable in beginning work with a new patient. If there has been a visit to the primary care doctor that involved obtaining laboratory data and having a physical examination, this information should also be brought to the initial appointment. This can avoid duplicating efforts and expenses by reordering tests that recently came back normal. It is also helpful to provide records regarding any medical illnesses that may be related to the depression, including thyroid or other endocrine problems, neurologic illnesses, heart disease, diabetes, hepatitis, and HIV. Think about each system of your body. Have there been significant illnesses or symptoms now or in the past? Importantly, report any chronic pain.

Medication List

Medical students are often taught that the most valuable diagnostic test is the "brown bag test." The patient is asked to take every medication and supplement in the medicine cabinet, put it in a brown bag, and bring it in to the appointment. By reviewing the medications, it is possible to determine what was given by previous doctors, ask about the benefits or side effects, and look for possible drug interactions.

A list of all psychiatric medications that have been taken in the past can be invaluable, even if they didn't work or were not taken for very long. The list should include any alternative medications, herbs, or other supplements that have been used. If a pharmacy has been consistently used over a long period of time, the records of drugs dispensed are often available from the pharmacist as a computer printout. We ask patients to try to generate this list by calling previous doctors, looking at pharmacy printouts, and looking in the medicine cabinet. The list of medications should be put in the form of a table that shows the name of the medicine, what you took it for (e.g., sleep, depression), the approximate dates of starting and stopping it, the maximum dose taken and for how long, whether there was a beneficial response and for which symptoms, whether side effects were problematic, and whether a blood level was ever obtained. Also note how adherent you were to taking the medications; you would not want to cross a potentially helpful medication off your list of possible treatments if it was not given a fair trial. The reason for stopping the medications is also important. Was there a nasty side effect, did the drug lose effect over time, or was there such an excellent long-term response that medicine no longer seemed needed? A sample Medication History Table is included at the end of this chapter for your convenience.

Life Chart

A life chart can also be very helpful. It allows the clinician to see the patient's longitudinal course of illness over time, analyze factors that may have influenced the illness, and note any patterns such as seasonal depression or anniversary reactions, such as the month a loved one was lost. A horizontal line is drawn across a grid representing several years. Each episode of depression or mania is placed along the timeline, associated with the month and calendar year in which it occurred. It is charted according to severity, including whether there was a hospitalization or suicide attempt. It is noted whether mania was dysphoric, how many mood switches there were in a given month, and if any daily (ultradian) cycling occurred during that month. Factors that may have influenced mood are charted, including new and ongoing medications, psychotherapy or other treatments and their impact, substance abuse, and comorbid psychiatric symptoms. For each episode, the life stresses are noted, as are any other helpful or harmful factors.

A sample Life Chart is included at the end of this chapter. Clearly the goals of this exercise and the previous one are to look for patterns of stressors that have triggered depressive episodes and patterns of treatment that are useful (or not) in treating the episodes.

Family History

Another extremely valuable piece of data is the family history of psychiatric problems, typically in first- and second-degree relatives. Often we see patients who say that they have a relative who has had depression, bipolar affective disorder, a suicide attempt, or substance abuse, but they don't know what treatments were tried and which were successful or made things worse. Often the first homework assignment for patients is to call every relative who has had problems similar to their own to find out what the most helpful medications were.

Symptoms

A great question for clinicians to ask during an initial interview is: "If I could give you the perfect medicine, what would it do for you? What symptoms would get better?" This question serves many purposes. It establishes that the doctor and patient are defining goals of treatment together. It brings out the most important symptoms. And it is also a reality check. If the answer is: "make my husband stop drinking and yelling at me," then you both know that something other than medicine will have to be a major component of the treatment plan. On the other hand, an answer like "help me to sleep and get my appetite and energy back" would indicate that medication may be useful.

Another excellent question is: "Which of your symptoms are 'loudest'? If those were to subside, might the others improve?" Again, the point is to target your most important symptoms. Drugs and psychotherapy treat symptoms, not disorders, and, although some doctors refer to "general templates" in their approach to treatment, these are seldom helpful to a client with his own individual clinical profile and set of priorities. Research, guidelines, and treatment algorithms may inform practice, but they do not determine the best recommendations for a specific patient. Open communication and careful record keeping are key.

To make an accurate diagnosis, your doctor will probably ask you about your symptoms at their worst, in addition to those you currently suffer most from. He will also want to know about any significant symptoms from illnesses—psychiatric or other—that may be related to the depression. These should be listed as well, but there should be a clear delineation in your records between past symptoms and those that are currently present. Some will show consistent patterns over time.

THE SYMPTOMS LIST

Major target symptoms—which are among the most important, distressing, disabling, or severe symptoms within the current episode—should be prioritized on the symptoms list. Additionally, minor symptoms that might be related to the depression or to medical problems should be listed so that they can later be distinguished from possible drug side effects. Again, indicate symptoms that are part of your history as well. For instance, it would be important to know if you've had mania in the past, and if symptoms within episodes have changed over time. Past events are important, too, such as the occurrence of several seizures 2 years ago. It's perfectly okay if the symptom list is lengthy, as long as the most important symptoms are clearly indicated.

Psychological symptoms of depression may include loss of pleasure or enjoyment, crying, hopelessness, worthlessness, helplessness, worry, irritability, sadness, pessimism, guilt, feeling overwhelmed or like nothing will get better, thoughts of death, obsessional intrusive recurrent thoughts, and others.

When developing the symptoms list, it is important to think about many categories. Physical symptoms of depression may include headaches, abdominal pain, back pain, diarrhea, constipation, bloating, nausea, sweating, shaking, feeling short of breath, tremor, palpitations, or feeling chills or hot.

Other biological symptoms of depression may include overeating or loss of appetite, weight gain or loss, oversleeping or insomnia, loss of sexual drive or responsiveness, low energy, and feelings of anxiety such as rapid heart rate, sweating, and others.

Behavioral symptoms of depression may include being very restless—with hand-wringing, pacing, rubbing oneself, or hair pulling—or the opposite, which may involve sitting like a bump on a log, thinking and talking in slow motion, or just "spacing out." Behavior changes may include social withdrawal: Patients will sometimes tell us that they don't answer the phone or get together with friends for dinner or a movie, or go to church the way they normally would. The extreme case is an individual who doesn't bathe or get dressed for weeks at a time and spends most of his day in bed or watching television. Behavior may also change in that the person who has normally gone to work regularly on time is now absent or late. The person who has been meticulous in taking care of hygiene and personal appearance, keeping the house neat, balancing the checkbook and paying the bills on time, and washing the car may now feel like these things don't matter and begin to neglect them.

Problems with thought and perception may include paranoid thoughts and feelings, visual or auditory hallucinations, or other psychotic symptoms.

If you believe you have symptoms of anxiety related to a traumatic experience, you may report intrusive memories, hypervigilance, a heightened startle response, situations you may be avoiding to avoid the anxiety, nightmares, or a feeling of numbness or detachment from yourself.

Symptoms of mania and hypomania include feeling very good, expansive, or irritable; having more energy or activity; being more social or outgoing; feeling more self-confident or grandiose; requiring less sleep; speaking so quickly others cannot keep up, or having the urge to keep talking; having racing or crowded thoughts; poor concentration or distractibility; increased sexual activity; impulsive activities with potential for painful consequences such as violent behavior, increased spending, or increased use of drugs or alcohol; and just general impulsivity that is different from your normal behavior patterns. Sometimes these symptoms are intermixed, or rapidly alternate with, the classic depressive symptoms in a "mixed episode."

If you have a history of substance use, list each substance and, for each, when you first used it, when you started using heavily, the last time you used it, and both how often and how much you currently use. If alcohol is your drug of choice, have you ever blacked out or gone into withdrawal? Had seizures? Have you had medical, legal, work, or family problems due to heavy drinking or drug use?

Important neurological symptoms that may indicate conditions related to depression include numbness or tingling anywhere, loss of balance, trouble with walking, double vision or vision problems, periods of amnesia, seizures, changes in coordination, speech difficulties, weakness in arms or legs, tremor, and fainting or dizziness. It is important to report any history of falls or head trauma, especially if you blacked out or were hospitalized. Endocrine symptoms may include a change in glove or shoe size, tremor, intolerance of heat or cold, sweating, thirst, craving sweets, frequent urination, or voice changes.

For each symptom, the magnitude, duration, and intensity are important. Is the symptom subjectively mild, moderate, or severe, and how much does it interfere with everyday functioning? Did it come on gradually or abruptly? How long ago? Was there an immediate trigger at the start of the symptom, such as a disruption in a major relationship, a new physical illness or medication, or a period of substance abuse?

Guides for compiling the review of symptoms—one for clinicians, another for patients—are included at the end of this chapter.

Questions to Ask the Doctor

Just as the doctor will have many questions for you, you should come to the appointment planning to gain some information as well.

Questions to Ask About the Diagnosis

If you are receiving a new diagnosis, or want more information about the one for which you are seeking help, you might want to ask the doctor or therapist a few questions. You may want to know about the nature of the particular illness and what is believed to be at the root of it. What biological, psychological, and social variables contribute? Ask the clinician how certain he is of the diagnosis, and what other possibilities he feels are most likely and why. If you have had a very difficult course of illness, would he recommend an independent opinion from another practitioner at this point? You can also ask what additional tests or exams would be recommended. If the current evaluation is a preliminary one, how soon will it be before the clinician is able to provide a more definite evaluation of your illness?

General Questions About Treatment

Ask the doctor what treatments he thinks might be helpful and how they will be expected to help. What does he expect the program to accomplish? Will his recommended treatment plan involve services by other specialists? If so, who will be responsible for coordinating those services? About how long does he expect this to take, how often will the plan be reevaluated, and how frequently will he and the other specialists be expecting you to attend appointments? What will be the best evidence that you are responding to the program, and how soon will this evidence appear?

A list of questions you may ask the doctor about your diagnosis and his approach to treatment is provided at the end of this chapter for your convenience. These questions are helpful when getting to know your psychotherapist as well.

Questions About Medications

When your new doctor or nurse practitioner offers you the option of medication, you will want to know why he has chosen this particular medicine. Find out both the trade and generic names it is known by and the class of drugs it belongs in (e.g., antidepressants), as well as the suggested dosage level, whether this will be increased, and how you will do this. Ask how it will be monitored and whether you will need any tests prior to starting it. How often will you need to repeat those tests? Find out how the medication is thought to work and what the clinician expects it to do for you. You may want to know what kind of a track record this medication has regarding effectiveness—both in the doctor's clinical experience and in terms of research findings. How long will it take to achieve that result? For example, Prozac may take 6 to 12 weeks to produce response in depression, but 3 months in some individuals (often at a higher dose) to treat OCD.

What symptoms indicate that the dosage should be changed or the medication stopped? Are there any risks associated with taking this medication? Find out about possible side effects: What are the short-term side effects, which might persist, and which, if any, are dangerous? What are the warning signs, and what can you do if you encounter them? Is there any way to minimize the chances of experiencing side effects? Does the doctor recommend any dietary or lifestyle changes when using this medication? MAO inhibitors, for instance, require a diet low in tyramine (a substance found in many foods, including smoked meats, aged cheese, and red wine). Some medications may make you more likely to get a sunburn, and others less able to regulate body temperature. Some should not be taken with grapefruit juice.

Consider using the convenient questions provided in the guide at the end of this chapter to ask about medication. Finally, ask your doctor or pharmacist where you can get more information on the medication, and whether they have any printed information you can have to study.

Working With Your New Clinician

Regular long-term follow-up appointments are essential for evaluation of treatment response and side effects, help coping with life stressors, and prescription refills. Their length and frequency will vary over time depending on the severity of illness, response to treatment, and life circumstances.

Follow-Up Appointments

Just as it is important to be prepared for the initial consultation, it is also important to be prepared for the follow-up medication management visits. At each visit, it is helpful to have a list of current medications, the dose of the medications, any changes in the medications, and additions or deletions of medications prescribed by other doctors. It is also helpful to list the symptoms and side effects that are currently most important, as well as how they have changed since the last appointment. A Report of Medication Response form is included at the end of this chapter for your use.

Usually a medication follow-up visit involves some general inquiry about the patient's work and home life to assess ongoing ability to function and deal with stressors, questions about the effectiveness of the psychiatric medication, questions about any ongoing symptoms or side effects, and joint decision-making concerning the next step in medication management. Examples would potentially include continuing the same medicine with the same dose or a dose adjustment, adding a second medicine to treat any residual (ongoing) symptoms or side effects, or changing medicines. You and your doctor may consider lifestyle changes such as decreasing alcohol use or increasing exercise or pleasurable activities. In this way, the collaboration between doctor and patient to optimize the medication management becomes a true partnership.

Follow-up appointments are usually set at 1- or 2-week intervals during the acute phase of treatment, when medications are being adjusted and acute life problems are being addressed. Most psychiatrists and patients can reach an agreement about when this intensity of treatment may no longer be necessary, usually when the symptoms become mild or resolve, the side effects are mild or tolerable, and the medication doses are stable. At this point, it is common to go to a long-term maintenance plan, typically setting appointments every 1 to 3 months for routine "med checks" that may be as short as 15 minutes. Most psychiatrists and patients know that regular review of medication response, doses, side effects, and perhaps laboratory monitoring can help to maintain a continuous, comfortable, trusting relationship. This is the foundation for prompt intervention if things get bad in the future.

Should doctors give refills of medication for patients they haven't seen in a long time? Sometimes a doctor will get a call from a patient who has not come to the office for several months or, more often, will get a fax from the pharmacist requesting authorization for a refill. This puts the doctor in a difficult position. If he says no, the patient will go without medicine and may decide to go off of it without discussing with the doctor how and when to do it. There may be an interruption in treatment until the patient makes an appointment. If the doctor says yes, he assumes liability for what happens to the person who is under his care, who is taking medications he has prescribed, and who might be falling apart with terrible stressors, heavy drinking, or planning an overdose. Every physician has his own policy about how to deal with this difficult situation. We suggest authorizing only a single short-term refill for the patient after he has set an appointment. At the appointment, the doctor can remind the patient that medication treatment must involve regular appointments during which the doctor can spend some time talking with the patient about how things are working.

Be Persistent!

Among adults who initiated antidepressant treatment for depression from 1996 to 2001, 42.4% discontinued medication within the first 30 days. This was most common among Hispanics, people with less than 12 years of education, and people with low family income (Olfson, Marcus, Tedeschi, & Wan, 2006). These people never really gave their medication a fair chance to work for them. Antidepressants may show some benefit by 2 weeks, but often take 1 to 2 months to be truly effective. Patient education about reasonably expected time to respond is essential.

Change One Thing at a Time!

During treatment of depression, it is very important to be patient. Despite the urgency of treating depression, only one drug change should be made at a time and each drug should be taken for a long enough time to decide that it is either very helpful, partially helpful, not helpful, or causing intolerable side effects. A critically important part of the doctor-patient collaboration is evaluating each intervention (medication or behavioral change) to determine if some or all symptoms have improved and if any new side effects have appeared. It is very important to not get discouraged and give up on a medicine before it has had a chance to work (typically 1 to 2 months). Once a decision on effectiveness has been made, the drug will either be continued (perhaps with dose adjustment) or stopped. This should be a very clear decision that is made before adding or switching to a second drug.

Sorting out cause-and-effect relationships between symptoms and medication, behavioral changes, and life changes can be extremely difficult when multiple treatments or activities have been started or changed at the same time. Consider the following, an extreme example: A perimenopausal 50-year-old woman presents for treatment of recent-onset depression. She has just started hormone replacement therapy, an antidepressant, a sleeping pill, and a blood pressure medicine. In addition, she has consulted her friends and begun an herbal supplement, as well as starting marital therapy to deal with long-standing issues in her relationship. At the same time, she has started meditation and yoga and gotten promoted to a new highly challenging job. She now wants to know which of these things is helping and which might be causing ongoing side effects and distress, but this is impossible to sort out because too many things were started at once. Sometimes it can take a period of several months or even years to achieve a regimen of medications that gives excellent control of symptoms with minimal side effects, and this ongoing process requires careful self-observation, patient-physician collaboration, and continuity of care.

Your Approach to the Working Relationship

In closing, we would like to say a few things about active and passive approaches to partnering with your doctor. We recognize that some patients—especially those who are acutely and severely ill—may be less inclined to advocate strongly for themselves and may benefit from a doctor with a take-charge attitude. For those of you who want to play a truly active role in your health care, however, we provide some thoughts on the difference between active and passive approaches.

Many people who have spent a long time in the health care system are accustomed to expecting a provider to take charge of their health. They might even feel helpless and lost in the system. They may rely completely on the provider's advice, seldom ask questions, and offer information only when asked. They may be complacent, demonstrating a fatalistic "what will be, will be" attitude, and they might not be interested in thinking about options. These patients may be hesitant to disagree with or confront their practitioner, worrying that their health care will be compromised if they ask questions or disagree.

More engaged consumers are active and assertive, not passive. They want and expect to work in partnership with clinicians, sharing decision-making about the treatment plan and sharing responsibility for choosing between options and alternatives. These patients select clinicians who will listen, who will involve them fully in decisions, who will seek to learn as much as possible about their health and well-being, and who will periodically seek updated information. Active patients are not embarrassed to stop the clinician if he is not communicating clearly or is using terms the patient does not understand.

Speaking out may keep you from an unnecessary or mistaken treatment, adverse drug reaction, or potential ongoing problem. By becoming informed and holding your own, you are using a health care professional as a consultant in helping you to heal, not as a person who holds the keys to your treatment. Clinicians have knowledge about the science of body and mind, but you are the only expert on you.

Psychiatric History—Clinician Version

Here we provide guide to writing a personal psychiatric history, in a commonly accepted format used by many clinicians when they write notes after an intake interview. The History consists of the History of Present Illness (HPI), which contains both current and historical data relevant to the patient's present symptoms and syndromes, followed by sections in which historical information on biological, psychological, and social factors not directly related to the present illness are recorded.

Identifying Data

- Name
- Age and birth date
- Ethnic origin
- Gender identification
- Employment or retirement status
- Influencing life circumstances
- How the patient was referred to the clinician, and for what purpose

An example:

"I am Jane Smith, a 47-year-old [date of birth] currently disabled, recently divorced African American female flight attendant, with no children. I come referred by John Barber, MD, my primary care practitioner, who feels I might benefit from seeing a specialist for my depression."

Chief Complaint

The "chief complaint" is the main reason the patient has chosen to visit the health care provider or therapist. It could be because she realizes how long it's been since she did not feel depressed, because her youngest son just moved to college and she is having difficulty coping, or because her husband has asked her to give medications a try. The chief complaint is a simple sentence or two, which is then explained in depth below.

History of Present Illness

Most of the data that will contribute directly or indirectly to the diagnosis and treatment of the patient's current problems should be included in the HPI.

The greatest focus of the HPI is a discussion of current symptoms and syndromes, as well as a chronologically organized history of exacerbations or remissions of illness. As many psychiatric illnesses are chronic or recurrent, knowledge of the course of illness from its onset is important in assessment and planning. Therefore, historical data of relevance to the present illness—such as that addressing medical illnesses, drug or alcohol use, sexuality, or financial troubles—is included.

To facilitate this review of psychiatric symptoms and associated factors, the Guide for Review of Symptoms, also at the end of this chapter, is provided. The Guide for Review of Symptoms, in turn, makes use of the Life Chart, which may also be used either within the Review of Symptoms and the Psychiatric History, or on its own.

Psychiatric History

As psychiatric illness is often chronic or recurrent, the HPI covers not only the current symptoms and their associated factors but the history of those symptoms or illnesses as well. The Psychiatric History therefore contains those past events, symptoms, diagnoses, and treatments that are not historically associated with information covered in the HPI. Examples would be an eating disorder in high school with no present residual symptoms, a brief period of psychosis related to a substance or medical condition, or ADHD that has not followed the patient into adulthood. If the history chronicles a lifelong struggle with depression, however, and the HPI focuses on just the past couple of years, more remote events may be recorded here.

- Description of the most recent period of stability.
- Chronology of past episodes or periods of mental illness regardless of whether they were diagnosed or treated.
- Medications: the format is provided in the Medication History Table. This should include all prescribed or over-the-counter medications, herbal products, vitamins and minerals, and other nutritional supplements.
- Other somatic therapies: provide the specifics for any past use of electroconvulsive therapy (ECT), vagus nerve stimulation (VNS), or transcranial magnetic stimulation (TMS), including when started, when stopped, number of sessions, technical parameters if known, helpfulness, any side effects, and name and contact information of the doctor who performed the treatment.
- Psychotherapy: type (e.g., psychodynamic, cognitive, behavioral, supportive), format (e.g., group, individual, couple), frequency, duration, attendance adherence to assignments, and patient's perception of the helpfulness of therapy and quality of relationship with the therapist.
- Alternative and complementary medical practices: describe use of massage, acupuncture, yoga, and other practices and how they have or have not been helpful.
- Psychiatric hospitalizations, ER visits, and periods of residential treatment, including the reasons, lengths of stay, total number, and most recent.
- Suicide attempts and acts of self-harm: precipitating factors, means (e.g., overdose, jumping), whether the threat or harm to self was impulsive or planned, whether there was any resultant injury (and its severity), and whether drugs or alcohol were involved.
- The same information for any acts of violence towards others.
- Names and contact information for previous outpatient psychiatrists, therapists, and case managers.

Substance Use History

Include details of the patient's use of:

- Alcohol (include type, e.g. beer, malt liquor, vodka)
- Opiates (prescription pain medication or heroin)
- Solvents and inhalants

Include details of the patient's use of:

- Cocaine (powder or crack)
- Methamphetamine
- Prescription stimulants
- Marijuana
- Anxiolytics and sedative-hypnotics (such as the benzodiazepines Klonopin, Ativan, Valium, Xanax, or prescribed sleeping medications)
- Hallucinogens
- MDMA (ecstasy)
- Androgenic steroids
- Tobacco
- Caffeine

For each substance used now or in past, provide the following data:

- Name of substance
- Route used (snorting, oral, smoking, or intravenous use)
- When use began
- When heavy use began
- Amount of current use (list by quantity or amount regularly spent)
- Pattern of use: binge/episodic versus chronic/continual; solitary or social
- Last use (e.g., last night)
- Number of times clean
- Longest time clean

For all drugs, cover also:

- Association of substance use with current psychiatric symptoms or pattern of illness.
- Any self-perceived benefits of use.
- Functional, interpersonal, legal, or financial consequences of use.
- Patterns of substance use within the family or living constellation.
- Factors contributing to being clean.
- Factors contributing to relapse
- Participation in peer support groups such as 12-Step and SMART.
- Chemical dependency treatment, including inpatient detox, residential treatment, or other programs.
- Tolerance and symptoms of withdrawal or delirium tremens (DTs, severe alcohol withdrawal), including: tremors, chills, nausea and vomiting, sweating, anxiety and agitation, headache, confusion or disorientation, diarrhea, fever, elevated heart rate or blood pressure, visual hallucinations or illusions (such as shadows or moving patterns in wallpaper), tactile hallucinations (formication, the sensation of something crawling on the skin), and seizures.

Here is an example of history of a patient's alcohol use, consequences, and treatment:

"Alcohol. Started drinking at 13 years old with kids at school casually, started drinking heavily at 18 with a pint of vodka and a 6-pack of 12-oz beers daily. I currently drink about that much daily, but much more heavily on the weekend or when I'm not working, or if I've had a fight with my girlfriend, who, by the way, uses a lot of meth. Last use this morning, 3 beers. The alcohol has caused problems in my relationships, was an issue in my divorce, and also caused legal problems in my 20's when I used to get into fights when drunk.

I still get kind of irritable but I can control that now. I think alcohol makes my anxiety and depression worse, although maybe the absence of it does, because it has always helped me to feel less nervous in social situations, and I express my feelings more easily when I'm drinking. I have been clean and sober for a few weeks to 9 months at the longest, which was 2 years ago. I tend to relapse with financial problems, and relapse affects my self-esteem and contributes to a sense of helplessness. Most helpful in staying clean has been attendance at AA meetings, though I don't currently have a sponsor. I have experienced blackouts and alcohol withdrawal numerous times when trying to quit cold turkey, managed this on my own by tapering my use with small amounts of alcohol, I have never been hospitalized for withdrawal, and fortunately have never had DTs."

General Medical History

While the HPI lists any medical illnesses and symptoms that are in some way related to the current psychiatric symptoms, the General Medical History and Review of Systems (ROS) are devoted specifically to medical illness. The General Medical History covers illnesses and their treatment chronologically from childhood, and the ROS (included near the end of the Psychiatric History) covers current physical symptoms not listed in the HPI.

- In chronological order list all operations, other hospitalizations, significant injuries, and significant illnesses (acute or chronic) not resulting in hospitalization. Of particular (but not exclusive) interest are the following:
  - Pertinent childhood illnesses or facts concerning growth and development.
  - Infectious processes including hepatitis, HIV, and any infection involving the neurologic system.
  - Head injury, neurologic disorders, endocrine disorders, sleep disorders, and conditions causing pain and discomfort.
- Complications of illness, injury and treatment are also noted.
- Information on past procedures, treatment and medications are helpful; current medical medications can also be listed along with current psychiatric medications on the Medication History Table.
- The following questions should also be considered:
  - Are undiagnosed illnesses causing the patient major distress or functional impairment?
  - Does the patient engage in high-risk behaviors that would predispose him or her to a medical illness?
- Sexual and reproductive history should be provided: matters related to sexual health, problems with sexual desire or performance, menstrual issues (including regularity and symptoms of premenstrual syndrome), obstetric history, or any sexually transmitted diseases.

Allergies and Sensitivities

An allergy is a reaction provoking an allergic immune response, including rash, hives, swelling, redness, itching, wheezing, and other symptoms. Sensitivities may include other reactions, such as nausea with some medications. Along with the name of the medication or allergen, the specific reaction should be listed.

- Allergies, sensitivities, and adverse reactions to medications or treatment (including contrast dye and latex)
- Reactions to environmental allergens
- Allergies and sensitivities to foods

Health Maintenance

If not already included elsewhere:
- Diet
- Exercise
- Sleep pattern and quality
- Last physical exam
- Regular complementary and alternative practices (e.g. massage, acupuncture, chiropractic)
- Contact information for the primary care provider and other practitioners

Family History

The family history chronicles both psychiatric and general medical illness in close (first- and second-degree) relatives. While information about family dynamics and cultural or ethnic values sometimes is recorded here; we prefer to include that information in the Social History, below, reserving the Family History for medical conditions of blood relatives only.

For each of the patient's first- or second-degree relative, provide the name, current age or age at time of death, and relationship to the patient. For second degree relatives, indicate whether the grandmother or aunt is maternal or paternal, and which of the patient's children gave birth to a particular grandchild.

Include information on the following psychiatric illnesses:
- Affective disorders, including depression, bipolar illness, and "nervous breakdown"
- Anxiety disorders, or "neuroses"
- Schizophrenia or psychosis
- Alcoholism and drug abuse
- Developmental disabilities including delay (retardation), autism, Aspergers, and learning disabilities
- Delinquency
- Legal difficulties
- Suicide or attempts
- Violence

Information known about the following should be included:
- Age of onset
- Course of illness
- Specific symptoms
- Medications and their effectiveness
- Psychotherapy
- Hospital care

Information on history of medical illnesses, particularly the following:
- Coronary artery disease
- Diabetes
- Hypertension
- Neurologic illness (e.g., stroke, epilepsy, tumor)
- High cholesterol
- Endocrine disorders
- Cancer
- Known familial diseases (genetic origin)

Sociocultural, Developmental, and Psychosocial History

Sociocultural History
- What are the patient's cultural, ethnic, spiritual, and religious beliefs, and how have these developed or changed over time?
- How do they relate to family of origin and other important relationships?
- Are there any traditions of particular importance to the patient?
- Does the patient hold any particular existential, moral, or interpersonal values or beliefs?

Upbringing
- With whom did the patient grow up, and what were the interpersonal relationships like within the household?
- Were cultural, ethnic, spiritual, and religious beliefs central during childhood?
- Did the patient move often, and were there any difficult cultural, social, economic or other transitions?
- Was there a history of adoption or foster care, or disruptions in the family environment due to divorce, remarriage, death, or prolonged absences of family members because of hospitalization, occupation or incarceration?

Developmental History
- Did the patient attain developmental milestones such as walking, talking, and toilet training at the expected times?
- Were there any childhood or adolescent behavioral problems such as tics, significant problems with temper, unusual or excessive separation anxiety, significant problems with sleep, disordered eating, deliberate self-harm, or wetting the bed?
- What was the patient's experience in school? Address grade completed or age when stopped, and for what reason.
- Describe academic ability and performance, including delays in learning to read, write or do math. Were there significant problems paying attention or finishing school work and completing homework?
- Were there frequent absences for medical or other reasons?
- Mention any behavioral problems or disciplinary action while in school.
- Were there problems in adolescence involving delinquency, drugs or drinking, or violence?
- Address the patient's satisfaction with social relationships in childhood and adolescence, including friendships (making and keeping), dating activity, and

relationships with siblings. Was severe shyness a problem with strangers or familiars? Were there problems with being bullied or bullying?
- What were the patient's hobbies and extracurricular activities? Were they social or solitary? Did the patient enjoy participation in athletics, clubs and other group experiences?
- Include a sexual history if this is pertinent.

Primary Relationships (With Partners and Children)
- Details of the current primary relationship, including length and quality.
  - What are the areas of agreement and disagreement, management of money, and role of "in-laws"?
  - What are the ages of children, relationships with children, and attitudes toward the raising of children?
  - Is the patient a member of a blended family?
- If the patient lives with people other than her partner or family, what is the description of persons living in the home?
- Describe details of previous relationships and relationship dissolution history.
- Have there been prolonged absences of current or former partners or children due to occupation, hospitalization, or incarceration?
- Has the patient suffered the death of a partner or child?
- What has the role of the patient's illness been in relationships with partners and children, and in the family dynamic?
- Describe the patient's sexual history, including sexual orientation, beliefs, practices, and past sexual experiences. Does the patient currently use a method of birth control? Do they practice safe sex?

Sociocultural Supports
- What are the patient's sociocultural supports (e.g., family, friends, work, and religious and other community groups)? Does the patient feel a sense of belonging in the community?
- What are the qualities of these contacts? Do they feel stable and gratifying?
- Have there been changes in the quality or frequency of contacts? What has been the patient's capacity to maintain friendships and acquaintances?
- Describe the patient's capacities for attachment, trust, and intimacy.
- Do things generally go well for the patient in her day-to-day contacts?
- Does the patient ever feel lonely? Is there a pattern to loneliness or isolation, and does this relate to the pattern of psychiatric illness?

Trauma and Stressors
- Is there a history of parental loss or divorce; physical, emotional, or sexual abuse; or exposure to other traumatic experiences? List the date and duration, description, persons involved, and whether the trauma was a threat, attempt, or event.
- Has the patient been the perpetrator of abuse to others? If so, what type and to whom?

- What have been the life stressors in the past year?
  - Relationship or marriage
  - Family or children
  - Social environment
  - Death
  - Housing or living arrangements
  - Financial
  - Employment or education
  - Legal problems
  - Abuse or neglect
  - Involvement with social agencies
  - Medical problems
  - Access to health care
  - Crime victim
  - War, disaster or civil unrest

Coping Styles
- Is the patient frequently tense, and how do they handle this?
- What strategies for coping has the patient used successfully during times of stress or adversity?

Personality Long-Term
- How would the patient describe her personality long-term?
- What changes in activities, interests, general mood and social patterns have occurred over time that might be a result of or contribute to psychiatric illness?

Future Goals and Plans
- What important changes or developments would the patient like to make in the future, in areas of self-development, education or occupation, social relationships, financial growth, or other important life areas?

Capacity for Self-Care
- Is the patient able to perform the expected activities of daily living (ADLs) of clothing, feeding, and providing shelter for herself?
- Is the patient able to eat a healthful diet and to get regular exercise?
- Is the patient able to manage money effectively?

Healthcare Values and Beliefs
- What are the patient's own interests, preferences, attitudes, expectations and values with respect to health care?
- Will treatment interfere with religious or cultural beliefs and practices, and how might this be addressed?
- Does the patient have an advanced directive or durable power of attorney for healthcare (DPOAH), and are there any particular health wishes the clinician should know about?

Occupational and Military History
Provide the following information related to each current and past occupation or job, in chronological sequence, beginning with most recent:

- Title of position held, and duration of time in that position
- Hours, tasks and responsibilities
- Work skills and strengths
- Job satisfaction

- Quality of work relationships with coworkers and supervisors
- Reasons for changing jobs
- Shift work, noxious or perilous environment, hazardous materials exposure risks, unusual physical or psychological stress, injury, or exposure to trauma
- Past or current experience with the workers' compensation system

List hobbies that are also important to the patient and/or carry exposure risk.

For military service, provide the following details:
- Which branch of the military did the patient serve in?
- What were the years of service?
- Was the patient a volunteer, recruit, or draftee?
- Was the patient ever rejected at time of enlistment?
- Was there combat exposure?
- Did the patient suffer injury, trauma, or exposure to chemical weapons?
- List awards, disciplinary actions, and discharge status.

Discuss retirement and disability:
- Is the patient unable to work due to disability?
- Describe any preparations for or adjustment to retirement, by choice, due to disability, or for other reasons.
- List the type of Income: pension from Social Security, disability, or past employer; General Assistance; military service connection; passive income or savings; or other.
- If on disability for psychiatric illness, does the patient have a conservator or payee? What is the conservator's contact information?

Legal History
- Does the patient have any past or current involvement with the juvenile or criminal justice system (e.g., warrants, arrests, jail or prison detentions, convictions, probation, parole)?
- If there has been detention, for how long was the patient incarcerated, and when were they released?
- Have there been interactions with law enforcement without formal arrest?
- Do past or current legal problems relate to aggressive behaviors or substance intoxication?
- Has the patient had other significant interactions with the court system (e.g., family court, workers compensation dispute, civil litigation, court-ordered psychiatric treatment)?
- Is past or current legal involvement a significant social stressor for the patient?

Review of Systems
The review of systems refers to the body's systems, including neurologic, cardiovascular, respiratory, and others. It includes current symptoms not already identified in the history of the present illness.

- Change in or difficulty with appetite, eating patterns, and sleep should be included.
- Indicate details of pain or discomfort, including quality (e.g., stabbing, dull, throbbing) and severity; pain is rated on a scale of 1–10, with 10 being the worst pain the patient has experienced, or the worst imaginable.
- Mention any systemic symptoms such as weight loss, fatigue, fever or sweating.
- Important are symptoms that may suggest neurologic involvement, including fainting, seizures, vertigo, problems with speech, walking or balance, tremor, muscle weakness, tingling, numbness, and headaches.
- Discuss symptoms that may signal endocrine involvement, including, heat or cold intolerance, excessive sweating, desire to drink or eat to excess, significant weight losss or gain that is not deliberate, frequent urination, changes in frequency of menstrual periods, and change in voice, glove, or shoe size.
- Describe any other symptoms suggestive of medical illness.

Health Teaching Assessment

To best help the clinician refer the patient to resources, he should know the following:

- Indicate the patient's preferred learning style(s): reading, discussion, lecture, demonstration, or audio visual.
- Does the patient have any physical or mental conditions that prevent her from learning about her own health care needs? Communication barriers may include hearing, vision, language, reading, or mental status.
- About which areas is the patient interested in learning more? Suggestions include but are not limited to medications, symptom management, relapse prevention, psychosocial skills, health maintenance and promotion, and pain management.

Psychiatric History—Patient Version

Here we provide version of the Psychiatric History designed to guide patients as they write a personal psychiatric history, in a commonly accepted format many clinicians are accustomed to reading. The history consists of the History of Present Illness (HPI), which contains both current and historical data relevant to the patient's present symptoms and syndromes, followed by sections in which historical information on biological, psychological, and social factors not directly related to the present illness are recorded.

Identifying Data
Name, age, sex, marital status, employment, and referral source

Chief Complaint
Main problem, symptom, or reason for seeking treatment

History of Present Illness
- Age of onset
- Number of episodes or recurrences
- Most troublesome symptoms
- Duration of symptoms in past episodes and currently
- Current and past treatments:
    - Medications: the format is provided in the Medication History Table. This should include all prescribed or over-the-counter medications, herbal products, vitamins and minerals, and other nutritional supplements
    - Include also ECT, VNS, TMS, or other treatments
    - Psychotherapy
    - Alternative and complementary medical practices such as acupuncture or massage
    - Support groups attended
    - What has been helpful or made things worse?

- History of psychiatric hospitalizations
- History of suicide attempts
- Names and contact information for current psychiatrists, therapists, and case managers

To facilitate this review of psychiatric symptoms and associated factors, the patient may optionally use the Guide for Review of Symptoms, also at the end of this chapter.
- This guide is helpful both for:
    - Integrating with this Psychiatric History
    - Use by those patients who wish to provide the clinician with basic information about their illness without writing a complete history
- The Guide for Review of Symptoms, in turn, makes use of the Life Chart, which may also be used either within the Review of Symptoms and the Psychiatric History, or on its own.

Substance Use History
- Have alcohol, street drugs, or abuse of prescription medications ever caused problems in the patient's work, school, or home life, or caused medical or legal problems?
- Have treatment been sought for substance-related problems, or has it been recommended by family or a healthcare professional?
- Periods clean and sober and factors that have been helpful in achieving and maintaining sobriety
- Include habitual use of tobacco and caffeine

General Medical History
- Have there been any major illnesses, operations, or hospitalizations?
- Are there any physical symptoms not satisfactorily evaluated & treated by the primary care physician?
- Is the patient taking any long-term prescription or over the counter medications or supplements?
  - Medical medications can also be listed along with psychiatric medications on the Medication History Table

Allergies and Sensitivities
Have there been any allergic or other negative reactions to medications?

Health Maintenance
- Does the patient get a routine annual physical exam and lab work?
  - Women: Pap and mammograms?
  - Men: prostate exam?
- Diet and exercise habits
- Contact information for the primary care provider and any specialists

Family History
- Have the patient's first- or second-degree relatives had any psychiatric problems, abused alcohol or drugs, had a nervous breakdown, or attempted suicide?
- If any close relative has been treated for psychiatric illness, what were the most helpful medications?

Sociocultural, Developmental, and Psychosocial History
- What was it like for the patient to grow up in her family? How were her relationships with parents, and siblings?
- How did the patient perform during school? How were relationships with peers and teachers?
- How many serious long-term romantic relationships have there been? How are the relationships with partner(s), and children? With current and former coworkers and superiors?
- Were there any major physical, emotional, or sexual traumas growing up?

Coping styles
- What helps the patient handle the stresses in her life?

Personality long-term
- How would the patient describe her personality long-term?

Future goals and plans
- What important changes or developments would the patient like to make in the future, in areas of self-development, education or occupation, social relationships, financial growth, or other important life areas?

Occupational and Military History
- Is the patient in school, working, unemployed, or retired?
- What have been the most successful, fulfilling or longest held jobs?

Legal History
- Is the patient facing any current legal stressors such as a lawsuit, divorce, criminal charges, or probation?

Guide for Review of Symptoms—Clinician Version

Here is a guide to recording pertinent data about current symptoms, their course over time, contributing and resulting factors, and what the patient has done to manage them. This guide may be used on its own, or inserted into the Psychiatric History form (also provided at the end of this chapter) under History of Present Illness.

Below is a list of symptoms common to a broad spectrum of psychiatric illnesses. They are not listed by association with any particular diagnosis both because many symptoms are listed in the criteria of a host of different disorders, and because diagnosis is not made on a list of symptoms alone.

The list of symptoms is followed by a selection of questions often asked by clinicians to elicit information about their character and quality, and to determine the relationship of the symptoms to time, medical illness, psychosocial and sociocultural factors, events, and other variables.

Symptoms

Negative thoughts, feelings and behaviors

- Depressed mood
- "Mood swings"
- Sadness
- Tearfulness
- Hopelessness
- Helplessness
- Worthlessness
- Poor self esteem
- Feelings of guilt
- Deep sense of shame
- Chronic feelings of emptiness
- Feelings of detachment or numbness
- Loneliness
- Isolative behavior
- Anhedonia (inability to experience pleasure)
- Decreased interest in activities once enjoyed
- Apathy (lack of motivation)
- Negative thoughts or pessimism
- Sense of a foreshortened future
- Diurnal pattern to mood (depression is more severe in the morning than in the evening)

Heightened thoughts, feelings and behaviors

- Expansive mood
- Feeling "hyper"
- More energetic than usual
- More social and outgoing than usual
- More active then usual
- Taking on more projects than usual
- Exaggerated sense of self-confidence
- Grandiosity
- Internal restlessness
- Racing thoughts
- Rapid speech
- Irritability
- Anger outbursts

Fears and anxieties

- Anticipatory anxiety
- Nervousness, or constant nervous tension
- Marked or persistent fear of a specific object or situation
- Anxiety about being in specific places or situations, such as crowds, standing in line, or certain modes of travel
- Avoidance of certain places, people or situations because of magical beliefs
- Fear of criticism, rejection, or inadequacy
- Fear of social or performance situations involving unfamiliar people or potential scrutiny
- Fear of abandonment
- Fear of losing control or going crazy
- Fear of gaining weight or becoming fat
- Intrusive, distressing memories
- Fear of persecution
- Fear of dying

Distorted thoughts and perceptions

- Paranoia (suspicion and mistrust or conviction that something bad will happen)
- Delusions (a fixed false belief)
- Auditory, olfactory, visual, or tactile hallucinations
- Command hallucinations (a voice commanding the patient to engage in a specific activity)
- Illusion (a misperception of real phenomena, such as an electrical cord being perceived as a snake)
- Belief that one has exaggerated power, importance, knowledge or ability
- Magical thinking: the belief that thinking equates with doing, or that one's thoughts, words, or actions will cause or prevent a specific implausible outcome
- The feeling of reliving a traumatic event (illusions, hallucinations, or flashbacks)

Obsessions, preoccupations and worry

Preoccupation with:

- Cleanliness
- Food or eating
- Perceived defect in appearance
- Details, rules, lists, order, organization, or schedules
- Jealousy, sin, sex, infidelity, perfect love
- Other preoccupation
- Persistent, uncontrollable worry
- Experience of recurrent, persistent, intrusive thoughts, impulses, or images that cause anxiety

Impulsive and compulsive behaviors

- Repetitive behaviors (e.g., hand washing, ordering, checking)
- Restrictive or binge eating; rituals involving food

- Repetitive mental acts (e.g., praying, counting, repeating words silently)
- Collection of objects that have neither useful nor sentimental value
- Pulling hair on the head or body, or eyelashes
- Compulsive picking or grooming
- Impulsive and problematic behavior involving stealing, shopping, gambling, sex, pornography, reckless driving, or internet use
- Other impulsive behavior
- Difficulty controlling anger

Dissociative phenomena

- Dissociation (emotional distancing, commonly, but not exclusively, experienced in traumatic or distressing circumstances)
- Derealization (feelings of unreality)
- Depersonalization (feelings of being detached from or of observing oneself)

Violence and self-harm

- Self-injurious behavior (e.g., cutting, burning)
- Thoughts of taking one's own life or of being better off dead
- Plan or intent to take one's own life
- Thoughts of, plans, or intent to hurt or kill others

Neuropsychological phenomena

- Difficulty concentrating or mind going blank
- Poor attention; easily distracted
- Reduced ability to focus, sustain, or shift attention
- Flight of ideas (the mind jumps from one idea to another unrelated idea)
- Memory impairment (impaired ability to learn new information or to recall previously learned information)
- Inability to recall important aspects or details of (or a particular span of time in) one's past
- Sitting and staring into space
- Disturbance in speaking, writing or understanding language
- Inability to put thoughts into words
- Disturbance of consciousness (i.e., reduced clarity of awareness of and response to the environment)
- Difficulty with in executive functioning (e.g., planning, organizing, sequencing, abstracting)
- Impaired ability to carry out motor activities

Peripheral nervous system activation

- Palpitations, pounding heart, or accelerated heart rate
- Tremor
- Paresthesias (numbness or tingling sensations)

- Chest pain or discomfort
- Feeling of choking
- Feeling dizzy, unsteady, lightheaded, or faint
- Chills or hot flushes
- Sweating
- Trembling or shaking

- Exaggerated startle response
- Hyperarrousal (heightened sensory activity)
- Hypervigilance (heightened sensory sensitivity accompanied by intensified response, the purpose of which it is to detect threats)

Other physical symptoms

- Headache
- Back ache
- Diffuse body aches
- Acute or chronic pain (severity on scale of 1–10)
- Muscle tension
- Fatigue after doing things
- Shortness of breath or smothering

- Nausea or abdominal distress, including diarrhea and constipation
- Increase or decrease in sexual drive, response, and activity
- Pelvic pain (or pain with intercourse)
- Menstrual changes
- Bruxism (grinding the teeth)
- Increased or decreased appetite
- Weight changes (up or down)

Sleep disturbance

- Insomnia (specify difficulty with getting to sleep, staying asleep, or early morning awakening)
- Daytime somnolence or oversleeping
- Restless, unsatisfying sleep
- Nightmares or recurrent, distressing dreams

Psychomotor activity

- Pacing or feeling that one has to keep moving
- Agitated or accelerated movement
- Slowness of movement
- Single or multiple motor or vocal tics (i.e., sudden, rapid, recurrent, nonrhythmic, stereotyped motor movements or vocalizations)

Questions About Symptoms, Course of Illness, and Related Factors
As you answer these questions, think not only of the symptoms themselves presently and over time, but also of other factors that may have contributed to or been affected by the illness, and those that have been helpful. Consider factors from:
- Psychiatric and medical history, including treatments
- Personality and temperament
- Substance use, current and past
- Habits of health maintenance (e.g., diet, exercise, massage)
- Family health history
- Relationships, current and past
- Sexual history
- Culture and community
- Religion and spirituality
- Childhood and developmental history
- Occupation, avocation and finances
- Legal history

Current symptoms and related factors
- What are the events or factors that led to help-seeking? And what led to those events? Tell a story, giving context to the list of symptoms below.
- What are the current symptoms? Which are most troublesome? Describe their character and quality, and severity.
  - Is there anything that makes them better or worse throughout the day?
  - Is the depression or are specific symptoms worse or better at a particular time of day?
- Of the symptoms, which are the "loudest"? In other words, which symptoms, if alleviated, would help to resolve others? Some people find, for instance, that panic symptoms, lack of appetite, and troubles with cognition are somewhat relieved if they are able to get restful sleep.
- Onset and duration: speaking of this particular episode, when did it start?
  - Did this episode develop abruptly, or did it seem to creep on over time?
  - How did the patient first come to realize she was depressed? Was she the first to notice, or did others comment?
- What has been the duration of this episode?
- What has been the course of this episode? Does the depression ebb and flow, or have specific symptoms become worse or better over time? Are there recognizable patterns to the course of this episode?

History of the illness
If this is not the first episode of depression, please describe the following:
- Describe the last period of wellness. How long did that last, and what contributed to stability?

- Onset of illness
  - When did the first episode or period of illness or instability occur (whether or not it was diagnosed or treated)?
  - Precipitants: what were the circumstances surrounding the first episode?
- Course and progression over time:
  - Frequency of recurrence: How many episodes has the patient had, about how long does each one last, and with what frequency do they occur? When the patient has periods of wellness, for how long to these last?
  - Have episodes of depression become longer, more severe, or more frequent over time? Have they been more spontaneous or required fewer triggers?
  - Are there any predictable precipitants or triggers (e.g., with trouble at work, or relapse to drinking), or do episodes seem to occur spontaneously? Have they become more spontaneous over time?
  - Do any particular symptoms precede a depressive episode? These are called prodromes. Some people find, for instance, and they feel more anxious in social situations, have more panic or anxiety, have trouble concentrating, or are more concerned about their physical health in the weeks or months leading up to an episode of depression.
  - Likewise, when depression has resolved in the past, which symptoms linger longer than others? Common residual symptoms include anxiety, trouble with concentration and short-term memory, insomnia, and fatigue.
  - How do the episodes relate to other illness factors over time? For instance, do the episodes of major depression seem to overlay an underlying, less severe depression (perhaps dysthymia) that does not resolve? If the patient has experienced mania, has it always been preceded or followed by depression?
  - Have symptoms changed over time, in their presence or prominence? For instance, has the patient become more isolative over time? Has she only recently experienced psychotic symptoms? Has her once euphoric manic episodes become more irritable, paranoid, or obsessional?
  - Consider using the Life Chart, found at the end of this chapter, to chronicle the history of past episodes and related events.

Patient's theory of causation

Think about any biological, psychological or social factors that may have contributed to the development of the current illness. Those from the past may include a family history of psychiatric or neurologic illness, for example, or traumatic childhood experience. Recent stressors or ways that the patient manages stress may also contribute. Does the patient have a theory of what may have caused her depression?

What makes it worse?

Which triggers or circumstances cause a worsening of symptoms, now and in the past? Are they certain people, specific settings, being out in public, perhaps light or sound? Are there particular memories or patterns of thinking that worsen the depression? These are just a few examples. Have the triggers listed been similar in past episodes, or have they changed over time?

What makes it better?

What has the patient tried during this episode and in the past that has been helpful? What has she tried that has not?

- Previous evaluation or diagnostic workup: has the patient seen another doctor or therapist for evaluation of the current illness?
  - What diagnoses were given?
  - Were any psychological tests, bloodwork, radiologic scans, or other evaluative tests done?
  - If they are different from those the patient has seen regularly for treatment, include contact information for the clinicians who have provided evaluations.
- Medications: Use the Medication History Table to provide information about prescribed and over-the-counter medications, vitamins, herbals, and other supplements that have been used. Include contact information for previous treating psychiatrists or general practitioners
- Describe use of electroconvulsive therapy (ECT), vagus nerve stimulation (VNS), or transcranial magnetic stimulation (TMS) for the current illness, including when started, when stopped, number of sessions, technical parameters if known, helpfulness, any side effects, and name and contact information of the doctor who performed the treatment.
- Psychiatric hospitalizations, ER visits, and periods of residential treatment.
- Psychotherapy: When has the patient seen a therapist for the current illness?
  - When did therapy begin, and when did it stop? With what frequency were sessions attended?
  - Was there a specific modality of therapy practiced (e.g., psychodynamic, cognitive, behavioral, supportive)?
  - Did the patient have a good relationship with the therapist?
  - What about the therapy was or was not helpful? If therapy was terminated, why?
  - Include contact information for previous therapists.
- Lifestyle and other factors: Does a certain diet, exercise, or meditation practice improve the depression? Getting out in the sun? Being around others?

Participating in a hobby, group, or church activity? List helpful factors other than medications and formal psychotherapy here.

Coping and stress tolerance

- Is the patient frequently tense or "stressed", and how does she handle this?
- Does she ever lose hope or feel like her life is out of control?
- What strategies for coping has she used during times of stress or adversity? Are these typically helpful?

Effect on functioning

- How has the evolving illness affected the patient's usual life functions and habits, including taking meals, sleeping, exercise, and other activities of self care?
- Has a marriage or partnership, education, occupation, or avocation been disrupted?
- Have relationships with or attitudes towards other people changed?
- Has the patient's personality, attitude towards self, coping strategies and activities, central beliefs, plans for the future, or general outlook been altered during the course of this illness?

Guide for Review of Symptoms—Patient Version

Here is a guide to providing the clinician with pertinent data about current symptoms, their course over time, contributing and resulting factors, and what the patient has done to manage them. This guide may be used on its own, or inserted into the Psychiatric History form (also provided at the end of this chapter) under History of Present Illness.

    The patient may write a narrative about symptoms, photocopy this guide and circle any symptoms that they would like to discuss with the clinician.

Symptoms

Negative thoughts, feelings and behaviors

- Self-critical, self-loathing, or self-destructive thought
- Sadness
- Hopeless
- Helplessness
- Shame or guilt
- Loneliness or isolative behavior
- Lack of motivation or apathy
- Decreased interest in activities once enjoyed, or inability to experience pleasure

Heightened thoughts, feelings and behaviors

- Symptoms of over-activation or excessive energy
- Expansive or euphoric mood
- More social, outgoing or active than usual
- Taking on more projects than usual
- Exaggerated sense of self-confidence
- Racing thoughts
- Rapid speech
- Internal restlessness
- Irritability or anger outbursts

Fears and anxieties

- Physical and mental symptoms of anxiety or "nervousness"
- Fear of specific objects or situations
- Fear of criticism, rejection or inadequacy
- Fear of abandonment
- Fear of gaining weight or becoming fat
- Intrusive, distressing memories
- Fear of persecution
- Preoccupation with worst-case scenarios

Distorted thoughts and perceptions

- Hallucinations (the experience of hearing voices or sounds, or seeing, feeling or smelling things others might not hear, see, smell or feel)
- Suspicion and mistrust or conviction that something bad will happen, such as the feat of being followed
- Other strange, frightening, or unusual thoughts

Obsessions, compulsions, preoccupations and worry
Thoughts, images, impulses, rituals, and repeated behaviors

- Preoccupation with any subject, such as food, rules or lists, cleanliness, or sin
- Repetitive behaviors, such as hand-washing, checking, or counting
- Hoarding paper or objects
- Obsessions or compulsions with food
- Problematic stealing shopping, gambling, sex, pornography, or internet use

Dissociative phenomena
- "Spacing out" under stress or when anxious
- Feelings of unreality
- Feelings of being detached from or of observing oneself

Violence and self-harm
- Injuring oneself to relieve anxiety or emotional pain
- Thoughts of, plans, or intent to hurt or kill oneself or others

Cognitive problems
- Difficulties with concentration, attention, memory, decision-making or planning

Physical arousal
Symptoms associated with feelings of fight or flight or adrenaline rush such as:
- Fast heartbeat
- Sweating
- Trembling
- Breathing hard
- Chest pain or discomfort
- Feeling of choking
- Feeling dizzy, unsteady, lightheaded, or faint
- Startling easily

Other physical symptoms
- Pain
- Headache
- Body aches or muscle tension
- Fatigue
- Appetite or weight changes
- Nausea or abdominal distress, including diarrhea and constipation
- Increase or decrease in sex drive, response, and activity

Sleep disturbance
- Difficulty getting to sleep or staying asleep (insomnia)
- Oversleeping or daytime sleepiness
- Restless sleep
- Nightmares or recurrent distressing dreams

Psychomotor activity
- Agitated, restless, or slow, sluggish movements

Course of Illness

Current episode

• Was there a trigger for the present episode?

• How long has it been going on?

• Is it getting better or worse?

• What are the most important or life-disrupting symptoms?

• What has been helpful and what has made things worse?

Past episodes

• If there have been previous episodes of similar symptoms
  - When did they start
  - What triggered them
  - What made them better or worse?
  - Did they resolve fully?

• Have episodes been getting more severe or frequent over time?

• Has the illness disrupted the patient's ability to work, study, or relate with family and friends?

• Consider using the Life Chart, also found at the end of this chapter, to chronicle the history of past episodes and related events

Medication History Table

Name of Medication			
Taken For			
Start Date			
Stop date			
Max Dose			
Time at Max Dose			
Response and Benefits			
Side Effects and Adjustments			
Blood Level?			
Taken as Directed?			
Why Stopped?			

Notes
Allergies and sensitivities to medications
Name(s) and contact information for prescribing clinician(s)
Pharmacies used

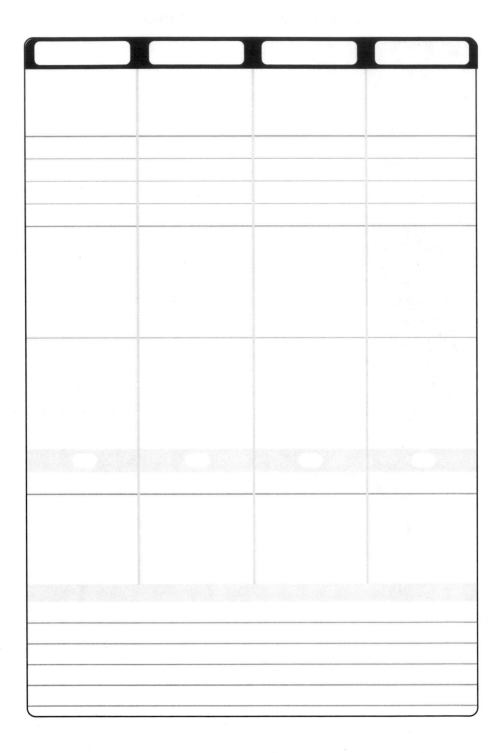

Medication History Table

The medication history table may be used to record data about medications the patient is currently taking and those she has taken in the past. It may be used for both psychiatric and medical medications.

- When filling out the form, be sure to include both **prescribed medicines and over-the-counter remedies.** Include all vitamins, herbal preparations, and any other alternative or complementary medicines.

- When writing what the medication was **taken for,** record the symptoms that were being targeted. The antidepressant Elavil, for instance, is used often for insomnia, chronic pain, irritable bowel syndrome, and headache prevention, in addition to depression.

- **Dates started and stopped** are preferable to simply stating the length of time the medication was taken, as the doctor can then see which drugs were taken at the same time. Start date should approximate the time the medication was first taken, and stop date the time it was last taken, even if there was a lengthy period of tapering. There is a column to record the **maximum dose taken**, and one for for **time at maximum dose**. If an antidepressant was taken for eight weeks but only two weeks at the highest dose before it was tapered and stopped, the patient may not have had an adequate trial on that medication.

- When recording **response and benefits**, record the particular symptoms that were helped, and the percent effectiveness the medication had overall. For instance: the patient may estimate her symptoms were 70% gone after a trial on the medicine, with sleep, appetite, motivation, and negative thinking being the most dramatically affected.

- When recording **side effects**, list also any **adjustments** that were made. Perhaps a medication causing nausea or daytime sedation was switched to bedtime dosing, Cogentin was added to an antipsychotic for tremor, or Ativan used for treatment-emergent anxiety when starting an SSRI.

- If a **blood level** was taken for the medication, this is helpful information. It is also helpful to know if a higher level produced side effects, but no additional benefit.

- Record whether or not the medication was **taken as directed**. If it was not, indicate whether doses were skipped, a lower or higher dose was taken, or other alteration to the prescriber's instructions. If the medicine was tolerable, the patient would not want to cross this potentially helpful medication off her list of possible treatments due to lack of a fair trial. It is also helpful to tell the doctor why directions were not followed, as he may know how other patients have overcome the same difficulty in the past.

- **Record why the medication was stopped**, whether for side effects, loss of effectiveness, the desire to try a drug with different properties, or other reasons.

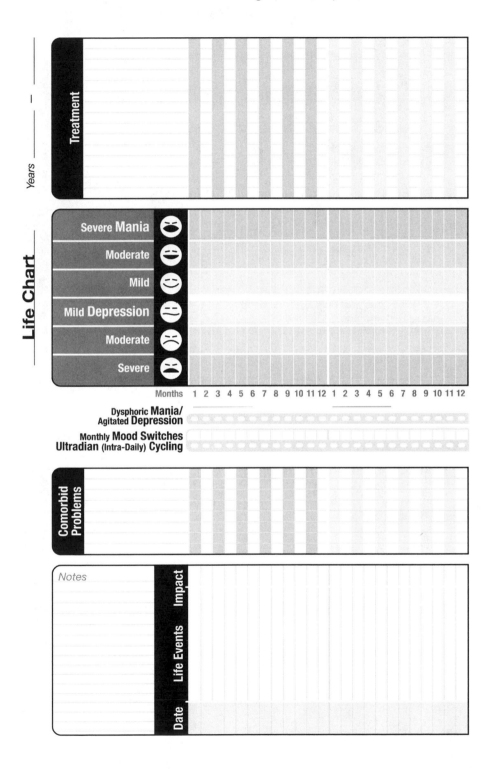

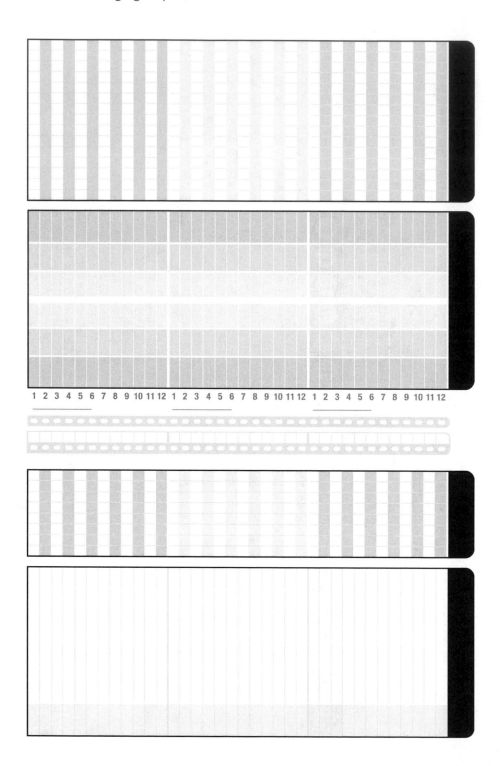

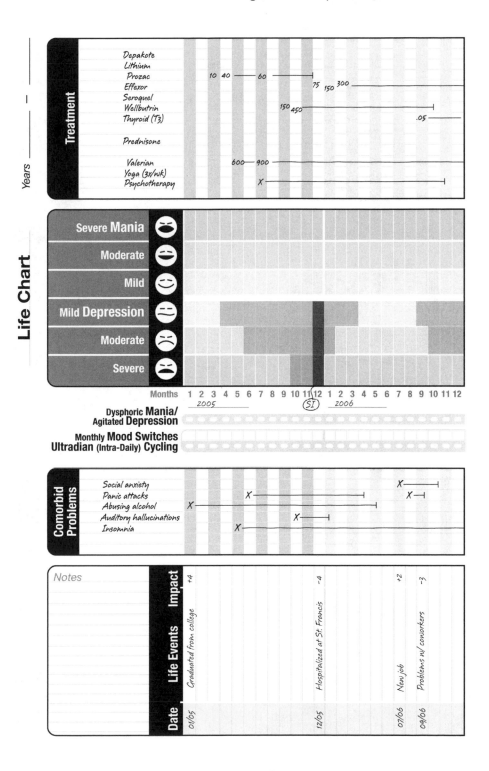

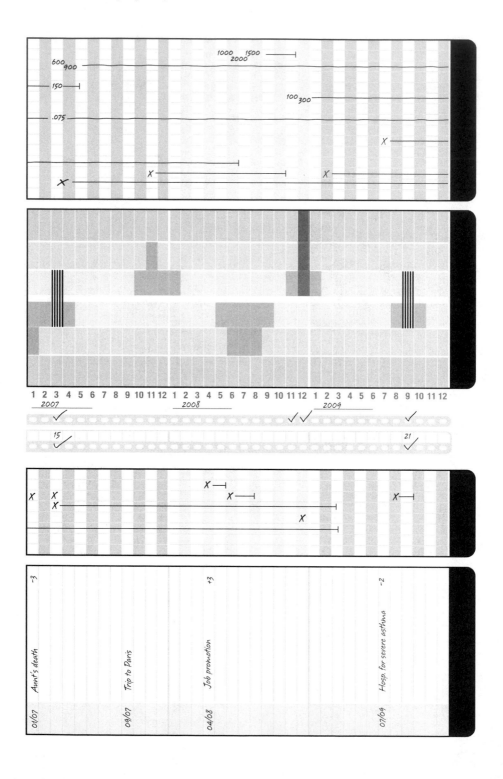

Life Chart

Instructions

A life chart allows your clinician to see how your illness has developed and changed over time, aiding in analysis of how mood and related symptoms may interact with life events, physical health, treatment, and overall functioning. It may demonstrate that episodes correlate to life events, or that they seem to occur spontaneously. A life chart may reveal a pattern of severity, duration, or seasonality. Manic episodes may consistently follow depressive episodes. A person may have a predoninantly depressive course of illness, or may frequently be hypomanic. Periods of rapid cycling (four or more mood episodes in a period of 12 months) may be revealed.

On the grid provided for charting mood, rate periods of illness by severity along a timeline. This chart allows mood to be charted by month over a period of five years.

Mild depression may include low mood, a feeling of distress, and perhaps some social isolation, with little or no decrement to functioning. **Moderate depression** may cause significant impairment in usual activity at work, school, or in relationships. You may miss days from work, school or other regular activities. When **severely depressed**, you may be thoroughly incapacitated at home or in the hospital, unable to perform usual occupational, educational or social functions. Eating or grooming may be difficult. Darken any periods of hospitalization, and note below any suicidal thinking or attempts.

Mild hypomania may include decreased need for sleep, increased energy, some irritability or elevated mood, and increase in racing thoughts, rapid speech, or social behavior. Impact of such symptoms may be minimal. At the **moderate level**, hypomania may include additional symptoms and impact productivity and ability to focus . Others may comment that your behavior is different from usual. **Severe mania** may include risky or uncontrolled behavior significant impact on work and relationships, concern for your safety and capacity for self-care, and perhaps hospitalization or even incarceration. Again, indicate hospitalization by darkening that period on your chart.

Depression is sometimes agitated, marked by anger, irritability, agitation or overactivity, or rapid thoughts and a sense of being driven. About 40% of people with bipolar illness experience **dysphoric hypomania**, where there may be symptoms of hypomania or mania marked by irritability or anger. If this is experienced, check the box under that episode to indicate this quality of mood.

Two other boxes are provided, one for indicating **switches in mood** occurring more than once within a given month, and one for marking mood switches occurring within a day.

A box is included for charting symptoms that are particularly distressing that happen within or between episodes, as well as any periods of **substance abuse**.

List any **medications** that have been taken, along with the strength in miligrams. Prescribed and over-the-counter medications should be listed, including herbals or other supplements and medications used for medical illness. You may also choose to list **psychotherapy** and any **complementary practices** such as yoga or accupuncture. Somatic treatments including ECT should be included.

Chart **life events** that were important or that affected (or were influenced by) any changes in mood. Include any hospitalizations and suicide attempts. Life events may be rated on a scale of -4 to +4 for negative and positive influence on mood.

Questions to Ask About Diagnosis and Treatment

The Diagnosis

What is my diagnosis? What is the nature of this illness and its course?

What is known about the cause of this particular illness?

How certain are you of this diagnosis? What else could it be?

The Diagnostic Process

Would a comprehensive physical exam, lab tests, or psychological testing be ecommend at this point?

Would seeing any other specialist help to reach a more certain diagnosis?

If your current evaluation of my illness is a preliminary one, when might you be able to provide a more definite opinion?

Treatment

What treatment(s) do you think would be most helpful? How will it be helpful?

Do you suggest medications, psychotherapy, a support group, intensive day treatment or residential/hospital treatment, or general medical treatments?

Will this program involve services by other specialists? If so, who will be responsible for coordinating these services?

About how long will this treatment program take, and how frequently will I be seeing you and the other specialists?

What are the best indications that I am responding to the program, and how soon will it be before these appear?

What percentage of your practice invoves treating patients with my kind of problem?

Questions to Ask About Medications

Medication Name _____ Drug Class _____

Is this an FDA approved or off-label use of the medication?

Is there an inexpensive generic available?

What are the usual starting and long-term doses?

Effectiveness

Among this class of medications, why did you choose this one for me?

How is this medication thought to work?

What symptoms usually improve first, and when may I expect to see some early response? When would I achieve the maximum response that I'll likely get from it?

What percent of patients with my diagnosis respond to this medication?

Adverse Reactions and Side Effects

What are the most common short and long-term side effects?

Are there any dangerous side effects? What is the chance I might experience them?

Is there any way to minimize the chances of experiencing any of these side effects?

Monitoring

Will I need blood tests before or during the time I take this medicine? How often?

Are there any lifestyle or dietary suggestions or restrictions to follow when using this medication?

Where can I get more information about this medication? Do you have any printed information?

Report of Medication Response

Report the following information to your clinician at each appointment:

Medication Administration

List the medications and doses you were prescribed, as well as the medications and doses you have actually taken.

Are you taking the medications as prescribed (e.g. morning or evening, with or without food or alcohol)?

Have you missed doses? Why?

Symptom Monitoring

Which symptoms have improved, and how?

Which symptoms have not changed or have worsened?

Have family, friends, or coworkers made comments regarding changes in your behavior or mood?

Side Effects

Are there any side effects? If so, which medication(s) do you believe may be causing them?

Are the side effects a tolerable nuisance, or are they severe enough to make you consider stopping the medicine?

tivities, central beliefs, plans for the future, or general outlook been altered during the course of this illness?

8

Psychotherapy Is More Than Talking to a Nice Person: Specific Approaches to Dealing With Depression

Never overlook the obvious! Depression occurs in people with psychological issues and relationship problems—it's not just about neurotransmitter abnormalities. Although drugs relieve symptoms, they do not necessarily do anything for difficult life situations and relationships; focusing solely on neurochemistry, and blinding oneself to the impact of childhood traumas and current stressful life situations, is a setup for missed treatment opportunities. Depression is considered a biopsychosocial illness, and addressing the psychological and psychosocial aspects of depression is just as important as treating its medical cause. Psychotherapy deals with this human side of depression—life's stresses, traumas, losses, and disappointments. Depression-specific psychotherapies focus on thoughts, behaviors, and interpersonal roles that may be maladaptive or disrupted and require active structured therapist involvement. Every good clinician with experience treating depressed patients goes beyond asking about symptoms to try to understand what their meaning is to the individual and what life situations might be contributing to ongoing unhappiness or clinical depression.

Psychotherapy—often referred to as talk therapy or counseling—addresses troubling symptoms, emotions, and patterns using psychological techniques. Unlike treatment with medicines, psychotherapy involves the hard work of self-examination and disclosure, acknowledging uncomfortable thoughts and painful feelings, and making changes in behavior that promote both physical and emotional health. Effective psychotherapy for depression often involves very specific treatment approaches and is far different from a friendly chat with a paid listener or best friend.

Given the range of approaches that are considered psychotherapy, arriving at a complete definition for the word is difficult. The emphasis and perspective placed on different components of therapy determines the distinctions among the various schools of psychotherapy. It can perhaps be summarily described as a process of discovery, the goal of which is to eliminate, control, or prevent troubling and painful symptoms so that a person can return to normal functioning. It also can be used to help a person overcome a specific problem or to stimulate overall emotional growth and healing. In regularly scheduled sessions—usually 45 to 50 minutes in length—a patient works with a therapist to identify, learn to manage, and ultimately overcome issues surrounding and underlying the depression.

Through these talk sessions, patients learn about the psychological, social, and environmental contributors to their condition so they can better understand it. They also may learn how to identify and make changes in troubling behavior or thoughts, explore relationships and experiences, and find better ways to cope, solve problems, and set realistic goals for their life. Psychotherapy can help patients regain a sense of happiness or well-being and control in their life, and it can help alleviate symptoms caused by depression, such as anger and hopelessness.

Although much of the therapy process hinges on communication between the therapist and the individual, it involves much more than just talking about problems. Family or friends can help a person feel better, provide an important sounding board and social support, or even give good advice for change, but this is not psychotherapy. People close to the patient may feel unable to respond frankly, may not be able to be neutral or objective about issues involving other family members or friends, and, without training and experience, may not recognize problems and subtle issues or know how to respond appropriately in a way that will facilitate change. Psychotherapy is a professional relationship between a therapist and patient that is based on therapeutic principles and structure and uses specific techniques that have been validated through research. It is an active process requiring concentration, energy, and commitment by both the patient and therapist.

Why Do Psychotherapy?

Most people seek therapy to relieve pain or distress. Experiencing emotional pain is part of being human, but sometimes this distress is persistent or severe and impairs daily life. Many people pursue psychotherapy because:

- They feel an overwhelming or prolonged sense of sadness, helplessness, or hopelessness.
- Their emotional difficulties make it hard for them to function from day to day—to concentrate at work, to care for themselves at home, to contribute to and enjoy their relationships.
- Their actions are harmful—they may drink or become overly irritable or aggressive.
- They perceive interpersonal problems between themselves and others.
- They suffer social isolation.
- Substance use has begun to affect their relationships and functioning.
- They are suffering grief over an overwhelming loss or over having a chronic illness.
- They feel that aspects of life have, for one reason or another, come to a standstill or a turning point.

Like medication, psychotherapy can provide patients with relief from symptoms, but it takes substantially more work. This work, however, is worth it—unlike medication, therapy provides patients with a toolkit, or a skill set, with which to understand the root of the problem, correct it, and prevent its recurrence. Skills can be acquired to understand and cope with relationships, or with excessive shyness, poor communication, lack of assertiveness, or poor anger control.

Psychotherapy also has the potential to help patients to maintain adherence to their therapeutic regimens and provides an opportunity for reality testing, as well as some motivation and psychosocial support. It can help a person to develop insight, become educated, learn to manage her symptoms, become a self-advocate, and generally improve the quality of her life. Psychotherapy may be useful in the context of stressful interpersonal, intrapsychic, or lifestyle factors or circumstances, lifetime history of adversity, maladaptive coping styles, and chronic disability. In each instance, poor coping skills and biological symptoms reinforce each other and both must be addressed.

Sexual dissatisfaction and dysfunction are common problems, especially in those experiencing depression, and therapists have made substantial progress in helping people obtain more enjoyment from their sexual functioning. Some have also developed expertise in focusing on healing the wounds caused by sexual, physical, or emotional trauma, helping patients regain a sense of control and move forward with their lives.

Psychotherapy and Depression

Of the many nonpharmacological approaches available for treating various mental conditions, none have been more thoroughly researched than those for depression, and some forms of depression-specific psychotherapy compare favorably with antidepressant therapy in terms of effectiveness. Findings have indicated that although psychotherapy may take slightly longer to begin alleviating specific and acute depressive symptoms, it appears to result in longer-lasting benefits and maintenance of a higher quality of psychological and social adjustment due to its ability to alter patterns of thought and behavior.

Depression-specific psychotherapeutic modalities include cognitive-behavioral therapy (CBT), behavioral therapy, interpersonal psychotherapy, and short-term or focused psychodynamic psychotherapy (each of these models is explored later in the chapter). Several of these modalities may be integrated in clinical practice in what is called an eclectic approach. What these approaches have in common is that they are problem-focused and goal oriented; patients with depression should be aware that therapies that seem open-ended or that have poorly defined goals may not be best suited to target recovery from depression.

No matter what the patient's specific goals are, psychotherapy offers an opportunity for those living with depression to gain insight and "test reality" when they have questions about whether fears or patterns of thought are reasonable. Psychotherapy helps one to become educated about depression or bipolar illness and teaches people how to talk to others about their condition. It can help patients come to terms with medication and side effects, learn to catch early warning signs of relapse or worsening symptoms, and recognize and cope with triggers that can lead to a return of symptoms. Depression aside, involvement in therapy can generally promote stress reduction and motivation, provide and model healthy social support, decrease defensiveness, increase a person's ability to express herself, and increase self-esteem.

How Psychotherapy Works

Psychotherapy helps to relieve depression in two ways: by encouraging the patient to change behaviors, and by promoting physiological changes (changes that occur in the brain).

Changing Behaviors

Rather than simply delivering damage-healing techniques, psychotherapy helps patients to build "buffering strengths." It stimulates development of interpersonal skills and teaches patients to approach things rationally and with honesty. Therapy promotes courage, optimism, realism, and perseverance. It can lend the depressed person perspective and help her to find pleasure in her experiences, be future-minded, and find purpose. The fostering of buffering strengths may be what makes psychotherapy so highly effective, especially where prevention of relapse and recurrence are concerned.

Changing Physiology

Depression is characterized by a decrease in metabolic activity (blood flow and energy consumption) in specific areas of the brain. Like other antidepressant treatments, CBT (and probably other forms of psychotherapy) seems to promote recovery from depression by modulating functioning of these specific sites in a way that is complementary to medication treatment. Before-and-after positron emission tomography (PET) scans in patients receiving CBT show increased blood flow in the limbic, or "emotional," system and decreased activity in certain "thinking" areas of the brain. Those on antidepressants show changes in the same brain regions that look surprisingly similar on the scans, though the changes in blood flow are in the reverse direction (decreased metabolism in the limbic system and increased activity in areas responsible for cognition). Treatment was effective in both conditions, producing a similar decrease in depressive symptoms.

This effect on metabolic activity may account for CBT's acute effects, which are typically more rapid than those seen from many other modes of therapy. The more lasting effects of psychotherapy, however, occur with intensive work over a period of time: When people make changes in behavior, attitude, approach, and response, reciprocal changes are made in their brains. As noted earlier, talk therapy is not just talking about your problems—it may involve homework, such as participating in social activities that have caused anxiety in the past, making lifestyle changes, tracking moods, or writing about thoughts. Patients are encouraged to look at things differently or to learn new ways of reacting to people and events. When people make changes in thought and behavior and practice them regularly, neurons fire in different patterns and sequences. The processes (extensions from the nerve cell bodies called axons and dendrites) that connect neurons in the brain grow and branch out, making many new connections. When behavioral or thought patterns are established, these connections are pruned back, leaving neural networks that have been reinforced and that are further strengthened with time and repetition of the new behaviors. The malleable brain literally rewires itself to accept and promote the new patterns, enabling people to literally "change their minds." This ability to rewire is called neural plasticity, or synaptic remodeling, and it is responsible for lifelong learning and change. This process of synaptic remodeling is similar to what happens when a person learns a new motor skill, like riding a bike or playing a musical instrument. The new skill is initially difficult and requires a lot of conscious effort, but it becomes far easier and more automatic after extended practice. Similarly, learning to think about and react to negative life events in a calm, accepting, creative, problem-solving way is a skill that requires hard work but becomes easier with practice.

Psychotherapy is linked physiologically not only to emotional health but to physical well-being as well—it can have a positive effect on the body's immune system; ameliorate the symptoms of pain, fatigue, and nausea experienced with depression; lengthen the lives of heart surgery and cancer patients; and improve a person's overall health status.

What Happens in the Process of Psychotherapy

It is impossible to predict what will happen during individual therapy sessions, how therapy will unfold over the course of time, and what kind of therapeutic relationship will be established between the patient and the therapist. Nor would you want to predict it! Though a seasoned therapist often sees similar themes, trends, and outcomes in work with different patients over time, each patient is unique. However, certain aspects of the patient-therapist relationship and of the first few sessions can be anticipated, and we discuss these here.

What to Expect During the First Sessions

During the first session, the therapist and the patient will spend some time clearly defining the reason the patient has sought therapy. This involves both a frank discussion of the patient's concerns as well as a careful history-taking, or interview, which may address emotional, physical, and sexual health, aspects of the patient's family history and occupational history, lifestyle, habits, and past experiences with therapy. The therapist will want to know what the patient has already tried, what she hopes to accomplish, and what has been most difficult about this problem for her. The therapist may explain some of his techniques and discuss what the patient thinks will be helpful and what will not. At the end of the hour, the therapist and patient will compare notes and discuss options. Hopeful accomplishments for the first session include deciding if there is a "good fit" between the patient and therapist, if the therapist is "getting it" relative to the patient's needs, and whether or not a second appointment should be pursued.

The second session usually picks up where the first left off—in areas that both parties feel are important but were not touched upon in the first session. Before that happens, however it is a good idea to review the patient's thoughts and reactions to the first session. An exploration of what most stands out from the first visit may help to shape the beginning of the therapeutic alliance and work. During this visit the therapist may reflect on strengths the patient has to fuel therapy: her motivation, degree of suffering, the stability and supportiveness of her social network, her level of insight, and so on. By the end of the second session, the therapist should feel comfortable explaining any diagnoses he has made and recommending a psychotherapeutic approach, its rationale, a frequency with which to meet, and perhaps an estimated length of time (or number of sessions) that may be expected. The hoped-for outcome of the treatment will be established (expressing optimism for realistic and attainable goals), as well as the likelihood of that outcome. Expectations will be reviewed: both what the patient should reasonably expect from the therapist and therapy process, and what work the patient should anticipate doing to encourage progress and improvement. Alternative treatments, their anticipated length and costs, and their risks and likely outcome may or may not be offered.

Session Length and Frequency

People often wonder why the typical "therapy hour" is 45 to 50 minutes. The therapist may use the remaining 10 minutes of the hour to take notes and reflect on the patient's progress. Group therapy sessions usually last longer and brief therapy interventions may take much less time. In some situations a therapist may offer longer sessions. For instance, a couple in therapy may find themselves just getting into a long-needed conversation. Added time may help them maintain the momentum.

A single hour can also be good because therapy can be emotionally intense and a patient may learn many things in a session. More time in session can be difficult to absorb mentally and emotionally.

A standard session time helps the therapist pace the session for the patient, for instance giving her time to pull herself together before going back to work. This predictable session length helps establish an expected emotional rhythm to even intense sessions. It instills a sense of emotional safety in that the patient knows when she can choose to open up difficult feelings and then contain them.

Emotional reactions or issues expressed in lateness or attempts to stay beyond the end of the session can be useful subjects of exploration. A phenomenon known as "doorknob therapy" emerges with some patients, who suddenly have an "ah ha" moment or a burning question or issue minutes before the end of a session. This can occur for many reasons. Sometimes it's because the issue is uncomfortable to talk about, but as the end of the session approaches, the patient realizes it's something she really wants to bring up. Exploring such attempts to go "outside the therapy frame" often gives the patient powerful and unexpected insights.

The frequency of sessions helps balance cost, intensity, and emotional containment. Patients most often attend sessions once weekly to balance cost and effectiveness and settle into an emotional rhythm provided by attending at the same time each week. Often seeing the therapist more frequently does not give the patient enough time to integrate the effects of the previous session. However, this option may be appropriate for patients immersed in intense emotional or life change; it may offer them the support to remain emotionally centered and assist them in activating coping skills. Patients also meet more often in psychoanalysis, which is a specialized type of long-term therapy designed to restructure the personality through a thorough exploration of life history and issues. Less frequent sessions may make maintaining continuity or momentum between sessions difficult. Meeting biweekly may offer less opportunity to accomplish changes at a steady pace.

Goals and Expectations

People approach psychotherapy with hopes and expectations, not all of which are conscious or realistic, and some of which are a function of pain, need, and knowledge deficit in areas in which they desire change. Through training and experience, therapists have acquired a notion of what is and is not attainable from psychotherapy; their blueprints and expectations may or may not be well matched at first with the patient's desired outcomes. The therapeutic process is therefore malleable, but it should be guided by clear goals: Patients and therapists should agree explicitly on the goals of the work they are performing mutually. If goals are not made explicit, they may become vague, unreasonable, and probably unattainable. That said, goals can be changed and developed over time, and it is good practice to compare notes from time to time, especially in a longer treatment, to make sure the patient and therapist are on the same page.

Although goals may change over time, they should reflect the patient's imperatives. If the patient feels that the therapist is setting goals that don't match her own, she should take note of this. At times, some therapists may unwittingly introduce their own unresolved issues, and this may influence their treatment decisions. For instance, if a patient mentions that she is in an unhappy marriage yet has sought therapy to resolve her fear of flying, and the therapist says she has to work on her marriage first, his insistence is out of line with her goals and will impede her progress. It will also create a relationship lacking trust.

The Focus of Therapy: On Past or Present?

Many people have stereotypic notions of therapy delving deep into their past and focusing on something vaguely related to their relationship with their mother. However, not everyone addresses her past in therapy. In fact, much of psychotherapy today is problem-centered and focused on current thoughts, feelings, and circumstances. When the past is addressed, the goal may be to understand what happened, its effects at the time, and its residual current influences, so that the patient can make changes in her response to this stimulus, better cope with the present, and feel better.

The Therapeutic Relationship

For therapy to proceed successfully, both the patient and therapist must be clear on what constitutes the role of each in this strictly professional relationship—not just literally, but in a way that may not be spoken yet is understood by each. Long ago, psychoanalytic theory raised our awareness of a process termed "transference," in which patients transfer feelings from other relationships in their life, past or present, onto the therapist. For example, the therapist may for a time represent (perhaps unconsciously) the patient's mother, father, or brother, with whom she is angry—or a once-dear friend whom she lost to betrayal. When this phenomenon occurs in the reverse—that is, when the therapist transfers his thoughts or emotions onto the patient—it is known as "countertransference." Transference is almost inevitable in the therapy process and is a powerful and desirable tool, though it can be confusing or even harmful if boundaries between the patient and therapist are blurred or ambiguous.

"Boundaries" are referred to by some as a construct that helps people to define themselves and their various roles and to maintain these roles in various social contexts. When appropriate boundaries are lacking, a child may become "parentified" (take on a parental role within a family), a person's right to autonomy within a given social system may be violated, or a person may not develop a sense of what parts of herself should be shared with others (with whom, when, and why) and what is best kept private. A lack of good boundaries engenders a poor sense of self and may also lead to one's being taken advantage of by others. Relationships that involve both a power differential and a sense of trust and vulnerability—such as those between teachers and students, religious leaders and the laity, or physicians and patients—may unfortunately be susceptible to boundary violations when codes of ethical conduct (such as those within the scope of licensing of therapists) are breached.

Boundaries are referred to by others to describe limits—agreements or conditions (such as the ground rules of therapy) that benefit both parties. Although boundaries are typically assumed or unspoken, agreements that describe the limits of the therapeutic relationship should be discussed at the first meeting with a new therapist. A set time and place of meetings, fee for services, policies regarding phone and e-mail contact, and what to expect if a session must be cancelled are pretty cut and dry. They allow the patient to know what she may reasonably expect, and they help to define a professional relationship that is mutually respectful, where the patient's needs are met without impinging on the therapist's time with other patients or personal relationships.

Other conditions of therapy that make the therapist comfortable working with the patient may be negotiated. These may include expectations about accepting sobriety, medications, or even hospitalization if the therapist feels that these are necessary. Another important agreement is whether the therapist is allowed or requested to talk to the patient's family or employer. For instance, the patient may request that information be shared if they choose to apply for state disability insurance (SDI) or supplemental security income (SSI) from the Social Security Administration. At other times, absolute privacy is necessary. Confidentiality is assumed in the therapeutic relationship, but it sometimes must be broken when there is imminent danger to self or others or suspicion of abuse of children or dependent elderly persons. A breach of confidentiality for these reasons is not boundary-crossing; it is required in compliance with the law. The therapist should provide, perhaps in a handout, this and other necessary information at the beginning of the working relationship.

In addition to providing a safe and mutually agreeable environment in which to work, professional boundaries may make it more comfortable for patients to answer embarrassing or difficult questions. The therapist is there to help, not judge, and confidentiality is built into the relationship. Getting to the core of issues is not always comfortable, but a fruitful working relationship should provide a "safe space" within which to approach and test that which engenders fear or brings up other uncomfortable feelings.

Different therapists have different ideas about what behaviors best represent them as a professional and best circumscribe their role. Some reveal little about themselves to patients; they may fear influencing how individuals present themselves or may have very firm beliefs or discomfort with self-disclosure. Others believe in "using themselves as a tool" and strongly feel that, as long as their disclosure is for a specific reason, is timely and appropriate, and is strictly for the good of the patient, it is useful. Likewise, some therapists feel more comfortable presenting themselves conservatively, in a way that asserts their position as the professional in the relationship, whereas others have a much more relaxed style, viewing the patient as the "expert" on herself. Different patients feel comfortable with different approaches—some prefer therapists who share a bit about themselves when appropriate, are casual, and who minimize any power differential, whereas others feel most secure with a more conservative, formal, guided therapy process.

Getting the Most Out of Therapy

When patients begin psychotherapy, they often ask what they can do to get the best results. One basic is choosing a therapist with whom one feels comfortable. Beyond that, defining goals, being open and honest, and applying oneself both during the time spent with the therapist and between sessions are important components of successful therapy.

Defining Goals

It is helpful for patients to ask themselves, "How would I like to be different by the end of therapy?" Patients should think specifically about changes they'd like to make in terms of their depression, their relationships, and their work or lifestyle. What would they like to eliminate—stress, symptoms, bad habits? What would they like to add—pursuing pleasurable activities, exercising, learning new interpersonal skills, improving management skills at work or at home? The therapist will help the patient evaluate and refine these goals and determine which goals they will work on in therapy.

Being Open and Honest

As trust develops between the patient and therapist, the patient should ask herself: Do I feel comfortable telling this person about my most sensitive issues? Do I feel like I am sharing, or simply telling? Am I open to feedback, and does this encourage me to further open up? As therapy proceeds, if patients find it difficult to trust the therapist, this is a valid issue to bring up for discussion.

Uncomfortable thoughts and feelings may carry the greatest leverage for growth. Once trust has been established with the therapist, issues that have great emotional charge or are being obsessed about may emerge more readily and often. Therapists can help patients to improve their awareness of these thoughts and feelings, to quiet them, and to find respite from them. Likewise, the patient's willingness to explore and challenge cherished beliefs and attitudes may enhance growth. When therapy reaches a level of intensity where it's really pushing emotional buttons, this is a powerful opportunity to make transformational decisions and changes. Patients who stick with it, pushing through and following through on the therapist's recommendations despite its being hard work, are generally rewarded with breakthroughs. The more difficult the work may seem, the more there is to gain from it.

Finally, therapy should be a safe place to face truths regarding addictions, self-destructive habits, or impulsive actions that encourage dissociation from or avoidance of uncomfortable feelings. Without attention, these issues will continue to block the process of healing and growth and will be damaging to the patient, her world, and those she cares about.

Within a trusting relationship, patients can let down their defenses and ask the therapist any question that crosses their mind—even "dumb" ones—without embarrassment. Patients are also able to share any frustrations with the therapy process, so such frustrations do not grow into resentments and block the therapeutic process. In the spirit of healing, the therapist may respond by taking the patient's concerns seriously, being open to a change of technique or approach, showing willingness to own any contribution to the patient's dissatisfaction, and helping the patient to understand her part in the exchange as well. Should a disappointing therapy encounter occur, welcome it—it can reveal relationship issues that need to be addressed and create a jumping-off point for further work.

Applying Oneself and Doing the Work

Some people greet a new therapist with an attitude that screams "fix me!" as if therapy were a procedure done by a therapist to—rather than in collaboration with—a patient. Although they may objectively know this isn't going to happen, some people have subjective resistance to "doing the work." Others are truly beleaguered by the experience of living with depression. It's a simple truth that passivity does not lead to wellness. No matter how painful, the best thing a depressed person can do is to "put one foot on the floor," drag herself to an upright position, and take action, whether or not she feels like it. It is a good idea to start with very small steps and work toward larger tasks, both in terms of therapy and in creating a more balanced lifestyle. The best daily schedule is one that includes activities the person wants to do as well as those she needs to do; discipline is powerful, and a task well done or commitment fulfilled gives a sense of accomplishment and helps to build self-mastery and self-esteem.

Therapy (and the rest of one's endeavors) will be more effective if time is spent reflecting on and working on the goals between sessions. Patients should think of therapy and treatment as parts of their lifestyle, not as separate activities they do for depression. Wellness is a lifestyle approach, and all aspects of one's life complement, support, or hinder effectiveness of the others. Eliminating stress is also helpful—perhaps by journaling, restructuring priorities, making time for pleasurable activities and recreation or exercise, and expressing feelings to people who are trusted. Patients should recognize negative thoughts, acknowledge them, and let them pass—and focus on and expect positive outcomes. As discussed earlier, "changing one's mind" happens not only through deliberate action such as repeated affirmations or substitutions of negative thoughts with more positive ones, but also by simply reminding oneself to find the positive in the everyday, to have a sense of gratitude, to find moments of peace or beauty or stillness, and to be mindful and reflective. All cognitive processes, even those that seem automatic, reinforce our patterns and affect our mental health.

People who actively participate in therapy recover more quickly and have fewer relapses. This means bringing therapy into one's everyday life—reflecting on the therapy between visits, evaluating thoughts and behaviors, identifying stresses that contribute to depression, and working to modify these. Patients should spend some time thinking about what success, and what wellness, mean to them on a personal level and how they plan to work toward these states—while enjoying the ride. Redefining and reinventing along the way are important. Keeping a journal of cognitive and emotional responses, experiences, and revelations can be a fantastic tool. Some weeks may provide many insights, ruminations, and expressive material; others may be dry, and that's okay, too. Gains from therapy may come in fits and starts.

Completing therapy "homework" the therapist has assigned is important. Homework is designed to help the benefits of therapy extend beyond the time spent in session, to carry therapy into the "outside" world, and to encourage growth that will fuel future sessions. Patients who are especially motivated can ask the therapist how they might supplement psychotherapy with readings, workbooks, client pamphlets, and the like. These are plentiful in CBT and available for other therapies as well.

Before attending an upcoming session, it is helpful for patients to collect thoughts they had about the previous sessions, insights that have come during the interval, and new ideas that are relevant to goals. The session should be planned to allow enough time to discuss what would be helpful to do during the coming week and to clarify the assignments and discuss difficulties that may arise with them before the session ends.

Taking notes at the end of each session or making a recording or summary of the session can be helpful in tracking progress, reviewing strategies to try during the week, and highlighting salient points that have emerged during the session.

Patients who are having difficulty applying themselves cognitively and emotionally between sessions need to ask the tough question: "What are my points of resistance?" Many people, no matter the degree of pain they experience, resist getting well. Depression may not feel comfortable, but it is familiar. It may also play a role in the patient's life, which therapists call "paradox." For example, a depressed person may fear the challenges she will face if she places herself in a new "well" context, such as a changing role in the family. Patients who have a paradoxical relationship with their depression will not get well until they discover and acknowledge this and decide to let it go.

Getting the Most From the First Session

Before going to a first therapy session, it is useful to spend some time on the telephone with the therapist. During this time of assessment, patients can ask the therapist if he would be willing to read over the patient's history before the first session. This not only provides the therapist with information that can jump-start the first session, but also demonstrates that the patient is proactive and wants to make the most of the therapy process. Most therapists will be willing to read a patient's history providing that it is neat, clear, and organized. The history should be typed if possible and marked "Confidential for [the therapist's name] Only!" Following are some suggestions of information that can be included:

- *Descriptive information.* Age, work and educational history, marital history/status.
- *Description of a typical day and week.*
- *History of the presenting problem.* The main reason therapy is sought, and a record of the history of the problem, including onset, duration, severity, characteristics/qualities, course over time, what makes it better or worse, and any associated context, problems, people, or events.

- *Thoughts of suicide.* Include pertinent information about thoughts of suicide, past and current, and any attempts. If there are current thoughts of suicide, highlight this part of the history and talk to the therapist directly about these thoughts.
- *Alcohol history.* Quantity and type of alcohol; frequency of drinking.
- *Drug history.* Any illegal drugs, for how often and how long.
- *Treatment history.* Any prescriptions taken, why they are taken, the name of the prescriber, dose, how often they are taken, and any side effects. List also medications that have been taken in the past, why they were started, why stopped, and notes about effectiveness and side effects.
- *Family tree or history.* Blood relatives only. Note whether living or dead, and any significant notes about the relationships, psychiatric symptoms or illnesses these relatives may have or have had, and best medication responses if known.
- *Relationship history.* Significant relationships, including partner/spouse, children, former partners, parents, and grandparents. List the ongoing effects of the sharing, learning, joys, traumas, and other experiences associated with these relationships. Include the length of relationships and the reason any of them have ended.
- *Emotional support system.* Describe self-care and outside supports.
- *Problem-solving history.* List attempts that have been made to deal with the problem. Also, include other significant problems that may have been solved and other accomplishments.
- *Objectives for therapy.* Describe current emotional state, desired emotional state, and how it might be achieved. What might be potentially helpful or unhelpful?

Again, this should be neat, clear, and organized, and the therapist should be alerted that it's on the way to allow ample time to review it before the first session. Modified for the particular purpose, histories are also very helpful for and appreciated by psychiatrists, general practitioners, and other health care professionals, especially when there is only a single visit or limited time scheduled with that person.

Assessing Progress

The therapy process begins with setting goals—perhaps regarding making changes in how the patient feels or how she approaches relationships and other important areas in her life, or regarding coming to terms with or gaining a better understanding of her circumstances. After some time has passed, patients should reflect on how they are coping with and viewing difficult thoughts, feelings, and situations, and ask themselves whether this has changed. The patient's progress (or lack of it) should be openly reviewed with the therapist.

The patient and therapist might agree on a time frame at which point they will discuss whether or not there has been any progress and how things are going in general. Three or four sessions after the initial session is generally a good time to review progress. It is important during this trial period for patients not to obsess over whether therapy is working, whether the patient really likes the therapist, whether the therapist can help, and so on. It's too early to know. That would be like going to the gym twice and then checking to see if your muscles are getting bigger!

Some patients find that progress comes in fits and starts; every few sessions or so they will have an "ah ha" moment, where a new level of understanding, resolve, or ability to act is reached—having entered therapy with a problem "this big," they emerge from a session with a better understanding and less anxiety regarding the issue. Therapy is working when symptoms improve, or perhaps when a better understanding and acceptance of a patient's thoughts and feelings is reached, or when the patient recognizes how various aspects and events of her life are related in ways she hadn't considered. Keep in mind that certain tasks require more time to accomplish than others. Some goals may need to be adjusted depending on how long the patient plans to be in psychotherapy. The patient will know when therapy is working, though this will take time.

Patients often feel a wide range of emotions during psychotherapy. Discussing painful and troubling experiences may be difficult and may leave them with questions about the purpose and process of therapy. Sessions may be erratic, inconsistent, and fraught with difficulties that make the patient want to quit. But this can actually be a positive sign indicating that the patient is starting to work through key thoughts and behaviors.

If, after some time, the patient finds herself feeling "stuck" or lacking direction, or hasn't begun to feel some relief or change, she should be open with the therapist. It may be that the patient's resistance is too great for psychotherapy at this point, or that the therapist in some way puts the patient on edge or on guard. It may be that the patient feels no connection to the therapist and can't get interested in the process. Patients should tell the therapist if they feel the match isn't a good fit, if they feel that rapport could be improved, or if they are questioning any aspects of the therapist's approach. It is sometimes wise to seek another opinion (as one would with any illness) from another therapist or mental health professional.

Therapy is an intensely individual process—not every therapist or technique, no matter how effective overall, is a good fit with every client. We sometimes hear complaints that the therapist listens too much and provides too little feedback. Sometimes therapists (typically psychodynamic ones) try to be an idealized "blank screen," hoping that the patient's transference reaction toward them will develop intensely so that it can be interpreted. (Transference is the projection onto the therapist of old feelings from past relationships that may have nothing to do with who the therapist is as a real person.) These therapists often incur the patient's wrath when no improvement in depression is seen after a month or two of psychotherapy.

Another complaint we sometimes hear is that, after a few months or even years, the visits to the therapist feel like having a friendly chat with a kind, understanding best friend or relative. This often happens when there is loss of a clear sense of the goals of treatment. At this point, either the patient or therapist (preferably both) should step back to examine the psychotherapy process and ask what it is that they are trying to accomplish and whether they are making progress on it.

Treatment Duration

The length of time spent in therapy, and the "efficiency" of a particular modality, may have something to do with the particular technique and with session frequency, but in large part it is determined by the issues being addressed and by factors ascribed to the individual.

Time-limited (12 to 20 sessions, depending on modality), manualized, goal-directed individual psychotherapies target rapid reduction of depressive symptoms specifically and have tight scope. CBT focuses on correcting cognitive distortions; interpersonal therapy (IPT) targets symptom relief and social functioning relative to relationships and role transitions (and usually targets a single problem); and dialectical behavior therapy (DBT) is skills-based, as is behavioral therapy. Therapies such as psychoeducation and social-rhythms therapy, which are usually wrapped into other approaches, are straightforward and education-based. There is a brief form of psychodynamic therapy, but it is not depression-specific or targeted at symptoms management; instead, it targets a single problem or behavior and does not address personality work as long-term approaches do. Within 12 to 15 sessions or so, an individual should be able to feel a change—a clear difference in how she thinks, feels, and acts, or in how things look to her—though not a "cure." If this isn't happening, a different type of therapy, a different therapist, or addition of medication may be in order.

Brevity of the course of therapy may be partially attributed to both the number and nature of issues addressed. Approaches that deal with the here and now and are solution-focused do not delve into the past to look for the solutions of problems or heal old wounds, as this is very time-consuming (though worthwhile for some individuals). If committed to a brief course, the therapist will assist the patient in selecting one or perhaps two issues to focus on.

A review of the research on brief treatments may give the impression that these approaches are especially effective in treating depression, but it should be noted that the people selected to participate in these clinical trials typically have "uncomplicated" major depression, without coexisting psychiatric, medical, or substance abuse conditions. The rapid symptomatic relief demonstrated in these trials may also be due to the acute nature of many episodes of depression; those who have been depressed for more than a year or two (depending on the individual study) are generally not enrolled in the trials. Select individual factors that affect depression treatment of any type include motivation, drive, persistence, insight, intelligence, stressors, social support, severity of symptoms, interpersonal skills, and existing adaptive coping mechanisms. These factors are also typically related to the complexity and chronicity of the illness. The depression, too, is a factor: Treatment can wax and wane, so to speak, with the depression, with periods of good days, weeks, or months and periods that are less productive.

We consider brief therapies to be of tremendous help to many people—but they aren't magic bullets for all patients. Even when brief therapy produces fantastic results, patients still may choose to continue therapy, not only to gain symptom relief but also to establish new behaviors and strengths, work on additional problems, and prevent relapse, especially when the patient's environment regularly presents challenges. Open-ended, "continuation treatment" options are structured adaptations of behavior therapy, CBT, and IPT that have less frequent sessions and are focused on maintenance of gains and prevention of relapse. This approach is specifically for people who have completed a course of brief therapy and have enjoyed benefit. Traditional analytic or dynamic therapies, which are typically open-ended and scheduled weekly, work on personality, character, and early-life relationships in addition to, and as reflected in, current issues. This therapy may be helpful alone or in combination with a structured approach. People with a history of trauma in childhood, with personality disorders, depleted self-esteem, long-standing depressive outlook, or history of difficulties in relating with others may gain benefit.

It is also important to understand that adequate "dose and duration" apply to psychotherapy as well as to medications. In a yearlong randomized STEP-BD trial for enhancement of pharmacotherapy in bipolar depression, intensive psychotherapy (up to 30 sessions of family-focused, interpersonal and social rhythm, or cognitive-behavioral therapies) demonstrated higher year-end recovery rates, shorter times to recovery, and more time well compared to three sessions of brief collaborative care (Miklowitz, Otto, Frank, Reilly-Harrington, Wisniewski, et al., 2007). These patients also accrued more benefit in areas of total function, relationship functioning, and life satisfaction, though no improvement was seen in work/role functioning and recreational activities.

In addition to factors related to the therapeutic approach and design, the individual, her environment, and the depression itself, there is the health care delivery system. Despite the benefits of psychotherapy, which has been demonstrated to be cost-effective in reducing mortality and morbidity (continued and complicated illness), many insurance firms and managed care companies have stringent limits on coverage and access to mental health care. If there is a limit to the number of visits a patient can afford, she must be sure to pace herself as she participates in therapy, keeping her goals in mind and communicating openly with the therapist about these concerns. The therapist must help the patient to maximize the time, focusing work on areas most in need of change. For patients who wish to continue therapy, there are several alternatives to sessions:

- Patients can start "tapering" therapy as they begin to feel better, scheduling visits once every 2 weeks, then once every 3 weeks. They can practice the skills they've learned in the meantime.
- Patients can see the individual therapist on an ongoing basis biweekly or monthly.
- Group therapy or a self-help support group can be added to individual therapy.
- Patients can plan a break of several weeks, make use of their gains, and then return to weekly therapy. This may also be viewed as intermittent brief psychotherapy—periods of therapy punctuated with breaks.
- Patients can terminate therapy with the option of resuming if needed. A scheduled follow-up session or phone contact can ease the transition.
- In CBT, booster sessions are recommended at 3, 6, and 12 months after therapy has ended. This can be considered regardless of theoretical framework.

The basic rule of thumb is to do therapy when it is needed and not when it isn't. After the patient has met goals and made significant gains, she can consult the therapist only when she faces a problem for which she needs professional help.

Therapy Doesn't Go On Forever
For many people, the first thing that comes to mind when thinking about therapy is a Woody Allen film, where characters go to their

analysts, year after year, for eternity. Although some patients do continue therapy indefinitely, most draw the line at some point and decide that, for one reason or another, they are ready to move on—which does not mean they won't return. Still, moving on is a process, and it happens for any number of reasons.

Knowing When It's Time to Stop

Many patients continue therapy for as long as it feels like it is helping, and others have limitations on the number of sessions they participate in. For patients in open-ended or continuation therapy, the following steps can help to determine a good end point:

- Determine whether the goals set at the beginning of therapy have been reached. If both patient and therapist feel that significant progress has been made, it may be appropriate to stop therapy.
- Review the therapy journal, if one has been kept. What progress has been achieved and what positive and negative aspects of various sessions and of the patient-therapist relationship stand out? It's helpful to keep a list in the journal of the specific changes that will signal that therapy may no longer be needed.
- Schedule a review session to examine the reasons for being in therapy, the progress made, and satisfaction with the therapeutic process.
- Discuss the therapist's ideas for reaching the desired therapeutic goal.

Flexibility is key as therapy progresses, as goals may change, but if financial or other reasons raise concern about when therapy should end, the patient should keep limitations clearly in mind and pace herself.

Other Reasons to Stop

The therapist's office must be a place where the patient feels free to talk about her most difficult issues. When a patient feels that there is something she just can't share, the implications of this should be examined. Patients should also be wary of advice. Certainly the therapist will offer many impressions, but unless the patient is simply unable to function, advice is not what she's there for.

A couple of reasons that may tempt patients to stop but that actually offer potential for growth are the stalemate and resistance. If a patient is dissatisfied with the therapy, making no progress, and feeling like she wants to quit, this may be resistance (related to something she is trying subconsciously to avoid or to fear related to the end of therapy), or it may indicate something inherent in the relationship with the therapist. In the former case, if the patient can let go and work through the resistance, therapy may make a leap forward. In the latter, interpretation may reveal that something wanted from the therapist perhaps isn't there. In this case, getting what is wanted may be far less helpful than discovering it and identifying its importance. For example, recognizing frustration over the therapist's lack of expression of empathy and validation when the patient repeatedly places herself in victim roles may offer her an opportunity to explore this frustration as it manifests in other relationships, and to challenge the lack of accountability and assertiveness that contribute to her feelings of helplessness and desperation. If the therapist can't help the patient through a stalemate or resistance, or if negative aspects of the experience are overwhelming the therapeutic work, it is a good time to plan termination. As always, patients should discuss their concerns with the therapist. Disagreements will inevitably arise, and this is part of the therapy process. A skilled therapist will be able to partner with the patient to find a satisfactory solution or end point. Therapists who are surprised and become defensive are lacking the skills to help the patient anyway. Patients should watch out for therapists who don't listen to their concerns or apologize for mistakes.

Unprofessional or Unethical Behavior on the Part of the Therapist
Therapy should always be terminated if the therapist acts in an unprofessional or unethical manner. Though the majority of therapists have their patients' best interests in mind, there are a few who may commit inappropriate actions. In many of these cases, respect and clear professional boundaries between the clinician and patient have not been maintained, or an unbalanced power differential has been erected and the

patient feels that she "needs" the relationship to continue. Damaging relationships are often the hardest to leave, but when a patient has even a hint of doubt about the therapist's practice, she should think it over carefully and discuss it with the therapist.

Following are some examples of unethical and unprofessional conduct:

- Sexual contact of any kind with a current patient, a patient's relative or significant other, or a former patient within 2 years after termination of therapy. Any sexual approach is unprofessional. Asking patients to remove any of their clothes or touching in any way without permission is unethical.
- Asking or agreeing to see a patient outside of therapy.
- Eliciting help from patients for the therapist's own problems, charities, or outside business interests. Therapists can bring up anecdotal information from their personal lives, but even this should be done judiciously and only to assist in the patient's therapy. The focus should not change to dealing with the therapist's problems.
- Violating a patient's confidentiality. Except for situations involving harm to self or others and specific insurance requirements, a therapist should never, without written permission, reveal what transpires during sessions or even the fact that the person is a patient.
- Providing services for which the therapist has no training, experience, or education, or advertising falsely regarding such services.
- Being under the influence of drugs or alcohol during a session.
- Committing fraud (billing for services not performed in order to reduce the amount the patient owes, or overbilling the insurance company to reimburse the patient for her copayment).
- Paying or accepting compensation for referral of patients.
- Assisting someone in the unlicensed practice of therapy.
- Raising the agreed-upon fee arbitrarily. Therapists may charge a reduced fee to accommodate a patient's financial situation. If the patient's situation improves, it is customary to reevaluate the circumstances, but therapists cannot increase the fee just because they believe the patient can afford it.

- Abandoning clients. If a therapist must suddenly terminate with a patient who still requires treatment, he must provide referrals to other practitioners who are prepared to assume the continuation of treatment.

In the Best Case, Termination Is a Process

The decision to end therapy is ideally made by both patient and therapist. It is a good idea to thoroughly discuss the issue prior to making a final decision. Ideally, the last session should be scheduled well in advance to allow the sessions preceding it to focus on discussing and "processing" the feelings of separation, loss, and mourning that are evoked during this time of saying good-bye. In psychodynamic or interpersonal therapies, further exploration and emotional growth may lead to important insights. In CBT, the process of termination is a good time to focus on consolidating gains.

In the best cases, the patient and therapist agree that therapy should end because the work has gone well and has had the desired effects. Termination is discussed, and a mutually agreeable ending date is set. During this ending phase, patients may experience a resurgence of symptoms and painful emotions, and both parties may experience the pain of loss of a relationship. The therapy ends with the recognition that good work was done through appreciated efforts by both the patient and the therapist, and that the patient is ready to move on. The therapeutic relationship and professional boundaries are left intact, and though the patient may never return, if the need should arise there would be no barriers.

In other cases, therapy may have to end (due to time-limited therapy design or lack of patient resources) despite a degree of dissatisfaction with what has been accomplished and a desire to continue the therapy. Both patient and therapist may agree that a hoped-for goal for the treatment will not be realized. The limitations of the experience are acknowledged, but there is still mutual appreciation, and the patient may choose to return at some point in the future.

After Therapy Has Ended

Although the therapy relationship is ultimately professional, it can feel intensely personal. It may seem odd or unnatural to spend hour after hour with an individual, sharing one's most intimate thoughts and feelings, and then actually plan for this relationship to formally "end." It is natural to have thoughts and feelings about what becomes of this relationship when therapy comes to a close. Although there are many different ways to manage this, it is not uncommon to allow for some kind of limited contact (such as occasional telephone calls) to occur after the formal therapy has ended, and many individuals and their therapists agree to arrange "booster sessions" for the future.

Psychotherapeutic Modalities

Of the dozens—perhaps hundreds—of forms of psychotherapy, the vast majority focus in one way or another on helping patients to reduce negative symptoms, gain insight into why these symptoms occurred, work through those issues, and reduce the reemergence of the symptoms in the future. The four major theoretical branches include cognitive, behavioral, dynamic (or analytic), and humanistic therapies. We focus here on the models that have been validated, through research, as successful in alleviating depression for many patients—specifically, CBT, which combines the classical schools of cognitive therapy and behavioral approaches, and IPT. We also discuss social rhythms therapy and psychoeducation, which are often blended with CBT and IPT. Several other forms, which have been less rigorously researched but may be helpful—especially to patients with complex, coexisting diagnoses or long-standing problems—are classic behavioral approaches, DBT (a specialized offshoot from CBT), and psychodynamic psychotherapy.

A specific type of psychotherapy may be chosen based on variables present in the patient's life. Unhealthy lifestyle habits including poor diet, lack of exercise, and poor sleep patterns may be addressed through psychoeducation and motivational interviewing. Heavy drinking, drug abuse, smoking, and other addictions, as well as complicated grief, may respond well to self-help groups. IPT or psychodynamic therapy may help those who remain in an abusive or demoralizing job or major relationship, are adjusting to role changes or stage-of-life issues, have a history of adversity, or experience social isolation. The person with housing or financial stress may benefit from coaching or case management. Those with symptoms complicated by poor coping mechanisms may benefit from skill-building and symptoms management. Family therapy may assist those who have assumed the "sick role" or "designated patient" status in a family system. Persons with severe, chronic, or recurrent illness may benefit from learning to self-monitor, use tools such as a mood diary, and engage in planning for wellness and prevention of relapse. A sense of community may come from joining a support group, church, or spiritual practice group. Whatever the approach, psychotherapy can provide education and support to maintain medication adherence, hope when side effects precede therapeutic benefit, and monitoring of suicidality.

Depression-Focused Psychotherapy

Many forms of psychotherapy, including some short-term (10 to 20 weeks) therapies, can help depressed individuals, with goal-directed modalities most likely to alleviate symptoms. Models of psychotherapy within this domain include various forms of behavioral therapy (BT), cognitive therapy, CBT, and IPT. Each draws its name principally from the objectives of treatment and from theories regarding the roots of psychopathology. The theories also carry predictions about specific outcomes, such as the effects of behavioral treatment on social skills, cognitive therapy on dysfunctional attitude, and IPT on measures of social adjustment. In each, model-specific formulations, psychoeducation, and procedurally guided interventions are employed to help patients learn to cope with and hopefully overcome depression.

What Goal-Directed Therapies Have in Common

Unlike traditional analytic or dynamic therapies, which are typically open-ended, none of these more structured therapies relies on the therapeutic relationship as the central force guiding the therapy process. Moreover, they deemphasize (though certainly validate the importance of) personality, character, and early-life relationships in the working process, and they do not view depression as the result of unconscious or neurotic conflicts. Unlike traditional therapies that were expected to last sometimes for years, each model of depression-specific treatment was initially developed as a short-term therapy, generally delivered over 2 to 4 months.

The time-limited nature of therapy is emphasized explicitly in terms of the goal to achieve rapid symptomatic relief, capitalizing on the acute nature of many episodes of depression. In clinical trials, psychotherapy is sometimes compared with pharmacotherapy in treatment of acute depression, typically in brief (12-week) trials. Its favorable results in these conditions argue for these therapies as cost-effective alternates or adjuncts to medication, but it is important to note three things in the evaluation of the generalizability of outcomes from clinical trials of time-limited therapies to real-world populations: First, the subjects enrolled in these trials are usually "pure" patients with "uncomplicated" major depression—they do not have many coexisting psychiatric, medical, or substance abuse conditions, and they do not demonstrate significant risk for suicide. Second, the subjects may or may not be newly diagnosed or experiencing their first depressive episode, but patients in chronic, long-standing episodes (more than 1 or 2 years, depending on criteria for the particular study) are generally not enrolled in the trials. Third, not only symptom relief is desired, but also long-lasting change made by establishing new behaviors and strengths. By necessity, longer-term models of treatment have been developed for BT, CBT, and IPT. These adaptations are generally less intense (in terms of frequency) and more focused on maintenance of gains and prevention of relapse than in traditional long-term psychotherapy. Well-being therapy (WBT) is a unique form of short-term maintenance therapy adapted from CBT. Focusing on residual symptoms of irritability, fatigue, hopelessness, diminished motivation, stress reactivity, and modifying lifestyles, while removing cognitive barriers to pleasurable experiences, this approach has demonstrated long-term decreases in depression recurrence after only 10 sessions of therapy.

Behavioral and Cognitive-Behavioral Therapies

Those with a history of depression are familiar with the concept of anhedonia. Literally translating as "without pleasure," this term describes a state in which people are unable to feel happiness or to enjoy activities they used to enjoy; some cannot remember ever having experienced enjoyment in the past. Feelings of hopelessness, worthlessness, failure, defeat, and loss are often central to the experience of depression, and they can lead to feelings of low self-esteem. When something bad happens to someone whose thinking has become distorted in this way, she responds by automatically assuming that it is her fault, a sign of personal inadequacy, and proof that nothing will ever work out right for her in the future. She further believes that if something good happens, it is just a coincidence. These thoughts may be perceived as being beyond the depressed person's control, reinforcing a feeling of helplessness. Once established, patterns of negative thinking can set a person up for chronic lack of well-being.

Whereas many schools of psychology consider negative thinking secondary to unhealthy emotions, cognitive theory posits that faulty thinking and perception, based on illogical and irrational beliefs, underlies and reinforces negative emotions. Adverse early experiences presumably cause a person to form pathological schemas or constructs of her relationship to herself, her world, and the future. When these schemas become triggered or activated, mood-dependent changes in memory, thought processing, and automatic negative thoughts (those occurring almost instantaneously with the worsening of depressed mood) result, as do dysfunctional attitudes, which are not only associated with more extreme or intense reactions to life stress, but also confer a greater risk of encountering new adversities.

A combination of approaches from both cognitive and behavioral theories, CBT provides techniques to help the patient establish control over negative thinking by correcting "cognitive distortions" or correcting thinking errors that abet such distortions. This process is called cognitive restructuring. CBT is certainly the best-studied and most often studied intervention for depression and bipolar illness. It is also among the most efficacious.

Whereas CBT approaches cognitive distortions with both cognitive and behavioral techniques, BT focuses on changing unwanted or unhealthy behaviors, without emphasis on cognitive processes. Developed by Albert Ellis, it has its roots in the principles of learning, including positive and negative reinforcement, conditioned reflexes, and others. From a behavioral perspective, depression is viewed as a consequence of insufficient reinforcement or poor conditioning. Though practiced in their "pure" form for persons suffering from phobias and other anxiety disorders, behavioral techniques are more likely to be incorporated into the cognitive-behavioral approach when used to treat depression. Depending on the nature of the problems, a therapist may choose to integrate more or less behavioral therapy into practice.

GOALS AND CHARACTERISTICS OF CBT

The goals of CBT are to alleviate depressive symptoms and prevent their recurrence by helping people to:

- Identify negative cognitions (thoughts, beliefs, ideas, attitudes, assumptions, mental imagery, and ways of directing their attention) regarding three areas: themselves and their circumstances, the world, and the future (known as the "cognitive triad").
- Discover what about these patterns is irrational or just not helpful, then test and reformulate.
- Develop new and more flexible, realistic, and validated alternatives.
- Test these new ways of thinking and rehearse cognitive and behavioral responses that are likely to have desirable results.

CBT asks patients to address their core beliefs, which are central ideas about the self that are formed early in life, activated at times of stress, and act as a filter through which interactions and other experiences are perceived. When these are maladaptive, they generally involve themes of unlovability and hopelessness, and they act as risk factors for future episodes. Unlovable core beliefs include believing one is unlikable, unwanted, bad, defective (and thus undeserving of love), or bound to be abandoned or rejected. Helpless core beliefs involve feeling powerless, vulnerable (to being hurt), inadequate, incompetent, disrespected, or not good enough (in terms of achievement). CBT also explores cognitive errors, also referred to as cognitive distortions (these are explored in more depth later). Cognitive errors involved in depression include all-or-nothing thinking, overgeneralization, disqualifying the positive, jumping to conclusions, and others. Cognitive errors in hypomania include positive fortune-telling or being overly optimistic about unknown outcomes, overreliance on luck, underestimating risk of danger, overestimating one's capabilities, disqualifying the negative or minimization of life problems, overvaluing immediate gratification, and misinterpreting intentions of others (e.g., misperceiving sexual or aggressive content or innuendo).

There are several approaches to CBT, including rational-emotive behavior therapy, rational-behavior therapy, rational-living therapy, cognitive therapy, dialectic behavior therapy, and the cognitive-behavioral analysis system of psychotherapy. Models have been designed especially for depression, chronic depression, shyness and social anxiety, panic attacks, phobias, obsessions and compulsions, chronic anxiety or worry, posttraumatic stress, eating disorders, personality issues, insomnia and other sleep problems, headaches, loneliness, insufficient self-esteem, inadequate coping skills, procrastination, passivity, substance abuse, smoking, overinhibition or expression of emotions, difficulties with career, job, or school, relationship issues, or being just plain stressed out. Most cognitive-behavioral therapies share the following characteristics:

- A theoretical basis in the scientific fact that our thoughts—not external things like people, situations, and events—contribute substantially to our feelings and behaviors.
- The premise that a sound therapeutic relationship is necessary for effective therapy but is not the focus. CBT is a collaborative effort between the therapist and the patient: The therapist assumes the role of a coach or teacher in addition to providing more nonspecific elements of support. CBT requires therapists to be active within sessions, which may foster a strong working alliance.
- An emphasis on teaching the benefits of feeling calm when confronted with undesirable situations. By reframing our outlook, we can change how we feel, even if the undesirable circumstances aren't malleable.
- A structured and directive nature. Each session has an agenda in which techniques and concepts are taught in an explicit way and goal achievement is always central.
- A theoretical basis in the assumption that most emotional and behavioral reactions are learned and that they can be unlearned or reformulated.

- Theory and techniques that rely on the inductive method, which encourages us to look at our thoughts as being hypotheses that can be questioned and tested against reality.
- Assigned homework. Exploring and establishing new cognitive schemas takes time, consideration, and rehearsal. Psychotherapy promotes change by "rewiring" the brain—which happens through repetition and reinforcement.

GOALS AND CHARACTERISTICS OF BEHAVIORAL APPROACHES

Behavioral treatments of depression include the social-learning approaches module of self-control therapy, social-skills training, and structured problem-solving therapy. Note the emphasis on learning and skills, in contrast to focus on cognitive distortions and core beliefs. Each module is time-limited (8 to 16 weeks), and all are built on and emphasize the following:

- A functional analysis of behavior, in which the relationship between the difficulty (e.g., poor social skills or inefficient problem-solving strategies) and the onset or maintenance of the depressive syndrome is defined.
- Specific stepwise strategies to improve recognition of problem areas and to begin to implement the targeted changes in thoughts, feelings, or behavior. Strategies include assertiveness training, modeling, role-playing, relaxation training, and behavioral distraction techniques such as thought-stopping, which can help patients to break the cycle of depressive ruminations.
- Self-monitoring and self-evaluation of mood and activity as part of daily routine, with logs kept daily so that the progress and effectiveness of the program can be reviewed.
- Decrease in or management of aversive events.
- Development of self-reinforcement patterns.
- Behavior change accomplished via education, observation, guided practice, social reinforcement, and individualized homework assignments, including scheduled increases in levels of general, social, and pleasurable activity and behavioral productivity.

- Behavior modification in which the patient is rewarded for engaging in positive behavior.

Like CBT, each form of BT emphasizes continued application of skills learned in treatment to reduce the risk of relapse. As in CBT, more specific attention to relapse prevention is provided for those with chronic or recurrent depression. In several models of BT, patients attend periodic booster sessions or monthly sessions for continuation therapy.

Behavioral techniques complement cognitive work by balancing the patient's inner experience with her behaviors and mode of relating in the outside world. They are components of other therapies, including DBT, IPT, and social rhythms therapy, in addition to CBT. It works best on very specific and circumscribed target symptoms or behaviors, and on conditioning new responses. For example, in depression, therapy may focus on increasing the number of pleasurable activities or social connections in a person's life. It would also involve conditioning responses of pleasure through repeated exposure to the enjoyable activities. Someone with a phobia may undergo gradual exposure to something they are afraid of, and may also be taught relaxation exercises and various kinds of practice for the real life situation.

BT is particularly effective for anxiety, panic, phobias, obsessive-compulsive problems, and various kinds of social or sexual difficulty. If these issues are the source of or coexist with the depression, BT may quite helpful.

DEPRESSION-FOCUSED CBT

CBT for depression involves several essential features: the identification and correction of inaccurate thoughts (from cognitive therapy), an emphasis on helping patients to engage more often in enjoyable activities from BT, and the enhancement of problem-solving skills. Along with the challenging of irrational beliefs, techniques commonly taught are relaxation education and training, self-monitoring, cognitive rehearsal, thought stopping, communication skills training, assertiveness skills training, social skills training, and bibliotherapy.

Early in the course of therapy, particularly with more severely depressed clients, behavioral techniques may be emphasized. Daily monitoring of moods and activities helps to increase participation in rewarding behaviors, like hobbies, seeing friends, reading, or enjoying a hike, which may have been woven into the patient's life before she became depressed. Relationships between moods and automatic thoughts may be charted. Similarly, assignments that encourage problem-solving, such as breaking tasks down into small steps, are used to address problems that are perceived as overwhelming or insurmountable (for the depressed person, these may include facets of daily living that were once routine).

Therapy moves on toward eliciting and testing the accuracy of automatic thoughts and developing rational alternatives. Strategies may include flash cards on which responses to automatic negative thoughts are written, or the helpful four-column Daily Record of Dysfunctional Thoughts (described later). Patients are also encouraged to keep their thought records as part of a journal or notebook so that a summary of the course of therapy is available. Each session ends with a new homework assignment that builds logically on the material covered in the session.

An additional focus used increasingly by therapists is psychoeducation. It is often wrapped in with the therapeutic processes in CBT and IPT. Psychoeducation focuses on educating patients about the aspects of managing their lives with an illness that is chronic or episodic and recurrent. Patients learn to understand cues and triggers for exacerbation and relapse, as well as coping and response strategies, and how they might best organize aspects of their lives for success.

One aspect of CBT that many find attractive is its time-limited design. Though uncomplicated problems may be helped in 2 to 4 months, patients with multiple or long-standing issues to work on, as well as those with chronic or recurrent depression, may require more time. Even after a patient has learned to recognize when and where her thought processes are going awry, it can take months of concerted effort to recognize an invalid thought on the fly and then substitute it with a more suitable one. Remember, too, that therapy works by rewiring the brain: As new networks formed by new, positive behaviors are reinforced, old, disused networks weaken. Repetition of new behaviors is key.

The following exercises are commonly used by CBT therapists to help patients recognize, challenge, and replace their cognitive distortions. The first is adapted from the highly recommended 1999 book *The Feeling Good Handbook* by David D. Burns. Burns begins by listing 10 common cognitive distortions.

COGNITIVE DISTORTIONS
- All-or-nothing thinking: Things are seen in black-or-white categories. If a situation falls short of perfect, it is seen as a total failure.
- Overgeneralization: A single negative event, such as a romantic rejection or a career reversal, is seen as evidence of a never-ending pattern of defeat. Words such as "always" or "never" are used when describing it.
- Mental filter: A single negative detail is dwelled on exclusively, so that the vision of all reality becomes bleak.
- Disqualifying the positive: Positive experiences are rejected by the insistence that they "don't count" for some reason or another. In this way, negative beliefs are maintained, even though they are contradicted by everyday experiences.
- Jumping to conclusions: Things are interpreted negatively when there are no facts to support such conclusions.
  - Mind-reading: A person's arbitrary conclusion that someone is reacting negatively to them, and they don't bother to verify this.
  - Fortune-telling: A person anticipates that things will turn out badly, and they feel convinced that their prediction is an already-established fact.
- Magnification and minimization: A person exaggerates the importance of their problems and shortcomings, or minimizes the importance of their desirable qualities. This is also called the "binocular trick."
- Emotional reasoning: A person assumes that their negative emotions reflect the way things really are ("I feel it; therefore it must be true"), which may lead to hopelessness and a sense of powerlessness over their circumstances ("I feel angry; this proves that I'm being treated unfairly").

- "Should" statements: A person tries to motivate themself with "should" and "shouldn't" statements as if they have to be whipped and punished before they can be expected to do anything. "Musts" and "oughts" are also offenders. All the "shoulds" and "musts" make them feel rebellious and they get the urge to do just the opposite. "Should" statements directed against oneself lead to guilt and frustration. When one directs them toward others, one feels anger, frustration, and resentment.
- Labeling and mislabeling: Labeling is an extreme form of all-or-nothing thinking or overgeneralization. Instead of saying, "I made a mistake," a person attaches a negative label to themself: "I'm a loser."
- Personalization: A person sees themself as the cause of negative external events that in fact they were not primarily responsible for or in control of.

Burns goes on to ask the patient: "Do any of these seem familiar? Which are long-standing patterns for you, and which are 'automatic thoughts'—those that dart immediately through your consciousness when you are feeling your worst?" The patient is then asked to dispute the negative thoughts by focusing on contrary evidence—to formulate explanations to dispute them. For example, the overgeneralization "I didn't get the job I interviewed for; I'm *never* going to get a job" could be disputed with "Even though I wasn't offered this job, I *have* been offered jobs in the past." Finally, the patient replaces the negative thought with an empowering positive thought and belief, such as, "I am good at what I do and my past employers have liked me. If I keep looking, I will be offered a job in the future."

A variation on this exercise is practiced by mindfulness-based cognitive therapists. In contrast to classical CBT, the mindfulness approach asks that the patient consider negative thoughts without challenging them. Patients are instructed to "allow the negative thought to enter your mind, turn it over, consider it, acknowledge that it's just a thought like any other, and let it go . . ." (Eisendrath & McLane, 2008).

The second exercise is the four-column Daily Record of Dysfunctional Thoughts. In this technique, the patient thinks of a situation or event that was distressing or depressing. She then creates a four-column table. In the first column, she records the objective situation—for example, "an argument with my boyfriend." In the second column, she lists the negative thoughts that occurred within the situation, such as "he hates me and is going to leave me." In the third column, ensuing negative feelings and dysfunctional behaviors are listed: "I am a failure and not worthy of his love." In the fourth column, she challenges her negative thoughts on the basis of objective evidence from her experience: "He didn't actually *say* that he hates me, and we've gotten through rough patches before. I'm not a failure and I can get through this just like I've done in the past."

This exercise is helpful in that it helps the patient to analyze the process by which she became distressed or depressed, illustrated in the first three steps. The negative thoughts of the second column are seen as a bridge between the situation and the distressing feelings. Finally, the fourth column allows her to test reality by comparing her negative thoughts to the objective evidence.

Dialectical Behavior Therapy

DBT is a form of CBT (largely grounded in behavioral theory) developed by Marsha M. Linehan specifically to treat borderline personality disorder; it is now used in clients with a wide range of other diagnoses as well. The primary objective of DBT is to teach behavioral skills to help patients tolerate stress, regulate emotions, and improve relationships with others. DBT offers an excellent method by which anyone—with or without a diagnosis—can gain better mastery over some valuable life skills. It is especially helpful, however, for those whose behaviors lean toward the impulsive or self-injurious—such as in substance abuse, eating disorders, deliberate self-harm (for example, cutting or burning oneself), and suicidality—and for people with a history of trauma.

DBT includes both an individual and a group component. In individual therapy, issues that come up during the week are addressed, with any self-injurious and suicidal behaviors taking first priority, followed by therapy-interfering behaviors and then quality-of-life issues, with the final goal being general improvement of one's life. Use of the skills developed in the group sessions, as well as their effectiveness, is discussed in individual therapy. In weekly group sessions, patients learn to use specific skills from four modules:

- *Mindfulness.* Many people engage in self-destructive behaviors, become numb or dissociate from their feelings, or become angered when they are "triggered" by events or conditions in their environment. Mindfulness, described as a calm, purposeful, and reflective presence, is a state of mind that assists in developing personal insight, realization, and self-awareness as the person focuses on experiencing the here and now rather than on the (potentially disruptive) theories, attitudes, judgments, and abstractions of what might be happening. Mindfulness is also the state of mind that allows for concentration. Core mindfulness skills help people to center themselves and remain in the present when stressed (rather than coping by some form of escape). Individuals learn to gracefully "feel the pain and do it anyway," which becomes easier as the person learns the difference between actual suffering and the perceptions and expectations of that suffering. Mindfulness skills are stressed at each DBT group session and are encouraged as a daily practice. Through mindful observation, one may learn to separate the helpful from the false, damaging, or misguided, and to be less judgmental, less reactive, and more self-accepting while observing, describing, and participating in group. The goal of group members is to integrate mindfulness into daily life between sessions.
- *Emotion regulation.* These skills include identifying and labeling emotions, identifying obstacles to changing emotions, reducing vulnerability to "emotion mind," increasing positive emotional events, increasing mindfulness to current emotions, taking opposite action, and applying distress-tolerance techniques.
- *Interpersonal effectiveness.* Similar to assertiveness and interpersonal problem-solving, this involves saying no, asking for what you need, and coping with interpersonal conflict.
- *Distress tolerance.* Rather than focusing on changing distressing events and circumstances, patients can learn to accept, find

meaning in, and tolerate distress, as well as bear pain skillfully while remaining in the moment.

Many participants attend group DBT but not individual therapy if combined treatment is not feasible or desired.

Interpersonal Psychotherapy

IPT, developed by Klerman and Weissman in the 1980s (and later adapted for use in bipolar disorders), is a structured, short-term (16 to 20 sessions) individual psychotherapy that focuses squarely on rapid reduction of depressive symptoms and improved social functioning, including more satisfying relationships and social contexts in the present. The targeted approach of IPT has demonstrated rapid improvement for patients with problems ranging from mild situational depression to severe depression with a recent history of suicide attempts. Along with CBT, IPT is among the most efficacious of psychotherapies studied for relief of depression and improvement of functioning in major life areas.

The IPT framework considers clinical depression as having three components: the development of symptoms, which arise from biological/genetic and/or psychological processes; social interactions with others, which are learned over the course of one's life; and personality, made up of more enduring traits and behaviors that may predispose a person to depressive symptoms. IPT emphasizes the functional role of depression, intervening at the levels of symptom formation and social functioning, and does not attempt to explore deep-seated sources of the symptoms or to alter aspects of the patient's personality. In IPT, patients are encouraged to assume the "sick role" in the context of their circumstances and relationships, which implies both that depression is a condition that "happens to" people (therefore relieving them of the need to assign guilt or blame to others) and that depression plays an active role in one's current relationships.

Central to IPT are four underlying interpersonal themes that appear to be involved in the onset and maintenance of depression: unresolved grief or loss, transitions from one social or occupational role to another, conflict between the patient and significant individuals in her life, and social isolation or deficiencies in the capacity to relate to others. Early in therapy, one or two problem areas in the patient's current functioning are identified. Emphasis is then placed on the ways in which these problems and their social context cause or maintain symptoms, as well as on ways in which problematic interactions develop when a person becomes depressed. Psychoeducation about depression or bipolar disorder and treatment is woven throughout, and social rhythms therapy (SRT), explained later in this chapter, is usually included for patients living with bipolar illness. Among therapies for bipolar illness, interpersonal social rhythms therapy (IPSRT) and CBT are the most efficacious psychosocial treatments studied.

The psychoeducational part of IPT includes discussion of the nature of depression and its treatment, as well as the ways it manifests in the patient's life and relationships. It offers techniques to better tolerate depressive symptoms, to improve symptom management, and to manage impairments associated with the depressed state, along with formulation of problem-solving strategies. These efforts also help lessen the demoralization and hopelessness experienced by most depressed people. Several techniques are utilized within the therapeutic process, many of which are modified interventions borrowed from other well-established therapies such as CBT and brief crisis intervention. Faulty thinking that prevents adequate communication may be challenged, and behavioral techniques to improve social skills are utilized.

In the past 20 years, IPT has been modified for a variety of conditions other than depression, including dysthymia, eating disorders, substance misuse, post-traumatic stress disorder, ADHD, several anxiety disorders, depression within pregnancy, and the condition of living with HIV/AIDS. There is also an IPT conjoint (couples) therapy for couples whose disputes contribute to depressive episodes, and a maintenance-therapy model aimed at preventing or reducing the frequency of further depressive episodes.

IPT and medication treatment have been shown to complement each other. In Ellen Frank's classic 3-year study, highly recurrent depressed patients treated initially with Tofranil (a tricyclic antidepressant) and IPT responders (those whose symptoms had been reduced by half during the trial thus far) were given 17 weeks of continued combined treatment, then randomized to 3 years of treatment with drug or placebo plus IPT or medication-management visits (the psychotherapy placebo condition). Continued medication showed a highly significant prophylactic (preventive) effect compared to placebo, and IPT increased the duration of wellness compared to no treatment.

Romantic Loss: Patricia

Patricia was a delightful 28-year-old woman with a master's degree in business. She worked for a large corporation and had recently separated from her husband of 2 years. She described her husband as an immature, happy-go-lucky man. He went to church weekly but never followed rules at work, did not show up on time, did not help at home, and did not relate to her on an emotional level. He did not have the level of drive, ambition, and willingness to work hard that Patricia so treasured in herself.

One evening, when socializing with colleagues after work, Patricia kissed a man whom she found very attractive. A private detective who had been hired by her husband saw this, and the husband immediately said he suspected her of having an affair and wanted a divorce. In addition to her acute depression triggered by the marital separation, Patricia reported long-standing irritability and feelings of not being good enough to be with her husband. This manifested in and was derived from long-standing behaviors Patricia had established. She realized, for instance, that during the marriage she had avoided asking for what she wanted and needed in terms of help around the house because she did not want to be seen as demanding, nagging, or like her husband's mother. Patricia's feelings about her divorce ran deep and involved other important relationships in her life. She was ashamed to tell her mother about her divorce out of a sense of failure. She viewed her mother as obese, self-sacrificing, chronically used and taken advantage of by her husband (from whom she was divorced), and not taking care of herself. Patricia realized parallels between her own marriage and that of her parents, and generalized some of the negative feelings about her parents to herself.

Patricia appeared to have a single episode of major depression that was triggered by the marital separation, superimposed on chronic mild depression and worry that were diagnosed as dysthymic disorder and generalized anxiety disorder. Much of this was triggered by her long-standing negative thought patterns and behaviors relative to her marriage. Patricia's IPT therapist helped her to work through these feelings of inadequacy, shame, and failure, and to analyze their contribution to her depression, as well as the price she was paying in her relationships by going through life with chronic dissatisfaction. I strongly recommended a divorce recovery group for her, and she was willing to attend to gain some additional support in processing the emotions that came with the end of the marriage.

Pharmacotherapy was started to complement the IPT and group therapy. I started Patricia on Paxil, but it did not produce adequate response and gave her increased appetite, so I suggested that she switch to Effexor XR. Her sleep and energy, as well as mood, substantially improved with this medication change. As she progressed in therapy, she began dealing proactively with selling the house that she and her husband had recently purchased. She also decided to begin an intensive personal fitness program and to date new people. She was able to recognize the recurrence of her unhealthy patterns when she met some men who were not taking care of themselves physically or financially and who abused alcohol or drugs. These relationships ended within a few months. Over the course of therapy, Patricia came to realize that her values, her goals, her healthy lifestyle, and her desire for a partner who would share these approaches to life were truly legitimate. She was no longer willing to settle for someone just to be in a relationship. She wanted, needed, and expected a life partner who could be emotionally supportive. A similar interpersonal approach was needed in helping Father John to face the major role transition that drastically impacted his sense of identity and security.

Case Example: Father John

Father John was a 53-year-old priest who, after 27 years of devoted service, experienced personality conflicts in his new parish assignment. He had insomnia, loss of interest in his usual activities, and felt less productive. He had been taking Paxil and Xanax long-term, prescribed by his primary care physician, but he said these were to treat immune problems, rather than depression.

John's problems began when he was brought into a new church that was known to have administrative problems; he was viewed as a heavy-handed administrator who would hold staff accountable for performing their jobs in a very efficient way. At his old church, John related to the bishop in a very direct and sometimes confrontational way when he disagreed with decisions. This approach did not work with the new bishop, however, who had made personnel changes that John disagreed with. John was also vocal about his feelings regarding what he perceived as mismanagement of church finances, which were being used to build an elegant house for the local leader despite the fact that there were massive legal settlements for previous abuse of parishioners.

I diagnosed John as having an adjustment disorder with anxious and depressive features, and because of some of the rigidity demonstrated in his interpersonal relationships, I suspected obsessive-compulsive personality traits, which include a very strong sense of right and wrong, a need to be in control, and a focus on details, rules over feelings, and work over play.

After disagreeing with the personnel changes and the church financial priorities and investments, John was very suddenly relieved of duties at the parish. He appealed the bishop's decision and lost his case in Rome. He was further upset when he was hospitalized and diagnosed as having a potentially chronic life-threatening disease and when the bishop's action relieving him of duty was upheld upon review in Rome. He was placed on medical disability, and suddenly his meager income was cut in half. The many priests whom he had considered close friends throughout years of church service shunned him. He felt terribly betrayed: When he had committed himself to his priestly vows, there was a clear understanding that the bishop and the church would take care of him in exchange for his devoting his life to the church. Suddenly, he viewed his relationship with the church as being like that of an employee who was laid off from his job and had no salable skills that would allow him to get another comparable job.

Throughout treatment, we attempted to find some understanding and appreciation of what had been meaningful in John's career as a priest and to encourage acceptance of the loss of this role so that he would not spend the rest of his life as an angry, resentful, bitter old man. John's life role transition was extremely difficult, and a spiritual advisor, psychiatrist, and close friends among long-term parishioners were all helpful in coping.

Parts of therapy dealt with how close John felt to his long-time parishioners, how they welcomed him into their homes and family life, and how this could continue beyond his years as their parish priest. John was a very bright man with a strong interest in the history of the Catholic Church and I encouraged him to write a book on the changes he saw and experienced in his church over the recent decades of lawsuits around issues of clergy sexual abuse. The goals were to get him to appreciate that his relationships with the people he served would always be with him and to get a sense of the historical context for what had happened to him. Writing might also help him to deal with some intense feelings. Teaching religion was another option that we discussed as a way of continuing meaningful work.

Social Rhythms Therapy

SRT, often a component of other therapies (especially IPT for bipolar disorders), focuses on behavioral features that appear to contribute to relapse in bipolar disorder. The central theory of SRT is that bipolar disorder is characterized by disturbed biological rhythms, most importantly the circadian cycle, a roughly 25-hour cycle within which we establish sleep-wake patterns. Some research indicates that people with bipolar illness may generally have a higher incidence of sleep disturbance or disorder (66%, even when not in a mood episode) and also a different circadian pattern in the expression of stress hormones (such as cortisol) than other people. Both of these represent vulnerabilities, and disruptions in social routine can push the envelope, resulting in stress, the triggering of symptoms, and perhaps relapse into mania or depression.

The reestablishment and maintenance of regular habits for personal and social routines occurring at least once weekly is a primary goal in treatment. A social rhythms chart is kept daily, on which wake and sleep times and sleep duration are recorded, as are eating patterns, social interactions and telephone use, computer and television use, work activities and patterns of these, activities of self-care, exercise, hobbies, and other events. Special attention is given to which activities are done alone, which are done with others present, or with others as active participants, and to the time the patient spends at home and away from home.

A sample Social Rhythms Chart is included at the end of this chapter. Though most people are already aware of areas in their lives that could be improved—improving eating habits and sleep patterns, and increasing time spent with friends, for instance—seeing them logged in black and white can be both surprising and instructive. Examining routine habits can help one to get a handle on ways to establish more regular and healthy patterns. Keeping a log makes this an active and dedicated process.

The component of the social rhythms chart considered most important concerns the sleep-wake cycle—chiefly the wake time, as the first morning exposure to bright light is the major signal to set the body's clocks. Sleep studies that manipulate the times at which subjects go to bed and rise have found wake times to be more than five times more influential than bed times in the maintenance of normal sleep patterns (Burgess, 2005). This is why getting up at the same time each morning and getting some sunlight is so critical in setting the sleep-wake clock, why bright-light therapy (used most often in seasonal affective disorder) is most effective if used upon awakening, and perhaps also why this therapy is often effective in bipolar depression. Although SRT appears to reduce the time to recovery of bipolar depression, it has not proved to be effective in relapse prevention on its own. This certainly does not discount the importance of its goals, however, or its utility in an overall treatment plan.

Though SRT is designed for people with bipolar illness, many people have dysfunctional social rhythms even when they're feeling well. These patterns are built and reinforced not during a single episode, but over a period of years. By exploring these patterns, making gradual stepwise changes, and monitoring progress, patients can use SRT as a valuable addition to their depression toolkit.

Psychotherapy for Addiction and Lifestyle Management
People struggling with addiction have approaches to managing their illness that may not involve going cold turkey. Abstinence, especially at the beginning of treatment, may not be a choice for all patients. Fortu-

nately, there are methods of working with one's therapist that can be quite successful, that are easy to learn, and that can be reinforced by all members of the treatment team.

The harm reduction approach (Giovino, 2004; Ritter & Cameron, 2006; Tatarsky, 2003) does what it says: helps patients to reduce the consequences of their addiction. Patients may be encouraged to "cut down to quit" (D. Wang et al., 2008). They might work with the therapist or doctor on identifying ways to work on the effects their substance use has on relationships, lifestyle, and work. For example, a man who becomes aggressive toward his wife when he drinks may choose to explore his impulsive reactions to his emotions, and to try behavioral interventions to minimize his feelings of aggression and the outbursts. This may be done independently of working on cutting down alcohol use. He can also work on more active coping skills and safety precautions to prevent infections and overdose.

Motivational interviewing uses the stages of change, or transtheoretical, model (Prochaska, DiClemente, & Norcross, 1992) to help individuals make improvements in chronic illness and lifestyle changes. This is an excellent complement to psychotherapy and can be used to address any area of the patient's life that requires growth or change, including chronic illness.

Psychoeducation

Every good therapist is also a teacher, in the broad sense of the word. They help patients to understand their illness and cope with life stressors in a growth-promoting way, and they encourage healthy diet, exercise, and self-help strategies. "Psychoeducation" focuses on teaching patients—and sometimes family and friends—about the illness. It also encourages them to become educated, proactive consumers of their own mental health care and to develop an attitude and behaviors that promote wellness and recovery. Psychoeducation stresses the idea that people get themselves well, using a bevy of tools available to them, only two of which are health care professionals and medications. It encourages people to pursue wellness as they uniquely define it. Psychoeducation is often wrapped into other therapies such as CBT, DBT, and IPT; it is also effectively taught as a single intervention in a group setting.

Through psychoeducation, patients learn about their illness and its natural history, both generally and with respect to the individual patient. This helps patients become aware of which symptoms (known as prodromes) appear before an episode occurs, which symptoms occur in clusters and when, and which personal triggers (e.g., romantic rejection, interpersonal conflict, substance abuse) bring these symptoms about. With this knowledge and insight, patients can learn to predict a new episode and head it off by pursuing appropriate treatment and by adjusting their lifestyle accordingly. They can learn what makes their depression better or worse and collect an arsenal of symptom management techniques, coping strategies, and problem-solving skills to "keep themselves safe." They learn about the medications they are taking, how they work, and what is reasonable (and not reasonable) to expect from them—as well as the differences between side effects and symptoms and how to effectively work through side effects with the doctor. Patients plan for the future, learning how to put supports in place and how to identify any barriers to treatment that may affect them. Psychoeducation may also connect patients with resources in their community, including support groups.

Family psychoeducation includes teaching coping strategies and problem-solving skills to families and friends of people with mental illnesses to help them relate and communicate more positively and effectively with their ill family member. This reduces distress, confusion, and anxieties within the family, which may in turn help the depressed person recover.

Psychodynamic Psychotherapy

Psychodynamic therapies of depression, though less well studied than CBT or IPT, and less efficacious in treatment of acute depression than more symptom-specific therapies, have clinical utility for patients who have tried pharmacotherapy and other forms of psychotherapy yet not attained relief from depression. These patients may benefit from in-depth exploration of unconscious conflicts, depleted self-esteem, and problematic internal object relations (mentally stored memories or representations of oneself "directing affect toward," or being emotionally engaged with, another).

Psychodynamic therapy, derived from psychoanalysis, includes insight-oriented, psychoanalytic, and explorative therapies, which share the belief that a person's feelings and behaviors are directly influenced by past events. Among the core beliefs of dynamic therapies are the assumptions that each stage in a person's life affects the next (beginning in infancy), that a large part of our mental functioning is "unconscious," and that internal conflicts between wants and needs and with societal norms are often hidden from consciousness (perhaps expressed in dreams). Depression and anxiety are viewed as resulting from these unresolved, generally unconscious conflicts, often stemming from childhood.

Psychodynamic approaches are particularly effective for personality work. People who have a long-standing depressive outlook on the world (distinct from dysthymia), as well as those with various personality difficulties (especially those with borderline or highly self-critical, perfectionistic traits), may not have benefited from other methods and may find psychodynamic therapy helpful. Characterological features and long-standing internal conflicts may not be apparent in a client who is acutely depressed, so therapy should be reserved for a period of at least partial remission of depression.

Psychodynamic work may be done in a brief format (12 to 20 sessions) or may be open-ended. In brief therapy, psychoanalytic principles are applied to the resolution of specific problems—perhaps a negative self-image that surfaces in certain social contexts or a problem behavior. In-depth personality work is not pursued.

Case Example: Lisa

Lisa was a middle-aged, divorced woman seen for consultation at the request of her insurance company due to concerns about her ability to work. A physician, she had been a faculty member of a medical school and had also developed a very successful private practice. However, recently she had become overwhelmed by some of her very needy patients and extremely upset when the spouse of a patient who had died filed a lawsuit against her; she felt that she had done everything right in treating the patient. She also felt used by her ex-husband. He had stopped working shortly after they got married, and after telling her for years that he wanted a divorce, he demanded a huge settlement and left her as the sole provider for their three children, one of whom had recently been suspended for selling drugs at school.

After the divorce, Lisa had an intense romantic relationship with another man, but after a few weeks he told her that he wanted to date other women. Two weeks later, Lisa attempted suicide by taking a potentially lethal overdose of drugs and was hospitalized. Word got around quickly in the community, and she promptly closed her medical practice and moved to another state.

When Lisa began seeing me, she was taking high-dose Effexor, Adderall, and Topamax, and the diagnostic impression was severe recurrent major depression that had a seasonal component. My impression was that Lisa was a woman who had learned early in childhood that her primary role was to take care of others and provide for their emotional needs. She did this by supporting an unemployed husband throughout the marriage, working very hard to provide the best possible private-school education for her children, who did not appreciate it, and giving as much as she could emotionally to her demanding patients. When things fell apart in her life, she made a serious suicide attempt. A neuropsychological evaluation was consistent with Lisa's own impressions and mine that she was quite bright but had impaired attention and concentration as well as existential self-image issues. Both the neuropsychologist consultant and I strongly recommended CBT to begin changing the behaviors that had allowed her to become so depleted in her chronic workaholic mode. After gaining depression-coping skills through CBT, Lisa began deeper work in psychodynamic psychotherapy to address the deep-seated thread that wound its way through her troubling relationships.

Mindfulness-Based Cognitive Therapy

The mindfulness-based cognitive therapy (MBCT) approach has three main ideas: decentering, mindfulness, and self-compassion. Decentering is the recognition that thoughts and feelings are mental events and not facts. Mindfulness involves paying attention to things, in the present, without judgment.

Unlike in CBT, thoughts are not labeled as positive or negative and are not challenged or tested. There is no attempt to look for evidence that the thought is true or false. The thought is simply noticed, like a passing cloud overhead, as something that is present but temporary. Patients learn that "my thoughts are not me" and are not "facts."

Mindfulness involves formal meditation practice, which may include focus on breathing, sounds, thoughts, and yoga positions and stretches, as well as the "body scan" to focus on physical sensations.

Because this approach allows negative thoughts and feelings to be viewed as temporary mental phenomena and not unchangeable facts, the negative ruminations that are often a central part of the depressed person's self-talk are viewed in a very different perspective. The focus is on being in the here and now and not replaying the past or predicting the worst-case scenario of the future. By tolerating unpleasant affect and reducing avoidance behavior, the suffering from depression is reduced. Self-compassion means acceptance of thoughts without judgment and softening self-criticism, which buffers negative feelings about the self and prevents the person from being overwhelmed with negative emotions. This approach has been proven to decrease depression recurrences in individuals with three or more episodes of depression (Williams, Teasdale, Segal, & Kabat-Zinn, 2007). It has also been shown to be helpful as an adjunctive treatment for treatment-resistant depression.

Problem-Solving Therapy

The central premise of problem-solving therapy is that weak problem-solving skills lead to vulnerability to depression. Life problems are harder to face when depressed, and having skills to deal with problems helps to increase the sense of self-control, which may prevent depression recurrences. The goals of treatment are to link depression to problems in living, define and set realistic goals for dealing with the problems, and teach a structured procedure for problem-solving that leads to positive experiences. Multiple solutions are evaluated and compared, and after a feasible solution is chosen and implemented, the outcome is evaluated. Generally a person will have several life problems. In these cases, it is best to make a hierarchy and start with easier problems in order to build positive success experiences. Like MBCT, this approach is usually done in a group setting, and a key role for the therapist is to make the group a safe place to experience and express thoughts, feelings, and problems.

Eclectic Approaches

"Eclectic" therapy approaches for depression integrate depression-specific techniques and approaches from dynamic, experiential-humanistic, cognitive, and behavioral schools and are enhanced by the therapist's clinical wisdom, expertise, and intuition. The goal is to sculpt an approach to psychotherapy that is specific to the patient as an individual.

Eclectic approaches can work well if the therapist is very knowledgeable on the nature and history of the patient's problems, what techniques the patient has previously tried, and the patient's personality and communication styles. The therapist should also utilize techniques grounded in approaches found efficacious for depression. It is important to note, however, that many therapists who call their approach eclectic have not organized a thought-out combination of specific modalities of psychotherapy—they simply practice a technique that is uniquely their own, developed over the course of their years in practice. With these therapists, it may be difficult to ascertain whether work will be of help to the patient in alleviating symptoms, learning new tools, and gaining new strengths.

Case Example: Refractory Depression With Overwhelming Stressors

Morton was a 56-year-old man who presented with a history of rapid-cycling bipolar I affective disorder that included seasonal features, as well as panic disorder with agoraphobia. In addition, he had degenerative disc disease in his spine and had been forced out of his job. Historically, his most helpful medications had been a complex combination of drugs with different mechanisms of action. Nardil, Sinequan, Klonopin, and lithium formed a long-term medication combination that helped him to minimize his depression over the next 2 years. Although this combination did quite well for him, he faced the massive stressors of dealing with a mother who required assisted living and a brother whose compulsive hoarding and refusal to move out of their mother's house led to major financial stressors and a sense of helplessness to deal with a very difficult situation. He dealt with numerous additional family stressors, had feelings of anger, helplessness, and frustration at dealing with the family issues, with his own forced retirement, and with never feeling consistently well enough to seek a new job, but due to the medication's stabilizing effect he was able to face these without becoming severely depressed. Though Morton had sought help through psychotherapy to deal with his feelings of anger and helplessness, which he connected to a long history of difficult relations with family, he found the past therapists' repeated attempts to deeply probe his core issues and feelings to be emotionally exhausting, arresting, and triggering. In his depressive state, he simply didn't have the coping skills and emotional strength to deal with these issues. Morton's new therapist employed an eclectic approach which involved psychoeducation to support adherence to medication: a present-oriented, supportive, directive, problem-oriented IPT intervention to support his stress over life role change as well as conflicts and helplessness associated with his family relations. CBT technique was used to counteract negative thought patterns. The therapist also supported Morton in approaching acceptance when facing a situation beyond his control. Mastery of what was changeable and acceptance of what wasn't changeable were the goals of therapy. The therapist made the active decision not to go into long-term psychodynamic issues from the past that would stir up painful traumatic memories.

Other Therapies

There are perhaps hundreds of other types of therapies, some of which are grounded in the schools of therapy described in this chapter, some of which are humanistic (a main branch of psychotherapy that focuses on self-actualization and on validation of the patient's feelings), and some of which stem from esoteric schools of thought and philosophy. As noted earlier, we chose to cover only therapies that are designed specifically for treatment of depression and have been shown to be clinically effective. Other models may or may not be helpful for certain patients, depending on their needs and personality.

Group Therapy

Group therapy provides treatment in a format with one or more therapists and six to ten participants, often with related problems. The participants improve not only from the interventions of the therapist, but also
from observing others in the group and receiving feedback from group
members. Widely used today, group therapy has been a standard treatment option since the 1940s. Evidence from controlled studies attests to
the usefulness of group psychotherapy, demonstrating its effectiveness
for patients with personality and anxiety disorders, substance-related
disorders, schizophrenia, depressive and stable bipolar disorders, and a
number of medical illnesses. Group psychotherapy has been found to be
as effective or even more effective than individual psychotherapy in
studies directly comparing the two methods for certain indications.

The group format, although not providing the one-on-one attention
of individual formats, has several advantages, including providing
increased feedback from different perspectives and the opportunity to
learn from others, to observe as they model behaviors, and to try out new
behaviors in the safety of the group. Group members can explore issues
in a social context that reflects real life and observe and reflect on their
own and others' social skills. They can increase self-awareness by
learning how others perceive them and by examining their response to
the feelings and experiences of others. Members can express feelings
they've been hesitant to share, learn to assert themselves, and feel freer
to take risks. They can choose to be verbally active or to spend some
sessions reflecting on the discussion and actions of other members.
Group therapy members benefit by helping each other to work through
personal issues in a supportive, confidential environment.

Similar to family therapy, group therapy is a style that can incorporate any of the psychotherapy schools, including those discussed in this
chapter. There are support groups for people in the same situation or
crisis, and groups that are heterogeneous in terms of age, sex, marital
status, and specific problems, more closely representative of real life. The
latter group constituency is especially effective for people with interpersonal difficulties and problems in relations, like intimacy, trust, and self-
esteem. Groups vary from classic psychodynamic psychotherapy groups,
where process is emphasized, to psychoeducational, which are closer to

a class and may focus on relationships, anger, stress management, and so on. Some are more didactic (structured, with specific techniques that are usually problem-centered and aimed at symptom reduction); others are more experiential. Goals may be achieved primarily through member interactions that stimulate discussion of interpersonal issues, or by approaches in which the projection of feelings onto the therapist (transference) is important. In some approaches, activities that occur in the group itself (here-and-now approach) become the material with which group is conducted, whereas other groups emphasize past events and activities that occurred outside the group. Issues and conflicts addressed in group psychotherapy may be categorized as affecting the entire group, or affecting an individual or part of the group. Group psychotherapy differs from a support group. For example, a therapy group made up of alcoholics differs from a meeting of Alcoholics Anonymous in that people in psychotherapy not only gain support and encouragement for sobriety but also focus on problems related to their alcoholism, such as maladaptive interpersonal relationships and intrapsychic conflict. Generally, psychotherapy groups have a designated paid, licensed professional as leader, whereas self-help groups have no designated leader or have a leader who has been successfully dealing with the problem personally over a relatively long period of time.

Most psychotherapy groups are discussion-oriented. Members are encouraged to divulge feelings, be open and honest, and listen to issues involving others. In other group psychotherapy approaches, a lecture format or videotape may be used during part of the session to stimulate discussion. Some psychotherapy groups are more action-oriented. In psychodrama, members assume roles (spouses, parents, etc.) in acting out a specific problem. In some groups aimed at resolution of symptoms, like behavior therapy and CBT, members practice specific techniques. In activity groups such as music or art therapy, members meet to learn about their intrapsychic and interpersonal worlds through engaging in activities.

Group therapy is working if the sessions bring patients personal insight and help them to learn something new. It may take several sessions, even months, to begin to see benefit from group therapy. Because resistance to therapy can be much higher in group than in individual therapy, therapists may require patients to commit to a certain number of sessions.

Group sessions can last from an hour and a half to 3 hours and meet once to twice a week. Some groups are short-term (6 to 20 weeks), structured, and goal-oriented, whereas others are more experiential and open-ended. For open-ended group therapy, members should wait 4 to 6 months before evaluating its effects.

Sometimes group therapy is used as the primary or single treatment approach; other times it's used along with individual therapy, often with a different therapist for each experience. The cost of group therapy is significantly less per session than that of individual therapy sessions.

Family Therapy

A common question is: "How do I get my husband/wife/child into therapy to deal with problems?" This is usually in the context of the family members not acknowledging the problem and not being particularly motivated to work on changing it. Common examples would be the college student who has stopped going to classes, is not seeking a job, stays in her room sleeping most of the day, and goes out socializing with friends most of the night. Another example is the person who is abusing alcohol, marijuana, or other drugs, saying, "It's not a problem to me. I can stop anytime I want to." Or the person who is quite depressed yet attributes it all to circumstances, saying, "If my husband would stop seeing other women and get a full-time job to support me and the children, I wouldn't be depressed." In such cases, family therapy is essential to change the situation. The first step is getting strong enough to tell the individual that her behavior is hurting her and the relationship, is unacceptable, and will not be tolerated long-term. The second step is recognizing that the family system has somehow allowed the behavior to go on without setting a clear, firm limit or consequence. The third step is to make the decision to work on changing the situation with a family therapist (and perhaps a group like Al-Anon) or to get out of it.

Sometimes a person with depression or bipolar disorder is marked as a "problem" in the family—or, in family-systems language, as the "identified patient"—when really the entire family is locked into some dysfunctional pattern of interaction. In these cases, while the identified patient is being treated expediently with medication, the dysfunctional family dynamic festers and continues to complicate the depressed person's ability to get well; the protracted depression, in turn, exacerbates the unhealthy family relational patterns. Although family therapy examines the role of the depressed member in the overall psychological well-being of the entire family, it also examines the role of the entire family in the maintenance of the depression.

THEORY AND GOALS

Family problems often involve blame, shame, and guilt associated with the attribution of problems to individuals. When discussing the topic of mental health within the family, doctors and therapists often refer to "high EE"—high expressed emotion. You may be picturing family members colliding with one another while expressing boundless joy, love, and gratitude, but unfortunately, high EE is used consistently to mean a high degree of expressed negative emotion, which is of course associated with the triggering or exacerbation of symptoms for people with depression or bipolar illness. These emotion-centered coping strategies are counterproductive and leave people feeling hopeless, powerless, and angry. Problem-centered coping, taught in family therapy, is associated with using resources to solve problems rather than to run from, yell about, and perpetuate them.

The concept of linear causality (action A leads to problem B) is not a part of the family therapy approach. Problems within a family are not ascribed to the "faults" of individual members but rather are considered external and arising from interactions in the family system. The family works together to creatively devise a solution to the problem. Family therapy is solution- rather than problem-focused: Therapists are not primarily concerned with the origins of dysfunction, which can only be guessed at, and are not amenable to change through psychotherapy. Emphasis is on the present and on the patterns of family interaction that sustain existing problems. The goal of family therapy is not to change the individual but to modify the system of relationships in which the individual is involved—which may then result in change in one or more family members.

Problems also may involve the labeling of family members, or ascribing stereotyped roles to them. This can lead to many forms of dysfunction in families, such as the person with mental illness being "infantilized": Having adopted the "sick role" in the family, the person may be catered to, not given responsibility or considered capable, and encouraged to regress and become dependent. The person may also become a scapegoat in the family system or have many of her "normal" actions pathologized (attributed to the illness). Family therapy avoids labels and diagnoses, which can put more (or less) importance on a specific individual and make it difficult to make progress. Some therapists consider diagnoses to be derogatory explanations that reinforce helplessness (internalized illness). The family and therapist may instead create a name that captures the experiential quality of the problem being worked with.

Family therapy practice is informed by a large number of theoretical perspectives. In treatment of depression and bipolar illness, the most helpful foci are family psychoeducation, communication training, and problem-solving/skills training. These may benefit the communication, interactions, and relationships of all family members, and, for the depressed person specifically, may help to prevent relapses, reduce interepisode symptoms, and encourage consistency with other aspects of the person's lifestyle (including maintenance of healthy habits and treatment regimens), as well as benefit social, occupational, and leisure performance. Although not studied well in unipolar depression, family therapies have shown excellent results in clinical trials of bipolar illness and schizophrenia. Though not generally viewed as a primary therapy for the treatment of any psychiatric illness, family therapy, like other therapies, indeed modifies the course of illness, often amplifying benefits of medication while promoting improvement in central relationships.

As a side note: We like to think of "family" as an individual defines it. A person's family may be her husband and children, her parents and siblings, a significant other, or the close friend she's shared a living space with for years—any social system (two or more people) that has effect on the individuals and vice versa.

THE FAMILY THERAPY PROCESS
A family therapist usually sees several members of the family concurrently, so that the ways different family members perceive mutual rela-

tions, as well as interaction patterns during the session (which frequently mirror interaction patterns at home), are apparent to both therapist and family. This material then provides fuel for discussion of patterns the members may or may not be aware of, and of ways to modify responses to other family members. At times, early relationships are examined to learn how current patterns developed. In goal-focused (versus open-ended) therapy, changes in current interactions are central. In family psychoeducation, communication training, and problem-solving/skills training, the approach is strictly solution-focused and strategic, minimizing personal history and subjective experience and focusing primarily on brief methods for solving present problems, whose solutions are developed by the family with the help of the therapist. Instead of dwelling on past failures or present difficulties, family members are urged to face the future with a new awareness of how best to tackle the problems as they recur. The roles played by various family members in reinforcing the depression within an individual are often examined as well.

Education about depression in general can also be an important role of therapy, which may address work on acceptance of the illness by the patient and family, as well as acceptance of treatment with medication. Some families must address alcohol or substance abuse, financial and employment difficulties, self-esteem injury, divorce, and relationship dysfunction that have arisen from a chronic course of depression or bipolar illness. The fear of recurrences and relapses, denial, anger, ambivalence, and anxiety may develop as a family adjusts to a diagnosis or discusses their feelings about an illness that has had a chronic course, and this is addressed. Family members learn about how they can help their loved one to recognize early warning signs of illness and about how to support the person in taking lifestyle measures to minimize risk.

Community Resources: Support Groups and Recovery Groups

A support group is a coming together of people with a common concern. People who have "been there" share their experiences, feelings, and perceptions. Though it is not psychotherapy, it can be a very powerful mediator of change. Organized around a specific issue, such as depression and bipolar disorder, bereavement, a particular illness, divorce, or recovery from addiction, support groups can help individuals or families confronted by circumstances or striving to maintain healthy behavior changes.

Support groups for people living with mental illness are quite common in most parts of the United States. Typically held in a model endorsed by a national advocacy association—such as the Depression and Bipolar Support Alliance (DBSA) or National Alliance on Mental Illness (NAMI)—these groups are not led by professionals, but rather are facilitated by an experienced group member. Members of support groups share frustrations and successes, referrals to qualified specialists and community resources, and information about what has been helpful in approaching recovery. They also share friendship and hope for themselves, their loved ones, and others in the group. DBSA has support groups in nearly every community, held for people with both depression and bipolar illness, usually weekly or occasionally biweekly. Some communities also have a group for teens or for partners and families. NAMI is primarily a family-support, education, and advocacy organization, though there are peer support groups offered by NAMI as well, typically geared toward people with more severe and chronic mental illness.

Some support groups, especially those for family members of people living with mental illness, focus not only on coping and shared experiences, but also on advocating for better hospital and community programs, as well as research and treatments—when people work collaboratively, they are often quite effective in local advocacy efforts and in fighting stigma.

Other organizations offering support groups are:

American Association of Retired Persons Grief and Loss Information
American Association of Suicidology (support for family and friends who have lost a loved one to suicide)
Anxiety Disorders Association of America
Child and Adolescent Bipolar Foundation
Depression After Delivery
Depression and Related Affective Disorders Association
Families for Depression Awareness
Federation of Families for Children's Mental Health (a parent-support and advocacy network)

Postpartum Support International
Recovery Inc.
Well Spouse Foundation

Support groups for people striving to end addictions often follow the 12-step approach and rely on faith in a higher power and support from others. Some people have been able to change their lives drastically with only their own readiness to do so and their commitment to a good 12-step group program.

One program of special interest to those with depression or bipolar illness is Dual Recovery Anonymous (DRA), a group approach designed specifically for those who are dually diagnosed with substance abuse and a mental illness. The group focuses on both issues, not just the addiction. Just a few of the other 12-step programs available are:

Alcoholics Anonymous
Narcotics Anonymous
Overeaters Anonymous
Gamblers Anonymous
Sex and Love Addicts Anonymous
Adult Children of Alcoholics (Al-Anon/Alateen)
Co-Dependents Anonymous
Debtors Anonymous
Emotions Anonymous

Not all abstinence-minded clients relate to the 12-step approach due to the faith-based component. Self-Management and Recovery Training (SMART) is a group-oriented program that is rationally oriented (versus faith-based) and employs a behavioral approach while eschewing the disease model of addiction. SMART welcomes people with any form of addiction, including eating disorders, compulsive gambling, and sexual addiction.

Selecting a Mode of Therapy

Different people will be attracted to different psychotherapy approaches. If the depression is influenced by relationships or a role transition, IPT may sound appealing. If persistent negative thought patterns are a problem, CBT might be especially effective. When selecting a mode of therapy, patients should think about the specific nature of their problems, how long they've had them, any concurrent diagnoses they may have, other treatments they have tried, their style of communication, how they like to work, their personality, and even insurance and affordability. They should consider the benefits of individual, group, and family approaches. There are many good sources available online and in bookstores for further research.

Regardless of the type of therapy pursued, a good therapeutic alliance between the patient and therapist is essential. Mutual respect, genuineness, and empathy must underlie the tasks and methods of therapy.

Considering Combined Treatment

Psychotherapy has historically been offered to those with mild to moderate depression as an effective alternative to medication. It is considered by some to be preferable in the context of personality disorders, pregnancy or lactation, presence of significant social stressors, and interpersonal or intrapsychic conflicts.

Depression-specific psychotherapy and pharmacotherapy are synergistic—that is, each enhances the other. There are several possible desired outcomes of combined therapy: It may increase the magnitude of response for an individual, may increase the probability of response (for those who may preferentially respond to one treatment or the other), or may enhance the breadth of response—producing a superior overall pattern. It's safe to say that drugs don't work if people don't take them; in addition to addressing difficult life situations and relationships, psychotherapy—through supportive and educational efforts to help patients understand their illness and treatment—helps some people to accept medication and work with side effects. In turn, medication may speed or enhance response to psychotherapy, especially for those whose depression is too severe to permit, without a little "push," the cognitive or emotional work necessary for effective participation in psychotherapy. Many large studies have looked at comparisons of pharmacotherapy, psychotherapy, and the combination—most using manualized approaches including cognitive-behavioral therapy or interpersonal therapy—with combination treatment generally demonstrating superior outcomes (Blom et al., 2007; Schramm et al., 2007).

As discussed earlier, pharmacotherapy and psychotherapy are usually performed by different professionals. This is often a result of economic realities; psychiatrists charge more than most other mental health professionals, and primary care physicians are often too heavily scheduled to take the time necessary to fully discuss problems with their patients. Collaborative treatment most often involves the psychiatrist or primary care physician prescribing medication while the psychologist, social worker, or couples or family therapist provides individual, family, or group psychotherapy. Sometimes the situation is complicated: The patient may be undergoing treatment for a chronic medical condition by the internist, receiving an antidepressant from the psychiatrist, participating in a support group, and getting individual and couples therapy from two different psychotherapists. The potential advantage for the patient is the availability of specialists in many different fields to help with her problems, often in more time-intensive, focused treatment modalities than any one of them could provide alone. The potential disadvantage is that roles may blur. For example, the psychiatrist may be asked to provide crisis psychotherapy when the therapist is on vacation and to prescribe pain medications when the internist is unavailable. The psychotherapist may advise for or against the use of a particular type of medication in a way that doesn't fit with the psychiatrist's treatment recommendations. Sometimes one approach is seen as curative and another is considered unimportant, based on the beliefs of the patient and her family about what caused the problems. For example, medications may be blamed for painful emotional states as well as side effects, and therapists may encourage getting off of them when stressors or conflicts are resolved. Most of these potential conflicts can be avoided by clear definition of roles and responsibilities, treatment goals, and who will do what during treatment. The most important part of collaboration is the actual contact (written or verbal) between the pharmacologist and psychotherapist, and it is essential that the patient authorize the sharing of information between them.

Research on Combined Treatment

The reason that psychotherapy and pharmacotherapy complement each other, encouraging a broader response than either approach alone, can be demonstrated both empirically (by measuring behavioral variables in individuals) and in brain-imaging studies. In studies that measure behaviors, drugs appear to work more rapidly than most types of psychotherapy and may depend less on the skill of the practitioner. Psychotherapy, however, appears to do more to enhance social functioning (particularly couples, family, and interpersonal therapy) and to reduce subsequent risk of relapse (particularly CBT) than does pharmacotherapy alone.

RELAPSE PREVENTION

In a study that looked at patients receiving either CBT or the antidepressant Paxil, both treatments produced a good response in patients (Goldapple et al., 2004). In a second study with Paxil and CBT, treatment was suspended for all patients for a year. Only a quarter of those receiving cognitive therapy suffered a partial relapse during this time, compared with 40% of those formerly on Paxil (Hollon et al., 2005). Essentially, medication appears to provide rapid relief from acute distress, where psychotherapy may engender broad, enduring change—with patients accruing the benefits of each with combined treatment.

PSYCHOTHERAPY AS AN AUGMENTATION STRATEGY

The Sequenced Treatment Alternatives for Depression (STAR*D) study (described later in more detail) allowed patients in both psychiatric and primary care settings to receive antidepressant treatment with the SSRI citalopram for up to 12 weeks. For those patients who did not achieve remission, second-, third-, and fourth-step strategies were sequentially available, which included both augmentation and switch options. For those STAR*D subjects not achieving remission after the initial trial on citalopram, second-step options included augmentation with CBT, bupropion, or buspirone, or switching to CBT, sertraline, venlafaxine, or bupropion. At 12 weeks, CBT alone or added to ongoing citalopram treatment produced remission rates similar to those seen in the medication augmentation and switch strategies. Where augmentation was concerned, medications were more rapidly effective than cognitive therapy. For those who chose to discontinue citalopram, switching to cognitive therapy was better tolerated than switching to a different antidepressant; remission rates among the several switch options were statistically similar (Thase, Friedman, et al., 2007).

Studies have repeatedly shown that psychotherapy and medication each increase the effect of the other. A recent study of chronic depression in the *New England Journal of Medicine* compared three groups of depressed patients: those who took nefazodone, those who participated in cognitive-behavioral analysis system of psychotherapy (CBASP, discussed later), and those who did a combination of both. While 52–55% of patients using either medication or psychotherapy responded to treatment, those on combined treatment enjoyed treatment response rates of 85% (Keller et al., 2000). What is more, this study suggests that medication may be effective in those unresponsive to psychotherapy, and vice versa (Schatzberg ct al., 2005). A comprehensive 2004 review published in the *Archives of General Psychiatry* also demonstrated synergy, and found that psychotherapy can help people stick with their drug treatment in the long term (Pampallona, Bollini, Tibaldi, Kupelnick, & Munizza, 2004).

The Treatment for Adolescents with Depression Study (TADS) compared the short- and longer-term effectiveness of medication and psychotherapy in depressed teens. Combination treatment with fluoxetine and CBT achieved a stable response (one without relapse) more quickly than did medication or psychotherapy alone, or placebo. Chances of this sustained early response were three times more likely with combination therapy than with placebo or CBT alone, and one and a half times more likely than with medication alone (Kratochvil et al., 2006). The combination was also found to have an antisuicide effect (Emslie et al., 2006; March, Silva, & Vitiello, 2006; March et al., 2007).

SUCCESS VARIES WITH INDIVIDUAL CIRCUMSTANCES

The success of single versus combined treatments varies with the individual circumstances of the patient. Though some guidelines suggest that those with milder, more transient depression may not require or respond to medications, other more recent studies have found that mild depression does benefit from pharmacotherapy. Some guidelines indicate that people with underlying anxiety disorders may rely more heavily on medication than on psychotherapy for response, as may those with a history of mood episodes or chronic depression, significant family history of mood disorders, severe symptoms, depression onset at a young age, and the risk of self-destructive behavior. A critical review by Hegerl questioning whether combination therapy is better than either psychotherapy or medication alone basically demonstrated an overall lack of evidence for the superiority of combination therapy, with the exception of patients with severe chronic depression and the elderly (Hegerl, Plattner, & Moller, 2004). However, most clinicians believe and behave differently, encouraging both medications and psychotherapy for their patients, especially those who have not had an expected, prompt, robust response to one of these treatment modalities. In support of this approach, studies cited by Nierenberg in his review of psychotherapeutic treatments demonstrated the benefit of psychotherapy (CBT specifically) in reducing residual symptoms and relapse rates in patients who had responded to antidepressants but not achieved full remission (Nierenberg, Petersen, & Alpert, 2003). In any case, the evidence just cited concerns response to treatment and not prevention of relapse; psychotherapy can be invaluable in providing the skills and tools to prevent relapse and enhance quality of life. There is currently no indication that pharmacotherapy does anything to reduce subsequent risk once medications are withdrawn.

The Cognitive-Behavioral Analysis System of Psychotherapy

One of the most important studies of psychotherapy versus medication therapy in chronic depression was carried out recently. Patients with at least a 2-year history of major depression (including those with both major depression and dysthymia or major depression with incomplete interepisode recovery) were randomized to receive Serzone (nefazodone), cognitive-behavioral analysis system of psychotherapy (CBASP), or both. This study examined acute antidepressant response in each condition, as well as the effect of crossing over from drug to psychotherapy or vice versa. It examined who had a preferential response to psychotherapy over drug therapy and, finally, it examined the role of psychotherapy in maintenance treatment (Klein et al., 2004; Nemeroff et al., 2003; Schatzberg et al., 2005).

First, what is CBASP? This is a manualized, structured, time-limited psychotherapy developed for the treatment of chronic depression. It combines elements of behavioral, cognitive, interpersonal, and psychodynamic psychotherapies. The goals are to help patients change patterns of coping, improve interpersonal skills, understand consequences of behavior, and interact more effectively with others. Social problem-solving skills are taught, homework is assigned, and the relationship with the therapist is used as a tool for increasing self-awareness of impact on others. The major technique is "situational analysis," involving examination with the therapist of a distressing interpersonal situation that occurred in the person's recent experience. This examination includes eliciting information about the event, interpreting it, looking at the person's behavior, identifying the actual outcome and the desired outcome, and determining whether the desired outcome was achieved. Remediation involves revising interpretations, behaviors, and desired outcome to increase the probability of achieving the desired outcome. Generalization of the analysis is discussed so that it can be applied to other similar situations.

The first phase of this study involved randomizing chronically depressed patients to treatment with Serzone (average 461 mg/day), CBASP (average 16 sessions), or the combination for a period of 12 weeks of acute treatment. The response rates for Serzone, CBASP, and combination treatment were 55%, 52%, and 85%, showing a very nice synergistic effect of medication and psychotherapy.

A careful look at the responders to the first phase of the study showed a very important finding: Among chronically depressed individuals, those with a history of childhood adversity (parental loss, physical or sexual abuse, or neglect) who completed the 12-week study showed a very high incidence of highly negative experiences. A third had lost a parent before age 15, 45% suffered physical abuse, 16% experienced sexual abuse, and 10% experienced neglect. More importantly, the subset of patients who had suffered childhood trauma showed a clear superiority of psychotherapy (with or without drug) over drug alone. In fact, among those with childhood adverse events, the chance of achieving remission was twice as high with psychotherapy as with antidepressant therapy. This was especially true among individuals with early parental loss, where the chance of achieving remission was 2.8 times higher with psychotherapy than with antidepressant medication alone.

The second phase of the study involved taking the nonresponders to Serzone and giving them CBASP, and vice versa, for 12 weeks, thus asking the very important question: Does psychotherapy work for drug nonresponders, and does medication work for psychotherapy nonresponders? When 12-week outcomes of study completers were analyzed, response rates were 57% among those who were randomized to receive CBASP and 42% for those who were randomized to Serzone. The difference between groups was not statistically significant, demonstrating that each intervention was a successful switch strategy for patients who had initially failed the other treatment. There were more dropouts among those switched to the drug from CBASP.

After the first phase of treatment, and the crossover phase for nonresponders, those who were responding to treatment were given 16 weeks of continuation with the same treatment (Kocsis et al., 2003). They were then randomized for 52 weeks of maintenance treatment. Those who were receiving Serzone alone or combined with CBASP were randomized to receive Serzone or placebo, and there was a clear advantage for continuation on Serzone over switching to placebo. Those who were receiving CBASP were randomized to CBASP (average 11 visits over 1 year) or assessment visits only. The group randomized to CBASP or assessment did not differ in any significant way from the original study population, though more women were randomized to receive CBASP than assessment only. One-year recurrence rates were 10.7% and 32% in CBASP- and assessment-only groups, demonstrating a significant protective effect of CBASP that emerged by 5 to 6 months of treatment in patients who were not receiving medication.

Regardless of whether it is conducted with or without pharmacotherapy, the work of psychotherapy involves trusting and sharing intimate secrets, thoughts, and feelings with another person, carefully examining the issues that contribute to the development and persistence of depression, and attempting to make major changes in thoughts, feelings, and behaviors. This is hard work, and it is a very active, collaborative learning process. The reward is often a sense of growth and greater ability to be strong in coping with the problems that life inevitably sends our way.

Social Rhythms Chart

	Activity				People		
Date _____	Time	Duration	Alone	With Others		Present	Involved
SELF-CARE							
Shower or grooming							
Physical exercise							
NUTRITION							
Morning beverage							
Breakfast							
Lunch							
Snack							
Dinner							
Snack or beverage							
ACTIVITIES							
Today's responsibilities:							
Today's leisure activities:							
SLEEP				Notes			
Out of bed							
Nap 1							
Nap 2							
Go to bed							
INTERACTION							
First contact with others							
Go outside (first time)							
Return home (last time)							

Social Rhythms Chart

Instructions

When sleep, nutrition, exercise, and other activities are in balance with each other and occur on a more or less regular schedule, they promote stable mood and wellbeing. Loosely adapted from the Social Rhythm Metric by Monk et al., this chart is used to track the patterning of routines. Used over time, social rhythms charting will provide data for exploration of how changes in the regularity of patterns and the amount or intensity of social interaction might interact with symptoms and general mood stability.

Charting your daily **activities** may be enlightening. Even if you know you don't eat as often as you should, or that you do spend a lot of time sleeping, seeing this in black and white may still surprise you! Charting can provide an objective record of your patterns, a tool that may help motivate you to make healthy changes and maintain good habits.

When charting responsibilities, include work, school, housework, childcare, family care, and volunteer activities. Leisure activities may include watching TV, participating in a hobby, reading, playing a game, or attending an event. The Nutrition and Sleep sections may be used variably; some people will wish for more lines to chart than others. Some people may run out of room when charting: if you find that your grooming, exercise or snacking habits are off the chart so to speak, there is a notes section for you to record your concerns.

For each activity, write the **time** you began it on a particular day, and the duration spent. Time is a most important factor where meals, duration of sleep (as well as bed and wake times), and the length of any activity—even enjoyable ones—you associate with worsening of symptoms are concerned.

Contact with other **people** is important to our daily rhythms. For your Self-Care, Nutrition and Activities, check the bubbles that indicate whether you were alone, in the presence of others, or involved with them in each activity. You may jot down the names of the family, friends or others inolved if you like.

Some **questions to consider** while looking over your charts:
• Which activities do you rarely perform? Which have become routine?
• Which activities may be contributing to your illness (e.g. being active late at night; compulsive showering, internet, gaming or exercise)?
• Is there balance to your responsibilities, leisure activities, and time for rest?
• Is there regularity to your mealtimes? Do you skip meals? Snack frequently?
• How much time do you actually spend in bed each day? Are your bed and wake times consistent?
• How much time do you spend with others, and who are they?
• Are others often present in your life, but rarely actually involved?
• Is much of your social life conducted by phone or email?
• Do you rarely leave the house, or avoid being home?
Consider putting a "+" by activities that you enjoyed or want to do more of, and a "-" by those you found difficult, unpleasant, or otherwise triggering.
Consider adding mood charting to this exercise, using the Personalized Daily Rating Scale or Core Symptom Severity Chart at the conclusion of chapter 10.

9

Choosing an Antidepressant for Major Depressive Disorder: Getting to Know the Drug Families

Antidepressant drugs are grouped into classes or families based on their mechanism of action. Some antidepressants increase levels of the neurotransmitter serotonin in the brain; some increase norepinephrine; some increase both. Others affect dopamine levels. Monoamine oxidase (MAO) inhibitors, an older family of antidepressants, work by blocking the degradation of these neurotransmitters, whereas the newer-generation selective serotonin reuptake inhibitors (SSRIs) work by blocking the reuptake of the neurotransmitters, leading to higher neurotransmitter levels in the synapse.

Antidepressant drugs suppress depression symptoms. They do not "cure" the underlying disorder, meaning that if they are discontinued, they no longer have an effect. Further, they only work when they are taken on a regular basis—they cannot be used on an as-needed basis for a few days at a time. We often explain to patients that some medications are truly appropriate for short-term use, whereas others correct a longstanding metabolic or physiologic abnormality. Examples of short-term medications include antibiotics for respiratory infection or narcotics for pain after an operation. Examples of long-term medications to correct ongoing physiologic abnormalities include drugs to lower blood pressure, reduce high levels of cholesterol, or control diabetes. As with antidepressants, the drug is used chronically and yields optimal results when it is combined with lifestyle changes.

Benefits

Antidepressants are often the first-line treatment for depression. This is especially true when the depression is severe or presents with many biological symptoms, when it has responded to medications in the past, is highly recurrent, or when multiple blood relatives have also had depression. Antidepressants tend to be more rapidly effective and less costly than psychotherapy. They can be prescribed by primary care physicians and have little risk of dangerous side effects. Often medication combined with psychotherapy is the optimal depression treatment.

Side Effects and Drug Interactions

All psychiatric drugs have side effects, but it can be very difficult to predict whether a particular individual will experience them or not. Most side effects are dose-dependent, meaning that a dose reduction will decrease their intensity. Sometimes the side effects decrease on their own over time, if the patient is willing to ride it out. In the case of SSRI antidepressants, for instance, several subtypes of serotonin receptors are initially involved, including those that may cause stomach upset. Within the first couple of weeks of treatment, adaptation of many serotonin receptors to the drug's presence leads to the fading of the side effects, while therapeutic effect increases.

One side effect seldom discussed is the risk of being involved in an automobile accident. The risk of a traffic accident is slightly higher among persons receiving an antidepressant than among those who do not receive them, regardless of whether a new-generation, nonsedating antidepressant or an older sedating antidepressant is used. It is not clear if this is due to the drug or the underlying depression (Bramness, Skurtveit, Neutel, Morland, & Engeland, 2008).

Another important consideration is drug interactions. All drugs may have drug interactions, so it is essential that the patient and doctor communicate about all medicines being taken, including herbal remedies.

Starting Antidepressants

One of the most common questions that patients ask when beginning antidepressant treatment is: "How long will it take to work?" With most antidepressant drugs, it takes about 2 to 6 weeks before some improvement in mood is seen; a more robust response takes longer. The STAR*D study described earlier showed that response to an SSRI antidepressant often occurs 6 or more weeks—indeed, as long as 12 weeks—after starting the medication. In double-blind controlled studies where some patients receive active drug and others receive the sugar pill (placebo), all of the antidepressants show significant delay between starting medication and statistically significant differences in depression severity ratings. Typically, the lag time between starting an antidepressant and seeing statistical separation between response rates of patients on the active drug and those on placebo is about 2 weeks, with a range of 1 to 4 weeks.

The first symptoms of treatment response generally include some decreased negativity, perhaps less frequent or persistent speaking about worries and fears, more motivation, and increased energy. This improvement is often more obvious to the patient's family, friends, and coworkers than it is to the patient, who may be more aware of the medication's side effects than its therapeutic effects. Fortunately these side effects often subside quickly, as noted earlier.

Attitude Toward Treatment

During the first few weeks of treatment, the patient's attitude toward medication is critically important. Stigma can damage the chances of success. If the patient, therapist, physician, and family members are all in agreement that a medication is needed, there is no real problem. However, if the patient or a family member views medication as unnatural, giving in to weakness, or a very short-term crutch analogous to taking an aspirin, the likelihood of the patient's using the medication long enough for it to be helpful is decreased. Similarly, if the therapist views medication as a powerful partner to psychotherapy, this attitude will strengthen the treatment plan, whereas the belief that beginning medication means the therapy is failing can be harmful.

One study that looked at attitudes toward antidepressants among 165 patients with major depression found that perceived necessity of medication was associated with older age, more severe symptoms, longer anticipated duration of symptoms, and belief that symptoms were due to a chemical imbalance (Aikens, Nease, & Klinkman, 2008). Perceived harmfulness of medication was highest among people who had not taken antidepressants before, attributed symptoms to random factors, and did not understand depression. Young people with mild, transient symptoms were most skeptical about taking antidepressants and would potentially benefit from education about treatment. Overall, age of first episode, sex, and level of education did not affect beliefs about antidepressant treatment.

Titration and Dose-Finding

Titrating the dose up gradually is essential, especially in individuals who have anxiety symptoms, because these drugs may worsen anxiety when they are started. With the SSRI antidepressants the randomized acute trials generally fail to demonstrate much advantage from dose increases, but a potential dose-response curve might exist in clinical practice (Baker, Tweedie, Duval, & Woods, 2003). For example, there doesn't appear to be much difference in response between patients who are randomized to take Prozac 20 mg or 60 mg for 5 weeks after failing to respond to 20 mg of Prozac at 3 weeks. The same is true of Zoloft 50 mg versus 200 mg daily (Schweizer et al., 2001). Another study of Zoloft also demonstrated this. Licht and Qvitzau (2002) took a group of 1,629 Danish patients with major depression and treated them with Zoloft 50 mg/day for 4 weeks. They then gave the nonresponders 100 mg/day for 2 more weeks. The 295 patients who remained in the study and had still not responded were randomized to one of three treatments for the next 5 weeks: Zoloft 100 mg/day, Zoloft 200 mg/day, or Zoloft plus mianserin (an antidepressant with a different mechanism of action and that is not available in the United States). The Zoloft 100 mg/day patients had a 70% response rate, the Zoloft plus mianserin patients had a 67% response rate, and the patients who received Zoloft 200 mg/day had a significantly lower response rate, 56%. Thus, a modest dose long-term resulted in the best response rate.

Staying on the drug longer makes far more difference in the response rate than the actual dose of the drug, within the usual therapeutic dose range. It is quite important to know what the usual therapeutic dose range for these drugs is. For treating depression, the following doses are typically adequate: Prozac 20 to 60 mg, Zoloft 50 to 200 mg, Paxil 12.5 to 50 mg, Celexa 20 to 60 mg, and Lexapro 10 to 20 mg. There will always be a few patients who require a lower or higher dose because they absorb or metabolize drugs a little differently from others, but the general guidelines are a good starting point. Often patients with obsessive-compulsive disorder (or bulimia, for which Prozac is FDA approved) require high doses of the SSRI drugs.

Effexor definitely has an ascending dose-response range, from 75 to 375 mg in the early trials that were performed with the immediate-release form of the drug (Rudolph et al., 1998). The higher dose is more effective for most patients. When the extended-release form of the drug was developed, the dose range found appropriate for most individuals was 75 to 225 mg daily. In some case reports of difficult-to-treat depression, doses of 450 to 600 mg were used and found safe with regular monitoring of blood pressure.

The newer SNRI Cymbalta is approved for doses of 40 to 60 mg/day for depression, although the dose-finding studies were done with doses up to 60 mg twice daily. The studies have not provided convincing evidence to persuade the FDA that 120 mg/day is better than 60 mg/day for depression, though there are undoubtedly some individuals who do better at the higher dose (Bech, Kajdasz, & Porsdal, 2006), which is FDA approved for generalized anxiety disorder and painful diabetic neuropathy. Clinicians commonly push the dose to 60 mg twice daily in depressed patients who have tolerated the drug well but failed to respond after several weeks.

The usual dose of Wellbutrin is 150 to 450 mg daily. When the drug is used in the immediate-release or slow-release form, each individual dose should not exceed 200 mg. With the new form of Wellbutrin XL it is possible to give 450 mg as a single morning dose. This drug should not be used above the recommended dose because of a clear increase in the risk of seizures.

Serzone is generally used in the dose range of 300 to 600 mg daily, and the dose may be split into morning and evening portions or may all be taken at night if the drug is too sedating. Monitoring liver functions is prudent, as is avoiding this drug in an individual with known liver disease.

Remeron is typically given in a dose of 15 to 45 mg daily, at night, with monitoring of weight and cholesterol. Weight gain, sedation, lack of sexual side effects, and anxiety reduction are characteristics of Remeron.

We have mentioned that blood levels are important for monitoring safe and therapeutic dosing of the tricyclic antidepressants; they are also very important in adjusting the dosage of lithium, Depakote, and Tegretol, for which use of guidelines helps to achieve usually beneficial doses with minimal side effects. Unfortunately, there does not appear to be a correlation between blood level and response for the SSRI antidepressants, Effexor, Pristiq, Cymbalta, Wellbutrin, Serzone, or Remeron.

Dosage and Side Effects

Side effects may also be relative to dosage. It is important to remember that drug doses recommended in the *Physician's Desk Reference* were determined by early studies funded by the manufacturer to determine the usual standard dose range for most people. Due to unusual metabolism of drugs, some individuals respond to a lower dose of the medication and experience intolerable side effects at average doses. Others will not respond to a medication until the dose is pushed higher than usual. In these cases, side effects help with dose-finding: The doctor will push the medication until effectiveness is achieved or side effects become intolerable.

Duration of Treatment

Another common question from patients who are starting antidepressants and beginning to feel well is: "How long do I need to take the drug?" Acute-phase treatment has a goal of response (symptom reduction of at least 50%) and remission (very few remaining symptoms), and this typically takes about 1 to 3 months. The long-term goal is full recovery, wherein the patient resumes normal activities and is able to get enjoyment and meaningful fulfillment from life. Continuation treatment typically goes on as long as the untreated episode would have gone; typical continuation treatment recommendations are 9 to 12 months after remission (Paykel, 2001), after which medication may be very slowly tapered. The goal is prevention of relapse (symptom reemergence) of the initial episode.

The next phase, long-term maintenance preventive treatment, depends on the number of episodes of depression the patient has experienced and on whether rapid deterioration occurred when antidepressants were stopped in the past. People who have had a single episode of major depression in their lifetime have approximately a 50% chance of having another episode. After two episodes, the chance of another is 70%, and after three the chance of recurrence is 90%. Often the time between the first and second episodes is fairly long, on the order of 2 to 5 years. Time between episodes can be very important for a woman who is just entering childbearing years and may want to try a prolonged period off of medications when planning a pregnancy.

A person with two episodes of depression is at intermediate risk of recurrence. If there is a history of very severe, suicidal, difficult-to-treat depression, or depression that recurred soon after a successful medication treatment was stopped, lifetime maintenance treatment should be considered.

The story is different for an individual who has had three or more major depressive episodes in his lifetime, because he has a 90% chance of future recurrences. An individual who has had three or more episodes of depression should consider lifetime antidepressant medication maintenance. There is no guarantee that lifetime medication treatment will prevent future episodes, yet data from 1- to 2-year trials of SSRI and SNRI antidepressants compared to placebo, and from a small but very important 5-year trial of imipramine (an older tricyclic antidepressant), consistently showed a reduction in risk of recurrences among those with a history of recurrent major depression who continued medication use compared to those who stopped it (Kupfer, 1993). Why try to prevent episodes? There is some evidence to suggest that each episode may be harder to treat than the prior ones, with a lower response rate to the previously successful treatments and a longer time to achieve response.

Stopping Antidepressants

Some patients stop drugs early in treatment. Common reasons include dislike of side effects, feeling that there is no longer a need for medication, feeling better, feeling that the medication was not working, and running out of pills. In primary care, 28% of patients stop within the first month, and 44% by the third month (Lin et al., 1995). This may be a case of self-sabotage, because medications suppress symptoms only when they are taken regularly, and the symptoms of a major depressive episode typically last for 6 to 12 months if untreated.

A frequent question is whether it is reasonable to consider trying a period off of medicines to see if they are no longer needed after 6 to 12 months of feeling well. The answer to this question is difficult and based on experience more than research literature. We ask patients to follow these simple rules in trying to discontinue medications:

- Do *not* stop taking medications abruptly because you ran out of them on vacation or forgot to pack them. That is asking for trouble!

- Only consider discontinuing medications after you have been free from all of your depressive symptoms for several months. If depression is chronic or there are still a few residual depressive symptoms, the risk of relapse or recurrence is high (Lin et al., 1998).

- Discontinue at a time when life is stable. A divorce, job change, or move to a new part of the country is not conducive to assessing a fair evaluation of whether medications are still needed. Timing is critical.

- If you are taking more than one medication, discontinue one at a time. Review all of the psychiatric medicines with your doctor and try to figure out which one of them is least important (for antidepressant response) or is causing the most side effects. Taper off of that one first; if you are still feeling well, then taper off of the next one.

- Discontinue each medicine gradually, typically over about 1 to 2 months (longer for benzodiazepine anxiolytics). There are two reasons for this. First, some medications, such as the benzodiazepine minor tranquilizers (Xanax, Klonopin, Ativan, Valium, Librium) and SSRI and SNRI antidepressants (Paxil, Luvox, Celexa, Lexapro, Zoloft, Effexor, Pristiq, Cymbalta), have withdrawal symptoms. A slow taper can minimize these. Prozac has a very long elimination half-life of 2 to 3 days for the parent drug and about 1 to 2 weeks for the active metabolite, so it is self-

tapering. It can also be used to taper other SSRI or SNRI antidepressants by switching to Prozac and then tapering. Abrupt discontinuation of lithium is associated with rapid relapse of manic or
depressive episodes; this is much less likely if lithium is tapered
over at least 1 to 2 months (Baldessarini et al., 1996; Suppes,
Baldessarini, Faedda, & Tohen, 1991). The second reason to taper
off gradually is that if the medication is really necessary and
helping maintain mood stability, a slow taper will allow you to
catch symptoms when they are mild and regain stability by
returning to the previous lowest effective dose.

- Review your initial target symptoms. These are your warning signs
  of the depression (or mania) coming back. Tell your significant
  other, best friend, or therapist that you are tapering medications
  with your doctor's agreement and ask that person to help monitor
  you for any signs of the illness returning.

- Be open to the possibility that you might need medications for the
  long haul. If you follow the process just outlined and recognize
  that you still need some or all of your medications, it will be based
  on a carefully planned evaluation and not on the doctor's authori-
  tarian pronouncement or your "forgetting" to pack them when
  going on vacation. It will truly be your thoughtful decision. You
  can always go back and retry these steps in another 6 to 12
  months.

Classes of Antidepressants

Each drug type or family has its advantages, side effects, risks, and
contraindications. Antidepressant drugs are often grouped into families
based on their mechanism of action. There are the SSRIs, SNRIs, MAO
inhibitors, norepinephrine reuptake inhibitors (NRI), reversible
inhibitors of MAO (RIMA), serotonin modulators, drugs with complex
mechanism of action on serotonin and norepinephrine, 5-HT2 antagonists, and norepinephrine and dopamine reuptake inhibitors. Although
these names describe the immediate test-tube effects of these drugs
(clinical response, by contrast, takes weeks), they are useful categoriza-
tions. If a patient is not responding to a given drug, he can be switched

to one in a different family, or if a drug has offered only partial benefit, another drug, again from a different family, can be added. The goal is to combine mechanisms of action for synergistic (more than additive) effect, not just to combine drugs that do the same thing.

Tricyclic Antidepressants

Among the older generation of antidepressants, the tricyclic antidepressants (TCAs) include Tofranil (imipramine), Norpramin (desipramine), Sinequan (doxepin), Surmontil (trimipramine), Elavil (amitriptyline), Pamelor (nortriptyline), and Vivactil (protriptyline). All are now available in inexpensive generic form.

The TCAs were a mainstay of treatment for many years, but are no longer considered first-line treatments because of their many side effects. They still have some role in treatment, however, and are especially useful for chronic daily headache, migraine headaches, neuropathic pain, irritable bowel syndrome, cancer, post-stroke depression, and postpartum depression. Depression in severely ill hospitalized patients may respond to these older drugs better than to the newer antidepressants. In the treatment of severely depressed inpatients, a comparison of imipramine given for 4 weeks (followed by lithium augmentation for 3 weeks for partial or nonresponders) versus fluvoxamine followed by lithium augmentation showed a clear advantage for the use of the TCA imipramine over the SSRI fluvoxamine (Birkenhager, van den Broek, Mulder, Bruijn, & Moleman, 2004a, 2006). A very similar earlier study comparing imipramine with lithium augmentation versus Remeron (mirtazapine) with lithium augmentation showed better response rates in severely depressed inpatients with imipramine than with Remeron (Bruijn, Moleman, Mulder, & van den Broek, 1998). They are less effective than the MAO inhibitor phenelzine, however, for treatment of atypical depression, and the TCAs have failed to demonstrate benefit in numerous studies of childhood depression.

Blood levels of the TCAs are important for optimizing the dose because some individuals metabolize these drugs quickly whereas others metabolize them slowly, due to genetics and other drugs being taken at the same time. These tests are also important for safety monitoring. Disadvantages of the TCAs are severe toxicity and seizures in overdose. Other serious side effects include the possibility of cardiac conduction abnormal-ities; antiarrhythmic effects make them contraindicated after a heart attack. If these drugs are used at very high doses in severely ill hospital-ized patients and blood levels are not checked, there is a substantial risk of causing confusion or even delirium in the elderly. There is risk of switch from depression into mania among patients with bipolar illness. Effects of adrenergic blockade include increased pulse rate and a drop in blood pres-sure upon standing up quickly (postural hypotension), which sometimes leads to dizziness or falls in the elderly. Because these drugs all share varying degrees of anticholinergic effect, therapeutic doses often cause dry mouth, blurred vision, constipation, urinary retention, and, especially in the elderly, the risk of memory problems or confusion. There are also discontinuation symptoms that relate to cholinergic rebound. Typically the drug that causes dry mouth and constipation when taken may precip-itate a flulike syndrome of nausea, diarrhea, and increased gastrointestinal motility when stopped. Several of the TCAs also have an antihistamine effect, which makes them sedating and leads to increased appetite, espe-cially for sweets, and a risk of weight gain. Sedation can be a problem or benefit, depending on the patient, with drugs such as Sinequan, Elavil, and Surmontil. Activation is a problem or benefit, depending on the patient, with drugs including Vivactil and Norpramin. In the middle of the activa-tion-sedation spectrum are Pamelor and Tofranil. The TCAs do have sexual side effects, but they were seldom discussed during the years these drugs provided the mainstay of depression treatment.

Monoamine Oxidase Inhibitors

The other family of older antidepressants is the MAO inhibitors. These drugs classically include Nardil (phenelzine), Parnate (tranylcypromine), and Marplan (isocarboxazid), which block the degradation of monoamine neurotransmitters such as norepinephrine, serotonin, and dopamine. Unfortunately, these drugs are nonspecific and irreversible, so that the enzyme molecules that they are locked onto become totally ineffective and have to be replaced over a period of a couple of weeks for the drug's effect to be eliminated.

The advantages of the MAO inhibitors are that they tend to work better than tricyclic antidepressants for individuals who have atypical depression characterized by mood that is reactive to environmental events, overeating, oversleeping, a sense of leaden paralysis (heaviness of the limbs), and a long-standing pattern of rejection sensitivity. They sometimes work in patients with very treatment-resistant depression or severe anxiety such as panic disorder or social phobia, when other antidepressants and minor tranquilizers have failed to work.

The biggest problem with these drugs is their significant risk of interactions with foods that are aged or prepared by fermentation (creating tyramine), such as red wine and aged cheese and, notably, draft beer and sauerkraut. They also have substantial drug interactions with cold medicine, diet pills, epinephrine used as topical anesthetic for dental or other minor surgical procedures, and Demerol when it is used for pain control. The MAO inhibitors also have substantial risk of weight gain, sleep disruption, and sexual side effects.

Eldepryl (selegiline) is an orally administered selective MAO-B inhibitor that is used in Parkinson's disease at low dose. It actually slows progression of the disease and has multiple neuroprotective effects (Magyar et al., 2004; Magyar & Szende, 2004; Palhagen et al., 2006). At higher doses, it is a nonselective MAO inhibitor and has antidepressant and anxiolytic effects, though it is not FDA approved for this use.

A very exciting development in the MAO inhibitor field is the availability of Emsam, a selegiline transdermal patch that allows the MAO inhibitor to be administered through the skin and thus bypasses the gut, greatly decreasing the risk of hypertensive crisis (high blood pressure reaction) when eating wine, cheese, or other tyramine-containing foods. Oral selegiline is only 4% bioavailable, whereas the transdermal form is 73% bioavailable, meaning that the skin patch is a much more efficient way of getting the drug into the bloodstream than pills are (Azzaro, Ziemniak, Kemper, Campbell, & VanDenBerg, 2007a, 2007b). Emsam has enough dopamine effect to increase energy, activity, and drive, has essentially no weight change associated with acute or long-term treatment (on average), and appears to have minimal sexual side effects. Analysis of four studies involving 800 patients enrolled in double-blind short-term studies demonstrated significant improvement in their baseline sexual function on this drug (A. H. Clayton et al., 2007). The starting (and usual target) dose is 6 mg every 24 hours via a skin patch (Bodkin

& Amsterdam, 2002). At this dose, there are no dietary restrictions and the drug has been shown effective for 1-year maintenance treatment after patients achieved acute response (Amsterdam & Bodkin, 2006). At higher doses of 9–12 mg every 24 hours, a low-tyramine diet is recommended to minimize the risk of the "cheese reaction" (sudden rise in blood pressure). It is interesting that although this risk is present, the original research studies did not note this problem occurring when patients were not advised to follow the low-tyramine diet (Amsterdam, 2003; Feiger, Rickels, Rynn, Zimbroff, & Robinson, 2006; Frampton & Plosker, 2007b, 2007c). Studies with healthy volunteers given Emsam and then asked to take pills containing tyramine (fasting or with food) showed a wide margin of safety between the dose of tyramine that would be ingested in a meal and the amount that caused elevation of blood pressure (Azzaro et al., 2006; Blob et al., 2007). Also, Emsam at 6 mg/day has minimal effect on the response to common cold pills (pseudoephedrine and phenylpropanolamine), although some patients studied had slight blood pressure elevation (Azzaro, VanDenBerg, et al., 2007).

Tegretol, an anticonvulsant often used as a mood stabilizer, increases Emsam levels and is contraindicated, as are SSRI and SNRI antidepressants (due to risk of serotonin syndrome) and Demerol (Goodnick, 2007). Unfortunately, the drug interactions of standard MAO inhibitors are still important. Diet pills, Demerol, Ultram, and cold medicines including dextromethorphan (cough syrup) and pseudoephedrine (Sudafed, a decongestant) should be avoided (Feiger et al., 2006; Frampton & Plosker, 2007b, 2007c; Goodnick, 2007).

The most common side effect is risk of local skin irritation, which is easily treated by the use of topical hydrocortisone and by varying the site of application of the patch. The other major side effect is insomnia, which can be treated with sleeping pills such as Ambien or Lunesta, or with low doses of the sedating antidepressant trazodone. The original studies that led to FDA approval of this drug did not look at issues of the dose-response curve (is more better?) or specific subtypes of depression (atypical, bipolar, seasonal, melancholic, or comorbid with an anxiety disorder) possibly having different response rates.

Is it safe to use an MAO inhibitor for treatment of a depressed stimulant abuser? The classic answer would be no, because of the risk of hypertension and because two of the nine metabolites of selegiline are 1-amphetamine and 1-methamphetamine (the relatively inactive forms of these molecules). However, a recent UCLA study of methamphetamine abusers demonstrated the interesting finding that intravenous methamphetamine was safely tolerated during oral selegiline treatment (Newton et al., 2005). A similar study of cocaine abusers demonstrated that intravenous cocaine was safely tolerated in volunteers who were using transdermal selegiline 20 mg/day (Houtsmuller et al., 2004). These two studies suggest safety for possible use of Emsam in treatment of stimulant abuse. Unfortunately, the drug was not effective in treating cocaine dependence (Elkashef et al., 2006).

The reversible inhibitor of monoamine oxidase A (RIMA) Aurorix (moclobemide) also appears to be a very safe drug, without dietary risks or sexual side effects, but it failed to demonstrate adequate antidepressant effect to get the approval of the FDA for marketing in the United States. It is available in Canada, Mexico, and many other countries.

Selective Serotonin Reuptake Inhibitors

The newer generation of antidepressants began to appear 20 years ago with the introduction of Prozac (fluoxetine). Initially, the SSRI antidepressants represented a class of drugs with a spectrum of action unknown beyond depression. Over time, Prozac was followed onto the U.S. market by Paxil (paroxetine), Zoloft (sertraline), Luvox (fluvoxamine), Celexa (citalopram), and Lexapro (escitalopram). These drugs were found clearly effective for the treatment of depression, panic disorder, obsessive-compulsive disorder (OCD), social phobia, generalized anxiety disorder, premenstrual dysphoric disorder, and post-traumatic stress disorder. Prozac was even found to have an antibinging effect in bulimia. The spectrum of benefit is quite dramatic. Although not every SSRI is FDA indicated for all of the anxiety disorders mentioned above, this is because data demonstrating efficacy were for various reasons not submitted for approval. Luvox, for instance, is indicated only for OCD. Since their mechanism of action on serotonin is identical, patients have their choice of several SSRIs that may be helpful for their symptoms. The safety of these drugs in terms of minimal cardiovascular effects and minimal anticholinergic effects, as well as their overdose safety, rapidly led to their becoming market leaders. The availability of some of these drugs as inexpensive generics has made them more widely available.

Peter Kramer's fascinating book *Listening to Prozac* showed us that the drugs clearly did more than treat depression, and people often felt reluctant to give them up when a depressive episode had been fully resolved for several months. Kramer raised the issue about whether this family of drugs was effectively allowing "plastic surgery" on personality traits, changing people in a way that made them less overreactive, more outspoken, more outgoing, and otherwise more socially adept. For some individuals, being less overreactive or shy was a true benefit, and anxiety reduction was part of a very nice treatment response that occurred after several weeks of taking the SSRI drugs.

Early in the development of Prozac it was thought that this drug might be a good appetite suppressant, but unfortunately the weight loss that was seen during the first 6 months of high-dose treatment of obesity was not sustained when people were followed out to a year of treatment with it. It appears that the SSRI family of drugs is weight neutral in short-term studies of about 2 months duration, but that most of these drugs can cause some weight gain over the longer term in studies of up to a year. Paxil may cause more weight gain than the other drugs in this family.

SIDE EFFECTS
Sometimes there is a full response to an antidepressant, and all the depression symptoms are resolved, but there are intolerable side effects. One approach to this is to simply lower the dose of the medication and determine if a slightly lower dose continues to provide good antidepressant effect and eliminates the side effects.

The primary disadvantage of SSRIs involves sexual side effects. Most commonly, this involves delay or inability to achieve orgasm, but it may also involve decreased sexual drive and excitement. Initial studies of the sexual side effects of Prozac indicated that these occurred in only about 2% of people taking the drug, but later studies that systematically asked more appropriate questions showed that approximately 50% of all patients receiving SSRI and SNRI antidepressants had some sexual side effects (Montejo, Llorca, Izquierdo, & Rico-Villademoros, 2001). Unfortunately, the sexual side effects do not go away over time in most cases, so numerous antidotes have been proposed, including adding Viagra, BuSpar, or Wellbutrin, and simply changing to a different drug outside of the SSRI class. For those lacking sexual responsiveness, but not desire, a delayed dose or "drug holiday" from Celexa or Lexapro (which have very short half-lives) may be helpful. The antidotes are not reliably effective. Sexual function returns to usual baseline when SSRI drugs are discontinued.

Sexual symptoms deserve a further special comment because human sexuality is so complex. Sometimes antidepressant drugs interfere with sexual drive, arousal, or orgasm, but they may be blamed inappropriately for sexual problems when other issues are involved. We believe that there are a number of questions that should be discussed around sexuality. First, does the patient like his partner? Sexual enjoyment is a very sensitive indicator of the quality of the relationship with the partner. If the partner has grown frail and medically ill, gained a great deal of weight, abused substances, stopped working and become financially dependent, or been physically or emotionally abusive, anger or resentment may get in the way of sexual pleasure. Occasionally, sexual enjoyment is minimal with the long-term partner but fantastic with a lover; this is not a medication side effect! Second, has depression robbed the patient of his enjoyment of favorite foods, hobbies, and recreation? Anhedonia (lack of pleasure) is a key symptom of a severe depression, where truly nothing is fun during the down times. Sexual pleasure will return when the depression lifts. Third, has the antidepressant affected sexual functioning? The most frequent sexual side effect is difficulty achieving orgasm, but sometimes loss of drive or difficulty with arousal (erection or vaginal lubrication) may also occur. If the antidepressant is causing a problem, the dose can be reduced, various antidotes can be tried (Wellbutrin, Viagra, or BuSpar), or the drug may need to be changed.

Gastrointestinal side effects (nausea and diarrhea), on the other hand, are usually short-lived and generally can be easily managed by dose reduction and taking the drug after a meal. Nausea usually resolves within a week or two.

Often the weight gain associated with SSRIs is very slow, gradual, and insidious, occurring over a period of many months. Counseling patients about diet and exercise from the beginning of treatment is very important.

Osteoporosis is a potential concern with both SSRI antidepressants and depression, and it is most commonly seen in individuals with numerous risk factors, including older women with a family history of osteoporosis and individuals with low weight, lack of calcium and vitamin D in the diet, substance use, low sex hormone levels, and thyroid or parathyroid disease. Apparently both depression and antidepressants increase fracture risk and the risk of loss of bone mineral density (Cooper et al., 2008; Diem et al., 2007; Haney et al., 2007; Spangler et al., 2008; Yazici et al., 2005; Ziere et al., 2008). Certain drugs—including antacids, anticoagulants, some anticonvulsants (e.g., Tegretol, dilantin, and phenobarbital), steroids, and SSRI antidepressants—may worsen the risk. We advise anyone at risk, especially postmenopausal women, to have bone density checked every 2 to 3 years.

SSRI drugs all have some interactions with drug-metabolizing enzymes in the liver known as cytochrome P450 enzymes. Each drug in this family has a slightly different profile and this may be important in the case of an individual who is taking many other medications. It appears that Lexapro, Celexa, and Zoloft have the least risk for drug interactions at this site. Most pharmacies have computer databases to check for these drug interactions and will gladly do so if a patient requests it because of a lengthy medication list.

Another problem with the SSRIs is discontinuation symptoms. The only SSRI that seems to have minimal or no discontinuation symptoms is Prozac and the reason for this is the very long half-life (slow elimination) of its active metabolite, norfluoxetine, which stays in the body for at least 1 to 2 weeks after the drug is discontinued. The other SSRI drugs have a half-life of approximately a day, so if the drug is abruptly discontinued it is quickly eliminated from the body and withdrawal symptoms including anxiety, insomnia, flulike symptoms, and strange electrical zings may occur within a few days of stopping the drug. These uncomfortable symptoms usually last only a week or two, and they are mostly preventable with gradual tapering off of the medication.

EFFECTIVE DOSING

A curious fact about SSRI antidepressants is the lack of any clear statistical correlation between the acute dose and the percentage of patients responding. Patients given a low dose of, say, Zoloft or Prozac are as likely to show a response by the end of a 6- to 8-week study as are patients given a high dose. There might be a potential dose-response relationship, but this is unclear (Baker et al., 2003). Similarly, studies evaluating blood levels of these drugs fail to show a relationship between levels and response. This puts the clinician in the unusual position of wondering whether early nonresponse is due to a dose that is too low for the individual patient or simply to the fact that the patient's response is slow and might be minimal at 2 to 4 weeks but become robust by 2 to 3 months. Most clinicians approach this dilemma by slowly increasing dose over time as tolerated, until the patient begins to show a response or side effects become bothersome.

Wellbutrin

After Prozac, the next new-generation antidepressant to be brought onto the U.S. market was Wellbutrin (bupropion). It appears to work via norepinephrine and dopamine reuptake inhibition, with no effect on serotonin. Wellbutrin is useful in treating major depression with reduced energy, pleasure, and interest (Jefferson et al., 2006), as well as cognitive retardation (slowing), fatigue, and anxiety when these are a component of the depression.

Wellbutrin is not specifically useful for the anxiety disorders, unlike the SSRI antidepressants, but people who have some anxiety symptoms can still have as good a response to Wellbutrin as they would to Zoloft. Studies largely attribute this to its effects on lifting depression and thereby secondarily attenuating anxiety. A recent UCLA study showed Wellbutrin to be as helpful as an SSRI (Lexapro) in generalized anxiety disorder (Bystritsky, Kerwin, Feusner, & Vapnik, 2008; Jamerson, Krishnan, Roberts, Krishen, & Modell, 2003). In comparison studies of Wellbutrin and Zoloft, the anxiety-reducing effect of both drugs was essentially the same (Trivedi et al., 2001). A recent meta-analysis suggested that SSRIs are more effective than Wellbutrin in treating major depression with anxiety, with the SSRIs having about a 6% advantage in response rates (Papakostas et al., 2008).

Wellbutrin has also has been found helpful in adults with ADHD. Wellbutrin or Strattera may be preferable to stimulants for treatment of

ADHD with comorbid substance abuse. An energizing and activating drug, it has some potential for weight loss, especially when it is used at the relatively high dose of 400 mg/day (Gadde & Xiong, 2007).

The surprising finding with this drug is that it helps people to stop smoking, whether or not they are depressed. Wellbutrin has been marketed under the name Zyban for this purpose. It is very important to remember that Wellbutrin and Zyban are the exact same drug under different names so the patient does not receive Wellbutrin from the psychiatrist trying to treat depression and Zyban from the primary care doctor hoping to provide assistance in smoking cessation. Such double prescribing could lead to an excessive dose and risk of a seizure. Chantix (varenicline), which acts on nicotinic acetylcholine receptors, is another pharmacologic aid to smoking cessation. It appears to be more effective than Wellbutrin for this purpose but has some risk of inducing depression or suicidal ideation (Gonzales et al., 2006).

Wellbutrin is sometimes used in combination with an SSRI. It is used as an augmenting agent in partial responders to an SSRI to try to convert them to full remitters. Lam, Hossie, Solomons, and Yatham (2004) reported that among patients who did not respond to Celexa or Wellbutrin over a period of 6 weeks, and were then randomized to either switch to the other drug or receive both drugs together, the combination was much better than switching. Wellbutrin is also sometimes used in combination with an SSRI to treat SSRI-induced sexual side effects, with variable results.

Wellbutrin has several advantages when compared to the SSRI antidepressants. Probably the most important advantage is that it is the antidepressant with the least risk of any sexual side effects; it may in fact actually be helpful for individuals with inhibited sexual desire. In an 8-week comparison study of Wellbutrin versus Lexapro (possibly least likely of the SSRIs to cause sexual side effects) versus placebo in depression, the effects of Wellbutrin on sexual function were indistinguishable from placebo, whereas Lexapro was associated with worsened sexual function and difficulty with orgasm; both drugs were comparably effective for depression (Clayton et al., 2006). The incidence of orgasm dysfunction was 15%, 30%, and 9% respectively. Worsened sexual function was reported by 20%, 36%, and 15% of patients on Wellbutrin XL, Lexapro, and placebo (Clayton et al., 2006).

Wellbutrin is not without side effects of its own. Unfortunately, its launch onto the market was delayed because the drug was tested in women with bulimia (binge eating and purging or using laxatives) and it was found to induce grand mal seizures in approximately 8% of them. The drug is now contraindicated in persons who have an eating disorder such as bulimia or anorexia, people with a history of head trauma or prior seizures, and people who would be at risk for seizures because of ongoing or recent substance abuse. Also, when the drug was being developed, it was used at doses up to 600 to 800 mg daily and the seizure risk was clearly higher in people who took doses greater than 450 mg/day. Sometimes Wellbutrin will worsen anxiety, insomnia, tremor, headaches, or constipation, and it is theoretically possible that it might activate psychosis because of its dopamine activity.

In summary, clinicians tend to choose Wellbutrin when they want to avoid sexual dysfunction and weight gain, but rarely choose it in the presence of anxiety symptoms or disorders (Zimmerman, Posternak, Attiullah, et al., 2005). Regarding who should receive an SSRI and who should receive Wellbutrin, a clinical adage is that the "undermodulated" person who has overly intense emotional swings and anxiety may find their emotional intensity toned down by the SSRI antidepressants, whereas the "underactivated," low-energy, lethargic patient who doesn't have much get up and go may be stimulated by Wellbutrin. Wellbutrin is perhaps the drug of choice for the patient who has depression along with ADHD, nicotine dependence, obesity, low energy, and failure to tolerate side effects or obtain optimal response to an SSRI, due to its broad spectrum of effects (Clayton, 2007; Clayton & Montejo, 2006; Dwoskin, Rauhut, King-Pospisil, & Bardo, 2006; Fava et al., 2003; Gadde & Xiong, 2007; Jamerson et al., 2003; Jefferson et al., 2006; Papakostas, Fava, & Thase, 2007; Papakostas, Kornstein, et al., 2007; Rush, Trivedi, Wisniewski, Stewart, et al., 2006; Tong, Carmody, & Simon, 2006; Trivedi, Fava, et al., 2006; West, Baker, Cappelleri, & Bushmakin, 2007; Wilens et al., 2005; Wilkes, 2006).

Wellbutrin is available as an immediate-release formulation, a slow-release (SR) formulation for twice-daily dosing, and an extended-release

(XL) formulation for once-daily dosing. All formulations are available in both generic and brand. The XL formulation is simplest to use because it allows for once-daily dosing in the morning. Some patients notice a real difference between generic and brand Wellbutrin XL and, for them, staying with the original brand name product is very important. The maximum dose of Wellbutrin is 450 mg/day. With all but the XL formulation, the maximum dose that should be given at any one time of day is 200 mg, so doses of 300 to 450 mg require split dosing with part of the dose in the morning and part in the afternoon; nighttime dosing may be tried but can cause insomnia. Occasional blood pressure elevation is a reason to monitor blood pressure at the beginning of treatment.

Serotonin Norepinephrine Reuptake Inhibitors

The main SNRIs prescribed in the United States for depression are Effexor (venlafaxine), Pristiq (desmethylvenlafaxine), and Cymbalta (duloxetine).

Effexor

Effexor is among the next generation of antidepressants with a dual mechanism of action involving reuptake inhibition of both serotonin and norepinephrine. It may also have a slight dopamine effect at very high doses. Its advantages include a higher remission rate than SSRIs (though this point is controversial), possibly slightly fewer sexual side effects than SSRIs, and less risk of drug interactions than some SSRIs. The dual action may make it better for individuals with chronic pain or frequent headaches than the SSRI antidepressants because serotonin and norepinephrine together affect the "tone" (set point) of spinal cord pain pathways. Effexor's disadvantages include risk of elevating blood pressure, especially at doses above 225 mg/day, and intense discontinuation syndrome if it is stopped abruptly rather than tapered slowly.

The most important difference between Effexor and the SSRIs is the ascending dose-response curve. Whereas the serotonin reuptake effect is clearly present at any dose of the drug, the norepinephrine reuptake effect requires a higher dose of perhaps 150 to 225 mg/day or more, and this dual action is associated with the increase in antidepressant response and remission. As noted earlier, if an individual in a study is randomized to receive Prozac 20 mg daily or 60 mg daily, or is randomized to receive Zoloft 50 mg daily or 200 mg daily, the probability of getting well over 2 months is essentially the same at low dose or at high dose (Preskorn, 1996; Schweizer et al., 2001). However, early studies with immediate-release Effexor spanning the dose range from 75 mg up to 375 mg daily demonstrated a clear dose-response curve, with a higher dose giving a greater probability of antidepressant response and a more rapid response—with very rapid dose titration as high as 375 mg/day in inpatients giving prompt response (Benkert, Grunder, Wetzel, & Hackett, 1996; Blier et al., 2007; Debonnel et al., 2007; de Montigny et al., 1999; Khan, Upton, Rudolph, Entsuah, & Leventer, 1998; Mendlewicz, 1995; Rudolph et al., 1998). In a more recent study of SSRI nonresponders, high-dose Effexor XR (average 309 mg/day) gave higher response rates than standard dose (average 148 mg/day) at 8 weeks, but by 12 weeks these differences disappeared (Thase, Shelton, & Khan, 2006).

Some researchers believe dual reuptake inhibitors to be more effective than those that work on serotonin alone. Dr. Michael Thase, a leading antidepressant researcher, has performed a pooled analysis of eight clinical trials in which patients were randomized to receive Effexor or an SSRI antidepressant or placebo (Thase, Entsuah, & Rudolph, 2001). He has shown that the probability of achieving full remission of depression symptoms is 25% for placebo, 35% for SSRI antidepressants, and 41–45% with Effexor at 8 weeks.

A subsequent larger meta-analysis called Comprehensive Analysis of Remission (COMPARE) included 34 randomized controlled trials of Effexor versus SSRI antidepressants and found that the Effexor remission rate was 5.9% higher than that for SSRI antidepressants (Nemeroff et al., 2008; Thase et al., 2001).

A similar meta-analysis by a German study group not affiliated with the drug's manufacturer has challenged the finding of Effexor's superiority (Weinmann, Becker, & Koesters, 2007), showing a small advantage in response but not remission rates for Effexor. The German group claims to have excluded from their analysis studies with methodological limitations, and those which were available as abstracts only (and not published reports and articles), and they did not "cherry pick" (selectively report) available data as other studies might have done.

Should Effexor indeed demonstrate the superiority of dual action, this may not extend to the entire class of SNRIs: one review demonstrated superiority of Effexor versus other SSRIs (with the possible exception of Lexapro) but indicated that there is no evidence of superiority of milnacipran (an SNRI with FDA indication in the United States for fibromyalgia and used for depression elsewhere) or Pristiq relative to SSRIs (Thase, 2008). There is some suggestion of superiority of Cymbalta versus SSRIs, though Lexapro appeared comparably effective and better tolerated (Thase, 2008). Indeed, discontinuation rates due to adverse events are shown to be 45% higher for those randomized to Effexor versus those subjects given SSRIs (Weinmann et al., 2008).

Effexor has some of the same side effects as the SSRI antidepressants, including short-term nausea, tiredness, and longer-term sexual side effects. There is some risk of blood pressure increase when the drug is used in doses over 225 mg/day, but most people don't require doses this high. Higher doses may have good tolerability, as was shown with average dose of 260 mg/day in one study of treatment resistant depression (de Montigny et al., 1999). Effexor has an unusually short half-life, so abruptly stopping the drug is more likely to lead to discontinuation symptoms than is stopping an SSRI, and gradual discontinuation is essential. Effexor has minimal effect on the cytochrome P450 enzymes and minimal protein binding, so it has a benign profile in terms of risks of drug interactions. This is especially important for patients taking digoxin or coumadin, and those who are on multiple medications from different doctors.

Summarily, the good news is that Effexor may get more people well. The bad news is that only about 41–45% of people taking the antidepressant with the highest published remission rate achieve full remission by 2 months. This is often the reason that augmentation strategies are implemented and that drugs are used in combination with psychotherapy to try to obtain a more frequent and robust response.

Pristiq

Effexor has a major metabolite that is in itself an active antidepressant. When a person is taking Effexor, about 70% of the drug found in the body is desvenlafaxine, which was was itself introduced to the market in 2008 under the brand name Pristiq.

Pristiq has the interesting property of not requiring cytochrome P450 2D6 oxidative metabolism prior to excretion, nor does it block that enzyme. It also is not a substrate of P-glycoprotein pumps, which are involved in maintaining the blood-brain barrier, and it has very low protein binding. These factors mean a very low risk of drug interactions in people taking many other drugs and potentially better safety in persons with liver disease or slow drug metabolism due to age, genetics, or other drugs taken at the same time. In addition, when used at its optimal dose of 50 mg/day (Clayton, Kornstein, Rosas, Guico-Pabia, & Tourian, 2009), it appears to have a rate of study dropouts due to side effects that is comparable to placebo.

The dose-response curve of Pristiq is very interesting: Unlike with Effexor, the advantage of drug over placebo on depression ratings in clinical trials does not increase with dose escalation. It was as great at 50 mg/day as it was at 400 mg/day, while the dropout rate was much lower at 50 mg/day than at 400 mg/day (Boyer et al., 2008; Clayton et al., 2009; Kamath & Handratta, 2008; Liebowitz et al., 2008).

Pristiq is currently FDA approved only for use in major depression. Studies are planned in perimenopausal vasomotor instability (hot flashes), fibromyalgia, and other forms of neuropathic pain. Pristiq occasionally raises blood pressure and cholesterol, so periodic monitoring of these is recommended. Like Effexor, it must be tapered gradually to minimize withdrawal symptoms.

Cymbalta

Cymbalta is FDA-approved for the treatment of depression, generalized anxiety, painful diabetic neuropathy, fibromyalgia, and, in many other countries, is approved for the treatment of female stress urinary incontinence.

Cymbalta is similar to Effexor in providing a mixed mechanism of action, but it has a more equal balance between serotonin and norepinephrine effects. The ratio of serotonin to norepinephrine potency of Effexor is about 30:1, whereas the ratio for Cymbalta is 9:1, implying that it is not necessary to go above the usual recommended dose (for depression) of 40–60 mg/day to achieve a dual mechanism of action. Generally, 60 mg/day of Cymbalta is the optimal dose in treating depression, but some individuals will require more or less than this amount (Bech et al., 2006). For the elderly a lower dose is often recommended. As some patients become anxious when first starting Cymbalta, most clinicians prefer to start a drug-naïve patient on 30 mg/day to minimize these tolerability issues.

When compared with Effexor, Cymbalta is considered equal in efficacy though a bit more difficult to tolerate when initiating, and has less of a withdrawal symptom burden when discontinuing. One study, sponsored by Cymbalta's manufacturer compared 6 weeks of treatment with Cymbalta 60 mg/day to Effexor XR 75–150 mg/day. The results showed greater initial tolerability of Effexor but comparable antidepressant efficacy. When the study was extended to 12 weeks with flexible dosing of up to Cymbalta 120 mg/day or Effexor 225 mg/day, the drugs still showed equal efficacy in reducing depression symptoms. At the study's end, Cymbalta caused fewer discontinuation symptoms than Effexor XR during 2- and 3-week taper periods (Perahia et al., 2008; Hartford et al., 2007).

Comparisons to SSRIs have been mixed. One study showed Cymbalta comparably effective to Lexapro and Paxil for treating depression (Frampton & Plosker, 2007a), while another found it better than comparator SSRI antidepressants in reducing total depression scores (on the Hamilton Depression Rating Scale), with specific improvement in work and activities, psychomotor retardation (slowing), genital symptoms, and hypochondriasis; insomnia improved more on SSRI antidepressants (Mallinckrodt et al., 2007).

In elderly populations, Cymbalta appears useful for those nonresponsive to Lexapro, but high dose (average about 90 mg/day) and long-term treatment (average 12 weeks) were necessary to see response (Karp et al., 2008). It may aid in limiting polypharmacy by treating multiple problems: Cymbalta given to a geriatric population of depressed patients (using 60 mg/day for 8 weeks in a group averaging 72 years of age) was demonstrated to improve cognition as well as depression and pain (Raskin et al., 2007), with improvements in cognition only partially explained by improvement in severity of depression.

In addition to its effects in acute illness, Cymbalta has demonstrated efficacy in long-term maintenance treatment of depression (Dunner et al., 2007), and also in relapse prevention (for 6 months) when compared with placebo (Perahia, Gilaberte, et al., 2006).

Like SSRIs, Cymbalta may be effective for premenstrual dysphoric disorder (Mazza, Harnic, Catalano, Janiri, & Bria, 2008) and for generalized anxiety disorder. A study comparing Cymbalta, Effexor, and placebo in generalized anxiety disorder showed both drugs to be comparable and better than placebo, as well as comparably tolerable (Hartford et al., 2007). As noted earlier, Cymbalta also appears to offer substantial benefit for women suffering from stress urinary incontinence (often after multiple pregnancies), as well as for male stress incontinence after prostatectomy (Fink, Huber, Wurnschimmel, & Schmeller, 2008; Ghoniem et al., 2005; Guay, 2005; Hurley, Turner, Yalcin, Viktrup, & Baygani, 2006; Jost & Marsalek, 2005; Mariappan, Alhasso, Ballantyne, Grant, & N'Dow, 2007; Millard, Moore, Rencken, Yalcin, & Bump, 2004; Oelke, Roovers, & Michel, 2006; van Kerrebroeck, 2004; van Kerrebroeck et al., 2004).

Cymbalta has demonstrated clear benefit for painful physical symptoms that occur either as part of major depression or generalized anxiety, or as experienced in the primary pain disorders peripheral neuropathy or fibromyalgia.

Cymbalta improves pain that occurs within the context of major depression, and this improvement contributes to overall depression remission rates (Fava, Mallinckrodt, Detke, Watkin, & Wohlreich, 2004). It appears to have an independent analgesic (pain-relieving) effect separate from its antidepressant effect (Perahia, Pritchett, Desaiah, & Raskin, 2006). It has also demonstrated clear benefit in pain associated with generalized anxiety disorder (Hartford et al., 2008; Russell et al., 2008).

Studies of chronic pain in nondepressed individuals with diabetic neuropathy have shown excellent response and won FDA approval for marketing of the drug for this use at a dose of 60 to 120 mg/day (Smith & Nicholson, 2007; Sultan, Gaskell, Derry, & Moore, 2008). One well-controlled study showed Cymbalta to be effective in fibromyalgia treatment of women, regardless of whether the patients had major depression, but its effect was not significant in the small number of men tested (Arnold, 2007; L. M. Arnold et al., 2004, 2005, 2007).

There is preliminary evidence of pain relief in osteoarthritis (Sullivan, Bentley, Fan, & Gardner, 2008) and Parkinson's disease (Djaldetti, Yust-Katz, Kolianov, Melamed, & Dabby, 2007).

The Cymbalta safety database includes almost 24,000 (predominantly female) adult patients ages 18–97 who have participated in clinical trials for a variety of indications (Gahimer et al., 2007). About 20% of patients discontinued the drug due to side effects. Common side effects (occurring in 5% or more of subjects) included nausea, headache, dry mouth, insomnia, constipation, dizziness, fatigue, somnolence, diarrhea, and sweating. Only 3.5% of patients had serious adverse events; no single serious problem was reported with a frequency of >0.1%. This drug at the recommended 60 mg is less tolerable than Lexapro 10–20 mg/day (Khan et al., 2007). Side effects that cause people to discontinue medications often occur early in treatment and are transient; as mentioned before, most clinicians prefer to start a drug-naïve patient on 30 mg/day and titrate the dose slowly.

Cymbalta appears to cause a lower rate of sexual dysfunction than the SSRI paroxetine based on systematic data gathered during depression treatment trials involving over 1,000 patients (Delgado et al., 2005; Nelson, Lu Pritchett, et al., 2006). It may make male orgasm more difficult to achieve, while not affecting other aspects of male sexuality or interfering with female sexual response. One study comparing it to Lexapro showed that overall response of the depression to treatment is also a very significant factor in sexual dysfunction and its resolution (A. Clayton, Kornstein, Prakash, Mallinckrodt, & Wohlreich, 2007). Unlike Effexor, Cymbalta does not appear to have any significant effect on blood pressure. In one study, only 2% of subjects dropped out of the trial due to weight gain (Dunner et al., 2007).

Like Effexor, Cymbalta has discontinuation symptoms if it is abruptly stopped, especially when using a high dose (120 mg/day).

These include dizziness, nausea, headaches, paresthesia (abnormal sensations, such as numbness or tingling of the skin), vomiting, irritability, and nightmares, so it should be gradually tapered at the end of treatment. Most of these symptoms resolve within 1 week (Perahia, Kajdasz, Desaiah, & Haddad, 2005; Perahia et al., 2008).

Cymbalta does have some cytochrome P450 2D6 enzyme inhibition and over 90% protein binding, so that it may show slightly more risk of drug interactions than Effexor does. People taking beta blockers in particular may have to have their dose adjusted. The drug also promotes loss of salt (and therefore water), a problem which may be more common in the elderly. Diuretic medications complicate this issue. Cymbalta should not be used in individuals with liver disease, severe kidney disease, or people who are heavy drinkers.

Desyrel and Serzone

Desyrel (trazodone) and Serzone (nefazodone) are in the class of serotonin modulators, acting primarily as potent antagonists at the 5-HT2 receptors, the effect of which is to increase availability of 5-HT1A. Desyrel has been developed and FDA approved as an antidepressant; however, the usual effective dose range of 200 to 600 mg daily is often so sedating that patients cannot tolerate it. Most use of Desyrel now is at 50 to 100 mg at bedtime to promote sleep, though studies of this use are lacking and there may be tolerance to the sedating effect over a few weeks.

Side effects of Desyrel include drop in blood pressure upon standing and occasional worsening of heart arrhythmias. About one in 10,000 males experience priapism (prolonged painful erections). If these last more than an hour, they must be treated in the emergency room.

Serzone (nefazodone), now available only in the generic form, is a closely related drug with less risk of oversedation and blood pressure drops on standing rapidly, as well as substantially less risk of prolonged painful erections. Serzone has the interesting advantages over the SSRI antidepressants of having no greater sexual side effects than placebo, no weight gain, and improvement in sleep quality (Hicks et al., 2002; Manber et al., 2003). It appears to be effective in PTSD and panic disorder, though it is not FDA approved for these uses (Hidalgo et al., 1999; Neylan et al., 2003). Serzone is no longer sold in Europe, and the manufacturer has stopped producing brand name Serzone for the United States, although several companies still produce generic nefazodone. There are apparently two reasons, one being a relatively low market share and the other being occasional reports of potentially fatal liver damage, usually in the first 6 months of treatment. The FDA estimates that this occurs very rarely, with only one in approximately 250,000 patients taking the drug for a year reporting severe liver damage. Serzone blocks the cytochrome P450 enzymes known as 3A3/3A4 and this can raise blood levels of the tranquilizer Xanax or the sleeping pill Halcion as well as many of the statin drugs (such as Lipitor or Crestor) that are used to lower cholesterol levels. The safest statin drug to use with Serzone is Pravachol (pravastatin), which is not metabolized through the 3A3/3A4 system.

Remeron

Remeron (mirtazapine) is another new-generation antidepressant. Its mechanism of action is complex and involves increased release of both serotonin and norepinephrine, as well as blocking of serotonin-2 and serotonin-3 receptors. Remeron is often used with SSRI or SNRI drugs for many reasons: its complementary mechanism of action may augment the antidepressant effect, it may block nausea and sexual side effects of the other drugs, and it may improve sleep and increase appetite. Its profile of increased appetite, weight, and sleep, as well as its antinausea effect, also make it particularly useful in some medically ill and geriatric patients. When used specifically in insomnia, a dose of 15 to 30 mg nightly is sufficient for sedation.

Side effects include substantial risk of weight gain and sedation in patients who may not desire these effects, and some risk of increasing cholesterol and triglyceride levels. Remeron does not appear to cause larger incidence of sexual side effects than placebo.

New Drugs on the Horizon

Many antidepressant drugs are still in development and some are expected to be on the market in the near future. Triple-action drugs that increase serotonin, norepinephrine, and dopamine simultaneously are among these (Millan, 2009). Also in development are drugs that effect glucocorticoids (cortisol) by blocking their production through brain signals or blocking their receptors peripherally and in the brain (Nihalani & Schwartz, 2007). These are thought to be particularly helpful in psychotic and melancholic subtypes of severe major depression.

Agomelatine is a promising new antidepressant that is an agonist at melatonin type 1 and 2 receptors and a serotonin 5-HT2C antagonist. The drug appears useful in severe depression, seasonal depression, and generalized anxiety disorder, with efficacy in depression appearing comparable to Effexor XR and sexual side effects less than with Effexor XR. The melatonin effects appear useful in synchronizing the body's circadian rhythms and normalizing sleep (Dolder, Nelson, & Snider, 2008; Kennedy, Rizvi, Fulton, & Rasmussen, 2008; Lemoine, Guilleminault, & Alvarez, 2007; Montgomery & Kasper, 2007; Pjrek et al., 2007; San & Arranz, 2008; Zupancic & Guilleminault, 2006).

Where anxiolytics are concerned, gepirone ER is an analogue of buspirone, which is sometimes used for the treatment of generalized anxiety disorder as an alternative or adjunct to the SSRIs. It is also an alternate to the benzodiazepines, which cause sedation, dependence, withdrawal symptoms, and may contribute to depression and poor sleep quality. Gepirone has been used successfully in Europe for many years but has failed twice to win FDA approval in the United States.

Researchers and drug companies who are working on developing these medications are very aware of the importance and potential competitive advantage of developing antidepressant drugs that act rapidly and bring a greater percentage of patients to the point of full remission from their depression symptoms, and can do so with minimal weight, sexual, and gastrointestinal side effects.

Selecting an Antidepressant

All antidepressants are not created equal. Some work much better than others for certain individuals and some have far fewer side effects than others in particular individuals. Part of the reason for obtaining a very detailed history of family members' drug responses (as well as the patient's drug responses) is to attempt to choose a drug with the best potential benefit and the least potential for side effects for an individual patient.

We are often asked if there is a test that will reliably predict which antidepressant will work best for an individual. Promising research is ongoing, with very sophisticated technology including computer-analyzed measures of the brain's electrical activity (EEG), PET and SPECT brain scanning to view areas of the brain that are relatively high or low in metabolic activity compared to the brain scans of people without psychiatric illness, and genetic analysis (for example, evaluating the serotonin transporter gene). All are expensive, available primarily in research clinics, and not yet reliable enough to substitute for systematic clinical trials of the medications. Sometimes a patient really does have to try a few different medications in order to find the one that both works well and has minimal side effects.

There is no ideal antidepressant. If we define antidepressant response as a 50% drop in depression severity as measured on a rating scale, all antidepressants have about a 60–65% response rate by 6 to 8 weeks of treatment. This contrasts with about a 25–30% response rate for an inert placebo (sugar pill). This means that if a person starts an antidepressant and continues to take it for 6 to 8 weeks, he has a 60–65% probability of getting significant improvement (response).

However, the true goal of treatment is remission—not just response. In remission, the depression rating scale shows a level of symptoms essentially the same as that of the nondepressed population, although perhaps with a few lingering symptoms. The person is more or less back to his old self and has resumed full normal activities. Unfortunately, remission only occurs in about 35–40% of patients on a single antidepressant for about 8 weeks. These numbers are derived from research-qualified patients who participate in double-blind studies designed to test the safety and efficacy of new drugs that are in development as part of the manufacturer's investigational new-drug application to the FDA. Such studies typically eliminate individuals with mild, treatment-resistant, bipolar, chronic, or suicidal depressions, individuals who are pregnant, and individuals who have any unstable medical illness or recent substance abuse, so their applicability to "real world" practice has been challenged (Zetin & Hoepner, 2007). In fact, anywhere from 75% to 91% of people applying to participate in an efficacy trial of antidepressants do not qualify. In the previously mentioned STAR*D study of patients who had real-world depression, including many patients with comorbid substance abuse or medical or psychiatric problems, the remission rate at 12 weeks on an SSRI was only 28–33%.

Again, different antidepressants work better for different people. When choosing an antidepressant, it is wise to consider the following factors:

- *Details of close relatives' response and the patient's response to previous medications.* If the mother, brother, or sister, for example, has done extremely well on a particular drug, that drug should be tried first for the new patient presenting for initial treatment. Similarly, if the patient comes in stating that several of his own past episodes of depression responded very well to a particular drug, that family of drugs should be tried again. On the other hand, if the patient says that he had a good response to a previous antidepressant but had terrible side effects such as extreme weight gain, loss of sexual responsiveness or drive, or feeling overly sedated or activated ("speedy"), that drug and others with similar side effects should be avoided.

- *Psychiatric comorbidity.* Psychiatric comorbidities, especially anxiety disorders, are common in depressed patients. The type of comorbidity should determine the medication selection. For example, obsessive-compulsive disorder, panic disorder, social anxiety (social phobia), and generalized anxiety disorder all respond nicely to the SSRI antidepressant family, including Prozac, Zoloft, Paxil, Celexa, Lexapro, and Luvox. The SNRI antidepressants Effexor and Cymbalta both have FDA-approved indications for major depression and generalized anxiety; Effexor is also approved for panic disorder and social anxiety. Cymbalta is approved for painful diabetic neuropathy, is helpful in fibromyalgia and other chronic-pain syndromes, and may also benefit women with stress urinary incontinence. Obesity would be a reason to avoid Elavil, Sinequan, and Remeron, and to consider Wellbutrin or an SSRI (with the exception of Paxil). Bulimia or anorexia nervosa would be a reason to avoid Wellbutrin (due to seizure risk) and consider an SSRI.

- *Medical comorbidity.* Patients who are medically ill may be on numerous drugs that could interact with an antidepressant. Effexor, Pristiq, Celexa, Lexapro, and Zoloft have the least risk of drug interactions due to blocking metabolism of other drugs at the cytochrome P450 enzyme system in the liver and gut.

- *Cost.* Another factor is the cost of the drugs. Some insurance plans cover only older generic drugs that are manufactured by several different companies and sold at competitive prices, whereas other insurance plans are willing to pay for the newer brand-name drugs. Tricyclic antidepressants are available as generics, as are some SSRIs (Paxil, Zoloft, Celexa, and Prozac) and other new-generation drugs (such as Wellbutrin and Serzone).

Some psychiatrists use the symptom profile to predict the best medication for a patient. Theoretically, dopamine deficiency is related to decreased ability to experience pleasure, decreased motivation, decreased attention, and cognitive slowing, and this may respond to Wellbutrin or a stimulant. Norepinephrine deficiency is associated with low energy, lethargy, or decreased alertness and may respond to Wellbutrin or Norpramin. Patients with low dopamine and norepinephrine may have decreased sense of reward and pleasure and become dependent upon nicotine or stimulants because of their temporary increase in these neurotransmitters. Serotonin deficiency may be associated with obsessive-compulsive behavior, panic, and anxiety, and may respond to SSRIs such as Prozac, Zoloft, Paxil, Celexa, or Lexapro. Patients with low serotonin may have a high level of harm avoidance, a trait commonly seen in people prone to anxiety or obsessive tendencies. Unfortunately, this scheme provides general guidelines but does not give a highly reliable profile of which symptoms respond to which type of antidepressant (Stahl, 2008).

The scheme does, however, help to predict which side effects are most likely with particular drugs. The dopamine drugs may worsen psychosis or cause activation or nervousness. The norepinephrine drugs may cause tremor, rapid pulse rate, dry mouth, constipation, urinary hesitancy, and insomnia. The serotonin drugs may cause sexual dysfunction, upset stomach or diarrhea, fatigue, and decrease in dopamine neurotransmission leading to decreased pleasure, apathy, decreased motivation, decreased attention, and cognitive slowing (Stahl, 2008).

Objectively Comparing Antidepressant Effectiveness

Clinicians often have a favorite antidepressant, but this preference is often biased, based on the doctor's initial impressions of responses of the first few patients he tried on a drug. A more reliable way of ascertaining antidepressant effectiveness is through pooled analysis, in which all data points from all patients in all available studies are reanalyzed. However, this requires access to original data, which study sponsors might not be willing to give. Another approach is meta-analysis of effect sizes. In this approach, multiple published studies are found through careful review of research publications. Then the change from baseline on drug versus placebo or other active comparator drug is analyzed and an "effect size" (difference divided by a measure of how scattered the data are) is calculated, so that the results of one study can be compared to those of another. The problem with this approach is that some negative studies never get published, so they can't be included in the analysis. The very best approach is a randomized head-to-head comparison study in which patients are assigned to one drug or the other and the double blind is maintained so that neither doctor nor patient knows which drug the patient is getting. This ensures that the pool of patients who may be assigned drug A is the same as the patients getting drug B, and that investigator bias is eliminated. The problem with this approach is that if both drugs are roughly equally effective, a very large sample size would be needed to show any significant differences between them.

Montgomery and colleagues (2007) asked which antidepressants have superior efficacy, based on direct head-to-head comparisons with other antidepressants, in moderate to severe depression. They concluded that Anafranil (clomipramine), Effexor (venlafaxine), and Lexapro (escitalopram) all had evidence of definite superiority, whereas Cymbalta (duloxetine) and Remeron (mirtazapine) had probable superiority.

Considering Nonpharmacological Treatments

Medications and psychotherapy are usually the first-line treatments in primary care and psychiatry for moderate to severe depression. Other treatments may be considered, however. Bright light may be helpful for seasonal depression, and brain stimulation may be considered in severe or treatment-resistant cases. Other complementary and alternative therapies are discussed later.

Psychotherapy

Psychotherapy is discussed at length in Chapter 8. It works well to increase insight, strengthen coping skills, challenge cognitive distortions, and allow change in behaviors and feelings over a long period of time. Psychotherapy requires a major commitment in time and effort to have significant impact. In return, there is the chance for lasting change in thought, feelings, and behaviors, and a potential for lowering the long-term risk of recurrence after treatment is stopped. Psychotherapy may be critically important alongside medications to deal with life stressors.

Light

Some individuals have a seasonal subtype of their mood disorder. Depression typically develops in the fall or winter and resolves in spring or summer, and a bright artificial light box is often helpful (Westrin & Lam, 2007). The typical light box costs about $200 to $300 and is covered by many insurance companies. It is used for about a half hour to an hour in the morning (when it is most effective) during the person's usual depression season. This treatment is very benign with minimal risk of side effects if there is no eye disease present. If eye problems are known to exist, it is essential to consult an ophthalmologist before attempting bright-light treatment. The most effective light boxes are those with compact LED units of 10,000 lux, or those with larger fluorescent units of 10,000 lux, with a wavelength of 470 nm. It is interesting that bright artificial light may also be helpful in premenstrual dysphoric disorder, bulimia, and bipolar depression, although there is a slight risk (1% in the general population) of bright-light treatment inducing mania. Some patients with nonseasonal depression also respond to this treatment, especially as an adjuvant added to an antidepressant (Even, Schroder, Friedman, & Rouillon, 2008; Wirz-Justice, 2006). Light therapy and cognitive-behavioral therapy may work very well in combination with each other in seasonal depression treatment (Rohan et al., 2007).

Brain Stimulation

Brain stimulation techniques are sometimes used in very difficult-to-treat depression. These include electroconvulsive therapy (ECT), vagus nerve stimulation (VNS), repetitive transcranial magnetic stimulation (rTMS), and deep-brain electrode stimulation. ECT is the most robustly effective treatment known for severe depression. It is appropriate for very acute, severe, life-threatening depressive episodes, especially with psychotic or catatonic features. It works quickly in the short term. VNS is an established treatment for epilepsy and has recently won FDA approval for treatment-resistant depression in individuals who have failed multiple other antidepressant medications. It may be used in unipolar or bipolar major depression with a history of failure on four different antidepressant treatments. Treatment response is slow, with benefit often occurring many months after the device is implanted, but the effect is often much more enduring than with ECT. The rTMS treatment was FDA approved for clinical use late in 2008.

Subtypes of Depression and Effects on Treatment Choice

As we have already suggested, some types of major depression influence the choice of antidepressant.

Psychotic Depression

Psychotic episodes of major depression involve hallucinations or delusions. Typically, the hallucinations are voices saying that a person is bad or deserves to suffer or should die. Delusions usually have to do with sin, evil, guilt, poverty, or devastating physical illness. When a person is suffering from psychotic symptoms, an antidepressant alone is often not enough. Studies performed many years ago that involved the typical antipsychotic drugs (such as Haldol, Stelazine, and Prolixin) and the tricyclic antidepressants clearly demonstrated that the combination of an antidepressant with an antipsychotic was far better than either drug alone. It has long been known that psychotic features can respond quite nicely to ECT. The current generation of antidepressants, especially the SSRIs, are often used in combination with atypical antipsychotics to treat individuals with psychotic major depressive episodes. Generally the antipsychotic is tapered over a period of a few months after there is good remission from the depression. The most important feature of psychosis is that it may go unrecognized if the depressed person does not reveal what is mentally going on inside to the treating psychiatrist. Patients may not want to report the strange thoughts or scary voices out of fear of being considered crazy. If these symptoms are not acknowledged openly, the psychiatrist has no chance to provide adequate treatment.

Melancholic Depression

Melancholic features may occur as part of a major depressive episode and generally represent the severe end of the biological symptom spectrum. These features involve extreme loss of pleasure in activities, loss of reactivity or enjoyment of pleasurable events, a distinct quality to depressed mood (different from grieving), worse mood in the morning (diurnal pattern), early morning awakening, severe psychomotor changes, and loss of appetite or weight along with extreme guilt. Melancholic features may respond to an SSRI antidepressant, but early studies that compared the tricyclic antidepressant Anafranil (clomipramine) against SSRI antidepressants in hospitalized melancholic patients showed that the tricyclic, with dual mechanism of action, gave a better response rate (Danish University Antidepressant Group, 1986, 1990). Many experts believe that the dual-mechanism drugs may work better than a single-mechanism drug in severe melancholic depression. This is why the tricyclic antidepressants and Effexor (and perhaps also Cymbalta) are often first-line treatments for severely ill or hospitalized melancholic individuals (Anderson, 1998, 2000).

Atypical Depression

Atypical features such as mood reactivity with mood brightening in response to positive events, increased weight or appetite, increased sleep, leaden paralysis, and rejection sensitivity were found many years ago to respond preferentially to MAO inhibitors rather than tricyclic antidepressants. Among the new-generation drugs, it appears that the SSRI antidepressants are quite effective for this group of patients. If an SSRI fails to be beneficial or well tolerated, many experts turn to Wellbutrin because of its energizing, activating effect. The MAO inhibitors, classically used in this subtype, are used as a third-line option only because of their side effect profile. Note that while Emsam (the transdermal selegiline patch) is the most recent preparation of an MAO inhibitor and the one with the fewest dietary restrictions, it has not specifically been tested in atypical depression. Bright artificial light may also be helpful.

Seasonal Depression

Seasonal affective disorder, most typically involving depressions beginning in the fall or winter, responds quite nicely to the use of a bright artificial light box (Westrin & Lam, 2007). This type of depression is often characterized by a hibernation response of overeating, oversleeping, social withdrawal, carbohydrate craving, and general lethargy. Early researchers made the analogy of seasonal depression to animal hibernation, which is triggered by shorter days in fall or winter. A study has shown that among Canadians with seasonal affective disorder, the use of a bright light box was about equally effective as the use of Prozac (Gaynes, 2007; Lam et al., 2006). The bright light box apparently tricks the body into thinking that it is time to energize for springtime rather than hibernate for winter. Wellbutrin has recently been shown effective in preventing recurrent episodes of seasonal affective disorder if started shortly before the usual time of the person's fall or winter depressions (Modell et al., 2005).

Bipolar Depression

Bipolar depression is sometimes helped by antidepressants, though the jury is out as to the extent of their utility. Although they may be useful for depression and anxiety in some, it is common for those with bipolar illness to have resistance to multiple antidepressants or to experience a loss of benefit over time. It is also possible for antidepressants to induce (hypo)mania or cyclicity in this population. One trial found that of those patients who did not develop hypomania on an antidepressant, only 23% achieved an antidepressant response (Ghaemi et. al., 2004). That said, antidepressants may prove invaluable for the patient who has anxiety comorbid to depression, which a large percentage do.

Because treatment of bipolar depression involves mood stabilizers as the mainstay, this topic is explored in Chapter 12.

Psychiatric Comorbidity and Medical Concerns

Depression often occurs with other psychiatric and medical conditions, and these may make diagnosis challenging and influence treatment selection. In the best case, the antidepressant may treat two or more conditions, but unfortunately there are some cases where the antidepressant may worsen or dangerously interact with treatment for the comorbid condition.

Anxiety Disorders

Sometimes depression and anxiety disorders go hand in hand and it is hard to differentiate the symptoms of each. Fortunately, the same medication may work to treat both.

Some individuals with depression have a history of, or a concurrent problem with, panic disorder, OCD, social phobia, premenstrual dysphoric disorder, post-traumatic stress disorder, or other anxiety disorders. The SSRI antidepressants are proven effective and many are also FDA approved for the treatment of these conditions, although for some individuals the drugs may initially cause a worsening of anxiety symptoms. It is therefore a good idea to start at a low dose that is very gradually built up. The use of liquid forms (for example, starting Prozac at 2 mg/day and increasing by 2 mg/day each week) allows a very gentle beginning of the drug without any noticeable increase in anxiety. Usually the full effect on the anxiety disorder is not seen until the SSRI has been used for about 1 to 3 months. The use of benzodiazepine minor tranquilizers (Klonopin, Xanax, or Ativan, for example) may help the person starting an SSRI to sleep and minimize the initial anxiety and jitteriness that these drugs sometimes cause. Antidepressants that may alternately be of some benefit in treating anxiety symptoms include Serzone and Remeron.

Case Example: Panic and Reluctance to Take Medications

Sally was a 47-year-old divorced saleswoman who presented with recent onset of panic attacks and depression. She had also had chronic worry and OCD (frequent checking), neither of which required treatment, for many years. Her internist found no medical problems that might cause her symptoms.

Sally was stressed by a new owner of the business she'd worked at long-term and by having her elderly, emotionally cold mother living with her. She had minimal benefit from 3 months of psychotherapy, and she was upset about having a psychiatric illness at this stage of her life and angry about having to take a psychiatric medication, so she rarely used Klonopin or Xanax for anxiety. I explained that Prozac might help her panic and other symptoms but she was reluctant to take it, so we used the liquid form to give her complete control over the dose adjustment. We started at 4 mg and worked up to 8 mg/day, and she had a response at this low dose. The liquid allowed her to fine-tune her dose to the point where it was tolerable and gave her body time to acclimate to the side effects. After a month of treatment, her panic attacks had become rare and people were commenting she was her old self again. Over the next few months, she gradually resumed visiting friends and practicing yoga and meditation, and she began dealing with unpleasant dreams in psychotherapy. She was also able to taper off of her previous very low dose of Klonopin. Thirteen years later she was taking Prozac weekly to minimize her frequency of ingesting medication, joking with me about my being her "drug dealer," and enjoying traveling on long cruises with her mother and friends. Psychologically, a medicine that she only had to take once a week seemed much less intrusive and serious than one that had to be taken daily.

Attention-Deficit/Hyperactivity Disorder

Individuals with a history of attention-deficit/hyperactivity disorder (ADHD) typically show problems beginning in childhood with being spacey, inattentive, a class clown, and repeatedly being told that they are not working up to potential or staying on task. The hyperactive component is more common in boys than in girls (ADD is the disorder minus this component) and sometimes fades during teenage years. Usually the individual with attention deficit will have difficulty in school by junior high or high school when native intelligence is no longer enough to allow them to do well. Often the child begins to lose interest in school and feels that he is a failure because he can't keep up with the academic demands. As a teenager, he is at greater risk for driving accidents, smoking cigarettes, and drug abuse. As an adult, he may have many job changes, relationship problems, and a history of impulsive decisions that are not thought out or in his best interest. When such an individual presents for treatment of depression, it is often in response to numerous work or relationship failures. The person may come across as angry, frustrated, having a short fuse, and irritable. There is often a gap between intelligence and lack of long-term accomplishments. The stimulant drugs such as Ritalin, Adderall, and Dexedrine may be effective for the attention problems, but they may not work as long-term antidepressants because their mood-elevating, energizing, and activating effects tend to fade over time. Wellbutrin is an effective antidepressant that appears comparable to Ritalin in its benefit on ADHD symptoms, and it is effective in adults with the disorder (Wilens et al., 200a). Strattera (atomoxetine), a norepinephrine reuptake inhibitor like the antidepressant Norpramin (desipramine), is FDA approved for ADHD. It has been demonstrated effective in both children and adults with ADHD. It appears to provide benefit for oppositional defiant behaviors, to have minimal effect on growth, and to have very rare risk of liver problems or seizures, though its effects might be slightly weaker than those of stimulants. It is useful for anxious patients, may be preferred for some substance-abusing patients with ADHD (Bangs et al., 2007; Bangs, Hazell, et al., 2008; Bangs, Jin, et al., 2008; Carlson et al., 2007; Chamberlain et al., 2007; Cheng, Chen, Ko, & Ng, 2007; Faraone et al., 2005; Gaillez, Sorbara, & Perrin, 2007; Geller et al., 2007; Gibson, Bettinger, Patel, & Crismon, 2006; Newcorn et al., 2008; Perwien et al., 2006; Prasa et al., 2007; Prasad & Steer, 2008; Spencer et al., 2005, 2006, 2007; Y. Wang et al., 2007; Wernicke et al., 2007; Wigal et al., 2005). Strattera has also demonstrated benefit for anxiety symptoms and affective lability (frustration intolerance, anger outbursts) but failed to demonstrate efficacy in early clinical trials as an antidepressant.

Case Example: Depression and ADHD

Ron was a 46-year-old, never married, Caucasian male with a PhD in an esoteric area of study. He was a university professor who complained of chronic depression that went as far back as grade school. He had lost a girlfriend because she could not deal with his depression, and he felt "sick to death" of work and was considering changing fields, even though he had a secure position at the university. Ron reported having felt depressed for at least half of the last 5 years. He felt a sense of worthlessness, meaninglessness, and lack of enjoyment of usual activities, like cooking. His mind would wander, and it was difficult to concentrate. Nothing—even receiving honors for his research papers—made a difference in how he felt.

My initial diagnostic impression was recurrent major depression. I asked Ron about his medication history, and he reported that he had had a brief positive response to Prozac at 20 mg daily but had stopped taking the medication due to severe sexual dysfunction. I decided to start him on very low-dose Prozac, but this led to some suicidal ideation, so we discontinued the drug.

A more thorough history-taking provided a breakthrough: Ron gave a history of childhood nervousness, restlessness, and decreased ability to concentrate, as well as adult difficulties with reading, listening to speeches, and focusing on his writing. He stated that when he had tried an amphetamine in the remote past, he could focus mentally much better. The additional diagnosis of ADHD was made, and when low-dose Ritalin was begun at his suggestion, Ron stated, "We've finally found something that works."

Ron did well on Ritalin alone for a year, but then his feelings of depression, meaninglessness, and existential angst returned. I suggested adding Wellbutrin to the Ritalin—a combination that proved enormously effective. Over the next 12 years, Ron continued to take Wellbutrin 300 to 450 mg daily, along with Ritalin about 30 mg daily, and during this time he was able to enjoy leading national symposia, testifying before Congress in his area of research expertise, and writing a major textbook. He met a woman who was very appropriate for him and got married. He continued his teaching job along with his profitable outside consulting work. His medication follow-up visits consistently involved reports that he was doing well and just needed medication refills. In 12 years of taking this medication combination, he appeared to be truly enjoying his work and marriage in ways that he had not been able to prior to the successful treatment. It was only when we had become partners and found a way to treat both depression and ADHD that Ron was able to achieve his full potential in both scholarship and home life.

Smoking

The relationship between smoking and depression is very interesting. Smoking may be a risk factor for development of depression, and quitting smoking may be a risk factor for development of depression in susceptible individuals. Simply having a mood disorder may decrease the likelihood of success in stopping smoking. It appears that Wellbutrin (also marketed as Zyban) may be effective for both the depression and smoking cessation; cognitive-behavioral therapy and the nicotine replacement transdermal patch are both alternatives and augmentation strategies to this approach (Evins et al., 2008; Gold, Rubey, & Harvey, 2002). Chantix, a partial agonist of nicotinic acetylcholine receptors, is also used for smoking cessation. Unlike Wellbutrin, it has a risk of inducing depression and suicidal ideation or behavior in some individuals. This makes Wellbutrin the preferred drug for individuals who have mood disorders and want to quit smoking.

Medical Comorbidity

Individuals who have epilepsy or seizure disorders should not be treated with antidepressants that lower the seizure threshold, such as Wellbutrin, Ludiomil (maprotiline), and Anafranil (clomipramine). Often the seizure disorder and the depression can be treated with one drug, such as the mood-stabilizing anticonvulsants Lamictal (lamotrigine) or Depakote (valproic acid). If an antidepressant is needed in addition to the anticonvulsant, the SSRIs probably are the safest choice.

Depression occurring after a heart attack is extremely important to spot, not only because it may interfere with rehabilitation but also because it is a risk factor for death over the next 6 months. The Sertraline Antidepressant Heart Attack Randomized Trial (SADHART) is a major study of depression occurring in the context of acute cardiac events (Glassman et al., 2002). People with major depressive symptoms after a heart attack were randomized to receive placebo or Zoloft. Those with previous depressive episodes and those whose current episode began before the cardiac event had an antidepressant benefit that exceeded that of placebo. The antidepressant did not have any adverse cardiac effects (e.g., on the heart's pumping ability). The patients who received the antidepressant lived longer than those who received placebo, although this difference was not statistically significant (Glassman, Bigger, Gaffney, Shapiro, & Swenson, 2006).

Similarly, post-stroke depression may interfere with rehabilitation, and interesting research has shown that Zoloft can decrease the likelihood of developing post-stroke depression and that Prozac and nortriptyline can actually increase the rate of survival after a stroke (Murray et al., 2005; Robinson et al., 2000; Spalletta & Caltagirone, 2003; Starkstein, Mizrahi, & Power, 2008). In the study that established this, Prozac was not given to individuals who had a hemorrhagic lesion (a burst blood vessel) within the brain, and nortriptyline was not given to individuals who had heart problems and might not tolerate it.

Pain

Another area of concern often faced by the psychiatrist is that of chronic pain. Here we are specifically concerned about chronic pain that does not have a clear-cut anatomic causal factor and thus is often considered functional pain or pain of unknown etiology. Fibromyalgia, migraine headaches, and lower back pain fall into these categories. Fibromyalgia is characterized by diffuse pain in multiple areas and a set of 18 tender points around the neck, shoulders, knees, hips, and other spots, as well as chronic fatigue; it is usually evaluated by a rheumatologist with a series of laboratory tests to help rule out more serious illnesses including autoimmune diseases. Fibromyalgia is often considered a disease of increased central (brain and spinal cord) pain sensitivity. There is no specific treatment for fibromyalgia, although many experts suggest a low dose of the tricyclic antidepressant Elavil for two reasons: It can help to consolidate fragmented sleep and it has some effect on decreasing pain. Because fibromyalgia so often involves deconditioning, aerobic exercise is frequently a part of the treatment.

Lyrica (pregabalin) was the first FDA-approved drug for the treatment of fibromyalgia. It acts on calcium channels of neuronal membranes that carry pain signals, but it does not significantly affect the heart or blood pressure. It appears to have excellent benefit for generalized anxiety as well. Cymbalta is also FDA approved for treatment of fibromyalgia and acts on descending pain-modulating fibers in the spinal cord. Because these two drugs have different mechanisms of action, they may well work synergistically, with the combination resulting in a more than additive effect on pain. Although clinicians often use them together, there are no studies on the combination published yet.

Migraine headaches are characterized by occasional warning signs such as flashing lights or other visual disturbance in the visual fields (known as "aura"), followed by a headache that typically starts on one side of the head and is pounding or throbbing. This is accompanied by sensitivity to light, sound, and smell, usually with a sense of nausea and sometimes vomiting. Migraines interrupt normal activities, making a person want to lie down in a dark, quiet room, and may last for many hours. The acute (episode-aborting) treatment of a migraine headache is achieved with a triptan like Imitrex, Treximet, Maxalt, Zomig, Frova, Amerge, or Relpax, and these are best given at the start of the migraine. When migraine headaches occur more than about twice a month, serious consideration should be given to preventive treatments. It appears that tricyclic antidepressants, Effexor, and some anticonvulsants such as Depakote and Topamax (topiramate), as well as beta blockers (such as propranolol, metoprolol, and timolol), have a preventive effect against migraine headaches (D'Amico, 2007; P. Gupta, Singh, Goyal, Shukla, & Behari, 2007; V. K. Gupta, 2007; Lampl, Katsarava, Diener, & Limmroth, 2005; Mulleners & Chronicle, 2008; Ramadan, 2007; Tomkins, Jackson, O'Malley, Balden, & Santoro, 2001; Yurekli et al., 2008). Sometimes chronic daily tension headaches are mixed in with migraines. These are typically characterized as being a tight band around the head that does not interfere with daily activities and often responds to aspirin or Tylenol and stress-reduction techniques such as meditation.

A study that compared placebo, the SSRI Celexa, and the tricyclic Elavil in chronic tension headaches showed that Elavil, but not Celexa, was better than placebo at headache prevention (Ashina, Bendtsen, & Jensen, 2004). Remeron is also effective in prevention of chronic tension headaches (Bendtsen & Jensen, 2004). In patients who have migraine with aura, Lamictal has benefit for headache prevention (Lampl et al., 2005).

Irritable bowel syndrome often occurs with depression or anxiety disorders. It is characterized by cramping, bloating, urgency to defecate, often diarrhea or constipation, and sensitivity to many specific foods. Sometimes drugs used to treat depression also treat irritable bowel syndrome by acting on the serotonin system. An example is Remeron, which blocks serotonin 3 receptors. Often low doses of the tricyclic antidepressants such as Elavil are used by gastroenterologists in an attempt to both exploit the anticholinergic effect that slows down bowel motility and to take advantage of the pain-decreasing effect.

Pain associated with various forms of arthritis that involve degeneration or inflammation of joints is best treated primarily with anti-inflammatory drugs such as aspirin or other nonsteroidal anti-inflammatory drugs (NSAIDs), but again the pain-reducing effects of the tricyclic antidepressants and the dual-action drugs such as Effexor and Cymbalta may be of benefit. Here a word of caution is warranted: The NSAIDs may cause stomach irritation or even an ulcer; the SSRI and SNRI drugs decrease stickiness of platelets (as do antiplatelet drugs) and have an anticoagulant effect so that blood clots more slowly. If an NSAID is used long-term with an SSRI or SNRI antidepressant, there is increased risk of dangerous gastrointestinal bleeding. Acid-suppressing drugs may limit this increased risk (de Abajo & Garcia-Rodriguez, 2008).

Painful peripheral neuropathy (a nerve disorder) may be idiopathic, meaning that there is no known cause, or it may be due to a vitamin deficiency, alcoholism, or diabetes. Neuropathies may respond to dual-action antidepressants like tricyclic antidepressants, Effexor, and Cymbalta, or to some anticonvulsants such as Neurontin (gabapentin) and Lyrica.

Case Example: Headaches and Bleeding Ulcer

Paul was a charming 55-year-old married man who traveled the country as a managing sales representative for a consumer product company. He had come under my care after his severe panic attacks forced him to run out of an airplane as its door was being shut in preparation for takeoff. He improved rapidly on a tricyclic and later SSRI antidepressants and soon could fly easily. We settled on a regimen of Lexapro, blood pressure medications (which both prevented most of his migraine headaches and lowered blood pressure), and Klonopin as needed for anxiety. He drank no alcohol.

One day, while attending a business meeting in Las Vegas, Paul had a headache and thought he had food poisoning. He was hospitalized and diagnosed with a bleeding ulcer leading to severe anemia. Afterward, he commented that he had been using a lot of aspirin for tension headaches around the time of the incident. He was warned by his internist to use no more aspirin or other NSAID drugs; Tylenol would be his medication for nonmigraine headaches from now on.

Stage-of-Life Considerations

Pregnant and breast-feeding women and geriatric patients present special challenges to the management of depression. Fortunately, a variety of useful data on treating people at these stages of life has allowed us to learn much more about safe and effective treatment.

Pregnancy

Because major depression occurs in peak reproductive years, the issue of antidepressants in pregnancy is quite important. Antepartum depression is quite common, and the postpartum period is the highest risk time in a woman's life for developing mood episodes of either depression or mania. This is probably due to the major hormonal shifts that occur abruptly at the end of pregnancy.

Although the purist would hope that a woman would be off of anti-depressants at the time of conceiving, this isn't always possible or practical. Over half of pregnancies in the United States are unplanned. The most typical scenario is for a patient to call the doctor saying that she just missed her period and purchased a home pregnancy test and the result turned out positive. She asks, usually in a state of anxious panic, what she should do. The first step is to decide whether she plans to keep the pregnancy. If she does want to keep it, the type of treatment is very relevant.

Some women find that pregnancy is protective against depressive episodes, although this long-held belief has been challenged recently and is probably a myth. It appears that risk factors for depression during pregnancy involve unplanned pregnancy, lack of psychosocial support (or an abusive or abandoning significant other), and prior history of depressive episodes.

RISK OF RELAPSE OF DEPRESSION IN PREGNANCY

A study of 201 women who became pregnant showed that depressive relapse occurred in 26% of women who remained on antidepressant medication and 68% of women who discontinued antidepressant medication (Cohen et al., 2006; Cohen, Nonacs, et al., 2004). The authors cautioned that women who are well on antidepressants are not protected by pregnancy; in fact, for women who go off their antidepressant during pregnancy, the risk of becoming depressed is five times higher than it is for women who continue their medication. Among women who discontinued antidepressants around the time of conception, 42% resumed taking them during pregnancy (Cohen, Altshuler, Stowe, & Faraone, 2004).

Other risks of discontinuing medication during pregnancy include the tendency of depressed women to get less prenatal health care (S. M. Marcus, 2009), and greater incidence of postpartum depression and its negative effect on mother-infant attachment (Seimyr, Sjogren, Welles-Nystrom, & Nissen, 2009). The chance of the physiologic effects on the mother's depression (including an increase in stress hormones; Oberlander, Weinberg, et al., 2008) presenting harm to the fetus may result in premature birth, lower birth weight, and smaller head circumference, among other problems (S. M. Marcus, 2009). It may affect the infant's stress response and temperament (E. P. Davis et al., 2007). A meta-analysis of studies of pregnancies that did or did not involve the mother taking an antidepressant (total 3,567 pregnancies) showed that the risk of spontaneous abortion was 12.4% on an antidepressant drug versus 8.7% off antidepressants. There were no differences among antidepressant classes, and the authors commented that the depression itself might account for some of this difference (Hemels, Einarson, Koren, Lanctot, & Einarson, 2005).

GENERAL APPROACH TO CARE

The general approach to planned pregnancy would be to try to taper off of all nonessential drugs prior to beginning the pregnancy. This is especially important with benzodiazepines (such as Klonopin and Ativan), as these drugs can take a long time to taper. Although generally safe in pregnancy, they are contraindicated in women who want to breast-feed. Whether a drug is essential is determined by how frequently and how severely ill the person gets, based on her prior history. An individual who has had only mild episodes of depression or hypomania that were widely spaced in time might choose to take the risk of having some symptoms early in pregnancy in order to be off of psychiatric medications, whereas a person who previously had very severe depressive episodes leading to tremendous self-neglect, malnutrition, substance abuse, or suicide attempts might choose to remain on her antidepressant and avoid the risks of depression throughout the pregnancy. The postpartum episode must also be evaluated in terms of whether there are or have been any psychotic features that involve the baby. If the mother believes that the baby is not hers or represents some very evil force, there is risk of harming the baby, and this can be a reason for immediate hospitalization or at least providing a protective and supportive significant other to take care of the baby during the woman's recovery.

The general approach to prevention of postpartum depression is to carefully inquire about what has worked in previous episodes of depression and use the same treatment again. One study looked at prevention of postpartum depression in women who had it at the conclusion of previous pregnancies. This study gave women the antidepressant that was previously effective for them immediately upon birth of the child and demonstrated that women treated this way had a much lower risk of developing postpartum depression than those who were given medicine only if the depression actually developed (Austin et al., 2008; Chabrol & Callahan, 2007; Daley, Macarthur, & Winter, 2007; Hanusa, Scholle, Haskett, Spadaro, & Wisner, 2008; Howard, Hoffbrand, Henshaw, Boath, & Bradley, 2005; Kidd, 2007; Lee & Chung, 2007; McQueen, Montgomery, Lappan-Gracon, Evans, & Hunter, 2008). Another approach to prevention of postpartum depression is cognitive-behavioral therapy (Cho, Kwon, & Lee, 2008). In one study, just a single cognitive-behavioral prevention session during hospitalization was found to have a robust preventive effect at 4 to 6 weeks postpartum (Chabrol et al., 2002).

SSRIs

Among antidepressant classes, SSRIs are the first choice. In a review of health plan databases including 118,935 births from 1996 to 2005, it was noted that SSRI use increased from 1.5% to 6.2% of pregnant women over this time period. Overall, 7.6% of pregnant women had taken some antidepressant medication during the last 2 years of the study (Andrade et al., 2008). This would imply that as the SSRI antidepressants have become first-line treatments, clinicians are considering the risk/benefit ratio more favorable.

BREAST-FEEDING

A common question is whether antidepressants can be taken by the mother while breast-feeding. Any antidepressant that is given to a woman during pregnancy will enter the fetal circulation and the baby will be born with some antidepressant in its system. Similarly, any antidepressant that is given to a breast-feeding woman will be present in the breast milk. The interesting and surprising fact is that sometimes an antidepressant is present in the breast milk yet undetectable in the breast-feeding infant. The probable explanation is that absorption of the drug from breast milk is very minimal because an infant's hepatic enzyme system is not mature enough to allow metabolism of the antidepressant. One expert consensus panel concluded that Zoloft appears to be one of the best-studied and safest antidepressants for the breast-feeding woman and her baby (L. L. Altshuler et al., 2001a, 2001b).

Case Report: A Model's Pregnancy

Kay was a beautiful 39-year-old former model with two healthy children ages 4 and 7 years. She had been treated for panic disorder by the neurosurgeon who had operated on her painful neuroma years earlier. Kay was doing well on Pamelor (nortriptyline) and Klonopin when she came in for her routine appointment 9 months after we had begun working together and announced that she was seeking a surrogate mother to have a baby for her and her husband. I was astonished and asked why, since she seemed youthful and healthy. She said that her obstetrician had told her she should never get pregnant while on her psychiatric medications. I begged to differ, and referred her for consultations with teratology experts who could further explain the slight risks of taking these medications while pregnant. She read many articles on pregnancy that I provided her, saw five expert physicians for detailed counseling, and decided to get pregnant. She was very proud to show off her new daughter and to have made a very well-informed decision to carry the baby herself with full awareness of the slight risks of taking medication during pregnancy.

CONCERNS REGARDING RISK

The data presented here are mixed, and controversy remains about the potential risks of antidepressant use in pregnancy, but overall, the majority of studies conclude that the increase in risk to the baby from the mother's use of antidepressants is small.

It appears that the tricyclic antidepressant drugs are quite safe in pregnancy, and there is extensive literature supporting this. Similarly, the SSRI antidepressants appear safe in pregnancy, with the largest database available for Prozac and smaller databases available for the other SSRI antidepressants. A recent warning recommended avoiding Paxil during pregnancy due to a higher risk of birth defects than with other antidepressants. There have been a few cases of pulmonary hypertension reported in infants whose mothers took Prozac during pregnancy. Wellbutrin was the only antidepressant that had an FDA category that was slightly better than the other antidepressants, but it is now designated as category C, comparable to the SSRIs.

ANTIDEPRESSANTS IN THE LATE GESTATIONAL PERIOD

The use of SSRI antidepressants after the 20th week of pregnancy has been associated with an increased risk of primary pulmonary hypertension in the newborn infant (C. Chambers, Moses-Kolko, & Wisner, 2007; C. D. Chambers et al., 2006). It is interesting that these drugs had been on the market for over 15 years before this association was found, and a hazard that takes this long to detect is obviously rare. Another study of SSRI-treated mothers suggested that the rate of congenital abnormalities is 1.4%, comparable to that of the general population, but that high-dose fluoxetine may be associated with low birth weight (Hendrick et al., 2003). Comparing depressed mothers who were not treated with medication to depressed mothers receiving SSRI antidepressants during pregnancy (and matching mothers for illness variables), Oberlander, Warburton, Misri, Aghajanian, and Hertzman (2006) found that the babies of mothers taking medication were more likely to have low birth weight and respiratory distress. Still another study suggested that SSRI exposure was a risk factor for atrial septal defect (a very specific heart defect), and that SSRI plus benzodiazepine use was a risk factor for congenital heart defects in general (Oberlander, Warburton, et al., 2008).

There is a neonatal behavioral syndrome associated with late-gestational SSRI exposure. This syndrome is usually mild and disappears within 2 weeks, but it can include nervous, motor, respiratory, and gastrointestinal symptoms. Rare serious symptoms may include seizures, dehydration, excessive weight loss, fever, or need for intubation (Moses-Kolko et al., 2005). In one study, the neonatal discontinuation syndrome was described as mild in 10 of 60 infants exposed to SSRI antidepressants and severe in 8 of those infants (Levinson-Castiel, Merlob, Linder, Sirota, & Klinger, 2006). Transient neonatal SSRI discontinuation symptoms are not associated with developmental problems at 2 or 8 months of age (Oberlander et al., 2004).

Three reviews concluded that there is no significant increased risk of malformations in infants exposed to newer antidepressants during the last trimester, compared to infants with no exposure in utero (A. Einarson, 2005; A. Einarson, Schachtschneider, Halil, Bollano, & Koren, 2005; T. R. Einarson & Einarson, 2005; Gentile, 2005a, 2005b, 2006).

Tricyclic or SSRI antidepressant use late in pregnancy is associated with a higher risk of preterm birth and perinatal complications (R. L. Davis et al., 2007). There was no difference in rates of major obstetrical or neonatal problems between SSRI and tricyclic antidepressants (Pearson et al., 2007).

The Motherisk Program in Canada assessed the effects of antidepressant exposure throughout pregnancy on the child's IQ, language, and behavior at ages 15 to 71 months. In utero exposure to tricyclic antidepressants or fluoxetine was compared with a nondepressed group not receiving antidepressants. No effects of drug exposure during pregnancy were found on any of these child outcome measures. It is interesting that maternal depression did have a significant adverse effect on the child's IQ and language (Nulman et al., 2002). In contrast, a small study of children born to mothers taking SSRIs during pregnancy compared to those who were drug-free showed some slowing of psychomotor development between 6 and 40 months of age (Casper et al., 2003). The length of time necessary for such children to show catch-up development has not yet been studied.

MOST CONCERNING MEDICATIONS
The drugs that appear more harmful in pregnancy include MAO inhibitors, Depakote, and Tegretol. The MAO inhibitors can interfere with drugs used to stop the progress of false labor. Depakote and Tegretol are associated with abnormalities in formation of the neural tube. Neural tube defects include spina bifida (an opening and deformation of the spine), anencephaly (the child is born without a brain), and encephalocele (defects in the infant's skull). Complications of these defects include hydrocephalus (fluid accumulating in the brain), paralysis of the legs, mental retardation or learning disabilities, and death. Lamictal is the anticonvulsant of choice in pregnancy in the opinion of many experts in epilepsy, though there is increased chance of cleft palate, a congenital malformation. Lithium is associated with cardiovascular abnormalities, but the risk of this is actually quite small: Although risk of Ebstein's anomaly is twice that in the general population (relative risk), the absolute risk is only 0.5%. Many doctors consider lithium one of the safer drugs in pregnancy.

INFORMATION AND HELP

Patients or clinicians who are facing the question of planning pregnancy in the context of psychiatric medication treatment are advised to contact a teratology (birth defect) information center or expert at a major university medical center for up-to-date information and counseling. Also, contacting the manufacturer of the current medication is a quick and easy way to get the latest pregnancy information that has been reported to the company.

Geriatric Depression

Depression is not a normal part of aging or being medically ill! Depression in the elderly deserves a very careful evaluation and should never be ignored or downplayed, because it may substantially worsen quality of life and even shorten life. Whereas 4.4% of older adults (people 65 years and older) meet full criteria for a mood disorder such as depression, up to 20% have significant symptoms of depression (NMHA, 2006). Only about half of these older adults who acknowledge that they may have mental health problems receive treatment from a health care provider, and only a fraction of those (3%) receive specialty mental health services—the lowest rate among any adult age group (NMHA, 2006).

Depression in people over 65 years of age involves several features that occur more frequently than in middle adult life. These include the diagnostic challenge of differentiating new-onset from recurrent depression, cumulative losses, traumatic events and other stressors, greater chance of medical causes of depression, and greater risk of both drug interactions and drug side effects. Depression in old age is also more likely to involve early insomnia, agitation, hypochondriasis, delusions, and atypical presentation.

In the STAR*D study mentioned earlier, a number of variables emerged as prominent features of geriatric depression: These patients reported longer durations of illness, a later age at onset of their first major depressive episode, more of these episodes, and, of course, more general medical comorbidity. Within an episode of depression, insomnia that occurs in the middle of the night with difficulties in getting back to sleep (middle insomnia), or that wakes them in the early hours of the morning without resumption of sleep (terminal insomnia), is more common in this age group. There is less irritability than in younger cohorts, and less of a tendency to oversleep. Older people are more likely to hold negative views of themselves, and to have symptoms consistent with generalized anxiety disorder, social phobia, panic disorder, and drug abuse. They are less likely to report prior suicide attempts. That said, according to the National Mental Health Association, the highest rate of suicide for any age group (19.4 per 100,000) is among people age 85 and older, and the second-highest rate of suicide (17.7 per 100,000) is among those between age 75 and 84 (NMHA, 2006). Single Caucasian males are at highest risk.

When an individual presents with depression after the age of 65 years, longitudinal course of illness is critically important. It is quite possible that there has been a highly recurrent illness beginning 20 to 50 years earlier. In that case, the pattern of factors triggering the episodes may be an important clue to treatment. For example, romantic losses, alcohol excess, or fall-winter onset may be clues to potentially beneficial interventions. If there has been treatment of previous episodes of depression, what was helpful before may be helpful now. If there was long-term preventive treatment of depression, was stopping it associated with the current episode? A new onset of depression in the elderly with no previous history of a mood disorder is a very strong reason to do a very thorough history, physical, and lab examination to look for possible medical problems that could be at cause.

Cumulative losses are a very challenging part of aging. As people approach old age, they have often had children move away, friends or close relatives die or move away, jobs end with retirement, and numerous other losses. Complicating these factors is the fact that many elderly individuals have losses in physical health. Sometimes these are catastrophic, such as stroke or heart attack. Sometimes they entail loss of function, such as inability to go running due to hip pain or inability to participate in an exercise class due to back pain. Sometimes erectile dysfunction or loss of sexual drive occurs in an individual who valued and enjoyed sexuality and has a partner who is still eager to be sexually active. The psychological reactions to these losses may trigger memories and feelings from earlier losses such as a parental death or divorce.

Case Example: Loss of Youth and Identity

Mimi was a very bright, charming, witty, youthful 76-year-old woman who was referred by her second husband (also my patient) and her therapist. She felt pushed into making the appointment by their saying that her medication of 10 years, Zoloft, was not working. She had taken this medication since the death of her first husband but reported that her depression history went back much further, probably to college days. She had a family history of depression in many relatives.

Mimi had enjoyed a very successful career as a prosecuting attorney before retiring at age 72. She remarried the following year and relocated to be with her husband. However, she felt isolated in her new community and was not making new friends or participating in her church. She had applied for local jobs but was not hired. "Four years ago I was a federal attorney," Mimi said in frustration. "Now when people look at me, all they see is a little old lady." She felt down, negative, and lost.

I hoped to boost Mimi's antidepressant effectiveness by switching her to a dual-mechanism drug and augmenting it if necessary. I knew, though, that the psychotherapist's contribution to her care was essential, as Mimi's sense of purpose in life was so clearly connected to her career. She would undoubtedly benefit from acknowledging the great accomplishments of her life, focusing on her new relationship and ways of enjoying retirement, connecting with a religious group, and possibly teaching a class at a nearby law school. It was important for her to develop a sense that life was not over when she stopped working.

Medical issues become more common in old age. The chances that a chronic infection, chronic pulmonary disease, heart disease, or cancer is developing or contributing to depression must be evaluated. Sometimes the earliest presentation of a dementia is depressed mood. Equally important, many elderly patients are on multiple medications at the time of presenting for treatment of depression. There are two important issues here. Did a medication contribute to the development of depression? The most important clue to this is when a person becomes depressed within a few months of taking a new medicine. The other issue is that of drug interactions. The chance of suffering an adverse drug interaction increases rapidly with number of drugs being taken. Computerized drug interaction programs (such as Epocrates) can help to warn of risks and are usually available to the physician and pharmacist.

Case Example: "Not My Usual Depression"

Stu was a very bright, friendly man who had a long-term career as an investigator. He first presented to me at age 50 with multiple symptoms of panic disorder, ADHD, mild alcohol abuse, and mild depression. We worked well together over a period of 8 years, during which time he used very minimal alcohol, sought work in his new home town, and dealt with some long-term issues of rejection from family, difficulty getting work assignments, and the implications of having had ADHD long-term. He did well taking dextroamphetamine and low-dose Xanax, with intermittent use of an SSRI or SNRI at times of increasing depression or anxiety. He was doing well off of antidepressants for about 5 years, but then started complaining of feeling like he was "falling apart," so we resumed his antidepressant.

Stu noticed some new symptoms that were not part of his usual depression. He was losing his self-confidence and sense of humor. He felt a little dizzy and confused. Since starting the antidepressant he noticed some dislike for the taste of his occasional cigarettes, some increased frequency of urination, occasional nausea, and some flank pain in the kidney areas, along with weight loss. I feared that a serious medical problem was causing his symptoms, but he had no health insurance and no primary care physician, and he did not feel particularly ill. Nevertheless, at my urging, he reluctantly agreed to borrow money from relatives for screening lab tests. A few days later, I called to tell him that his prostate-specific antigen (PSA) was more than 400 times the upper limit of normal. I told him he needed to be hospitalized for a diagnostic workup and, a short time later, tests revealed metastatic prostate cancer. He took the news well and, in his usual investigative style, learned all he could about the disease, its treatment, and how to get indigent medical services at the local university hospital. He thanked me for insisting that he get the medical tests and for getting him into the medical care system so quickly. I was glad that I had listened to the new physical complaints and acted on the suspicion that medical problems could be involved.

Physiological reserves decrease with age. The ability of the cardiovascular system to adjust to changes in circulatory demand decreases. The body composition changes so that there is more fat and water and less lean muscle mass. The brain's ability to tolerate drugs that may cause sedation or confusion lessens. The ability of the liver and kidneys to metabolize and excrete drugs decreases. It is important that psychiatric medications are started at low dose then gradually titrated until benefit or side effects appear. Simplifying the drug regimen and eliminating nonessential drugs, preferably with once- or twice-daily dosing of each medication, are important for adherence.

For many reasons, the older tricyclic antidepressants present more hazards than the newer drugs. Among tricyclics, nortriptyline and desipramine are often considered safest. The anticholinergic effects of some tricyclics include dry mouth, blurred vision, constipation, and in extreme cases may include delirium. The postural hypotensive risks of the tricyclics may lead to light-headedness and falling when a person gets up quickly. For these reasons, the newer drugs such as SSRIs, Effexor, Remeron, and Wellbutrin are generally considered first-line; Norpramin (desipramine) and Pamelor (nortriptyline) are second-line; and other tricyclics, such as Elavil, Anafranil, and Sinequan, and the oral MAO inhibitors (Parnate and Nardil) are third-line drugs (Janicak et al., 2006; Kennedy, Lam, Nutt, & Thase, 2007). A caution about the SSRI and SNRI drugs in the elderly is the risk of hyponatremia, or low sodium in the blood, which may occur within a few weeks of starting an antidepressant and may be worsened by diuretics (water pills). Symptoms may include lethargy, disorientation, weakness, muscle cramps, anorexia, nausea, headaches, memory impairment, difficulty concentrating, confusion, and even seizures. If these symptoms occur, a physician can order a blood test of electrolyte levels and make a diagnosis so that the situation can be corrected quickly.

Electroconvulsive therapy is also safe, highly effective, and sometimes life-saving in elderly individuals with severe depression (Sherman, 2009; Stoppe, Louza, Rosa, Gil, & Rigonatti, 2006).

10

Evaluating the Success or Failure of Pharmacotherapy

The success or failure of antidepressant treatment is evaluated somewhat differently in clinical studies versus clinical practice. Clinical studies of drugs, often performed by the drug manufacturer, usually look at the relatively short-term effect of the drug on a homogeneous population of study participants. Clinical practice, on the other hand, is much messier, with a diverse population being treated and the ultimate goal being long-term remission of symptoms, as well as recovery: the return to a satisfying, meaningful life.

This chapter discusses the difference between response and remission and defines the important concepts of relapse and recurrence. It also outlines the common causes of nonresponse to treatment, offers guidelines for improving tolerability of drugs, and addresses treatment-resistant depression.

Defining Response and Remission

Antidepressant response is the standard by which drugs are tested for marketing. A standardized depression rating scale is used to measure the severity of the depression every week during a clinical trial testing a new drug, and a 50% drop in symptom severity is considered a drug response; this typically occurs at a time point of 6 to 8 weeks, although investigational drugs typically show statistical gains on placebo much earlier. The Hamilton Depression Rating Scale (HAM-D) and Montgomery Asberg Depression Rating Scale (MADRS) are the most widely used ratings. Both focus on depression symptoms. Patient self-rating scales, such as the Beck and Zung depression rating scales, often complement the clinician-rated scales.

For many years, a 50% drop in depressive symptoms on clinician-rated scales such as the HAM-D or the MADRS has been the gold standard for U.S. Food and Drug Administration approval for marketing of antidepressant drugs. The result of two decades of antidepressant research, using the 50% drop in symptom intensity by 6–8 weeks to signify antidepressant "response," has been that all marketed antidepressants have been shown essentially equal in their effectiveness, all better than placebo, and that they differ from one another primarily in terms of side effects. Typically new drugs such as SSRI antidepressants have shown fewer side effects and fewer dropouts due to intolerability than the older tricyclic antidepressants.

If response is getting better, is remission getting well? In clinical practice (contrasted with drug studies), remission is defined as a time when the individual no longer has any depression symptoms persisting beyond a very mild level. Some argue that depression is such an all-pervasive illness that additional long-term functional (in contrast to symptomatic) outcome measures should be considered, such as social and occupational functioning, health-related quality of life, and subjective sense of physical and mental health or disability (Bech, 2005). This more rigorous standard—known as recovery—has more recently been proposed as the ideal target of treatment (Zimmerman, Posternak, & Chelminski, 2005). Even symptom-free, a person with no plans for the future or healthy interpersonal relationships might not consider herself "well." Relationships with self and others, as well as future-mindedness, are excellent indicators of well-being. Clinicians should ask patients about their relationships—how many close friends they have, how often they see them, how their relationships with family are going. How do they feel about their future? Do they have plans? Are they motivated and is there evidence of follow-through? How do they describe their relationship with themselves? Do they have a healthy self-concept? Global quality of life is the ultimate goal of aggressive treatment of mood disorders. Where remission can take a month or two (or even longer) to achieve, full recovery may require still more patience.

Methodology of Clinical Trials

In order to gain FDA permission to market a drug, a pharmaceutical company must provide data on at least two independent, double-blind, placebo-controlled studies demonstrating a moderate effect size, a statistical measure demonstrating difference between ratings (in this case, ratings of response) of patients taking the new drug and those on an inert placebo, which is usually a sugar pill. Often three to five trials are actually performed to demonstrate success in two or more of the studies because some studies have high placebo-response rates (due to very nice researchers treating patients kindly) or low drug-response rates (due to initial uncertainty about appropriate drug-dosing and side effect management). Some of these studies have a third arm of randomization to an old established drug and are not adequately powered statistically to see if the new drug is truly better or not as good as the old drug; the old drug is there to demonstrate that the study population is responsive to some drug. This active comparator drug is a requirement for many European drug submissions for marketing.

Antidepressant efficacy trials usually show a placebo response rate at 6 or 8 weeks of about 25–30% and a drug response rate of about 65–70%. Remission rates, unfortunately, are substantially lower, typically being about 25% for placebo, 35% for SSRI antidepressants, and approximately 41% for mixed-mechanism drugs such as Effexor.

Such clinical drug trials enroll outpatients who are willing to be randomized to drug or placebo in order to receive free treatment. Typically, these volunteers for trials must meet very stringent criteria to get into a study—they must meet a minimum level of depression severity and duration, and they must not meet criteria for bipolar illness, have psychotic features to their depression, significant suicidal ideation, or substance abuse within the 6 months previous to study entry. Some trials also exclude for various anxiety disorders or other Axis I and II disorders. They must have no significant laboratory abnormalities and must not be taking any psychiatric medications. Questionable criteria, not widely used, include brief (less than a month) or lengthy (more than 2 years) episodes, selected nonsevere Axis I disorders including dysthymia, and medical illnesses. Patients are not allowed to start psychotherapy while participating in the study, though continuation of ongoing psychotherapy is permissible in most; in these cases, the therapy must be continued to minimize the effect of change on treatment response.

The use of such rigorous inclusion and exclusion criteria represents an attempt by the pharmaceutical company to have very well-defined patient samples that are likely to demonstrate homogeneity and to have a reasonable chance of drug-responsive illness. Such criteria may contribute to overestimation of the drug's performance. Study patients are not typical of clinical practice patients; 75–90% of patients who come to a psychiatrist for treatment of depression do not qualify for participation in studies (depending on the number of exclusion criteria employed), yet most benefit from antidepressant medications (Zetin & Hoepner, 2007). The STAR*D study, reported later, attempted to enroll the types of patients that primary care providers and psychiatrists actually see and treat, and its results are therefore more generalizable to real-world practice.

Patients who *do* qualify for drug studies are typically given a placebo for the first week or two (known as the lead-in period) without their knowledge so that individuals who have a placebo response are eliminated from the double-blind phase of the study. The assumption is that they do not really need a drug to get better, and their inclusion in the study may confound meaningful results by minimizing effect size between drug and placebo. Also, during this placebo lead-in time, many blood tests are analyzed to make sure that the depression is not due to a major medical problem and to keep people with significant lab test abnormalities out of the study.

After the placebo lead-in period, patients remaining are given a baseline depression rating and then randomized to active drug or placebo. Typically, the drug is given at a fixed dose, so that doses are not changed for patients who may require a higher dose to demonstrate efficacy or a lower dose to minimize side effects. Efficacy may be compromised in this practice.

After the trial has run for 6 to 8 weeks (depending on study design), with data having been gathered weekly, response and remission rates are calculated by a statistical analysis technique known as intent-to-treat last-observation-carried-forward. Intent-to-treat means that any patient who attends a baseline evaluation of their depression after the placebo lead-in phase is counted as a subject in the study, even if they drop out before the next study visit. Patients who drop out during the study then have their last observation carried forward; that is, they are treated statistically as though they had stayed in the study, with their last depression measurement assumed not to have changed over the time that they were not seen. Occasional studies attempt to predict what would have happened to those patients based on their initial ratings and the longer term course of the completers who were assigned to the same treatment (mixed model for repeated measures method of analysis). This effectively means that dropouts are counted as not responding to treatment because most dropouts have either failed to respond or had unacceptable side effects.

Relapse and Recurrence

The difference between relapse and recurrence has to do with when the symptoms reemerge relative to how long the depression would have lasted if left untreated. For example, if a patient whose depression would have lasted a year if untreated experiences the reemergence of symptoms (despite ongoing treatment) sometime before a year has passed, that would be considered a relapse. If the depression symptoms reemerge at a time beyond the normal duration of the average untreated depressive episode, this is considered a new episode or a recurrence.

There has been some confusion in the definition of these terms because each has been "operationalized" (defined in terms that can be objectively measured) inconsistently for use in various clinical trials of antidepressants and psychotherapeutic modalities. However, an excellent description of the terms has been provided by the American College of Neuropsychopharmacology (ACNP). According to the ACNP, relapse may occur after a patient has achieved remission (but before she has achieved recovery), and recurrence may occur following recovery from a depressive episode. Remission "should be ascribed after 3 consecutive weeks during which minimal symptom status (absence of both sadness and reduced interest/pleasure along with the presence of fewer than three additional symptoms) is maintained," and recovery "after 4 months following the onset of remission, during which a relapse has not occurred" (Rush, Kraemer, et al., 2006, p. 1841). This is supported by naturalistic data on long-term outcome of major depression, which suggested that 4 to 6 months of no more than one or two mild depressive symptoms is a reasonable time point for declaring a person to have achieved recovery from a depressive episode (Furukawa et al., 2008).

Relapse and recurrence carry discrete risk factors. Those for recurrence include residual symptoms, two or more prior depressive episodes, chronicity of depression lasting over 2 years, family history of mood disorders, coexisting anxiety disorders or dysthymia (a low-grade depression for 2 years or longer), and onset of first depressive episode prior to age 20 or after age 60. Predictors of relapse (in addition to those listed for recurrence) include residual symptoms such as sleep disturbance, fatigue, or low energy and cognitive problems, the heightened emotional sensitivity that often accompanies improvement of depression, and a slow return of physiologic variables to their normal state, such as cerebral blood flow and cortisol secretion. Other factors affecting relapse and recurrence include temperament, personality structure and type (such as a depressive, anxious-sensitive, or "neurotic" personality), stressful life event characteristics, and poor change in dysfunctional attitudes and in extreme thinking.

Personalized Rating Scale

Many clinicians do not use rating scales, but they can be invaluable in predicting signs of relapse or recurrence. We recommend that patients create their own personalized daily rating scale. It can be very helpful to put the most important symptoms on a graph so that symptom intensity over time can be followed during treatment. A placebo response (to your medication) might be very brief, showing quick improvement of symptoms with return of the symptoms after a few days, while true drug response usually comes on gradually over a period of a few weeks and is lasting. It is also very important to use this graph to look at whether brief worsenings of symptoms are related to premenstrual days, life stressors, or possibly times of missing prescribed medications or using too much alcohol or abusable drugs. This Personalized Daily Rating Scale charts and rates the same items and variables as the Life Chart does, but differs in that it is prospective rather than retrospective, is charted by days of the month rather than months of the year, and symptoms rather than episodes are the focus. A sample is included at the end of this chapter, as is a simplified version, the Core Symptom Severity Chart.

On the Core Symptom Severity Chart, the patient can chart three target symptoms over the span of 31 days, assigning a severity rating ranging from awful to bad, fair, good, or excellent. This chart also notes what medications are being taken and their doses, and there is a space for recording dates of the menstrual period, any changes in medication or missed doses, use of alcohol or drugs, and positive or negative life stressors. This chart is most helpful when begun just before starting or changing medications.

Patients can also get the Quick Inventory of Depression Symptoms Self Report (QIDS-SR) and present it to their doctor. Used in the STAR*D trial, it is the most modern and comprehensive self-rated depression rating scale designed for outpatient use, and is available online (www.ids-qids.org).

As mentioned earlier, it is very important to prepare a list of depression symptoms as well as any other potential symptoms that might later be confused with side effects. Depression symptoms may include changes in sleeping, energy, appetite, movement, enthusiasm, sexual drive or response, thinking, or feeling. Potential physical symptoms that might later be confused with side effects could include indigestion, nausea, abdominal pain, diarrhea or constipation, insomnia or daytime sleepiness, problems in sexual functioning, headaches, tremor, coordination or muscle problems, joint pain, and skin rashes. Simply having a baseline list of what the symptoms are before starting medication can be very helpful in deciding whether a new symptom is due to the drug or might be the worsening of something that was there before drug was started. You may choose to use the Guide for Review of Symptoms, found at the conclusion of Chaspter 7, and the Core Symptom Severity Chart, provided at the end of this chapter.

Potential Causes of Nonresponse

Only 20% of patients experience true resistance to treatment with medications. For the rest, there are several common causes of drug failure, most of which can be worked with by the doctor. The most common are inaccurate diagnosis, inappropriate treatment, and inadequate dose or duration of treatment, to which patients often contribute by not taking medications as prescribed and adhering to the agreed-upon treatment plan. Co-occuring psychiatric diagnoses (especially anxiety and personality disorders) and substance abuse complicate treatment, as do comorbid medical illnesses and some of the medications used to treat them. Certain subtypes of depression are difficult to treat, as is depression owing largely to difficult life circumstances. For this psychotherapy may be a necessary component. Some patients have individual physiologic differences, including poor gastrointestinal absorption of the medication, a tendency toward delayed response, and rapid metabolism, leading to very low and possibly ineffective drug levels (Kornstein & Schneider, 2001).

Inadequate dose was a much greater problem when tricyclic antidepressants were in widespread use. At that time, the strategy of dosing was to "start low, and go slow, but go." This meant that often the drug dosage initially had to be kept very low to allow accommodation and make the side effects tolerable, with the dose eventually being increased to approach a therapeutic level. The most common mistake was failing to increase the dose to the point where the person was either getting substantial benefit or having side effects. This problem sometimes happens with Effexor now, because it has an ascending dose-response curve, but it doesn't often happen with the SSRI drugs or Wellbutrin. The SSRI antidepressants are usually started at full therapeutic dose. If they aren't (usually because the patient has panic or other anxiety symptoms or some initial nausea), they are usually titrated to adequate dose fairly easily. A therapeutic dose of a drug typically falls within the range described in the FDA package insert. Remember, though, that this dose range was determined by the manufacturer and is based on large population statistics. The lower end of the dose range typically represents the point at which the drug separates from placebo statistically, and the upper end indicates the point at which side effects outweigh benefit and above which additional benefit is not likely: Some individuals respond to less than usual doses because they are "slow metabolizers" of drugs; a small dose accumulates in their body to a full therapeutic level because they cannot efficiently metabolize and excrete the drug. Others may absorb the drug poorly from the intestine or be "fast metabolizers" who break down and excrete the drug quickly, so they need an unusually high dose of the same drug to experience any effect.

Inadequate duration of a medication trial is another cause of nonresponse. The patient may take longer to respond to an average dose of medication than others due to physiologic differences. Most antidepressant efficacy trials run for 8 weeks because this is often the amount of time it takes to demonstrate a good effect size between active drug and placebo. Some patients may take as long as 12 weeks to respond, however, and indeed the STAR*D trial allowed 12 weeks for each treatment step. Typically in clinical practice a couple of weeks will determine if a medicine is tolerable and a period of about a month or two will determine if it is effective, but some patients do require more time. The doctor and patient must weigh benefit versus risk in either quitting a medication at about 8 weeks after reaching full therapeutic dose if there is not a robust response at that time, or waiting until 12 weeks or so before making that decision. In the first scenario the patient may discontinue a potentially helpful medication, adding it to a possibly growing list of things that didn't work, feeling less hopeful, and having to start over again with a new medication, all the while remaining depressed. In the second scenario, the patient spends 4 or so additional weeks miserably depressed, knowing that if he has not enjoyed good response by 8 weeks, chances are even less likely with each additional week that passes. To help the doctor and patient make this decision, they should look for early signs of improvement. Patients who go on to respond favorably to a medication often enjoy some lifting of mood in as little as 2 weeks, typically with increased energy, more motivation or ability to make decisions, and a less negative attitude. These changes may be very subtle, and often those close to the patient will notice them before the patient does. Another reason medication trials may be of inadequate duration is that the amount of time allowed for good response should begin once the patient has reached a full therapeutic dose, and not during the period of titration to that dose. Some patients take more time than others to titrate to full therapeutic dose because they require an unusually high dose due to metabolic differences, as described above. Others need to titrate very slowly due to treatment-emergent anxiety or other problems with initiating the medication.

Psychiatric illness may also contribute to drug failure. Commonly, there is an incorrect diagnosis. If a person with bipolar illness is diagnosed with unipolar major depression, they may be given an antidepressant without a mood stabilizer, which at best will not stop their mood cycling, and at worst may exacerbate it. Someone with borderline personality disorder misdiagnosed with bipolar illness may find that medications take the edge off their symptoms but little else; this patient may need to add intensive trauma-specific or psychodynamic psychotherapy, or specialized cognitive-behavioral work like dialectical behavior therapy. Some subtypes of depression are more difficult to treat than others, including atypical subtype, "double" depression (major depression superimposed on dysthymia), psychotic depression, bipolar depression (particularly if rapid-cycling), and severe and/or melancholic depression. While symptoms of anxiety are normally experienced in depression and resolve with the mood episode, comorbid anxiety disorders—including panic disorder, post-traumatic stress disorder, obsessive-compulsive disorder, social phobia, and generalized anxiety disorder—may complicate depression treatment and often require individual attention. Other conditions requiring special attention include somatoform and eating disorders, and personality disorders.

There are a few factors that the pharmacologist can do little to compensate for, and this is because antidepressants are not antimisery pills. Psychotherapy is a better option for addressing many personality issues, as well as certain temperaments (stable patterns present since very early childhood) including cyclothymic, anxious-sensitive, and depressive temperaments. It can help with life circumstances such as relationship difficulties, stage-of-life issues, poor economic or social circumstances, poor social and occupational functioning, or adjusting to a devastating medical diagnosis or chronic and disabling condition. Psychotherapy can also boost medication treatment by improving adherence to a therapeutic regimen, and helping the patient to improve lifestyle patterns and habits (Nemeroff, 2004).

Substance abuse is often hidden or denied. As we have discussed elsewhere, the person who is actively abusing alcohol, street drugs, stimulants, or narcotics is only adding fuel to the fire of depression and making it less likely that she will benefit from antidepressants.

Medical problems or drugs used to treat them may cause depression. Some medical problems such as cancer or HIV infection absolutely must be treated with life-saving (or -prolonging) drugs, and the doctor and patient must acknowledge that antidepressant treatment plus supportive counseling on accepting the implications of the disease will help but may not completely resolve the depression. Other times, the depression may be due to something as simple as hypothyroidism, estrogen deficiency (in perimenopausal women) or testosterone deficiency (in late-onset male depression), or vitamin deficiency, which can easily be treated.

Low folate levels, for example, are a risk factor for depression across several observational epidemiologic studies involving 15,315 participants (Gilbody, Lightfoot, & Sheldon, 2007), and low serum folate (but not low vitamin B12 or high homocysteine levels) are associated with lower response rates to fluoxetine (Prozac) initially and when fluoxetine is combined with augmentation agents. Folic acid is an inexpensive, safe, and well-tolerated supplement to other treatments for depression (Fava, 2007; M. J. Taylor, Carney, Geddes, & Goodwin, 2003). Since there is a genetic variant involving folate metabolism that is found more commonly among persons with depression, schizophrenia, and bipolar disorder (Gilbody, Lewis, & Lightfoot, 2007), a fully methylated form of the vitamin, called Deplin, bypasses this genetic defect. It may boost antidepressant effect with very little risk of side effects.

It is also possible for medications to cause depression. Reglan (metoclopramide), which is used for stomach problems, blood pressure medications that act on the brain (such as beta-blockers and clonidine), cancer drugs, interferon, and others may cause depression. The usual clue is the onset of depression within a month or two of starting a new medication. An "index of suspicion" is critical in making this diagnosis; it can be missed if the doctor and patient do not consider the possibility. Often the offending drug can be changed to one that has a much lower risk of affecting mood.

More than 50% of responders do not achieve remission, and residual symptoms are almost as common as nonresponse. Delayed remission is a significant cause for perceived drug failure. Risk factors for delayed remission include chronicity, longer length of episode, number of previous episodes, medical comorbidity, older age, Axis I or II psychiatric comorbidity, and severity.

Tolerability

Sometimes poor tolerability interferes with an adequate trial of antidepressant medication. If there is a side effect in the first week or two of treatment, the patient may decide to stop the drug rather than working with the doctor on managing it, by temporary dose reduction, for example, or taking the medication after food or at a different time of day. Cutting the initial drug dose in half for a week and then retrying the standard effective dose will substantially reduce most drug side effects. Sometimes impatience leads patient and doctor to change a drug before a 4- to 8-week trial has been completed, so no one knows if the drug would have been effective if it had been taken for a full trial.

There are several ways to make an antidepressant drug more tolerable. The first is to lower the dose, often to a tiny "baby dose" that the clinician believes is unlikely to make a substantial difference in the symptoms yet is very tolerable. After a few days at this very low dose, the medication can be gradually increased toward a standard therapeutic dose over a period of a few weeks. Sometimes splitting the drug dose into morning and evening portions or taking it at a different time of day (such as in the evening for a drug that causes drowsiness or in the morning if it causes insomnia) can be helpful. If there is some nausea, taking the drug after food or with a lot of fluids may help. A truly concerned doctor will often help to provide support and frequent visits or phone consultations during the early phase of the medication trial in order to try to make it as tolerable as possible. If the drug has been carefully tried and truly causes side effects that are not acceptable, it is quite reasonable to discontinue it and try something else.

Switching Medication

Sometimes a drug produces no response even when it is given an adequate trial. If there is truly no improvement in the main target symptoms after a month or two of taking medication at a proven effective and recommended dose, it is reasonable to give up on that drug and go on to a new class of drug. Some patients do require as many as 12 weeks at full dose to respond, but this is not very common. The chance of response peaks at around 6 to 8 weeks and begins to decrease after about 8 weeks.

There is a distinction, however, between improvement and response. Response indicates significant improvement and contributes to the decision to continue treatment with that medication. In the case of some improvement but nothing significant after several weeks, the doctor and patient must weigh the benefit of holding out for full response versus switching medications. This is where carefully charting symptom intensity comes into play, so that any signs of improvement will be noticed and this decision can be made in the best possible way.

If the drug is abandoned as being truly not helpful, we believe it is worthwhile to consider changing to a drug with a different mechanism of action. This is discussed in the next chapter.

Treatment-Resistant Depression

As many as 15% of patients diagnosed with a mood disorder eventually present with treatment-resistant or refractory depression (Berlim & Turecki, 2007). Having tried two or more medications from different pharmacologic classes for a reasonable duration (at least 4 weeks), they have failed to show adequate response, typically defined as 25% decrease in symptom severity (Hirschfeld et al., 2002; Souery et al., 1999). Thase and Rush (1997) outlined the following stages of treatment resistance:

Stage 1. Failure of a trial on one antidepressant for adequate dose and duration

Stage 2. Failure of a trial on a second antidepressant of a different class (mechanism of action)

Stage 3. Stage 2 plus failure on a tricyclic antidepressant

Stage 4. Stage 3 plus failure on an MAO inhibitor antidepressant

Stage 5. Stage 4 plus failure after a course of ECT

This approach could be criticized for not accounting for augmentation strategies that might place patients at intermediate levels of treatment resistance—for example, the patient who fails a trial on Prozac (stage 1) and then fails to respond to Prozac plus augmentation with lithium or thyroid hormone might be considered at a stage 1.5 level of treatment resistance. It must also be considered with the understanding that the tricyclic antidepressant and MAO inhibitors are not always reserved for more resistant cases, but may be selected at any stage with severity or subtype of depression in mind. Though this staging is perhaps imperfect and oversimplified, it at least provides some structure for researchers trying to describe patient populations for treatment resistance or "next step" studies.

Some individuals who have full response to an antidepressant and do quite well on it lose response over time. This may be part of the natural course of the illness, such as with rapid-cycling bipolar affective disorder in which spontaneous improvement and spontaneous worsening may occur several times a year regardless of the medication being used. Sometimes the full response is achieved and then pharmacologic tolerance, known as tachyphylaxis (loss of benefit), occurs. This was first described as "Prozac poop-out" in individuals who had taken that antidepressant for 1 to 3 years and found that it stopped working at that point. There have been several approaches to this, one of which involves increasing the dose of the antidepressant. Another approach involves the theory that long-term use of an SSRI may turn down the brain's dopamine system, leading to less sense of drive and reward. In this case, the addition of Wellbutrin or a stimulant such as Ritalin or Dexedrine can restore the dopamine function. Sometimes SSRI tachyphylaxis is treated by switching to a dual-acting drug such as Effexor; dual reuptake inhibitors generally carry less of a chance of tachyphylaxis than the SSRIs do.

__Personalized Daily Rating Scale__

Instructions

Similar to creating a retrospective Life Chart, **mood charting** increases awareness of how treatment, social rhythms, and life circumstances relate to mood. It also provides your clinician with a snapshot of your mood between visits.

On the grid provided for charting mood, rate your mood daily by severity. You may use two checkmarks if necessary to indicate highest and lowest mood on a particular day.

Mild depression may include low mood, a feeling of distress, and perhaps some social isolation, with little or no decrement to functioning. **Moderate depression** may cause significant impairment in usual activity at work, school, or in relationships. You may miss days from work, school or other regular activities. When **severely depressed**, you may be thoroughly incapacitated at home or in the hospital, unable to perform usual occupational, educational or social functions. Eating or grooming may be difficult.

Mild hypomania may include decreased need for sleep, increased energy, some irritability or elevated mood, and increase in racing thoughts, rapid speech, or social behavior. Impact of such symptoms may be minimal. At the **moderate level**, hypomania may include additional symptoms and impact productivity and ability to focus . Others may comment that your behavior is different from usual. **Severe mania** may include risky or uncontrolled behavior significant impact on work and relationships, concern for your safety and capacity for self-care, and may result inhospitalization or even incarceration.

Depression is sometimes agitated, marked by anger, irritability, agitation or overactivity, or rapid thoughts and a sense of being driven. About 40% of people with bipolar illness experience **dysphoric hypomania**, where there may be symptoms of hypomania or mania marked by irritability or anger. If this is experienced, check the box under that episode to indicate this quality of mood.

Two other boxes are provided, one for indicating the number of **switches in mood** occurring on a given day, and one (for women) indicating whether the day occurs during a **menstrual period.**

A box is included for charting symptoms other than depression, hypomania, or mania that are worrisome or distressing; any **substance abuse**. Symptoms may include:

• Insomnia, oversleeping or daytime sleepiness	• Fatigue	• Anxiety
	• Changes in appetite	• Agitation
• Paranoia or Hallucinations	• Impulsivity	• Irritability
	• Panic	• Other symptoms

List any **medications** and other treatments, along with the strength and how many units (e.g., pills taken; sessions of psychotherapy, ECT, exercise, or complementary therapies). Prescribed and over-the-counter medications should be listed, including herbals or other supplements and medications used for medical illness.

Chart **life events** that influence any changes in mood. Include any hospitalizations and suicide attempts. Life events may be rated on a scale of -4 to +4 for negative and positive influence on mood.

Years

Personal Daily Rating Scale

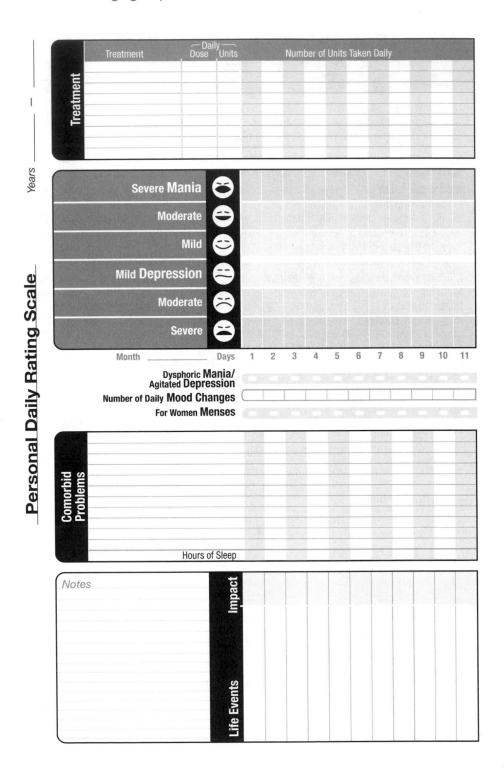

Personal Daily Rating Scale

Years

Treatment	Daily Dose	Units	Number of Units Taken Daily										
Lithium	300 mg	3	3	3	3	3	3						
Seroquel	25 mg	1 prn	1	1			1						
Lamictal	200 mg	1	1	1	1	1							
Lexapro	10 mg	1	1	1		1	1						
Provigil	200 mg	1/2	1/2	1/2	1	1/2	1/2						
Ativan	1 mg	1 prn	3		2	3							
Yoga	1 hr	3x/wk	1		1								
Psychotherapy	1 hr	1x/wk			1								

Personal Daily Rating Scale											
Severe **Mania**											
Moderate											
Mild	✓	✓		✓							
Mild **Depression**				✓	✓						
Moderate											
Severe											

Month _____ Days   1   2   3   4   5   6   7   8   9   10   11

Dysphoric Mania/ Agitated Depression   ✓

Number of Daily **Mood Changes**	0	1	1	2	0						

For Women Menses ✓ ✓

Comorbid Problems											
Insomnia	X	X			X						
Headache		X									
Anxiety	X	X	X	X	X						
Irritability				X							
Agitation			X								
Impulsivity			X	X							
Panic			X	X							
Fatigue											
Hours of Sleep	6	3	12	8	8						

Notes	Impact		+2	-3							
	Life Events		New roommate	Bad review at work							

Core Symptom Severity Chart

Instructions

This chart helps you to monitor the severity of your core symptoms on a daily basis. It is a tool you and your clinician can use to help guide your treatment.

List the **medications** you are currently taking in the spaces provided, including the total daily dose for each. Include any complementary medicines used.

Record each of your three most frequent, severe, or bothersome **symptoms** next to a symbol (o,+,x) in the Target Symptoms legend.
Frequently charted symptoms include:

- Mood
- Energy
- Sleep
- Anxiety
- Agitation
- Irritability

Using the symbols, chart the severity of each symptom daily, before or after taking your evening medication. Severity may be rated on a scale of 0–4, ranging from awful to bad, fair, good, and excellent.

A rating of excellent denotes a symptom status contributing to stability with excellent functioning and wellbeing.

Symptoms that contribute to severe decrement to functioning, suicidal ideation, or hospitalization may be rated as awful.

Where mood and energy are concerned, high mood or energy may be rated poorly if they are associated with discomfort, poor outcomes, or symptoms such as impulsivity, irritability, agitation, anxiety, or disorganization.

Throughout the month, make notes in the space provided regarding the occurrence of:

- Dates of menstrual period
- Use of alcohol or drugs
- Positive or negative life stressors
- Changes in medication
- Missed doses
- Hospitalization

Core Symptom Severity Chart

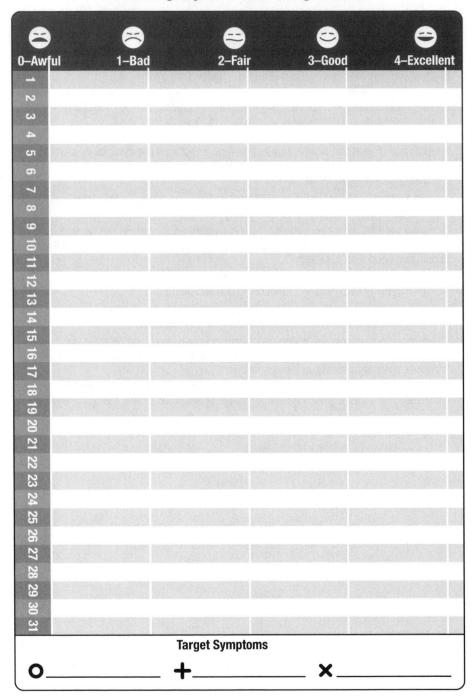

	0–Awful	1–Bad	2–Fair	3–Good	4–Excellent

Target Symptoms

O _____ +_____ ✕_____

Medication	Daily Dose

Notes

Name   **Month**

_____   _____

11

My Antidepressant Isn't Working. What Now? Sophisticated Approaches to Augmenting, Combining, and Switching Medicines

If a drug trial leads to an inadequate or partial response, the most frequent question facing the clinician and patient is whether to augment, combine, or switch drugs, or simply continue for a longer time on the current drug. *Augmenting* refers to adding a second medication that is not usually used as an antidepressant. *Combining* means adding a second antidepressant with a different mechanism of action while continuing the first drug. *Switching* implies discontinuing the first drug and trying a different drug, usually one with a different mechanism of action. Adding psychotherapy, if it is not already ongoing, is another option.

Many patients have to try several drugs, or combinations of drugs, to find the one that works best for them. How does one decide which strategy is best? As you read you may refer to the Algorithm for Augmentation and Switch Strategies, a decision tree illustrating steps in treatment adjustment that may be taken over time. This tool may be found at the end of the chapter.

Antidepressant Augmentation

Augmenting employs multiple mechanisms of drug action in the hope of achieving a more robust response. In an academic specialty clinic practice, major depression patients who are antidepressant nonresponders are most likely to have their antidepressant switched, whereas those who are partial responders are most likely to have their antidepressant augmented. Partial responders receiving augmentation do better than partial responders who have their medication switched (Papakostas, Petersen, Green, et al., 2005).

Partial response is more common than complete nonresponse in the outpatient setting, and augmenting is a reasonable approach for a partial responder because it means continuation of the first drug for a much longer trial, allowing it a better chance of working. Compared with switching, augmenting also has the advantage of avoiding discontinuation symptoms. The disadvantage of augmentation is that it may involve a more complex regimen, more drug cost, more risk of drug interactions, and perhaps more risk of side effects, although sometimes the side effects of the first drug are reduced by the addition of the second drug.

Mechanism of Action

It is important to understand that there are only a few basic mechanisms of action used by the currently available antidepressant drugs. Further, our understanding of that mechanism of action is compromised by the fact that humans do not participate in experiments involving basic science, thus the mechanism of action as we understand it is really what the drug does to a normal animal brain (in the living animal or test tube), which may be different from what it does in the brain of an ill human.

It is also helpful to consider that drug targets and true mechanism of action may not be one and the same. Whereas antidepressants target the transporters responsible for reuptake of neurotransmitters and the receptors to which these neurotransmitters bind, actual antidepressant effect happens "downstream" of the initial action of the drug. Chemical reactions known as second messenger systems inside the neuron result in the expression of new proteins. Indeed, research is consistently demonstrating that antidepressants may act through expression of new genetic material (Musazzi et al., 2009; Racagni & Popoli, 2008; Tardito et al., 2009). Science has not yet discovered how to target and manipulate these intracellular mechanisms directly.

The tricyclic antidepressants block reuptake of norepinephrine and, to a lesser degree, may also block reuptake of serotonin. They also have other effects such as anticholinergic and antiadrenergic effects, which mostly relate to side effects. The MAO inhibitors block breakdown of neurotransmitters such as norepinephrine, serotonin, and dopamine. The SSRI antidepressants block serotonin reuptake into the presynaptic synapse and make more of this neurotransmitter available at the receptors. The mixed-reuptake drugs Effexor, Pristiq, and Cymbalta block serotonin and norepinephrine reuptake. Effexor also has some dopamine reuptake blockade activity at high doses. Serzone blocks serotonin-2 receptors and causes a milder reuptake inhibition of serotonin-1A and norepinephrine. Wellbutrin and its active metabolite block reuptake of norepinephrine and dopamine, which makes this drug quite different from all the other antidepressants. Remeron increases release of norepinephrine and serotonin and blocks serotonin-2 and serotonin 3-receptors, which means that it is less likely to cause sexual side effects or nausea than the SSRI drugs. Lithium has many proposed mechanisms of action and is often used in bipolar affective disorder as well as unipolar depression for its augmenting effects and also as its antisuicide effects.

Augmentation Strategies

As mentioned earlier, augmentation usually involves adding a drug that is not an established antidepressant when used alone, such as lithium, thyroid hormone, Lamictal, stimulants (Dexedrine, Adderall, or Ritalin), estrogen or testosterone, omega-3 fatty acids, BuSpar, or others. The strongest data for augmentation support the use of lithium and Cytomel, a pharmaceutical preparation of the thyroid hormone triiodothyronine, or T3 (referring to the fact that the molecule has 3 iodine atoms).

AUGMENTATION WITH LITHIUM

Lithium augmentation appears to affect serotonin as well as the adrenal axis in animal experiments. There are no consistently identified predictors of response to lithium augmentation, but of the commonly used augmentation strategies, it is the best-studied and most consistently effective, and it is considered a first-line strategy for patients with major depression who do not respond to an antidepressant (Bschor & Bauer, 2006; Bschor et al., 2002; Carvalho, Cavalcante, Castelo, & Lima, 2007; Crossley & Bauer, 2007). There is very strong evidence that lithium is an effective augmentation agent and modest evidence that it may accelerate early antidepressant response (Crossley & Bauer, 2007). In placebo-controlled acute studies, 45% of lithium-augmentation patients responded, whereas 18% of placebo patients responded (Bauer, Adli, et al., 2003; Bauer et al., 2000; Bauer, Forsthoff, et al., 2003).

Occasionally patients will notice response within 2 or 3 days of adding lithium to their previously ineffective antidepressant; typically response occurs within 1 to 6 weeks. Lithium augmentation should be given for at least 2 weeks to determine if it is effective, and continued for at least 12 months if it helps (Bschor et al., 2002).

Lithium blood levels must be monitored to ensure a concentration that is high enough to be effective yet not so high that it causes unnecessary side effects. Typically levels of 0.5–0.8 mEq/l or higher are used for augmentation, but occasionally lower levels are effective. Because lithium may slow thyroid gland function, it is routine to obtain a baseline thyroid-stimulating hormone (TSH) level and to check this every 6 to 12 months. Lithium may also affect the kidneys, so urinalysis and serum blood urea nitrogen (BUN) and creatinine should also be obtained (Bauer, Adli, et al., 2003; Bauer, Forsthoff, et al., 2003; Bschor et al., 2003). Long-term lithium treatment is associated with gradually increasing creatinine levels (a blood test for kidney function). If used with care to avoid toxicity, it is quite safe relative to kidney function even in elderly patients (McCann, Daly, & Kelly, 2008).

The toughest task in adding lithium to an antidepressant is convincing the patient to take it, as many patients believe the drug is used only in cases of extremely severe illness.

Case Example: Dramatic Lithium Augmentation Response

Sarah was a 50-year-old woman from India, living with her husband and three children. She was on medical leave from her job. She had been terribly upset when her son received a neurologic diagnosis, and she was afraid that, within her culture, her two daughters would have great difficulty finding someone to marry because there was a family history of a genetic illness.

Sarah was not motivated to do anything; even taking a shower and brushing her teeth were an effort. She was unable to follow the storyline of a television show, took sleeping pills every night, had very low energy, and had had no sexual relations with her husband for 6 months. She felt that her body was not moving well, and she had lost 30 pounds in 2 months. She was feeling worthless, guilty, and unable to make decisions, and she had thoughts of her own death.

Sarah had been tried on full therapeutic doses of Remeron, Seroquel, and Effexor. My diagnostic impression was severe major depressive episode and I was concerned about possible psychotic features. Lithium augmentation was started in addition to her Remeron and Effexor, which were maintained at maximal doses. Two weeks later, Sarah reported that she was cleaning, cooking, shopping, and feeling like doing things again. A month later, she reported that her worries were "stupid," and she no longer needed her nightly sleeping pill. She was feeling like she was back to her normal self within 2 months, and she was getting back to her normal weight and resuming sexual activities with her husband. Sarah gradually tapered her medications over the next year and continued to do quite well, now accepting that her son's neurologic disorder was not going to be a major handicap or get in the way of his being successful in life.

THYROID AUGMENTATION

Another well-studied approach is the use of an antidepressant plus thyroid hormone such as Cytomel (also known as triiodothyronine, or T3), most often used in unipolar depression, or Synthroid (levothyroxine, or T4), thought more useful for bipolar depression.

Depressed patients may manifest subtle thyroid abnormalities (overt dysfunction is uncommon), or activation of an autoimmune process (Fountoulakis et al., 2006). Hypothyroidism at even mild, subclinical levels is significantly associated with refractory depression, with 52% of patients in six clinical studies demonstrating subclinical hypothyroidism (Howland, 1993). Indeed, even the mildest hypothyroidism can make a person nonresponsive to antidepressants. For this reason it is wise to get a TSH level on any patient presenting with difficult-to-treat depression. If the TSH is even slightly above the normal range, it means that the thyroid is working overtime to try to compensate and make just enough thyroid hormone for the brain and pituitary to sense it as being adequate. Even though an endocrinologist might not choose to treat the patient with a mildly elevated TSH and no other symptoms of hypothy-roidism, a psychiatrist might view it differently and say that treatment-resistant depression can be a manifestation of the mildest degree of hypothyroidism. For reference, the normal range for TSH was for many years set at 0.5–5.0 (with hypothyroidism above 5.0). In 2002, however, the American Association of Clinical Endocrinologists narrowed the range significantly to 0.3–3.04 (Johns Hopkins Urban Health Institute, 2001). Still, many textbooks and some of the medical literature refer to the older figures. Since low thyroid function is defined as serum TSH concentrations equal to or above the upper 25th percentile of normal range (Corruble, Berlin, Lemoine, & Hardy, 2004), it is especially impor-tant that a depressed person's TSH level be at 2.28 or lower.

While thyroid treatment may be used to correct thyroid abnormali-ties, it is also useful in some patients with normal thyroid function at supraphysiologic (levels above that normally occurring in the body) doses (Nirenberg, Fava, et al., 2006). For these patients, it may boost the effectiveness of antidepressant treatment.

An early study showed that lithium and T3 were comparably effec-tive for augmenting tricyclic antidepressants in unipolar refractory depression (R. T. Joffe, Singer, Levitt, & MacDonald, 1993). The STAR*D trial showed similar results. Of patients failing two previous trials, 15.9% and 24.7% reached remission with lithium and T3 augmen-tation respectively (Nirenberg, Fava, et al., 2006), a statistically similar result. Compared with lithium, T3 augmentation involves lower side effect burden and greater ease of use.

A meta-analysis that evaluated eight studies including 292 patients who failed to respond on tricyclic antidepressants (TCAs) and who were then given T3 augmentation showed that they were twice as likely as patients given placebo to get a response; this corresponded to a 23% increase in response rate compared to placebo (Aronson, Offman, Joffe, & Naylor, 1996).

A study of 20 patients who had failed to respond to at least 8 weeks of SSRI antidepressant treatment showed that T3 at 50 mcg/day for 4 weeks was beneficial for 35% of patients. It was especially helpful in atypical depression but worsened the symptoms of the melancholic patients (Iosifescu et al., 2005).

Abraham, Milev, and Stuart Lawson (2006) studied 12 patients who had failed to respond to at least 6 weeks of an SSRI and who had normal thyroid functions by giving them 25–50 mcg/day of T3; 42% responded within 3 weeks. In another study, 17 females with either unipolar or bipolar depression who had failed to respond to serotonergic antidepressants were given T4 100 mcg/day; 4 weeks later, 94% were improved (Lojko & Rybakowski, 2007).

For bipolar patients, high-dose Synthroid, average 320 mcg/day, was given to 10 women with normal thyroid function but ongoing depression despite mood stabilizer and antidepressant treatment. During 7 weeks of treatment, 7 patients remitted while 3 showed partial response (Bauer et al., 2005).

AUGMENTATION WITH DOPAMINERGIC AGENTS

Mirapex (pramipexole), a dopamine-agonist drug approved for use in Parkinson's disease, may be helpful in treatment-resistant depression. When added to TCA or SSRI antidepressants for bipolar or unipolar depressed patients who had failed to respond, it was helpful for 61% of patients at an average dose of 1 mg/day and at an average time to remission of 10 weeks. No sleep attacks were reported, but 3 of 23 patients developed hypomania or mania in long-term followup (Cassano et al., 2004). A small study of the Parkinson's drug ropinirole (average 1.3 mg/day) showed benefit when added to SSRI or TCA treatment in depression (Cassano et al., 2005).

Another way of boosting dopamine is by adding a stimulant such as Dexedrine, Adderall, or Ritalin (methylphenidate); unfortunately, a double-blind controlled study of adding slow-release methylphenidate (Concerta, mean dose 34 mg/day) to ongoing antidepressant medication in treatment-resistant major depression failed to demonstrate benefit (Patkar et al., 2006). Not only do these drugs assist with lethargy, fatigue, tiredness, or difficulty with focus and concentration while taking an antidepressant, but they also improve the response to the antidepressant medication by allowing the antidepressant to work better. An alternative for this purpose is Provigil (modafinil), an alerting drug with a different mechanism of action, possibly via histamine at the cerebral cortex and on the hypocretin/orexin system in two nuclei of the hypothalamus. Early studies showed it to have little effect on dopamine activity in the striatum, and therefore far less risk of abuse than the psychostimulants (Menza, Kaufman, & Castellanos, 2000). It is now known that dopamine figures prominantly in the drug's effect on wakefulness and vigilance (Dopheide, Morgan, Rodvelt, Schachtman, & Miller, 2007; Madras et al., 2006), which may account for its ability to lower depression scores in unipolar (Konuk, Atasoy, Atik, & Akay, 2006; Thase, Fava, Debattista, Arora, & Hughes, 2006) and bipolar (Frye et al., 2007) depression independent of its action on excessive sleepiness and fatigue.

Wellbutrin also allows the opportunity to augment with a dopaminergic agent; this is discussed later with other antidepressant combination approaches.

AUGMENTATION WITH ATYPICAL ANTIPSYCHOTICS

The atypical antipsychotics, which include Zyprexa, Seroquel, Risperdal, Invega, Geodon, Abilify, and Clozaril, are widely used in the treatment of schizophrenia, where they have generally replaced the typical antipsychotics due to their much better tolerability and potential for benefit for cognitive impairment and negative symptoms, which include blunted affect and emotion, poverty of speech (alogia), inability to experience pleasure (anhedonia), lack of motivation, and lack of desire to form relationships. All atypical antipsychotics (with the exception of Clozaril) have now been FDA approved for the treatment of acute mania (either alone or added to a classic mood stabilizer such as lithium or Depakote), and several have indications for treatment of depression as well. Because of its unique risk of bone marrow suppression and need for frequent blood tests, Clozaril has been used almost exclusively in schizophrenia or schizoaffective disorder that is very treatment-refractory. The role of atypical antipsychotics in treatment-resistant depression is still evolving but overall looks very promising. All of these medications affect serotonin receptors in ways that would suggest antidepressant and antianxiety effects. Geodon blocks reuptake of serotonin, norepinephrine, and dopamine in a way that suggests it should act very much like the majority of antidepressants.

Zyprexa. A large study of patients who had failed to respond to a trial of an SSRI and a trial of Pamelor (nortriptyline) randomized 482 patients to continuing Pamelor, starting Prozac or Zyprexa monotherapy, or starting the combination of Prozac and Zyprexa together. There didn't appear to be much difference among these groups in their responses, although the combination group had a more rapid onset of benefit than other groups (Shelton et al., 2005).

Another study gave patients Prozac for 8 weeks, then randomized the nonresponders to an additional 8 weeks of Prozac, Zyprexa, or the combination; patients receiving the combination did better than those receiving either drug alone, with an 8-week remission rate of 27.3%, but there was more weight gain among patients receiving Zyprexa or the combination than those receiving Prozac (Thase, Corya, et al., 2007).

Originally indicated for depressive episodes associated with bipolar I disorder, Symbyax (the combination of Zyprexa with Prozac) was approved by the FDA for treatment-resistant unipolar depression in April 2009.

Abilify. Three studies of patients who had inadequate response to one to three previous antidepressants gave these patients 8 weeks of an SSRI or SNRI (Effexor) antidepressant. After the 8-week period, the nonresponders received their ongoing antidepressant plus Abilify at 2–20 mg/day or placebo in double-blind fashion. The studies showed benefit for Abilify augmentation (Berman et al., 2007; R. N. Marcus et al., 2008) and led to its becoming the first drug to be FDA approved (Berman et al., 2009) for augmentation of antidepressants in treatment-resistant unipolar depression, with remission rates of 26% at 6 weeks. The average dose in the studies was about 11 mg/day, but many clinicians would choose to start at 2 mg/day to minimize side effects, then increase to 5 mg/day the second week and to 10 mg/day if needed in the third week. All subtypes of depression examined appeared to respond equally well. However, there was a surprising gender difference in response in one of the three studies but not in the other two. In the first Berman study, men did not respond differently to Abilify versus placebo, but women did. Since the major efficacy trials, a small short-term open study suggested that Abilify may be useful as an augmenting agent in patients receiving but not responding to Wellbutrin (Sokolski, 2008).

In elderly patients who failed to respond to sequential trials of 16 weeks on escitalopram followed by 12 weeks on either duloxetine or venlafaxine, 2.5 to 15 mg/day of adjunctive aripiprazole brought 50% remission; in those patients continuing treatment over a median of 27.6 additional weeks, none relapsed (Sheffrin et al., 2009). It was also helpful in patients with anxious or atypical features when added to standard antidepressant therapy (Trivedi et al., 2008).

Seroquel. Seroquel XR (extended release) is FDA-approved for augmentation in antidepressant nonresponders at 150–300 mg/day. The standard release preparation of Seroquel has also shown to be helpful. The addition of Seroquel 200–600 mg/day to SSRI antidepressants showed antidepressant benefit in a small open study (Olver, Ignatiadis, Maruff, Burrows, & Norman, 2008). A randomized controlled study of depressed patients who had failed to respond to 6 weeks of an SSRI or SNRI antidepressant and who also had anxiety symptoms showed that Seroquel at an average dose of 182 mg/day was beneficial for both anxiety and depression symptoms beginning within the first week and continuing through the eighth week of the study (McIntyre, Gendron, & McIntyre, 2007). A small open-label study of antidepressant nonresponders at 4 weeks showed that Seroquel 400 mg/day and lithium were both beneficial augmenting agents, and suggested that Seroquel gave more benefit than lithium (Doree et al., 2007). In patients who had failed at least two 8-week antidepressant trials and then failed 3 weeks of lithium augmentation, cognitive-behavioral therapy with Seroquel at a dose of 25–375 mg/day (average 148 mg/day) demonstrated benefit over cognitive-behavioral therapy plus placebo (Chaput, Magnan, & Gendron, 2008).

Adding Seroquel 25–100 mg to fluoxetine did not result in greater depression relief but did help insomnia in depressed patients receiving the combination (Garakani et al., 2008). Another small open-label study showed that add-on Seroquel (average 315 mg/day) was beneficial in treatment-resistant depression with insomnia improving by 2 weeks and mood improving by 5 weeks (Sagud, Mihaljevic-Peles, Muck-Seler, Jakovljevic, & Pivac, 2006). Seroquel added to venlafaxine or escitalopram for 4 weeks improved measures of major depression, motor activity, sleep quality, and daytime sleepiness, even at high mean daily doses and despite the sedative effects of quetiapine (Baune, Caliskan, & Todder, 2007). So effective is quetiapine in treatment of insomnia, it is frequently used at low doses of 25–50 mg at bedtime for just this purpose, and research into its utility has followed this trend independent of its study in mood and psychosis. In healthy male volunteers, objective and subjective sleep quality were measured by polysomnography and patient questionnaires in double-blind, placebo-controlled, randomized crossover fashion under standard and noisy sleeping conditions. At 25 mg and 100 mg, Seroquel significantly improved sleep induction and continuity, and also increased total sleep time, sleep efficiency, percentage sleep in stage 2 (slow-wave sleep) and subjective sleep quality (Cohrs et al., 2004). It improved sleep disturbances in a prospective open-label study of combat veterans with PTSD (Robert et al., 2005), and insomnia during 3 months of treatment in nonpsychotic patients with Parkinson's disease at a mean dose of 31.9 mg/day (Juri, Chana, Tapia, Kunstmann, & Parrao, 2005).

Seroquel's manufacturer is seeking FDA approval for treatment of major depression and generalized anxiety disorder.

Risperdal. Risperdal augmentation for antidepressant nonresponders was better than placebo (Mahmoud et al., 2007). A study of Celexa nonresponders at 6 weeks showed that the addition of open-label Risperdal for 4 weeks substantially raised the remission rate, but then double-blind discontinuation (so that some patients continued on both medications while others received Celexa plus placebo) demonstrated no benefit over 6 months of continuation treatment in terms of preventing relapse back into depression (Rapaport et al., 2006).

In evaluating the studies reviewed here, the reader should note that as in most all efficacy trials of depression, stringent inclusion and exclusion criteria apply. If a trial does not study psychotic major depression specifically, it most likely excludes for it. For this reason, it is still not clear which patients are most likely to benefit from antipsychotic augmentation.

In weighing the risks and benefits of the atypical antipsychotics, it is important to realize that all of them have some risk of neuroleptic malignant syndrome (a rare syndrome of high fever and muscle rigidity) and tardive dyskinesia (late-onset involuntary movements, mostly of facial muscles). Of the atypicals, Zyprexa and Seroquel are the most likely to cause sedation and weight gain, Risperdal is intermediate, and

Geodon and Abilify are the least likely to cause these problems. They also may increase triglyceride and cholesterol levels, blood sugar, and risk for diabetes, although Abilify and Geodon are least likely to cause these side effects as well. All of the atypicals may increase the risk of death in elderly patients by about 1.2% (Schneider, Dagerman, & Insel, 2005). This does not mean that the drugs should not be used; it means that they should be carefully monitored and benefit versus side effects should be assessed carefully during their use.

LESS COMMON APPROACHES

Riluzole. Riluzole is a glutamate-modulating agent approved for the treatment of amyotrophic lateral sclerosis (ALS; Lou Gehrig's disease). It was given open-label at a dose of 50–100 mg twice daily to a group of 19 medication-free, treatment-resistant major depression patients; at 6 weeks 46% of completers showed response. Side effects included headache, nausea, vomiting, and decreased salivation. Another small open-label study of treatment-resistant depression showed rapid benefit from riluzole augmentation (Sanacora et al., 2007; Zarate, Payne, Quiroz, et al., 2004).

Pindolol. A rather controversial augmentation strategy is the use of an antidepressant plus pindolol. Pindolol is a beta-blocker occasionally used for its blood pressure-lowering effects. There have been many reports about pindolol either hastening initial antidepressant response or providing additional benefit in individuals who failed to respond initially to their antidepressant. Pindolol 2.5 mg three times daily did not benefit SSRI nonresponders in one study but the same drug given 7.5 mg in a single morning dose was beneficial for another small group of SSRI-refractory patients (Perry et al., 2004; Sokolski, Conney, Brown, & DeMet, 2004). Unfortunately this literature appears to be very mixed and the efficacy of this approach remains in question.

SAM-e. S-adenosyl-L-methionine (SAM-e tosylate, by Nature Made) was added to SSRI or Effexor in 30 partial or nonresponders in a dose of 400 mg twice daily for 2 weeks and then 800 mg twice daily for 4 more weeks. Of the original study group, 50% showed a response by 6 weeks, with most of the improvement occurring by 1 to 3 weeks (Alpert et al., 2004). A more detailed discussion of this and other treatments employed in alternative and complementary medicine may be found in Chapter 15.

At the end of this chapter you will find a chart summarizing augmentation and combination strategies, their benefits, and their risks.

Combining Antidepressants

The combining of antidepressants has the same potential advantages and disadvantages as augmenting, but because each drug is an antidepressant in its own right, it may have the theoretical advantage that each drug could have an impact on different components of the depression symptom profile (or brain circuits).

Combination Strategies

Among the most popular combination strategies are using an SSRI with Desyrel (trazodone) for insomnia, an SSRI with Wellbutrin or Norpramin for the patient with low energy, and an SSRI with Remeron for nausea, insomnia, or weight loss. Although very low-dose trazodone will not improve response to depression directly, the relief from insomnia and improvement in sleep quality go a long way toward helping depression treatment. Due to differences in mechanism of action, both Wellbutrin and Remeron, in addition to their own unique properties, serve to augment (improve the effectiveness of) the SSRI.

AN SSRI WITH WELLBUTRIN

A very popular approach is the combination of an SSRI with Wellbutrin. It was, in fact, the most popular of several augmentation strategies in a survey of psychiatrists attending a Harvard psychopharmacology course. The theoretical appeal is that Wellbutrin works by complementary mechanism of action, often helps to increase energy and decrease weight, and may be helpful in treating SSRI-induced sexual side effects. Lam and colleagues (2004) did a study of patients who had failed one previous antidepressant and then failed a 6-week trial of either Celexa or Wellbutrin. In the study, the patients were assigned to either switch to the other drug or combine the two drugs for 6 weeks. The combination strategy brought 28% of patients into remission, compared to 7%

for the switching strategy. A small open-case report series also showed benefit from giving treatment-resistant patients the combination of the SNRI Cymbalta and Wellbutrin (Papakostas et al., 2006).

AN SSRI WITH TRICYCLIC ANTIDEPRESSANTS

Other approaches involve an SSRI plus the TCA desipramine (which is a norepinephrine reuptake blocker), again with the hope of increasing energy. The caution in this case is that Prozac and Paxil may block metabolism of desipramine (far more than Zoloft, Celexa, or Lexapro would), so levels may be much higher than they would be otherwise with a typical therapeutic dose of the TCA. For this reason, the use of TCA blood levels is an important safety monitoring issue.

Nelson, Mazure, Jatlow, Bowers, and Price (2004) demonstrated that inpatients with major depression who were randomized to receive the SSRI Prozac, Norpramin (a TCA norepinephrine reuptake inhibitor), or the combination for 6 weeks had much higher remission rates on the combination than on either drug alone, demonstrating the advantage of using a dual mechanism of action in achieving remission.

AN SSRI OR SNRI WITH REMERON

An SSRI or SNRI is sometimes used with Remeron both because Remeron may augment effectiveness of the other medication, and because it may help to induce sleep as well as decrease nausea and perhaps sexual dysfunction caused by the other drug. Remeron is helpful for sleep at lower doses (15–30 mg). At 45 mg norepinephrine effect increases and the sedative effect is lost for many patients.

AN SSRI WITH REBOXETINE

A study confirming this approach involved patients who were nonresponders or partial responders to SSRI antidepressants and then had Reboxetine (a European norepinephrine reuptake inhibitor) added for 6 weeks; 47% of patients remitted in this open-label study (Rubio, San, Lopez-Munoz, Garcia-Garcia, & Alamo, 2003).

MAO INHIBITOR COMBINATIONS: A WORD OF CAUTION

There is one combination that is absolutely forbidden because of the risk of serotonin syndrome: If an SSRI, SNRI, or Anafranil is combined with an MAO inhibitor antidepressant, a potentially lethal interaction involving very high fever may occur. The antibiotic Zyvox (linezolid) is an MAO inhibitor and can have similar reactions with serotonergic antidepressants (Bijl, 2004; Gillman, 2005; Isbister, Buckley, & Whyte, 2007; Izumi et al., 2006, 2007; Packer & Berman, 2007; Sola, Bostwick, Hart, & Lineberry, 2006; J. J. Taylor, Wilson, & Estes, 2006). Another relatively contraindicated combination is an MAO inhibitor with a stimulant, although some researchers have successfully (but cautiously) used low-dose stimulants with MAO inhibitors in patients who are refractory, have postural hypotension or daytime sedation while taking an MAO inhibitor, or have ADHD with depression; careful blood pressure monitoring is essential with this combination (Feinberg, 2004).

Case Example: Combining Antidepressants

Sister Dee, a 74-year-old retired religious sister, was referred by her superiors because of a history of depression going back as far as age 21. She had been given low-dose Stelazine, a typical antipsychotic, to use intermittently for her excessive crying spells. She had told her primary care doctor of feeling chronically tired and had been given Wellbutrin 5 years earlier. She had never been hospitalized and had never experienced a manic episode.

Dee's complicated medical history included high blood pressure, hypothyroidism, osteoporosis, fibromyalgia, hearing difficulties, and hypoglycemia, and her medication list included eight nonpsychiatric prescription medications. I diagnosed chronic major depression and added Lexapro to her Wellbutrin. She called the new antidepressant her "crying pill" because it had relieved the crying episodes she had been experiencing, but she continued to have low energy, for which Provigil was added. This helped her to have more energy for social activities and outings with her friends, and she remained stable on this combination over the next two and a half years. She clearly demonstrated the benefits of combining two antidepressants with different mechanisms of action and adding in a stimulating medication for the fatigue. As mentioned previously, a chart of augmentation and combination strategies has been included for your review at the end of this chapter.

Switching Antidepressants

Compared with augmentation strategies, switching antidepressant drugs has the advantage of simplicity, less cost and risk of drug interactions, and fewer side effects. Switching may mean that the patient is taking only one psychiatric medication, probably only once a day, and this makes medication adherence much more likely. Switching is the most appealing strategy if the first antidepressant tried has intolerable side effects even after a gentle buildup to the lowest usually effective dose, or if the first antidepressant has truly given no benefit after a 4- to 6-week trial. This is a situation in which rating scales, such as the Hamilton Depression or Montgomery-Asberg Depression Rating Scale, might be helpful, because a 20% drop in a rating scale at about 2 weeks is a hopeful sign that more benefit will follow, whereas no drop or worsening on a rating scale would confirm the lack of benefit. The rating scales may demonstrate subtle changes that could be missed by simply asking, "Do you feel better?" Sometimes the patient says yes just to try to please the doctor.

Should one ever switch within the same class of drugs? Switching from one SSRI to another may be reasonable, as often individuals may respond to one but not another. Studies that have looked at this issue typically take nonresponders to one SSRI, switch them to the study sponsor's SSRI openly, and show that there is some benefit from doing so. This methodology leaves much to be desired because there is always a question as to how much simply staying on the SSRI drug class longer helped and how much investigator suggestion and enthusiasm in a nonblind study might have contributed to the response to the second medication. Going on to a third or fourth drug within this class, however, seems like beating a dead horse. If a person's serotonin system has not responded to two different SSRI drugs, the chances of response to yet another are rather slim, so switching out of this family makes the most sense.

The exception to this is the case of obsessive-compulsive disorder (OCD). It appears that OCD responds only to the SSRIs or Anafranil (and possibly Effexor) because OCD involves a serotonin abnormality. Noradrenergic antidepressants clearly do not work for OCD. Other disorders, including panic, posttraumatic stress, bulimia, social phobia, and premenstrual dysphoric disorder, may also show a very preferential response to serotonin antidepressants.

If the patient does not have OCD, is being treated for difficult depression, and has gotten no benefit from the first antidepressant, generally the approach is to switch to a second antidepressant from a different family. Examples would be a switch from an SSRI to Wellbutrin, Effexor, Pristiq, Cymbalta, Remeron, Serzone, or a TCA. If several of these have been tried and found unsuccessful, switching to an MAO inhibitor may be worthwhile.

Switching Strategies

A patient who has failed to respond to two SSRI antidepressants still has many switch options open to him or her. These include dual-acting drugs (Effexor, Pristiq, or Cymbalta), serotonin modulators (Serzone), an atypical drug (Remeron), dopamine norepinephrine drug (Wellbutrin), tricyclic drugs (e.g., Tofranil, Pamelor), or MAO inhibitor drugs (Emsam, Nardil, or Parnate).

Poirier and Boyer (1999) demonstrated that switching treatment-resistant patients from an unsuccessful TCA or SSRI trial over to Paxil or Effexor demonstrated a significantly higher response and remission rate for Effexor than Paxil. The ARGOS study showed that when SSRI nonresponders (or intolerant patients) were switched to another SSRI, Remeron, or Effexor, there was a higher response rate at 24 weeks with Effexor than with the other drugs (Baldomero et al., 2005). Fava and colleagues (2003) showed that Prozac nonresponders had about a 60% chance of responding when switched to Wellbutrin.

A Dutch study examined switching to MAO inhibitor antidepressants in psychiatric inpatients with a history of failure to respond to a TCA (with adequate blood level) or Luvox (fluvoxamine, an SSRI only approved for OCD in the United States but used in depression elsewhere). Of these patients, 30% had mood-congruent psychotic features. Fifty-two percent of the patients who completed 5 weeks of taking Nardil (average dose 79 mg/day) or Parnate (average dose 60 mg/day) responded; side effects included dizziness, agitation, and insomnia. The percentage of patients who responded and the percentage with severe side effects were the same for both drugs. Among the few patients with preserved mood reactivity (capable of being "cheered up" by external events or interactions with people), 83% of patients were MAO inhibitor responders (Birkenhager, van den Broek, Mulder, Bruijn, & Moleman, 2004b). Thus, this symptom so characteristic of atypical depression predicted good MAO inhibitor response in treatment-resistant depression.

N-methyl-D-aspartate may represent a receptor that is altered in depression and potentially responsive to drugs. The anesthetic ketamine was given intravenously to a group of patients with treatment-resistant depression and shown to have an immediate antidepressant effect that lasted for up to a week after the drug was given (Zarate et al., 2006). This approach currently is unavailable outside of the research setting.

The role of Lamictal, FDA approved for prevention of mania and depression in bipolar illness, is not yet well defined relative to treatment of either recurrent major depression or acute bipolar depressive episodes. This drug does appear promising in both of these areas, however. Lamotrigine appeared helpful for treatment-resistant unipolar depression in an open-label study (Gutierrez, McKercher, Galea, & Jamison, 2005). It also appears to decrease frequency of migraine headaches in patients who suffer from migraine with aura (Lampl et al., 2005).

SWITCHING ANTIDEPRESSANTS AFTER SSRI "POOP-OUT"
Switching antidepressants is a necessary option not only when a patient fails to respond, but also when a medication fails to continue its benefit. "Prozac poop-out," technically called tachyphylaxis, is a phenomenon occasionally seen by clinicians. It is more common in bipolar than unipolar patients. The patient does well on an SSRI antidepressant such as Prozac for a while (often a few years but sometimes as little as a few months), but then it stops working. Posternak and Zimmerman (2005) looked at patients treated long-term with an SSRI, Effexor, or TCAs and showed that tachyphylaxis was more frequent with SSRIs than with Effexor or TCAs.

Case Example: Shawn

Shawn was a charming Irishman with a history of alcoholism and active A.A. participation. He had been using high doses of the sleeping pill Restoril, typically 60 mg each night, along with Xanax 1 mg/day. Prozac was his long-term antidepressant of choice. The initial diagnostic impression was one of alcohol abuse in stable long-term remission and benzodiazepine (minor tranquilizer or sleeping pill) dependence, which did not involve abuse. Although A.A. would never approve of the use of the sleeping pill and tranquilizer, I believe it was medically justified based on his substantial improvement in sleep, pain, and mood, lack of any observable or subjective impairment in memory, and lack of history of abusing the tranquilizers. Stressors included having survived a serious automobile accident and the breakup of his marriage. He had diverticulosis as well as fibromyalgia pain that interfered with his life at many times. He required surgery for an abdominal aortic aneurysm, and that went quite well. Seven years into treatment, Shawn reported that he was "in a funk," depressed, anxious, sleeping poorly, having a hard time getting up in the morning to go to his A.A. meeting, and bothered by the past and scared about the future at age 69 with only a few friends and minimal income. He felt isolated and that his glory days as a professional athlete were far behind him. He felt a lack of goals, meaning, and purpose in his life. Prozac was pushed to 80 mg/day, and Wellbutrin was added, but about 3 weeks later, there was no improvement, and so the Prozac and Wellbutrin were switched to Effexor. By 3 weeks later, he was reporting that Effexor 225 mg/day was doing a nice job of cutting the edge on both the depression and anxiety. Over the next 4 years, Effexor provided stable antidepressant effect at a dose of 300 mg daily, and his Restoril dose remained stable at 60 mg/day.

Real World Treatment: The STAR*D Study

The Sequenced Treatment Alternatives to Relieve Depression (STAR*D) is the largest, most expensive, most comprehensive study of treatment steps for depression. It enrolled 2,876 patients in both psychiatric and primary care settings, and treatment was carefully monitored with both depression and side-effect rating scales. The goal was to demonstrate response and remission rates for a series of treatments for depression, with the primary outcome measure being remission. How many patients would get better on a first-line SSRI antidepressant, and how many would reach remission after trying more complex next-step strategies involving augmenting, switching, or adding psychotherapy? The other goal of this study was to demonstrate that measurement-based planned treatment steps for depression could be accomplished in "real world" patients who had other medical or psychiatric disorders, substance abuse issues, and other conditions that would disqualify them from most randomized controlled trials of antidepressants. The study was "equipoise randomized": At each of the three steps of treatment beyond the initial one, patients could tell their doctors that they would not accept randomization to a specific treatment. Some patients did not want to accept psychotherapy, for example, as a sole treatment (without medications) if the initial medication trial was unsuccessful.

Demographic and Clinical Characteristics of Participants

Many interesting features of depression emerged from the STAR*D study. We will describe these in some detail, because they paint a fascinating picture of how many life areas are affected by depression and how complex this illness is when viewed in terms of the problems associated with it.

Twenty-one percent of the patients who entered the STAR*D study had chronic episodes lasting 24 months or longer, and factors associated with chronicity included old age, low income, no insurance, unemployment, medical illnesses, lower physical quality of life, comorbid generalized anxiety disorder, few prior episodes, history of suicide attempts, being black or Hispanic, and being treated in a primary care rather than a psychiatric setting (Gilmer et al., 2005). The duration of the presenting episode of depression did not affect the likelihood of remission during the initial treatment, which was a trial on the SSRI Celexa (citalopram) (Gilmer et al., 2008).

Depression recurrences were associated with earlier onset, older age, and positive family history of depression compared with first-episode patients (Hollon et al., 2006). Older patients had longer illness duration, larger number of depressive episodes, more medical comorbidity, and more insomnia than younger patients (Husain et al., 2005). Family history of mood disorder was more common in women than in men and was associated with younger age of depression onset (Nierenberg et al., 2007).

Onset before age 18 years was associated with the female sex; longer duration of illness and episodes; more suicidality; greater severity; more comorbidity; sadness, irritability, and agitation; atypical features; and lower educational attainment and marriage rates (Zisook et al., 2004).

Atypical depression features were present in 18% of the STAR*D patients and were more likely to be present in females, those with early onset, those with more anxiety comorbidity, and those with greater symptom severity (Novick et al., 2005).

Comparing men and women with major depression, the women had younger age of illness onset and more anxiety, somatoform features (psychosomatic illness), bulimia, and atypical symptoms than men. Men had more alcohol and drug abuse (S. M. Marcus et al., 2005).

Among premenopausal women not taking contraceptives, 64% reported premenstrual worsening of depression (Kornstein et al., 2005).

A significant effect of maternal depression, and its remission or persistence, was shown on the rates of symptoms and diagnoses among 7- to 17-year-old children of the study participants, implying that children of depressed women should be evaluated because a third will have some psychiatric symptoms (Pilowsky et al., 2006; Weissman et al., 2006).

A history of suicide attempts was reported by 16.5% of study participants. Those who had made attempts were compared to those who had not. The suicide attempters had earlier age of onset of their illness, more medical conditions, more alcohol/substance abuse, more work hours missed, and more depressive episodes. In other words, they had a greater burden of illness, and this implied to the researchers that they could potentially benefit from ongoing aggressive care including long-term maintenance pharmacotherapy (Claassen et al., 2007). Two genetic markers were found to be associated with risk for suicidal ideation during the Celexa (citalopram) treatment (Laje et al., 2007). Other markers were associated with treatment response (Lekman et al., 2008).

Among patients in the STAR*D study, comorbidity with other disorders was common: 29.3% had social anxiety, 20.8% had generalized anxiety, 18.8% had post-traumatic stress disorder, 12.4% had bulimia, 11.9% had alcohol abuse/dependence, 13.4% had obsessive-compulsive disorder, 11.1% had panic, 9.4% had agoraphobia, 7.3% had drug abuse/dependence, 3.7% had hypochondriasis, and 2.2% had somatoform disorder (Kornstein et al., 2005; Rush, Zimmerman, et al., 2005).

Significant medical comorbidity was common (52.8%) and was associated with older age, lower income, unemployment, limited education, longer episode of depression, more physical symptoms, and absence of family history of depression (Yates et al., 2004).

Depression severity was similar among patients presenting to primary care and to specialty care settings (Gaynes et al., 2005).

Interestingly, a genetic marker (serotonin 2A receptor) was associated with response to the citalopram (McMahon et al., 2006).

Step 1: A Trial on Celexa (Citalopram)

In the STAR*D study, researchers initially gave patients with major depression a trial on Celexa (citalopram) in gradually increasing doses. This was chosen for Step 1 of the study because most patients received an SSRI as the first-line depression treatment in clinical practice. Symptoms and side effects were measured at each visit. If there was no response at lower doses, the dose could be raised as high as 60 mg/day. Patients received a very long trial on this medication—up to 14 weeks. About 28–33% showed remission while 47% showed response; many patients required at least 8 weeks to achieve these. Caucasian, female, employed individuals, and individuals with higher education or income had higher remission rates, whereas those with longer episodes of depression, more comorbid psychiatric disorders (especially anxiety and substance abuse), medical illnesses, and lower functioning had lower remission rates (Trivedi, Rush, et al., 2006). Patients with public insurance or no insurance had more chronic, severe, disabling depression than those who had private insurance (Lesser et al., 2005). Of patients who ultimately responded to citalopram, 65% demonstrated the response by week 6 and 35% responded later. Of patients who ultimately remitted, only 53% had done so by week 6 and 47% did so later (Trivedi, Rush, et al., 2006).

Step 2, Step 3, Step 4: Augmentation or Switch to a Second Treatment
After the Celexa (citalopram) (Step 1) phase of the study, patients were
offered a series of three additional sequential steps of treatment. Patients
who failed to remit after completing a particular treatment sequential
step were offered their choice of treatments in the subsequent step. The
overall remission rate was 36.8% at Step 1, 30.6% at Step 2, 13.7% at
Step 3, and 13% at Step 4, based on the QIDS-SR self-report of
symptom severity (Rush, Trivedi, Wisniewski, Nierenberg, et al., 2006).
Thus, there was a significant drop in remission rates after two treatments
had been given. Overall, 66% of patients who persisted through all
necessary steps long-term got well at some point, but when those with
relapses were tallied, only 43% of the patients had gotten well and
stayed well (Nelson, Portera, & Leon, 2006).

Step 2

Step 2 took patients who had failed to remit after as many as 12 weeks
of treatment with Celexa (citalopram) and offered them either augmentation or switch to a different drug or to cognitive-behavioral therapy
(CBT). Those who chose augmentation received Wellbutrin SR (bupropion) up to 400 mg/day, BuSpar (buspirone) up to 60 mg/day, or CBT
along with their citalopram (average 55 mg/day). Remission was
achieved, based on the Hamilton Depression Rating Scale, in 29.7% of
the Wellbutrin patients, 30.1% of the BuSpar patients, and 23.1% of
those participating in CBT. The Wellbutrin group had better self-
reported symptom reduction and lower dropout rates than the BuSpar
group (Trivedi, Fava, et al., 2006; Wisniewski et al., 2007).

Those who chose the switch option were offered random assignment
off of citalopram and onto Zoloft (sertraline up to 200 mg/day), Wellbutrin (bupropion SR up to 400 mg/day), or Effexor (venlafaxine up to
375 mg/day), or were offered nonpharmacologic treatment with CBT.
Remission rates on Zoloft were 18–27%, Wellbutrin 21–26%, and Effexor
25%, with self-rated response rates of 26–28% for all three drugs. Twenty-
five percent of those switched to CBT attained remission. The three
drugs did not differ significantly with respect to outcomes, tolerability, or
adverse events (Rush, Trivedi, Wisniewski, Stewart, et al., 2006).

It is interesting that these results showed that continuing on an SSRI (Zoloft), or switching to an SNRI (Effexor) or to a norepinephrine-dopamine drug (Wellbutrin) all gave approximately equal probabilities of response or remission. Thus the theoretical advantages of changing to a drug with a different mechanism of action did not translate into a clinically meaningful difference to the patients; some clinicians chose to switch out of class only after adequate dose and trial of two SSRIs.

Switching to CBT worked approximately as well as medication switch at Level 2, but medication augmentation (two medications) beat medication plus CBT for probability of remission. Only about a fourth of the patients entering Step 2 treatment were willing to be randomized to CBT (Thase, Friedman, et al., 2007).

The Step 2 study did not really answer the question of whether switching or augmenting was the better strategy, because the "equipoise stratified randomized" design allowed patients to make the decision about which strategy to pursue. Because this decision was not randomized, the results could not yield a scientifically valid answer to the question of which was the better strategy.

Step 3

STAR*D Step 3 offered a third treatment trial to patients who had failed to remit after up to 12 weeks of citalopram treatment and then also failed to remit after augmentation with buspirone, bupropion, or CBT or switching to another antidepressant or CBT. This third trial again offered the patients choice of a switch or augmentation. The patients who switched medication received either Remeron (mirtazapine) up to 60 mg/day or Pamelor (nortriptyline) up to 200 mg/day. The rates of remission after a 14-week treatment trial, based on the Hamilton Depression Rating Scale, were Remeron 12.3% and Pamelor 19.8%. There were no statistically significant differences in efficacy or tolerability between these two treatments (Fava, Rush, et al., 2006). Among those in the augmentation group, some received lithium and others received Cytomel (triiodothyronine, a synthetic thyroid hormone). The remission rates were 15.9% and 24.7%, respectively, and the Cytomel was better tolerated than lithium (Nierenberg, Fava, et al., 2006).

Step 4

Step 4 enrolled patients who had failed three prior treatments and randomly assigned them to treatment with Parnate (tranylcypromine, an MAO inhibitor, average 37 mg/day) or Effexor XR plus Remeron (venlafaxine average 210 mg/day plus mirtazapine average 36 mg/day), a combination strategy christened "California Rocket Fuel" by psychopharmacologist and clinical investigator Stephen Stahl. Remission rates were 6.9% and 13.7%, which were not statistically significantly different. Parnate gave less symptom reduction and caused more dropouts due to intolerance than Effexor plus Remeron (McGrath et al., 2006).

Clinical Implications

The STAR*D study demonstrated clearly that measurement- and protocol-based treatment of depression could be delivered with comparable results in both the psychiatric and primary care settings. It showed us that patience is important in giving patients adequate medication trials, and that persistence in trying many different treatment approaches often pays off

Useful as the STAR*D study may have been, however, it will not be the last word on depression treatment. Even before the study, it was known that aggressive sequential antidepressant trials could help patients who did not respond to their first treatment. Quitkin and colleagues (2005) showed that 65–66% of outpatients with depression could achieve remission if they continued in treatment long enough to receive up to three adequate 6- to 12-week medication trials. Further, the STAR*D study failed to show clinicians much that would guide treatment decisions at different stages of treatment resistance because the various choices had outcomes so similar to one another at each treatment step. Other studies, although generally smaller, have shown some important differences between treatments.

One such study, on geriatric refractory depression, randomized 53 elderly nonresponders to paroxetine 40 mg/day plus interpersonal therapy to receive augmentation with bupropion, nortriptyline, or lithium (a patient could be tried on more than one augmenting agent if necessary) or switch from paroxetine to venlafaxine. Each augmentation strategy was tried for about 7 weeks. The average time from start of augmentation to response was about 6 weeks. The study showed that 31–45% of patients responded to each of the augmentation strategies. Overall, 60% of patients responded to one of the three augmenting strategies. Some patients switched to Effexor XR (venlafaxine) with or without trying augmentation strategies, and 42% responded at an average dose of 244 mg/day and at an average of 6 weeks on this medication. Overall, the authors concluded that their patients had similar benefit from any of the three augmentation strategies or switching to Effexor, but the Effexor was better tolerated than the augmenting strategies (Whyt et al., 2004).

Many augmentation and combination strategies are used by clinicians, with drug choice often based on the patient's ongoing (residual) symptoms. Some strategies have data supporting efficacy from large trials including the STAR*D study, while others are supported by smaller studies. More often than we would like to admit, there is an intuitive, creative, experience-based "educated guess" made by the clinician as part of finding the best combination of medications for a patient who is difficult to treat.

Case Example: Antidepressant Poop-Out

This particular case study tells the story of a man whose treatment involved several of the strategies this chapter has covered, implemented in various creative ways, some of them successful. Dave was a 52-year-old married commercial pilot at the time that I first saw him. He had taken the TCA Tofranil, prescribed by his primary care doctor, for only about 8 months and reported that it had the uncomfortable side effects of sedation and dry mouth. After trying an alternative TCA without improvement, he returned to the Tofranil, but he began to have breakthrough depression. A switch to Prozac provided no benefit, but then, when lithium was added, Dave commented that he felt the best and most normal he had in years. He stayed on that combination during the next 2 years as I continued to work with him and then he sought treatment with two other psychiatrists.

Thirteen years after I had originally seen him, Dave came back for reevaluation. At that point, he was retired, and he reported that one of the other psychiatrists who had been working with him also treated his wife. His wife and the doctor did not get along, however, so Dave transferred his care to a university geriatric psychiatrist who seemed too busy to spend much time with him.

Dave said that Tofranil had stopped working for him several years ago. He had switched to Prozac, which worked for a while but then also lost its effectiveness. The same subsequently happened with Effexor and Paxil. Lithium augmentation had been tried on a few occasions without much lasting benefit. At this point, I again diagnosed recurrent major depression and noted the frequent loss of effectiveness of his antidepressants. I started Dave back on Effexor with instructions to push the dose up as quickly as possible to combat his sense of hopelessness and depression. I then planned aggressive augmentation strategies. Lithium was added but it caused swelling and no benefit, so we tried Zyprexa 5 mg, which proved quite helpful. Dave continued with Effexor 150 to 300 mg daily and Zyprexa 2.5 to 5 mg daily, and the lithium augmentation was terminated in favor of a trial with the thyroid hormone Cytomel (T3). Unfortunately, the Cytomel made Dave feel extremely nervous, and he requested evaluation for ECT or repetitive transcranial magnetic stimulation. While investigating these possibilities we continued the Effexor and Zyprexa, and Dave began feeling better.

This combination worked well for 2 years, but then the depression returned again. We pushed the Effexor up to 450 mg daily, with the Zyprexa remaining at 5 mg, and we tried Adderall and then Provigil for the low energy, without much benefit. When this did not work, we switched from Effexor plus Zyprexa to Cymbalta plus Zyprexa. Cymbalta had just been released and appeared to be a little more energizing than Effexor. This turned out to work well, and over the next year Dave's mood and energy were quite stable and he was able to enjoy the extensive travel that his retired-pilot status provided for him.

Although Dave's other psychiatrists and I never observed a hypomanic or manic episode that would suggest bipolar disorder, and Dave never really experienced sustained benefit from lithium, he did have the

classic cycle of repeated antidepressant response and then loss of
response that is suggestive of bipolar spectrum. It is quite significant that
the Zyprexa that was usually required along with his antidepressant has
a role as a long-term mood stabilizer in bipolar affective disorder. I
would have preferred using Lamictal for preventing his recurrences of
depression, but it was very poorly tolerated within Dave's first few days
of trying it. His excellent self-discipline with extremely healthy diet and
exercise habits allowed him to remain on the Zyprexa long term,
without substantial weight gain or metabolic problems.

When vagus nerve stimulation (VNS) became FDA approved, Dave
decided to have this treatment in addition to his medications because it
offered substantial hope of preventing recurrences long term. At 6
months after receiving VNS, Dave reported that he felt a more complete
response than he ever had experienced with medications alone.

Treatment of Residual Symptoms: Sleep Problems and Fatigue

Sometimes patients experience a partial response to an antidepressant
trial. Their mood is better but inconsistently so, or their mood is better
but other symptoms such as insomnia or fatigue have worsened. Sometimes one symptom, such as insomnia, has improved but mood has not
improved. In such cases the symptoms that are remaining are considered
residual symptoms. Although some have held that these symptoms
might resolve along with the depression, it is now well known that
depression does not completely resolve without aggressive treatment
targeted specifically at those individual symptoms, and sometimes they
can be treated by a second medication that is very specific.

For example, a patient who has had a good antidepressant response
but remains fatigued or sleepy during the day may benefit from the
addition of a stimulant such as Ritalin. A person who has significant
improvement in depression but persisting insomnia may be treated with
a sleeping medication such as Lunesta, Ambien, or Sonata, or with a low
dose of Desyrel, which has sedating effects and can improve sleep architecture. Some patients report that Ambien and Lunesta increase their
depression, so their use should be monitored with this in mind.

However, a study involving giving Prozac with either placebo or Lunesta to patients with major depression and insomnia both showed benefit for the insomnia and more rapid global improvement in depression in the Lunesta group. There were no apparent withdrawal symptoms when the sleeping pill was discontinued after 8 weeks of nightly use (Fava, McCall, et al., 2006; Krystal et al., 2007).

Provigil (Modafinil) augmentation of SSRI antidepressants improves fatigue and sleepiness as well as overall mood (Fava, Thase, & DeBattista, 2005; Fava et al., 2007; Konuk, Atasoy, Atik, & Akay, 2006; N. A. Rasmussen et al., 2005; Thase, Fava, et al., 2006). Although this "wakefulness-promoting agent" is not FDA approved for augmentation in depression, it is clearly safer than the use of stimulants (such as Adderall, Dexedrine, or Ritalin) because Provigil has minimal risk of abuse or raising blood pressure.

Case Example: Insomnia in Depression

Tom, a 40-year-old married man who described himself as a workaholic, ran a very successful financial consulting business and lived with his family. He was referred by another psychiatrist for difficult-to-treat depression. Tom experienced repeated episodes of depression and his brother had died of suicide. However, cognitive therapy had helped him so that despite his depressed mood, he was able to run his business quite nicely and maintain a positive relationship with his wife and children; his catastrophic thoughts were unlikely to be realized.

Tom had a therapeutic blood level of his antidepressant, Norpramin, but was still occasionally cycling into depressions. Because Norpramin is a purely noradrenergic drug and he was having breakthrough depressions while on a therapeutic level of this, his other psychiatrist added Zoloft, a purely serotonergic drug. The combination generally worked well. Adding lithium was of no benefit. Later, the Norpramin was switched to Wellbutrin in an attempt to minimize side effects and improve energy, and Zoloft was switched to Celexa with slightly better tolerability. BuSpar was added as a boosting agent, and when mild subclinical hypothyroidism was detected, a low dose of Synthroid was added. Tom reported only very brief mild depressions on this combination over a period of several years, but when he became depressed, early-morning awakening was one of his most bothersome symptoms. He added in the very short-acting sleeping pill Sonata to be taken only if he awoke early in the morning and commented that this allowed him to "cheat the depression out of a few hours of sleep." Feeling well-rested made a world of difference in his daytime functioning; he no longer had to fight exhaustion as a component of his depression, and the episodes gradually became rarer, milder, and shorter in duration.

Case Example: Sleep Disruption in Depression

Emerald was a 26-year-old graduate student with a history of depression that went back 4 years, the first episode having begun after an affair with a fellow student working in the same research lab. Symptoms included distractibility, anxiety, sleep difficulties, fatigue, poor time management, and difficulty focusing. Emerald also reported ongoing anxiety with muscle tension, restlessness, fatigue, worry, irritability, and history of some panic attacks. She had obsessive thinking but no compulsive behaviors. She reported a vague history of premenstrual syndrome, as well as intermittent extreme difficulties falling asleep and waking up. A sleep study had shown abnormal sleep architecture with frequent arousals. Work stress contributed to her insomnia. Emerald had a history of high-energy periods that typically lasted for 2 days, during which she was more cheerful, talkative, energetic, and distractible. She would spend more money during these periods, purchasing things that she would later return. She also had racing thoughts and started lots of projects.

Emerald had a history of poor response to Serzone, Prozac, and Wellbutrin, and optimal response to Effexor XR. My initial diagnostic impression was bipolar II affective disorder and generalized anxiety disorder; Lamictal provided some additional mood stability when added to the Effexor. The concern about insomnia with difficulty awakening was addressed: Neurontin, Desyrel, and Remeron did not adequately control her insomnia, and low-dose Ritalin and Adderall did not do much for her inability to wake up at a reasonable hour and focus her mind. Provigil 200 mg in the morning, however, was quite helpful in helping her to wake up early in the morning and get to work at her research position on a more regular basis. This was still a very difficult challenge for her, though, and ongoing attempts were made to normalize her sleep-wake cycle. A second sleep study again showed repeated arousals through the night. Stabilizing her daytime alertness and promoting regular sleep-wake habits were essential for her ability to complete her graduate program.

The key concept to remember when deciding between augmentation and switching is that one should never settle for partial response before aggressive attempts have been made to get a better, more complete response in resolving depression symptoms. Sometimes something as "simple" as improving sleep can have a huge impact on daytime functioning and overall antidepressant response.

Algorithm for Augmentation
and Switch Strategies

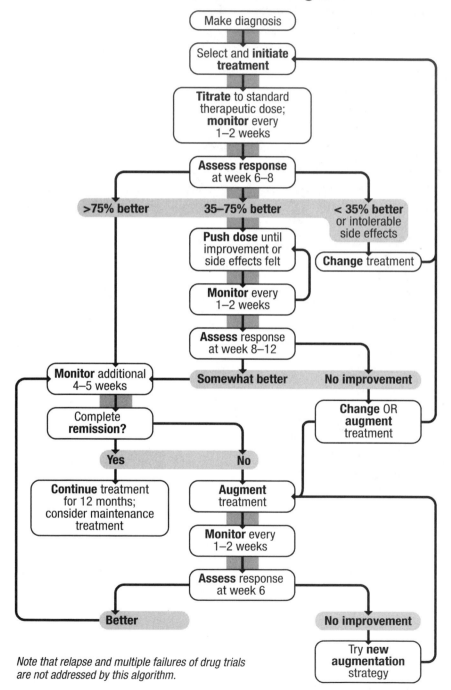

Note that relapse and multiple failures of drug trials
are not addressed by this algorithm.

Augmentation and Combination Strategies

Medications	**Best-Studied**	lithium
		thyroid hormone— T3 for unipolar depression / T4 for bipolar depression
	Anxiolytic	buspirone
	Antidepressant*	SSRI, SNRI, NDRI (bupropion), TCA, MAOI, receptor modulators (nefazodone, mirtazapine)
	Atypical Antipsychotic	aripiprazole, quetiapine, olanzapine
	Anticonvulsant	lamotrigine
	Novel Strategies	pramipexole, pindolol, ropinirole; less-often-used strategies
	Deplin	L-methylfolate, a fully methyated form of folic acid
	Complementary Medicines	omega 3 fatty acids, inositol, vitamin B6, vitamin B12, folic acid, SAM-e†, L-tryptophan†, 5-HTP, DHEA†, others
Other Somatic Treatments	**Prescribed**	ECT, VNS, rTMS
	Non-prescribed	Exercise, bright light therapy
	Mind-Body Therapies	tai chi, qi gong, yoga, meditation, others
Psychotherapy	**Structured**	CBT, CBASP, DBT, MBCT, IPT, IPSRT
	Non-structured	psychodynamic psychotherapy, supportive therapy, problem-solving therapy, family therapy
	Educative	psychoeducation, social rhythms therapy
	Format	Individual and group formats

5-HTP=5-hydroxytryptophan; CBASP=cognitive behavioral analysis system of psychotherapy; CBT=cognitive behavior therapy; DBT=dialectical behavior therapy; DHEA=dehydroepiandrosterone; ECT=electroconvulsive therapy; IPSRT=interpersonal and social rhythm therapy; IPT=interpersonal therapy; MAOI=monoamine oxidase inhibitor; MBCT=mindfulness-based cognitive therapy; NDRI=norepinephrine dopamine reuptake inhibitor; rTMS=repetitive transcranial magnetic stimulation; SAM-e=S-adenosyl-L-methionine; SNRI=serotonin norepinephrine reuptake inhibitor; SSRI=selective serotonin reuptake inhibitor; T3=triiodothyronine; T4=L-thyroxine; TCA=tricyclic antidepressant; VNS=vagus nerve stimulation

Choose an antidepressant of a different mechanism of action from the initial antidepressant agent.

†*May cause a switch to (hypo)mania or mood cycling in persons with bipolar illness.*

Note that concomitant therapy with a mood stabilizing medication (lithium, atypical antipsychotic, certain anticonvulsants) is recommended for all patients with bipolar illness who are taking antidepressants.

12

Bipolar Depression Requires Different Approaches

Recognizing bipolar affective disorder and distinguishing it from recurrent major depression is very important, as the treatment for this diagnosis is different from that for major depression. Mood stabilizers, rather than antidepressants, are the mainstay of treatment, as antidepressants may increase mood cycling or cause a "roughening" of mood. Tachyphylaxis (loss of effectiveness) is also more common in this population than in unipolar depression. Due to all-too-frequent misdiagnosis, however, the most commonly prescribed first drug in the treatment of patients with bipolar affective disorder is an antidepressant (Baldessarini et al., 2007). This is most often because these patients are frequently misdiagnosed with unipolar major depression. In fact, the average person with bipolar affective disorder may have 10 years of illness and see four different physicians before an accurate diagnosis and appropriate treatment plan are made (Hirschfeld, 2002, 2007; Hirschfeld, Calabrese, et al., 2003; Hirschfeld et al., 2000, 2005; Hirschfeld, Holzer, et al., 2003; Hirschfeld & Vornik, 2004).

Bipolar I affective disorder involves a history of mania that lasts for at least a week or requires hospitalization, causes major functional impairment, or includes psychotic features. Bipolar I depression has some empirical data to guide its treatment. Bipolar II disorder involves hypomanic periods where symptoms are milder and do not involve psychosis, but during which other people can tell the patient is not his usual self. Hypomanic episodes require a minimum of 4 days duration, although some European experts say that 1 or 2 day duration is adequate to make the diagnosis.

Bipolar disorder is very frequently misdiagnosed. The fluidity of some diagnostic constructs may lead to confusion, as may the subtlety and variety of symptoms present in depressive and (hypo)manic episodes that do not necessarily fit neatly into commonly recognized notions of mood states.

Some diagnostic models place bipolar affective disorder on a spectrum: Along with the *DSM-IV* diagnoses of bipolar I and II disorders and cyclothymic disorder, antidepressant-induced manic episodes are recognized by some as an indicator of underlying bipolar illness, as is a "hyperthymic" temperament (high energy at baseline) with depressive episodes. Recurrent depression in a patient with bipolar disorder in relatives is often placed on this spectrum. Some Europeans look at multiple episodes of unipolar major depressive disorder occurring more frequently than every 2 years as a sign of bipolar illness even in absence of family history, and would use mood stabilizers to help these cyclic patients even if hypomanic symptoms have never been present. This might be a relevant issue for individuals who have had frequent episodes of depression that break through despite long-term antidepressant treatment. Mood episodes marked by frequent cycling are hallmarks, including recurrent or sporadic brief episodes of hypomania lasting less than 4 days, highly recurrent unipolar depressive episodes, and recurrent brief depression. As seasonal pattern and atypical features are so common in bipolar illness, some researchers place seasonal affective disorder and atypical depression among bipolar spectrum disorders. Due to these various diagnostic models and constructs, the precise boundary between bipolar and recurrent major depressive disorders is sometimes unclear.

The very nature of depression and of (hypo)mania within a given diagnosis may also confound diagnosis. Bipolar II patients typically suffer a more depressive course than their type I counterparts, and they also may show an anxious-sensitive personality type, with more fear, anxiety, and risk of suicide. Such patients may have hypomania marked by irritability rather than elated mood, and often anxiety, obsessionality, or panic as well. They are very often misdiagnosed with unipolar depression. Classical hypomania may also confound diagnosis as these episodes may go unrecognized altogether: For many, function appears to improve during these periods of elevated mood because the person experiences a sense of elation, increased energy and creativity, and increased sexual intensity;

because these are enjoyable and viewed as positive aspects of life, they are often not recognized as part of an illness. This lack of awareness may be on the part of both the clinician and the patient, who typically will not present to the psychiatrist when he is hypomanic and feeling well. Perhaps because of this lack of recognition, bipolar II depression has had very little empirical research on its optimal pharmacologic treatment. The mania present in bipolar I disorder may also become blurred and less recognizable when depressive symptomatology is also present. Although classic euphoric mania is quite easy to distinguish from depression, a mixed state involving agitation and symptoms meeting criteria for depression and mania concurrently may look to one observer like a severely agitated depression (which occurs in both unipolar and bipolar depression) and to another observer like dysphoric mania.

Along with confusion surrounding the definition of diagnoses and discrete episodes, the prominence of depression in the long-term natural history of bipolar disorder presents a third contributing factor to misdiagnosis. Bipolar I patients treated in university clinics for an average of 12.8 years were found to be asymptomatic (well) 53% of the time, depressed 32% of the time, hypomanic or manic 9%, and cycling or mixed 6%. Among bipolar II patients, 46% of their follow-up time (average 13.4 years) was spent asymptomatic, 50% depressed, 1% hypomanic, and 2% cycling or mixed (Judd & Akiskal, 2003; Judd, Akiskal, Schettler, Coryell, Endicott, et al., 2003; Judd, Akiskal, Schettler, Coryell, Maser, et al., 2003; Judd et al., 2002; Judd, Schettler, et al., 2003). For both groups, the vast majority of time ill is spent in depression.

While bipolar depression may seem indistinguishable from unipolar depression to some, there are subtle cues that in aggregate can lead the clinician to an accurate diagnosis. Comparing 477 bipolar depressed patients against 1,074 unipolar depressed patients, differences emerged. Bipolar patients had a family history of bipolar disorder, earlier age of onset, and greater number of episodes. Bipolar patients also had more fear. Unipolar patients had more sadness, insomnia, depressed behavior, and cognitive-intellectual, muscular, respiratory, and genitourinary symptoms (Perlis, Brown, Baker, & Nierenberg, 2006). Compared with unipolar recurrent major depression, bipolar depression is more likely to be associated with oversleeping, motor retardation (slowing), mood lability (for example, anger outbursts), early onset, and family history of bipolar affective disorder (Bowden, 2005).

The nature of response to antidepressant treatment (or lack of it) may in itself be diagnostic. Fast onset of depressive episodes, in the absence of acute critical life events, is common in bipolar depression and rare in unipolar depression; development of an episode over a period of a week or less occurred in 58% of bipolar depression episodes and only 7.4% of unipolar major depression episodes (Hegerl et al., 2008). It is also common for bipolar depression to last about 3 months whether an antidepressant or placebo is added to an ongoing mood stabilizer (Frankle et al., 2002). A study by Sharma, Khan, and Smith (2005) showed that 61 patients referred to a specialty center for treatment-resistant major depression with a history of "escape of response" to adequate trials of at least two antidepressants for a previous episode, when carefully diagnosed, appeared to include 35% bipolar patients (mostly bipolar II). When these patients were followed up for a year with structured diagnostic interviews, interviews of at least one close family member, review of all previous treatment, and careful observation of symptoms, the prevalence of bipolar affective disorder was 59%. When the broader concept of bipolar spectrum was applied to these patients, 80% of them met the criteria. In this group, 93% of patients were using antidepressants upon presentation, but only 52% were using them at 1 year of specialty clinic treatment. Mood stabilizers and atypical antipsychotics were frequently substituted for the antidepressants. The authors suggested that several treatment-related factors may indicate that a patient really has a bipolar spectrum disorder rather than pure major depression. These factors include treatment-resistant depression, loss of a good antidepressant response over time, and antidepressant-induced anxiety, insomnia, agitation, and racing thoughts (Sharma et al., 2005).

Treatment Guidelines

According to the 2002 American Psychiatric Association treatment guidelines, bipolar I depression is best treated with a mood stabilizer such as lithium or Depakote in mild cases. In more severe cases, lithium or Depakote may be combined with an SSRI antidepressant or Wellbutrin. Sometimes an MAO inhibitor is also used for treatment-resistant cases. An antidepressant should not be used without a mood stabilizer in bipolar I depression because of the risk of inducing cycling, such as a swing into mania, or more frequent mood instability. Lithium may be more effective in individuals who have fewer than four previous episodes and who have a classic bipolar course of illness (manic-depressed-well longitudinal course; euphoric rather than irritable mania) and a family history of positive lithium response and bipolar features. Lithium is probably less effective in psychotic patients, rapid-cycling patients, and patients whose depression follows mania (rather than the mania following the depression). It appears that Depakote may be better for rapid-cycling bipolar patients who have had numerous episodes in the past, have more than four episodes per year, or suffer drug-induced mania or episodes of mixed mania (where depressive symptoms are featured). As mentioned, rapid-cycling course is difficult to treat, and Depakote is only marginally more effective than lithium. Both drugs have rather poor response rates of around 50–55%.

Unfortunately only 40% of bipolar patients respond to Depakote or lithium in depression. Although Depakote is recognized in the American Psychiatric Association treatment guidelines for preventive use in bipolar disorder, it is not FDA approved for this because the main long-term preventive trial seeking FDA approval failed to show that Depakote was better than placebo. Depakote is, however, FDA approved for treatment of acute manic episodes. A study of rapid-cycling bipolar affective disorder in which patients who had responded to the combination of lithium and Depakote were assigned double-blind to either lithium or Depakote in monotherapy failed to show a difference between these treatments over a 20-month maintenance period (Calabrese, Rapport, et al., 2005; Calabrese, Shelton, et al., 2005).

There is another, more recent, set of expert treatment guidelines for bipolar depression. The Texas Implementation of Medication Algorithms update on bipolar I disorder (Suppes et al., 2005) indicated that the approach to bipolar depression differs based on the patient's status when presenting for treatment. The patient who is taking lithium should have her serum level adjusted to at least 0.8 mEq/l. This is because lower lithium levels may be less effective for depression, although some patients are stable on lower doses long term. The usual serum level of lithium that is therapeutic is 0.5 to 1.2 mEq/l with the blood drawn 10 to 12 hours after the last dose of lithium and very consistent dosing (no missed doses) for at least 4 to 7 days before the lab visit.

If there is a history of severe or recent mania, the first-line choice is an antimanic drug (lithium, Depakote, or an atypical antipsychotic) plus Lamictal. If the patient is not taking a drug shown to be very effective in mania and does not have a history of severe or recent mania, Lamictal monotherapy is the first choice. Though not effective for acute treatment, Lamictal is FDA approved for prophylaxis (prevention) of both manic and depressive episodes. A partial or nonresponse may then lead to the use of Symbyax (fluoxetine olanzapine combination) or Seroquel. Continuing nonresponse would lead to further steps that may include lithium, Lamictal, Symbyax, or Seroquel, and still further the addition of Tegretol, an SSRI, Wellbutrin, Effexor, or ECT. Tricyclic antidepressants (added to a mood stabilizer), MAO inhibitors, pramipexole, Trileptal (oxcarbazepine; Tegretol with an additional oxygen molecule attached), and stimulants or thyroid hormones are reserved for the most treatment-resistant patients. Setting priorities for which treatment to use first and which to reserve for greater treatment resistance involve efforts to minimize risk of destabilizing (cycle induction) by tricyclic antidepressants or the hypertensive risk of diet and drug interactions of the classic oral MAO inhibitor antidepressants.

Medications for Bipolar Depression

Medications used to treat and to prevent depression and mania in bipolar illness are called mood stabilizers. While lithium, several anti-seizure medications, and all of the newer antipsychotics have been called mood stabilizers, the true meaning of the term refers to an agent that can both treat and prevent both poles of the illness. To date, only Seroquel has indications for use in mania, bipolar depression (in monotherapy), and maintenance, though several others are indicated for mania and either acute depression or acute mania. Clinically, this means that while an individual may do very well on Lamictal (predominantly antidepressant) for prevention of episodes at either pole, a breakthrough of acute mania may best be treated by adding something known to work well in mania rather than increasing the dose of Lamictal. Likewise, however, it is important to remember that a medication may be useful in areas for which it does not have FDA approval: lithium, for instance, is indicated only for mania and maintenance, but historically has been found extremely helpful in depression as well.

Medications have not been specifially designed to treat bipolar illness, as they have been for depression and schizophrenia. Whereas those medications are designed to target the receptors on the surface of the cell that bind to neurotransmitters, the protein and enzyme systems thought to be responsible for the instability and cycling seen in bipolar illness (protein kinase C [PKC] and cyclic adenosine monophosphate [cyclic AMP]) are intracellular (they reside within the cells), they are activated through "second messenger systems" (i.e., effects downstream of the drug's target), and modern science has not found a predictable way of targeting these directly. The usefulness of existing central nervous system medications has been "discovered" in clinical practice, and later tested in scientific studies. The anticonvulsants Depakote and Tegretol, for instance, were seen to improve mood in people with epilepsy. Since then, manufacturers of a host of medications in this class have run trials to see if their drugs might be found efficacious. While the sodium channel-gated drugs (such as Depakote, Lamictal, and Tegretol) seem to be helpful, those that modulate calcium channels (Topamax, Neurontin, Keppra, and others) are not. The same trend of clinical discovery and subsequent experimentation and FDA approval has taken place with the atypical antipsychotics, all of which are indicated now for acute mania, and several of which have indications for depression or maintenance therapy as well.

Lithium

In 1948, John Cade, a researcher in Australia, discovered that lithium produced a docile effect in his guinea pigs. Thus began the experimentation with lithium as a medication. Lithium was shown over 30 years ago to have a statistically significant antidepressant effect in bipolar disorder, and one advantage over other therapies is its antisuicide effect

(Baldessarini et al., 2006; Baldessarini, Tondo, & Hennen, 2001, 2003; Tondo & Baldessarini, 2000; Tondo, Hennen, & Baldessarini, 2001; Tondo, Isacsson, & Baldessarini, 2003; Tondo, Jamison, & Baldessarini, 1997; Tondo, Lepri, & Baldessarini, 2007). In fact, the risk of suicide and attempted suicide during long-term lithium treatment is lowered by 80% in both bipolar and unipolar mood disorders, and lithium is the only drug used for mood disorders that has this effect. In addition, it appears to protect neurons from apoptosis (programmed cell death, to which bipolar individuals are biologically predisposed), encourage their growth, and reduce anger and irritability.

Anticonvulsants

Lamictal (lamotrigine) is clearly beneficial in long-term prevention of recurrent bipolar affective disorder, and it has FDA approval for this use. It has a stronger effect in preventing depression than in preventing mania, which is opposite to lithium in long-term maintenance (Bowden et al., 2003; Calabrese et al., 2003; Goodwin et al., 2004). It is not yet clear whether it has a true acute antidepressant effect: The latest tally of acute bipolar depression studies showed benefit in one study and failure in four studies of acute bipolar depression (Calabrese et al., 2008). Still, many clinicians use Lamictal for this purpose and the expert consensus recommendations previously described give it a high priority for treating bipolar depression.

Adolescents with bipolar depression showed mood improvement with Lamictal in a small open study (Chang, Saxena, & Howe, 2006), and in an open-label comparison study of lithium versus Lamictal as monotherapy for bipolar II depression, both drugs were equally effective at 8 weeks, although lithium had more side effects (Suppes et al., 2008). Lamictal is modestly effective in treating rapid-cycling bipolar disorder (Calabrese et al., 2000). In the large STEP-BD study, patients receiving Lamictal from their clinicians were likely to have had a history of rapid cycling or antidepressant-induced mania (Marangell et al., 2004).

Lamictal has a lesser side effect burden than some other medications. When patients in the Lamictal studies of recently manic or recently depressed bipolar patients were switched from their prior medications to Lamictal for 8 to 16 weeks, self-reported cognitive symptoms were significantly improved, independent of initial mood or mood improvement (Calabrese et al., 2002; Khan et al., 2004). Lamictal is weight neutral and is associated with weight loss in obese patients (Bowden et al., 2006).

Many clinicians fear the potentially very serious rash associated with Lamictal, called Stevens-Johnson syndrome, yet the risk of this among more than 2,000 patients treated with Lamictal in studies was 0–0.1% (Calabrese et al., 2002). The risk of benign rashes was about 8%. Because of the risk of serious rash, the dose of Lamictal must be increased very gradually; some experts prefer to avoid using it in patients currently taking Depakote (which doubles serum Lamictal levels), though this combination treatment approach may safely be initiated by taking 10 (as opposed to the usual 5) weeks to titrate Lamictal to a therapeutic dose of 200 mg/day. Dermatologic precautions are usually recommended: for the first couple of months on Lamictal, no new skin-contact products (e.g., hair coloring or shampoo, shower soap, laundry detergent, deodorant, lotions, perfumes), no new herbal or supplement products or foods, and avoidance of sunburn and poison ivy. Whatever has been used long-term before starting Lamictal is considered safe to continue (Ketter, Greist, et al., 2006; Ketter et al., 2005). It is important that the warning signs of serious rash be explained to the patient: Swollen lymph nodes, involvement of mucus membranes (eyes, nose, mouth, vagina), fever, or general systemic illness are major warnings to seek urgent medical evaluation and consider stopping the medication.

Depakote (valproic acid), another anticonvulsant, appeared to offer some acute antidepressant and antianxiety effects in a small study of bipolar depression (Davis, Bartolucci, & Petty, 2005). Another study indicated that patients who were on lithium or Depakote and had a breakthrough depression would do equally well if the other mood stabilizer were added to the regimen or if the antidepressant Paxil was added (Young et al., 2000). A third trial compared the effects of lithium and Depakote in pediatric bipolar affective disorder. Children with bipolar I or II disorder, average age 10.8 years, were first stabilized on the combination of lithium and Depakote, and then were randomized to either of the drugs alone. There was no significant difference in time until relapse between the two drugs (Findling et al., 2005).

A major review of the use of the anticonvulsant Topamax (topiramate) in bipolar affective disorder, conducted by the Cochrane Collaboration, concluded that there is insufficient evidence to recommend its use in either phase (depression or mania) as monotherapy or as an adjunctive treatment (Vasudev, Macritchie, Geddes, Watson, & Young, 2006). This is a useful medication, however, in treatment of post-traumatic stress disorder. It also has utility where impulsivity is concerned (as in treatment of binge eating or alcoholism) and may help to reduce appetite in patients who have gained weight on antipsychotic or other medications. Because obesity contributes to depression, you might say that Topamax can have secondary antidepressant effects.

A study of Zonegran (zonisamide) in various phases of bipolar disorder showed some benefit for both mania and depression, as well as weight loss, but 32% of patients dropped out of the study due to worsening of mood symptoms (McElroy et al., 2005).

ATYPICAL ANTIPSYCHOTICS

Symbyax (olanzapine-fluoxetine combination), a combination of Zyprexa and Prozac, is an FDA-approved drug for the treatment of bipolar I depression. Unfortunately, it has the weight-gain risk and the possibility of increased cholesterol or precipitating diabetes that are associated with Zyprexa, as well as the risk of sexual side effects frequently associated with Prozac. Many antidepressants that treat bipolar depression appear to increase the risk of switching into mania, though this effect is often counteracted by concomitant administration of a mood stabilizer. The most interesting feature of Symbyax, when it was tested and found effective in bipolar depression, was that the rate of switching from depression into mania was identical to that of placebo. Thus depression could be treated without increased risk of inducing mania.

A large 7-week study of Symbyax versus Lamictal in depressed bipolar I patients showed greater improvement on rating scales with Symbyax, but the overall response rates of Symbyax (68.8%) and Lamictal (59.7%) were not statistically significantly different. Unfortunately, the side-effect burden was greater with Symbyax than Lamictal in terms of sedation, weight gain, and lipid elevation (Brown et al., 2006).

Seroquel (quetiapine), another antipsychotic, has been tried and found effective for bipolar depression in both bipolar I and bipolar II disorders, as well as in rapid-cycling and non-rapid-cycling patients when given as monotherapy at doses of 300 to 600 mg/day for 8 weeks. Like Symbyax, Seroquel relieved depression, decreased anxiety symptoms, and had a switch rate into mania comparable to that of placebo. There was no advantage of 600 mg compared to 300 mg/day, so the usual target dose is 300 mg/day. Some sedation is an expectable side effect upon starting treatment (Calabrese, Keck, et al., 2005; Hirschfeld, Weisler, Raines, & Macfadden, 2006; Thase, Macfadden, et al., 2006). Symbyax patients had side effects including sleepiness, weight gain, increased appetite, and increased blood sugar and cholesterol. Seroquel patients had side effects including dry mouth, sedation, dizziness, and constipation. No other atypical antipsychotic drugs have such large, double-blind, well-controlled, randomized studies in bipolar depression (Calabrese, Elhaj, Gajwani, & Gao, 2005). Both Symbyax and Seroquel are now FDA approved for the treatment of bipolar depression.

Monotherapy trials of Abilify (aripiprazole), also an antipsychotic, failed to demonstrate efficacy in treatment of bipolar depression. There is some suggestion that Abilify may be a useful adjunctive treatment in patients with treatment-resistant bipolar depression (Ketter, Wang, Chandler, Culver, & Alarcon, 2006), however, and the drug is FDA indicated for adjunctive use in treatment-resistant unipolar depression.

Stimulants

Stimulants may be used in bipolar disorder to treat residual depression and medication-induced sedation without significant risk of switching to mania according to a small case-report series (P. J. Carlson, Merlock, & Suppes, 2004). These drugs include but are not limited to Ritalin (methylphenidate) and various preparations of amphetamine.

Provigil (modafinil) is a wakefulness-promoting agent originally designed for use in narcolepsy; technically it is not a psychostimulant. A case report of two patients with bipolar depression in remission but with ongoing daytime oversleeping demonstrated benefit from Provigil (Fernandes & Petty, 2003). In an 85-patient 6-week controlled study of bipolar depression, Provigil was shown effective in improvement of depressive symptoms when added to a mood stabilizer (and, in some cases, an antidepressant) at a dose averaging slightly under 200 mg/day (Frye et al., 2007). A large private-practice case review of the use of Provigil in both unipolar major depression and bipolar depression in 191 patients demonstrated benefit for fatigue and sleepiness without risks of mood switching, tolerance, or abuse (Nasr, Wendt, & Steiner, 2006), and Frye has also demonstrated a low risk of mood switch. Others recommend caution in using this drug in bipolar illness (Plante, 2008; Wolf, Fiedler, Anghelescu, & Schwertfeger, 2006).

Antidepressants

Antidepressants should not be used without a mood stabilizer in bipolar I depression and generally are not recommended by experts in the field because they may lead to a roughening of the course of illness with more short-term mood fluctuations, increased cycling into future episodes of mania or depression, or even an acute switch out of depression into mania (Ghaemi et al., 2004; Leverich et al., 2006). In refractory bipolar patients, antidepressants may ignite a switch from depression into a mixed episode of dysphoric mania. Antidepressants that have been demonstrated to present least chance of switching include the SSRIs and Wellbutrin; dual-action drugs that act on serotonin and norepinephrine, including Effexor and some TCAs, present higher risk.

Sometimes an antidepressant is inadvertently given without a mood stabilizer because the doctor didn't take a careful history and ask about past mania, or the patient didn't tell the doctor about past manic episodes. In clinical practice, 56% of initial monotherapies for bipolar depressed patients are antidepressants (Baldessarini et al., 2007; Ghaemi et al., 2004; Leverich et al., 2006). Doctors can minimize this problem by encouraging patients and families to report past manic episodes, explaining that antidepressant monotherapy can actually make such symptoms worse.

Some clinicians believe antidepressants should not be used, with or without a mood stabilizer, under any circumstances in bipolar disorder, and this is unfortunate. There is a prominent anxiety component to many bipolar presentations, and serotonergic agents are first-choice in these conditions. Although benzodiazepines may be helpful, they have their drawbacks, including increased risk of accidental injury, problems with memory formation, disruption of sleep quality, dependence, and the risk of worsening depression long-term. Removing antidepressants from the shelf narrows a person's range of choices for treatment of a wide range of symptoms, including the following:

- Depression, mood swings, and symptoms associated with borderline personality disorder (all antidepressants)
- Augmentation of other antidepressants (Wellbutrin, Remeron, and Norpramin)
- Diffuse symptoms of anxiety, panic disorder, generalized anxiety disorder, social anxiety disorder, and anger (SSRIs, SNRIs)
- Body dysmorphic disorder, OCD, obsessive-compulsive spectrum disorders (those involving impulse control), and eating disorders (SSRIs)
- Insomnia (Remeron, Desyrel, and Elavil)
- Intentional weight gain and control of nausea (Remeron)
- Weight loss and sexual side effects of SSRIs (Wellbutrin)
- ADHD and smoking (Wellbutrin and Pamelor)
- Energy/fatigue (Wellbutrin and Norpramin)
- Headache and chronic pain (Elavil)
- Hot flashes, peripheral neuropathy, and fibromyalgia (SNRIs)
- Stress urinary incontinence (Cymbalta)

CONSIDERATIONS REGARDING BIPOLAR II DISORDER

Bipolar II depression has been minimally studied in terms of treatment responses and long-term stability, yet it deserves special attention due to its significantly depressive and anxious course, posing increased risk for suicide. Jay Amsterdam has suggested that Prozac may be a useful antidepressant and might have a mood-stabilizing effect in bipolar II depression (Amsterdam & Brunswick, 2003; Amsterdam et al., 1998; Amsterdam & Shults, 2005; Amsterdam, Shults, Brunswick, & Hundert, 2004). Wellbutrin may also share these properties (Haykal & Akiskal, 1990). Such recommendations have considerations: Bipolar II patients may suffer a chronically depressive course despite treatment with mood stabilizers. They are also particularly prone to anxiety comorbidity (more than 60%). For these reasons, antidepressants show much utility. The question, however, is whether increased mood cycling will occur in a person who may not demonstrate clear full symptomatology associated with hypomania or a classic profile of hypomania. Some bipolar II patients express mood disturbance secondary to use of an antidepressant as an increase in episodes of depression, as a "roughening" of mood, or as subsyndromal hypomania, with few symptoms, but typically character- ized by overactivity and irritability. Most experts agree that long-term mood stabilizers are the preferred treatment and that they should accompany antidepressants when the latter are used.

BENEFITS AND RISKS

For those bipolar patients taking an antidepressant with a mood stabi- lizer, the question of how long to continue antidepressant therapy after resolution of depression may arise. Some authors believe that an indi- vidual suffering a breakthrough episode of depression while taking a mood stabilizer should continue a beneficial antidepressant for a year; others argue that the antidepressant should be discontinued within a month or two of achieving remission from the depression. Working in collaboration with the Stanley Bipolar Network of researchers, Lori Altshuler, in the UCLA Mood Disorders Clinic, has shown that an anti- depressant that has been helpful in a bipolar depressive episode should be continued for at least a year rather than stopped quickly, because there is less risk of recurrence of depression and no increased risk of mania with a long-term antidepressant added to the mood stabilizer (L. Altshuler et al., 2001; L. Altshuler et al., 2003). A very important study of treating bipolar I and II depression involved 366 patients with depres- sion who had Wellbutrin, Paxil, or placebo added to their ongoing mood stabilizer treatment for up to 26 weeks and were followed to determine if they would obtain 8 weeks of sustained normal mood or switch into mania or hypomania. Results demonstrated that 23.5% of those receiving mood stabilizer plus antidepressant had a durable recovery, whereas 27.3% receiving a mood stabilizer plus placebo had a durable recovery. The rates of switches were similar on antidepressants or placebo (10.1–10.7%). In this study, the addition of an antidepressant neither helped nor harmed patients compared to placebo (Sachs et al.,

2007). Others argue that adding an antidepressant to a mood stabilizer and continuing it after remission of the depression may cause cycling out of the current depression quickly and into the next one more quickly.

Regarding rates of switching to mania with acute treatment, there is no clear answer. This is partially due to the fact that studies such as those already mentioned have not operationalized hypomania or mania in any consistent fashion. Some use DSM-IV criteria; others use less stringent criteria. Due to differences in definition and methodology, iatrogenic (treatment-induced) mania is reported at rates ranging from 3% to 33%. It is interesting that there is a trend for investigators from the East Coast to report higher incidence of iatrogenic mania, possibly reflecting effect of bias on study design. Some very large studies have found antidepressants to be helpful with low risk of switch: Gijsman, Geddes, Rendell, Nolen, and Goodwin (2004) analyzed 12 acute trials of antidepressants in 1,088 bipolar depression patients and found that antidepressants were more effective than placebo for bipolar depression and that tricyclic antidepressants had a 10% switch rate, compared to 3% for other antidepressants. The STEP-BD study reported on a group of 335 patients with bipolar depression who had two or more manic symptoms during their depressive episodes. These patients were given their mood-stabilizing medication with or without an antidepressant. The use of an antidepressant was associated with a higher mania symptom rating at 3-month follow-up, and the addition of an antidepressant neither hastened nor prolonged time to recovery from the depression (Goldberg et al., 2007).

Unfortunately, there are no studies of the effects of antidepressants on the long-term longitudinal course of bipolar illness, although we know that rapid cycling, if induced, may continue for an average of 2 years. Finally, there are very few studies on the effect of antidepressants on frequency of depression. We know of only one small study, which involved questionnaires and was therefore not representative of the scientific evidence produced by experimental studies.

PSYCHOTHERAPY

Medications are not the only available augmentation strategy. Miklowitz added intensive psychosocial intervention to medication treatment of depressed bipolar patients in the STEP-BD study and found that 30 sessions over 9 months of interpersonal and social rhythm therapy, cognitive-behavioral therapy, or family-focused therapy were beneficial compared to brief psychoeducational treatment. The form of therapy was not specific, and the outcome variables that showed benefit from psychotherapy included functioning (overall), relationships, and life satisfaction, though there was no significant effect on work/role function or recreational activities. Those receiving intensive psychotherapy had shorter times to recovery and higher rates of recovery at a year than those who did not (Miklowitz, Otto, Frank, Reilly-Harrington, Kogan, et al., 2007; Miklowitz, Otto, Frank, Reilly-Harrington, Wisniewski, et al., 2007).

Numerous studies have pointed to the failure of prophylaxis (prevention of recurrence) with medications alone in the treatment of bipolar I disorder. In a randomized controlled trial of interpersonal and social rhythm therapy (IPSRT) and intensive case management (ICM) in 175 clinically ill bipolar I patients who were already taking medication, patients were randomly assigned to either IPSRT or ICM or an acute phase of the trial, and then randomized again to either intervention for a 2-year maintenance phase. A subject could therefore be treated under one of four conditions; there was no difference between groups in time to stabilization, though in the 2-year maintenance phase patients assigned to IPSRT in the acute treatment phase survived longer without a new episode of either mania or depression irrespective of assignment for maintenance treatment. After controlling for other factors, it was discovered that participants in the IPSRT group had higher regularity of social rhythms, and the ability to increase this regulation during the acute phase of treatment was what reduced likelihood of recurrence during the maintenance phase (Frank et al., 2005).

Case Example: A Bipolar Family

Mike, a successful 53-year-old real estate broker in a stable relationship, presented with a history of long-standing depression. His mother had depression, his father had bipolar affective disorder, and his daughter also had bipolar affective disorder. He said that the tricyclic antidepressant Vivactil had been helpful, but it made him feel hyper and "weird." Zoloft and Prozac had both given him sexual side effects, and he did not want to try them again. He had experienced a fall while taking lithium. Despite Mike's history of very chronic major depression with some anxiety and occasional excess alcohol use, I decided that another try on an antidepressant would not be worthwhile and used the family history as a guideline to try him on the mood stabilizer Lamictal, to which he responded well. Mike was very happy to have a medicine that both helped his depression and, unlike the antidepressants, did not cause any sexual side effects. Was he bipolar? His history was one of depression without mania, but his genetics suggested a trial on a medication usually used in bipolar affective disorder, and this was successful.

Case Example:
Bipolar Affective Disorder With Long-Term Nonadherence

Nina was a very slender, attractive, quiet 35-year-old who was on conservatorship at the time that I saw her (a conservator is a court-appointed person who can make decisions about treatment, including medication, hospitalization, and placement, for an individual whom a judge considers too ill to do this for herself). Nina had a childhood history of attention-deficit disorder, though in school she had been popular and enjoyed being a cheerleader, after which she had completed college and had been very successful in her career. In her late 20s she was diagnosed with bipolar affective disorder, and within a span of 8 years Nina had been hospitalized 10 times for manic and depressive episodes.

When manic, Nina became irritable, delusional, grandiose, and hyper-religious. She would make foolish investments and go on spending sprees, most recently amassing $100,000 in credit card bills. She sometimes went for days without sleeping, and became highly productive at work. Her episodes lasted anywhere from a week up to 3 months. Complicating the mood disorder was hypothyroidism, which can present with many symptoms that resemble depression, including fatigue, poor memory, weight gain, constipation, and additional physical symptoms including cold intolerance, irregular menstrual periods, hoarse voice, and dry skin. The low thyroid was easily diagnosed with a blood test and treated with replacement thyroid hormone.

When Nina felt well, she would lie to her doctors and stop taking medicines. She told me that she did not tolerate them because she could not tolerate the tremor, jerking, and weight gain. Throughout my year of treating her, there were frequent appointments focused on minimizing side effects, as well as on controlling her chronic background depression. It was only because she trusted me to pay close attention to her concerns about weight and other side effects that she was willing to take medications long term. In addition to medications, Nina had just started very intense psychotherapy with a psychiatric social worker who placed a strong emphasis on dealing with the illness and working with the family. In psychotherapy, Nina realized the importance of limiting the stresses that she subjected herself to, at her new job, for instance. At one point, she was able to clearly assert herself with her therapist and with me and say that there was a lot more to her life than her illness, and she wanted to work on other issues. By that time, she was about to get off of the conservatorship, she was working steadily at a full-time job, and she was taking good care of herself, both physically and emotionally.

Case Example:
Bipolar Depression With Antidepressant-Induced Mania

Deena was a 49-year-old unemployed woman referred by another psychiatrist for chronic depression that began when her manager at work would not allow her to take time off for classes. She began a medical leave of absence, and over a 2-year period of depression she lost weight, lost muscle tone, had insomnia, felt dizzy, and described 1-week trials on Lexapro and Celexa, both of which led to her staying up all night, making a lot of phone calls, and feeling out of control, agitated, and irritable. Those episodes occurred 2 years before I first saw her. Her two previous episodes of depression had begun after the deaths of a brother and her father. In her present episode, Deena felt that she had lost her successful career as a saleswoman and her sense of independence when she moved in with her mother. When I saw her, she was taking Risperdal and Xanax and was still having insomnia. She failed to receive benefit from brief trials of Depakote, Neurontin, and low-dose Seroquel and Zyprexa, but she had never tried lithium or Tegretol. She had been withdrawing from all of her friends, had stopped working, and was afraid that she might have to sell the home that she had owned for 10 years. She said that during her brief manic periods, while on antidepressants, she would not sleep for a couple of nights at a time, was more talkative and impulsive, and experienced racing thoughts and distractibility. Her mother told me that Deena's paternal grandmother had committed suicide, and her father had had bipolar affective disorder. I was the first doctor to make the diagnosis of bipolar affective disorder, depressed. Clues including there being a bipolar relative and a history of antidepressant-induced mania led me to use primarily mood stabilizers and attempt to taper away antidepressant medications. After I obtained normal laboratory data, I treated Deena on lithium and Lamictal. When these were not sufficient to clear the depression, and she was unwilling to consider electroconvulsive therapy, I suggested that we add Symbyax. By about 10 weeks of treatment, Deena was starting to come out of the depression. Over the next year, the lithium and Lamictal were maintained at full therapeutic doses, and the individual components of Symbyax (Prozac and Zyprexa) were given at progressively tapering doses. As she got better, with fewer depressive symptoms, I took a much more active and directive role in telling her to begin contacting friends, going out shopping, and visiting her own home. She was also able to get a volunteer job helping a major organization that serves the mentally ill. She began working part-time in a retail store and found that this built her self-confidence, and she would occasionally venture out of her mother's home to visit her own home in Los Angeles. At 4 years of treatment, Deena was feeling a great sense of accomplishment and gratitude for treatment. She said, "I guess I'm bipolar. You've given me back my life." Her treatment was one in which accurate diagnosis and change in medication management were the first steps, and ongoing behavior changes were the necessary next steps to achieve recovery.

Case Example: Mania With Psychotic Features

Eliza, a 41-year-old woman, was brought to the emergency room by her husband after he found her walking through the neighborhood with a loaded gun, saying that she thought the gun was a beer and she was going to put it in her mouth. She had a 2-day history of increased energy, decreased sleep, and "acting crazy," with pressured speech and being critical, explosive, labile, and irritable. She had experienced similar episodes roughly once a year for the last several years. Her father had a history of depression and alcoholism, and her mother also had depression.

My initial diagnostic impression was bipolar mania with psychotic features. Eliza rapidly stabilized on Depakote, but she preferred to take lithium for the next 3 months. I did not see her again until 2 years later, when she reported having restarted lithium on her own a few days earlier when she was dealing with some family stresses and her husband thought she was becoming "high" again. Three years later, she presented for an urgent appointment. Her husband was concerned that she was impatient, not sleeping, arguing, restless, becoming more outgoing than usual, and cleaning the house in the middle of the night, and he asked her to resume medication. Again, I diagnosed a manic episode and this time gave her Zyprexa with lithium, which she took for 2 months before discontinuing them on her own.

Eliza had very obvious bipolar affective disorder and was unwilling to tolerate the side effects of long-term preventive medication. However, she was able to avoid disastrous consequences because she was willing to listen to her husband and her psychiatrist when the first signs of mania recurred. This was not my idea of optimal treatment because Eliza was not on any long-term preventive medication; we were putting out fires rather than preventing them. But this was the compromise treatment that Eliza could accept for her manic episodes.

13

Child and Adolescent Depression

Childhood depression differs from adult depression, and it often goes unrecognized. Childhood and adolescence are periods of rapid development, and depression may present differently depending on the child's developmental stage. Children may become easily upset, disappointed, and frustrated, expressing their feelings through behavioral changes that may be socially or developmentally appropriate. As a result, parents can have difficulty recognizing depressive symptoms, or they may minimize such symptoms, viewing them as appropriate responses to social stressors. Parents may also be concerned about having a child "labeled" with depression, due to the fear of stigma in educational, familial, and social environments. Frequently, parents exhibit a tremendous amount of guilt themselves, believing that their role in parenting or creating the child's environment is solely responsible for the onset of depressive symptoms in their child. This, too, may interfere with the identification, acceptance, and treatment of depression in children.

Developmentally, the adolescent period serves as a rite of passage into adulthood, marked by puberty, self-exploration, identity formation, and abstract and existential thought. Teens have more pressures to negotiate than children do, from academics to work, friends, and family life. Inherently, teens will be apt to experiment and test parental limits, frequently resulting in adversarial relationships within the family. Alternatively, some teens may become either withdrawn or overly dependent on parents and family members. In either case, depressive symptoms may be overlooked or attributed to the adolescent's "just being a cranky teen," or "being close" to mom or dad, or "living in his own world."

Prevalence of Childhood and Adolescent Depression
Childhood is defined as the period after infancy (1 year of age) to the

onset of puberty, which varies from individual to individual. Girls tend to enter puberty anywhere from 9 to 13 years of age, whereas boys reach puberty around 13 to 15 years of age. Most of the literature and research defines these populations using the terms prepubertal (childhood) and pubertal (adolescence).

The most recent studies show that up to 2.5% of children and 8.3% of adolescents in the United States suffer from depression. The incidence of major depression increases in adolescence; the likelihood of having an episode by age 18 is approximately 20%. Additionally, more than 50% of depressed adults report having had their first episode of major depression by 20 years of age. Screening this age group is therefore very important, as roughly 20–50% of adolescents and young adults may have unrecognized symptoms of depression. Diagnosing and treating depression earlier may improve the overall course of the illness.

In adulthood, women are twice as likely as men to suffer from major depression. In childhood, males and females are equally affected by depression, but in adolescence, females are more vulnerable to it than their male counterparts. There are many theories about why this may be, relating to biological, psychological, and social factors. Biologically, girls enter puberty earlier than boys, which may contribute to an earlier onset of symptoms. Psychologically, girls are more likely to discuss and process emotional stressors, which may result in a greater identification of a persistent sad, irritable, or angry mood. Also, girls have higher rates of body-image disorders, which can be exacerbated during puberty. Socially, girls are at greater risk for sexual abuse, which can significantly affect mood and self-esteem. When adolescent males are stressed, they more frequently cope by distracting themselves with social, academic, and athletic activities. This manner of coping, although helpful, may distract from identification of mood and therefore may stall recognition of depressive symptoms.

Current research indicates that the onset of depression is occurring earlier in life. According to a study in the *Journal of the American Medical Association (JAMA)*, early-onset depression persists, recurs, and continues into adulthood, often being predictive of a more severe course of illness. Though some evidence points to genetic markers and "familial loading" (having many relatives with depression) as being responsible for both childhood onset and for a severe course of illness, the literature is also clear that repeated episodes of depression in and of themselves may yield a more chronic, recurrent, and treatment-resistant course.

Untreated depression may result in damage to self-esteem, family life, and relationships. Without effective treatment, a depressed child may overidentify with his illness, coming to view the depressed state as normal or internalizing it as if it were part of him. Depression may thwart a child's ability to excel in major life areas and to meet important social and intellectual developmental milestones; children may have trouble playing catch-up if certain critical periods in development are missed due to a depressive episode. Indeed, the nature of the course of depression may heavily influence the quality and magnitude of a child's experiences, positive and negative, as he transitions into adulthood.

Maternal Depression

As noted previously, one aspect of the large-scale STAR*D study was to assess mothers with depression and their children. It was observed that mothers who were depressed had a significant likelihood of having children who demonstrated depressive symptoms as well. It was concluded from the study that when the mother's depression was treated, the children's depressive symptoms resolved as well. This study suggests that recognizing and treating symptoms of parental depression can have a significant impact on the child's symptoms of depression (Weissman et al., 2006).

Clinical Course of Depression

Child and adolescent depression is more frequently an episodic disorder, with high rates of recurrence that may exceed those of adult depression. For kids, the average duration of a depressive episode is 1 to 9 months. About 1 out of every 10 cases will have a course longer than 1 to 2 years. There are quite a few factors associated with clinical course in depression. The first of these factors is the child's cognitive style and temperament. Children who tend to think negatively and are more avoidant and withdrawn are more likely to process life stressors in a less adaptive way and become depressed. Children who have an increased genetic risk may be more likely to develop depression when faced with environmental stressors. Likewise, children with early adverse experiences, exposure to negative life events, and stressful family relationships are more likely to develop depression, as are children who are very hard on themselves or attribute external problems to themselves. If a child is faced with a stressful environmental circumstance where he feels lack of control, he may adopt a style of self-blame to gain control, which may eventually turn into increased guilt and perception of responsibility for external events, which may contribute to depression. Functioning at school is also critically connected to the clinical course of depression. Children measure themselves by their achievements at school, and their self-esteem can be strongly affected by poor school performance. Not succeeding in school may contribute to chronic frustration and low self-esteem, which may foster the development and progression of depression. When a child is struggling in school, parents and teachers must make every effort to get them the accommodations they need so they can participate.

Bipolar Disorder in Children and Adolescents

When evaluating depression in children and adolescents, it is important to consider the diagnosis of bipolar disorder (an in-depth discussion of diagnosing appears later in this chapter). As previously mentioned, bipolar disorder in adults is characterized by depressive, manic or hypomanic, or mixed (symptoms of both mania and depression) episodes, with a peak age of onset between 15 and 19 years old. Studies in bipolar adults have reported that up to 60% experienced symptoms prior to 20 years of age, and 10–20% reported them prior to age 10. There are few studies on rates of bipolar disorder in adolescents. One community study evaluated youths ages 14 to 17 and demonstrated a lifetime prevalence of approximately 1% in this population (Lewinsohn, Klein, & Seeley, 1995).

The subject of childhood bipolar disorder is currently in hot debate among researchers and clinicians. In the past, it was thought that bipolar disorder was extremely rare in children, with peak onset being in the mid-teenage to early adulthood years. More recently, many clinicians have begun diagnosing children with bipolar disorder, and researchers are working to determine the validity of this diagnosis in children. In addition to this, greater consideration is being given to the course of the illness across the life span. Many questions have yet to be answered.

Children who have frequent mood swings, temper tantrums, inattention, hyperactivity, and grandiosity are often potential candidates for a diagnosis of bipolar disorder. These children require careful assessment, as there may be many underlying factors and alternative diagnoses contributing to the presentation of symptoms. Making a diagnosis of bipolar disorder without careful consideration of the influence of other potential psychiatric illness, psychological factors, and social and environmental stressors can lead to inadequate treatment or pharmacologic overtreatment.

Suicide

Children and adolescents with unipolar or bipolar depression are at risk for suicide. Risk factors for suicide include previous attempts, concurrent substance abuse, family history of suicide, HIV or other illness, feelings of hopelessness, running away, serious family disturbances such as abuse, isolative and stressful social environments, and significant anger and agitation. Signs of worsening depression include increased guilt, boredom, and difficulty concentrating; decreased self-care; changes in appearance; changes in sleeping and eating habits; decreased pleasure from previously enjoyable experiences; decreased school performance; and preoccupation with suicide or death in conversation, even jokingly. Children and teens with suicidal intent and plans may exhibit dramatic changes in their behavior or personality. For example, they may give away prized possessions or purchase weapons or firearms. It is important to seek emergency services if a child or teen is suicidal. Intensive treatment is required to ensure safety.

The SSRI Paxil (paroxetine) has been the subject of much of controversy, as a review of the literature on this medication sparked the FDA's concern about antidepressant medication possibly increasing risk for suicidal thoughts. Paxil is less likely to be used as a treatment for this reason. The FDA began to look into this concern about suicidality and conducted a large-scale study of short-term treatment of depression with a wide range of antidepressants. An expert group of child and adolescent psychiatrists was asked to very carefully reexamine the data obtained during this large series of studies that randomized consenting patients with depression into groups that would receive an investigational new antidepressant drug or a placebo. Such studies are an FDA requirement before a drug can be marketed in the United States. The placebo group had a 2% suicide signal (suicidal thoughts or behaviors) compared to 4% in the treatment group. No completed suicides occurred during the studies. The results were statistically significant, and the FDA proceeded to place a black-box warning of increased risk of suicidal thinking and behavior on all antidepressants. The only medication in the study that seemed more likely than others to increase suicidal behavior was Effexor; otherwise, there were no significant differences among the medications. It is important to consider the risks and benefits of treatment, and to ensure that close monitoring is in place when a child is started on antidepressant medication.

Several long-term observational studies have found a correlation between increasing antidepressant use and a decreasing rate of completed teen suicides. The risks, as outlined by the FDA, of antidepressants causing suicidal thoughts indicate that this may occur at the beginning of treatment; long-term studies suggest, however, that use of antidepressant medications may decrease overall suicide rates by decreasing the burden of depression over the full course of treatment. The risk-to-benefit ratio of using antidepressant medication to treat child and adolescent depression needs to be assessed prior to starting treatment. Parents should discuss this with their child's psychiatrist so that they can learn about how suicidal thoughts may manifest behaviorally, and so that they can be active participants in monitoring and reporting side effects.

Diagnosing Depression and Bipolar Disorder

The *DSM-IV* criteria for a diagnosis of depression in children and adolescents are the same as those for depression in adults: 2 weeks of consistent change in mood, either depressed or irritable; loss of interest or pleasure; and changes in sleep, appetite, energy level, activity, and concentration. Additional symptoms include feeling hopeless and having decreased self-worth, low self-esteem, excessive guilt, and thoughts of death or suicide. Five of these criteria must be met for most of the day, nearly every day, for a full 2-week duration of time to make the diagnosis of major depressive disorder.

Likewise, the *DSM-IV* criteria for bipolar disorder in children and adolescents are the same as those for adults. To make a diagnosis of bipolar I disorder, one must have discrete episodes of depression and mania. Bipolar II disorder is marked by episodes of depression and hypomania (symptoms not as severe as mania). Bipolar disorder "not otherwise specified" (NOS) is a diagnosis for individuals who demonstrate severe symptoms that do not fit the usual time course as described later in this chapter.

The *DSM-IV* defines mania as being a distinct period of abnormally elevated, expansive, or irritable mood that lasts at least a week or that requires hospitalization. If the mood is elevated or expansive, the person must also have at least three of the following symptoms, and four of the symptoms if mood is just irritable: inflated self-esteem or grandiosity, decreased need for sleep, more talkativeness or pressure to continue talking, racing thoughts, distractibility, agitation or increased goal-directed activity, and excessive involvement in high-risk behaviors. In younger children these symptoms present in age-appropriate contexts. For example, hypersexuality in children may present as increased masturbation, exposing oneself in public, or grabbing other children inappropriately. Grandiosity may present as the child's behaving like he is the "king of the world" or as believing that he has special powers, such as being able to fly, and actually acting on those beliefs. These thoughts and behaviors must represent a change from baseline and be present with other symptoms, so as to differentiate mania or hypomania from normal fantasy and imaginative play.

Of course, many teens are naturally irritable, demonstrate inflated self-esteem, and engage in high-risk behaviors. In teens with mania, however, these symptoms represent a change from the adolescent's previous functioning and can be so intense that the consequences threaten the individual's well-being. High-risk behaviors can be things such as running away from home, bingeing on drugs or alcohol, increased sexual interest and activity, or excessive spending. In addition to these symptoms, adolescents will present with decreased need for sleep in manic episodes, as well as increased goal-directed behavior. For example, a teen may get involved in numerous new activities in school, increase participation in social events, or begin multiple complex projects but not have the concentration or organization to complete them. Manic teenagers may appear more talkative than normal, not allowing others to get a word in, and they may be hard to follow in conversation. They may report that their thoughts are moving very rapidly. They may appear more distractible, unable to sustain attention on one topic or task for very long. In addition, they may appear more agitated, having difficulty sitting still or staying in one place for a sustained period of time. A sudden change in self-identity, such as style of dress or makeup, interest in a radically different religion or style of music, or drastic change in ideals and life goals may be a clue to a mood disturbance, either mania or depression.

Hypomania can be harder to recognize, as the episode may not involve any major behavioral change. This makes diagnosing hypomania more difficult. As in adults, the symptoms do not cause significant impairment, but are noticeable to people other than the child as being different from their usual behavior. As in adults, the most common symptoms are psychomotor acceleration (more physically active), increased energy and goal-directed activities, talkativeness or pressured speech, and varying moods (either euphoric or irritable). In children, these symptoms typically occur in the late afternoon to evening, and sometimes into the early morning hours. These children may not fall asleep until the wee hours of the morning, and may wake feeling depressed, lethargic, and wanting to sleep throughout much of the day.

In youth with bipolar disorder, the more frequent first episode is depression (rather than mania or hypomania). A striking finding is that 20–40% of depressed children and adolescents go on to develop bipolar disorder 5 years later. Therefore, even if a child's first presentation is for symptoms of depression, it is important to keep bipolar disorder on the radar in the future.

Childhood bipolar disorder differs slightly in presentation from adult bipolar disorder. In children, the episodes of mania and depression tend to switch (or cycle) more rapidly, making discrete episodes harder to detect. Also, children frequently present with more mixed episodes, where symptoms of depression and mania appear at the same time. As one may guess, this makes for a confusing set of circumstances. Children often have mood changes over the course of a day, on a continuous basis. The key in making the diagnosis of bipolar disorder is recognizing the cluster of symptoms that cause distress or a change in functioning. These symptoms must be significant enough to interfere with the child's overall well-being.

Youth with bipolar disorder can experience psychotic symptoms while in a depressed, mixed, or manic episode. (These psychotic symptoms are very different from those involved in schizophrenia. In schizophrenia, teens tend to have chronic psychotic symptoms with few to no mood changes.) Psychotic symptoms include hallucinations or delusions. Hallucinations can involve any of the human senses, but they are most often auditory or visual. Delusions are fixed false beliefs that are not consistent with reality. Delusions can fall anywhere on the spectrum from small deviations from reality to really far-off beliefs. For example, a large deviation from reality would be a patient who believes the FBI is after him; a small deviation might be believing in magical occurrences. To be considered delusions, these beliefs must be very different from those of the family, community, subculture, or religion in which the person has been growing up. In bipolar disorder, if psychotic symptoms are present, they will resolve as the mood symptoms improve.

Like adults, children and adolescents may have depressive symptoms outside of the context of major depressive disorder. Depression may occur within an adjustment disorder, disruptive behavior disorder, learning disorder, or anxiety disorder—or as part of bipolar disorder or psychosis. Additionally, depression may be concurrent with chronic medical problems in children, commonly with many types of cancers, epilepsy, organ transplant, cystic fibrosis, and diabetes. Depression may occur as a result of substance abuse in older children and adolescents. Children and adolescents who have been abused or victimized are at greater risk for major depression and post-traumatic stress disorder;

nearly 4% of boys and more than 6% of girls have symptoms of post-traumatic stress disorder caused by violence they have endured or witnessed (NMHA, 2006). The more mild but chronic form of depression known as dysthymia can occur in children and adolescents as well, but the criteria for diagnosis differ from those for adults. With children and adolescents, the symptoms must be present for just a year instead of 2 years. If a child doesn't meet the exact criteria for major depression but still has a significant mood change with an overall change in functioning, he may have a depressive disorder not otherwise specified.

History-Taking

A thorough history-taking is just as important in diagnosing children and adolescents as it is in diagnosing adults. With children, this also includes inquiring about functioning at school.

Family Psychiatric History

Children and adolescents with family histories of mood disorders are at greater risk for having depression. If a child has one depressed parent, he is three times more likely than the average child of the same age and sex to have a major depressive episode. Children have the highest risk for major depressive disorder if a single parent has a history of recurrent major depressive disorder or early-onset mood disorders, or if both parents have anxiety disorders or mood disorders.

Children of parents who have a history of other psychiatric disorders are also at greater risk for developing psychiatric conditions. A study of bipolar parents found that their children had elevated rates of major depression, bipolar disorder, anxiety, and disruptive-behavior disorder (Birmaker et. al., 2009). In another study, parents with a history of drug or alcohol abuse and anxiety had children with increased rates of conduct disorder and depression (Ohannessian et al., 2004). It is unclear to what degree this risk is due to genetic factors and how much environment may play a role.

Social and Educational History

Children and teens grow and develop under the influences of their families, schools, and communities. Understanding these microenvironments is of great importance when assessing mood and behavior. There are many environmental influences that can shape a child or teen's behavior.

First and foremost, it is necessary to understand who the legal guardian is so that consent for psychiatric evaluation and treatment can be obtained. It is also important to know the details of the family constellation and how the child or teen has developed relationships within this context. Understanding family stressors is critical. In our culture, divorce and nontraditional families are common, and families may experience challenges in balancing career and family and high living expenses. It is common for families to move frequently or to experience times of economic hardship. Also, living in rural, suburban, and urban environments can influence a child's experience growing up. This information is vital for a mental health professional to make a diagnosis.

Abusing substances such and drugs and alcohol can directly and indirectly influence mood and behavior. In making a diagnosis of depression, it is important to understand if a child or teen is actively abusing substances. Many substances themselves can cause depression, as was discussed in earlier chapters. Children and teens may grow up in households where parents are abusing substances, putting them at greater risk for depression. This also puts them at greater risk for neglect and abuse, which in turn can lead to depression. Child abuse is common and often undisclosed. It has been estimated that 3.25 million children are reported each year for alleged abuse (Administration for Children and Families, 2006). This is an important piece of a child's history to understand, recognize, and treat. Understanding if a child or teen's safety is being compromised is an essential part of diagnosis. At times it may be necessary to involve child protective services to provide a child or teen safety and support.

General household safety is also important for families. Locking up potentially lethal household items—most obviously, weapons, but also over-the-counter medications, household cleaners, and sharp objects—is of vital importance in preventing accidental or intentional injury. It may be difficult for parents to think of their child or teen potentially engaging in actions of self-harm, let alone suicide, but if a child or teen is depressed, he is more prone to having thoughts of suicide and may engage in self-harming behaviors. Parents should talk with their mental health professional about safety plans tailored to the child and family. The mental health professional will be able to make specific recommendations.

School is the childhood version of work. Children and teens who are depressed often have a history of decline in academic performance and may demonstrate changes in behavior with peers and in interests and activities. The school staff can provide extremely helpful information to clinicians assessing a child or teen. Teachers can provide valuable reports on classroom behavior and academic performance. School counselors may have a sense of the child's personality, interests, and achievements over a larger scope of time. This information can be useful in diagnosing not only depression, but also a variety of psychiatric conditions that often accompany depression, such as attention-deficit/hyperactivity disorder (ADHD) or language and learning disorders.

It is essential for a child or teen to have positive and rewarding experiences at school. This alone may produce positive change in a child or teen's self-esteem and identity formation. It is very helpful for parents to stay in close contact with their child's school. Often problems at school are the first indicator of a psychiatric condition in a child.

Considering the Patient's Developmental Stage

The challenge in making the diagnosis of depression in children and adolescents is recognizing the previously mentioned *DSM-IV* symptoms of depression in the context of different developmental stages.

Younger children may be limited in their ability to put feelings into words. Therefore, depressive symptoms are often demonstrated behaviorally. Irritable or depressed mood may appear as increased temper tantrums, crying episodes, or emotional responses out of proportion to environmental stressors. Frequently, children demonstrate extreme emotional sensitivity to rejection or failure. Irritability may manifest as a disruption in the child's current relationships with friends—for example, in frequent fighting or losing friends. Irritability may also cause an increase in behavioral problems at school, resulting in phone calls from teachers. Anhedonia (the inability to experience pleasure) in this age group may be characterized by a child's lack of interest in playing with favorite toys or games, or in engaging in other activities the child once enjoyed.

Frequent remarks about "being no good," not being "good at anything," or "not being able to do anything" may be suggestive of a sense of worthlessness or low self-esteem. Just like adults, children may have difficulties with sleep (too much or too little), or changes in appetite (eating too much or too little). Children may also have changes in their energy level, often complaining of "being bored," and depression frequently manifests in physical complaints such as headaches, stomachaches, and muscle pains.

Adolescents demonstrate depressive symptoms through their behavior as well, but they may be better able to put their emotional state into words. The way depression looks in adolescents depends on their personality and on whether their affective state is primarily irritable or melancholic. Irritable adolescents may demonstrate anger with outbursts of shouting, often fighting with parents and peers. They also may have more frequent crying spells, often out of proportion to stressors. Their physical appearance might change drastically—yet another mode of communicating of emotions. As noted earlier, they may engage in more reckless, risk-taking behavior. Other adolescents may appear more melancholic and withdrawn: These teens may "somatize" their depression, making complaints about physical symptoms like headaches, stomachaches, and pain that interfere with their daily activities and often result in absences from school or lack of participation in social events. Additionally, these teens may be more isolative and withdrawn, with poor communication styles. Symptoms common to affectively irritable and melancholic teens would be sleep and appetite changes, changes in weight and physical appearance, and poor self-esteem. Adolescents who are depressed may talk of running away, complain of being bored, or engage in alcohol, nicotine, and drug use. All of these symptoms are red flags for depression in adolescents, especially if the aggregate result is an overall decline in functioning from the past.

Case Example:
Emergency Evaluation of Physical Complaints in a 14-Year-Old Boy

I first met Charles, a 14-year-old, in the emergency room. He had been brought in by his mother due to complaints about headaches and persistent numbness and tingling in the back of his neck, forehead, and hands. After the thorough evaluation by the emergency medical doctor revealed no acute medical concerns, it was noted on further interview that Charles had been sad lately, not interacting with friends, and doing poorly in school. The emergency room physician decided to consult psychiatry to consider a diagnosis of depression.

When I met Charles, he was lying in bed and appeared quite thin. His voice was soft and his speech mumbled. He reflected on having felt down for the past 2 months, with decreased energy, low appetite, and increased sleep. His older sister, who was present for part of the interview, stated that she heard him complain of "not having any friends," "being a loser," and having chronic body pain. She reported that she would ask him to come out and join their friends for dinner, and he would say he was too tired. Charles further reflected on the decline of his grades at school. He was a former A/B student, but for the last 3 months he had been getting Ds and Fs. He said he had been trying to do his work but had been distracted and unable to concentrate. He had stopped turning in assignments and hadn't been able to focus during exam time. Charles denied any recent stressors in his life. He lived at home with his parents, and there had been no recent changes in their lifestyle. Charles also denied any tobacco, alcohol, or drug use and said he was not involved in any gang activity or criminal or reckless behavior. He was not dating, and identified himself as heterosexual but not sexually active.

Charles's mother was a homemaker, and his father worked as a tradesman. When I met with his mother, she was very concerned about Charles's current state of emotional and physical health. She was quick to describe how he had lost weight and had not been eating despite her daily cooking. She was initially focused on something being medically wrong with him, as there had been no real diagnosis for his numbness. When we began to discuss his depressive symptoms, she immediately became tearful. She went on to talk about how she had tried to be the best mom for her son. She reflected on times they had spent together talking about feelings and how she had been there to help boost his self-esteem. We talked about how depression might occur sporadically, and that there did not have to be a life event to trigger it. I tried to make it very clear to her that no flaw in her attentive and loving parenting had caused him to become depressed. We went on to discuss how untreated depression may lead to worsening of symptoms and even suicide. We also discussed Charles's risk for future depressive episodes, either triggered by stressful life events or appearing as sporadic occurrences. I described how timely intervention and treatment might help prevent future episodes and result in improvement in his overall functioning.

Charles and his mother seemed relieved by my diagnosis of major depression, and a plan for treatment was set forth. Charles in particular was relieved to know that I had seen other teens with his symptoms and that, like the others, he would benefit from treatment.

This case example illustrates how important it is to recognize that nonspecific physical complaints can be the first clue in considering a diagnosis of depression. With children and adolescents, it often can be easier to discuss what physically ails them, which can be used by the clinician to begin a discussion about emotions. For example, many children who have anxiety or depression about going to school will have headaches or stomachaches only in the morning. A clinician can talk about the stomachaches with the child and then begin a discussion about why mornings may be stressful for the child and what is going on at school to cause stress. This can be an effective way to understand what the physical symptoms mean for the child, and it also creates a common language to discuss stressors when emotional vocabulary may not be developed enough to do so. Also, kids who have physical complaints may feel invalidated when the medical workup is negative, because their physical symptoms are very real to them; talking with the child about the physical symptoms may help make him feel more validated. It is very important not to minimize the physical complaints, but rather to help reframe why they are occurring. For example, telling a kid he is having a headache because he does not want to go to school is very invalidating. A way to reframe that for the child may be, "I know school can cause stress, and stress can cause headaches. Let's focus on how to manage the stress so your head doesn't hurt."

Another important issue illustrated in this example is the mother's experience of Charles's symptoms. She was very preoccupied with the physical symptoms, as the emotional symptoms were difficult for her to acknowledge due to her guilt. It is much harder for parents to accept a mental health disorder than it is to accept a physical illness because they feel responsible for "creating the emotional illness" in their children. This sense of shame can become a barrier to seeking treatment for the child's depression. This is a very common phenomenon and it is important to address it immediately, so the parent is at ease and more open to diagnosis and treatment.

Case Example: Emergency Evaluation of an 8-Year-Old Girl With Suicidal Ideation

Angela was an 8-year-old girl who presented with her parents to the emergency room with a history of worsening temper tantrums over the previous 2 months, increasing in duration and frequency, and a 1-day history of suicidal ideation. Angela's parents reported that they had moved 5 months ago but could not identify any other recent stressors. They described Angela as always being very "sensitive." They stated that she had a history of being easily upset, and that she had been seen by a therapist in the past for anxiety. Angela had always been fascinated by the cable programming centered on weather and natural disasters and was preoccupied with this material to the point of not interacting with friends as she had before. Angela's parents also reported that over the last 2 months, Angela had not been sleeping well, waking frequently in the middle of the night as well as having difficulty falling asleep. She had been eating less at breakfast and dinnertime. Her mother reported increased difficulty in getting Angela to school due to irritability and crying episodes. Angela had frequently complained of headaches and had not been as eager to play games with her parents or friends as she had been in the past.

During the interview without her parents, Angela said she was sad but didn't know why. She claimed that she was ugly and not good at anything, and said that she was going to take a kitchen knife, run away from home, and kill herself. She was able to describe what it means to be dead and stated yet again that she didn't want to live anymore. She said that she had been more restless inside lately and reported some difficulties with friends at school. Her mother agreed that Angela had seemed more agitated lately.

Angela's parents worried that they were "overreacting" in bringing their daughter to the emergency room, but they realized that her behavior was getting out of control. I reassured them that bringing Angela to the emergency room was an appropriate and necessary response to her current emotional state. We decided that an inpatient admission to psychiatry was the next best step in Angela's treatment, to ensure her safety as well as clarify any other additional psychiatric diagnoses, and to start medication treatment.

In this example, we can see how difficult it can be for parents to distinguish depressive symptoms from a kid's "just having a difficult time" lately. As illustrated in the example, Angela had classic symptoms of depression, including decreased appetite, anhedonia, isolation, sadness and irritability, hopelessness, guilt, and suicidal thinking. Kids may also take a new interest in material that is depressing or destructive. In this example, Angela's intense preoccupation with natural disasters may have been a way of projecting her negative worldview or reflective of her negative emotional state. Of course, this is only a hypothetical explanation, but it is common to see kids, when depressed, become preoccupied with these types of themes.

Differential Diagnoses

Children and adolescents may have symptoms that look like depression but are in fact indicative of other psychiatric disorders or are occurring as a feature within another psychiatric disorder. When considering depressive symptoms in a child, it is important to assess the presence or absence of these other conditions.

There is an adage in medical practice that certain medical problems tend to run in packs. Basically, one condition is often seen with others. For example, people with diabetes may have problems with high blood pressure and high cholesterol. The same is true in psychiatry. About 40–90% of children and adolescents with major depressive disorder have other psychiatric diagnoses. Specifically, dysthymia, anxiety disorders, and disruptive behavior disorders can occur simultaneously in about 10–80% of children and teens diagnosed with depression.

Children and adolescents with ADHD, other learning disabilities, pervasive developmental disorders (PDD), and speech and language disorders can feel demoralized and demonstrate low self-esteem. Children who are anxious may get easily overwhelmed and frustrated, which can go hand in hand with depression. Depression may be underlying an eating disorder or may be a first episode in the course of bipolar disorder. Youth who abuse substances can be depressed as well.

Full Medical Exam

Prior to any psychiatric exam, it is helpful to have a complete physical examination. This is especially important with mood symptoms that are accompanied by physical complaints. Identifying and treating coexisting medical problems may alleviate psychiatric symptoms and vice versa. This is discussed in further detail later.

Vision and hearing screens are done routinely in childhood. But children may subsequently develop poor vision or hearing, with resultant academic, behavioral, and emotional changes. Vision and hearing screens are often worth repeating when children and teens present for psychiatric evaluation. A full physical exam may reveal laboratory findings of hypothyroidism, hepatitis, anemia, kidney disease, diabetes, or other medical problems that could present with depressive symptoms. It will also sometimes reveal signs of trauma, such as bruises, abrasions, self-cutting or burning scars, or even broken bones in various states of healing. These may raise the suspicion of physical abuse.

Pervasive Developmental Disorder and Communication Disorders

Children who have PDDs meet criteria for diagnosis by demonstrating impairment in development of social reciprocity, verbal or nonverbal communication with stereotyped or restricted interests, thoughts, behavior, and activities. These children may or may not have mental retardation as well. They may have a more difficult time interacting socially as a result of their inability to read social cues. They also may have more difficulty playing and interacting with peers due to their restricted interests, thoughts, and behaviors. Socially, it can be challenging for these children to express themselves if they have a communication disorder. Consequently, children may feel rejected by others, which may wear on their self-esteem. Also, they may be irritable and have low frustration tolerance when they are unable to match the social pace of those around them, or when they cannot express or pronounce the words needed to communicate effectively. This can result in behavioral changes, mood swings, and temper tantrums. It may take these children a longer time to accomplish tasks and understand directions, which in turn can result in frustration for both parent and child. This can greatly affect the parent-child relationship and have an impact on the child's self-image and mood. Therapeutic interventions may include social skills training, occupational therapy, speech and language therapy, parent support groups, parenting strategies, and individual and family therapy.

Communication disorders in children can take a variety of forms. Children can have problems with expressive language, receptive language, or both, as well as problems with stuttering or pronouncing words correctly. Communication problems may exist alone or in the context of a PDD. Communication and language disorders require a thorough speech and language evaluation to make the diagnosis. A neuropsychologist will often use specialized tests to estimate receptive and expressive language abilities, memory for verbal and nonverbal materials, ability to do reading and math, ability to reason and plan, and general intelligence (IQ).

For both PDDs and communication disorders, it is important to have a complete medical evaluation as well to rule out any hearing loss or medical problem that may be contributing to the delays. Working with a speech and language pathologist is essential for the treatment of any language or communication disorder.

Case Example: Eric

A 9-year-old boy named Eric was admitted to a day treatment program for increased aggression and temper tantrums. Eric had undergone previous neuropsychological testing and speech and language testing through the school where he currently had an individualized educational program (IEP). This testing revealed slowed cognitive processing speed as well as receptive and expressive language difficulties.

Upon admission to the program, Eric's interactions with peers and staff were odd. He had very poor eye contact and could not play well with peers. He had difficulties with expressive language, being unable to respond appropriately to questions and unable to give any coherent or logical history of recent events or stories. He was preoccupied with superheroes. His mother was very frustrated with him because he had been having difficulty getting ready to get to school on time and difficulty following directions; he also appeared disinterested in her instructions and efforts to motivate him. In fact, she found it hard to talk with him about most things, and this compounded her frustration. For example, when she once asked him what he wanted to eat for dinner, he responded by talking about something else and then minutes later said he was hungry for pizza. She thought he was doing this to be oppositional. In addition, at family parties, she would ask him to tell his relatives about school, and again he would appear to ignore her questions and focus on something else. Eric himself was clearly frustrated as well, which he expressed through temper tantrums and becoming aggressive.

During the day treatment program, our team worked with Eric on feeling identification and on using coping tools to manage feelings of frustration. We also encouraged the use of a behavioral modification program at home, using sticker charts with visual cues to help motivate Eric to get to school in the morning. We encouraged communication with visual prompts for times when it appeared Eric was having difficulty with language. The development of this treatment plan also helped to educate Eric's mother about his language disorder and slow cognitive processing so she could appropriately shift her communication style. Further speech and language therapy, individual therapy, and occupational therapy were recommended. The goal was to make Eric feel like a success, which would boost his self-esteem.

Eric did not demonstrate any sleep, appetite, or energy problems, and therefore did not meet criteria for depression. His low self-esteem and low frustration tolerance were in the context of his language disorder and slow cognitive processing, and they were improved by the treatment of these primary psychiatric conditions. Educating Eric's mother about coping with his handicaps allowed her to feel less angry at his lack of responsiveness.

As this case example shows, it is important to do a thorough evaluation of a child's cognitive functioning, gathering data from multiple sources and getting testing when indicated to appropriately understand symptoms and make a diagnosis. It is very common for kids with speech and language problems, learning disabilities, and developmental delays to feel sad and frustrated. These kids have difficulty communicating, which is frustrating, and often they are not at the same level as their peers, which can affect their self-esteem. It is important to recognize this when developing a treatment plan. Treatment focused on improving the child's ability to communicate will help the child's self-esteem and frustration tolerance. A treatment plan focused on improving the child's mood alone would be detrimental, as the main skill deficit is in communication.

Anxiety Disorders

There are a variety of anxiety disorders that can be diagnosed in children and teens. Children with generalized anxiety disorder may present with symptoms of decreased sleep, increased worries or fears, feeling keyed-up or on edge, feeling easily fatigued, muscle pain, or difficulties concentrating or feeling as if their mind is going blank. Obsessive-compulsive disorder (OCD) can occur in children as well, with similar symptoms as adults. Kids with OCD have intrusive, disturbing thoughts (or images or impulses) that result in either emotional distress or compulsive, repetitive behaviors. Social phobia can occur in kids and teens as well, where social activities are avoided due to excessive fear of scrutiny by others. Children and teens who have been victims of trauma and abuse can develop symptoms of post-traumatic stress disorder. These children may reexperience the trauma through flashbacks, nightmares, and imaginary play. Children and teens may appear detached emotionally or have a sense of foreshortened future. They may also have an exaggerated startle response as well as difficulty sleeping and increased irritability.

Depression is common in children with anxiety disorders. In children with anxiety disorders, 28–69% also experience depression. It is therefore important to screen for depression in children with anxiety disorders and vice versa.

Eating Disorders

Eating disorders—anorexia, bulimia, binge eating, and eating disorders not otherwise specified—most frequently develop during early adolescence. Up to 2% of all college-aged women have bulimia nervosa, and nearly 4% of females will have anorexia at some point during their lifetime (NMHA, 2006). It is important to screen for eating disorders in depressed teens, and vice versa.

Methods of controlling caloric intake include restricting diet by eating less or eating only certain types of low-calorie foods and purging or eliminating ingested food by inducing vomiting or abusing laxatives. Extreme exercise is common to control overall daily caloric balance. A feature common to all these disorders is that self-esteem is associated with body weight and shape. Anorexics are often very thin and by definition have a failure to maintain 85% of their ideal body weight. They have an intense fear of gaining weight or becoming fat without recognizing that they are underweight. They do not recognize the seriousness of their weight loss, which frequently results in missed menstrual periods. Anorexia is frequently seen in teenagers who have perfectionistic, obsessive-compulsive personality styles. They frequently are over-achievers in all areas of their lives.

Bulimia can be more insidious and less obvious, as teens with this disorder frequently maintain normal body weight. Bulimia is marked by binge eating and then compensating by purging, taking laxatives, or exercising excessively. Binging is defined by eating an amount of food that is larger than most people would eat during a 2-hour period of time. Bulimia has a higher comorbidity in teens who abuse substances and demonstrate more risk-taking behaviors.

Eating disorders not otherwise specified is a category that encompasses eating disorders that do not meet the strict criteria for anorexia or bulimia.

The same disturbance in body image is evident, with efforts to control caloric intake by restriction or compensatory behaviors. This category also includes binge eating disorder. Binge eating disorder does not have validated criteria at this time, but it is described by repeated episodes of overeating that are not associated with compensatory behaviors.

If the eating disorder is severe, malnutrition alone may cause low energy and disturbance in sleep and mood. One theory regarding the attempt to control caloric intake is that it is a means of coping with stressors. By controlling calories, the patient is controlling something in his or her life. As with the other eating disorders, self-image is strictly influenced by body weight and shape. With this vulnerable self-esteem, teens with eating disorders can have comorbid depressive disorders. Anxiety disorders are also common in eating-disordered patients. In binge eating disorders, there may be an element of emotional eating, using eating to cope with stressors or anxiety.

Eating disorders are complex: There are new biologic theories for why they occur, as well as a long history of psychological factors involved with their development. These disorders usually require intensive treatment, including medical, nutritional, psychiatric, and psychological evaluations with ongoing followup. Medical intervention is of paramount importance, as eating disorders can be life-threatening. Severe malnutrition can lead to osteoporosis, hormonal changes, electrolyte imbalances, and cardiomyopathy that can result in heart attacks, stroke, or death. Also, self-induced vomiting over time can result in erosion of the esophagus and teeth and rupture of the esophagus where it meets the stomach. Abuse of laxatives can result in chronic problems with constipation and electrolyte disturbances that can lead to kidney damage, heart attack, or death. Binge eating disorders can result in obesity, which is associated with development of diabetes, high blood pressure, sleep apnea, and heart disease over time. Having a nutritionist involved is important to guide the patient in how to resume a healthy diet to obtain optimal body weight. Some hospitals have programs dedicated to the treatment of eating disorders. Often there are a variety of services available, from outpatient to day treatment to inpatient hospitalization, based on the severity of the disorder.

Substance Abuse Disorders

Older children and teenagers may experiment with drugs and alcohol. Kids may even attempt to get high from inhaling household chemicals and glue or taking over-the-counter cold medicines and cough syrups. Of particular interest, kids often overdose on coricidin tablets, called the "triple-C," in order to get high. It has also become popular for kids to smoke or steep (make tea from) certain wildflowers, such as salvia. These substances can dramatically affect mood and behavior. Youth with undiagnosed psychiatric conditions may abuse substances in an effort to ameliorate their symptoms, but after the withdrawal symptoms and reality set back in, they are at risk for developing severe lows and even more significant depressive symptoms. As we have already described, substance-abuse disorders can cause depression as well as exist in combination with depression.

Learning Disorders

Children can have learning disabilities in the areas of reading, mathematics, and written expression, or difficulties with processing information. Learning disorders are diagnosed by formal neuropsychological testing. If a learning disorder is suspected in a child due to failure to meet academic standards or severe emotional or behavioral problems, a parent can request in writing that the school complete an evaluation for an IEP. This evaluation usually includes psychological testing. A parent can also pursue neuropsychological testing through a private neuropsychologist who does this type of work.

Children with learning disorders may clearly present with academic problems, but if there are associated behavioral difficulties, these kids stand out to parents and teachers alike. Specifically, children may engage in many behaviors—often oppositional or defiant—to avoid facing what is difficult for them. They may selectively participate in class or complete only certain kinds of homework. When asked to complete certain types of assignments or participate in class, children may feel humiliated if they simply cannot do it. This can result in chronic demoralization and fragile self-worth. Children may feel that they are constantly spinning their wheels, trying to keep up with others, and feeling chronically unsuccessful. Peers may ridicule them, and adults trying to give direction and instruction may get frustrated with them. It is not surprising, therefore, that these children may become depressed.

A very important part of the treatment in these cases is implementing strategies at school and home to improve the child's academic success. This alone can boost the child's mood and self-esteem. Individual therapy can be very beneficial in teaching a child or teen about his learning disorder and in outlining his strengths so that he can effectively develop strategies for problem-solving.

Disruptive-Behavior Disorders and Attention-Deficit/ Hyperactivity Disorder

Disruptive behavior disorders are divided, according to the DSM-IV, into oppositional-defiant disorder and conduct disorder. Oppositional-defiant disorder is a pattern of negative and hostile behavior that occurs for at least 6 months in duration, during which children meet at least four of the following criteria: losing temper often; arguing with adults often; defying rules; deliberately annoying people; blaming others for their mistakes; becoming easily annoyed, angry, and resentful; and being spiteful and vindictive. Conduct disorder is more severe, must be ongoing for 12 months or longer, and is marked by aggression toward people and animals, destruction of property, deceitfulness, theft, and serious violation of rules (for example, running away, truancy).

Children with ADHD demonstrate inattention—with or without hyperactivity or impulsivity. These children frequently get behind in school due to problems with concentration, and they frequently demonstrate irritability. They may develop behavioral problems both at home and at school because of their impulsivity and hyperactivity. These children often feel disliked by teachers, parents, and peers due to their behavior problems or need for frequent instruction and redirection. Academic and social problems that evolve may lead to decreased self-esteem.

When thinking of psychiatric disorders in youth, practitioners often use the analogy of an onion. Once one disorder exists, other disorders begin to layer one on top of another as time passes. The idea is that the initial disorder, if left undiagnosed and untreated, can be so debilitating that children then become anxious or depressed. If children are anxious or depressed, they may develop disruptive behaviors or engage in substance abuse. Such is often the case with ADHD. About 30% of youth with ADHD develop depression. Thus, a careful differential diagnosis is essential, because what initially looks like depression might actually be untreated ADHD. Likewise, when kids have ADHD or learning or language disorders, it is important to keep symptoms of depression on the radar screen.

Case Example: 6-Year-Old Boy With ADHD Combined Type and a Possible Language Disorder

Jack was a very handsome, intelligent 6-year-old boy who initially presented with ADHD symptoms. His mother and teacher described him as "driven by a motor"; he had difficulty remaining seated at school as well as at home for mealtimes. He had often been nonadherent with rules and verbal requests, and he had been getting into fights at school with peers.

The current working diagnosis for Jack was ADHD combined type (meaning that he exhibited both inattentive and hyperactive symptoms), and he was started on Ritalin. The stimulant improved Jack's performance in school, but there still were continued mood symptoms. During our weekly therapy sessions, Jack consistently picked out "sad" and "angry" from the feelings sheets we used. He spoke of getting picked on by peers and of other social problems at school.

I also noticed that Jack often responded oddly to simple questions. For example, when I asked him what his teacher's name was, he said "sixty." Another time, when I inquired about what he'd had for lunch, he started talking about the sewers near his home. This prompted me to wonder about his having a receptive language disorder. Jack's problems may have been partly due to difficulty processing language—hearing sounds, interpreting them as words, and understanding the meaning of them—rather than simply due to his being distracted.

I arranged for a speech and language evaluation and in the meantime worked with the school to help Jack's teachers understand this child's difficulties so that adjustments could be made to make him feel more successful. I also helped his parents create sticker charts for use at home and explained how to use visual aids when giving directions to ensure Jack's understanding of them. The parents were also educated on the use of praise and positive rewards for positive behavior. In session, Jack and I began working on feeling identification and using tools to cope with anger and sadness, such as taking deep breaths, counting to 10, and "changing channels."

The sticker charts proved very helpful, as did giving Jack more time to accomplish tasks in school. Jack also responded well to positive rewards for positive behavior. My encouraging Jack to "stay in his bubble" helped him to be aware of his personal space, discouraging physical aggression.

Although Jack did not meet the criteria for depression at the time I saw him, he was certainly at risk for it, as are all children with ADHD, and I did notice mood changes in him. I continued to monitor him for depression during the time I saw him, and I educated his mother about the risk for depression and asked her to monitor for it herself as well. My hope was that effectively treating Jack's ADHD, gaining a full understanding of his speech and language capabilities, devising behavioral modification programs for school and home, and maintaining our course of individual therapy and parent education would help to minimize Jack's risk for developing depression.

Case Example: Joey

Joey was a 13-year-old boy who presented because his mother was concerned that he looked depressed. She reported that he never talked about his feelings and had been doing poorly in school. He had been having some sleep disturbance, but no appetite problems. The sleep problems seemed chronic in nature.

During our first session Joey was unresponsive to questions about his feelings and showed no facial expressions whatsoever. He said that he had always had difficulty in school, particularly with concentrating and paying attention, and that he frequently daydreamed. His mother described problems with attention at home, usually manifested by her son's seeming to "not be present" during conversations and by his not following directions when asked to complete a chore or task. Joey had always had few friends. He had gotten by with average grades until this year, when he started failing classes. The schoolwork had become more demanding and required greater mental effort, detail, and organization for completion.

Joey denied any hopelessness, energy changes, or suicidal thoughts, though he did talk about feeling "like a failure" at school and how frustrated he had been trying to get schoolwork completed. He felt humiliated when the teachers reprimanded him for not paying attention. The other kids picked up on this and teased him for it as well.

It seemed like Joey's difficulties were chronic in nature, primarily stemming from his problems with attention. We decided to pursue treatment for ADHD inattentive type with Concerta (a sustained-release preparation of Ritalin or methylphenidate), and we continued psychotherapy and modifications to his academic program. Joey responded well to this, showing significant improvement in his schoolwork, which resulted in improvement in his self-esteem. He also was able to stay on task in class, which reduced the amount of negative attention he received. Overall, his mood improved and he felt better, which in turn helped him develop relationships with peers. Additionally, through this process, his mother gained a better understanding of her son, learning that his inattention was due to his ADHD and not to being oppositional. It is important to separate the child from his behavior, recognizing that the child is good and capable of making better behavioral choices.

Chronic Illness and Depression

Serious chronic medical problems can either occur with depression or result in depression. Any chronic medical problem requiring close monitoring and intensive treatment may be very stressful for children to deal with. Medical problems frequently associated with depression include lupus, epilepsy, cancer, hypothyroidism, anemia, organ transplant, and AIDS. There is the inherent expectation for these children to be active participants in their care, which may include complex and tedious daily treatments. This alone requires a lot of patience and strength on the child's part, as he is often sacrificing physical comfort and playtime to participate in such treatment. Depression in these children may manifest as nonadherence with treatment and a more complicated course in their medical conditions. It is important to be aware of this, as some research done in adults suggests that treatment of depressed mood associated with medical problems may improve the course of medical illness.

Treatment

Before discussing treating depression in children and adolescents, it is important to talk about untreated depression. For a variety of reasons, many parents and teens are resistant to treatments for depression. Obstacles to treatment can vary widely. Often, teens and older children refuse treatment as they do not recognize their depressive symptoms or don't want to take medications or participate in therapy. Parents may align with their child in these circumstances. Parents, too, may have personal reservations about therapy and medication, or they may be reluctant to argue about treatment adherence with the child, thinking this will upset him further. Bad experiences with previous therapists and medication side effects—particularly weight gain—may make it hard for children and teens to see the benefit of treatment. Therefore, it is prudent to discuss the risks of untreated depression with both child and parent at the time of diagnosis. In medicine, treatments are recommended based on the research to support them, as well as on the risk-to-benefit ratio. The risks associated with lack of treatment are, of course, worsening symptoms, which relate to an overall decline in functioning. Older children and particularly teenagers are at greater risk for suicide and substance abuse with untreated depression, and worsening overall course is associated with lack of treatment in children of all ages. In adults, the clinical course of untreated depression results in more frequent depressive episodes, with greater severity of symptoms with each relapse. Depression may result in poor judgment, which may ultimately have an effect on physical health and increase risk of illness. It may result in academic and work failure, contributing to lower achievement in life and risk for lower socioeconomic status in adulthood. Family and friends may change from being supportive and helpful to frustrated, angry, and withdrawn when their best efforts to help "cheer up" the depressed person aren't well received.

Medication

Children are not small adults. Treatment of child and adolescent depression with medication has similarities to treatments for adult depression, but also significant differences. There are far fewer studies done in children and adolescents due to the desire to "protect" vulnerable populations from the risks of research. Often data from adult literature are extrapolated to the child population, but this may be an unreliable strategy, as children may respond differently to adult treatments and their illness may not follow the same epidemiological trends as seen in adults. This suggests an even greater need for continued research.

MEDICATIONS FOR UNIPOLAR DEPRESSION

Treating depression with antidepressant medication is common in adult practice and can be an important part of treating child and adolescent depression as well. Selective serotonin reuptake inhibitors (SSRIs) have demonstrated overall safety and efficacy in treating depression. Among them, Prozac (fluoxetine) has been most studied and has demonstrated the greatest efficacy in clinical trials for treatment of depression. It is also the only drug that is FDA approved for depressed children and adolescents ages 7 to 17 years. In a recent meta-analysis, fluoxetine was the only individual SSRI that showed a response significantly better than placebo, with an associated greater reduction in depression scores (Tsapakis, Soldanin, Tondo, & Baldessarini, 2008). Other SSRI medications such as Celexa and Zoloft have been shown to be effective for use in child and adolescent depression (Wagner, 2005; Wagner, Jonas, Findling, Ventura, & Saikali, 2006; Wagner et al., 2003, 2004).

Non-SSRI medications that have been studied in children and adolescents include tricyclic antidepressants (TCAs), serotonin norepinephrine reuptake inhibitors (SNRIs), tetracyclic antidepressants (Remeron), and the atypical antidepressants (such as Serzone and Wellbutrin). The clinical trials for TCAs do not demonstrate efficacy for the treatment of child and adolescent depression. Similarly, clinical trials of Serzone demonstrated no efficacy, and neither did trials of Remeron and Effexor (an SNRI).

MEDICATIONS FOR BIPOLAR DEPRESSION

There are very few studies on treatment of bipolar disorder in children. The studies that have been done suggest that mood stabilizers and atypical antipsychotic medication may be helpful for short-term stabilization. Children with bipolar disorder and ADHD may benefit from mood stabilizers and stimulants. There are limited studies regarding the treatment of pediatric bipolar depression and treatment of bipolar disorder with other psychiatric conditions. There is a need for further research in this area, as well as for studies that address long-term treatment.

It is important to recognize that pediatric depression may be part of an underlying bipolar disorder. This is important when treating depression with antidepressant medication. If there is an underlying bipolar disorder, the child may be more likely to become agitated or maniclike while on the antidepressant medication. A diagnosis of bipolar disorder cannot be made based on this response to treatment, however. Even if a child does not have an underlying bipolar disorder, he may become agitated on antidepressant medication for reasons that are not yet completely understood. It is extremely important to watch for behavioral and mood changes at home while having a psychiatrist closely monitor treatment after an antidepressant medication is started. If the child does become agitated or maniclike, other treatments can be considered.

Major Trials in Adolescent Depression

The Treatment for Adolescents with Depression Study (TADS) is one of the most recent large-scale studies of depression treatment in adolescents. This multicenter study looked at 439 adolescents from ages 12 to 17; participants were of evenly mixed gender and cultural backgrounds. The average age was 14.6 years; 45.6% were male, 73.8% white, 12.5% African American, and 8.9% Hispanic (Herman, Ostrander, Walkup, Silva, & March, 2007; Kratochvil et al., 2006; Treatment for Adolescents

With Depression Study Team, 2005). The most common concurrent diagnoses were generalized anxiety, attention-deficit hyperactivity, oppositional-defiant, social phobia, and dysthymia. Of the patients in the study, 86% were in their first episode (Treatment for Adolescents With Depression Study Team, 2005). The study team compared cognitive-behavioral therapy (CBT) only, medication (with Prozac-fluoxetine 10–40 mg/day) only, both psychotherapy and medication, and placebo. The group that demonstrated greatest safety and improvement was treated with Prozac and therapy. The trial also demonstrated that Prozac alone was more effective than therapy alone, and that therapy alone was no different from placebo (March et al., 2004). Response rates at 12 weeks were: fluoxetine plus CBT 71%, fluoxetine alone 60.6%, CBT alone 43.2%, and placebo 34.8% (March et al., 2004). An important finding was that CBT appeared to have a protective effect against suicidal events (March et al., 2006).

There were some predictors of acute 12-week outcome that were present at the start of study participation. Younger age, less chronic depression, higher functioning, less hopelessness, less suicidal ideation, fewer melancholic features, fewer comorbid diagnoses, and greater expectation for improvement were all associated with better outcome. Combined treatment with fluoxetine plus CBT was more effective than fluoxetine alone for mild to moderate depression and for patients with high levels of cognitive distortion, but not for severe depression or patients with low levels of cognitive distortion. Adolescents from high-income families did as well with CBT alone as with combined treatment (Curry et al., 2006). There was a broader range of improvement (compared to placebo) at 12 weeks with combination therapy than fluoxetine alone. Combination therapy improved functioning, global health, and quality of life, whereas medication without therapy improved only functioning compared to placebo (Vitiello et al., 2006). Time to response also differed among treatment groups, with fluoxetine and combination therapy showing accelerated response relative to placebo, and combination therapy showing faster response than CBT alone (Kratochvil et al., 2006).

Suicidal thinking improved in all treatment groups, but greatest improvement was in the fluoxetine plus CBT group. Side effects reported by at least 2% of patients receiving fluoxetine or the combination of fluoxetine and CBT, and occurring at least twice as often as in patients receiving placebo, included sedation, insomnia, vomiting, and upper abdominal pain. As depression improved, physical complaints and suicidal ideation decreased in proportion to treatment benefit (Emslie et al., 2006). Remission, the real goal of treatment, was achieved at 12 weeks by 37% of patients in the combination group, 23% in the fluoxetine group, 16% in the CBT group, and 17% in the placebo group. Among patients who responded but were not fully well, half still had some symptoms such as sleep or mood disturbance, fatigue, or poor concentration (Kennard et al., 2006).

By 36 weeks, the combination therapy was still slightly better than either fluoxetine or CBT alone, and the use of CBT with fluoxetine decreased the risk of suicidal ideation and attempts. Table 13.1 summarizes the response rates. Note that the group who received placebo during the first 12 weeks were treated openly afterward and are not included in this analysis. The results are striking: Longer duration of treatment gives higher response rates, and combined treatment is better than medication or CBT alone.

Table 13.1
Response Rates in the Treatment for Adolescents
With Depression Study (TADS)

Week	12	18	36
Combination	73	85	86
Fluoxetine	62	69	81
CBT	48	65	81

Source: March et al., 2004.

Another very large study was the Treatment of Resistant Depression in Adolescents (TORDIA) study, which involved a group of 334 patients 12 to 18 years old who had major depression that had failed to respond to an SSRI during 2 months of treatment. They were given a different SSRI or Effexor (venlafaxine 150–225 mg/day) with or without CBT. The response rate with CBT and a switch to either another SSRI or Effexor yielded a higher response rate—54.8% over 12 weeks—whereas medication switch alone yielded a 40.5% response rate. There was no difference between response rates of SSRI and Effexor, and there were more side effects with Effexor than the SSRI drugs (Brent et al., 2008; March et al., 2004).

Psychotherapy

Studies of therapy as a treatment are more difficult to conduct than are trials of medications, but specific therapies such as CBT, interpersonal therapy (IPT), and family therapy have demonstrated efficacy in short-term treatment of child and adolescent depression. Overall, psychotherapy is an important part of treatment for depression, but it alone has not been shown to be as efficacious as medication treatment. The best outcomes are usually when patients receive both therapy and medication treatment. There is some evidence that CBT and IPT may be effective for treatments of early-onset depression.

Individual Therapies

CBT focuses on the association between thoughts, feelings, physical reactions, and behaviors. Specifically, it addresses how certain thoughts, or cognitive distortions, can affect the types of feelings one has. The goal is to teach kids coping tools for feelings and to learn more about what thoughts may be associated with certain feelings. It is thought that shifts in thinking will help feeling management, which in turn can alter physical reactions and behavior. IPT focuses on identified problems with role transition, grief, interpersonal disputes, and interpersonal deficits. By using role-playing, analysis of communication style, and the therapeutic relationship, the patient gains a greater understanding of himself and how he relates to the world around him. He learns how to negotiate relationships in a more adaptive fashion.

CBT and IPT are short-term therapies that utilize a manualized structure in their administration. They are primarily aimed at symptom reduction, working on one or two problems during the course of treatment. There are longer-term therapies available for children and teens with more chronic or complex symptoms and stressors. These longer-term therapies are effective in preventing relapse, building self-esteem, and developing strategies to help a child or teen utilize his strengths in problem-solving.

Family Therapy

As mentioned, there are many factors associated with depression, both biological and psychosocial (having to do with thoughts, emotions, and the child's external world). Therapy is a very important part of treatment in that it helps to address some of these psychosocial factors. Through therapy, children can also learn more about themselves. They can learn to use coping skills to help them manage their feelings. They can learn to use their strengths to strategize around difficult situations and solve problems. This can be extrapolated into the family system as well.

Family therapy is an important treatment intervention focused on helping families with problem-solving, conflict resolution, and building positive family interactions. Families can be very important sources of support for kids battling depression. Teaching families about the signs and symptoms of depression can help them understand the child's moods and behavior. Families can provide a safe home environment, restricting a child's access to lethal medications, substances, or firearms. Enlisting families as part of the treatment team can benefit patients as well. Families can help teach coping skills at home. They can also help to monitor effects of treatments and overall changes in symptoms, which is of great help to the treating physician.

Sometimes a child of divorcing parents feels in the middle of a battle, being emotionally pulled to be the ally of one parent over the other in disputes over custody, who was "wronged" by the other spouse, or how much child support is really needed to allow continuing after-school activities such as music or sports. Sometimes a child blames one parent for the breakup. The child may fear the complete loss of a parent and not be allowed by the court or the custodial parent to see one parent for a very long time. Direct interventions with the divorcing family may help the parents to minimize the damage to the child by decreasing overt hostility and blame and by encouraging simple, direct explanations to the child of visitation and custody plans.

Parents are an integral part of the treatment process. Sometimes small shifts in parenting styles may help produce great change in a child's mood. In younger children, catching them being good is a great strategy for parents. Praise and positive rewards for good behavior can boost a child's self-esteem. In addition, parents can help coach children to use their coping tools to manage their emotions, as well as remind them to focus on the positive when they are stuck in a negative thinking cycle.

With adolescents, parents often have a more difficult role in treatment. It is important for parents to keep tabs on the teen's depressive symptoms. This is a difficult task, as depressed adolescents more frequently are irritable and often deny that they are depressed. In this case, parents may need look at other signs, such as school performance, persistent physical complaints, sleep patterns, appetite changes and subsequent weight changes, and change in previous level of activity and personal interests. Other adolescents may be more tearful and report sadness or feelings of personal failure. In this case, it is important for parents to encourage the teen to develop strategies to manage his feelings, as well as to recognize thought patterns that may contribute to those feelings. For example, if a teen has repeated thoughts that he is "not good enough," sooner or later he may feel sad because of this thought. It may be helpful to coach him to test evidence for such a negative belief. For instance, if he is getting great grades in school but makes a mistake on an assignment, clearly the evidence is greater for his success than for his failure.

These are just a few suggestions for the many ways parents can help. Working with a child and adolescent psychiatrist or therapist on developing an individual treatment plans is recommended in any circumstance. This will ensure that the child's unique needs are addressed, and it can help the parents to adapt their parenting style so that it complements and contributes to the value of therapy, both benefiting the child and strengthening family relationships.

Involving the School

School has a critical role in the lives of children and teens. The importance of the school's feedback was discussed in the earlier section on diagnosis. A child or teen's school can be a very integral part of the psychiatric assessment and treatment plan. If a child or teen has significantly poor academic functioning due to a medical or psychiatric condition, parents can request that the school conduct an evaluation for an IEP. The school may accept or decline this request, but it must do so within a certain time frame. Legally, the request must come from a parent, but having the added support of a psychiatrist or psychologist can often be helpful. At that point, if the school accepts the request, it will proceed with its evaluation. At the end of the evaluation, parents will be invited to join a meeting at the school to discuss the findings and recommendations. Again, a mental health professional can support parents through this process. Depending on a school's resources, it may be able to provide supportive services such as social work, speech therapy, occupational therapy, and individual aids in the classroom. These resources are usually provided if a child qualifies for an IEP.

A child or teen may already have an IEP in place. In this case, it may be helpful to have the mental health professional collaborate with the school staff. It is helpful for the school to know what the treatment plan is so that it can help monitor symptoms and do its part in implementing changes. Schools can be great at helping reinforce coping strategies for children who have difficulty with mood and behavior in the classroom. Also, schools can report on side effects of medications as well as complete behavior checklists to help a psychiatrist monitor treatment efficacy.

If a child or teen does not appear to need a complete IEP, it may be helpful to have the mental health professional work with parents and teachers. Behavioral modification strategies that are consistently enforced at home and school can be very helpful for younger children. For any age child, working with the teacher to understand reasons for poor academic performance can help in developing strategies to improve this. The teacher may have recommendations for work that can be done with the parent's help outside the classroom. In addition, if a teacher understands a child's special circumstances, she too may have suggestions and be willing to implement new classroom strategies to help the child better manage his behavior and emotions.

Any change that can be made to make a child successful at school will help build his self-esteem and morale. This helps treat depression and decreases further risk of developing depression, while providing a foundation for the child to reach his maximum academic potential.

Treatment Course

Response rates to treatment for child and adolescent depression were discussed earlier in this chapter. Based on data from 13 trials and 2,910 participants, pooled absolute rates of treatment response were 61% in participants treated with antidepressants and 50% in participants treated with placebo (Bridge et al., 2007). In the TADS study discussed earlier, 60% of patients treated (with fluoxetine, CBT, or the combination) were in remission at week 36. Longer-term outcomes, from reviews of the literature, report that around 50% of children and adolescents remain clinically depressed at 12 months, and 20–40% at 24 months (Birmaher et al., 1996; Harrington, 2001; Kovacs et al., 1984). Around 30% of children and adolescents have recurrences within 5 years, and many of these children and adolescents develop episodes into adult life (Fombonne, Wostear, Cooper, Harrington, & Rutter, 2001a, 2001b; Lewinsohn, Rohde, & Seeley, 1998; Weissman, Wolk, Goldstein, et al., 1999; Weissman, Wolk, Wickramaratne, et al., 1999). In the longer term, those children and young people who develop a recurrent or chronic disorder extending into adulthood are likely to suffer considerable disability and impairment, high rates of comorbid disorders with poor academic functioning, difficulties in peer and family relationships, and increases in substance use and attempted and completed suicide (Brent & Birmaher, 2002; Fleming, Boyle, & Offord, 1993; Harrington, Fudge, Rutter, Pickles, & Hill, 1990). These statistics overall suggest there is a 50% chance of response to treatment and a 30% chance that another episode may occur. It is essential to discuss this treatment process with kids and parents, emphasizing that it may take a few medication trials to get a response, as it is a 50/50 chance.

Lack of Response to Treatment

There are several things to consider if there is little to no response to treatment. First, increasing the frequency of visits to the psychiatrist or therapist may provide more intensive assessment and treatment. This may encourage the child to open up about life stresses that are hard to discuss. The doctor may collaborate with the patient and parents in considering other contributory psychiatric diagnoses and in making sure those are being treated as well. Of course, reconsidering the initial primary diagnosis may be necessary, with subsequent shifts in the treatment plan. Another consideration in teens is whether they are abusing substances, which may sabotage treatment. Finally, whether or not the child or teen is actually taking the medication or participating in treatment must be questioned.

There are many predictors of poorer outcome and failed response to an antidepressant. Children who inherently have anxious or sensitive temperaments may be less responsive to treatment. The more severe or complex the psychiatric condition, the more difficult it may be to treat. This includes severe depressions and bipolar disorder, psychotic depression, and multiple psychiatric diagnoses. Depression that occurs with medical conditions can be less responsive to treatment as well. If children have difficulty with gut absorption due to a medical condition, this too can result in limited response to treatment. If a child or teen has depression with complex psychosocial stressors or poor family support, this can also be a predictor of poorer outcome.

Unfortunately in some circumstances, a child's temperament may clash with his environment, resulting in a vicious circle. A child born with a more sensitive temperament may be more emotionally and behaviorally reactive to stimuli. Often this can elicit strong frustration from parents. Unfortunately, over time these children may suffer from being teased by others or neglected by family members or peers who feel defeated because they cannot soothe them. These children are vulnerable to abuse due to the frustration they may elicit from parents and caretakers. These cycles can be very complex and adversely affect the parent-child relationship, which can result in poorer response to treatment.

If a First Medication Trial Is Unsuccessful

There have not been any large-scale studies to support strategies for treatment of depression in children and adolescents after first-line strategies fail. There is very little research in these populations on whether to switch or add medications; some suggest trying an alternative SSRI medication prior to considering adding other medications. If one of these strategies is tried and there is still a poor response, another strategy may be to add lithium or Wellbutrin (bupropion). The currently ongoing TORDIA trial hopes to address this very issue. The results will be very important in guiding treatment in the future. So far, they have shown the benefit of adding CBT to antidepressant medication treatment (Brent et al., 2008).

In all cases, it is important to remember that each child is unique, requiring treatments to be tailored to his specific needs. Comprehensive treatment for depression in children requires a team approach, addressing both medication and therapy and considering family and school environments as well as any social concerns or special needs. Understanding what depression can look like—or not look like—is essential. Early recognition of depression symptoms and treatment to help improve overall functioning can help children master develop-mental tasks and maximize their potential in life.

14

Extreme Measures: Electroconvulsive Therapy, Vagus Nerve Stimulation, and Repetitive Transcranial Magnetic Stimulation

There are many ways to stimulate the brain physiologically. The most common are electroconvulsive therapy (ECT), repetitive transcranial magnetic stimulation (rTMS), and vagus nerve stimulation (VNS). ECT is the oldest and most effective treatment for severe, life-threatening depression, and modern anesthesia has eliminated most of the complications except memory complaints. rTMS, a more tolerable alternative, has now been approved by the FDA. VNS involves a surgically implanted device, like a pacemaker, that stimulates the brain via the vagus nerve. Deep-brain stimulation, involving the implantation of electrodes on both sides of the brain, is used in only a few research centers.

Why these treatments help depression, how their mechanisms are similar to or different from drugs, and why some people respond to brain stimulation when drugs have not been helpful are profoundly important questions that have led to extensive speculation and no clear answers.

Electroconvulsive Therapy

The incorrect notion that schizophrenia and epilepsy never occurred together gave way to an 18th-century theory that there was a biological antagonism between schizophrenia and epilepsy. This gave doctors the idea that seizures could be artificially induced in psychiatric patients to "undo the insanity." Methods involved the injection of insulin, camphor (originally used in the 16th century!), or metrazol (a circulatory and respiratory stimulant) to induce seizures or coma (Pearce, 2008).

In the 18th century, Benjamin Franklin sustained two electric shocks to the brain during his own experimentation with "shock-induced amnesia," which left him with the impression that "shocks to the cranium could be therapeutic," after which he suggested "trying the practice on mad people." Jan Ingenhousz, in consultation with Franklin, was the first to apply electricity in a clinical setting (Finger & Franklin, 2006). Over a century later, the popularity of electric stimulation and success of insulin and convulsive therapy led Italians Ugo Cerletti and Lucio Binito to begin research into the electrical induction of convulsions in psychiatric patients (Endler, 1988). Beginning with a method that had been used by slaughterhouse workers on pigs, they shocked their first human subject in 1938. Electroshock was easier to deliver than metrazol or insulin, and it had fewer complications. More than 40% of United States psychiatric hospitals were using electroshock just 3 years after the first human trial (Accornero, 1988).

Early ECT treatments were not without drawbacks. They were given without general anesthesia or muscle-relaxing drugs, and patients were often terrified of the "lightning bolt" going through their brain, the broken bones that could result from intense muscle contractions, and the profound confusion and memory loss that resulted from the seizure and sometimes from hypoxia (inadequate oxygen supply to the brain during intense activity of a seizure). Sometimes, in cases of schizophrenia, "regressive ECT" was done in an attempt to make an adult function at the level of a very young child (due to extreme confusion) and then "reparent" him. Historically, ECT was used as a treatment for most major forms of mental illness (including depression, mania, catatonia, and schizophrenia) before effective psychiatric drugs were available. In those days, the alternatives were hydrotherapy ("continuous baths" and the "wet sheet pack"), the insulin- or metrazol-induced coma, barbiturate- or opiate-induced sedation, "prolonged sleep therapy," and frontal lobotomy. Fortunately, we've since come a long way in treating mental illness.

Modern Electroconvulsive Therapy

Modern ECT is typically given in a postoperative recovery suite with an anesthesiologist and psychiatrist working as a team. The anesthesiologist starts an IV and gives oxygen via a face mask. He then gives a short-acting barbiturate to put the patient to sleep. When the patient is asleep, succinylcholine is given to cause muscle paralysis. In this way the patient is not aware of receiving the electrical stimulus, and the massive muscle contractions that can cause fractures are prevented. A mouthpiece is placed in the mouth to protect the tongue and teeth. Oxygen is given via a face mask, because the muscle paralysis prevents the person from breathing spontaneously for a few minutes. During the electrical stimulation, the current is set a little above seizure threshold and is delivered for a few seconds. Typically the seizure is monitored via electroencephalogram (EEG) leads. Sometimes a blood pressure cuff is placed on the arm and kept inflated from just before the time of giving the succinylcholine until after the seizure is completed. This leaves the forearm mobile, and the seizure can be monitored by watching for finger-twitching in this arm. Typically the whole procedure is completed in less than a half hour, and often it is done on an outpatient basis if the patient has a supportive family member to drive her home afterward. Remission rates for patients receiving ECT for depression range from 55% to 86% (Kellner et al., 2006; Prudic, Olfson, Marcus, Fuller, & Sackeim, 2004). Factors associated with efficacy of ECT include catatonic features, melancholic features, delusions, and history of prior ECT response.

ECT is now reserved for the most severe, urgent, treatment-resistant cases of depression and is used when a very rapid response is potentially life-saving—for example, with a patient who is lying in bed all day, refusing to eat or dress herself, having hallucinations or delusions of sin, guilt, or punishment, and talking of wanting to be dead. ECT is used primarily for treatment of major depressive episodes (either unipolar or bipolar) and occasionally for mania or schizophrenia. It is rarely used for delirium, Parkinson's disease, neuroleptic malignant syndrome, or intractable epilepsy (where the electrically induced seizures actually raise the seizure threshhold for future seizures). It is generally avoided in patients with brain tumors, aneurysms, or stroke, as well as in those with recent myocardial infarction (heart attack).

The 2006 book by Kitty Dukakis and Larry Tye, Shock: The Healing Power of Electroconvulsive Therapy, illustrates the potential for dramatic benefit from ECT. The authors raise the questions of why this treatment modality is not offered sooner to patients suffering from very chronic or recurrent depression and why it is not offered more often for maintenance treatment. The book also describes factors that may make ECT more or less tolerable and educates readers on how to communicate with their doctors to receive the best possible outcome.

Technique

ECT may be administered to both sides of the brain (bilateral) or to the hemisphere that is not dominant for speech. Most right-handed people, and some left-handed ones, are left-hemisphere speech-dominant, so the ECT electrodes are placed on the right side of the head for unilateral nondominant ECT. Unilateral treatments are associated with less confusion and memory loss, so many clinicians start with this approach and switch to bilateral ECT only if there is no response after several treatments. Other clinicians believe that bilateral treatments are more rapidly effective and begin with these.

Unilateral placement is not the only aspect of ECT technique that is important in minimizing memory impairment: Brief pulse stimuli are less disruptive than sine wave stimuli, unilateral is less disruptive than bilateral electrode placement, bifrontal electrode placement offers advantage over bitemporal placement, and stimulus intensity slightly above seizure threshold is optimal. The Mecta Corporation now makes ECT equipment that, when applied bifrontally (where seizure threshold will be higher), produces "nonconvulsive seizures," where EEG seizure activity is manifested in absence of motor convulsive activity, indicating prefrontal seizure activity without motor-strip involvement in the brain (Teman, Perry, Ryan, & Rasmussen, 2006). A series of ECT treatments that is both effective and tolerable typically involves no more than 10 to 12 sessions, given three times weekly; this acute series may be followed by maintenance treatments spaced at longer time intervals over several months. Note that benzodiazepines, anticonvulsants, and lithium may need to be decreased or stopped during a course of ECT in some cases, as anticonvulsants raise the seizure threshhold and lithium levels may climb into the toxic range. Lithium may also prolong the effect of muscle-relaxing drugs. Common acute side effects of ECT include muscle aches, posttreatment confusion, and headache; these typically subside quickly.

A Few Considerations

There are some problems with ECT, the most prominent complaint being its effect on memory. Apparently, it takes a while for recent events to be consolidated into long-term memory, and since ECT disrupts this process, some events from the recent past might not be stored in long-term memory after ECT has begun. A visit from friends or a phone conversation with family during the course of ECT, for example, might not be remembered the next day. A person who hid the jewelry or safe deposit box key prior to going to the hospital for ECT might not remember where he put them after the ECT treatments begin. After the course of ECT is completed, a patient may be challenged by learning and remembering new material. The total duration of time when memory is functioning poorly before, during, and after the ECT series is often estimated by patients as longer than what is estimated by clinicians and reported in the medical literature (Fraser, O'Carroll, & Ebmeier, 2008; Ingram, Saling, & Schweitzer, 2008). Long-term follow-up testing of memory function after ECT shows that residual depression is an important predictor of memory complaints. Sometimes depression itself, medication, or dementia coexisting with depression contributes to memory problems. Amnesia is greater for recent events than for remote events.

The second problem with ECT is that it doesn't work for everyone, and when it does work, its effects are time-limited, making relapse possible. Predictors for ECT nonresponse in depression include chronicity (current episode duration over 2 years) and medication resistance, defined as a lack of response to several medication trials of therapeutic dose and reasonable duration (Dombrovski et al., 2005). Substance abuse and personality disorder may also make ECT less likely to be helpful (Feske et al., 2004; Prudic et al., 2004).

When ECT is successful, the acute course must be followed by an attempt to prevent relapse back into depression. There are two approaches to this. One is the use of medications with the hope that they will be more effective after acute recovery than they were in the acute phase of illness. One study demonstrated the acute benefit of receiving Tofranil (imipramine) with ECT, but showed that after completing ECT, Paxil (paroxetine) 30 mg/day was more helpful than Tofranil in preventing relapse (Lauritzen et al., 1996). Another study demonstrated that Tofranil was far better than placebo at preventing relapse after successful ECT treatment of drug-resistant depression (van den Broek, Birkenhager, Mulder, Bruijn, & Moleman, 2006). A large controlled study of patients who had successfully responded to ECT demonstrated that relapse rates at 6 months in patients receiving Pamelor (nortriptyline) plus lithium were 39%; relapse rates on Pamelor alone were 60%, and relapse on placebo occurred in 84% of patients (Tew et al., 2007).

The other option after the acute series of ECT has resolved the severe depression is maintenance ECT, in which the treatment is repeated, even though the person is feeling well, at intervals that are progressively longer between treatments. Maintenance treatments are usually given every week, then every 2 weeks, and then monthly for about 6 months. A group of medication-resistant patients who had responded acutely to ECT was given continuation ECT without medications and the 6-month relapse rate was 50% (Wijkstra, Nolen, Algra, van Vliet, & Kahn, 2000).

It is interesting that failure to suppress (turn off) cortisol secretion when given dexamethasone appears to be a predictor of post-ECT relapse (Bourgon & Kellner, 2000) but it also may predict response to ECT (McElroy et al., 1992); melancholic and psychotic depression, both marked by cortisol nonsupression, may respond well to ECT.

The conclusion from these studies is very clear: Anyone who receives ECT treatment for treatment-resistant severe depression should realize that the immediate relief of symptoms is no guarantee of ongoing mood stability. There is a very high risk of relapse, and aggressive treatment with antidepressants, mood stabilizers, maintenance ECT, or some combination of these is essential.

ECT use is still subject to some sociological variables. It is easier to get this treatment in Europe and the eastern United States than in the western United States, and it is easier to get in a private practice than in a public hospital. Patients generally have the right to refuse ECT. Many states require that a second psychiatrist who is not treating the patient be called in for a consultation. He must agree that the patient both needs the ECT treatment and is competent to give informed consent (understand risks, benefits, and alternatives). In the case of a patient who is involuntarily hospitalized or refuses the treatment, a judge may decide whether the patient is to be given ECT. In California, ECT must be explained to the patient 24 hours before informed consent documents are signed, and a second board-certified psychiatrist must certify that the patient has the capacity to consent (understands risks and benefits and alternatives and is willing to accept the treatment recommendation) and that ECT is the least drastic alternative available. Family must be notified unless the patient rejects this, and ECT is banned for patients younger than 12 years of age.

Obviously there is a need to improve upon ECT so that the cost in terms of memory and hospital expenses can be lessened. Sackeim's group of researchers at Columbia University is actively developing modifications in ECT techniques that may improve efficacy and decrease memory problems.

Case Example: Linda

Linda was a 38-year-old single woman living with a small dog and working as a librarian. She came to me complaining of feeling depressed, tired, and chronically tearful. The triggers were having her sister and brother move out of the area. She found herself crying at her job and took a medical leave of absence. Her coworkers became very concerned about her well-being when she was seen researching legal issues around her possible death.

Linda reported that she had lost interest in things, gained weight, felt worthless and guilty, and had repeated thoughts about her own death. Her brief "bursts of energy," which involved compulsive shopping on eBay and rearranging furniture, never lasted more than a day. Linda also reported a history of depression and suicide attempts beginning at age 11. She had recently been diagnosed with diabetes and hypothyroidism; the hypothyroidism was being adequately treated but Linda was not carefully monitoring her blood sugar.

I tried Linda on various combinations of Prozac, Norpramin, BuSpar (for anxiety), lithium (for augmentation of antidepressant effect), occasional trazodone (for insomnia), and Provigil (for daytime alertness), and her therapist worked with her on accepting her new diagnosis of diabetes and learning how to manage it. This helped a little, and Linda was able to return to work part-time. By 5 months into treatment, she was able to work full-time. After 17 months, however, the depression was back, for no apparent reason, and Linda was not bathing, paying bills, sleeping, or going to work. Her mother was taking care of her dog and wanted Linda to move in with her. The therapist and I both recommended ECT. Linda consented to an acute series of ECT treatments, followed by 3 weeks of outpatient treatment to maintain her gains. She had a hard time remembering new information at her job, but she was able to resume part-time work. The ECT was far from perfect, because it interfered with her ability to learn new material and she still had to fight the depression, but she was making progress.

Case Example: Sue

Sue first came to see me with complaints of depression, nervousness, and anxiety. She was a very slender, lively, retired elementary school teacher who seemed much younger than her 76 years of age. She had a history of two prior depressive episodes, and the present depression seemed to have been triggered by medical problems. She had developed diffuse muscle pain (polymyalgia rheumatica) 4 years earlier and recently had an immune system problem causing inflammation of the scalp arteries (arteritis) with some loss of vision in one eye. This had required treatment with prednisone, a steroidal immune suppressant that can contribute to depression with chronic use. Sue's list of past tried and failed antidepressants was extensive. I tried Effexor, Remeron, lithium augmentation, Serzone, BuSpar, Zyprexa, Prozac, Lamictal, and Wellbutrin over the next 8 months. When these treatments failed, and Sue continued to suffer despite the resolution of her medical problems, I resumed the Effexor plus low-dose Zyprexa and asked her to see two other psychiatrists for consultations about ECT.

I was amazed when Sue came in one day saying that she had talked to the psychiatrists and still had a few questions about ECT, but was starting to feel less depressed. She was enjoying doing things with her family, knitting, visiting friends, and doing her volunteer work at the library. She was wondering if she still had to go the hospital for ECT, and of course my answer was no. We continued her antidepressant and about 3 years after her recovery she completed a very slow, gradual taper off of the Effexor and was consistently feeling well and enjoying life.

A few months later, however, Sue accidentally fell and broke her right arm. Her depression returned, with terrible insomnia, and she resumed Effexor, getting up to the full dose that had been helpful to her at the time of her previous recovery. By a month into the episode, constipation, body jerking, insomnia, inability to concentrate, and inability to use her right arm had become overwhelming. I recommended hospitalization but she declined. Several days later she overdosed on sleeping pills and was admitted to the hospital intensive care unit. This time around, we wasted no time. As soon as Sue was medically stable, she was transferred to the psychiatric hospital and ECT was started. Nine unilateral nondominant ECT treatments pulled her out of the depression with no confusion, and she agreed to have a few maintenance treatments and stay on the antidepressant.

What made me recommend ECT for Sue so slowly the first time and so quickly in the next episode? The first time we worked together, she appeared able to tolerate the depression without hurting herself. There was a good therapeutic alliance and she knew we were working together to try many different treatment options and would keep trying until she got well. The second time was different. I knew that her depression would be extremely hard to treat and probably slow to respond. I also knew that she had made a suicide attempt, so clearly her psychological reserves to cope with the depression were far less than they had been a few years earlier. I was very grateful that the sleeping pills I had given her had a very wide therapeutic index (difference between therapeutic dose and toxic dose) and it was almost impossible to take a fatal overdose, but I did not want to risk her possibly becoming more "creative" in another suicide attempt if she remained depressed.

Sue stabilized after the ECT and reluctantly agreed to stay on medication even after the depression symptoms resolved. I didn't want to take the chance of discontinuing maintenance treatment to see if it was still needed. At 79, life is too short to risk a recurrence.

Repetitive Transcranial Magnetic Stimulation

Because ECT is costly in time, money, and memory impairments, newer and better treatment is needed. Many researchers have attempted to develop rTMS for this purpose, and late in 2008 rTMS received FDA approval for treatment of depression. This treatment is a 40-minute outpatient procedure that is performed in a psychiatrist's office. Patients typically receive daily treatment for 4 to 6 weeks. The huge advantage of rTMS over ECT is the lack of seizure, making anesthesia unnecessary and confusion unlikely to occur.

Like any very new technique, the details of how best to use it are still being explored; placement of the magnetic coils, stimulus parameters, frequency and duration of treatment, and efficacy are still being evaluated. Generally, improved outcome occurs with greater course duration, pulse intensity, and pulse quantity.

Reviews of multiple studies have demonstrated benefit compared to sham (fake) treatment (Gershon, Dannon, & Grunhaus, 2003; Holtzheimer, Fawaz, Wilson, & Avery, 2005; Kozel & George, 2002). A review by Lam, Chan, Wilkins-Ho, and Yatham (2008) included 1,092 patients and concluded that the response rate was 25% and remission 17% with rTMS, versus 9% and 6% with sham treatment. Postmenopausal women may not respond to rTMS as well as men and premenopausal women (Huang, Wei, Chou, & Su, 2008). In one largely representative trial, transient headache and scalp pain were common, but incidence of this side effect declined markedly after the first week of treatment. Changes in hearing and cognitive ability were not seen, and overall there was a less than 5% discontinuation rate due to adverse events. There were no deaths or seizures in over 10,000 treatment sessions, and no new safety observations emerged during 6 months of followup (Janicak et al., 2008).

Some studies have been very promising in their attempt to compare rTMS with ECT for treatment-resistant depression, whereas other studies fail to demonstrate efficacy. High-frequency left prefrontal rTMS has been shown effective in a series of 26 antidepressant-refractory patients with major depression (Yukimasa et al., 2006). A similar study of left dorsolateral prefrontal cortex rTMS failed to show a difference between high- and low-frequency stimulation (Miniussi et al., 2005).

Before rTMS got its final FDA approval, other countries (including Canada and Israel) had already approved it for clinical use. It remains to be seen how useful or available it will be over the next few years; the equipment is expensive, treatment times are extensive, and, as with ECT, some form of maintenance treatment is required. Only a single trial has been performed on the efficacy of antidepressant treatment in maintaining benefit gained from rTMS. It was found that Remeron (mirtazapine) was able to further improve the clinical response to rTMS and that responders to rTMS monotherapy should receive subsequent medication treatment without delay to avoid a return of symptoms (Schule et al., 2003).

Vagus Nerve Stimulation

Another approach to brain stimulation is the vagus nerve stimulator. This technology has been used in the treatment of drug-resistant epilepsy in the United States since 1997, and it was FDA approved for treatment-resistant depression in 2005.

The vagus ("wandering") nerve goes from the brain to the heart and gut, and its descending paths control heart rate variability and gastrointestinal motility. It was discovered many years ago that 80% of its fibers go upward from the periphery to the brain, where there are many projections to areas thought to be involved in mood regulation. This led to attempts to stimulate the vagus nerve in order to suppress seizures, and subsequently to observations that this approach improved mood in many epileptic patients. This is quite similar to the observations that led to the use of many anticonvulsants in treatment of mood disorders.

A VNS stimulator device, about the size of a silver dollar, is surgically implanted in the upper left anterior chest wall, just under the collarbone. The wire from the device goes under the skin up into the left side of the neck, and the nerve-stimulating electrode is placed there around the left vagus nerve. The surgical procedure takes about an hour, and the main risk is of infection at the site of surgery, occurring in about 1% of cases. Neurosurgeons and ear, nose, and throat (ENT) surgeons are most familiar with operating in this area. After a couple of weeks for healing, the stimulator is turned on by a wand held over the stimulator, which communicates with it through the skin. Programming, which is done by a trained psychiatrist or neurologist in the office, is done using a hand-held computer with a wand attached and takes only a few minutes for each session. The stimulus parameters are very gradually adjusted over a period of months to those that are optimal for the patient. Side effects of hoarse voice, sore throat, and a sense of air hunger may occur; they are minimized by adjusting the stimulus parameters. Typically the stimulator is on for 30 seconds and off for 5 minutes, 24 hours a day, unless the patient places a magnet over the stimulator to turn it off temporarily, which may be important at times of public speaking or singing. The battery life is typically from 3 to 8 years, and the device is surgically replaced when the battery dies.

VNS works much more slowly than antidepressant drugs and ECT do. It is not unusual to have to wait 3 to 6 months or more to see some response; median time to response in 1-year trial with 74 subjects was 9 months (Schlaepfer, et al. 2008). The initial VNS trial in depression failed to demonstrate efficacy. The device was implanted and, after allowing 2 weeks for healing, the stimulus parameters were adjusted over the next 10 weeks in some patients and the stimulator was left off in others. There was minimal difference in depression response in this study between those with active stimulation and those with the stimulator implanted but not turned on (Rush, Marangell, et al., 2005).

The next set of studies were designed to look for response out to 1 to 2 years, and the group of patients who received the VNS implant was compared to a group of patients with treatment-resistant depression who were treated as usual in the community. Both groups were allowed to continue on medications at their doctors' discretion. Both groups had failed to have a good sustained response to four or more antidepressant trials before entering the study, and both included patients with both recurrent major depression and bipolar depression. By the end of a year, the response rate for the VNS group was 27% and that for the treatment-as-usual group was 13% (George et al., 2005; Rush, Sackeim, et al., 2005). Patients who got to the point of response with the VNS usually maintained the response long term. Unfortunately, a careful statistical search for predictors of who would respond long term failed to yield any strong clues in terms of illness or drug treatment characteristics.

A 2-year outcome study of 59 treatment-resistant depression patients receiving VNS treatment reported 1- and 2-year response rates of 44% and 42%; impressively, 81% of patients were still receiving VNS at 2 years. A larger group was subsequently reported, showing 157 evaluable patients with 2-year response rates of 27–32%. Among the 3-month and 12-month responders, the percentage maintaining response at 2 years was 69–70% (George et al., 2005, 2007; Nahas et al., 2005; Sackeim et al., 2001, 2007).

Clearly VNS was an option that offered hope of response to these highly treatment-resistant patients, but the 2-year study was neither double-blind nor based on random assignment of who would receive VNS and who would receive treatment as usual, and there was no control group for comparison. The "quasi-experimental" nature of this study led to controversy within the FDA and delay in approval of this treatment. The company that makes the device is now committed to performing a large-scale registry study of treatment-resistant depression patients who will be followed from 2 to 5 years to observe their responses to VNS or treatment as usual in the community. In the meantime, Medicare has declined to pay for treatment, which in 2008 cost about $20,000 to $40,000 for the device, surgeon, anesthesiologist, and hospital fees. Following suit, many private insurance companies also refused to pay for this FDA-approved treatment on the grounds that proof of efficacy in trials that are not randomized, double-blind, and controlled is insufficient. The lessons learned from the VNS studies are that this is a treatment that will produce response (defined as a reduction of symptoms of around 50%) in about 30–40% of patients over a period of 1 to 2 years, and remission (very few remaining symptoms) in around 17–33% of patients (Corcoran, Thomas, Phillips, & O'Keane, 2006; Marangell et al., 2002; Schlaepfer et al., 2008). As mentioned, its benefit occurs very slowly, but the benefit is usually persistent for individuals who have not had benefit from multiple drug trials: Sustained response (without relapse) at 12 months is typically 40–46% (Marangell et al., 2002; Schlaepfer et al., 2008). Predictors of nonresponse to VNS are having received ECT (3.9 times less likely) and being resistant to multiple (more than 6) antidepressant trials (Sackeim et al., 2001).

Case Example: Vagus Nerve Stimulation

Candy was a very bright and charming 24-year-old woman attending a local college. She viewed herself as smart, creative, introspective, quiet, spiritual, eager to learn, and an independent thinker. She reported a history of depression since age 13, when her mother had begun dating a man who, a year later, became Candy's stepfather. Candy's relationship with her stepfather had been stormy since her mother married him.

Candy had never been manic, but she did notice seasonal worsening that lasted for months and involved fall and winter fatigue, crying, and feeling the world was empty, with nothing good or exciting to do. She would sleep a lot, crave carbohydrates and chocolate, gain weight, lose interest in sex, and withdraw socially. She had been seeing a psychiatrist but reported that he "didn't know what to do next" to treat her. A research PET scan had indicated a pattern suggestive of atypical depression that would not respond to SSRI antidepressants but might respond to anticonvulsants or stimulants; however, combinations of Wellbutrin, high-dose Effexor, Zyprexa, Lamictal, and trials on Provigil and Adderall (amphetamines) and lithium had all failed to pull her out of her depression.

Candy's family and I felt she was getting worse, so I suggested a course of ECT, which had showed some benefit 4 years earlier when Candy first tried it as a treatment. She felt better after 11 treatments but had confusion and needed to stay with her elderly grandmother. Over the next several months she had approximately 50 ECT treatments, which helped temporarily but did not keep her out of the depression long term despite aggressive medication therapy. We tried an MAO inhibitor and she was cooperative with the special diet but still didn't improve.

Life stressors added to Candy's struggle to overcome her depression. She had lived with a boyfriend she had met in the hospital for a while, but conflicts with him never resolved to the point where the relationship felt truly supportive and satisfying to either of them. Her grandmother died and her elderly cat was sick. She experienced ongoing joint pain and was diagnosed with fibromyalgia by a rheumatologist. She was unable to keep up with schoolwork and had to drop out of college.

A year into treatment, Candy got a consultation with a world-famous psychopharmacologist in San Diego, and he supported evaluation for a vagus nerve stimulator. I rallied two of her previous psychiatrists, and we wrote four letters recommending that Candy be considered for this treatment. At that time, the FDA had not yet approved VNS for use in treatment-resistant depression. Although we found a local neurosurgeon willing to implant the device, we faced an insurance company refusing to pay about $25,000 for it. The family took the chance that, if they paid for it, the insurance company would eventually reimburse them, and they proceeded with the treatment.

Eight months after the VNS implant, I got a letter from Candy's father saying that she seemed much better. She was more energetic, animated, and involved with the world. She had tried going off of her antidepressant medications and didn't crash. She and her family felt that the vagus nerve stimulator was finally starting to work. Candy came in a few weeks later to tell me that she had stopped all of her medicines a month before. She had published an article in a support-group newsletter and was back to doing some creative writing. She appeared bright, animated, and energetic. I saw her again 2 months after she had gone off her medicines, and then 10 months after the VNS surgery, and she continued to do quite well without medications.

15

Complementary and Alternative Medicine: Herbs and Supplements

Some people who have not found antidepressants to be tolerable or effective may turn to alternative medicines and practices to treat their depression. Others desire to treat themselves to save money or to avoid doctors or the stigma of taking prescribed psychiatric medicines.

This chapter discusses the treatments available at local health food stores: "dietary supplements" (vitamins and minerals, herbs and other botanicals, amino acids), hormones such as DHEA, neurotransmitter precursors (tryptophan, SAM-e, inositol), omega-3 fatty acids, and homeopathy. It also offers guidelines to finding professional help in the area of alternative and complementary medicine.

What Is Complementary and Alternative Medicine?
Complementary and alternative medicine (CAM), as defined by the National Center for Complementary and Alternative Medicine (NCCAM, a component of the National Institutes of Health), is a group of diverse medical and health care systems, practices, and products that are not currently considered to be part of conventional medical practice. *Alternative medicine* refers to unconventional treatments as an alternate to allopathic treatments (conventional medical modalities); *complementary medicine* refers to unconventional treatments as adjuncts or cotherapy to usual medical care. There are high rates of CAM use (36–42%) among the general public in the United States. (Barnes, Powell-Griner, McFann, & Nahin, 2004; Eisenberg et al., 1998). Emotional distress predicts a higher use of CAM (Druss & Rosenheck, 2000; Unutzer et al., 2000)—around 13–22% in depressed persons (Kessler et al., 2001; Unutzer et al., 2000) and 41–54% in severe depression (Eisenberg et al., 1998; Kessler et al., 2001)—and CAM use is posi-

tively associated with seeking conventional mental health care (Kessler et al., 2001; Roy-Byrne et al., 2005; Unutzer et al., 2000).

The NCCAM classifies CAM therapies into five categories:

- Biologically based therapies including herbs, foods, and vitamins
- Complete alternative medical systems such as homeopathic and naturopathic medicine in Western cultures, traditional Chinese medicine, and Ayurveda, from India
- Mind-body interventions, designed to enhance the mind's capacity to affect bodily function and symptoms, including meditation, biofeedback, hypnosis, and guided imagery, and therapies that use creative outlets such as art, music, or dance
- Manipulative and body-based methods, including chiropractic or osteopathic manipulation, and massage
- Energy therapies, including biofield therapies (e.g., Qi Gong, Reiki, and therapeutic touch) and bioelectromagnetic-based therapies (the unconventional use of electromagnetic fields)

Of depressed persons who seek CAM, 34% take mind-body therapies, 10% seek spiritual healers, 8% use manipulative therapies, and 7% try herbs and other supplements (Kessler et al., 2001). This chapter chiefly addresses biologically based therapies. The following chapter introduces several mind-body interventions, body-based methods, and energy therapies as potential additions to a healthy lifestyle.

When considering natural remedies, it is important to remember that something's being "natural" does not guarantee it's good for you! Many natural treatments come with side effects and may interact with prescription medications or other over-the-counter products, causing serious problems. For example, the herbs kava and comfrey have been linked to serious liver damage; alcohol, tobacco, and opium are all natural, and their hazards are obvious in people who overuse them. In some cases, people have experienced negative effects even though they took the supplement as the label suggested.

CAM use is typically not disclosed to physicians and this can be a problem (Druss & Rosenheck, 2000; Eisenberg et al., 1998). Patients should inform each of their providers about all remedies being taken and ask their pharmacist about potential drug interactions. This is especially important with prescription medications.

People who should use extra caution or completely avoid taking supplements include:

- Women who are pregnant or nursing
- Women taking birth control pills (some herbs can make these ineffective)
- People with kidney, liver, or heart problems or certain other medical conditions
- People planning to have surgery (because certain supplements may increase the risk of bleeding or affect anesthetics and painkillers)
- People with HIV infection
- People taking prescription or over-the-counter medications
- Children (many supplements have not been tested for use in children)
- People who have had organ transplants

Interactions of the supplement with prescribed medications, via enzyme induction or blockade, may make the prescribed drugs ineffective or induce intolerable side effects.

Because pharmacists may have more information than prescribers on interactions, it is important to involve them. Consultation with a practitioner of alternative and complementary medicine is also a good idea.

Furthermore—and this is an important distinction—there is a significant difference between what a substance is "used for" and what it might "work for." Popular literature and opinion often takes precedence over quality research where supplements are concerned. For example, many people use ginkgo biloba for minor memory deficits but there is no rigorous scientific evidence that ginkgo provides improvement. Just as health care providers evaluate the research on prescription medications before offering them to patients, people considering alternative therapies also benefit from learning to evaluate claims and research.

Evaluating Alternative Remedies

The Internet is a good place to find both reliable and false information on which supplements might work in depression, sleep, or other problems. When evaluating Web sites, the following questions may be asked: Who runs the site? Is it government, a university, or a reputable medical or health-related association? Is it sponsored by a manufacturer of drugs or other products? What is the purpose of the site? Is it to educate the public or to sell a product? What is the basis of the information? Is it based on scientific evidence with clear references? Advice and opinions should be clearly set apart from the science.

A good way to find reliable information is to use sources such as those provided by the National Institutes of Health (NIH), including the afore-mentioned NCCAM (www.nccam.nih.gov) and the Office of Dietary Supplements (ODS; www.ods.od.nih.gov), which helps coordinate NIH research on supplements. From their "research" portal one can access the databases of the International Bibliographic Information on Dietary Supplements (IBIDS, http://ods.od.nih.gov/health_information/ibids.aspx) and Computer Access to Research on Dietary Supplements (CARDS, http://dietary-supplements.info.nih.gov/research/cards_database.aspx).

Abstracts (brief summaries) of research articles are also available through NIH's Medline, accessible to the public through PubMed (www.pubmed.com). To read reviews of the evidence systematically and rigorously compiled by trusted sources, the Cochrane Library (www.cochrane.org/reviews/clibintro.htm) seeks to provide "up-to-date, accurate information about the effects of health care." Abstracts of these reviews can be read online without charge, and subscriptions to the full text are offered at a fee and are carried by some libraries. The Agency for Healthcare Research and Quality has produced a number of evidence-based reviews of dietary supplements, available at http://www.ahrq.gov/clinic/epcindex.htm#complementary.

For further information on surfing the Web for information on CAM, a Web page hosted by the FDA titled Tips for Savvy Supplement Users includes very thorough information on how to safely and effectively search the Web for information on dietary supplements. It may be found at http://www.fda.gov/Food/DietarySupplements/ConsumerInformation/ucm110567.htm, and includes many links to other sites that will help the reader to find information on the Internet, evaluate research, and answer questions about product claims and labeling.

When choosing what to read, remember that primary sources trump secondary sources; for example, a clinical trial provides more scientifically rigorous information than does a review of many trials. Often secondary sources are all quoting the same single piece of primary evidence. We recommend locating at least three trials, each including a relatively good number of human subjects, that have demonstrated similar results before believing their claims. There are many trials to be read, and it's the accumulated weight of evidence that matters.

Another helpful resource is Herbalinks, from the University of Iowa (http://www.uiowa.edu/~idis/herbalinks/). It was created by pharmacists, for pharmacists, to assist them in finding useful and trustworthy information. They list and systematically rate sites—including those containing monograms and full databases—they believe to be useful and of highest quality, many of them available to the public free of charge.

When researching supplements on the Internet, remember that reliable sources will list their references after the article. Keep in mind, however, that research can usually be found to substantiate just about any claim an author wants to make, so healthy skepticism is of value. Choose Web sites published by reputable organizations, and know that their information often is provided by or licensed from a secondary source.

For general information, some insurance plans offer health and wellness sites to their members, such as www.miavita.com from Blue Cross.

One extensive and preferred provider of health education is www.aisle7.net/, which provides easy-to-read information on many health problems, news, articles, Q&A, and toolkits. They include a free and quite extensive interaction checker for medications, herbs, and supplements. A rare and valuable feature is their inclusion with the listing of each treatment the nutrients that are depleted by various medications, and those that may help with side effect control. Their information is licensed from the trusted sources Lexicomp and A.D.A.M. Though you may not access the information on Aisle7's Web site, you may look through it on sites that license their information. Enter "healthnotes" or "aisle7" in your favorite search engine to find Web pages from many hospitals, online retailers, and others that purchase the right to host information from Aisle7, including University of California at San Diego's MyHealth site, the University of Michigan Health System, Quest Diagnostics, the Bastyr Center for Natural Health, GNC, and Albertson's markets.

To assist in choosing a product of good quality and standards, ConsumerLab (www.consumerlab.com), a privately held laboratory, does rigorous independent testing of alternative products—more than 2,100 products by 350 brands to date—and offers their trusted results on the Internet. Easy to read and to navigate, the Web site offers a natural-products encyclopedia and includes recalls, warnings, and news. ConsumerLab is recommended by the American Academy of Family Physician and others.

The nonprofit site www.quackwatch.org was created to "combat health-related frauds, myths, fads, and fallacies," and it focuses on information that is difficult to get elsewhere. Provided by a worldwide network of volunteers and expert advisors, this easy-to-navigate site includes a 16-source search engine and lets readers in on what clinicians are saying about, for instance, that widely marketed brand of "natural" lithium that is nonstandardized and does not recommend blood monitoring or that complicated herbal blend that makes impressive claims about its use in depression.

To research CAM without access to the internet, we recommend you visit your local library or a medical library (universities with medical schools have one). There a librarian can assist you with finding scientific articles published in books and journals. The NCCAM Clearinghouse is an information servide that provides information on complementary and alternative medicine to practitioners and the public. They can be reached by phone at 1-888-644-6226, by email at info@nccam.nih.gov, or on the web at http://nccam.nih.gov/health/clearinghouse/.

These are just a few of the Web sites we recommend. Please see the extensive list in Chapter 17 for more information.

Quality Research

When evaluating any research, keep in mind the following: Much of the research on supplements comes from reputable scientists in Germany (where the government standardizes herbal remedies) and elsewhere in Europe, where supplements have been regularly used for decades. Those studies are not designed, however, with the same scientific methods required by the FDA when attempting to demonstrate efficacy and safety. Due to lack of funding sources, there is a dearth of high-quality evidence on herbs and other supplements for depression. Whereas good-quality studies of medications are randomized, placebo-controlled, double-blind (neither the researcher nor the subject knows whether the subject is taking the medication being studied or the comparison compound/placebo), and have a good number of patients enrolled, many trials of supplements are not: They may be "open label" (not blind), have a "small n" (few subjects), a nonrandom sample in some cases, and no control group in others. These options greatly limit cost and generalizability of the studies.

Further, unlike the trials presented to the FDA to request permission to bring drugs to market, "continuation studies"—studies of about a year, performed after the compound is demonstrated to be effective acutely, and designed to demonstrate long-term safety—are rarely performed with supplements. Without this additional time, safety and tolerability data are unknown or inconclusive at best.

Understanding How Supplements Work

There is more to research than determining whether a substance is effective for a given application: The "mechanism of action" (MOA; how the supplement works) and delivery (how the substance is made available to the body) are also important to know. Knowing the MOA allows the patient and doctor to rationally choose further treatments—without this information, one runs the risk of trying a new treatment with a mechanism similar to that which previously did not produce response. The MOA of many supplements is either unstudied or unknown. There may be dozens or even hundreds of compounds in an herbal supplement; identification of the active ingredients in herbs is an area of research at the NCCAM.

Unlike medications regulated by the FDA, manufacturers of over-the-counter dietary supplements do not have to perform tedious and expensive testing on the effectiveness of the delivery system of the supplement. Many supplements are not "bioavailable"—that is, they are not absorbed into the bloodstream and made useable by the body in the form they are sold. Folic acid, for instance, goes through four steps of metabolism before it can be made useful for the brain, and many people with medication-resistant depression do not efficiently perform the final step (Stahl, 2007). In a trial of four delivery systems for coenzyme Q10, some had good bioavailability and others did not (Weis et al., 1994).

Standards

Finally, whereas the FDA establishes rigorous standards for the efficacy, safety, purity, dosage, and manufacturing of drugs, supplements (regulated by the FDA as food products, not as drugs) are not held to the same standards. They are not subject to premarket approval or a specific postmarket surveillance period.

A large percentage of herbals and other supplements available over the counter do not contain the amount of active ingredients claimed. Supplement labels might refer to the product's quality being "standardized," "certified," or "verified." There is no legal definition for these terms, so they don't guarantee quality: In an analysis of Saint John's wort commissioned by the *Los Angeles Times*, ten products labeled as "standardized" or having "certified potency," "high potency," or "guaranteed potency" were purchased from six retail health food stores and analyzed by spectrophotometry for hypericin levels. Seven of the 10 products contained 75–135% of the labeled hypericin level; three had no more than half of the labeled potency. Some of the variation in potency reflected a natural decay of hypericin (which is sensitive to light and temperature) after the product had left the factory (Monmaney, 1998).

Indeed, sometimes contents are quite dissimilar to those in the list printed on the bottle and may even contain harmful additives or contamination, including metals, unlabeled prescription drugs, microorganisms, or other substances. Other unregulated details about botanical products specifically include species or parts of plant used, influences of climate and soil, optimal growing, harvesting, and storage conditions, method of extraction, and bioavailability of the formula.

Unlike other supplements, vitamins and minerals may carry the United States Pharmacopoeia (USP) seal. Many quality products don't undergo the testing to obtain the label, however, so its absence does not indicate lack of quality.

A Word on Effectiveness

It is important to remember that even a well-manufactured, quality product produces the desired results in only a percentage of the people who take it. Just as carefully developed and targeted antidepressant medications fail to induce response and remission in some of the people who take them, herbal and other supplements do not bring relief to all consumers. They are generally more effective in those with mild to moderate illness. Severe, melancholic, and psychotic types of depression are very unlikely to respond to alternative therapies alone. For perspective, consider also that 25% of those given placebo on an antidepressant trial do rather well (Walsh, Seidman, Sysko, & Gould, 2002), as do 19% of those on a waiting list to get onto a trial (Posternak & Miller, 2001). Consider the rates of response and remission claimed by quality clinical trials before investing in an alternative regimen.

For reference, it is not possible to compare the aggregate outcomes of several trials of a supplement to the trials of an antidepressant. There are many "negative trials" of antidepressants (trials in which the study drug was not found efficacious), and these are rarely published. Thus the apparent efficacy of these medicines may seem more optimistic than accurate due to publication bias. Reports on trials of complementary therapies, when funded by sources other than a manufacturer (e.g., NIH), are published in reports regardless of outcomes. Additionally, when comparing a supplement to a marketed drug, only head-to-head studies are instructive. Trials of supplements designed to augment rather than replace an antidepressant (e.g., Deplin, or L-methyl folate) are an exception.

Dietary Supplements

This section catalogues a number of nonprescription treatments, along with their reputed effects, the research behind the claims, and any drug interactions, warnings, and contraindications. Although some alternative therapies have good data indicating they may be helpful for certain groups of clients, others have not been rigorously studied and may have caveats. Of the many therapies available, only those with a base of scientific evidence were considered for inclusion in this chapter.

As defined by Congress in the Dietary Supplement Health and Education Act, which became law in 1994, a dietary supplement is a product (other than tobacco) that:

- Contains a "dietary ingredient" intended to supplement the diet, which contains one or more of the following: vitamins; minerals; herbs or other botanicals; amino acids; and dietary substances such as enzymes, organ tissues, and glandulars
- Is intended to be taken in tablet, capsule, powder, softgel, gelcap, or liquid form
- Is not represented for use as a conventional food or as a sole item of a meal or the diet
- Is labeled as being a dietary supplement
- Is taken by mouth

Vitamins

Essential to life, vitamins help to regulate the metabolism and assist in the release of energy from the food we digest. As coenzymes, vitamins work with enzymes to catalyze the chemical reactions continually taking place in our bodies. Having the proper balance of vitamins and minerals is very important—be skeptical of any advice or program that suggests very large doses of any one nutrient. Excesses of isolated vitamins or minerals can produce the same symptoms as their deficiencies, or may deplete other vitamins; folate, vitamin B12, and vitamin B6 are all good examples (Balch, 2006).

VITAMIN B12

Vitamin B12 (also called cobalamin), acting as a cofactor ("helper molecule") of folate, helps to produce a form of folate necessary to make DNA, which in turn is necessary for maintenance of red blood cells and healthy nerve cells (Zittoun & Zittoun, 1999).

Depression is one of the many signs of vitamin B12 deficiency, as are confusion, dementia, and poor memory (Office of Dietary Supplements,

2006). The combination of low folic acid and vitamin B12 with high homocysteine levels has been suggested to predict depression both in the general population and in studies of depressed patients (Coppen & Bolander-Gouaille, 2005). Although some studies suggest B12 deficiency is causally related to depression (Tiemeier et al., 2002), others do not (Sachdev et al., 2005).

Vitamin B12 is found in animal-based foods (fish, meat, poultry, eggs, milk, and milk products); vegetarians and vegans can get B12 from fortified cereal products (Institute of Medicine & Food and Nutrition Board, 1998). As people in the United States generally consume the recommended amounts of vitamin B12 (Institute of Medicine & Food and Nutrition Board, 1998), deficiencies generally result from an inability to absorb it (due to a stomach or intestinal disorder) or a strict vegan diet. As up to 30% of adults age 50 and older may have an increased growth of intestinal bacteria (atrophic gastritis) and be unable to normally absorb vitamin B12 in food, the Institute of Medicine (IOM) recommends that this population receive most of their B12 from supplementation and fortified foods (Institute of Medicine & Food and Nutrition Board, 1998). Younger people may be at the same risk for deficiency but be less likely to exhibit symptoms, and those who do not take supplements are twice as likely to be deficient as supplement users are, regardless of age group (Tucker et al., 2000). Medications that interfere with B12 absorption include (but are not limited to) metformin, used in diabetes, several antibiotics when used long-term, and some anticonvulsants (including phenytoin). Chronically used salicylates (including aspirin) have been shown to reduce blood concentrations of vitamin B12. Medications that interfere with B12 absorption from food sources (though not supplements) include the proton pump inhibitors (PPIs, including Nexium, Prevacid, Prilosec, Aciphex), which treat peptic ulcer disease and gastroesophageal reflux disease, both common in depression.

Some researchers suggest that vitamin B12 deficiency should be suspected in all patients at risk for deficiency (the elderly and those with intestinal disorders) and in those with unexplained anemia or neurological symptoms (Hvas & Nexo, 2006). A doctor can order a blood test for serum B12 levels. If it is low, the Schilling test can be used to determine the body's ability to absorb the vitamin.

Whereas dietary B12 can be replaced with supplements in case of deficiency, however, there is no evidence that "supraphysiologic" doses (those resulting in higher-than-normal blood levels) of B12 help depression. Recommended daily allowances for adult men and women, pregnant women, and lactating women are 2.4, 2.6, and 2.8 micrograms daily, respectively, and the IOM claims that "no adverse effects have been associated with excess vitamin B12 intake from food and supplements in healthy individuals" (Institute of Medicine & Food and Nutrition Board, 1998). Intramuscular shots every 2 to 3 months may be helpful for those whose health conditions make absorption of oral supplements difficult (Hvas & Nexo, 2006). People over age 50 should consume vitamin B12 in its crystalline form, which is included in fortified foods, as it is most easily absorbed. For most people, 1 mg oral or sublingual B12 supplementation (as methylcobalamin, rather than the more common and less effective cyanocobalamin; Balch, 2006) is sufficient (Hvas & Nexo, 2006). One excellent systematic review suggests 2-mg doses of oral vitamin B12 daily, then 1-mg doses daily, tapering to a weekly and finally a monthly dose (Vidal-Alaball et al., 2005).

FOLIC ACID

Folic acid, also known as vitamin B9, or folacin, is the synthetic form of folate. Among its many functions, folate assists with the synthesis of genetic material, making it important during periods of rapid cell division and growth. Lack of folic acid during pregnancy can lead to neural tube defects (which cause central nervous system birth defects). Folate allows us to produce healthy red blood cells and avoid anemia. Along with vitamins B6 and B12, folate lowers homocysteine levels, mediating the inflammatory response, which plays a role in depression and heart disease. Folate deficiency is twice as likely to be linked to depression as is B12 deficiency (Reynolds, Preece, Bailey, & Coppen, 1970).

Depressed persons are as much as 38% more likely to have low serum folate levels as are normal controls (Bottiglieri et al., 1992; Carney, 1967; Carney et al., 1990; Morris, Fava, Jacques, Selhub, & Rosenberg, 2003; Reynolds et al., 1970), and those with low folate levels due to malabsorption (M. Botez, Botez, & Leveille, 1979), use of anticonvulsants for epilepsy (Edeh & Toone, 1985), anemia (Shorvon, Carney, Chanarin, & Reynolds, 1980), and dietary folic acid restriction (Herbert, 1962) show neuropsychiatric symptoms including the apathy, fatigue, insomnia, impaired ability to concentrate, and irritability that are so common in depression.

There are many links between folate deficiency and depression. Folate plays an important part in the synthesis and metabolism of neurotransmitters. Along with B12, it is essential in the synthesis of SAM-E (Bottiglieri, 1996) and of phenylalanine and tryptophan (Bottiglieri et al., 1992), and the amino acids discussed below that are involved in the biosynthesis of norepinephrine, serotonin, and dopamine. Patients with low red blood cell folate levels have lower concentrations of the important serotonin metabolite 5-HIAA in their cerebral spinal fluid, and of the dopamine metabolite HVA (M. I. Botez & Young, 1991; M. I. Botez, Young, Bachevalier, & Gauthier, 1979; Bowers & Reynolds, 1972; Surtees, Heales, & Bowron, 1994).

Where treatment is concerned, high folate values predict better acute (Wesson, Levitt, & Joffe, 1994) and long-term (Coppen, Chaudhry, & Swade, 1986) outcomes. Low levels may hinder response to antidepressant treatment with fluoxetine (Fava et al., 1997), nortriptyline, or sertraline (M. Alpert, Silva, & Pouget, 2003), and folate augmentation may greatly improve response to antidepressant treatment (J. E. Alpert et al., 2002; Bottiglieri, 1996; Coppen & Bailey, 2000; Roberts et al., 2007). A 2003 review from the Cochrane Collaboration concludes that is currently unclear if this is the case both for people with folate deficiency and for those with normal levels (Caspi et al., 2003).

Patients may augment their antidepressant treatment with folate to help achieve response, to help partial responders toward remission, or to alleviate residual symptoms. The recommended daily allowance of folate for adults if it is naturally occurring in food is 400 mcg daily for men and women, 600 mcg if pregnant, and 500 mcg if lactating. Fruits (especially citrus), leafy green vegetables (like spinach, romaine lettuce, and turnip greens), and legumes (such as dried beans and peas) are all natural sources of folate. If folate is taken in the synthetic form (folic acid) from supplements and fortified foods, the RDA is 240, 360, and 300 mcg respectively. For those with depression, 2 mg of folic acid daily (Abou-Saleh & Coppen, 2006) is recommended during acute, continuation, and maintenance treatment.

As already mentioned, folate deficiency is not uncommon in those who suffer from depression. Even in deficient individuals who are not depressed, apathy, fatigue, insomnia, irritability, and impaired concentration are common. Other signs of deficiency include glossitis (inflammation of the tongue) and diarrhea. Megaloblastic anemia may result. Deficiency may be tested with blood levels of vitamin B12 and folate, as well as a complete blood count, which may differentiate megaloblastic anemia from B12 deficiency.

There are several causes of deficiency. Inadequate intake is common in those with alcoholism, eating disorders, and other conditions linked with malnutrition. Alcoholism also affects folate levels by interfering with metabolism, renal excretion (too much is excreted too quickly), hepatic reabsorption, and absorption. Malabsorption may also result from diseases including celiac disease, sprue or other malabsorption syndromes, and congenital or acquired folate malabsorption, as well as a number of medications (including phenytoin and barbiturates). Increased excretion is common in diabetes and renal dialysis. Deficiency can also result from inadequate bioavailability and increased excretion.

Importantly, inadequate metabolism may be caused by a number of medications, including methotrexate, metformin, oral contraceptives, lithium, isotretinoin, and most anticonvulsants, including those commonly used as mood stabilizers: Tegretol, Depakote, and Lamictal. A congenital or acquired enzyme deficiency may also be the cause. While dietary and supplemental folate is effective in reversing most forms of deficiency, even in the case of malabsorption, inadequate metabolism or utilization cannot be treated with supplemental folic acid. Folate goes through four steps of metabolism.

Enzyme deficiency interrupts the fourth and final step that converts folate to L-methylfolate—the only active form of folate that can cross the blood-brain barrier—which regulates synthesis of the monoamine neurotransmitters serotonin, dopamine, and norepinephrine (Stahl, 2008). While L-methylfolate is necessary to correct a neurotransmitter imbalance linked to depression, and is especially common in those whose depression has not responded to medications (Stahl, 2007), 7 of 10 people with depression may have a genetic enzyme deficiency (Kelly et al., 2004; Papakostas et al., 2004). For these patients, Deplin (L-methylfolate), a fully methylated form of folate, corrects folate deficiency, thereby boosting antidepressant effectiveness (J. E. Alpert et al., 2002; Bottiglieri, 1996; Coppen & Bailey, 2000; Roberts et al., 2007) with very little risk of side effects (Coppen & Bailey, 2000; Papakostas et al., 2004). A single 7.5 mg tablet of Deplin is equivalent to taking 66 800-mcg folic acid pills (Willems, Boers, Blom, Aengevaeren, & Verheugt, 2004). This large dose of L-methylfolate will not result in folate overdose, but may lower levels of carbamazepine, fosphenytoin, phenytoin, phenobarbital, primidone, or valproic acid, so patients taking these medications may need to adjust their dose.

Folate intake from food is not associated with any health risk. The risk of toxicity from folic acid intake from supplements and fortified foods is also low (Hathcock, 1997). Still, for those taking dietary folic acid in the form of a supplement, the upper limit for healthy adults is 1 mg daily, unless otherwise directed. Higher doses may mimic (trigger symptoms of) vitamin B12 deficiency (Institute of Medicine & Food and Nutrition Board, 1998). Where folic acid supplements can correct the anemia associated with B12 deficiency, it will not correct any changes in the nervous system, and masking this disorder may result in permanent nerve damage. Persons 50 years of age or older especially should have their B12 levels checked before beginning folic acid supplementation.

VITAMIN B6

Vitamin B6 (pyridoxine, pyridoxal, and pyridoxamine), a water-soluble vitamin, is required for a wide variety of functions, including efficient nervous and immune system function. It is needed for the synthesis of neurotransmitters, including serotonin and dopamine (Leklem, 1999). The recommended daily amount of vitamin B6 is easily provided by a healthy diet; supplementation in higher doses is recommended only in those with deficiency (rare in the United States), such as in alcoholics and some older adults (Leklem, 1999), or those taking Nardil (phenelzine, an MAO inhibitor; Malcolm et al., 1994; Stewart, Harrison, Quitkin, & Liebowitz, 1984).

Though B6 deficiency has been linked to depression (Leklem, 1999), it is not yet known whether supplementation improves symptoms of depression (Hvas, Juul, Bech, & Nexo, 2004) or premenstrual syndrome (PMS; Macdougall, 2000; Wyatt, Dimmock, Jones, & Shaughn O'Brien, 1999). Some people have used megadoses of vitamin B6 to treat depression and PMS, but this is not advisable. In a review describing subjects who used high-dose B6 in PMS, 40% of those with higher-than-normal blood levels exhibited peripheral neuropathy (damage to the nerves in the arms and legs; Dalton, 1985). This can result from supplementation at doses lower than 500 mg daily (Institute of Medicine & Food and Nutrition Board, 1998); the damage is reversible when supplementation is stopped (Selhub et al., 1995). The upper tolerable intake level for vitamin B6 for all adults is 100 mg daily (Institute of Medicine & Food and Nutrition Board, 1998).

INOSITOL

Regarded by some as "vitamin B8" (Parfit, 1999), inositol (a sugar alcohol, and a form of niacin) affects the action of serotonin, acetylcholine, and norepinephrine, and it has a therapeutic profile similar to SSRI antidepressants (Mishori, 1999). Those with depression may have lower-than-normal levels of inositol in their spinal fluid (Barkai, Dunner, & Grss, 1978), as may people who ingest large amounts of caffeine.

Small double-blind studies have found inositol helpful (Levine, 1997; Levine, Barak, Kofman, & Belmaker, 1995); a double-blind study of 42 people with severe depression that was not responding to standard antidepressant treatment, however, showed no improvement (Levine, 1997; Levine et al., 1995). A trial adding inositol to ongoing medications for bipolar depression also failed to show significant benefits (Chengappa et al., 2000). Inositol supplementation has been found to trigger manic episodes (Gelber, Levine, & Belmaker, 2001), and one therapeutic action of lithium is to cause a relative inositol deficiency (Barkai et al., 1978). Those with bipolar illness may have an excess of inositol when manic (Belmaker, Benjamin, & Stahl, 2002).

Inositol has also been studied for panic disorder (Benjamin, Levine, & Fux, 1995; Palatnik, Frolov, & Fux, 2001), bulimia (Fux, Levine, & Aviv,

1996; Gelber et al., 2001), and obsessive-compulsive disorder (Gelber et al., 2001), but there have been only a few small trials with mixed results.

Whereas the typical American diet provides around 1,000 mg daily, doses of up to 18 g (typically 12 g) have been used in trials for depression (Levine, 1997). Imagine taking 24 500-mg capsules daily, and spending around $115 monthly to do so!

Serious adverse events have not been reported even with high doses of inositol (Belmaker, Bersudsky, & Benjamin, 1995), but long-term safety studies have not been performed. Also, any contaminant present in a supplement that is taken in large quantities may represent a health hazard, so a reputable product should always be used.

A Few Minerals Worth Mentioning
Though not mainstays of treatment, several minerals have a definite influence on depression.

IRON

Iron works alongside vitamin B12 and folic acid in the formation of red blood cells, binding oxygen to hemaglobin in red blood cells and bringing them to brain and all other tissue (Koury & Ponka, 2004). Iron deficiency is more common among depressed people than nondepressed people (Bodnar & Wisner, 2005). In a population of 250 female medical students, experimentally changing the status from normal to low ferritin (iron) levels nearly doubled the rate of depression, before the occurrence of anemia (Vahdat Shariatpanaahi, Vahdat Shariatpanaahi, Moshtaaghi, Shahbaazi, & Abadi, 2007). Multivitamins can be purchased with or without around 10 mg of iron per daily dose, though it is not prudent to supplement with iron unless one is deficient, as iron overload has been linked to liver (Kew, 2008) and breast (Toyokuni, 2009) cancers, as well as to cognitive dysfunction and neurodegeneration (Youdim, 2008). Ferritin levels can be determined with a simple blood test. The body retains iron for quite a while, so many people who use iron do not need to do so long term. Some women, for instance, take it for just 4 to 5 days during menstruation to make up for lost blood, or, alternately, once weekly (Februhartanty, Dillon, & Khusun, 2002).

MAGNESIUM

The electrical conductivity of nerve cells relies on calcium, magnesium, and glutamate. Too much calcium and glutamate activity unchecked by a balance of magnesium may lead to dysfunctional cell signaling at N-methyl-D-aspartic acid (NMDA) receptors and neuronal injury that contributes to depression (Eby & Eby, 2009). Antidepressants have been shown to raise magnesium in the brain (Eby & Eby, 2009).

Depressed patients exhibit significantly lower serum levels of magnesium than nondepressed persons (Zieba et al., 2000), though there is no correlation between blood or serum magnesium levels and depression severity (Zieba et al., 2000). Low brain magnesium has been found in magnetic resonance spectroscopy imaging of treatment-resistant depressed patients (Eby & Eby, 2009). Symptoms associated with deficiency range from apathy to psychosis (H. H. Rasmussen et al., 1989) and include confusion, asthenia, insomnia, headache, delirium, hallucinations, agitation, anxiety, and irritability (Eby & Eby, 2006). Magnesium depletion is also involved in systemic inflammation (Jacka et al., 2009) and thyroid dysfunction (Hasey et al., 1993; Joffe et al., 1996), and is caused by an increase in stress hormones (Eby & Eby, 2006), all of which may be challenges in depression.

Supplementation may be indicated when a specific medication or a health problem causes excess loss of magnesium (e.g., diuretic treatment, excessive dietary calcium, diabetes, alcoholism), or limits absorption (intestinal conditions) (Kelepouris & Agus, 1998; Wester, 1987), or when there are symptoms consistent with magnesium deficiency. In several cases, recovery from major depression has been brought about in fewer than 7 days using 125–300 mg of magnesium (as glycinate and taurinate) at mealtimes and bedtime (Eby & Eby, 2006).

The IOM recommends 400 mg for males and 310 mg for females for daily magnesium intake, some to all of which comes from a diet of largely unprocessed foods. The modern Western diet poses a challenge here as calcium, glutamate, and aspartate are added to processed foods, where magnesium is removed. If taken as a supplement, the consumer will accrue higher and more equal absorption and bioavailability with the glycinate, chloride, taurinate, or lactate preparations of magnesium than with the more commonly manufactured magnesium oxide or magnesium hydroxide (Eby & Eby, 2006; Firoz & Graber, 2001). Glutamate and aspartate preparations may be neurotoxic. Supplemental magnesium is best consumed on an empty stomach and at bedtime. It is best taken in divided doses, especially if diarrhea is experienced as a side effect.

ZINC

Zinc is an essential trace mineral that is nearly as abundant in the human body as iron. It has structural, enzymatic, and regulatory roles, including those in the activity of neurons and of memory. Zinc has the same function as magnesium in the NMDA receptors, but to a lesser extent. Lower serum zinc in major depression is predictive of treatment-resistant depression and plays a regulatory role in the immune and inflammatory response, alterations of which are associated with major depression (Maes et al., 1997). Similarly to antidepressants, zinc induces brain-derived neurotrophic factor gene expression (Nowak, Szewczyk, & Pilc, 2005). It also has protective antioxidant properties (Nowak & Szewczyk, 2002). As with magnesium, low serum zinc levels are normalized in antidepressant treatment (Nowak, Siwek, Dudek, Zieba, & Pilc, 2003; Nowak et al., 2005).

Zinc supplementation to antidepressant therapy with tricyclic drugs or SSRIs showed improvement at 6 and 12 weeks when compared with placebo, hypothetically due to modulation of the glutamatergic or immune systems (Nowak et al., 2003). Interestingly, in a 12-week study of zinc supplementation in imipramine therapy of unipolar major depression, no significant differences were demonstrated between treatment with zinc and placebo in treatment nonresistant patients, though there was robust increase in efficacy and decreased time to response in those with treatment resistance (Siwek et al., 2009).

Persons susceptible to zinc deficiency include children, the elderly, and pregnant or lactating women; malnourished persons; those with a variety of lower GI problems; people with alcoholic liver disease; persons with sickle cell anemia; and strict vegetarians whose food sources largely include grains and legumes, foods high in phytic acid, which reduces zinc absorption (King & Cousins, 2006). Persons taking anticonvulsant drugs, especially valproic acid, may be deficient in zinc, as may those using diuretics for prolonged periods.

The U.S. RDA for adults ages 19 and older is 11 mg daily for males and 8 mg for females. Women who are pregnant or breast-feeding require 11 and 12 mg respectively. The recommended upper limit for zinc intake is 40 mg/day. National dietary surveys in the United States suggest that adult women should consume 9 mg/day, and men 13 mg/day (Food and Nutrition Board Institute of Medicine, 2001). Zinc is found in shellfish, eggs, beef, and other red meats, where its bioavailability is relatively high because of the presence of certain amino acids (cysteine and methionine) that improve zinc absorption, and the relative absence of phytic acid, which inhibits absorption. The zinc in whole grain products, legumes, and other plant proteins is less bioavailable due to their relatively high content of phytic acid (King & Cousins, 2006).

If supplementation is desired, a daily multivitamin is a good source and may contain zinc in any of several of its salt forms. Picolinate has been shown to be more absorbable, though this may be offset by increased elimination. Zinc is regarded as relatively safe and generally well tolerated when taken at recommended doses, with few studies reporting side effects. There are interactions between zinc and the metabolism of a large number of medications, particularly the quinolone and tetracycline classes of antibiotics; separating administration of zinc and a medication by 2 hours should prevent the interaction ("Minerals," 2000). Zinc may also augment or interfere with drugs, herbs, and supplements that contain caffeine or have antibiotic, hormonal, blood pressure-altering, or diuretic effects, or that act on insulin levels.

VANADIUM
Vanadium, a mineral that assists with the uptake of glucose in muscle tissues and helps to regulate energy balance, is found in small quantities in most multivitamins. Those with bipolar illness should avoid ingesting supplements containing more than 10 mcg per daily dose (amount contained in a typical multivitamin). Manic individuals have significantly raised vanadium levels in hair (Naylor, Smith, Bryce-Smith, & Ward, 1984a, 1984b) and bipolar depressed patients have raised blood levels of vanadium; both normalize with recovery (Naylor, 1984). Some implicate vanadium in the cause of bipolar illness (Naylor & Smith, 1981). Vanadate (a compound containing an oxoanion of vanadium)

inhibits an enzyme (Na, K-ATPase) necessary to regulation of certain cellular activity. Lithium reduces this inhibition, and both phenothiazine antipsychotics and MAO inhibitors convert vanadate to a less active ion, vanadyl. Further, several therapies based on decreasing vanadate levels in the body have been reported effective in both mania and depression (Naylor, 1984).

Too Much, Too Little, or Just Right: A Word on Megadosing and on Deficiencies Associated With Treatment

Vitamins and minerals are required in sufficient quantity by the human body, and many medications—including those used in psychiatry—may induce deficiency. Attempting to compensate or to treat disease with megadoses of vitamins or minerals can lead to toxicity, however.

ADDRESSING VITAMIN AND MINERAL DEFICIENCIES ASSOCIATED WITH DRUG THERAPY

A number of psychiatric medications may compete for absorption of, decrease synthesis of, or increase metabolism of a number of nutrients. Carbamazepine (Tegretol) may interact with biotin, L-carnitine, folic acid, vitamin D (leading secondarily to reduced calcium absorption), and vitamins K, E, and B6. Valproic acid (Depakote) interferes with folic acid, L-carnitine, vitamins D and B6, niacin, and zinc. Not as much data are available on lamotrigine (Lamictal), though the FDA package insert warns of development of folate deficiency, and problems with increased vitamin D metabolism run across all anticonvulsants. The patient who takes anticonvulsants of any type should consider supplementing with vitamin D and folic acid (Johnson, 2007; Natural Standard, 2010b; NMCD, 2010b). Other nutrients that may be variably interfered with by anticonvulsants include selenium and phosphorous (Natural Standard, 2010b). Thyroid supplements may increase loss of calcium when used in supraphysiologic doses (Natural Standard, 2010b; NMCD, 2010b). Tricyclic antidepressants may cause deficiency of riboflavin (Johnson, 2007; Natural Standard, 2010b) and coenzyme Q10 (Natural Standard, 2010b), and phenothiazine antipsychotics with vitamin D (Johnson, 2007), DHEA, and riboflavin (Natural Standard, 2010b). Clozapine is associated with reduced serum levels of selenium, and some antipsychotics may reduce the natural production of coenzyme Q10. Diazepam and temazepam may alter synthesis or release of melatonin. SSRI antidepressants may reduce melatonin and sodium levels (Natural Standard, 2010b).

ORTHOMOLECULAR THERAPY: TOO MUCH OF A GOOD THING?
Orthomolecular psychiatry has been defined by its proponents as "the treatment of disease by varying the concentrations of substances normally present in the human body" (Pauling, 1968, p. 265). This type of megavitamin therapy dates to the early 1950s, when a few psychiatrists began adding vitamin B3 to their patients' regimens. Later on, this approach was expanded to include other vitamins, minerals, hormones, and diets, alone or in combination with medications and ECT.

In the early 1970s, a task force appointed by the American Psychiatric Association investigated the claims of psychiatrists who espoused the orthomolecular approach, noting the use of unconventional treatments and diagnostic methods as well. The scientific review published by this group concluded that, based on the quality of the research reviewed, "the credibility of the megavitamin proponents is low." They went on to criticize the "massive publicity which they promulgate via radio, the lay press and popular books, using catch phrases which are really misnomers like 'megavitamin therapy' and 'orthomolecular treatment,'" (Lipton, 1973).

Following on this investigation, the National Institute of Mental Health Research Advisory Committee reviewed all studies conducted through 1979 and agreed that megavitamin therapy was ineffective and potentially harmful. They, too, found that virtually all trials showed serious shortcomings in the number of participants, the presentation of baseline characteristics and outcomes, and other aspects of methodology.

Claims that megadoses of vitamins and minerals are effective against mental retardation, learning disabilities, and psychoses in children were debunked by the American Academy of Pediatrics (Nutrition, 1976) and the Canadian Academy of Pediatrics (CAP Nutrition Committee, 1990). These groups warned against the potentially toxic effects and lack of proven benefit in the conditions studied.

Although the human body requires vitamins and minerals in its metabolic activities, it has limited capacity for their use. Toxicity is a risk with fat-soluble vitamins and all minerals. Many micronutrients taken in larger-than-recommended doses may cause deficiencies of other nutrients, and they also may interact poorly with medications and other supplements.

Amino Acids

Protein is the second most abundant substance in our body. Only water is more plentiful. The 100,000-plus proteins are composed of various combinations of 22 amino acids, linked together by peptide bonds. When the body is functioning normally, it breaks down proteins from foods like meat and dairy or selected combinations of plant proteins and reassembles the amino acids into whatever substance it needs.

Some amino acids can be manufactured in the body from others and are thus called nonessential. Tyrosine is an example. Those that the body cannot produce, such as phenylalanine and tryptophan, need to be taken in through the diet and are called essential. Prefixes are often appended to the names of these compounds, as in L-tyrosine or DL-phenylalanine. Because these compounds are racemic, they come in two forms: L (*levo*, Latin for left) and rarely D (*dextro*, Latin for right). The L form is the naturally occurring molecule, which plants and animals use to form proteins. The D forms are generally synthesized molecules and with very few exceptions are not used by animals.

The amino acids discussed here are the ones most commonly used in treatment of depression. Of these, systematic reviews of several such interventions have found only SAM-e in monotherapy (Ravindran et al., 2009) and SAM-e or L-tyrosine adjuvant to antidepressants (Sarris, Kavanagh, & Byrne, 2010) to be recommendable, based on the quality of studies and availability of safety and long-term data. Though several of the amino acids we have included have not been shown effective in quality clinical trials, we cover them here as they are often tried by consumers, and anecdotally have been helpful to many people. Below you will find information on phenylalanine, tryptophan, 5-hydroxytryptophan (5-HTP), tyrosine, SAM-e, taurine, and GABA.

The two most widely held biochemical models of depression—the catecholamine and indoleamine hypotheses—explain depression as a result of deficient transmission of the catecholamines norepinephrine and dopamine, or the indolamine serotonin, respectively. Until recently, drugs used to treat depression appeared to enhance neurotransmission in one or both of these systems, and this was thought to be their method of action (Gelenberg & Klerman, 1978). In fact, our current models of depression sprang directly from this purported action of antidepressants (Gelenberg & Gibson, 1984). Phenylalanine, tryptophan, 5-HTP, and tyrosine are used in treatment of depression as they are precursors to neurotransmitters implicated in this illness. In the body tryptophan is converted to 5-HTP, which is converted to serotonin. From there, serotonin can be converted to N-acetylserotonin and finally to melatonin. The chemical cascade for the catecholamines procedes from phenylalanine to tyrosine, then to dopa, before conversion to dopamine, then norepinephrine, and finally epinephrine, also known as adrenaline. The thyroid hormones triiodothyronine (T3) and thyroxine (T4) also are derived from tyrosine.

SAM-e—while not itself an amino acid—is considered to be a metabolite of the essential amino acid L-methionine, and must be present as a methyl donor for conversion processes that allow the indolamine and catecholamine pathways to function properly (A. L. Miller, 2008). Taurine is an inhibitory amino acid that increases the effects of GABA by enhancing receptor binding (Jia et al., 2008) and slowing its degradation. Taurine is also thought to attenuate anxiety by decreasing the effects of the stimulatory amino acid N-methyl-D-aspartate (NMDA) (Saransaari & Oja, 2000) and inhibiting release of norepinephrine (Mizushima, Nara, Sawamura, & Yamori, 1996). GABA is an amino acid and also itself a neurotransmitter, rather than a precursor. Though there is little empirical evidence on its use in mood and anxiety disorders, we include it because it is so widely used and anecdotally it has been of help to a number of our clients.

A nutritionist who uses amino acids to treat mood and anxiety symptoms takes a full health history just as a psychiatrist does. He will choose the amino acids based on the client's individual symptom profile and then complement them with other nutrients based on what he feels the client might lack, and also to encourage optimal conversion, absorption, and function of the amino acids. Dietary changes are typically made as well.

Julia Ross, author of *The Mood Cure* and *The Diet Cure*, gives four symptom profiles in her books and suggests amino acids that might be appropriate for each. For people whose depression is accompanied by worry, anxiety, irritability, phobias, panic or obsessionality, with trouble initiating or maintaining sleep, and afternoon or evening cravings for carbohydrates or alcohol, she recommends tryptophan or 5HTP to stimulate serotonin. For those whose depression is marked by boredom, lack of energy and motivation, inability to concentrate or focus, and cravings for stimulants such as chocolate or caffeine, she recommends L-tyrosine to stimulate production of dopamine and norepinephrine. Those who feel overwhelmed, burned out, and stiff or tense from the effects of stress, and who might also crave food, alcohol, or drugs when feeling stressed, are recommended to take GABA combined with L-taurine and/or glysine. Those who have chronic physical pain or are "sensitive to emotional pain," cry easily or are often sad, and are prone to crave comforting or numbing behaviors and substances are recommended to try DL-phenylalanine, which slows the brain's destruction of endorphins (Ross, 2003). Another particular dosing protocol calls for 5-HTP and tyrosine taken in specific ratios four times daily, with the addition of several cofactors and sulfur amino acids for optimal results, including vitamin C, calcium, B6, folic acid, selenium, and cysteine.

Though books such as *The Mood Cure* (Ross, 2003) give suggestions for do-it-yourself supplementation, consulting a nutritionist is wise to improve effectiveness and safety. Amino acid regimens can be quite complex. In addition to the few amino acids that are central to the creation of neurotransmitters, a number of others play smaller but important functions, and as a single amino acid can be insufficient in isolation or create imbalance in others if used alone, regimens often include more than one. Amino acids are often taken with other nutrients necessary for their synthesis into neurotransmitters. Vitamin B6 or a B complex are recommended with all amino acids given for depression, for instance. Serotonin production will be interrupted in those deficient in niacin, and neither tryptophan nor 5-HTP can convert to serotonin without B6, though there is concern that in its presence 5-HTP may convert too quickly to serotonin and not be allowed across the blood-brain barrier. (The last few sentences may be more confusing than helpful to the reader.) To further complicate matters, such complex regimens are often based on theories and animal research without supporting data from trials in depressed humans. Collaboration with a professional who has many years of clinical experience treating individuals with mood disorders is recommended.

The profile of each amino acid below begins by explaining the theoretical action of the substance from basic science studies, and about the effects of its blood concentration or depletion on mood in humans. However, outcomes of clinical trials often don't align with theory: Though tyrosine depletion has been found to attenuate dopamine function, which has theoretical bearing on some symptoms of depression, interventions with supplementation have not found it to be helpful (Gelenberg et al., 1990). Though some research suggests that phenylalanine is deficient in patients with ADHD (Bornstein et al., 1990), it has not been found efficacious in this disorder (Wood, Reimherr, & Wender, 1985b; Zametkin, Karoum, & Rapoport, 1987). No significant relationships were found between the plasma levels of taurine or seven other amino acids and the levels measured in brain cortex (Wright & Gaull, 1988). Remember also that what a substance is used for and what it is shown to be efficacious in can be very different.

PHENYLALANINE

Phenylalanine (D, L, or DL-phenylalanine; DLPA; 2-amino-3-phenyl-propanoic acid) is an essential amino acid. L-phenylalanine is converted preferentially to L-tyrosine, and from there to the catecholamines dopamine and norepinephrine. It may also be converted to phenylethylamine (PEA), a compound similar to amphetamine that occurs normally in the human brain (as well as in chocolate and marijuana), and has been shown to have mood- elevating effects. D-phenylalanine— which does not normally occur in the body or in food—enhances pain relief by inhibiting enkephalinase, the enzyme that metabolizes endorphins. It is preferentially converted to PEA but also to L-phenylalanine in the body (Natural Standard, 2010g).

Orally, phenylalanine is used for psychiatric conditions including depression, ADHD, Parkinson's disease, and alcohol withdrawal symptoms (NMCD, 2010e).

Studies have shown that phelylalanine depletion increases vulnerability to lowered mood (Leyton et al., 2000; Sabelli et al., 1986) and that depressed people commonly have low levels of PEA (Moises, Waldmeier, & Beckmann, 1986; Nakagawara, 1992; Sabelli et al., 1986), while it may be elevated in (hypo)manic persons (Karoum et al., 1982; Moises et al., 1986). Limited and preliminary clinical research performed in the 1970s suggests L- or DL-phenylalanine might be useful for depression (Beckmann, Athen, Olteanu, & Zimmer, 1979; Beckmann, Strauss, & Ludolph, 1977; Birkmayer, Riederer, Linauer, & Knoll, 1984; Fischer, Heller, Nachon, & Spatz, 1975), but this research requires replication adherent to current methodologic standards. Though some research suggests that patients with ADHD have lower levels of amino acids including phenylalanine (Bornstein et al., 1990), neither D- nor DL-phenylalanine has sustained effect in symptoms of this disorder (Wood et al., 1985b; Zametkin et al., 1987).

If you're considering phenylalanine, 250 mg L-phenylalanine (Birkmayer et al., 1984) and 150 to 200 mg DL-phenylalanine (Beckmann et al., 1979) per day have been studied in unipolar depression, though Balch's *Prescription for Nutritional Healing* and Ross's *Mood Cure*, popular with the lay public, recommend doses of 600–1,200 mg daily for anxiety (Balch, 2006) and 1,500 mg in the morning or 500 mg/day taken with 500 mg/day L-tyrosine for depression (Balch, 2006; Ross, 2003). One trial dosed L-phenylalanine as high as 14 g daily with no adverse events, though this dose was held no longer than a week (Sabelli et al., 1986). Phenylalanine should be taken at least half an hour before or after a meal. To get more phenylalanine in your diet, choose cottage cheese, fish, seafood, meats, poultry, peanuts, sesame seeds, lentils, sunflower seeds, black beans, watercress, and soybeans.

Common side effects include constipation, heartburn, and nausea, and sometimes headache. Increase in anxiety, hypomania, insomnia, and sedation have occurred in clinical studies. Individuals with phenylketonuria should not take phenylalanine, and theoretically the supplement should be used cautiously in persons with hypertension, as this supplement is a precursor to catecholamines (Natural Standard, 2010g).

Concomitant use of L-phenylalanine and antipsychotics can contribute to the development and severity (Gardos, Cole, Matthews,

Nierenberg, & Dugan, 1992) and exacerbation (Mosnik, Spring, Rogers, & Baruah, 1997) of tardive dyskinesia. DL-phenylalanine with levodopa can exacerbate tremor, rigidity, and the "on-off" syndrome in patients with Parkinson's disease (NMCD, 2010e). Theoretically, L-phenylalanine might increase the risk of hypertensive crisis when used with MAO inhibitors (Silkaitis & Mosnaim, 1976). Theoretically, phenylalanine may inhibit absorption of baclofen and make antihypertensive drugs and herbs less effective. There may be interactions with immunomodulators, as PEA may inhibit synthesis of antibodies (Natural Standard, 2010g).

TRYPTOPHAN AND 5-HTP
Tryptophan [L-tryptophan; L-2-amino-3-(indole-3-yl) propionic acid], synthesized in the body from L-phenylalanine, is a nonessential amino acid that converts first to 5-HTP and then to the indolamines serotonin and melatonin.

In psychiatry, orally administered L-tryptophan and 5-HTP are used for sleep disorders, depression, anxiety, premenstrual syndrome, ADHD, smoking cessation, and Tourette's syndrome (Natural Standard, 2010a; NMCD, 2010h). 5-HTP is used for migraine and tension-type headaches, fibromyalgia, binge eating associated with obesity, and premenstrual dysphoric disorder (PMDD), and as adjunctive therapy in seizure disorder and Parkinson's disease (Natural Standard, 2010a; NMCD, 2010a). Research has not borne out its utility in all of these disorders.

There is convincing evidence that tryptophan depletion primarily and selectively affects serotonergic transmission, reduces the effects of SSRIs, and contributes to depression (Neumeister, 2003; Salomon, Miller, Delgado, & Charney, 1993). Depletion of tryptophan can cause a relapse in treated depression and precipitate depressive symptoms in patients with a history or family history of depression, as well as in healthy volunteers (C. Bell, Abrams, & Nutt, 2001; Murphy, Smith, Cowen, Robbins, & Sahakian, 2002). However, tryptophan depletion does not seem to worsen symptoms in people with untreated depression (Delgado et al., 1994). Additionally, dietary L-tryptophan depletion has been associated with bulimia relapse (K. A. Smith, Fairburn, & Cowen, 1999), and deterioration of schizophrenia symptoms (R. P. Sharma et al., 1997).

Taking 5-HTP orally seems to significantly improve symptoms of depression (Nakajima, Kudo, & Kaneko, 1978; Shaw, Turner, & Del Mar, 2001), and there is evidence that it might be comparable to the antidepressants Luvox and Tofranil (Coppen, Whybrow, Noguera, Maggs, & Prange, 1972; Poldinger, Calanchini, & Schwarz, 1991). Some preliminary clinical research suggests that L-tryptophan in combination with conventional antidepressants might improve their effectiveness (Nardini, De Stefano, Iannuccelli, Borghesi, & Battistini, 1983; Walinder, Skott, Carlsson, Nagy, & Bjorn-Erik, 1976) and might be helpful in seasonal affective disorder (SAD) (Ghadirian, Murphy, & Gendron, 1998), insomnia (Hartmann & Spinweber, 1979; Korner et al., 1986), and in PMDD (Steinberg, Annable, Young, & Liyanage, 1999). Of 108 trials of tryptophan or 5-HTP for depression reviewed by the Cochrane Collaboration, however, only two were judged of sufficient quality to be included in their systematic review, and they found the evidence of insufficient quality to be conclusive (Shaw et al., 2001). Evidence for all indications is sparse and considered preliminary (NMCD, 2010h).

One may do best to try 5-HTP before tryptophan as tryptophan has difficulty crossing the blood-brain barrier. Also, the body uses 5-HTP only for serotonin production, whereas tryptophan has other functions. Compared with L-tryptophan, less 5-HTP is required to make a given quantity of serotonin. 5-HTP is typically dosed at 50–100 mg per day, but higher doses are used, and side effects are dose dependent. Clinical trials of 5-HTP for depression have studied doses as low as 50 mg/day and as high as 500 mg/day (van Praag, 1981), and 25–350 mg daily has been used for anxiety (Natural Standard, 2010a). Tryptophan dosages are 1,000–4,000 mg/day. Taking a 5-HTP supplement with a high-carbohydrate food or drink, like juice, is thought to increase its absorption. 5-HTP effects in depression may be potentiated by tyrosine (van Praag, 1984). To increase your intake of tryptophan at mealtime, choose chicken, turkey, fish, beef, and dairy products.

Tryptophan and 5-HTP can cause gastrointestinal side effects such as heartburn, stomach pain, belching and flatulence, nausea, vomiting, and diarrhea (Byerley, Judd, Reimherr, & Grosser, 1987; Natural Standard, 2010a), and tryptophan may lead also to headache, lightheadedness, dry mouth, visual blurring, ataxia, drowsiness, and anorexia (Shaw et al.,

2001). These supplements also may cause mood disturbance and should be used cautiously in bipolar illness (Natural Standard, 2010a). In 1989, more than 1,500 cases of eosinophilia-myalgia syndrome (EMS) and 37 deaths were associated with L-tryptophan use in the United States, 95% of which were traced to a single manufacturer in Japan (Kilbourne, Philen, Kamb, & Falk, 1996). In 1990, L-tryptophan was recalled in the United States. It is currently available over the counter, and cases of EMS are considered rare. There is also concern that 5-HTP, like L-tryptophan, can (rarely) cause asymptomatic eosinophilia and EMS (FDA, 1998, 2001).

Tryptophan and 5-HTP should not be taken together or with St. John's wort and SAM-e. They should be used with serotonergic antidepressants such as SSRIs or TCAs only under supervision, and may be dangerous when combined with MAO inhibitors due to risk of serotonin syndrome. Caution should be used with other serotonergic medications including dextromethorphan, Demerol, Tramadol, Talwin, and (with 5-HTP only) carbidopa. Taking L-tryptophan with phenothiazines (such as Thorazine, Prolixin, Stelazine, and Melaril) can cause movement disorders. Tryptophan may increase the effects of central nervous system depressants, including benzodiazepines and some herbal supplements. 5-HTP may give false positive results on 5-HIAA screening for carcinoid tumors (NMCD, 2010a, 2010h).

Both 5-HTP and tryptophan have multiple other side effects and drug interactions. A thorough consideration of the available data should be undertaken if the supplements are to be used.

TYROSINE

Tyrosine [L-tyrosine; 2-amino-3-(4-hydroxyphenyl)propionic acid], an amino acid that can be synthesized in the body from phenylalanine, is a precursor to dopamine, norepinephrine, and the thyroid hormones.

In psychiatry tyrosine is used for ADHD, PMS, Parkinson's disease, alcohol and cocaine withdrawal, Alzheimer's disease, loss of libido, schizophrenia, stress and fatigue, and narcolepsy, improving alertness following sleep deprivation (NMCD, 2010i).

Many studies implicated the tyrosine hydroxylase gene in predisposition to bipolar disorder, though two large meta-analyses did not find an association (Furlong et al., 1999; Turecki, Rouleau, Mari, Joober, &

Morgan, 1997). Tyrosine depletion has been found to attenuate dopamine function in healthy individuals (Harmer, McTavish, Clark, Goodwin, & Cowen, 2001; McLean, Rubinsztein, Robbins, & Sahakian, 2004) and in euthymic women with a history of recurrent depression (McTavish, Mannie, Harmer, & Cowen, 2005), which has implications for the pathogenesis of a disruption in affect relative to reward-based processing in depression (McLean et al., 2004).

Andrew Gelenberg and colleagues (1990) treated outpatients in a double-blind study with L-tyrosine 100 mg/kg/day, imipramine, 2.5 mg/kg/day, or placebo for 4 weeks and found "there was no evidence that tyrosine had antidepressant activity." This was also the bottom line of his review on theoretical background and clinical experience with L-tyrosine for depression (Gelenberg & Gibson, 1984). As mentioned, tyrosine depletion does attenuate dopamine in humans, though this does not seem to cause depressive relapse in people with a history of depression (McTavish, Mannie, & Cowen, 2004; McTavish et al., 2005; Roiser et al., 2005).

Though these results on depression as a syndrome have been negative, it is possible that certain depressive symptoms will respond to L-tyrosine, or that your nutritionist will choose to augment 5-HTP or another nutrient with this amino acid. If you are thinking of adding L-tyrosine to your regimen, N-acetyl-L-tyrosine is a more rapidly absorbed and bioavailable form. It is used in doses of about 150–1,000 mg/day. Dosages of L-tyrosine are higher at 500–1,500 mg daily; 500 mg three times daily is recommended (Balch, 2006) and is typically suggested by manufacturers. Reduced levels of dopamine may result from high doses (Chinevere, Sawyer, Creer, Conlee, & Parcell, 2002), and high or chronic doses may reduce absorption of other amino acids. Tyrosine may be found in dietary proteins in dairy products, meats, seafood and fowl, eggs, various nuts and legumes (including soy), avocados, bananas, seaweed, oats, and wheat. When dietary intake of tyrosine is inadequate, phenylalanine is converted to tyrosine (Food and Nutrition Board, IOM, 1999). Dietary needs of tyrosine are dependent on phenylalanine intake.

Tyrosine has FDA Generally Regarded As Safe status in the United States. Side effects may include nausea, headache, fatigue, heartburn, and arthralgia (NMCD, 2010i; Wood, Reimherr, & Wender, 1985a).

There is some concern that tyrosine might decrease the effectiveness of L-dopa when administered within 2 hours. There may be additive effects with thyroid hormone medications, and it may also decrease TSH results on blood tests. Theoretically, tyrosine might exacerbate hyperthyroidism and Graves' disease (NMCD, 2010i).

SAM-E

S-adenosylmethionine (SAM-e, S-adenosyl-L-methionine) has been available as a dietary supplement in the United States since 1999, but it has been used as a prescription drug in Italy since 1979, in Spain since 1985, and Germany since 1989. While not itself an amino acid, SAM-e is formed by the union of the amino acid methionine when bonded with adenosine triphosphate (ATP), the major source of energy in the body. SAM-e works through three biochemical pathways. It donates molecules, called methyl groups, to other substances, helping to form genetic material, components of the cell membrane, myelin (the insulating coating on nerve fibers), and neurotransmitters. It helps to form sulfur-containing amino acids like the antioxidant glutathione. SAM-e also helps to regulate gene expression through the formation of polyamines, keeping cells growing and replicating at the proper rate (Natural Standard, 2010h; NMCD, 2010f). SAM-e works synergistically with folate, B6, and B12 in reducing homocysteine levels (Friedel, Goa, & Benfield, 1989), which has implications for depression.

Psychiatric uses of SAM-e include depression, anxiety, PMS, PMDD, ADHD, and improving intellectual performance. Other neurologic uses include Parkinson's disease, Alzheimer's disease and other dementias, multiple sclerosis, spinal cord injury, seizures, and migraine headache (NMCD, 2010f).

Supplementing the diet with SAM-e can result in increased levels of serotonin, dopamine, and phosphatides, improve binding of neurotransmitters to receptor sites by increasing membrane fluidity (Bottiglieri, 2002; Rosenbaum et al., 1990), increase serotonin turnover, and elevate dopamine and norepinephrine levels (Bottiglieri, 2002; Bottiglieri, Hyland, & Reynolds, 1994; Rosenbaum et al., 1990). Depression is associated with lower than normal steady-state concentrations of SAM-e, and mania may result from elevated serum concentrations (Cantoni,

Mudd, & Andreoli, 1989). Neuroimaging studies indicate that SAM-e affects the brain similarly to conventional antidepressants (O. Arnold et al., 2005; Saletu, Anderer, Di Padova, Assandri, & Saletu-Zyhlarz, 2002).

Compared with many other nonpharmaceutical supplements, SAM-e has been extensively studied, with three decades of literature suggesting its efficacy and safety in depression (Cantoni et al., 1989; Nguyen & Gregan, 2002; Papakostas, Alpert, & Fava, 2003; Vahora & Malek-Ahmadi, 1988; A. L. Williams, Girard, Jui, Sabina, & Katz, 2005). Compared to standard antidepressant agents, SAM-e has fewer side effects and shorter time to onset of benefit (Vahora & Malek-Ahmadi, 1988), especially when used parenterally (intravenously or intramuscularly). Controlled trials have found SAM-e to be more efficacious than placebo and equal in efficacy to the tricyclic antidepressants for treating major depressive disorder when administered parenterally; less evidence supports the use of oral SAM-e, although some trials have demonstrated its efficacy as well (Papakostas, 2009). Questions remain about mechanism of action, bioavailability, and absorption of oral SAM-e (A. L. Williams et al., 2005). There is only preliminary (though no controlled) evidence examining whether oral forms of SAM-e can be safe, tolerable, and efficacious when used adjunctively with antidepressants (Papakostas, 2009).

For depression monotherapy, an oral or parenteral (Friedel et al., 1989) dose of 400–1,600 mg/day has been used, with 1,600 mg/day the most commonly used dose for oral administration in clinical trials (Bressa, 1994). SAM-e 200 mg intramuscularly has been used safely for the first 2 weeks of TCA therapy to speed response (Berlanga, Ortega-Soto, Ontiveros, & Senties, 1992). SAM-e can cause nausea and vomiting in some people, so it is important to start low and go slow. An example of a titration schedule would be to start at 200 mg twice daily for the first two days, increase to 400 mg twice daily on day 3, to 400 mg three times daily on day 10, and then to a maximum dosage of 400 mg four times daily after 20 days, if needed. Betaine (trimethylglycine, TMG) may increase the synthesis of SAM-e (A. J. Barak, Beckenhauer, Junnila, & Tuma, 1993; A. J. Barak, Beckenhauer, & Tuma, 1994) and is often given with it (Balch, 2006). A deficiency in B12 and folate levels may result in low serum levels of SAM-e (Friedel et al., 1989), so supplementing with these may be prudent. SAM-e supplements should always be taken on an empty stomach and separate from other amino acids, to maximize absorption.

Side effects of orally administered SAM-e are more common with higher doses and include flatulence, nausea, vomiting, diarrhea, constipation, dry mouth, headache, mild insomnia, anorexia, sweating, dizziness, and nervousness (NMCD, 2010f). SAM-e methylates levodopa, which might worsen Parkinsonian symptoms (Charlton & Crowell, 1992). SAM-e has been associated with (hypo)mania in case reports and clinical trials of both oral and parenteral formulations; this supplement should not be used by persons with bipolar illness (Cantoni et al., 1989; Carney, Chary, Bottiglieri, & Reynolds, 1989; Carney, Toone, & Reynolds, 1987; Goren, Stoll, Damico, Sarmiento, & Cohen, 2004; Kagan, Sultzer, Rosenlicht, & Gerner, 1990). Use cautiously in patients with anxiety disorders or a prominent anxiety component to their depression (Natural Standard, 2010h).

SAM-e should not be coadministered with St. John's wort, tryptophan, or 5-HTP. Combination with serotonergic antidepressants such as TCAs and SSRIs may cause additive serotonergic effects and serotonin syndrome-like effects. It should be used with these only under careful supervision. SAM-e may be dangerous when combined with MAO inhibitors. Caution should be used with other serotonergic medications including dextromethorphan, Demerol, Tramadol, and Talwin (NMCD, 2010f). Theoretically, SAM-e might reduce the effectiveness of levodopa in Parkinson's disease (Charlton & Crowell, 1992).

TAURINE

Taurine (L-taurine; 2-aminoethane sulfonic acid) is an organic acid found in bile, the lower intestine, and in the tissues of many animals, including humans (Brosnan & Brosnan, 2006). In the strict sense, it is not an amino acid (Carey, 2006), but it is often called one.

Despite its inclusion in energy drinks such as Rockstar (100 mg per serving) and Red Bull (1,420 mg), it is actually an inhibitory chemical known for having a calming effect. It also has antioxidative and anti-inflammatory properties (Dincer, Babul, Erdogan, Ozogul, & Dincers, 1996; Wright & Gaull, 1988). Taurine has neuroprotective (El Idrissi &

Trenkner, 1999; Louzada et al., 2004; Wu et al., 2005) and anticonvulsant properties (El Idrissi & Trenkner, 1999) due to its ability to reduce glutamate-induced increase in calcium influx in neurons. Theoretically it would benefit people suffering from mania in this way. Taurine may attenuate anxiety by inhibiting release of norepinephrine (Mizushima et al., 1996).

Psychiatric and neurologic uses of taurine are limited to ADHD, seizure disorders, autism, alcoholism, and improvement of mental performance (NMCD, 2010g).

Major depression is characterized by higher plasma taurine levels than normal controls (Altamura, Maes, Dai, & Meltzer, 1995; Lima et al., 2003), though not in all studies (Maes, Verkerk, Vandoolaeghe, Lin, & Scharpe, 1998). Lower baseline serum taurine levels may predict a clinical nonresponse to treatment with antidepressants with a serotonergic mode of action, such as trazodone in monotherapy or combined with fluoxetine or pindolol (Maes et al., 1998), which in turn may lower serum levels of taurine (Lima et al., 2003; Maes et al., 1998). No significant relationships could be found between the plasma levels of taurine and the levels measured in brain cortex, however (Wright & Gaull, 1988).

Though theoretically taurine has potential effects on mood and anxiety states, there is not one clinical trial in humans indexed in the National Library of Medicine. Its popularization in books (Balch, 2006; Ross, 2003) and by practitioners as a complementary or alternative treatment rests on theory and anecdotal evidence.

Taurine is found abundantly in animal proteins such as meat and fish. If you decide to try adding supplemental taurine to your regimen, it should be taken at least half an hour before or after a meal to maximize absorption. Many product manufacturers recommend taurine be taken in one dose of 1,000 mg daily; it may also be taken at 1,500 mg/day in three divided doses. The best dose is not known from studies of depression in humans.

Orally, side effects have not been reported in clinical trials using taurine for up to a year. Taurine is thought to have diuretic properties, and so theoretically may reduce excretion and increase levels of lithium, necessitating a reduction in dose (NMCD, 2010g). Use cautiously in patients with high cholesterol or triglycerides and those taking statins.

Taurine may have hypotensive, hypoglycemic, antiplatelet, and anticoagulant effects. A single case of mania was reported in a man who consumed several energy drinks containing taurine, caffeine, B vitamins, and other ingredients (Red Bull Energy Drink) over a period of four days (Natural Standard, 2010i).

GABA

Unlike the other amino acids covered here, GABA (gamma-aminobutyric acid) itself serves as neurotransmitter, not a precursor. It is related to the mechanism of action of anticonvulsants, benzodiazepines, and many other medications.

In psychiatry, GABA is used orally or sublingually for relieving anxiety, elevating mood, relieving PMS, treating ADHD, and for increasing feelings of well-being (NMCD, 2010d).

Once again, what something is used for and what it has shown utility for are often different. There is little research on GABA's effectiveness in mood and anxiety and so it is not possible to provide a review of the literature on its effectiveness and safety. We nonetheless felt compelled to include it here as GABA supplements have brought significant relief anecdotally to a number of our patients who suffer physiologic symptoms of anxiety, including a number of people living with PTSD. They find it calms their anxiety and can be helpful for sleep if the supplement does not contain a small amount of tyrosine, which is often included to prevent daytime sleepiness.

Excess GABA can cause anxiety, seizures, shortness of breath, numbness around the mouth, and tingling in the extremities. Theoretically it can interact with sedatives and antianxiety agents, antidepressants, pain relievers, muscle relaxants, alcohol, and antiseizure medications.

As doses have not been tested, we cannot list recommendations, though some manufacturers recommend at least 2 g daily for effectiveness, with 5 g being more effective, and 18 g an upper limit. GABA is sold in capsules, tablets, or as a powder. It is best absorbed when taken between meals. As very little GABA crosses the blood-brain barrier, the patient may do well to purchase picamilon (nicotinyl-y-aminobutyric acid), a form of GABA combined with nicotinic acid as a carrier that was developed by the All-Union Vitamin Research Institute in 1970 and is now available from a variety of manufacturers. Studies in animals suggest it exhibits the properties of a tranquilizer with a stimulating component, and does not induce muscle relaxation, drowsiness, or lethargy (Akopian, Balian, & Avetisian, 2006).

GENERAL TIPS FOR ADMINISTRATION

In addition to the information on each individual supplement, some tips apply to supplementation with any amino acid. Amino acids have a high rate of turnover in the body, and if a necessary amino acid is not found in food, the body will break down its own tissue to get it, one of the many reasons eating small frequent meals is recommended for good health. Your supplement regimen will likely include dosing with amino acids two to four times daily.

Amino acids are best absorbed when taken on an empty stomach, as proteins in food may compete for absorption. They are often taken first thing in the morning with juice, however, as the carbohydrates can aid absorption. When considering whether to supplement with amino acids, ask yourself if this is a schedule you can maintain: you may be taking amino acids two to four times daily between the four to five meals and snacks already in your daily schedule.

As amino acids are digested, ammonia is produced. The normal amount produced from digestion of the food we eat is managed by the liver, but high doses of amino acids can create toxicity that may leave you feeling agitated and edgy, and perhaps give you a headache. Certain amino acids are more likely to be toxic in excessive amounts—including aspartic acid, glutamic acid, homocysteine, cysteine, serine, and tryptophan—but very high doses are not recommended for any amino acid, especially in persons with impaired liver or kidney function. The B and C vitamins and others can be helpful for detoxification. Your nutritionist or other clinician will aid you in choosing appropriate nutrients to optimize use of your supplements.

Another safety note is that pregnant women should only consume amino acids under supervision. There is a paucity of data on their safety in this population.

As with traditional antidepressants, each individual responds differently to treatment. Just as there are early and placebo responders with conventional medications, improvements in mood are noticed by some in just a few days on amino acids. Others don't notice any improvements for a few months, then notice steady and growing improvement over time. Similar to those taking antidepressants, the average patient begins to notice gradual improvements beginning after 1 month of treatment, and they then continue to improve. If an individual amino acid supplement is taken alone for longer than 1 month, an amino acid complex should be added to the protocol to prevent imbalance and any resulting deficiency of other amino acids.

Note that to check levels of amino acids, many nutritionists will want to use blood profiles, urine samples, and hair analysis. As there are so very many reasons why an individual might have high or low concentrations of these nutrients as reflected on a given test, it is our opinion that they may not be worth your investment.

Omega-3 Fatty Acids

Omega-3 fatty acids (polyunsaturated fatty acids, PUFA) that are used in psychiatry include eicosapentanoic acid (EPA) and docosahexanoic acid (DHA). A third is alpha linoleic acid (ALA), which has not been shown useful in treatment of mood disorders. The omega-3s are classified as essential fatty acids (EFA) because they must be derived from food sources; the body cannot synthesize them.

There are historical arguments for increasing our intake of omega-3 fatty acids. Almost 4 million years ago, *Australopithecus afarensis*—the oldest widespread hominid—roamed the Rift Valley in Kenya. Two and a half million years ago *A. afarensis* gave rise to three species. While *A. boisei* and *A. robustus* lived in forested areas and along the river margins, evidence of *Homo habilis* has been found almost exclusively around lakes, where its diet consisted largely of fish. This is the species that is thought to have developed into humans (Andrews & Martin, 1991; Broadhurst, Cunnane, & Crawford, 1998). These early hominids evolved eating a 1:1 ratio of omega-3 to omega-6 PUFAs. Humans once ate freeranging buffalo, deer, and other game that fed on wild plants. We ate wild plants that contained abundant quantities of omega-3 EFAs. We currently receive omega-6 oils from similar food sources, as cows and farmed fish are fed grains. As omega-6 fatty acids are proinflammatory and omega-3s are anti-inflammatory, our modern diet literally feeds diseases involving inflammatory processes (Stoll, 2001). Humans in Westernized countries now eat a 1:10 to 1:20 ratio, depending on where they live (Brooks et al., 2000). EPA has anti-inflammatory properties, increases high-density lipoproteins (HDL; "good cholesterol"), and lowers low-density lipoproteins (LDL; "bad cholesterol"). Omega-6 oils are inflammatory. Where the diet of our ancestors kept them in balance, our current diet has given rise to many inflammatory illnesses, including hypertension, coronary artery disease, rheumatoid and osteoarthritis, inflammatory bowel disease, and depression (Stoll, 2001).

In psychiatry, fish oil is used for mood stabilization and depression in mood disorders, ADHD, schizophrenia, Alzheimer's disease and other dementias, and aggressive or violent behavior (Natural Standard, 2010f; NMCD, 2010c). In addition to modulating inflammation, EPA modulates signaling cascades within neurons—including those responsible for glutamatergic activity and calcium influx, implicated in bipolar cyclicity and "excitotoxicity"—and regulates gene expression. Its neuroprotective properties further include benefit to the composition and plasticity of the cell's lipid membrane, where it also increases electrical conduction and neurotransmitter responsivity (Decklebaum, Worgau, & Seo, 2006; Kidd, 2007). Although DHA neither has anti-inflammatory properties nor does it perform any of the functions listed above, omega-3 EFAs are beneficial not only in their action but also simply in their presence; the ratio of omega-6 to omega-3 fatty acids in and of itself is implicated in disease (Frasure-Smith et al., 2004; Jacka et al., 2004).

A number of epidemiologic studies conducted by Joseph Hibbeln have demonstrated the effect of omega-3 consumption in large populations: less seafood consumption predicts increased annual prevalence of major depression (Hibbeln, 1998), postpartum depression (Hibbeln, 2002), and homicide mortality rates (Hibbeln, 2001). Omega-3 fatty acids are related to serotonin activity in healthy volunteers (Hibbeln et al., 1998).

There is an acute need for well-designed and executed randomized controlled trials. The Cochrane Collaboration found only five studies of omega-3 fatty acids in bipolar illness that met inclusion criteria for systematic review, with highly variable methodological quality. Only one study showed a benefit for depression symptom severity but not for mania in adjunctive depression of bipolar disorder (P. Montgomery & Richardson, 2008). A second review agreed that current data on the efficacy of EPA and DHA in the treatment of bipolar disorder are insufficient to support conclusions that can guide clinical practice (Sempels & Sienaert, 2007). Studies in monotherapy and adjunctive therapy in unipolar depression have similar limitations, and results regarding efficacy are mixed (M. P. Freeman, 2009). A systematic review of studies that examined the efficacy of omega-3 fatty acids in the depressed mood of both bipolar and unipolar patients included 12 RCTs in a meta-analysis and commented that trial evidence that examines the effects of omega-3 PUFAs on depressed mood is limited and difficult to summarize and evaluate because of considerable heterogeneity of methods and quality. It concluded that "the evidence available provides little support for the use of n-3 PUFAs to improve depressed mood," recommending larger trials with adequate statistical power to detect clinically important benefits (Appleton et al., 2006). Numerous other reviews have concluded that the evidence implies promise of a treatment effect of omega-3 fatty acids for depression in adults, though further study in larger trials with greater methodologic quality is needed (Appleton, Rogers, & Ness, 2008; Kraguljac et al., 2009; Severus, 2006; A. L. Williams et al., 2006), as is more sophisticated investigation of dose response in particular populations (Osher, Belmaker, & Nemets, 2006; A. L. Williams et al., 2006), the length of time required for significant response, and the relationship between EPA and DHA (Osher et al., 2006).

Though available data do not conclusively support omega-3 fatty acids for use in treatment of mood disorders, augmentation should still be considered, as they are simply far less present than they should be in the human diet, and general health benefits are well established and adjunctive use has low risk. Health benefits of omega-3 EFA may be especially important in patients with psychiatric disorders, due to high prevalence rates of smoking and obesity and the metabolic side effects of some psychotropic medications (M. P. Freeman et al., 2006).

The best source of omega-3 fatty acids is from oily fish with dark meat, such as salmon, mackerel, sardines, menhaden, anchovies, and herring. These fish store the oil in their muscles, whereas white fish (like cod) store it in their livers. The oils are essential to fish as well, which derive theirs from algae, plankton, and tiny, brightly colored crustaceans called krill, which give salmon their pink color. To get sufficient omega-3 to benefit health from fish alone, one would have to eat a lot of fish. A typical 3.5-oz serving of fish contains between 1.2 (for Atlantic salmon) and 3.3 (sardines) grams of omega-3, which consists of both EPA and DHA. To achieve sufficient doses of EPA, once would have to eat still more. It would take between 6 and 32 average-sized cans of tuna (depending on species) to achieve the 9.6 g/day dose used in Andrew Stoll's initial study of bipolar illness.

Fresh wild-caught fish are perhaps not the best source because of safety: Fish can be loaded with contaminants. Freshwater fish is the most highly contaminated, and ocean fish are not regulated by the FDA. Anchovies, sardines, and menhaden have shorter lives and are lower on the food chain and hence are less likely to be polluted, as are fish from deep, cold waters, such as those near Norway. Fish can also be expensive: Wild-caught salmon, when in season, can cost as much as $30 per pound. Farmed salmon is not an acceptable option. It costs less certainly, but has far less concentration of omega-3 fatty acids, as these fish are fed "salmon chow." In Western Europe, salmon chow may contain krill meal, but in the United States and elsewhere it is grain-based and hence increases rather than decreases the ratio of omega-6 to omega-3. Furthermore, salmon raised in close quarters take on sea lice, which are then killed with pesticides. Antibiotics are used to control diseases in farm populations. Higher concentrations of cancer-causing pollutants and toxins are found in farmed salmon than in their wild counterparts. Note that "Atlantic salmon" account for over 95% of the farmed salmon produced, mostly on the Pacific coast of Canada and Chile. If it's inexpensive and says Atlantic on the label, it's farmed (Stoll, 2001).

There are plant-based alternatives to fish and fish oil supplements for vegetarians. Flaxseed, purslane, walnut, perilla, and other plants contain ALA, though there have been no trials of ALA in psychiatric illness, and stable-isotope tracer studies indicate that less than 1% is metabolized to EPA or DHA in humans (Pawlosky, Hibbeln, Novotny, & Salem, 2001). Still, some people use flaxseed oil in lieu of fish oil: 1–2 tablespoons per day of flaxseed oil will provide 7–14 g of ALA. Liquid oil must be refrigerated; capsules may stay on the shelf but are as expensive as fish oil. Flaxseed oil has a strong taste but can be taken with an orange juice chaser, added to smoothies, or to salad dressings. No more than 2–3 tablespoons of flaxseed or meal should be taken daily, as seed husks contain several chemicals that may be toxic at higher doses. At these doses it may interrupt iodine uptake by the thyroid gland. Husks also contain lignans, which have estrogenic, antiestrogenic, and steroidlike activities (Hoepner, 2006; Stoll, 2001).

Remember that the ratio of omega-3 to omega-6 is important. All oils and fats a person consumes compete for receptor sites and inclusion in cell membranes. As well as supplementing with omega-3, reducing sources of omega-6 may be helpful; omega-9 oils such as canola and olive oil may be substituted in cooking, for instance (Hoepner, 2006).

Supplementing with fish oil capsules is a simple way to get omega-3 into one's diet. For mood disorders and illnesses involving inflammation, EPA and not DHA is desired, so dose should be determined by the number of milligrams of EPA contained in the capsules. Be sure to read labels carefully: some will list number of milligrams by capsule, and others by recommended serving. Dosage in mood disorder studies varies (Hoepner, 2006; Stoll, 2001). The Inuit (indigenous people of Alaska) eat up to 19 g daily, and Greenland Eskimos up to 14 g/day of EPA. Andrew Stoll's (2001) seminal study in bipolar illness supplemented with 9.6 g/day of EPA. When Stoll's book *The Omega 3 Connection* was published in 2001, his recommendations were for 1.5–4 g of EPA daily for those with mood disorders, and 1 g for cardiac health, mild mood symptoms, or mood enhancement. For cardiac health, the American Heart Association also recommends 1 g of omega-3 EFS daily, but does not specify EPA or DHA (Leaf & Hatcher, 2009). One large, well-designed trial achieved good results results with 1 g daily of EPA (Peet & Horrobin, 2002). Results for the group receiving 1 g were better than those seen in the subjects taking more. Like any treatment, every client will respond differently. It's likely wise to start with 1–2 g/day as the patient feels comfortable (Hoepner, 2006).

When choosing a supplement, concentration matters: more highly concentrated oils tend to have less of a "fishy" taste or "repeat". Most brands have a concentration of around 50%. Ratios of EPA:DHA may also be important, as it means taking fewer pills, and anecdotally (in case studies) some patients switched from a high-EPA formulation to one with high DHA have experienced worsening of mood (Hoepner, 2006; Stoll, 2001).

Quality is important. Look for a high concentration and ratio of EPA:DHA, low omega-6 and saturated fat concentration, low cholesterol concentration, molecular distillation process (to remove impurities), pharmaceutical-grade purity, and "winterization" (which solidifies and removes saturated fats). Oil should be light in color and clear, and should not have a strong odor. Manufacture and encapsulation under nitrogen prevents oxidization. Peroxide value at time of manufacture should be less than 5. Look for presence of vitamin E (mixed tocopherols) as antioxidants. Fish from deep, cold waters are less likely to contain toxins and impurities, as are smaller fish (lower on the food chain). Cod liver oil is not recommended, as vitamin A is potentially toxic at the doses one might be taking (Stoll, 2001). As much of this information is not on the label, fact gathering may be time consuming. Brands we recommend, which meet these requirements, include Trader Joe's (which is quite inexpensive), Nordic Naturals, and Andrew Stoll's brand OmegaBrite (Hoepner, 2006).

It is recommended that the antioxidant vitamins C and E be taken along with the EFA supplement (Stoll, 2001). For vitamin E, look for 400–600 mg of mixed natural tocopherols. More than 600 mg of vitamin E daily may contribute to heart failure, so the amount present in a daily multivitamin should be factored into the dose (Saremi & Arora, 2009). With vitamin C, the brand Ester C has good bioavailability, and many manufacturers incorporate this into their supplements. Antioxidants last only about 4–6 hours in the body, so divided doses are recommended. A general multivitamin is also recommended, containing B vitamins (including folate), zinc, magnesium, and selenium (Hoepner, 2006; Stoll, 2001).

Changes in mood and other markers of health status may take several weeks or months to occur, depending on an individual's neurochemistry and stores or depletion status of omega-3 fatty acids (Stoll, 2001).

Orally, fish oils are generally well tolerated at doses of 3–4 g/day or less for EPA and DHA combined (NMCD, 2010c). Fish oil supplements can cause a fishy aftertaste or repeat, and in some people have caused halitosis, heartburn, dyspepsia, nausea, loose stools, and rash (Natural Standard, 2010f; NMCD, 2010c). To avoid nausea or fishy repeat, choose supplements containing a 50% or higher concentration of omega-3. Nordic Naturals makes a lemon-flavored oil. Some people have had good results with taking the majority of the capsules at night or storing them in the freezer. To avoid diarrhea (which is not common with moderate doses), the supplements may be taken with meals to improve fat absorption (Hoepner, 2006). Extremely high doses of ALA from flaxseed oil (more than 20–40 g/day) have been associated with reports of iatrogenic mania. It is unknown whether this was part of the normal pattern of illness (Stoll, 2001). Doses greater than 3 g/day of fish oil or high dietary intake of fish can inhibit platelet aggregation, increasing the risk of bleeding, so caution should be taken when coadministering with other supplements and drugs that have antiplatelet or anticoagulant constituents including aspirin, many herbal products, and high doses of vitamin E. Caution should also be used with SSRI antidepressants, which carry GI bleeding risk. As an anti-inflammatory, very high doses of fish oil might affect immunoreactivity, which might be detrimental to elderly people and people with suppressed immune function There is some evidence that contraceptive drugs might interfere with the triglyceride-lowering effects of fish oils, and the fat absorption blocker orlistat (Xenical, Alli) blocks absorption of the oils (Natural Standard, 2010f; NMCD, 2010c).

For a wealth of additional information and tips on everything related to omega-3s and mood disorders, we recommend *The Omega-3 Connection* (Stoll, 2001). Though published in 2001, much of the data behind its content has not changed (with the exception of outcomes data from clinical trials). It is perhaps the most comprehensive and informative sourcebook on the subject for the lay public.

Neuroactive Hormones

Two neuroactive hormones found helpful in depression are DHEA and melatonin. Although known as a vitamin, the naturally-occurring form of vitamin D is actually a prehormone that affects depression in several ways.

DEHYDROEPIANDROSTERONE

Dehydroepiandrosterone (DHEA), an adrenal corticosteroid and neuro-hormone that converts to estrogen and testosterone, has been studied since the 1950s and was made available as a dietary supplement in 1994 (O. Wolkowitz & Reus, 2002). The supplement became wildly popular due in part to mass-marketed books promoting it as an immune booster and mood enhancer that could also increase sex drive, improve energy, and lengthen one's life span (Callahan, 1997; Cherniske, 1998). The ensuing widespread unregulated use of DHEA concerns medical professionals because studies on related factors, behaviors, and traits have been only quasi-experimental, and there are no data on long-term use (Katz & Morales, 1998; van Vollenhoven, 1997).

When one undergoes chronic stress, DHEA and allopregnanolone decrease as cortisol (a stress hormone) increases. In animal models, depression is associated with an increase in cortisol and related harm to neurons in the hippocampus (a brain structure associated with forming memories). Predictably, reduced hippocampal volume is seen mainly in patients with major depression who also have a history of early life trauma, which caused cortisol to be overexpressed chronically during this time in their lives. Animal studies have suggested that DHEA stimulates creation of new neurons in this area and also helps them to survive (O. Wolkowitz, 2008).

Thus, it's not surprising that supplemental DHEA may improve mood, as it was shown to do in a small 6-week, double-blind, controlled trial in which patients took the hormone alone or added it to their ongoing antidepressant (O. M. Wolkowitz et al., 1999). In another small trial sponsored by NIH, people age 45 to 65 with new-onset major or minor depression took 90 mg DHEA for 3 weeks and then 450 mg for another 3 weeks. They, too, were able to attain a 50% or greater reduction in scores on a measure of depressive symptoms (Schmidt et al., 2005). There have been other successful studies in elderly populations as well as in teens (women who are undergoing hormonal adjustments or have low levels of estrogen), and in patients with disorders other than depression, including Alzheimer's dementia and anorexia nervosa (O. Wolkowitz & Reus, 2002).

Due to the need for more adequately controlled studies, long-term studies, and those with safety data, DHEA cannot be recommended for clinical use at this time (Arango, Ernsberger, Sved, & Mann, 1993; Katz & Morales, 1998; van Vollenhoven, 1997). Those interested in trying it despite these caveats should choose a product from a large, reputable manufacturer that assays its DHEA by high-performance liquid chromatography. Over-the-counter supplements contain 0–150% of the DHEA content they claim, and products derived from Mexican wild mountain yams contain diosgenin, a source of steroid product that has been found ineffective. Ideally, a prescription written to a compounding pharmacy is recommended (O. Wolkowitz & Reus, 2002).

Dosing for depression is recommended at 25 to 100 mg daily (although trials have used doses ranging from 5 mg to several grams daily). Doses should be given twice or three times daily, with a larger portion in the morning dose to mimic the body's natural circadian rhythm (O. Wolkowitz & Reus, 2002). The physician can order a baseline serum level of DHEA-S to assess relative appropriateness of supplementation and for comparison purposes during treatment; there is no clear dose-response relationship, however, and effective serum levels may vary with age, sex, and other factors (van Vollenhoven, 1997). If 3 months elapse with high-normal to supraphysiologic (higher than normal) blood levels and symptom reduction is not satisfactory, further improvement is unlikely and DHEA should be discontinued (O. Wolkowitz & Reus, 2002).

MELATONIN

Melatonin (MLT; N-acetyl-methoxytryptamine) is an indole neurohormone produced in the brain from tryptophan by the pineal gland. Its synthesis and release are stimulated by darkness and repressed by light. It regulates our circadian clock, and its levels in the blood rise to their peak just prior to bedtime (Axentsev et al., 2010).

Melatonin is thought to control the circadian pacemaker and promote sleep by resetting disturbed circadian rhythms and their associated disorders. It is used also in primary and secondary insomnia, various diseases that may benefit from its antioxidant properties, and cancer, among other problems (Buscemi et al., 2004).

Melatonin may be effective when used in the short term to treat delayed sleep phase syndrome and to decrease sleep onset latency—but not sleep efficiency or quality—in persons with primary sleep disorders such as insomnia, although the magnitude of the effect appears to be limited. In people with sleep disorders comorbid to other illness, melatonin may modestly increase sleep efficiency and total sleep time, but does not appear to decrease sleep latency or improve sleep architecture. No evidence suggests that melatonin is effective in alleviating the sleep disturbance aspect of jet lag and shiftwork disorder, and evidence for treatment of sleep disturbance in patients with mood disorders was found to be sparse, and contradictory. The NIH's Agency for Healthcare Research and Quality and the Natural Standard Research Database's monograph on melatonin have found evidence suggesting limited or no benefits (Axentsev et al., 2010; Buscemi et al., 2004).

Melatonin's role in mood disorders has a theoretical basis. Patients with winter depression are suggested to have a phase delay in their circadian rhythms, and the phase-shifting effect of light is thought to be associated with the efficacy of light treatment. Melatonin and serotonin can also cause phase shifts of the rhythms and may underlie the antidepressant effect independently of time of day or an individual's circadian phase (Partonen, 1994). Supersensitivity to light suppression of melatonin is thought to be a marker for genetic vulnerability in bipolar patients, though this was seen only in those with bipolar I disorder (Nurnberger et al., 2000).

Endogenous levels of melatonin have been compared between patients with and without mood disorders, in various mood states and levels of severity, during various times of day, and on and off antidepressant treatment. Melatonin levels have been shown to be similar (L. A. Carvalho, Gorenstein, Moreno, & Markus, 2006; Voderholzer et al., 1997) or higher (Szymanska, Rabe-Jablonska, & Karasek, 2001) in unipolar depressed patients and lower in depressed, manic, and euthymic bipolar patients (S. H. Kennedy, Kutcher, Ralevski, & Brown, 1996) than in healthy control subjects. Studies have found depressed people to have diminished (Voderholzer et al., 1997) or elevated (Rabe-Jablonska & Szymanska, 2001; Varma, Kaul, Varma, Kalra, & Malhotra, 2002) melatonin levels during the evening, but that patient, illness, and treatment variables influence these results. A pattern of increased melatonin secretion in depressed patients is inconsistently related to the severity of their depression (Rabe-Jablonska & Szymanska, 2001; Szymanska et al., 2001). Antidepressants are shown to have an effect on endogenous melatonin levels irrespective of improvement of symptoms (L. A. Carvalho, Gorenstein, Moreno, Pariante, & Markus, 2009; Varma et al., 2002).

If trials of melatonin supplementation for sleep in mood disorders have been mixed, those for its use in improving depression have been decidedly poor. Melatonin does not substantially augment light treatment in winter depression (Danilenko & Putilov, 2005) or existing antidepressant therapies in patients with treatment-resistant depression (E. J. Dalton, Rotondi, Levitan, Kennedy, & Brown, 2000) or in those 3 months post-ECT (Grunhaus, Hirschman, Dolberg, Schreiber, & Dannon, 2001). It does not sustain beneficial effects of total sleep deprivation in winter depression (Danilenko & Putilov, 2005). It had no significant effects on mood or sleep in rapid-cycling bipolar patients, though its withdrawal delayed sleep onset time (Leibenluft, Feldman-Naim, Turner, Wehr, & Rosenthal, 1997).

Based on available studies and clinical use, melatonin is generally regarded as safe in recommended doses for short-term use, with adverse effects being similar to placebo. These include fatigue (especially with morning use and high doses), headache, hypothermia, pruritus, abdominal cramps, and tachycardia (Avery, Lenz, & Landis, 1998; Brzezinski, 1997; Sack, Lewy, & Hughes, 1998; Shamir et al., 2001). Irregular sleep-wake cycles, confusion, sleepwalking, vivid dreams, nightmares, and mood changes have also been noted, as have changes in blood pressure, increase in cholesterol, and abnormal heart rhythms. There have been case reports of blood clotting (particularly in patients taking blood-thinning medications). Melatonin use may lead to reduced glucose tolerance and insulin sensitivity. Melatonin may alter levels of sex, thyroid, and growth hormones, as well as prolactin, oxytocin, vasopressin, and cortisol. Melatonin supplementation should be avoided in women who are pregnant—based on possible hormonal effects increasing the risk of developmental disorders—and during breast-feeding. There have been reports of increased breast size, as well as decreased sperm count and motility in men who use melatonin. It may increase or decrease intraocular pressure and risk for glaucoma. Psychotic symptoms and increased seizure risk have been associated with overdose (Natural Standard, 2010e).

There are many complex interactions with medications, supplements, and laboratory tests. They include calcium channel blockers, beta-blockers, the SSRI fluvoxamine, blood-thinning medications, nonsteroidal anti-inflammatory inhibitors, hormonal agents including oral contraceptives and DHEA, loop diuretics, several benzodiazepines, echinacea, and caffeine.

This list of adverse events, physiologic influences, and drug interactions is far from complete. An exhaustive monograph on melatonin (Natural Standard, 2010e) including details on efficacy, side effects, and interactions is available at medical libraries that subscribe to the Natural Standard Research Collaboration database. The NIH's MedlinePlus has produced a summary of this document for the lay public (MedlinePlus, 2009a).

We feel that the poor evidence for improvement of sleep disturbance and mood coupled with the numerous and complicated interactions and contraindications gives melatonin a poor benefit versus risk profile. We do not recommend its use to our patients, though we have included it in this chapter due to its popularity as a "natural" sleep aid.

To those readers who will want to try this supplement based on anecdotal evidence, we must say that optimal dose, length of therapy, and effect on endogenous melatonin are as yet unknown. Studies of synthetic melatonin supplements have evaluated as little as 0.5 mg and as much as 50 mg of melatonin taken nightly. There is no widely accepted standardization for melatonin, and a number of different formulations have been used in clinical trials, but no comparison exists on how they differ in terms of content, quality, and effectiveness. Many brands contain impurities and dissimilar amounts of actual hormone, and melatonin derived from the pineal gland of animals should not be used due to risk of viral illness. Time of administration varies by application and we urge the reader to seek professional advice on how to use melatonin for best and safest results.

VITAMIN D AND DEPRESSION

Although vitamin D is referred to as a vitamin, foods we normally consume do not have significant amounts of it. Vitamin D has two main forms: vitamin D2 (ergocalciferol) and provitamin D3 (cholecalciferol, or calciol), the latter of which is the naturally occurring form, a prehormone, and the form used for low-dose supplementation. It is made in the skin by the action of sunlight, hydroxylated by the liver to 25(OH)D (calcifediol, the form most readily detected in the bloodstream), and further converted by various organs to steroid hormones, including 1,25(OH)2D3 (calcitriol), the most metabolically active form of vitamin D (Johnson, 2007).

The major functions of vitamin D are to increase the efficiency of intestinal calcium and phosphorus absorption, to maintain normal serum concentrations of these minerals, and to promote normal bone formation and mineralization. It regulates genes and may provide protection from hypertension, osteoporosis, cancers, autoimmune diseases, and mental illness (Johnson, 2007; Natural Standard, 2010j).

Vitamin D may be related to depression and other forms of mental illness in several ways. It appears to be crucial for brain development and function (Eyles, Brown, Mackay-Sim, McGrath, & Feron, 2003; Garcion, Wion-Barbot, Montero-Menei, Berger, & Wion, 2002; J. C. McCann & Ames, 2008). Certain brain cells contain receptors for vitamin D and make enzymes that convert 1,25(OH)D to the steroid 1,25(OH)2D3. Vitamin D assists in biosynthesis of neurotrophic factors. It is involved in brain detoxification pathways and has neuroprotective effects (Garcion et al., 2002). Vitamin D may contribute to increased brain serotonin levels (Partonen, 1998; Puchacz, Stumpf, Stachowiak, & Stachowiak, 1996). Vitamin D levels are inversely related to those of melatonin, another mood-regulating hormone, which helps to regulate insomnia, mood swings, and food cravings. Sun exposure shuts down production of melatonin while triggering release of vitamin D. It should then come as no surprise that vitamin D may be the link between seasonal change in mood and photoperiod (Berk et al., 2007), and has been implicated in seasonal affective disorder (SAD) (Schlager, Schwartz, & Bromet, 1993). Supplementation has improved symptoms of SAD in some (Gloth, Alam, & Hollis, 1999; Lansdowne & Provost, 1998) but not all studies (Dumville et al., 2006; Harris & Dawson-Hughes, 1993).

Low serum 25(OH)D levels have also been associated with reduced cognitive function (Przybelski & Binkley, 2007; Wilkins, Sheline, Roe,

Birge, & Morris, 2006), anxiety (Armstrong et al., 2007), and nonseasonal depression (Armstrong et al., 2007; Jorde, Sneve, Figenschau, Svartberg, & Waterloo, 2008; Schneider, Weber, Frensch, Stein, & Fritz, 2000; Wilkins et al., 2006), and the apparent positive effect of vitamin D supplementation may indicate a causative relation (Jorde et al., 2008). Depression and vitamin D deficiency may have a bidirectional relationship, of course, with depression leading to fewer outdoor activities (and less sun exposure) and decreased vitamin intake, with vitamin D deficiency then completing the circle by helping to maintain the depressed state (Hoogendijk et al., 2008).

Finally, depression has significant comorbidity with illnesses associated with vitamin D deficiency, such as decreased bone mineral density and osteoporosis, diabetes, heart disease, hypertension, multiple sclerosis, cancer, rheumatoid arthritis, and increased mortality, especially cardiac mortality (Cannell, 2010; Holick, 2003; Zittermann, 2003).

Though it is too early to say conclusively that repletion of vitamin D levels will improve psychiatric symptoms, there is growing evidence that it may. A therapeutic role for vitamin D supplementation in the treatment of mood disorders could provide a safe, low-cost therapy with additional advantages to general and bone health (Berk et al., 2007). Important questions persist concerning precisely how vitamin D may affect monoamine function and the HPA axis response to stress, whether vitamin D supplementation can improve depression in the moderate-to-severe range, and whether optimizing vitamin D levels is protective against both incidence and recurrence of depression (Bertone-Johnson, 2009).

Clinical deficiency typically results from inadequate direct sunlight exposure (or sunscreen use) in combination with inadequate dietary intake. Vitamin D-deficient diets are associated with milk allergy, lactose intolerance, and strict vegetarianism. The application of sunscreen with an SPF factor of 8 reduces production of vitamin D by 95%. Susceptible people include the elderly, dark-skinned individuals, those with malabsorption, abnormal hepatic metabolism, chronic renal disorder, disease of the small bowel, and obesity. Many anticonvulsants (including Depakote, Lamictal, Tegretol, Topamax, and others) and all steroids increase need for vitamin D supplementation (Higdon, Drake, & DeLuca, 2008; Johnson, 2007; National Institutes of Health ODS, 2009).

In adults, severe vitamin D deficiency can lead to osteomalacia, characterized by bone pain and muscle weakness. Serum concentration of 25(OH)D is the best indicator of vitamin D status. Recent research suggests that >32 ng/ml (>80 nmol/L) is a health-based cutoff for overall health maintenance and disease prevention (Higdon et al., 2008; National Institutes of Health ODS, 2009). Parathyroid hormone level and calcium absorption are not optimized until this level is reached.

The IOM Food and Nutrition Board (FNB) has found that recommended dietary allowance (RDA) cannot be determined as sunlight accounts for such a large (and variable) amount of one's intake. In 1997 an adequate intake (AI) was therefore set at 200–600 IU (depending on age) daily, though as of 2005 the Dietary Guidelines for Americans recommend 1,000 IU/day for healthy older adults (Johnson, 2007), and physiological human requirements (from all sources) may be 10 times higher than the AI listed in 1997 (Heaney, Davies, Chen, Holick, & Barger-Lux, 2003; Holick, 2001; Vieth, 1999; Zittermann, 2003). Most vitamin D experts now say that humans should get about 4,000–5,000 units of vitamin D per day (Cannell, 2010; Vieth, 1999). Though the FNB reports an upper limit of just 2,000 IU/day (Heaney et al., 2003), trials in healthy adults suggest that doses up to 10,000 IU/day are safe (Hathcock, Shao, Vieth, & Heaney, 2007). Toxicity is rare and may occur at serum concentrations of 25(OH)D >200 ng/ml (>500 nmol/L).

If you're interested in boosting your daily dose of vitamin D, it is available in the diet chiefly in fish liver oils and fatty saltwater fish such as salmon and mackerel. In some developed countries, milk and other foods are fortified with vitamin D2 or D3, as are some breads and cereals, and some egg yolks (Johnson, 2007). Vitamin D is much more readily obtained through sun exposure or dietary supplementation, however.

Cholecalciferol is the preferred form of vitamin D, as it is the compound your skin makes naturally when exposed to UVB. In the absence of exposure to sunlight, at least 5,000 IU per day will be needed to ensure serum 25(OH)D levels in the desirable range (Vieth, Chan, & MacFarlane, 2001). Note that cholecalciferol is 1.7 times more efficient at raising 25(OH)D levels and perhaps even safer than the more commonly used synthetic analog, ergocalciferol (Trang et al., 1998;

Vieth et al., 2001), or calcitriol—a steroid converted from cholecalcif-erol—which is costly and both fails to address low stores of 25(OH)D and may cause hypercalcemia (Vieth, 2005).

Those who do not mind sun exposure may judiciously expose arms, and legs, or face, arms, and hands, to direct midday sunlight three times weekly. A good dose is about 25% of the time it takes for one's skin to turn red (suberythemal dose; about 5–15 minutes), at which point vitamin D production is maximized (Holick, 2003; Johnson, 2007). More is not better, as one may risk skin cancer, and the sun will begin to destroy any excess vitamin D, a natural safeguard against toxicity (Cannell, 2010). Depending on skin type, dark-skinned people may need 5–10 times longer in the sun than white patients (Cannell, 2004; Holick, 1995). Several months of judicious sun exposure should restore optimal vitamin D levels (Cannell, 2010), depending on how far you live from the equator, how dark your skin is, and how much you weigh.

Note that vitamin D interacts with a number of medications. Certain antiseizure drugs and rifampin may accelerate the conversion of vitamin D to inactive metabolites. Both stimulant laxatives and Orlistat (an obesity drug) can reduce vitamin D absorption; fat-soluble vitamins should not be taken within 2 hours of its administration. Use of corti-costeroids can cause osteoporosis and calcium depletion over time, creating greater need for supplemental calcium, and vitamin D for its absorption. Use of vitamin D and calcium together may decrease the inflammatory response. Hypermagnesemia may develop with use of magnesium-containing antacids. Excess vitamin D may lead to hypercal-cemia and abnormal heart rhythms, and so should be avoided in patients taking digoxin or herbs with similar properties.

Herbal Medications

Two herbal medicines used to treat depression are St. John's wort and rhodiola. While the former has been studied throughout the world for many years, the latter is just beginning to receive attention.

SAINT JOHN'S WORT

People have used Saint John's wort (SJW; *Hypericum perforatum*) to treat depression for centuries. It is licensed in Germany and other European countries as a treatment for mild to moderate depression, as well as for anxiety and sleep disorders. Though the active ingredients hypericin and hyperforin have been isolated, postulated mechanisms of action remain hypothetical. Those involving serotonin appear to be the most critical.

Studies show that SJW extracts are more effective than placebo and that they are equally effective to active controls based on a number of double-blind, placebo-controlled studies and comparator studies, all conducted in Europe since 1979 (Linde et al., 1996, 1996; Mischoulon & Rosenbaum, 2002). Most of the studies, however, have flaws in their methodology, and the longest trials to date are 12 weeks (with one 26-week exception), making maintenance and safety data unavailable. In many well-designed trials conducted in the United States, SJW has not proven effective when compared to antidepressant or placebo (Shelton, 2002). A 26-week NIH study found response to SJW, antidepressants, and placebo for moderately severe major depression to be both similar and poor (23.9%, 24.8%, and 31.9% respectively), though the rate of overall functioning appeared better for those using the antidepressant (Hypericum Depression Trial Study Group, 2002).

Common side effects (many transient) with SJW include gastrointestinal symptoms, dizziness or confusion, fatigue, dry mouth, restlessness, headache, allergic skin reactions, sexual dysfunction, frequent urination, swelling, and phototoxicity (sensitivity to natural or artificial sunlight; P. A. DeSmet, 2004). In accordance with an FDA warning in 2000, SJW is contraindicated in those taking many medications for HIV, cancer treatment, organ transplant, and oral contraception, as it induces a liver enzyme required to convert these drugs and many others (approximately 60% of pharmaceutical agents!) to their active metabolites, causing these medications to be more rapidly metabolized and therefore quickly cleared from the body (Willson & Kliewer, 2002; Yue, Bergquist, & Gerden, 2000). Another important drug interaction can lead to serotonin syndrome, a potentially fatal condition characterized by confusion, agitation, restlessness, sweating, shivering, tremor, diarrhea, incoordination, fever, muscle spasms, overactive or overresponsive reflexes, and other symptoms. Serotonin syndrome may occur when SJW is taken in large doses with antidepressants or other drugs (including cough syrup) that affect serotonin levels and whose metabolism is inhibited by SJW. Finally, although SJW may be shown helpful in mild to moderate unipolar depression, it may induce mania—and thereby pose a risk for increased mood cycling—in those with bipolar illness. Anxiety is also a side effect in these individuals.

Dosage of SJW is based on hypericin concentration in a given extract. Various clinical trials have used 0.17 to 2.7 mg of standardized 0.3–0.5% hypericin daily by mouth, or 900 to 1,800 mg of SJW extract. Starting at the lower dosage and working up slowly is suggested. Three times daily dosing is recommended, though if insomnia occurs, the supplement can be taken in the morning. SJW should be stored in a dark, dry, cool place. Refrigeration or freezing is recommended but not necessary.

RHODIOLA

Rhodiola rosea, which influences levels and activity of monoamine neurotransmitters and opioid peptides such as beta-endorphins (G. S. Kelly, 2001), has been shown superior to placebo in a randomized clinical trial in mild to moderate depression (Darbinyan et al., 2007) and in an open-label trial for generalized anxiety disorder (Bystritsky, Kerwin, & Feusner, 2008). This Russian folk medicine was also well-studied in many classified trials during the cold war (Prathikanti, 2008). In addition to having antidepressant effects, rhodiola has been touted as an "adaptogen" for its ability to promote resilience under a variety of chemical, biological, and physical stressors, helping the user to avoid decline in work performance, poor appetite, poor sleep, irritability, fatigue, and headaches that might develop after intense physical or intellectual effort (G. S. Kelly, 2001). It has been shown to enhance cognitive performance under stress and to reduce mental fatigue (as demonstrated by improved scores on exams), as well as improve overall well-being (Olsson, von Scheele, & Panossian, 2008; Prathikanti, 2008).

A generally safe and effective dosing range is 300 to 900 mg daily (Prathikanti, 2008). Those with bipolar disorder should take caution, as rhodiola may provoke hypomania. Those who have suffered a heart attack should not use rhodiola due to its potential to cause mild tachycardia (heart rate greater than 120 beats per minute).

HERBAL MEDICINES FOR INSOMNIA, ANXIETY,
MEMORY, AND DETOXIFICATION

Next to St. John's wort, the three most widely studied herbs that have been popularized for those with psychiatric illness help with its comorbidities: valerian for insomnia and anxiety, kava kava for anxiety, and ginkgo biloba for memory problems. Milk thistle is worth mentioning as some believe it has utility in cleansing the liver of toxins, including medications.

Valerian

Valerian (*Valeriana officinalis*), a plant native to Europe, has been used for both insomnia and nervous tension since the times of ancient Greece and Rome. Valerian extracts (made primarily from the root of the plant) became popular in Europe and in the United States in the mid-19th century and were used widely until prescription benzodiazepine sedatives and anxiolytics (such as Ativan, Klonopin, Restoril, and Valium) became available. As these drugs may induce dependence and rebound insomnia, adversely impact sleep quality, and are associated with hangover and poor cognitive functioning the day after administration (none of which occur with single or repeated use of valerian; Taibi, Landis, Petry, & Vitiello, 2007), alternatives are often sought.

There is no agreement as to the active constituents of valerian; as with many plants, interactions among many compounds are likely responsible for its effects (Russo, 2001). Valerenic acids and valepotriates are included in extracts. Valerian extract may cause sedation and ease anxiety by increasing the amount of GABA available to brain cells by promoting GABA release and blocking its reuptake (Santos, Ferreira, Cunha, Carvalho, & Macedo, 1994).

Outcomes of clinical trials of valerian for primary insomnia and other sleep problems have been mixed, and meta-analyses and systematic review of these studies have found the evidence inconclusive. A 2007 meta-analysis of 29 controlled trials found valerian safe but ineffective (Taibi et al., 2007). In a systematic review of nine randomized, placebo-controlled, double-blind clinical trials of valerian for insomnia (Stevinson & Ernst, 2000), three of the more highly rated studies found it to be helpful for sleep, though findings were contradictory. A meta-analysis of 16 studies examining a total of 1,093 patients showed statistically significant benefit for improvement of sleep quality on several measures (including time to fall asleep, wake after sleep onset, sleep efficiency, and self-rated sleep quality), but this summary measure showed evidence of publication bias (Bent, Padula, Moore, Patterson, & Mehling, 2006). All three of these reviews found significant variability among studies in subjects, sources, preparation and doses of valerian, outcome measures, and general quality of both methodology and reporting.

Few studies of valerian in anxiety have been undertaken, and only a single study of valerian in any disorder in which anxiety was the primary symptom met the stringent criteria required to be included in a systematic review from the Cochrane Collaboration (Miyasaka, Atallah, & Soares, 2006). Among published studies, the group found mixed, contradictory outcomes predominantly from small trials with nonrigorous methods and reporting.

Despite lack of conclusive evidence supporting valerian's use in sleep difficulties and anxiety, quite a number of patients have reported anecdotally to us that it has been helpful for them. Its good tolerability profile and lack of interactions with drugs, foods, and other herbs and supplements make for low risk for patients who want to try it. We also appreciate that valerian doesn't cause the dependence, poor sleep quality, rebound insomnia when discontinued, or next-day impairment of functioning, which may accompany many medications used to treat sleep and anxiety problems.

Valerian is on the FDA's Generally Regarded as Safe list. Studies lasting 4–6 weeks have demonstrated it to be tolerable and safe in recommended doses, with occasional reports of headache, stomach upset, itching, and dizziness (De Smet, 2004), though similar effects have also been reported for placebo. Use for more than 2–4 months may result in insomnia for some patients, and a hangover may result if high doses are used. Although valerian has not been reported to interact with any drugs, this has not been rigorously studied (Office of Dietary Supplements, 2008). Valerian will not synergistically increase drowsiness caused by barbiturates, narcotics, benzodiazepines, or alcohol, but may add to these effects. Valerian tinctures may contain high alcohol content (15–90%), and should not be used when alcohol is contraindicated.

Valerian tinctures and capsules are more palatable than the tea, and standardized forms are available, including Alluna Sleep, Valerian-400, and Sedonium, the dosage recommendations of which have been tested in clinical trials where they were used. There may be significant variation in amounts of valerenic acids and valepotriates among commercial products (De Smet, 2004), and many are blended with other herbs such as hops, lemon balm, and passionflower. Common recommended doses include 1–3 gr of dried root and rhizome (German Commission E, 1995), 450 mg of extract for sleep 1 hour before bedtime (study doses have ranged 400–900 mg), and 200–300 mg of extract in the morning for anxiety. Doses of 300–1,800 mg of valerian may also be taken in capsule form (Medlineplus, 2009b). One may also use 1–3 ml of tincture or infusion of 2–3 g per cup of valerian root daily; the use of tea has not been studied. Sleep improvement may increase with nightly use rather than on an as-needed basis, results peaking after 14 days (Vorbach & Gortelmeyer, 1996).

Kava Kava

Kava (*Piper methysticum*) is a flowering shrub from the pepper family indigenous to South Pacific islands. A beverage made from the roots of *P. methysticum* has been used to induce relaxation both medicinally and in social and ceremonial settings since the beginning of recorded history in that part of the world.

The herbal remedy, also known as kava kava, is derived from the root of the plant; the chemical and pharmacologic properties of its active phytochemicals—known as kavalactones or kavapyrones—have been studied since the 1960s (Hänsel, 1968). The remedy has been used for a great many applications but is most widely applied today in treatment of anxiety, insomnia, and menopausal symptoms; it shows clear efficacy in clinical trials only for anxiety. It has the advantage over benzodiazepine anxiolytics of calming without disrupting mental clarity, impairing memory, or leading to dependence.

The majority of evidence shows that kava extracts (standardized to 70% kavalactones) are superior to placebo (Pittler & Ernst, 2003; Sarris, Kavanagh, Adams, Bone, & Byrne, 2009; Sarris, Kavanagh, Byrne, et al., 2009) and possibly comparable to low-dose benzodiazepines (Malsch &

Kieser, 2001) in those suffering from symptoms of anxiety, and similar to buspirone (Boerner et al., 2003) in generalized anxiety disorder. There is some evidence to the contrary as well (Connor, Payne, & Davidson, 2006). The data reviewed by the Cochrane Collaboration suggested that the preparations and dosages used in those studies reviewed were relatively safe for short-term treatment (up to 24 weeks) (Pittler & Ernst, 2003).

Safety concerns regarding kava have been significant, and for this reason we cannot recommend the supplement to our patients or readers. Though kava extracts have been safely used in clinical trials under medical supervision for up to 6 months, there still is concern that it may lead to hepatotoxicity and liver failure in susceptible patients taking relatively normal doses, short term. There are at least 68 such reported cases, including hepatitis, cirrhosis, fulminant liver failure, and reports of death (Natural Standard, 2010d). Liver transplants have resulted from as few as 4–12 weeks of use. Skin changes, neurotoxicity, and possible pulmonary hypertension are possible as well. In 2002, sales of products and preparations containing kava were suspended or withdrawn in Canada, Germany, Switzerland, Australia, France, and Spain, though it may now be had in Germany by prescription only. The U.S. FDA has issued warnings to consumers and physicians (Parkman, 2002; U.S. FDA, 2002a, 2002b), yet has not withdrawn the supplement from the market.

Ginkgo Biloba

Ginkgo biloba, known to scientists as *Gingko biloba L.* and commonly as kew tree and maidenhair tree, can be found in the Far East, Europe, and the United States. It has survived for 200 million years and has been used medicinally for thousands (Van Beek, Bombardelli, Morazzoni, & Peterlongo, 1998). In traditional medicine, ginkgo has been used to treat respiratory diseases, circulatory disorders, sexual dysfunction, and loss of hearing. Today, extracts of the ginkgo leaf are used chiefly by those hoping to improve memory, to treat or help prevent Alzheimer's and vascular dementias, to manage intermittent claudication, and to treat tinnitus, altitude sickness, PMS symptoms, and other health conditions (Natural Standard, 2010c).

Many people with psychiatric illness seek to improve their memory and concentration. Though there have definitely been positive trials, the largest and most well-designed studies—as well as meta-analyses—do not demonstrate significant findings. In a systematic review of 15 trials, neither acute nor long-term administration of ginkgo to young (under age 60) healthy subjects showed improvement of any of several aspects of cognitive function (Canter & Ernst, 2007). Similarly, ginkgo also failed to improve memory in a rigorous 6-week trial, sponsored by the National Institute on Aging, of more than 200 healthy adults over age 60 (Solomon, Adams, Silver, Zimmer, & DeVeaux, 2002). Another study funded by the National Center for Complementary and Alternative Medicine followed 3,069 72–96-year-old community-dwelling participants with normal cognition or with mild cognitive impairment for an average of 6 years, and found 240 mg standardized ginkgo leaf extract to be ineffective in lowering the overall incidence of dementia and Alzheimer's disease (DeKosky et al., 2006, 2008; Snitz et al., 2009).

Evidence for ginkgo's usefulness in other areas of interest to people with depression—including tinnitus (Rejali, Sivakumar, & Balaji, 2004) and antidepressant-induced sexual dysfunction (Kang, Lee, Kim, & Cho, 2002; Wheatley, 2004)—is no more promising than the memory research, and for this reason we do not include information on its use, side effects, and potential drug interactions, of which there are several.

Silymarin (Milk Thistle)

The fruit and seeds of milk thistle (*Silybum marianum*) have been used for more than 2,000 years as a treatment for disorders of the liver, bile ducts, and gallbladder. Most research has studied silymarin or silybin, its major component, rather than the plant in its whole form (DerMarderosian, 2009). Silymarin is thought to act through antioxidant activity (by increasing levels of intrahepatic glutathione), toxin blockade, and stabilizing cell membranes, as well as by limiting fibrosis and modulating the immune system and inflammatory process (AHRQ, 2000).

Many people who take medications that are hepatically metabolized use silymarin (the herb's active compound) in an effort to cleanse the liver, hoping to protect or support it. Its typical use, however, is to treat cirrhosis, chronic hepatitis (liver inflammation), and gallbladder disorders, and, although some studies indicate silymarin may improve liver function, both study designs and reporting have been weak and flawed, and results mixed (Barrette et al., 2010). Of the few trials that have been undertaken to determine whether silymarin protects the human liver from toxicity resulting from medications, most have been negative. These include a 90-day trial in 60 women whose liver disease presumably resulted from long-term therapy with phenothiazine or butyrophenone antipsychotics, which demonstrated that 800 mg of daily silymarin plus or minus antipsychotic medications did not significantly improve liver transaminase levels when compared with placebo (Palasciano, Portincasa, & Palmieri, 1994). Silymarin (420 mg daily) was used for 3 months to prevent liver toxicity in 217 Alzheimer's patients taking the drug tacrine. Liver function tests were statistically similar between those randomized to silymarin and those taking placebo at 12 and 15 weeks (Allain et al., 1999).

To date, there is no conclusive evidence to prove the claimed uses of silymarin for treatment and prevention of liver disease, and we therefore do not recommend it to our readers. If it is to be used, doses ranging from 160 to 800 mg have been used safely in clinical trials (Barrette et al., 2010). Legalon is a pharmaceutical-grade extract that may be used by various supplement manufacturers. We caution against the use of liver-cleansing products that include multiple herbs without first asking your doctor or pharmacist to check for drug interaction. Silymarin itself has interactions with a number of medications, including some hormonal agents (Mulrow, Lawrence, & Jacobs, 2000), and theoretically may decrease the clearance of glucuronidated agents, such as Ativan (lorazepam) and Lamictal (lamotrigine) (Venkataramanan et al., 2000). Adverse reactions include gastrointestinal symptoms that are generally mild, and there are rare cases of anaphylaxis.

Homeopathy

Homeopathy—also known as homeopathic medicine—seeks to stimulate the body's "vital force" or self-healing response, to promote wellness and prevent disease by giving very small doses of highly diluted substances. It is most commonly used for such ailments as allergies and rashes, asthma, fatigue, anxiety, depression, gastrointestinal distress, ear infections, and headaches.

German physician Samuel Christian Hahnemann developed this therapeutic method more than 200 years ago in an effort to heal without harm: at the time, common medical treatments included purging, blistering, bloodletting, and the use of sulfur and mercury. Medications were few, and knowledge of their mechanisms and effectiveness very limited (Bell & Pappas, 2007). With this individualized, holistic approach that caused almost no side effects, Hahnemann was one of the first to humanely treat mentally ill patients (Winston, 1999). Homeopathy made its way to the United States in the early 19th century. By the turn of the 20th century, Dr. Charles Frederick Menninger, an American psychiatrist, considered homeopathy to be "wholly capable of satisfying the therapeutic demands of this age better than any other system or school of medicine" (Menninger, 1897).

A central principle of homeopathy is the "law of similars," which postulates that like cures like: Symptoms can be treated by (very small amounts of) a substance that produces similar problems in healthy individuals. Indeed, in Greek *homeo* means similar, and *pathos* is suffering or disease.

The principle of dilutions (or "law of minimum dose") states that the lower the dose of the medication, the greater its effectiveness. Substances are diluted by "potentization," which is meant to transmit some form of energy or information from the original substance to the final diluted remedy. Though typically no molecules of the original substance remain, it has theoretically left an imprint on or "essence" in the remedy, and it is this essence that stimulates the body to heal itself.

Homeopathic remedies are derived from natural substances found in minerals, animals, and plants. Common remedies are derived from arnica, nettle, sulfur, and red onion, which are processed in the form of small tablets (most common), powder, granules, liquid tinctures, ointments, or creams. Those remedies commonly called on to treat depressed individuals include pulsatilla for tearfulness, ignatia to ease grief, sulfur for despair, and aurum metallicum for suicidal ideation. Several remedies may be used concurrently by a given individual, and may be differently chosen for diverse individuals with the same ailments. Homeopaths treat holistically, sometimes taking several hours to tailor individualized treatment regimens while keeping in mind a person's genetic and personal health history, lifestyle, and body type, as well as current physical and emotional symptoms.

Homeopathy is controversial in the scientific world because a number of its key concepts are not consistent with established laws of science, particularly chemistry and physics (van der Watt, Laugharne, & Janca, 2008). It is debated how a highly diluted substance could be effective. It is implausible to some that something that can cause illness might also cure it. Some believe that homeopathy does work, but modern scientific methods have not yet explained how. Science also fails to elucidate the true mechanism of many allopathic medications; despite this fact, well-designed clinical trials are able to show whether the medications treat symptoms of disease in humans. The demonstration of efficacy of homeopathy is, however, fraught with difficulty.

Clinical trials often are methodologically flawed: Homeopathic treatments are highly individualized, so individual trial subjects may each be receiving different treatments, chosen from literally hundreds of different homeopathic remedies. Ultrahigh dilutions cannot readily be measured, making design and replication of studies difficult. Many trials are not blinded, placebo-controlled, or properly statistically powered, and they may enroll very few research subjects. Studies of good quality sometimes contradict each other. Owing to these and other factors, most analyses of the research on homeopathy have concluded that there is little scientific evidence to support its efficacy in any specific condition (Bell, Ernst, Mansky, & Khalsa, 2009), including depression and anxiety (Pilkington, Kirkwood, Rampes, Fisher, & Richardson, 2005, 2006).

Finding Professional Help

We encourage those who choose to explore supplementation to involve a practitioner of CAM treatment in their care. The practitioner may be able to customize the treatment and assist in selecting a safer and more effective regimen. Not everyone who calls himself a nutritionist or naturopath has ample knowledge of and experience with mood and anxiety disorders, even if he is certified. As we have seen, there are treatments that may be helpful to some while harmful to others. Supplements such as SAM-e, Saint John's wort, and DHEA, for instance, may cause those with bipolar illness to have increased mood cycling.

There are a number of ways to research qualified practitioners. Start by asking a doctor, other health professionals, or someone knowledgeable about CAM for a recommendation or referral. A nearby hospital or medical school may maintain a list of area CAM practitioners. Some medical centers have a CAM center or practitioners on staff. Professional organizations for the type of practitioner being sought may provide referrals. They are likely to have standards of practice and publications explaining the treatment their members provide, and they may offer information on training, licensure, and certification of practitioners. The American Psychiatric Association keeps a list of trusted CAM practitioners in some areas. The Internet can be used to search for such professional organizations, or a librarian can be asked for help in searching directories. One directory is the Directory of Information Resources Online (DIRLINE), compiled by the National Library of Medicine (www.dirline.nlm.nih.gov). It contains information about a variety of health organizations, including those representing CAM practices. Finally, many states have regulatory agencies or licensing boards for certain types of practitioners, and they may offer helpful information. These agencies or boards may be found on the Internet; asking the state, county, or city health department if it has contact information is another option.

Before meeting with a practitioner, it is wise to make a list of questions to ask about the person's practice, training, credentials, and fees. Ask if it is possible to have a brief consultation in person or by phone with the practitioner, as speaking with the person directly is important. This initial consult may or may not involve a charge. Following is a list of questions that can be asked.

- Where did you receive your education, and do you have any additional training? What licenses or certifications do you have?
- In which health conditions do you specialize, and how frequently do you treat people with mood disorders?

- Do you believe my complaint can be effectively addressed by your therapies? Can you reference scientific research supporting the treatment's use for my condition?
- What is involved in the treatment? Will there be an initial workup, with testing involved? Is there a minimum number of visits or treatments required? Are any necessary products provided or available at your office?
- What will be involved in the first visit or assessment? Is there anything I need to bring, or any necessary preparation?
- How many patients do you typically see each day? How much time do you spend with each client?
- What expense is involved? Are services billed per visit or as a package of services? Will there be testing involved? Products? Can you give me an estimate of expenditure for the initial workup and course of treatment?
- Are your services covered by my insurance? Do you have a list of practitioners who will accept my insurance? (Unfortunately, whereas acupuncture and chiropractic treatments are covered by many insurance companies, nutritionists and naturopaths, and much of their laboratory testing, typically are not.) The U.S. FDA has a helpful Web page on how to pay for alternative and complementary care (http://nccam.nih.gov/health/financial/).
- When are appointments offered? How long is the wait for an appointment? Where is the office located?
- Is there a brochure or Web site that can tell me more about the practice?

In choosing a practitioner, patients should assess how comfortable they felt during these first interactions with each practitioner consulted. Which practitioners responded most thoughtfully to the questions and inspired the patient's confidence? To prepare for the first visit, the patient should gather information about his health history—including not only his mental health but also any injuries, surgeries, and major illnesses—as well as about prescription drugs and any supplements or over-the-counter medicines being taken.

During the first visit, a second list of questions should be asked:

- What benefits I can expect from this therapy?
- Can you share any scientific articles or references about using the treatment for my condition?
- Are there any associated risks, and do the benefits outweigh these risks for my condition?
- Are there any conditions for which this treatment should not be used?
- Are there any side effects I may experience? .
- Are there possible interactions with other treatments or medications I am using?
- How much time will I invest in this treatment? Will the therapy interfere with any of my daily activities?
- How long will I need to undergo treatment? How often will my progress be assessed, and treatment reevaluated?
- Will I need to buy any equipment or supplies?
- Will you collaborate with my psychiatrist or internist regarding any tests or treatments that will be required?

After the first visit, patients should ask themselves whether they felt comfortable with the practitioner. Did he invest time in getting to know the patient and his specific concerns? Did he demonstrate knowledge about the patient's condition? Did the patient feel comfortable asking questions, and did the practitioner respond satisfactorily? How satisfying was the overall interaction? Was the practitioner open to how his therapy might work together with conventional medicine? Was he clear about the costs, time, and effort associated with treatment? Overall, does the treatment plan seem reasonable and acceptable?

As with any professional consulted for your care, the patient may get a second opinion, look for a different practitioner, or stop treatment altogether if he is dissatisfied or uncomfortable. As it may not be advisable to stop some treatments midcourse, however, patients should talk with the practitioner before stopping to make sure that it is safe to do so. They should openly discuss with the practitioner the reasons they are not satisfied or comfortable with treatment. If they decide to seek another practitioner, this information will be valuable to the first practitioner. Communication is the key to the best possible outcome and satisfaction with health care.

Finally, clinical trials are a potential source of CAM therapy. Though they require specific entrance criteria and that patients follow strict treatment protocols, treatment is provided without cost. NCCAM supports clinical trials of CAM therapies, which take place in many locations worldwide. To find trials that are recruiting participants, visit www.nccam.nih.gov/clinicaltrials, where one can search for trials by the type of therapy being studied or by disease or condition. The NCCAM Clearinghouse can also be called toll-free in the United States at 1-888-644-6226 and internationally at 301-519-3153. A second source of information on clinical trials is http://clinicaltrials.gov, developed by the NIH to provide information to the public on over 6,200 clinical studies sponsored by NIH, other federal agencies, and the pharmaceutical industry in more than 69,000 locations worldwide. People interested in participating in clinical trials should be aware that they often exclude individuals who are taking conventional treatment already; it is important discuss with the treating physician the risks and benefits of stopping medications before deciding to enter a study.

16

Living a Healthy Life While Living
With a Psychiatric Illness

As clinicians, we sometimes notice that the more drugs we give patients, the more passive they often become. It reminds us that a positive and proactive attitude is extremely important on the journey to wellness.

Now that we've covered a full range of treatment options that can be provided by doctors, therapists, and other people in the world of health care, it's time to examine what people can do to take care of themselves. This involves adopting a lifestyle that brings peace, health, and enjoyment in life—a life that is an expression of who one is as an individual: One's own version of wellness, and their unique understanding of "normal."

This chapter is written for patients who want to take charge of their own recovery and wellness by integrating lifestyle modification, self-care, advocacy, and modes of treatment or activities other than psychotherapy and medications into their personal plan for recovery from depression. This chapter has value for clinicians as well, who may wish to introduce their patients to these options encouraging and supporting their use. It begins with an orientation on developing a healthy mindset from which to launch the journey toward wellness. We discuss the meaning of recovery, and we look at various ways you can help yourself to stay well, including the creation of a recovery action plan. We talk about compiling a "wellness toolbox," which includes charting your mood, establishing healthy diet and exercise, and getting a good night's rest, and we cover some complementary health practices known to be helpful in depression.

Finally, we look at your relationships—with yourself, with those you love, and with the community.

Becoming Recovery-Minded

Recovery is rediscovering meaning and purpose in life after living with the traumatic experience of mental illness. It is a journey, a process, and a way of life. It is an approach to the challenges that come your way. It is not a linear process, but rather one that allows movement in various directions and the imperfection of sometimes taking a few steps backward.

Recovery is the development of a goal to work, live, and make a contribution to the world. It involves new discovery of meaning and purpose, and it comes in stages. The first requirement is a sense of hope—of knowing things will get better. Then there is the process of becoming empowered, confident, and proactive, of rejecting stigma, of reaching out to others, and of learning to express your emotions and learn from them. It is a way of honoring yourself. Responsibility for yourself and the way you live in the world then follows. The goal of recovery is to continue the journey—and to enjoy it because you've found a meaningful role in life.

Kindness

The first step is learning to be kind to yourself. Becoming well is not about "getting rid" of symptoms. This is not a war, and it's not about control. It's about making peace with your symptoms by listening to them and understanding them. Once you set fear aside and listen to what your illness has to say to you, you might find a profound wisdom that will be a great blessing to your life. For many people who live with a mood disorder, recovery is a lifelong process. It helps to make a friend of your perceived enemy.

A Proactive Approach

Over the time you've spent in treatment, you've been given much advice and have been told many things, some of which may have been conflicting or puzzling. Through this process, you may have lost your way when it comes to finding your own answers. Living with chronic or recurrent depression or identifying with your illness may have made you beleaguered and then passive.

Here are some things to think about: When another person suggests you try something, make sure it feels right before acting on it. Notice your emotions. What are they telling you? Have a responsible, take-charge attitude when receiving advice, even if this person is your doctor. Remember that you are the expert on you, and the clinician is a helpful consultant who has knowledge and tools that may be of use to you. Together, you are a team. Take a proactive approach to this relationship.

Educate yourself so that you know all there is to know about the issues at hand. Remember that just because you've read information in a book by a prestigious author, it may not be right for you. Familiarize yourself with the topic and build a well-rounded database of information on your topic. Involve various sources of information in your search, including the opinions of people you trust.

Before making a decision about your treatment or another area of your life, sit back and wait for a moment. Let it settle. Often, after reflection, you will change your mind. Journaling may be helpful in understanding how you really feel about something. Take time to pause and reflect, and don't allow others to pressure you into making important decisions.

Recovery focuses on valuing and building on your many capacities and talents, as well as your resilience and ability to cope in a healthy way. It also means valuing the inherent worth of individuals. It emphasizes your roles as a partner, caregiver, friend, student, or employee, not the role of a depressed individual. The process of recovery moves forward through trusting and supportive interaction with others.

In taking this kind, proactive, patient approach with yourself, and in thinking about recovery as a journey rather than a finite goal, you may find that the quality of your life improves and that the wisdom you gain adds richness to your life.

Illness Self-Management: A Tool for Recovery

Illness self-management is a toolkit comprising four components. Educating yourself about your illness and its management has been found to improve knowledge and thus is a proactive approach. Behavioral tailoring to address medication nonadherence helps you to learn to participate regularly with your treatment. Developing a relapse-prevention plan helps to prevent relapse. Finally, learning coping strategies for dealing with persistent symptoms reduces both the severity of these symptoms and the distress that comes from feeling a lack of control in their presence.

These four treatment components are included in the illness management and recovery implementation kit, developed as part of the evidence-based-practices project sponsored by the Substance Abuse and Mental Health Services Administration (SAMHSA). Visit http://mental-health.samhsa.gov/cmhs/communitysupport/toolkits/illness for more information.

Following is a more in-depth discussion of some of the techniques that are used within this framework, including social rhythms therapy, mood charting, and the recovery action plan.

Wellness Recovery Action Planning

People with mental health difficulties were self-managing and functioning in the community long before the idea of recovery became popularized. Studies show that self-management (the determination to manage the illness, take action, feel better, and face problems) facilitates recovery (Allott, Loganathan, & Fulford, 2002).

Techniques common to all self-care strategies include exercising, praying or meditating, practicing good nutrition, writing down or talking about problems, contacting or visiting with friends, undertaking creative endeavors, and engaging in self-advocacy (Rogers & Rogers, 2004). Seeking mental health services and taking medications are aspects of self-managed care for many people as well.

Mary Ellen Copeland's Wellness Recovery Action Planning program, known as WRAP, is one of the most popular manualized self-management programs. There are WRAP workshops and classes available through a variety of services. WRAP is something people can do on their own as well. Here we introduce you to its principles and practices.

While engaging in WRAP, participants create their own individualized plans for healthy and creative living, based on internal and external resources they identify and develop. The first step in the WRAP plan is creation of a personal "wellness toolbox," which outlines simple, low-cost or free self-management strategies like healthy diet and exercise, healthy sleep patterns, and relationship skills. The wellness toolbox is inclusive of a daily maintenance plan, as well as action plans based on identification of triggers and early warning signs: WRAP explores how people can learn to recognize and manage their prodromal symptoms (early warning signs of relapse), as well as develop a crisis plan to bring resources into play to prevent an episode and to specify how they would like to be treated in times of crisis. Then comes the postcrisis plan for getting back on the road to recovery. Having identified the components of the toolbox, the person then makes a plan for bringing each item outlined on line in their life.

WRAP is designed and managed by the mental health consumer who will be using it. It is meant to increase personal empowerment, improve quality of life, decrease and prevent troubling or intrusive behaviors and feelings, and assist people in achieving life goals and dreams. People who use WRAP say that they feel better and enjoy more quality in their lives. They report faster rates of recovery. They feel prepared to handle the challenges that come up in life, and in this way they have improved self-esteem, an internal locus of control, better self-efficacy, and reduced anxiety.

Values and ethics employed in WRAP include maintaining hope with the knowledge that people with mental illness live full and successful lives on their own terms; valuing self-determination, personal responsibility, self-advocacy, and empowerment; recognizing that one's capacity for recovery is without limits; and knowing that a person's participation in any program or aspect of treatment is as an equal to any clinician or other caregiver. The consumer is an expert on herself. There are many other positive, affirmative, and inspiring aspects of the WRAP approach that include honoring and involving others in one's recovery process.

Copeland provides many products to help people do their own WRAP program on her Web site. Interested readers can visit www.mentalhealthrecovery.com.

Social Rhythms Therapy

Social rhythms therapy (SRT), discussed in Chapter 8, involves regulation of daily activities, which promotes mood stability. In the context of recovery, the Social Rhythms Metric (SRM) chart is especially useful. To complete the chart, you list 17 daily life activities, noting the time at which you participated in each of the activities. This includes the time you got out of bed, your first contact with another person (in person or by phone), when you had your morning beverage, and when you ate breakfast. It then asks you to chart when you went outside for the first time that day and when you started work, school, housework, child or family care, or volunteer activities. Then it's time for lunch, and perhaps an afternoon nap. You also chart any physical exercise, dinner, an evening snack or drink, leisure activities such as watching a program on television, and the time you returned home that evening. Importantly, you also chart when you go to bed at night. A sample chart is available at the end of Chapter 8 for your use.

Using the SRM chart can teach you a lot about the presence or absence of ritual and of healthy activities in your life, and it also improves mood stability by regulating sleep and wake times, regular meal times, and exercise, all of which have effects on the production of hormones, neurotransmitters, and energy. Regulation of social activities discourages isolation, which is common in depression.

Mood Charting

Charting your mood helps you become more familiar with the patterns of your ups and downs and what is associated with them. This is a helpful tool for you and your doctor or therapist to review together.

A daily diary is kept, monitoring your mood on a daily basis and assigning any feelings of depression or mania a score from 0 to 10 each day. You can indicate whether your mood was irritable or dysphoric, whether there were any other uncomfortable associated symptoms, such as a panic attack, and any important events, such as a hospitalization. There is a place to indicate the number of significant mood shifts that day. You also chart the medications you took that day. Did you forget to take some? How many hours of sleep did you get? Are you on your menstrual period? There is a place to indicate the effect your mood had on your activities that day and, in turn, any significant events that may have affected your mood. There are a couple of versions of this type of mood chart, and they are available in the public domain. Good ones are available at www.bhicares.org/pdf/manual/indepthassessment/daily%20 mood%20charting.pdf and at http://measurecme.com/resources/ MEASURE_Mood_Diary.pdf. You may also use the personalized Daily Rating Scale or the simpler Symptoms Severity Chart provided at the end of Chapter 10.

A Healthy Lifestyle
A healthy diet and regular exercise are vital components of a healthy lifestyle.

Diet and Nutrition
Adjusting both diet and nutrition may help some people with mental illnesses manage their symptoms and promote recovery. Dietary changes affect your brain's physiology, and making a few dietary changes can go a long way in improving your mental outlook. The topic of nutrition for mental health has filled entire books on its own. Below are just a few salient tips to build upon.

We recommend a diet high in nutrients, including the macronutrients of carbohydrates, protein, and fats, and the full complement of vitamins and minerals you receive from a well-balanced diet. The Mediterranean diet is one such healthy eating pattern, including plenty of fruits, nuts, vegetables, cereals, legumes, and fish. All of these are important sources of nutrients linked to preventing depression.

You should eat plant-based foods that provide you with antioxidants, such as deeply pigmented fruits and vegetables. The brain is at risk for free radical damage; antioxidants fight free radicals, which contribute to aging and disease.

Protein-rich foods boost alertness. Foods like turkey, tuna, and chicken, as well as other animal- and plant-based sources, are rich in the amino acid tyrosine, which is a precursor to dopamine and norepinephrine, neurotransmitters associated with alertness and concentration. You should include protein in each meal. Eating foods like fruit or sugar alone can spike your blood sugar, only to have it drop shortly after. Enjoy a piece of cheese or some peanut butter with your apple, or add yogurt to your snack. The brain uses around 50% of the glucose (form in which the body stores sugars) in your body, and it functions best when blood sugar levels are even.

Understand the connection between carbohydrates and mood. Foods high in carbohydrates, such as breads, cereal, and pasta, raise the level of serotonin in the brain. When serotonin levels rise, we feel less anxious. Make smart choices: Reach for some fruit, grains, vegetables, and legumes, and limit sugary snacks. Diets high in sugar are known to be associated with depression.

Deficient omega-3 fatty acids are associated with depression. Joseph Hibbeln and colleagues (Hibbeln, 1998; Hibbeln, Niemenen, Blasbalg, Riggs, & Lands, 2006; Tanskanen et al., 2001) have determined that societies that eat a small amount of omega-3 fatty acids have a higher prevalence of major depressive disorder than societies that get ample omega-3 fatty acids. Other epidemiological studies show that people who infrequently eat fish, a rich source of omega-3 fatty acids, are more likely to suffer from depression. As humans were evolving, we consumed a 1:1 ratio of omega-3 to omega-6 fatty acids. Omega-6 is a pro-inflammatory fatty acid, which is abundant in our diet. We now consume a 1:10 to 1:20 ratio in Westernized countries. Not only are omega-3 fatty acids beneficial to the heart, brain, and other organ systems in and of themselves, but also the very act of balancing the ratio of 3 and 6 helps to control inflammatory processes. Sources of omega-3 fatty acids include fatty fish (anchovy, mackerel, salmon, sardines, shad, and tuna), flaxseed, and nuts. Only eicosapentanoic acid has anti-inflammatory properties, however, and these cannot be obtained from nuts and seeds. The body converts less than 1% of alphalinoleic acid (ALA, from walnuts or flaxseed) to EPA.

Caffeine may be your favorite morning beverage, but it can also be your drug of choice. People become dependent on caffeine, which can adversely affect mood when not taken moderately. If you are drinking more than two to three cups of coffee daily (or the equivalent), or if caffeine in any amount gives you the jitters or makes you rev up and then crash, you might consider cutting back or eliminating caffeine altogether. Because caffeine dilates blood vessels, cutting back can cause withdrawal effects such as headache in a person accustomed to having a steady drip of her favorite brew. Note that, without caffeine onboard, you may feel any sedative effects of your psychiatric medications more keenly.

Following is a good plan for cutting back on caffeine: First, estimate your daily caffeine intake by number of servings. A serving is a 12-oz can of soda or a 10-oz mug of coffee, for instance. Next, begin to decrease your intake by replacing your coffee, tea, or soda with a decaffeinated one, and gradually continue the taper for about 6 weeks or so, replacing one serving per week. For instance, a person who drinks two cups of coffee in the morning, two sodas in the afternoon, and a cup of tea in the evening would require 5 weeks to become caffeine-free. You might want to evenly space your caffeinated beverages throughout the day as you cut back. You may, for instance, first cut the evening tea to improve your sleep, then one of the morning beverages, then an afternoon can of coke, and so on.

Exercise

Exercise has been referred to as the least expensive and most available antidepressant. Regular physical exercise can help people reduce stress, depression, and anxiety and enable them to better cope with adversity (NMHA, 2006). People who have major depression and anxiety disorders are significantly (60%) less likely to relapse if they exercise regularly—and continue exercising over time—than if they take medication alone (NMHA, 2006).

BENEFITS OF EXERCISE

People who exercise have reported that they sleep better, think more clearly, have less nervousness and anxiety, feel happy and content more often, feel better about themselves, lose weight, develop strength, and enjoy a sense of well-being. If easing depression isn't enough of a motivator to exercise, here are several others:

- Aerobic exercise (walking, running, or biking, for instance) increases oxygen consumed, providing you with the ability to fight free radicals, which are associated with cellular aging. Just a 15–25% increase is like shaving 10 to 20 years off your age. Aerobic exercise may also stimulate the growth of new brain cells.

- Studies lasting many years have consistently shown that being active cuts the risk of premature death by about 50% for men and women.
- When you exercise, your body releases chemicals called endorphins. These endorphins interact with the receptors in your brain that reduce your perception of pain.
- Endorphins also trigger a positive feeling in the body, a type of euphoria referred to by some as "runner's high." This can be accompanied by a positive and energizing outlook on life, which means that self-esteem is improved.
- Improved self-esteem is a key psychological benefit of regular physical activity and in and of itself can improve depression!
- Being overweight is correlated with depression and also with fatigue. Physical activity is a natural and pleasurable way to keep your weight within a healthy range.
- Endorphins act as analgesics, which means they diminish the perception of pain. They also act as sedatives. They are manufactured in your brain, spinal cord, and many other parts of your body and are released in response to brain chemicals called neurotransmitters. The neuron receptors that endorphins bind to are the same ones that bind some pain medicines. However, unlike with morphine, the activation of these receptors by the body's endorphins does not lead to addiction or dependence.
- Moderate workouts temporarily increase the aggressiveness or capacity of immune cells. Have you ever noticed that people who exercise regularly catch fewer colds?
- Not only does exercise raise "good" HDL cholesterol and lower blood pressure, but new research shows it also reduces arterial inflammation, a risk factor for heart attacks and strokes.
- Do you have asthma? Exercise may reduce your need to use an inhaler.
- Like regularly spaced meals containing a balance of nutrients, exercise helps maintain a healthy blood sugar level by increasing the cells' sensitivity to insulin and by controlling weight. Risk of developing type 2 (sugar) diabetes can be significantly lowered with regular exercise.

- Exercise may protect against breast and prostate cancer by regulating hormone levels. It may also reduce colon cancer risk by speeding wastes through the gut and lowering the insulin level.
- Women who are going through menopause may find that fitness relieves their "vasovagal" symptoms (hot flashes and night sweats). Both walking and yoga have been shown to be helpful.
- Pelvic exercises help prevent erectile dysfunction and possibly benign prostate enlargement, a common cause of urinary problems.

Note that there is a dose-response relationship to exercise as well, meaning that more is better! Level of cardiorespiratory fitness correlates to relief of depression as measured on a scale, with increasing benefit with more miles walked, peaking at 11 to 19 miles per week.

WHAT FORMS OF EXERCISE ARE BENEFICIAL?

So now that you're ready to dig in and go for it, what sorts of exercise may be beneficial? Obviously, getting your heart rate up is a goal, and this can be accomplished by running, walking, biking, rowing, playing singles tennis, low-impact aerobics, rollerblading, or other moderately strenuous activities. Other activities that are less strenuous but still beneficial include dancing, swimming, yoga, housework (especially sweeping, mopping, and vacuuming), and gardening. If you play golf, try carrying your clubs and walking around the green rather than using the cart.

Because strong social support is important for those with depression, joining a group exercise class may be beneficial. Or you can exercise with a close friend or your partner. Forms of exercise that involve a social component include yoga, aerobics, basketball, golfing, or walking with a buddy.

In choosing an activity, ask yourself what physical activities you enjoy. What sorts of programs best fit your schedule? Are there physical conditions that may present limitations? Are group activities attractive to you, or would you rather go solo? Consider your goals, also. Are you interested in weight loss, strengthening muscles, improving flexibility, or simply mood enhancement?

Walking is an exercise that deserves special attention. It's easy, free, requires no special equipment, and is convenient. You can walk in whatever you are wearing, so you don't have to change clothes, and you don't need to shower after walking. You can walk anytime and anywhere that is safe, and, if there are trails near your home, you may enjoy spending time in nature. Walking is noncompetitive, so old feelings of not being as good as others don't come up. It is very unlikely that you will sustain the type of overuse injuries that may occur with other types of exercise, such as running.

GETTING STARTED

For most people, checking in with a health care provider is not necessary before starting a new exercise program. However, if you have not exercised in a while, are over age 50, or have a medical condition such as diabetes or heart disease, it is advisable.

When you first start your exercise program, you should plan a routine that is easy to follow and maintain. Any new project or endeavor can feel overwhelming when you are depressed. When you begin feeling comfortable with your routine, you can start varying your exercise times and activities. To get started, make sure you choose an activity you enjoy. Exercising should be fun. Put your routine into your schedule, even on your calendar if you need to be reminded. You may want to vary your exercises so you don't get bored. Try biking a couple days a week and playing basketball with friends on the weekend, for instance. Avoid buying expensive equipment or health club memberships until you're sure that exercise is something you can commit to. Stick with it. If you exercise regularly, it will soon become part of your lifestyle and will help reduce your depression.

Frequency of exercise for depression has been studied, and at minimum you should try to exercise at least 20 to 30 minutes, three times a week. Studies indicate that exercising four or five times a week is best. Take it easy if you are just beginning. Start exercising for 20 minutes. Then you can build up to 30 minutes. But do start with three times weekly to see benefits.

STICKING WITH IT

Some people experience difficulty getting started on or maintaining an exercise program. Actually, "most people" might be a more accurate statement! You may feel that you don't have time, that it interferes with other activities and responsibilities, or that you won't enjoy it. One or several of the following suggestions might help you solve this problem.

Consider your exercise time as fun or "play" time, not as work. Everyone needs and deserves to have time to play. Ask friends or family members to exercise with you. It's easier to get out if a friend is expecting you. Schedule exercise at the same time each day to provide structure. It may help you to stick to your exercise regime if you keep a record of your exercise and how it makes you feel. Reward yourself each time you exercise or after you have followed your exercise plan for a specific length of time. For example, you could put aside a couple of dollars each time you exercise to save for a treat!

To save time and also boost effectiveness of other strategies in your wellness plan, you can combine exercise with focusing on positive thoughts, connecting with social support, and getting light exposure.

Avoid sabotaging yourself. If you miss a day, or even weeks, of exercising, just start in again. If you've been away from exercise for a while or have had to stop because of an injury or illness, start again gradually.

Restful Sleep

One of the items measured on the social rhythms metric is regular sleep patterns. Many people with depression and bipolar disorder suffer from insomnia or other difficulties with getting a good night's rest, and lack of sleep or too much sleep can worsen moods.

We recommend keeping a regular sleep schedule whenever possible. It is more important that you wake up at the same time each day than that you go to bed at around the same time each night (Burgess, 2005), but both are important. If you are depressed, try not to go to bed very late (after midnight), and try not to sleep in past around 8:30 in the morning, as this can disrupt your body's natural rhythms, including the expression of regulatory hormones like cortisol, necessary in managing stress.

If you have insomnia, try to avoid taking naps during the day because they can interfere with nighttime sleep.

Sleep Hygiene

The following suggestions for nonpharmacologic approaches are what is known as "sleep hygiene."

THE BEDROOM
- The room should be cool dark, and well-ventilated.
- Block distracting noise and as much light as possible; cover any light sources (even small ones).
- The bedroom should be for sleep and sex only (no TV or reading).
- Cover the alarm clock so that you cannot keep checking to see what time it is.

BED AND WAKE TIMES
- Get up and go to bed at same time daily—wake time is especially important.
- Early to bed and early to rise—make bedtime no later than midnight.
- Don't go to bed unless you are sleepy.

BEFORE SLEEP
- A light snack before bed is okay. Warm milk and foods high in tryptophan may help: yogurt, eggs, turkey, meat, nuts, beans, fish, cheese (especially cheddar, Gruyerè, and Swiss), soy products.
- Practice relaxation techniques before bed: yoga, deep breathing, progressive relaxation.
- Television and computer use (especially games and the Internet) can be stimulating; avoid if possible for the 2 hours before bedtime.
- Presleep rituals are helpful: a warm bath, a few minutes of reading (not in the bedroom).
- A hot bath 90 minutes before bed will raise the body temperature; the drop in temperature thereafter may leave you feeling sleepy.

GETTING TO SLEEP
- If it takes you more than 15 to 30 minutes to get to sleep, get up, go into another room, and read until you are sleepy (nonstimulating material).

- You can also try mindfulness meditation.
- If this doesn't work, it's time for medication, although medication should be a last resort.
- The advice for waking during the night is similar: If you wake and can't get back to sleep after 15 to 20 minutes, don't "try hard" to sleep. Leave the bedroom and:
  - Read, have a light snack, take a bath, or engage in a quiet activity.
  - Then go back to bed, typically in about 20 to 30 minutes.
  - Don't engage in activities such as housework, office work, computer use, or watching TV.
  - Alternate idea: Practice mindfulness relaxation in bed for 20 minutes. See your doctor, nurse, or therapist to learn how.

DURING THE DAY
- Get out for some natural light for about 15 minutes first thing in the morning, or try a light box.
- Maintain good nutrition, including folate and iron supplementation if your doctor suggests you need it.

Things to avoid:
- Daytime napping (or limit it to 30 to 45 minutes).
- Lying in bed (get into bed only when you are sleepy).
- Alcohol 4 to 6 hours before bedtime.
- Caffeine 4 to 6 hours before bedtime.
- Nicotine before bedtime.
- Exercise 4 hours before bed (earlier aerobic exercise, however, helps insomniacs)
- Heavy, spicy, or sugary foods 4 to 6 hours before bedtime.
- Going to bed hungry.
- Don't take worries to bed—assign a "worry period" during the evening or late afternoon. Write the worries down and tell yourself you've done all you can do about them today. They'll still be there tomorrow; you can worry about them then.

Complementary Health Practices

In the last chapter we discussed complementary and alternative dietary supplements. Here we focus on exercises for the mind, body, and spirit that have been shown to be helpful for people living with depression, anxiety, and other mental and physical health challenges.

Before engaging in any complementary technique, you should be aware that many of these techniques have not been evaluated in scientific studies. Often, only limited information is available about their safety and effectiveness. Each state and each discipline has its own laws and rules about whether practitioners are required to be professionally licensed. If you plan to visit a practitioner, it is recommended that you choose one who is licensed by a recognized national organization and who abides by the organization's standards. It is always best to speak with your primary health care provider before starting any new therapeutic technique.

For the Body

Mind-body therapies are used by 16.6% of adults in the United States (Barnes et al., 2004). They are used most often by individuals suffering from anxiety, depression, and various pain syndromes, particularly musculoskeletal pain, such as low back pain; 68–90% of people who give them an adequate trial find them to be helpful. While half of people surveyed use these therapies along with conventional medicine, others give it a try when they no longer believe traditional medical care can help them (Bertisch, Wee, Phillips, & McCarthy, 2009).

YOGA

The word *yoga* comes from the Sanskrit word *yuj*, which means "yoke" or "union." It is believed that this describes the union between the mind and the body. Practitioners of this ancient Indian system of health care use breathing exercises, posture, stretches, and meditation to balance the body's energy centers. Yoga is used in combination with other treatment for depression, anxiety, and stress-related disorders.

A study found that of 31,000 U.S. adults surveyed in 2002, yoga was one of the top 10 CAM modalities used, with 8% of those surveyed participating in some form of yoga during their lifetime (Barnes et al., 2004).

Yoga was originally developed as a method of discipline and attitudes to help people reach spiritual enlightenment. The Sutras outline eight limbs or foundations of yoga practice that serve as spiritual guidelines:

- Yama (moral behavior)
- Niyama (healthy habits)
- Asana (physical postures)
- Pranayama (breathing exercises)
- Pratyahara (sense withdrawal)
- Dharana (concentration)
- Dhyana (contemplation)
- Samadhi (higher consciousness)

The numerous schools of yoga incorporate these eight practices in varying proportions. Hatha yoga, the most commonly practiced in the United States and Europe, emphasizes postures (asanas) and breathing exercises (pranayama). Major styles of hatha yoga include Ananda, Anusara, Ashtanga, Bikram, Iyengar, Kripalu, Kundalini, and Viniyoga.

People use yoga for a variety of health conditions including anxiety disorders or stress, asthma, high blood pressure, and depression. It is also helpful for general physical fitness and relaxation. Research suggests that yoga might improve mood and sense of well-being, counteract stress, reduce blood pressure and heart rate, increase lung capacity, improve overall physical fitness, strength, and flexibility, and improve muscle relaxation and body composition. It has also been shown helpful in relieving symptoms of anxiety, depression, and insomnia, and to have a positive effect on central nervous system chemistry.

ACUPUNCTURE

This Chinese practice of inserting needles into the body at specific points manipulates the body's flow of energy to balance the endocrine system. Physiologic processes affected include heart rate, body temperature, and respiration, as well as sleep patterns and emotional changes. Acupuncture has been used in clinics to relieve stress and anxiety, to assist people with substance abuse disorders through detoxification, to treat attention-deficit/hyperactivity disorder in children, to reduce symptoms of depression, and to help people with physical problems. A meta-analysis of eight small randomized controlled trials comparing a total of 477 subjects found acupuncture to be efficacious for depression (Wang et al., 2008).

There are independent practitioners of acupuncture, or you may find clinics where Chinese medicine is practiced by a number of clinicians. Low-cost acupuncture services may be found at schools, where students in the later part of their training work with you. In some cities, acupuncture is on the menu at free clinics for the poor. Some health insurance covers acupuncture.

MASSAGE

Massage therapy has been used to treat trauma-related depression and stress, as well as a host of other health-related problems. A 2002 national survey found that 9.3% of 31,000 U.S. participants had used massage therapy, with 5% having used it in the preceding 12 months (Barnes et al., 2004).

According to recent reviews, people use massage for a wide variety of health-related intents, including to relieve pain (often from musculoskeletal conditions, but from other conditions as well), rehabilitate sports injuries, reduce stress, increase relaxation, address feelings of anxiety and depression, and promote general wellness.

There are over 80 types of massage therapy, all involving manipulation of the muscles and other soft tissues of the body, often varying pressure and movement. A few examples include: Swedish massage, which uses long strokes, kneading, and friction on the muscles to aid flexibility; deep-tissue massage, which uses patterns of strokes and deep finger pressure on parts of the body where muscles are tight or knotted, focusing on layers of muscle deep under the skin; trigger-point massage, which involves deeper, more focused pressure on myofascial trigger points, or "knots" that may form in muscles; and shiatsu massage, which involves rhythmic pressure from the fingers on parts of the body that are believed to be important for the flow of a vital energy called qi (pronounced "chee," it means "air" or "power").

The training and experience of massage therapists runs the gamut. We recommend that you ask the person for his credentials and experience before engaging his services. Find out if he attended a certified training program, the length of that program, and whether he is certified in massage therapy. Also ask about his technique, what sorts of ailments he has treated, and the changes he has seen in his clients. Massage therapy can cost upwards of $150 per session, and regular sessions may be required to see benefit.

TAI CHI

Tai chi is a mind-body practice that originated in China as a martial art. It is practiced through breath and meditation while moving the body slowly.

In traditional Chinese medicine, illness is believed to be the result of imbalance between two opposing life forces, yin and yang. Many practitioners believe that tai chi helps the flow of qi throughout the body. Tai chi aims to reestablish balance, create harmony between body and mind, and orient a person within his surroundings and the world.

Tai chi is widely practiced in China (including in its hospitals and clinics) and in other countries with a substantial native Chinese population. In the United States, a 2002 national survey of 31,000 adults found that 1.3% of people who participated had practiced tai chi within the preceding 12 months (Barnes et al., 2004).

Preliminary evidence suggests that when practiced regularly, tai chi may increase muscle strength and improve cardiovascular health, coordination, and balance. Practitioners believe that tai chi acts through massaging the internal organs, aiding gas exchange within the lungs, helping the digestive system to work more efficiently, improving balance, and increasing calmness and awareness.

Tai chi may also be seen as a beneficial form of physical exercise. It is low-impact, weight-bearing, and aerobic; it increases physical condition through muscle strength, coordination, and flexibility, and it eases pain and stiffness. Sleep may be improved, both in elimination of insomnia and in improvement of sleep efficiency and quality. It lowers the risk of falls in the elderly. People practicing tai chi also gain the benefits that can be had through meditation.

QIGONG
Qigong, a traditional Chinese medicine technique, is sometimes described as "a way of working with life energy." There are three main branches of qigong: medical (used for healing), spiritual (for self-aware-ness), and martial art (for self-protection). Qigong can be practiced daily with the aim of health maintenance and disease prevention. Medical qigong can be an active (internal) or passive (external) noninvasive tech-nique that involves meditating, cleansing, strengthening/recharging, and circulating and dispersing qi.

Qigong is considered beneficial for a large variety of medical condi-tions, including chronic conditions like cancer, chronic fatigue syndrome, osteoporosis, high blood pressure, stomach ulcers, and asthma. There is also evidence of its adjunctive use (in addition to medications) in treat-ment of high blood pressure, as well as reports that it may be used in management of pain and anxiety or depression associated with pain and chronic illness.

For the Mind
Stress is intimately related to symptoms experienced by those who live with mood and anxiety disorders. Ways of coping with stress are many and varied, and they include some of the techniques covered here, namely hypnotherapy, meditation, relaxation, and visualization and guided imagery.

STRESS MANAGEMENT
Some suggestions for stress management that can be incorporated with any of the following techniques include recognizing your signs of stress and trying to recall how your body feels during times of stress. Do you get a queasy feeling before taking an exam? Do arguments give you headaches? Do you have difficulty sleeping when under pressure at work? Write down your signs of stress so you can reflect on them later. Then notice your reactions to stress: How do you typically deal with these situations, and are your coping methods or strategies (or simply

reactions) helpful? Are there times when you recall having dealt with stress very well or poorly?

How do you manage anger? Some people use a pen and paper to write about everything they feel angry about and then burn the paper. Others turn up music and then say out loud what they'd really like to express to someone with whom they are very angry. Some people get their anger under control with exercise.

Time management is very helpful in managing stress, and this includes getting a handle on lateness and on procrastination. If you need to, make lists and prioritize. Ask a friend to hold you accountable for your responsibilities and to report to them on your progress. There are many books on time management.

Set goals and work toward them—a sense of accomplishment imparts well-being and eases depression. Keep in mind, however, that there is only so much you can accomplish at any one time. Be realistic, and also remember to take breaks and do things you enjoy.

Positive self-talk can help you to deal with stress—and to eliminate its opposite, negative self-talk and cognitive distortions (see Chapter 8). Have positive affirmations that you think about or even verbalize to yourself. Sometimes writing them on Post-it notes and putting them on the refrigerator or bathroom mirror is reinforcing. Make sure to update them and move them around so they don't become just part of the scenery. Some people choose to make flash cards of them and carry them around to reflect on throughout the day. Try picturing yourself in a positive situation—for instance, being calm during a test and doing very well. Remind yourself of times you have done very well in the past. Also, look at the big picture: Will a stressful situation really matter in 5 years? If the thing you're concerned about does happen, will the sky fall? Like the Serenity Prayer says, try to accept the things you cannot change, change the things you can, and have the wisdom to know the difference.

HYPNOTHERAPY

Hypnotherapy, or hypnosis, derives from the Greek word *hypnos*, meaning sleep. The Austrian physician Franz Anton Mesmer is responsible for the popularity of hypnosis in modern Western society—hence the word mesmerize. Mesmer believed that illness was caused by an imbalance of magnetic fluids in the body and that this could be corrected by "animal magnetism"; the hypnotherapist could heal the patient by transferring his own personal magnetism. In the early 20th century, the British and American Medical Associations and the American Psychological Association endorsed hypnotherapy as a medical procedure, and in 1995, the U.S. National Institutes of Health issued a consensus statement noting the scientific evidence in favor of the use of hypnotherapy for chronic pain, particularly pain associated with cancer.

The mechanism of action of hypnotherapy is not well understood. Some research reports that changes in skin temperature, heart rate, intestinal secretions, brain waves, and the immune system occur; the same changes are reported with other forms of relaxation. Other body systems believed to be affected include the endocrine glands and the limbic system (the emotional center of the brain).

The goals of hypnotherapy vary. They can include behavior change or treatment of a psychological condition. It is important that the person being hypnotized is under his own control at all times and is not controlled by the hypnotherapist or anyone else. Self-hypnosis is sometimes used in addition to sessions with a hypnotherapist, although study of self-hypnosis is limited. Books, audiotapes, and videotapes are available for training in self-hypnosis, but they have not been scientifically evaluated. Group sessions may also be offered. Hypnotherapy can be used with other techniques such as cognitive-behavioral therapy.

MEDITATION

Meditation is believed to be very helpful for people with depression, and it is considered a vital part of recovery for many people, who often continue to practice when they are well. The various health problems that may be helped by meditation include anxiety, pain, mood and self-esteem problems, stress, insomnia, and physical and emotional symptoms associated with chronic illness. Meditation is also used for overall wellness. In 2004, it was found that nearly 8% of people had used meditation specifically for health reasons during the preceding year (Barnes et al., 2004).

Resting the mind also has a dramatic effect on brain activity. When an alpha wave state is induced in the brain, many physiological changes occur, starting with the autonomic nervous system. Functions such as the heartbeat, sweating, breathing, and digestion may be affected. Through this influence, meditation induces changes such as that in the body's fight-or-flight response.

In meditation, a person learns to focus her attention and to clear her mind of the thoughts that usually occupy it. The state achieved is believed to be associated with greater physical relaxation, mental calmness, and psychological balance. Meditation is practiced both on its own and as a component of some other therapies, such as yoga, tai chi, and qigong. Most types of meditation take place in a quiet location with a specific, comfortable posture (which varies depending on the type of meditation practiced). There is a focus of attention and an open attitude.

In order to clear the mind and remain quiet, a number of techniques may be practiced. Some focus on the breath. Others may focus on an object, such as a candle or an object in nature. You may use a mantra, a word or phrase that you repeat internally to create focus. Some people choose to chant in unison with others in group meditation practice. In yoga or tai chi, movement is used as a point of concentration to the exclusion of other thoughts. In mindfulness meditation, one focuses on the present and on being aware of one's surroundings, or simply on allowing thoughts and perceptions to enter the mind but then gently pass without resistance.

RELAXATION

Relaxation can be as simple as taking a warm bath, taking the dog out for a stroll, or listening to music that helps you feel relaxed and positive or upbeat. It may also involve more controlled techniques, such as progressive muscle relaxation. Dancing, art-making or art appreciation, fishing, reading, drinking a warm cup of tea, shopping, visiting with friends, or playing a sport are all forms of relaxation many people enjoy.

During stressful situations, the sympathetic nervous system increases activity, leading to the fight-or-flight response. Heart rate, blood pressure, breathing rate, blood supply to the muscles, and dilation of the pupils often increase, and these may be relieved to varying degrees with relaxation techniques.

Some forms of relaxation can be practiced anywhere, such as taking a moment to calm your thoughts when you are feeling stressed during the day. Pausing for a few moments to stretch your muscles and joints even while remaining seated at your desk at work can be very helpful. Rhythmic, deep, visualized, or diaphragmatic breathing can be used, and this is part of many relaxation techniques, as well as a helpful practice in and of itself. You can begin by breathing deeply through the nose, letting the air fill the bottom of your lungs first, all the way down to the stomach, and then breathe out slowly, concentrating on muscle relaxation. Try repeating a positive statement to yourself as you do this.

There are forms of relaxation exercise that take a little longer and involve a quiet space. One is Jacobson muscle relaxation, also called progressive muscle relaxation. First, sit or lie down comfortably, perhaps listening to some soothing music, and close your eyes. Then, starting with your toes, tense each muscle group tightly for 30 seconds and then relax it. Feel the reaction of your muscles: Which are the most tight? Is there any pain? Having this awareness will help you to recognize times during the day when you are feeling stress. If you are interested in this type of progressive relaxation, there are tapes that can guide you through it.

Relaxation techniques are taught by many types of health care professionals, including complementary practitioners, medical doctors, psychotherapists, hypnotherapists, nurses, and sports therapists. They may be brief or involve many sessions, and include guided imagery (covered shortly), meditation, and autogenic training.

Other types of relaxation therapy include mind/body interaction, music- or sound-induced relaxation, biofeedback, desensitization, cognitive restructuring, and adaptive self-statements (positive reinforcement and affirmation).

GUIDED IMAGERY OR VISUALIZATION
This process involves going into a state of deep relaxation and creating a mental image of recovery and wellness. Physicians, nurses, and mental health providers occasionally use this approach to treat alcohol and drug addictions, depression, panic disorders, phobias, and stress.

Imagery has been said to cause many types of changes in the body, including alterations in breathing, heart rate, blood pressure, metabolism, cholesterol levels, and functions of the gastrointestinal, immune, and endocrine systems. In guided imagery, you use the senses of touch, smell, sight, and sound to achieve a tranquil state that may help you to reduce or better cope with your psychiatric or physical symptoms.

Therapeutic guided imagery is believed to allow patients to enter a relaxed state and focus attention on images associated with issues they are confronting, or simply to take a pleasant trip away from their worries or pain. An experienced practitioner may help patients to tap into latent inner resources and find solutions to problems. It is an exercise that you can practice on your own, however. Books and audiotapes are available, as well as interactive guided imagery groups, classes, workshops, and seminars.

Scientists have studied guided imagery for many health problems, including the following:

Guided imagery has been shown to improve depression in older adults (McCaffrey, 2007). It has shown to improve both depression and cortisol levels with (McKinney, Antoni, Kumar, Tims, & McCabe, 1997) or without (Freeman et al., 2008) the addition of soothing music. Guided imagery has been found helpful for anxiety and depression in the post-partum period (Rees, 1993, 1995), and for anxiety during pregnancy (Jallo, Bourguignon, Taylor, & Utz, 2008). In people with bulimia, regular use of guided imagery is self-soothing (Esplen & Garfinkel, 1998; Esplen, Garfinkel, Olmsted, Gallop, & Kennedy, 1998), decreases bingeing and purging, and improves attitudes toward eating and body image (Esplen et al., 1998). Individuals have used it to quit smoking (Wynd, 1992, 2005). Imagery has been used successfully to improve the mental health and well-being of the caregivers of chronically ill children (Hernandez & Kolb, 1998), and mentally ill persons (Yip, 2003), and of those caring for loved ones in hospice (Moody, Webb, Cheung, & Lowell, 2004).

Imagery is helpful in people living with medical illness. It is helpful for preoperative anxiety (Norred, 2000; Walker, 2002), and decreases depression in people who have undergone surgery (Leja, 1989) or are in rehabilitation (Collins & Rice, 1997). Further, it has been shown to decrease postoperative pain and length of hospital stays (Halpin, Speir, CapoBianco, & Barnett, 2002; Tusek, 1999; Tusek, Cwynar, & Cosgrove, 1999).

When used by cancer patients, imagery eases anxiety (Cameron, Booth, Schlatter, Ziginskas, & Harman, 2007; Nunes et al., 2007; Roffe, Schmidt, & Ernst, 2005; Rossman, 2002), depression (Bakke, Purtzer, & Newton, 2002; Nunes et al., 2007), and pain with associated anxiety (Moore & Spiegel, 2000; Sloman, 1995). Trials pairing imagery with progressive muscle relaxation (PMR) showed effects on anxiety, depression, and the side effects of chemotherapy (Yoo, Ahn, Kim, Kim, & Han, 2005), and on anxiety and cancer pain (Kwekkeboom, Hau, Wanta, & Bumpus, 2008).

Remarkably, the meaning of pain, as noted in verbal descriptions, may change with the use of guided imagery. Patients who once had described pain as never-ending, relative, explainable, torment, and restrictive, were able to describe it as changeable after participating in an intervention, and they no longer referred to it as never-ending (W. Lewandowski, Good, & Draucker, 2005). Guided imagery and visualization have been helpful for both adults (Stevensen, 1995) and children (Rusy & Weisman, 2000) with acute pain, and for patients with chronic pain (Lecky, 1999; W. A. Lewandowski, 2004), including people suffering from osteoarthritis (Baird & Sands, 2004; Morone & Greco, 2007) and juvenile rheumatoid arthritis (Walco, Varni, & Ilowite, 1992) long term. It brings relief to those suffering from fibromyalgia (Fors, Sexton, & Gotestam, 2002; Menzies & Kim, 2008; Menzies, Taylor, & Bourguignon, 2006). When implemented with PMR, it soothes children with functional abdominal pain (Miranda & Sood, 2006; Weydert et al., 2006; Youssef et al., 2004). Guided imagery may provide added benefit for migraine (Baumann, 2002; Ilacqua, 1994; Narduzzi et al., 1998; Olness, Hall, Rozniecki, Schmidt, & Theoharides, 1999; Peters, Plohn, Buhk, & Dahme, 2000) or tension headache (Astin, 2004; Mannix, Chandurkar, Rybicki, Tusek, & Solomon, 1999; Narduzzi et al., 1998; Zitman, van Dyck, Spinhoven, & Linssen, 1992) when used along with standard medical care. Some studies show that relaxation therapies may also reduce the frequency of migraine (Baumann, 2002; Olness et al., 1999; Peters et al., 2000).

Interestingly, imagery may help those suffering from test anxiety (Wachelka, 1999), performance anxiety (Speck, 1990; Suk, Oh, & Kil, 2006), and problems with working memory (Hudetz, Hudetz, & Klayman, 2000; Hudetz, Hudetz, & Reddy, 2004), which for some persons is associated with anxiety. In medical students undergoing stress it relieved depression and anxiety while also boosting immune function (Gruzelier, 2002). Improved immunity has been found in patients living with breast cancer as well (Gruzelier, 2002), though a 3-month study found that this effect was not sustainable in their subjects (Bakke et al., 2002).

For the Spirit

In health care, spirituality is identified with experiencing a deep-seated sense of meaning and purpose in life, together with a sense of belonging. It is about acceptance, integration, and wholeness. This desire for wholeness of being is not an intellectual attainment but rather lies in the essence of what it means to be human. It holds that life is a perpetual journey of discovery and development, during which maturity is often gained through adversity. The relief of suffering remains a primary aim of health care, but it is by no means the whole story.

Spirituality may be a component of religion, but it is experienced on its own for many people. It is inclusive and unifying, and it applies to everyone, including those who do not believe in God or a "higher being."

SPIRITUAL PRACTICE

Spirituality may be experienced in an activity such as art-making or enjoyment of nature. It may involve reading material that allows you to better understand how you integrate and move through the world. It may involve goals, such as developing a better relationship with yourself, learning to love yourself, feeling more universally connected, or asking yourself for forgiveness and releasing guilt and shame.

Some people who have a faith-based religious spiritual practice choose to become involved in community activities and attend a place of worship where they commune with others. There are ritual and symbolic practices. Some people make pilgrimages or go on retreats, read scripture or listen to sacred music, practice acts of compassion (including volunteerism), or take part in deep reflection.

SKILLS GAINED

Skills gained through spirituality may include being self-reflective and honest; being able to remain mindful and in the present; remaining alert, unhurried, and attentive throughout the day; and being able to rest, relax, and create a still, peaceful state of mind. Some people find they develop a greater empathy for others, are able to give without feeling drained, find hope and courage within distress, and are able to grieve and let go.

An important principle of the spiritual approach to mental health care is reciprocity. This means that the giver and receiver both benefit from the interaction. Provided that exhaustion and burnout are avoided, caretakers naturally develop spiritual skills and values over time as a result of their devotion to those with whom they engage. Those benefiting from care are often, in turn, able to give help to others in distress.

People with health problems who seek to become more spirituality connected find that they have improved self-control, self-esteem, and confidence. Their recovery may be easier and may happen more quickly. They may be able to move through a grieving process and benefit through the exploring of their loss. They may find that their relationship with themselves, others, nature, or God is improved. They may find a new sense of meaning, resulting in a peace of mind and reawakening of hope. Spirituality may help people to accept and gracefully live with problems not yet resolved.

The subject of spirituality has filled thousands of books. Rather than go into explicit detail here, we encourage you to visit a bookstore that has a good section on spirituality or religion and take an unhurried period of time to just browse and acknowledge the thoughts and feelings that flow through you as you explore.

Relationships

The word "relationship" conjures thoughts and images of people we spend time with. We also relate in the context of social structures; that is, in families and groups, communities, and the world at large.

A Relationship With Yourself

Of all the people you know, you spend the most time with yourself. For people with mood disorders, this is not always a healthy relationship. There are a large number of activities and techniques that foster self-worth, self-esteem, and a sense of well-being.

SELF-ESTEEM

Low self-esteem is a symptom of depression, and improvement in this area may help you to lift your mood. Listen to yourself and to your body. What is it telling you? Make a list of things that make you feel bad about yourself, and then make a list of things you could do to counteract these negative feelings.

Some practices that may boost self-image include eating healthy food and exercising, keeping up with your personal hygiene, and finding new things to do each day. Make a list of things you've always wanted to do, then pick just one, and plan how you might approach it. When you begin to move forward on tasks that are important to you, and when you begin to maintain your health and treat yourself as someone special each day, self-esteem is sure to improve.

Some ideas for improving self-image include activities that are pretty small and basic. Clean your bathroom. Clean out that drawer. Write those thank-you notes you've been putting off for 6 months. Yes, taking care of tasks that have been dwelling in the back of your mind for a long time can bring a sense of release. Try doing something that reflects your own special talents and abilities—for instance, making gifts for friends or playing with someone's pet.

Try on a new image. If you can't afford to buy new clothing in retail stores, have fun thrift shopping. Take a friend. Make a living space that honors the person you are. Decorate your home with small items that give you pleasure when you see them, or clear an area of your home that is used simply for meditation, writing, or art-making. Make a ritual of meals and enjoy them leisurely with others.

Doing something nice for other people is an important self-image booster. Get the focus off of yourself and onto others. Help a friend out at his home or volunteer for a worthy organization.

You may be doing some of these things now. See how good it feels to recognize that? Give yourself a moment to feel good. Now it's time to find other things you can work on. As you find new ways to care for and honor yourself daily, your self-esteem will surely improve.

SELF-FORGIVENESS

Forgiveness is important to your recovery. Lack of self-forgiveness can result in a loss of love for yourself and indifference to your needs, as well as disrespectful treatment of yourself, including self-destructive behaviors. You may engage in ruminative thinking about past failures, and respond to this with self-pity or with hostility, sarcasm, and cynicism toward yourself. You may be suspicious of others' motives and behaviors toward you when actually they like you very much and wish you well. You may live in an emotional vacuum and then experience chronic attacks or angry outbursts against yourself. All of this self-defeating thinking and behavior may lead you to be unwilling to change or to seek the help necessary to change.

All people have the capacity for change. In order to forgive yourself and let go of past hurt and pain, learn to trust in your inherent goodness. If you follow the lead of a higher power, let go and allow it to care for you in times of pain. Let go of fears of the future and allow yourself to be vulnerable to growth, knowing that you are human and therefore likely to have a few faults and make mistakes.

In order to increase your ability to forgive yourself, ask yourself what "self-forgiveness" means to you. Have you ever forgiven yourself before? How did it feel? How is your lack of forgiveness affecting your emotional stability? How does lack of forgiveness for yourself affect your relationship with others? What is blocking you from forgiving yourself, and what would you need to do to change these beliefs? There are many other questions to ask yourself. It may be useful to explore these painful feelings with your therapist.

Relationships With Others

Social support is a key ingredient in dealing with emotional pain that goes along with unremitting anxiety and depression. Regular contact with friends and family who are supportive helps in recovery and keeps you well.

KEEPING A CIRCLE OF SUPPORT

When we ask our patients what represents the most pain in their lives, they often answer "loneliness." Loneliness may cause you to lose the motivation to change, to forget the reason for changing, or to lose interest in your efforts. You may get to a point where you feel there is no visible change in your life. Having good reciprocal relationships in your life will help you to feel good about yourself, feel good about the effort you are making, and be more conscientious in your effort to change.

A good friend is someone you respect and trust—someone who shares with you without judgment or criticism, is open and honest, and helps you work through things when you are having a hard time. You can tell a friend anything and he will not betray your confidence. This friend or family member would never take advantage of you.

Make a list of the people in your life whom you feel closest to—those people whom you would turn to in times of need. You will find that some friends meet some needs and others meet other needs. Is there something you could do to improve your relationships with these people? It's tough sometimes to reach out when you have depression. Many people are tempted to isolate. It helps to make plans with a friend and ask him to hold you to the commitment. Consider inviting him to your home to play a game or share a meal. Stop in and visit if he is having a hard time. Do something for him that expresses your caring. Find more enjoyable activities the two of you can share.

You may find it helpful to reach out to make new friends. Making new friends is not easy. Try to ignore those feelings that it may be difficult, as well as your fears of rejection, and participate in activities in the community where you can meet other people. You might choose to attend a support group for people with similar life challenges or health issues, or one for people of the same age or sex. You might consider joining a church or civic group or taking a class. Volunteering is an excellent way to meet others while working on projects you both care about. There are group activities you can find online through www.meetup.com. This is a way to meet others who are also there specifically to make new friends who share their interests. There are activities ranging from hiking to eating fried chicken to sharing interest in science fiction, and many of them cost little or no money to participate in. After you meet new friends, you may find that you are becoming more comfortable with someone, that you have things in common and are able to share. Some effort may be required to make this happen; you might want to suggest a casual activity like taking a walk together, or meeting for coffee, or calling to discuss something you think may be of interest to the person. If you are shy and just want to test the waters a bit, try sending a short, friendly e-mail and watch for a response.

RELATIONSHIPS AND COMMUNICATION WITH FAMILY

The following suggestions are adapted from material written by one of our colleagues. After losing her home and business to a particularly devastating period of depression, she moved back home to live with her parents. These were the thoughts, actions, and attitudes she and her family adopted to help them love and grow together while the depressed woman healed.

Communication. "Above all, respect, trust, and love are key. Know each other as people, not simply as father and son, sister and brother." Try to remove role disparities that may exist between you and your loved one. Level the playing field, so to speak. Also, while your family knows you love them, hearing you express this to them will be meaningful. Encourage open expression of love and caring between you and your family. Importantly, "give physical affection when you feel like it, and encourage your loved one to do the same—hugs can feel really good!"

"Allow for emotions and expression. Create a space in which it's safe to share." You or your loved one may express negative emotions from time to time. When someone speaks to you in anger or fear, try not to "mirror" them. Emotions are infectious—make an attempt not to allow fear, anger, or other negative emotions to creep into your expressions when your loved one expresses them. If you must, try to do so thought-fully. With anger, focus on how you feel, not on what you believe someone is making you feel. You are responsible for your own reactions and behavior, and so is your loved one.

People with mood disorders can be very reactive, especially when they are not feeling well. This is especially true of those who have bipolar disorder, or who have a history of traumatic experiences. Reactions may be very positive or very negative, black or white. The news is wonderful, or it is devastating. A friend is evil, mean, and bad because he didn't answer an e-mail in the span of 2 days. The person may express this quite dramatically, or may obsess over it. She may feel emotive about an event or issue for a longer period of time than others may. She may "overread" meaning into situations, or become mildly paranoid. Rejection sensitivity is also common—reality checks are helpful! Depressed or anxious people may sometimes think with their feelings more than with their heads. And watch out for the famous "double *I*'s": irritability and impulsivity. They strike in pairs.

Remind your family members of the effort you are making and the importance to you of effective communication with them. What psychologists call "high EE" (expressed emotion) creates negative and even abusive communication patterns. It is a significant trigger for the person with mental illness, and has been shown to exacerbate symptoms and worsen illness severity of the depressed individual. Avoid discussions when they become heated. Emotions are necessary to express, but there are productive and positive ways to do so. Learn when to refuse to continue the discussion until later. It is okay to be assertive and set limits. Silence is a wonderful tool and should be used more often.

When you have something to say but are afraid of becoming overwhelmed by emotions, or that it just won't come out right, consider writing it instead. We are often more thoughtful when we express ourselves in writing. We spend the time to get it down just so. Delivering a written message may help the recipient to be less reactive than if the message were discussed. He will have time to reread, to consider, and to respond. He will appreciate the time and effort spent on writing it and may realize that you are truly serious about the issue and mean what you say. Other family members can do the same: Writing about a sensitive topic can help greatly to alleviate the anxiety surrounding it. Everyone will be more likely to be rational and, if people do vent it may be more therapeutic than damaging. Waiting for the reply encourages patience and reflection.

Spend time and have fun together. Plan family discussion time. An establishment of rituals within the family can be important and helpful. Plan regular family dinners, and do fun things—hike, bike, take a day trip, go to an antique car show or out to hear some jazz. Play board games, or do a puzzle. Our depressed colleague and her parents did many such activities together. In addition to bringing her and her family closer, participating in social activities and getting out of the house discouraged isolation. "When I was really deeply depressed I felt like I was around 8 years old, and my parents must have sensed this, because they took me to all sorts of places I hadn't been to since I was small. We went to the county fair to ride the carnival rides and pet the animals. We went to old restaurants near the town I grew up in, and one I used to go to with my grandmother when I was little. Sometimes this was overstimulating, so we did things at home, too. My mom and dad got out scrapbooks and old pictures and slides. We piled in bed together, ate popcorn, and watched comedies. One of the positive things I got from my depression was a renewed sense of closeness with my family."

Your family can support you in maintaining healthy daily patterns. "One doesn't have to *want* to do things in order to do them. One tip my therapist gave me that I now suggest to my depressed patients is that each day should include both things a person wants to do and things she has to do—at least one small task of each. Discipline builds on successes and fosters self-esteem." Infantilization and spoiling are damaging. The depressed person should have responsibilities of her own, and should try to accomplish small tasks each day, pushing herself to accomplish more or to take on more complex tasks as she recovers. The depressed person should be encouraged to get up and get moving. "It was easy to find something useful, like washing the dishes. Sometimes I would do favors for my mom or dad. Finding something I wanted to do was more difficult, as nothing seemed fun at the time, but my therapist encouraged me to find 'five minutes of joy' each day. I practiced being mindful, getting my mind off of myself and onto things in my surroundings, like sitting near a fish pond, playing with my parents' cat, or seeing how many colors of green I could count in a tree."

Establishing mutual agreements. If you are going to live with your family, work with them to set limits and house rules. Our colleague suggests that expectations should be made concrete rather than vague, or, worse, unexpressed. "Fences are bad news; they create tension. Don't sit on one." Each member of the household should make up her mind regarding what she expects, and follow through assertively. Flexibility is good, but if one is not consistent in approach, the results won't be, either.

Any consequences to lack of observance of house rules should be made very clear and should be perceived as fair to all parties. Mutual agreement rather than control should be the goal here. People with mood disorders may become quite reactive when they feel pushed into a corner, and this isn't healthy for anyone. To avoid anyone's tendency to be coercive when a limit is pushed, it is helpful to have a clear and mutually agreeable verbal "contact"—everyone should be ready to deliver, hold herself and others accountable, and maintain her credibility. The contract should be one everyone will be able to make good on.

Your family can help you to manage your illness. Come up with a plan together. Tell your family and friends what your warning signs are for mania and depression; find subtle and acceptable ways in which they can remind you that you are "doing it again."

You and your family should make an effort to normalize the illness: not in a way that ignores or denies it, but don't blame every good and bad event each day on the illness. Those with bipolar illness, for instance, are able to have genuine anger and joy and to be highly productive or a bit down just as "normal" people are. Normal is defined by an individual, on his own terms—encourage your loved one to do the same. If others compare your expression of well-being and normality with their own or with a perceived societal expectation, you may feel that your individuality is not being honored. If they use this comparison to support a tendency to define you by your diagnosis, this may encourage you to fulfill their expectations by falling into a sick role within the family structure.

Your loved ones can support you in positive thinking. "When I was depressed I did some things that felt sort of embarrassing but really were helpful. I papered my bathroom and the fridge in Post-it notes with embarrassing reminders, sayings, and affirmations. It's actually made me laugh when people came over to visit and I had to explain. I also asked my mother to remind me of positive things often. I couldn't always do it for myself, and found that even if she repeated something 50 times a day I didn't find it demeaning, but rather found it helpful, and it was a constant reminder that she cared about how I felt. My therapist encouraged me to write reminders of positive things, and of gratitude, on flashcards and to carry these with me, and this was somewhat helpful as well."

Your family can work with you to encourage healthy relationships with others, ensuring that they are not the only source of support. They can help you to encourage growth versus chaos. Ask them to remind you about social rhythms (sleep, eating patterns, exercise, social activity, work patterns, leisure activities, self-care, chores, a rhythm to one's day and week, etc.). They can help you to improve your executive function (tasks performed by the prefrontal cortex of the brain) by encouraging decision making, planning and follow-through, and discouraging stagnation or impulsive, unplanned actions.

To hospitalize or to stay home with family? "Twice my psychiatrist asked if I wanted to go to the hospital, and I was at first confused by this until I realized he was making this suggestion simply because he judged my symptoms to be severe. Once he met my family and they expressed their commitment and ability to care for me, and talked about my mother's experience caring for my grandfather during his several periods of depression, my doctor understood I was better off at home with them." At some point you may be in the position to consider hospitalization, which is appropriate for anyone who is a danger to themselves or others, or is incapable of caring for themselves and hasn't sufficient personal resources to obtain care at home.

Hospitals provide safety, treatment, structure to one's day, and a few marginally palatable meals. It is difficult to sleep, however, as hospitals can be noisy, and there is little that is comforting about the atmosphere. Depending on the hospital there will be more or less structure in terms of activities. It may be more or less engaging, satisfying, or productive than being at home. There is little continuity of care: clinicians come and go, and care with them ends when you leave. Treatment may not agree with what your regular clinician would have you do, and that person may not have influence while you're in the hospital. Treatment may be more aggressive than you like, and will be planned by people who do not know you well. Many therapeutic agents may be started at once.

If your family can provide appropriate structure and care in a supportive way that neither infantilizes you nor sets up an antagonizing situation for both parties, you may be better off at home. This is of course realistic in depression; those with psychosis or florid mania may require more structure and professional care.

Your Relationship With the World
Deciding whether to reveal your illness to others is difficult for some. While keeping it a secret may seem to limit risk of stigma expressed by

others, it can foster self-stigma, and may present a barrier to closeness in relationships. Revealing your illness at work present its own challenges.

SELF-DISCLOSURE

Steele and Berman (2001) put it best: "A bold but necessary move, self-disclosure is a first step toward successfully addressing the stigma associated with being mentally ill. Before we can reveal ourselves to others, we have to come out of our own dark closets." The stigma associated with mental illnesses is one of the most persistent problems individuals face. It is fundamental to discrimination in housing, employment, and insurance. It prevents treatment, and it impedes recovery.

Self-disclosure fights stigma. Many people stigmatize mental illness because it is foreign to them, perhaps even frightening. It is something that can happen to anyone, yet they may believe they do not know anyone who lives with a mental illness. People's attitudes improve when they have direct contact with individuals with mental illnesses—when they can get to know people beyond labels and myths.

Self-disclosure also relieves tension for the person living with mental illness. Hiding information and worrying that someone will discover your secrets consumes a lot of personal energy. Telling your story can feel like "coming out of the closet." It also can help give others hope, increase public awareness, and make it easier for others to reveal their own experiences and truths. Self-disclosure may help you to connect with peers and aid in the recovery process.

If you decide to disclose your mental illness, there are a few things to keep in mind. First, it is a good idea to become educated about your illness so that you can educate others. Second, always disclose first to someone you trust, and make sure you feel safe while doing so. Third, remember that sharing can be more or less revealing depending on the individual you are sharing with. You are in control of how much to tell; you will not allow others to manipulate you.

Self-disclosure may have risks. You may doubt your ability to maintain a secret. You may know of people who have had negative ramifications, including discrimination, when they have shared their experiences with others. Indeed, others may label you or make false assumptions about you, and this can damage self-esteem.

Some benefits of disclosure include not having to worry about hiding experiences, and the relief that comes from being more open about your day-to-day experience of living in the world. You may find that others express acceptance, including those with similar experiences, and this can be heartening. You may find allies who can help you in the future. You will be able to increase your sense of personal power and help to fight stigma. Following are some important facts about mental illness that you can mention when talking to other people.

- Mental illness is not contagious.
- Mental illnesses are brain disorders, and they have a strong biological component.
- Mental illness is very common! Psychiatric patients take up more hospital beds than patients with cancer, diabetes, arthritis, and heart disease combined. One out of four families is touched by mental illness, and 20% of the population will experience it within their lifetime. Statistically speaking, this makes mental illness normal!
- Mental illness affects thinking, behavior, feeling, and judgment. The course is unpredictable, and symptoms often fluctuate on a daily basis for some individuals.
- Mental illness is eminently treatable, though it is not curable.
- Individuals with mental illness are rarely dangerous; rather, they generally tend to fear people and be quite introverted. In fact, in the absence of drugs and alcohol, people with mental illness are associated with fewer acts of violence than are people in the general population.

GOING TO WORK

Many people who live with mood disorders have extremely successful careers. Many work and live normal lives. Work is a healthy activity that can increase well-being and give a sense of self-worth. Coping with a mental disorder at work can be challenging, however, so many people choose not to disclose to their supervisor or coworkers.

In considering how you will navigate the workplace while living well with your illness, know that disclosure is within your purview, and you have no obligation to discuss your personal health matters with anyone if you do not wish to do so.

Make sure your job matches your coping skills, however. Arrange to take frequent breaks, or perhaps work a flexible shift. If your job is sometimes challenging for you emotionally, you may consider having at least one person at work whom you trust enough to talk to when times are tough and who can tap you on the shoulder when he noticed symptoms you are not yet picking up on. This is especially important for those living with bipolar disorder, who may not have insight into a hypomanic episode. Have a strong support system outside of work as well, and don't make work your life. It is an important part of your life, but putting all your eggs in one basket may set you up for devastation should you experience disappointment on the job.

17

Learning More:
Books and Web sites

We know that our book can't teach you everything you might want to know about depression, and perhaps you are at a point where you really want to develop a deeper understanding and knowledge of the illness. The reference list here includes books we believe to be some of the most outstanding and newest in a rapidly growing field.

For Psychiatrists

Gabbard, G. (2007). *Gabbard's treatments of psychiatric disorders* (4th ed.). Washington, DC: American Psychiatric Publishing.

Goodwin, F., & Jamison, K. (2007). *Manic-depressive illness: Bipolar disorders and recurrent depression.* New York: Oxford University Press.

Hales, R., Yudofsky, S., & Gabbard, G. (2008). *The American psychiatric publishing textbook of psychiatry* (5th ed.). Washington, DC: American Psychiatric Publishing.

Janicak, P., Davis, J., Preskorn, S., Ayd, F., Marder, S., & Pavuluri, M. (2006). *Principles and practice of psychopharmacotherapy* (4th ed.). Philadelphia: Lippincott Williams & Wilkins.

Saddock, B., & Saddock, V. (Eds.). (2005). *Kaplan and Saddock's comprehensive textbook of psychiatry* (8th ed.). Philadephia: Lippincott Williams & Wilkins.

Schatzberg, A. F., & Nemeroff, C. B. (2009) *The American Psychiatric Publishing textbook of Psychopharmacology* (4th ed.). Arlington, VA: American Psychiatric Publishing.

Stein, D., Kupfer, D., & Schatzberg, A. (2006). *The American Psychiatric Publishing textbook of mood disorders.* Washington, DC: American Psychiatric Publishing.

Stern, T., Rosenbaum, J., Fava, M., Biederman, J., & Rauch, S. (2008). *Massachusetts General Hospital comprehensive clinical psychiatry*. Philadelphia: Mosby Elsevier.

For Everyone

Akiskal, H., & Tohen, M. (2006). *Bipolar psychopharmacotherapy: Caring for the patient*. West Sussex, England: John Wiley & Sons.

Brown, R., Gerbarg, P., & Muskin, P. (2009). *How to use herbs, nutrients and yoga in mental health care*. New York: Norton.

El-Mallakh, R., & Ghaemi, S. (2006). *Bipolar depression: A comprehensive guide*. Washington, DC: American Psychiatric Publishing.

Golant, M., & Golant, S. K. (1998). *What to do when someone you love is depressed: A practical, compassionate, and helpful guide*. New York: Holt.

Greenberger, D., & Padesky, C. (1995). *Mind over mood: A cognitive therapy treatment manual for clients*. New York: Guilford.

Higgins, E., & George, M. (2007). *The neuroscience of clinical psychiatry: The pathophysiology of behavior and mental illness*. Philadephia: Lippincott Williams & Wilkins.

Kelsey, J., Newport, D., & Nemeroff, C. (2006). *Principles of psychopharmacology for mental health professionals*. Hoboken, NJ: John Wiley & Sons.

Kennedy, S., Lam, R., Nutt, D., & Thase M. (2007). *Treating depression effectively: Applying clinical guidelines* (2nd ed). London: Martin Dunitz Informa Health care.

Ketter, T. (2005). *Advances in the treatment of bipolar disorder*. Washington, DC: American Psychiatric Publishing.

Kramer, P. (2005). *Against depression*. London: Viking Penguin.

Miklowitz, J. (2002). *The bipolar disorder survival guide: What you and your family need to know*. New York: Guilford.

Patterson, J., Albala, A., McCahill, M., & Edwards, T. (2006). *The therapist's guide to psychopharmacology: Working with patients, families, and physicians to optimize care*. New York: Guilford.

Phelps, J. (2006). *Why am I still depressed? Recognizing and managing the ups and downs of bipolar II and soft bipolar disorder.* New York: McGraw-Hill.

Post, R., & Leverich, G. (2008). *Treatment of bipolar illness: A casebook for clinicians and patients.* New York: Norton.

Preston, J., O'Neal, J., & Talaga, M. (2008). *Handbook of clinical psychopharmacology for therapists* (5th ed.). Oakland, CA: New Harbinger.

Schatzberg, A., Cole, J., & DeBattista, C. (2007). *Manual of clinical psychopharmacology* (6th ed.). Washington, DC: American Psychiatric Publishing.

Stahl, S. (2008). *Stahl's essential psychopharmacology: Neuroscientific basis and practical applications.* New York: Cambridge University Press.

Williams, M., Teasdale, J., Segal, Z., & Kabat-Zinn, J. (2007). *The mindful way through depression: Freeing yourself from chronic unhappiness.* New York: Guilford.

Web sites

Comprehensive Health Information Sites

FEDERALLY SPONSORED SITES
MedlinePlus, health information from the National Library of Medicine:
www.medlineplus.gov
Healthfinder.gov: *www.healthfinder.gov*
Centers for Disease Control and Prevention: *www.cdc.gov*

COMMERCIAL SITES
WebMD: *www.webmd.com*
MerckMedicus, patient education:
www.merckmedicus.com/pp/us/hcp/templates/tier2/patientEdu.jsp
MerckSource: *mercksource.com/pp/us/cns/cns_home.jsp*
UpToDate Inc., complete and current medical information:
www.uptodate.com/patients/index.html
RealAge, health and wellness:
http://healthlibrary.epnet.com/GetContent.aspx?token=1edc3d6e-4fec-4b20-baca-795e48830daa

Wrong Diagnosis, symptom-based differential diagnosis:
www.wrongdiagnosis.com/

FOR CHILDREN, SENIORS, AND FAMILIES
Familydoctor.org: *http://familydoctor.org/online/famdocen/home.html*
American Association of Retired Persons (AARP):
http://www.aarp.org/health/conditions
American Academy of Pediatrics: *www.aap.org*

Mental Health Information Sites

PRIVATELY HOSTED BY PROVIDERS AND CONSUMERS
Psych Central: *http://psychcentral.com*
Internet Mental Health: *www.mentalhealth.com/*
Psyplexus, mental health information portal: *http://psyplexus.com*
Dr. Ivan's Depression Central: *www.psycom.net/depression.central.html*
Psycheducation.org: *www.psycheducation.org*
Mental Health Today: *www.mental-health-today.com/index.htm*

INFORMATION SPECIFICALLY ON BIPOLAR DISORDERS:
Bipolar Disorder Today, research:
www.mental-health-today.com/bp/network.htm
Pendulum.org, bipolar disorder news, information, and support:
www.pendulum.org
McMan's Depression and Bipolar Web: *www.mcmanweb.com*

COMMERCIAL SITES
Medscape, psychiatry and mental health resource centers:
www.medscape.com/psychiatry/resource
MerckMedicus, psychiatry specialty page:
*www.merckmedicus.com/pp/us/hcp/sp/hcp_sp_template.jsp?specialty-
Name=Psychiatry*
In Psychiatry: *www.inpsychiatry.com*
HealthyPlace.com, mental health information and support:
www.healthyplace.com
Mentalhealthchannel, a mental health community:
www.mentalhealthchannel.net
Merck Manual Home Edition, mental health disorders:
www.merck.com/mmhe/sec07.html?WT.z_section=Mental Health Disorders

Patient-Centered Guides, bipolar disorders center:
www.patientcenters.com/bipolar

FROM SAMHSA
Substance Abuse and Mental Health Services Administration
(SAMHSA), mental health information center:
http://mentalhealth.samhsa.gov/
SAMHSA, mental health links:
http://mentalhealth.samhsa.gov/links/default2.asp

CULTURALLY COMPETENT PSYCHIATRY
EthnoMed:
http://ethnomed.org
National Center for Cultural Competence:
http://nccc.georgetown.edu/index.html
National Alliance on Mental Illness (NAMI), cultural competence:
www.nami.org/Content/NavigationMenu/Find_Support/Multicultural_Su
pport/Cultural_Competence/Cultural_Competence.htm

INSTITUTES, FOUNDATIONS, AND MENTAL HEALTH
ADVOCACY AND SUPPORT ORGANIZATIONS
American Psychiatric Foundation: *www.psychfoundation.org*
National Alliance on Mental Illness (NAMI), mental health
support, education, and advocacy:
www.nami.org
Depression and Bipolar Support Alliance (DBSA):
www.dbsalliance.org/site/PageServer?pagename=home
International Society of Bipolar Disorders, Education Center:
www.isbd.org/edcenter/edcenter.asp
National Alliance for Research on Schizophrenia
and Affective Disorders (NARSAD):
www.narsad.org/
Postpartum Support International: *www.postpartum.net*
Anxiety Disorders Association of America (ADAA):
www.adaa.org/
National Anxiety Foundation: *www.lexington-on-line.com/naf.html*
Dana Foundation, information about brain research:
www.dana.org

CHILD AND ADOLESCENT MENTAL HEALTH
National Institute of Mental Health (NIMH),
child and adolescent mental health:
www.nimh.nih.gov/health/topics/child-and-adolescent-mental-health/index.shtml
National Federation of Families for Children's Mental Health:
www.ffcmh.org
It's Allright, real stories about mental illness for adolescents:
www.itsallright.org
Child and Adolescent Bipolar Foundation (CABF): *www.bpkids.org*
Juvenile Bipolar Research Foundation: *www.bpchildresearch.org*

Substance Abuse

INFORMATION
Federally Sponsored Sites
Substance Abuse and Mental Health Services Administration
(SAMHSA):
http://samhsa.gov
SAMHSA's National Clearinghouse for Alcohol and Drug Information:
http://ncadi.samhsa.gov/
National Institute on Alcohol Abuse and Alcoholism:
www.niaaa.nih.gov
National Institute on Drug Abuse: *www.nida.nih.gov/*
National Council on Alcoholism and Drug Dependence (NCCAD):
http://ncadd.org/
Partnership for a Drugfree America: *www.drugfree.org/*

Commercial Sites
Streetdrugs.org: *www.streetdrugs.org*
The Good Drugs Guide:
www.thegooddrugsguide.com/

Harm Reduction
Harm Reduction Coalition: *www.harmreduction.org*
International Harm Reduction Association: *www.ihra.net/*

ADDICTION RECOVERY
Support for Recovery
Faces and Voices of Recovery, mutual support resources:
www.facesandvoicesofrecovery.org/resources/support_home.php
SoberRecovery: *www.soberrecovery.com/*

12-Step Organizations
Alcoholics Anonymous (AA): *www.aa.org*
Narcotics Anonymous (NA): www.na.org
Alanon and Alateen www.al-anon.alateen.org

Directories of Self-Help Recovery Groups
12 Step Cafe: *www.12steps.org/*
Save OurSelves (SOS), secular sobriety: *www.sossobriety.org/*
Open Directory, health/addictions: *www.dmoz.org/Health/Addictions*
Addiction and Substance Abuse Organizations:
*http://en.wikipedia.org/wiki/Category:Addiction_and_substance_
abuse_organizations*

Trauma
International Society for the Study of Trauma and Dissociation
(ISSTD): www.isst-d.org
The International Society for Traumatic Stress Studies (ISTSS):
www.istss.org
Sidran Institute, traumatic stress education and advocacy:
www.sidran.org
Child Trauma Academy: *www.childtrauma.org/*
Gift From Within, information on PTSD and healing:
www.giftfromwithin.org
Adult Survivors of Child Abuse (ASCA): *www.ascasupport.org*
Survivors Art Foundation, healing through art, art through healing:
www.survivorsartfoundation.org

PTSD SPECIFIC
National Center for PTSD: *www.ptsd.va.gov*
Post Traumatic Stress Disorder Gateway: *www.ptsdinfo.org*
National Center for PTSD: *http://ncptsd.va.gov/ncmain/index.jsp*

Post Traumatic Stress Disorder Today:
www.mental-health-today.com/ptsd/

Suicide and Self-Injury

SUICIDE
Societies and Foundations
American Foundation for Suicide Prevention (AFSP): *www.afsp.org*
American Association of Suicidology:
www.suicidology.org/web/guest/home

Prevention
Stop a Suicide Today: *www.stopasuicide.org/*
National Suicide Prevention Lifeline: *www.suicidepreventionlifeline.org*
Mental Health Today, suicide prevention and hotline:
www.mental-health-today.com/suicide
Suicide Awareness Voices of Education (SAVE): *www.save.org*
Suicide, read this first: *www.metanoia.org/suicide*

DELIBERATE SELF-HARM
American Self-Harm Information Clearinghouse:
http://selfinjury.org/indexnet.html
S.A.F.E. Alternatives, self abuse finally ends: *www.selfinjury.com*
Secret Shame, self-injury information and support: *www.selfharm.net/*
Self-injury.net, a support community for self-injurers:
http://self-injury.net
Dialectical Behavior Therapy (DBT) Self Help: *www.dbtselfhelp.com/*

Treatment

MEDICATIONS AND PSYCHOTHERAPY
Sites Specific to Medications
Dr. Bob's Psychopharmacology Tips: *www.dr-bob.org/tips/intro.html*
Dr. Bob's Psycho-Babble, discussion board: *www.dr-bob.org/babble*
The United States Pharmacopeial Convention: *www.usp.org*
National Council on Patient Information and Education (NCPIE):
www.talkaboutrx.org/index.jsp
SafeMedication.com, from the American Society of Health-System
Pharmacists (ASHP): *www.safemedication.com*

Consumer Reports, Best Buy Drugs:
www.consumerreports.org/health/best-buy-drugs/index.htm
WorstPills.org, expert, independent second opinion for prescription
drug information: *www.worstpills.org/*

Sites Specific to Psychotherapy
American Psychological Association (APA): *www.apa.org*
Fenichel's Current Topics in Psychology:
www.fenichel.com/Current.shtml
A Guide to Psychology and Its Practice, consumer information about
clinical psychology: *http://www.guidetopsychology.com*

ECT
ECT.org, electroconvulsive therapy information and support:
www.ect.org/
Mental Health America, Position Statement 34, ECT:
www.mentalhealthamerica.net/go/position-statements/34

TREATMENT GUIDELINES
National Guideline Clearinghouse: *www.guideline.gov*
American Psychiatric Association Practice Guidelines:
psych.org/psych_pract/treatg/pg/prac_guide.cfm
Expert Consensus Guidelines: *www.psychguides.com*
Texas Implementation of Medication Algorithms:
www.dshs.state.tx.us/mhprograms/TIMA.shtm
American Academy of Child and Adolescent Psychiatry (AACAD),
practice parameters: *www.aacap.org/page.ww?section=Practice+Parame-*
ters&name=Practice+Parameters

Accessing Treatment
FIND A DOCTOR OR TREATMENT CENTER
American Medical Association (AMA), Doctor Finder:
www0.ama-assn.org/apps/captcha/verify.cgi?reason=nocookie&
method=GET&url=https://extapps.ama-assn.org/doctorfinder/home.jsp
U.S. Department of Health and Human Services, Health Resources and
Services Administration (HRSA), Find a Health Center:
http://findahealthcenter.hrsa.gov

SAMHSA's National Mental Health Information Center,
mental health services locator:
http://mentalhealth.samhsa.gov/databases
SAMHSA, substance abuse treatment facility locator:
http://dasis3.samhsa.gov

FIND A THERAPIST
American Psychological Association, find a psychologist:
http://locator.apa.org
American Association for Marriage and Family Therapy, therapist
locator: *www.therapistlocator.net/*
GoodTherapy.org: *www.goodtherapy.org*
1-800-therapist.com: *www.1-800-therapist.com/about-us*
4therapy.com Network: *www.4therapy.com/*

JOIN A CLINICAL TRIAL
ClinicalTrials.gov: *www.clinicaltrials.gov*
Centerwatch Clinical Trials Listing Service: *http://centerwatch.com/*
Trials Central: *www.trialscentral.org/*
Search Clinical Trials, center for information and
study on clinical research participation:
www.searchclinicaltrials.org/fastsearch/searchform.asp

AFFORDING TREATMENT
Medicaid and Medicare Insurance Plans
Medicare.gov, the official U.S. government site for people with
medicare: *www.medicare.gov/*
Medicare.gov, premiums and coinsurance rates:
http://questions.medicare.gov/cgi-bin/medicare.cfg/php/
enduser/std_adp.php?p_faqid=2100
Centers for Medicare and Medicaid Services: *www.cms.hhs.gov*
American Assoication of Retired Persons (AARP):
www.aarp.org/health/insurance

Medications: Coverage and Guidance
Medicare Prescription Drug Plan Finder:
www.medicare.gov/MPDPF/Public/Include/DataSection/Questions/MPDPF
Intro.asp?version=default&browser=Firefox%7C3%7CMacOSX&language=
English&defaultstatus=0&pagelist=Home&ViewType=Public&PDPYear=20
09&MAPDYear=200

Centers for Medicare and Medicaid Services,
prescription drug coverage:
www.cms.hhs.gov/PrescriptionDrugCovGenIn
MSNBC, ten tips to spend less on prescription drugs:
www.msnbc.msn.com/id/24490488

Medications: Assistance Programs
NeedyMeds: *www.needymeds.org*
Partnership for Prescription Assistance: *www.pparx.org*
RxAssist: *www.rxassist.org*
PatientAssistance.com: *www.patientassistance.com*
RxHope: *www.rxhope.com*
Access2wellness.com: *www.access2wellness.com/a2w/index.html*
Free Medicine Program: *www.freemedicineprogram.org*
Mental Health Today, guide to prescription assistance programs:
www.mental-health-today.com/rxassist.htm
Mental Health Today, state and local prescription assistance programs:
www.mental-health-today.com/statemeds.htm

Drug Discount Card Programs
Mental Health Today, drug discount card programs:
www.mental-health-today.com/rxcards.htm
AARP Prescription Discount Program:
www.aarphealthcare.com/products/rxdiscounts/default.aspx
Peoples Prescription Plan: *www.peoplesrxcard.com*
Walgreens Prescription Savings Club:
https://webapp.walgreens.com/MYWCARDWeb/servlet/
walgreens.wcard.proxy.WCardInternetProxy/RxSavingsRH?
AARP Prescription Discount Program:
www.aarphealthcare.com/products/rxdiscounts/default.aspx

COMPLEMENTARY AND ALTERNATIVE MEDICINE
National Institutes of Health, National Center for
Complementary and Alternative Medicine:
http://nccam.nih.gov/health
MedlinePlus, complementary and alternative medicine:
www.nlm.nih.gov/medlineplus/complementaryandalternativemedicine.html

MedlinePlus, complementary and alternative therapies:
www.nlm.nih.gov/medlineplus/complementaryandalternativetherapies.html
SAMHSA, alternative approaches to mental health care:
http://mentalhealth.samhsa.gov/publications/allpubs/ken98-
0044/default.asp
BioMed Central (BMC) Complementary and Alternative Medicine:
www.biomedcentral.com/1472-6882
Alternative Medicine Foundation: *www.amfoundation.org/index.htm*
ConsumerLab.com, independent tests of herbal, vitamin, and mineral
supplements: *www.consumerlab.com/tnp.asp*
Medfinds, holistic medicine directory: *www.medfinds.com*

Dietary Supplements
National Institutes of Health, Office of Dietary Supplements (ODS):
http://dietary-supplements.info.nih.gov
ODS, dietary supplement fact sheets:
http://ods.od.nih.gov/Health_Information/Information_About
_Individual_Dietary_Supplements.aspx
MedlinePlus, all herbs and supplements:
www.nlm.nih.gov/medlineplus/druginfo/herb_All.html
National Library of Medicine, Dietary Supplements Labels Database:
http://dietarysupplements.nlm.nih.gov/dietary
American Botanical Council:
http://abc.herbalgram.org/site/PageServer?pagename=Homepage

Information From the U.S. Food and Drug Administration (FDA)
FDA, consumer information on dietary supplements:
www.fda.gov/Food/DietarySupplements/ConsumerInformation/default.htm
FDA, dietary supplements: *www.fda.gov/Food/DietarySupplements*
FDA, dietary supplement alerts and safety information:
www.fda.gov/Food/DietarySupplements/Alerts/default.htm

Information From the Food and Nutrition Information Center (FNIC)
FNIC, dietary supplements:
http://fnic.nal.usda.gov/nal_display/index.php?tax_level=1&info_center=4
&tax_subject=274

FNIC, dietary supplement information for consumers:
*http://fnic.nal.usda.gov/nal_display/index.php?info_center=4&tax_level=3
&tax_subject=358&topic_id=1611&level3_id=5964&level4_id=0&level5
_id=0&placement_default=0*
USDA Nutrient Data Laboratory, search the USDA
National Nutrient Database for standard reference:
www.nal.usda.gov/fnic/foodcomp/search

Interaction Checkers
Medfinds Interaction Checkers, data from Healthnotes by Aisle7.com:
www.medfinds.com/healthnotes.php?contentid=2411003
ConsumerLab.com, interaction checker:
www.consumerlab.com/tnp.asp?chunkiid=33801

Accessing Treatment
NCCAM, paying for CAM treatment:
http://nccam.nih.gov/health/financial
NCCAM, clinical trials: *http://nccam.nih.gov/research/clinicaltrials*

Research Databases
NCCAM Clearinghouse: *http://nccam.nih.gov/health/clearinghouse/*
NCCAM, CAM on PubMed:
http://nccam.nih.gov/research/camonpubmed
ODS, International Bibliographic Information on
Dietary Supplements (IBIDS) database:
http://ods.od.nih.gov/Health_Information/IBIDS.aspx
ODS, Computer Access to Research on
Dietary Supplements (CARDS) Database:
http://dietary-supplements.info.nih.gov/Research/CARDS_Database.aspx
Division of Drug Information Service, University of
Iowa College of Pharmacy, herbal links:
www.uiowa.edu/~idis/herbalinks

Buyer Beware
National Council Against Health Fraud: *www.ncahf.org*
Quackwatch, Guide to Quackery, Health Fraud,
and Intelligent Decisions: *www.quackwatch.org*

Prominent Mood Disorders Research Projects
Sequenced Treatment Alternatives to Relieve Depression (STAR*D):
www.edc.pitt.edu/stard/public/index.html
Stanley Medical Research Institute:
www.stanleyresearch.org/dnn/CenterforPsychiatricResearch/
tabid/103/Default.aspx
Systematic Treatment Enhancement Program for
Bipolar Disorder (STEP-BD): *www.stepbd.org*
Bipolar Genetics Collaboration: *www.bipolargenes.org*

Self-Help and Recovery-Oriented Sites

EMPOWERMENT, EDUCATION, ADVOCACY, COMMUNITY
National Mental Health Association's Mental Health
America, advocacy, public education, support:
www.mentalhealthamerica.net
National Empowerment Center: *www.power2u.org/*
Center for Psychiatric Rehabilitation, Boston University,
Repository of Recovery Resources:
www.bu.edu/cpr/repository/index.html
Psybersquare, strength and health through community and self-help:
www.psybersquare.com
National Mental Health Consumers' Self-Help Clearinghouse:
www.mhselfhelp.org
Harbor of Refuge, bipolar disorder support: *www.harbor-of-refuge.org*
Bipolar Significant Others: *www.bpso.org*

ILLNESS SELF-MANAGEMENT
Recovery Inc., Abraham Low Self-Help Systems:
www.recovery-inc.com
Wellness Recovery Action Plan (WRAP), Mary Ellen Copeland:
www.mentalhealthrecovery.com
Bipolar Happens: Straight Talk on Managing Bipolar Disorder:
www.bipolarhappens.com

SUPPORT GROUP LISTINGS
Mental Help Net, self-help sourcebook online:
www.mentalhelp.net/selfhelp

MedHelp, American Self Help Clearinghouse Support Groups:
www.medhelp.org/support-groups/index.html
MerckMedicus, patient support groups:
www.merckmedicus.com/pp/us/hcp/hcp_patient_support.jsp

PUT AN END TO STIGMA
SAMHSA's Resource Center to Promote Acceptance, Dignity and
Social Inclusion Associated With Mental Health (ADS Center):
www.adscenter.org

Disability, Employment, and Legal information
Disability.gov, connecting the disability community to
information and opportunities: *Disability.gov*
The Arc of the United States:
www.thearc.org/NetCommunity/Page.aspx?pid=183
American Disability Association: *www.adanet.org*
National Disability Rights Network: *www.napas.org*
The Disability Online Resource Centre: *www.disability-online.com*

DISABILITY AND THE LAW
Bazelon Center for Mental Health Law, advocating for the
civil rights and human dignity of people with mental disabilities:
www.bazelon.org
American Bar Association, Commission on Mental and Physical
Disability Law: *www.abanet.org/disability*
National Resource Center on Psychiatric Advance Directives:
www.nrc-pad.org
National Special Needs Network, Inc., supplemental needs trusts:
www.nsnn.com/frequently.htm

DISABILITY AT WORK AND AT SCHOOL
AHEAD (Association on Higher Education and Disability):
www.ahead.org/
Health Resource Center, online clearinghouse on
postsecondary education for individuals with disabilities:
www.heath.gwu.edu
Social Security Online, The Work Site: *www.ssa.gov/work*

The U.S. Equal Employment Opportunity Commission,
The Americans With Disabilities Act (ADA),
employment rights as an individual with a disability:
www.eeoc.gov/facts/ada18.html
The Job Accommodation Network: *www.jan.wvu.edu*
Patient-Centered Guides, Bipolar Disorders at Work:
www.patientcenters.com/news/bipolar_work.html

News Sources
AGGREGATED MENTAL HEALTH NEWS
Mdlinx.com: *www.mdlinx.com/psychlinx/*
Medscape Psychiatry and Mental Health: *www.medscape.com/psychiatry*
PsychiatryMatters.MD:
www.psychiatrymatters.md/index.asp?C=29874400556936805556
MedWire News, Psychiatry:
www.medwire-news.md/47/Psychiatry.html
In Psychiatry, Psychiatry News: *www.inpsychiatry.com/news/default.aspx*
American Psychological Association, Psychology Newswire:
www.apa.org/news/psycport/index.aspx
ScienceDaily, Mind and Brain News:
www.sciencedaily.com/news/mind_brain
Mental Health Matters: *www.mental-health-matters.com*

PERIODICALS
The Carlat Psychiatry Report: *www.thecarlatreport.com*
Psychiatric Times, American Psychiatric Association's newspaper:
www.psychiatrictimes.com/home?verify=0
Bipolar Disorder Magazine: *www.bphope.com/*

EXCELLENT RADIO SHOWS ON MENTAL HEALTH
The Infinite Mind programs: *www.lcmedia.com/mindprgm.htm*
All in the Mind: *www.abc.net.au/rn/allinthemind/*

Reference
DSM DIAGNOSTIC CRITERIA AND CODES
Psych Central, *DSM-IV* codes/diagnoses:
http://psychcentral.com/disorders/dsmcodes.htm

Psych Central, *DSM-IV* Mental Disorders Index:
http://psychcentral.com/disorders
Psychnet, complete list of *DSM-IV* codes:
www.psychnet-uk.com/dsm_iv/_misc/complete_tables.htm
Psychnet, *DSM-IV* Disorder Information Index:
www.psychnet-uk.com/dsm_iv/dsm_iv_index.htm

SYSTEMATIC REVIEWS AND EVIDENCE REPORTS
The Cochrane Collaboration, Home of the Cochrane Library and
Cochrane Reviews: *www.cochrane.org/reviews/clibintro.htm*
Cochrane Library, advanced search:
http://mrw.interscience.wiley.com/cochrane/cochrane_search_fs.html
Agency for Healthcare Research and Quality (AHRQ),
EPC Evidence Reports: *www.ahrq.gov/clinic/epcindex.htm*

GUIDES TO EVALUATION OF WEB SITES AND SCIENTIFIC LITERATURE
HON Code, Health on the Net Foundation: *www.hon.ch/*
Healthfinder.gov, quality of health information:
www.healthfinder.gov/scripts/SearchContext.asp?topic=14310&section=5
World Health Organization, Medical Products and
the Internet—A Guide to Finding Reliable Information:
http://apps.who.int/medicinedocs/en/d/Js2277e/
National Institutes of Health, National Center for Complementary and
Alternative Medicine, Evaluating Web-Based Health Resources:
http://nccam.nih.gov/health/webresources/
National Institutes of Health, Office of Dietary Supplements, How to
Evaluate Health Information on the Internet:
*http://ods.od.nih.gov/Health_Information/How_To_Evaluate_Health_Infor
mation_on_the_Internet_Questions_and_Answers.aspx*

LIBRARY, DICTIONARY, GLOSSARY, LEXICA
National Library of Medicine, National Institutes of Health:
www.nlm.nih.gov
PubMed: *www.ncbi.nlm.nih.gov/pubmed*
Online Dictionary of Mental Health: *http://human-nature.com/odmh*
American Psychological Association, Glossary of Psychological Terms:
www.apa.org/research/action/glossary.aspx

FDA, acronyms and abbreviations:
www.accessdata.fda.gov/scripts/cder/acronyms/index.cfm
MediLexicon, medical dictionary, medical abbreviations, and other
search engines: *www.medilexicon.com*

HEALTH STATISTICS
Mental Health, A Report of the Surgeon General:
www.surgeongeneral.gov/library/mentalhealth/home.html
World Health Organization Statistical Information System (WHOSIS):
www.who.int/whosis/en/
Office of Disease Prevention and Health
Promotion, Healthy People 2010:
www.healthypeople.gov
U.S. Department of Health and Human Services,
National Center for Health Statistics:
www.hhs-stat.net/scripts/orgurl.cfm?orgabb=NCHS

Epilogue

Mental health clinician and patient are a team battling depression together. Sometimes they may need to call on the psychotherapist, psychiatrist, internist, pastor, significant other, family members, close friends, and depression support group for their support and guidance. A second opinion may also be sought and is worthwhile if things are not improving as expected. A good clinician welcomes and learns from this to the benefit of his patient.

Ingredients essential to achieving wellness and lasting good benefit from treatment include getting off on the right foot with a full data set. The more information a clinician has to work with, the better she can know the patient and make informed decisions. There should be no hidden secrets from the clinician, or important pieces of information forgotten. The patient may utilize the tools provided in this book to create a comprehensive history for the clinician, who should also have full access to past treatment records, family history, and awareness of all problem areas, whether or not they are the focus of treatment.

Patience and persistence are essential. There are no drugs without side effects, and often successful treatment requires a series of medication trials. More than one medication may be required to get better, and to stay well. An attitude toward maintaining wellness as well as treating acute depression is essential. Please don't change or stop medications when feeling better, especially without discussing it with the psychiatrist, because lifelong disorders usually require lifelong treatment. You now understand also how important psychotherapy can be in this journey. You know that it is more than talking; it is an active process of working on self-discovery and changing thoughts, feelings, and behaviors that requires hard work. To complement medications and psychotherapy, a healthy lifestyle combining diet, exercise, stress management, rest, spiritual life, meaningful relationships, and work are all part of minimizing the lifelong impact of depression or bipolar affective disorder.

Getting and staying well can be a cathartic and rewarding experience. It may offer you challenges but also rewards you had not anticipated. We sometimes ask patients to think about what their illness has done for them. Beyond the pain there lie gifts.

Never give up hope! The approaches we have outlined in this book may be skillfully combined to improve depression and regain a fulfilling quality of life.

References

Abou-Saleh, M. T., & Coppen, A. (2006). Folic acid and the treatment of depression. *Journal of Psychosomatic Research, 61*(3), 285–287.

Abraham, G., Milev, R., & Stuart Lawson, J. (2006). T3 augmentation of SSRI resistant depression. *Journal of Affective Disorders, 91*(2–3), 211–215.

Accornero, F. (1988). An eyewitness account of the discovery of electroshock. *Convulsive Therapy, 4*(1), 40–49.

Administration for Children and Families. (2006). National Child Abuse and Neglect Data System. In D.o.H.a.H. Services (Eds.). Available from http://www.acf.hhs.gov/programs/cb/pubs/cm06/cm06.pdf

AHRQ. (2000). Milk thistle: effects on liver disease and cirrhosis and clinical adverse effects. Summary, Evidence Report/Technology Assessment: Number 21 Retrieved February 2, 2010, from http://www.ahrq.gov/clinic/epcsums/milktsum.htm

Aikens, J. E., Nease, D. E., Jr. , & Klinkman, M. S. (2008). Explaining patients' beliefs about the necessity and harmfulness of antidepressants. *Annals of Family Medicine, 6*(1), 23–29.

Akiskal, H. S. (1996). The prevalent clinical spectrum of bipolar disorders: Beyond DSM-IV. *Journal of Clinical Psychopharmacology, 16*(2 Suppl 1), 4S–14S.

Akiskal, H. S., & Benazzi, F. (2003). Family history validation of the bipolar nature of depressive mixed states. *Journal of Affective Disorders, 73*(1–2), 113–122.

Akiskal, H. S., Benazzi, F., Perugi, G., & Rihmer, Z. (2005). Agitated "unipolar" depression re-conceptualized as a depressive mixed state: Implications for the antidepressant-suicide controversy. *Journal of Affective Disorders, 85*(3), 245–258.

Akopian, V. P., Balian, L. S., & Avetisian, N. A. (2006). [The effect of hypokinesia on depression and on the central GABA-A receptor complexes in the rat brain]. *Eksperimentalnaia i Klinicheskaia Farmakologiia, 69*(2), 10–13.

Allain, H., Schuck, S., Lebreton, S., Strenge-Hesse, A., Braun, W., Gandon, J. M., et al. (1999). Aminotransferase levels and silymarin in de novo tacrine-treated patients with Alzheimer's disease. *Dementia and Geriatric Cognitive Disorders, 10*(3), 181–185.

Allott, P., Loganathan, L., & Fulford, K. W. M. (2002). Discovering hope for recovery. *Canadian Journal of Community Mental Health, 21*(2), 13–34.

Alpert, J. E., Mischoulon, D., Rubenstein, G. E., Bottonari, K., Nierenberg, A. A., & Fava, M. (2002). Folinic acid (Leucovorin) as an adjunctive treatment for SSRI-refractory depression. *Annals of Clinical Psychiatry, 14*(1), 33–38.

Alpert, J. E., Papakostas, G., Mischoulon, D., Worthington, J. J., 3rd, Petersen, T., Mahal, Y., et al. (2004). S-adenosyl-L-methionine (SAMe) as an adjunct for resistant major depressive disorder: An open trial following partial or nonresponse to selective serotonin reuptake inhibitors or venlafaxine. *Journal of Clinical Psychopharmacology, 24*(6), 661–664.

Alpert, M., Silva, R. R., & Pouget, E. R. (2003). Prediction of treatment response in geriatric depression from baseline folate level: Interaction with an SSRI or a tricyclic antidepressant. *Journal of Clinical Psychopharmacology, 23*(3), 309–313.

Altamura, C., Maes, M., Dai, J., & Meltzer, H. Y. (1995). Plasma concentrations of excitatory amino acids, serine, glycine, taurine and histidine in major depression. *European Neuropsychopharmacology, 5*(Suppl), 71–75.

Altshuler, L., Kiriakos, L., Calcagno, J., Goodman, R., Gitlin, M., Frye, M., et al. (2001). The impact of antidepressant discontinuation versus antidepressant continuation on 1-year risk for relapse of bipolar depression: A retrospective chart review. *Journal of Clinical Psychiatry, 62*(8), 612–616.

Altshuler, L., Suppes, T., Black, D., Nolen, W. A., Keck, P. E., Jr. , Frye, M. A., et al. (2003). Impact of antidepressant discontinuation after acute bipolar depression remission on rates of depressive relapse at 1-year follow-up. *American Journal of Psychiatry, 160*(7), 1252–1262.

Altshuler, L. L., Cohen, L. S., Moline, M. L., Kahn, D. A., Carpenter, D., & Docherty, J. P. (2001a). The Expert Consensus Guideline Series. Treatment of depression in women. *Postgraduate Medicine* (Spec. No.), 1–107.

Altshuler, L. L., Cohen, L. S., Moline, M. L., Kahn, D. A., Carpenter, D., Docherty, J. P., et al. (2001b). Treatment of depression in women: A summary of the expert consensus guidelines. *Journal of Psychiatric Practice, 7*(3), 185–208.

Amsterdam, J. D. (2003). A double-blind, placebo-controlled trial of the safety and efficacy of selegiline transdermal system without dietary restrictions in patients with major depressive disorder. *Journal of Clinical Psychiatry, 64*(2), 208–214.

Amsterdam, J. D., & Bodkin, J. A. (2006). Selegiline transdermal system in the prevention of relapse of major depressive disorder: A 52-week, double-blind, placebo-substitution, parallel-group clinical trial. *Journal of Clinical Psychopharmacology, 26*(6), 579–586.

Amsterdam, J. D., & Brunswick, D. J. (2003). Antidepressant monotherapy for bipolar type II major depression. *Bipolar Disorders, 5*(6), 388–395.

Amsterdam, J. D., Garcia-Espana, F., Fawcett, J., Quitkin, F. M., Reimherr, F. W., Rosenbaum, J. F., et al. (1998). Efficacy and safety of fluoxetine in treating bipolar II major depressive episode. *Journal of Clinical Psychopharmacology*, *18*(6), 435–440.

Amsterdam, J. D., & Shults, J. (2005). Fluoxetine monotherapy of bipolar type II and bipolar NOS major depression: A double-blind, placebo-substitution, continuation study. *International Clinical Psychopharmacology*, *20*(5), 257–264.

Amsterdam, J. D., Shults, J., Brunswick, D. J., & Hundert, M. (2004). Short-term fluoxetine monotherapy for bipolar type II or bipolar NOS major depression—low manic switch rate. *Bipolar Disorders*, *6*(1), 75–81.

Anderson, I. M. (1998). SSRIS versus tricyclic antidepressants in depressed inpatients: A meta-analysis of efficacy and tolerability. *Depression and Anxiety*, *7*(Suppl. 1), 11–17.

Anderson, I. M. (2000). Selective serotonin reuptake inhibitors versus tricyclic antidepressants: A meta-analysis of efficacy and tolerability. *Journal of Affective Disorders*, *58*(1), 19–36.

Andrade, S. E., Raebel, M. A., Brown, J., Lane, K., Livingston, J., Boudreau, D., et al. (2008). Use of antidepressant medications during pregnancy: A multisite study. *American Journal of Obstetrics and Gynecology*, *198*(2), 191–195.

Andrews, P., & Martin, L. (1991). Hominoid dietary evolution. *Philosophical Transactions of the Royal Society of London, Series B*, *334*, 199–209, discussion 209.

Angelucci, F., Aloe, L., Jimenez-Vasquez, P., & Mathe, A. A. (2003). Lithium treatment alters brain concentrations of nerve growth factor, brain-derived neurotrophic factor and glial cell line-derived neurotrophic factor in a rat model of depression. *International Journal of Neuropsychopharmacology*, *6*(3), 225–231.

Angst, J. (1998). The emerging epidemiology of hypomania and bipolar II disorder. *Journal of Affective Disorders*, *50*(2–3), 143–151.

Appleton, K. M., Hayward, R. C., Gunnell, D., Peters, T. J., Rogers, P. J., Kessler, D., et al. (2006). Effects of n-3 long-chain polyunsaturated fatty acids on depressed mood: Systematic review of published trials. *American Journal of Clinical Nutrition*, *84*(6), 1308–1316.

Appleton, K. M., Rogers, P. J., & Ness, A. R. (2008). Is there a role for n-3 long-chain polyunsaturated fatty acids in the regulation of mood and behaviour? A review of the evidence to date from epidemiological studies, clinical studies and intervention trials. *Nutritional Research Review*, *21*(1), 13–41.

Appleton, K. M., Rogers, P. J., & Ness, A. R. (2010). Updated systematic review and meta-analysis of the effects of n-3 long-chain polyunsaturated fatty acids on depressed mood. *American Journal of Clinical Nutrition*, *91*(3), 757–770.

Arango, V., Ernsberger, P., Sved, A. F., & Mann, J. J. (1993). Quantitative autoradiography of alpha 1- and alpha 2-adrenergic receptors in the cerebral cortex of controls and suicide victims. *Brain Research, 630*(1–2), 271–282.

Armstrong, D. J., Meenagh, G. K., Bickle, I., Lee, A. S., Curran, E. S., & Finch, M. B. (2007). Vitamin D deficiency is associated with anxiety and depression in fibromyalgia. *Clinical Rheumatology, 26*(4), 551–554.

Arnold, L. M. (2007). Duloxetine and other antidepressants in the treatment of patients with fibromyalgia. *Pain Medicine, 8*(Suppl. 2), S63–S74.

Arnold, L. M., Lu, Y., Crofford, L. J., Wohlreich, M., Detke, M. J., Iyengar, S., et al. (2004). A double-blind, multicenter trial comparing duloxetine with placebo in the treatment of fibromyalgia patients with or without major depressive disorder. *Arthritis and Rheumatism, 50*(9), 2974–2984.

Arnold, L. M., Pritchett, Y. L., D'Souza, D. N., Kajdasz, D. K., Iyengar, S., & Wernicke, J. F. (2007). Duloxetine for the treatment of fibromyalgia in women: Pooled results from two randomized, placebo-controlled clinical trials. *Journal of Women's Health, 16*(8), 1145–1156.

Arnold, L. M., Rosen, A., Pritchett, Y. L., D'Souza, D. N., Goldstein, D. J., Iyengar, S., et al. (2005). A randomized, double-blind, placebo-controlled trial of duloxetine in the treatment of women with fibromyalgia with or without major depressive disorder. *Pain, 119*(1–3), 5–15.

Arnold, O., Saletu, B., Anderer, P., Assandri, A., di Padova, C., Corrado, M., et al. (2005). Double-blind, placebo-controlled pharmacodynamic studies with a nutraceutical and a pharmaceutical dose of ademetionine (SAMe) in elderly subjects, utilizing EEG mapping and psychometry. *European Neuropsychopharmacology, 15*(5), 533–543.

Aronson, R., Offman, H. J., Joffe, R. T., & Naylor, C. D. (1996). Triiodothyronine augmentation in the treatment of refractory depression. A meta-analysis. *Archives of General Psychiatry, 53*(9), 842–848.

Ashina, S., Bendtsen, L., & Jensen, R. (2004). Analgesic effect of amitriptyline in chronic tension-type headache is not directly related to serotonin reuptake inhibition. *Pain, 108*(1–2), 108–114.

Astin, J. A. (2004). Mind-body therapies for the management of pain. *Clinical Journal of Pain, 20*(1), 27–32.

Atack, J. R., Broughton, H. B., & Pollack, S. J. (1995). Inositol monophosphatase—a putative target for Li+ in the treatment of bipolar disorder. *Trends in Neuroscience, 18*(8), 343–349.

Austin, M. P., Frilingos, M., Lumley, J., Hadzi-Pavlovic, D., Roncolato, W., Acland, S., et al. (2008). Brief antenatal cognitive behaviour therapy group intervention for the prevention of postnatal depression and anxiety: A randomised controlled trial. *Journal of Affective Disorders, 105*(1–3), 35–44.

Avery, D., Lenz, M., & Landis, C. (1998). Guidelines for prescribing melatonin. *Annals of Medicine, 30*(1), 122–130.

Axentsev, S., Corrado, M., Basch, E., Boon, H., Grimes Serrano, J., Hammerness, P., et al. (2010). Melatonin, Monograph. Retrieved February 2, 2010, from Natural Standard Database: http://www.naturalstandard.com/monographs/herbssupplements/melatonin.asp?printversion=true

Azzaro, A. J., Vandenberg, C. M., Blob, L. F., Kemper, E. M., Sharoky, M., Oren, D. A., et al. (2006). Tyramine pressor sensitivity during treatment with the selegiline transdermal system 6 mg/24 h in healthy subjects. *Journal of Clinical Pharmacology, 46*(8), 933–944.

Azzaro, A. J., VanDenBerg, C. M., Ziemniak, J., Kemper, E. M., Blob, L. F., & Campbell, B. J. (2007). Evaluation of the potential for pharmacodynamic and pharmacokinetic drug interactions between selegiline transdermal system and two sympathomimetic agents (pseudoephedrine and phenylpropanolamine) in healthy volunteers. *Journal of Clinical Pharmacology, 47*(8), 978–990.

Azzaro, A. J., Ziemniak, J., Kemper, E., Campbell, B. J., & VanDenBerg, C. (2007a). Pharmacokinetics and absolute bioavailability of selegiline following treatment of healthy subjects with the selegiline transdermal system (6 mg/24 h): A comparison with oral selegiline capsules. *Journal of Clinical Pharmacology, 47*(10), 1256–1267.

Azzaro, A. J., Ziemniak, J., Kemper, E., Campbell, B. J., & VanDenBerg, C. (2007b). Selegiline transdermal system: An examination of the potential for CYP450-dependent pharmacokinetic interactions with 3 psychotropic medications. *Journal of Clinical Pharmacology, 47*(2), 146–158.

Baird, C. L., & Sands, L. (2004). A pilot study of the effectiveness of guided imagery with progressive muscle relaxation to reduce chronic pain and mobility difficulties of osteoarthritis. *Pain Management Nursing, 5*(3), 97–104.

Baker, C. B., Tweedie, R., Duval, S., & Woods, S. W. (2003). Evidence that the SSRI dose response in treating major depression should be reassessed: A meta-analysis. *Depression and Anxiety, 17*(1), 1–9.

Bakke, A. C., Purtzer, M. Z., & Newton, P. (2002). The effect of hypnotic-guided imagery on psychological well-being and immune function in patients with prior breast cancer. *Journal of Psychosomatic Research, 53*(6), 1131–1137.

Balch, P. (2006). *Prescription for nutritional healing* (4th ed.). Garden City Park, NY: Avery.

Baldessarini, R. J., Leahy, L., Arcona, S., Gause, D., Zhang, W., & Hennen, J. (2007). Patterns of psychotropic drug prescription for U.S. patients with diagnoses of bipolar disorders. *Psychiatric Services, 58*(1), 85–91.

Baldessarini, R. J., Tondo, L., Davis, P., Pompili, M., Goodwin, F. K., & Hennen, J. (2006). Decreased risk of suicides and attempts during long-term lithium treatment: A meta-analytic review. *Bipolar Disorders, 8*(5 Pt 2), 625–639.

Baldessarini, R. J., Tondo, L., Faedda, G. L., Suppes, T. R., Floris, G., & Rudas, N. (1996). Effects of the rate of discontinuing lithium maintenance treatment in bipolar disorders. *Journal of Clinical Psychiatry, 57*(10), 441–448.

Baldessarini, R. J., Tondo, L., & Hennen, J. (2001). Treating the suicidal patient with bipolar disorder. Reducing suicide risk with lithium. *Annals of the New York Academy of Sciences, 932,* 24–38; discussion 39-43.

Baldessarini, R. J., Tondo, L., & Hennen, J. (2003). Lithium treatment and suicide risk in major affective disorders: Update and new findings. *Journal of Clinical Psychiatry, 64*(Suppl. 5), 44–52.

Baldomero, E. B., Ubago, J. G., Cercos, C. L., Ruiloba, J. V., Calvo, C. G., & Lopez, R. P. (2005). Venlafaxine extended release versus conventional antidepressants in the remission of depressive disorders after previous antidepressant failure: ARGOS study. *Depression and Anxiety, 22*(2), 68–76.

Bangs, M. E., Emslie, G. J., Spencer, T. J., Ramsey, J. L., Carlson, C., Bartky, E. J., et al. (2007). Efficacy and safety of atomoxetine in adolescents with attention-deficit/hyperactivity disorder and major depression. *Journal of Child and Adolescent Psychopharmacology, 17*(4), 407–420.

Bangs, M. E., Hazell, P., Danckaerts, M., Hoare, P., Coghill, D. R., Wehmeier, P. M., et al. (2008). Atomoxetine for the treatment of attention-deficit/hyperactivity disorder and oppositional defiant disorder. *Pediatrics, 121*(2), e314–e320.

Bangs, M. E., Jin, L., Zhang, S., Desaiah, D., Allen, A. J., Read, H. A., et al. (2008). Hepatic events associated with atomoxetine treatment for attention-deficit hyperactivity disorder. *Drug Safety, 31*(4), 345–354.

Barak, A. J., Beckenhauer, H. C., Junnila, M., & Tuma, D. J. (1993). Dietary betaine promotes generation of hepatic S-adenosylmethionine and protects the liver from ethanol-induced fatty infiltration. *Alcoholism, Clinical and Experimental Research, 17*(3), 552–555.

Barak, A. J., Beckenhauer, H. C., & Tuma, D. J. (1994). S-adenosylmethionine generation and prevention of alcoholic fatty liver by betaine. *Alcohol, 11*(6), 501–503.

Barak, Y., & Aizenberg, D. (2006). Association between antidepressant prescribing and suicide in Israel. *International Clinical Psychopharmacology, 21*(5), 281–284.

Barkai, A., Dunner, D., & Grss, H. (1978). Reduced myo-inositol levels in cerebrospinal fluid from patients with affective disorder. *Biological Psychiatry, 13,* 65–72.

Barnes, P. M., Powell-Griner, E., McFann, K., & Nahin, R. L. (2004). Complementary and alternative medicine use among adults: United States, 2002. *Advance Data,* (343), 1–19.

Barrette, E.-P., Basch, E., Basch, S., Boon, H., Conquer, J., Foppa, I., et al. (2010). Milk thistle (Silybum marianum). Monograph. Retrieved February 2, 2010, from Natural Standard Database: http://www.naturalstandard.net/index-abstract.asp?create-abstract=/monographs/herbssupplements/milkthistle.asp

Bauer, M., Adli, M., Baethge, C., Berghofer, A., Sasse, J., Heinz, A., et al. (2003). Lithium augmentation therapy in refractory depression: Clinical evidence and neurobiological mechanisms. *Canadian Journal of Psychiatry,* *48*(7), 440–448.

Bauer, M., Bschor, T., Kunz, D., Berghofer, A., Strohle, A., & Muller-Oerling-hausen, B. (2000). Double-blind, placebo-controlled trial of the use of lithium to augment antidepressant medication in continuation treatment of unipolar major depression. *American Journal of Psychiatry, 157*(9), 1429–1435.

Bauer, M., Forsthoff, A., Baethge, C., Adli, M., Berghofer, A., Dopfmer, S., et al. (2003). Lithium augmentation therapy in refractory depression-update 2002. *European Archives of Psychiatry and Clinical Neuroscience, 253*(3), 132–139.

Bauer, M., London, E. D., Rasgon, N., Berman, S. M., Frye, M. A., Altshuler, L. L., et al. (2005). Supraphysiological doses of levothyroxine alter regional cerebral metabolism and improve mood in bipolar depression. *Molecular Psychiatry, 10*(5), 456–469.

Bauer, M., & Whybrow, P. (1990). Rapid cycling bipolar affective disorder II. Adjuvant treatment of refractory rapid cycling with high dose thyroxine. *Archives of General Psychiatry, 47,* 435–440.

Bauer, M., & Whybrow, P. (2001). Thyroid hormone, neural tissue, and mood modulation. *World Journal of Biological Psychiatry, 2,* 59–69.

Bauer, M. S., Wisniewski, S. R., Marangell, L. B., Chessick, C. A., Allen, M. H., Dennehy, E. B., et al. (2006). Are antidepressants associated with new-onset suicidality in bipolar disorder? A prospective study of participants in the Systematic Treatment Enhancement Program for Bipolar Disorder (STEP-BD). *Journal of Clinical Psychiatry, 67*(1), 48–55.

Baumann, R. J. (2002). Behavioral treatment of migraine in children and adolescents. *Paediatric Drugs, 4*(9), 555–561.

Baune, B. T., Caliskan, S., & Todder, D. (2007). Effects of adjunctive antide-pressant therapy with quetiapine on clinical outcome, quality of sleep and daytime motor activity in patients with treatment-resistant depression. *Human Psychopharmacology, 22*(1), 1–9.

Bech, P. (2005). Social functioning: Should it become an endpoint in trials of antidepressants? *CNS Drugs, 19*(4), 313–324.

Bech, P., Kajdasz, D. K., & Porsdal, V. (2006). Dose-response relationship of duloxetine in placebo-controlled clinical trials in patients with major depressive disorder. *Psychopharmacology, 188*(3), 273–280.

Beck, A., Rush, A., Shaw, B., & Emery, G. (1979). *Cognitive therapy of depression.* New York: Guilford.

Beckmann, H., Athen, D., Olteanu, M., & Zimmer, R. (1979). DL-pheny-lalanine versus imipramine: A double-blind controlled study. *Archiv für Psychiatrie und Nervenkrankheiten, 227*(1), 49–58.

Beckmann, H., Strauss, M. A., & Ludolph, E. (1977). Dl-phenylalanine in depressed patients: An open study. *Journal of Neural Transmission, 41*(2–3), 123–134.

Bell, C., Abrams, J., & Nutt, D. (2001). Tryptophan depletion and its implications for psychiatry. *British Journal of Psychiatry, 178,* 399–405.

Bell, I., Ernst, E., Mansky, P., & Khalsa, P. (2009). *Homeopathy: An introduction.* NCCAM Publication No. D439.

Bell, I., & Pappas, P. (2007). Homeopathy. In J. Lake & D. Speiegel (Eds.), *Complementary and alternative treatments in mental health care.* Arlington, VA: American Psychiatric Publishing.

Belmaker, R., Benjamin, J., & Stahl, Z. (2002). Inositol in the treatment of psychiatric disorders. In D. Mischoulon & J. Rosenbaum (Eds.), *Natural medications for psychiatric disorders: Considering the alternatives* (pp. 111–124). Philadelphia: Lippincott Williams & Wilkins.

Belmaker, R., Bersudsky, Y., & Benjamin, J. (1995). Manipulation of inositol-linked second messenger systems as a therapeutic strategy in psychiatry. In G. Gessa, W. Fratta, L. Panni, & G. Serra (Eds.), *Depression and mania: from neurobiology to treatment* (pp. 67–84). New York: Raven Press.

Benazzi, F. (2001). Is 4 days the minimum duration of hypomania in bipolar II disorder? *European Archives of Psychiatry and Clinical Neuroscience, 251*(1), 32–34.

Benazzi, F. (2003a). Frequency of bipolar spectrum in 111 private practice depression outpatients. *European Archives of Psychiatry and Clinical Neuroscience, 253,* 203–208.

Benazzi, F. (2003b). Improving the Mood Disorder Questionnaire to detect bipolar II disorder. *Canadian Journal of Psychiatry, 48*(11), 770–771.

Benazzi, F. (2003c). Major depressive disorder with anger: A bipolar spectrum disorder? *Psychotherapy and Psychosomatics, 72*(6), 300–306.

Benazzi, F. (2004). Agitated depression: A valid depression subtype? *Progress in Neuro-psychopharmacology and Biological Psychiatry, 28*(8), 1279–1285.

Benazzi, F. (2005). Family history validation of a definition of mixed depression. *Comprehensive Psychiatry, 46*(3), 159–166.

Benazzi, F., & Akiskal, H. (2005). Irritable-hostile depression: Further validation as a bipolar depressive mixed state. *Journal of Affective Disorders, 84*(2–3), 197–207.

Benazzi, F., Koukopoulos, A., & Akiskal, H. S. (2004). Toward a validation of a new definition of agitated depression as a bipolar mixed state (mixed depression). *European Psychiatry, 19*(2), 85–90.

Bendtsen, L., & Jensen, R. (2004). Mirtazapine is effective in the prophylactic treatment of chronic tension-type headache. *Neurology, 62*(10), 1706–1711.

Benjamin, J., Levine, J., & Fux, M. (1995). Double-blind, placebo-controlled, crossover trial of inositol treatment for panic disorder. *American Journal of Psychiatry, 152*, 1084–1086.

Benkert, O., Grunder, G., Wetzel, H., & Hackett, D. (1996). A randomized, double-blind comparison of a rapidly escalating dose of venlafaxine and imipramine in inpatients with major depression and melancholia. *Journal of Psychiatric Research, 30*(6), 441–451.

Bent, S., Padula, A., Moore, D., Patterson, M., & Mehling, W. (2006). Valerian for sleep: A systematic review and meta-analysis. *American Journal of Medicine, 119*(12), 1005–1012.

Berk, M., Sanders, K. M., Pasco, J. A., Jacka, F. N., Williams, L. J., Hayles, A. L., et al. (2007). Vitamin D deficiency may play a role in depression. *Medical Hypotheses, 69*(6), 1316–1319.

Berlanga, C., Ortega-Soto, H. A., Ontiveros, M., & Senties, H. (1992). Efficacy of S-adenosyl-L-methionine in speeding the onset of action of imipramine. *Psychiatry Research, 44*(3), 257–262.

Berlim, M. T., & Turecki, G. (2007). Definition, assessment, and staging of treatment-resistant refractory major depression: A review of current concepts and methods. *Canadian Journal of Psychiatry, 52*(1), 46–54.

Berman, R. M., Fava, M., Thase, M. E., Trivedi, M. H., Swanink, R., McQuade, R. D., et al. (2009). Aripiprazole augmentation in major depressive disorder: A double-blind, placebo-controlled study in patients with inadequate response to antidepressants. *CNS Spectrums, 14*(4), 197–206.

Berman, R. M., Marcus, R. N., Swanink, R., McQuade, R. D., Carson, W. H., Corey-Lisle, P. K., et al. (2007). The efficacy and safety of aripiprazole as adjunctive therapy in major depressive disorder: A multicenter, randomized, double-blind, placebo-controlled study. *Journal of Clinical Psychiatry, 68*(6), 843–853.

Bertisch, S. M., Wee, C. C., Phillips, R. S., & McCarthy, E. P. (2009). Alternative mind-body therapies used by adults with medical conditions. *Journal of Psychosomatic Research, 66*(6), 511–519.

Bertone-Johnson, E. R. (2009). Vitamin D and the occurrence of depression: Causal association or circumstantial evidence? *Nutrition Reviews, 67*(8), 481–492.

Bijl, D. (2004). The serotonin syndrome. *Netherlands Journal of Medicine, 62*(9), 309–313.

Birkenhager, T. K., van den Broek, W. W., Mulder, P. G., Bruijn, J. A., & Moleman, P. (2004a). Comparison of two-phase treatment with imipramine or fluvoxamine, both followed by lithium addition, in inpatients with major depressive disorder. *American Journal of Psychiatry, 161*(11), 2060–2065.

Birkenhager, T. K., van den Broek, W. W., Mulder, P. G., Bruijn, J. A., & Moleman, P. (2004b). Efficacy and tolerability of tranylcypromine versus phenelzine: A double-blind study in antidepressant-refractory depressed inpatients. *Journal of Clinical Psychiatry, 65*(11), 1505–1510.

Birkenhager, T. K., van den Broek, W. W., Mulder, P. G., Bruijn, J. A., & Moleman, P. (2006). [Comparison of the effectiveness of two treatment strategies in inpatients with a depressive disorder. A double-blind study of imipramine followed by lithium addition versus fluvoxamine followed by lithium addition]. *Tijdschrift voor Psychiatrie, 48*(4), 271–281.

Birkmayer, W., Riederer, P., Linauer, W., & Knoll, J. (1984). L-deprenyl plus L-phenylalanine in the treatment of depression. *Journal of Neural Transmission, 59*(1), 81–87.

Birmaher, B., Axelson, D., Monk, K., Kalas, C., Goldstein, B., Hickey, M. B., et al. (2009). Lifetime psychiatric disorders in school-aged offspring of parents with bipolar disorder: The Pittsburgh Bipolar Offspring study. *Archives of General Psychiatry, 66*(3), 287–296.

Birmaher, B., Ryan, N. D., Williamson, D. E., Brent, D. A., Kaufman, J., Dahl, R. E., et al. (1996). Childhood and adolescent depression: A review of the past 10 years. Part I. *Journal of the American Academy of Child and Adolescent Psychiatry, 35*(11), 1427–1439.

Blier, P., Saint-Andre, E., Hebert, C., de Montigny, C., Lavoie, N., & Debonnel, G. (2007). Effects of different doses of venlafaxine on serotonin and norepinephrine reuptake in healthy volunteers. *International Journal of Neuropsychopharmacology, 10*(1), 41–50.

Blob, L. F., Sharoky, M., Campbell, B. J., Kemper, E. M., Gilmor, M. G., VanDenberg, C. M., et al. (2007). Effects of a tyramine-enriched meal on blood pressure response in healthy male volunteers treated with selegiline transdermal system 6 mg/24 hour. *CNS Spectrums, 12*(1), 25–34.

Blom, M. B., Jonker, K., Dusseldorp, E., Spinhoven, P., Hoencamp, E., Haffmans, J., et al. (2007). Combination treatment for acute depression is superior only when psychotherapy is added to medication. *Psychotherapy and Psychosomatics, 76*(5), 289–297.

Bodkin, J. A., & Amsterdam, J. D. (2002). Transdermal selegiline in major depression: A double-blind, placebo-controlled, parallel-group study in outpatients. *American Journal of Psychiatry, 159*(11), 1869–1875.

Bodnar, L. M., & Wisner, K. L. (2005). Nutrition and depression: Implications for improving mental health among childbearing-aged women. *Biological Psychiatry, 58*(9), 679–685.

Boerner, R. J., Sommer, H., Berger, W., Kuhn, U., Schmidt, U., & Mannel, M. (2003). Kava-kava extract LI 150 is as effective as opipramol and buspirone in generalised anxiety disorder—an 8-week randomized, double-blind multicentre clinical trial in 129 out-patients. *Phytomedicine, 10*(Suppl. 4), 38–49.

Bornstein, R. A., Baker, G. B., Carroll, A., King, G., Wong, J. T., & Douglass, A. B. (1990). Plasma amino acids in attention deficit disorder. *Psychiatry Research, 33*(3), 301–306.

Botez, M., Botez, T., & Leveille, J. (1979). Neurological correlates of folic acid deficiency: Facts and hypothesses. In M. Botez & E. Reynolds (Eds.), *Folic acid in neurology, psychiatry and internal medicine* (pp. 435–461). New York: Raven Press.

Botez, M. I., & Young, S. N. (1991). Effects of anticonvulsant treatment and low levels of folate and thiamine on amine metabolites in cerebrospinal fluid. *Brain, 114*(Pt 1A), 333–348.

Botez, M. I., Young, S. N., Bachevalier, J., & Gauthier, S. (1979). Folate deficiency and decreased brain 5-hydroxytryptamine synthesis in man and rat. *Nature, 278,* 182–183.

Bottiglieri, T. (1996). Folate, vitamin B12, and neuropsychiatric disorders. *Nutrition Reviews, 54*(12), 382–390.

Bottiglieri, T. (2002). S-adenosyl-L-methionine (SAMe): From the bench to the bedside—molecular basis of a pleiotrophic molecule. *American Journal of Clinical Nutrition, 76*(5), 1151S–1157S.

Bottiglieri, T., Hyland, K., Laundy, M., Godfrey, P., Carney, M. W., Toone, B. K., et al. (1992). Folate deficiency, biopterin and monoamine metabolism in depression. *Psychological Medicine, 22*(4), 871–876.

Bottiglieri, T., Hyland, K., & Reynolds, E. H. (1994). The clinical potential of ademetionine (S-adenosylmethionine) in neurological disorders. *Drugs, 48*(2), 137–152.

Bourgon, L. N., & Kellner, C. H. (2000). Relapse of depression after ECT: A review. *Journal of ECT, 16*(1), 19–31.

Bowden, C. L. (2005). A different depression: Clinical distinctions between bipolar and unipolar depression. *Journal of Affective Disorders, 84*(2–3), 117–125.

Bowden, C. L., Calabrese, J. R., Ketter, T. A., Sachs, G. S., White, R. L., & Thompson, T. R. (2006). Impact of lamotrigine and lithium on weight in obese and nonobese patients with bipolar I disorder. *American Journal of Psychiatry, 163*(7), 1199–1201.

Bowden, C. L., Calabrese, J. R., Sachs, G., Yatham, L. N., Asghar, S. A., Hompland, M., et al. (2003). A placebo-controlled 18-month trial of lamotrigine and lithium maintenance treatment in recently manic or hypomanic patients with bipolar I disorder. *Archives of General Psychiatry, 60*(4), 392–400.

Bowers, M. B., Jr., & Reynolds, E. H. (1972). Cerebrospinal-fluid folate and acid monoamine metabolites. *Lancet, 2*(7791), 1376.

Boyer, P., Montgomery, S., Lepola, U., Germain, J. M., Brisard, C., Ganguly, R., et al. (2008). Efficacy, safety, and tolerability of fixed-dose desvenlafaxine 50 and 100 mg/day for major depressive disorder in a placebo-controlled trial. *International Clinical Psychopharmacology, 23*(5), 243–253.

Bradley, R. G., Binder, E. B., Epstein, M. P., Tang, Y., Nair, H. P., Liu, W., et al. (2008). Influence of child abuse on adult depression: Moderation by the corticotropin-releasing hormone receptor gene. *Archives of General Psychiatry, 65*(2), 190–200.

Bramness, J. G., Skurtveit, S., Neutel, C. I., Morland, J., & Engeland, A. (2008). Minor increase in risk of road traffic accidents after prescriptions of antidepressants: A study of population registry data in Norway. *Journal of Clinical Psychiatry, 69*(7), 1099–1103.

Braverman, J., & Roux, J. F. (1978). Screening for the patient at risk for postpartum depression. *Obstetrics and Gynecology, 52*(6), 731–736.

Brent, D., & Birmaher, B. (2002). Clinical practice. Adolescent depression. *New England Journal of Medicine, 347*(9), 667–671.

Brent, D., Emslie, G., Clarke, G., Wagner, K. D., Asarnow, J. R., Keller, M., et al. (2008). Switching to another SSRI or to venlafaxine with or without cognitive behavioral therapy for adolescents with SSRI-resistant depression: The TORDIA randomized controlled trial. *JAMA, 299*(8), 901–913.

Bressa, G. M. (1994). S-adenosyl-l-methionine (SAMe) as antidepressant: Meta-analysis of clinical studies. *Acta Neurologica Scandinavica, 154*(Suppl.), 7–14.

Bridge, J. A., Iyengar, S., Salary, C. B., Barbe, R. P., Birmaher, B., Pincus, H. A., et al. (2007). Clinical response and risk for reported suicidal ideation and suicide attempts in pediatric antidepressant treatment: A meta-analysis of randomized controlled trials. *JAMA, 297*(15), 1683–1696.

Broadhurst, C. L., Cunnane, S. C., & Crawford, M. A. (1998). Rift Valley lake fish and shellfish provided brain-specific nutrition for early Homo. *British Journal of Nutrition, 79*(1), 3–21.

Brooks, T. J., Wall, G. W., Pinter, P. J., Jr., Kimball, B. A., Lamorte, R. L., Leavitt, S. W., et al. (2000). Acclimation response of spring wheat in a free-air CO_2 enrichment (FACE) atmosphere with variable soil nitrogen regimes. 3. Canopy architecture and gas exchange. *Photosynthesis Research, 66*(1–2), 97–108.

Brosnan, J. T., & Brosnan, M. E. (2006). The sulfur-containing amino acids: An overview. *Journal of Nutrition, 136*(6 Suppl), 1636S–1640S.

Brown, E. B., McElroy, S. L., Keck, P. E., Jr. , Deldar, A., Adams, D. H., Tohen, M., et al. (2006). A 7-week, randomized, double-blind trial of olanzapine/fluoxetine combination versus lamotrigine in the treatment of bipolar I depression. *Journal of Clinical Psychiatry, 67*(7), 1025–1033.

Bruijn, J. A., Moleman, P., Mulder, P. G., & van den Broek, W. W. (1998). Comparison of 2 treatment strategies for depressed inpatients: Imipramine and lithium addition or mirtazapine and lithium addition. *Journal of Clinical Psychiatry, 59*(12), 657–663.

Brzezinski, A. (1997). Melatonin in humans. *New England Journal of Medicine, 336*(3), 186–195.

Bschor, T., & Bauer, M. (2006). Efficacy and mechanisms of action of lithium augmentation in refractory major depression. *Current Pharmaceutical Design, 12*(23), 2985–2992.

Bschor, T., Berghofer, A., Strohle, A., Kunz, D., Adli, M., Muller-Oerlinghausen, B., et al. (2002). How long should the lithium augmentation strategy be maintained? A 1-year follow-up of a placebo-controlled study in unipolar refractory major depression. *Journal of Clinical Psychopharmacology, 22*(4), 427–430.

Bschor, T., Lewitzka, U., Sasse, J., Adli, M., Koberle, U., & Bauer, M. (2003). Lithium augmentation in treatment-resistant depression: Clinical evidence, serotonergic and endocrine mechanisms. *Pharmacopsychiatry, 36*(Suppl. 3), S230–S234.

Burgess, H. (2005). *Wake time influences circadian clock more than bed time.* Paper presented at the Associated Professional Sleep Societies 19th Annual Meeting, Denver.

Burns, D. (1999). *Feeling good: The new mood therapy.* New York: Collins Living.

Buscemi, N., Vandermeer, B., Pandya, R., Hooton, N., Tjosvold, L., Hartling, L., et al. (2004). Melatonin for treatment of sleep disorders. Summary, Evidence Report/Technology Assessment: Number 108. AHRQ Publication Number 05-E002-1. Rockville, MD: Agency for Health care Research and Quality.

Byerley, W. F., Judd, L. L., Reimherr, F. W., & Grosser, B. I. (1987). 5-Hydroxytryptophan: A review of its antidepressant efficacy and adverse effects. *Journal of Clinical Psychopharmacology, 7*(3), 127–137.

Bystritsky, A., Kerwin, L., & Feusner, J. D. (2008). A pilot study of Rhodiola rosea (Rhodax) for generalized anxiety disorder (GAD). *Journal of Alternative and Complementary Medicine, 14*(2), 175–180.

Bystritsky, A., Kerwin, L., Feusner, J. D., & Vapnik, T. (2008). A pilot controlled trial of bupropion XL versus escitalopram in generalized anxiety disorder. *Psychopharmacological Bulletin, 41*(1), 46–51.

Calabrese, J. R., Bowden, C. L., Sachs, G., Yatham, L. N., Behnke, K., Mehtonen, O. P., et al. (2003). A placebo-controlled 18-month trial of lamotrigine and lithium maintenance treatment in recently depressed patients with bipolar I disorder. *Journal of Clinical Psychiatry, 64*(9), 1013–1024.

Calabrese, J. R., Elhaj, O., Gajwani, P., & Gao, K. (2005). Clinical highlights in bipolar depression: Focus on atypical antipsychotics. *Journal of Clinical Psychiatry, 66*(Suppl. 5), 26–33.

Calabrese, J. R., Huffman, R. F., White, R. L., Edwards, S., Thompson, T. R., Ascher, J. A., et al. (2008). Lamotrigine in the acute treatment of bipolar depression: Results of five double-blind, placebo-controlled clinical trials. *Bipolar Disorders, 10*(2), 323–333.

Calabrese, J. R., Keck, P. E., Jr. , Macfadden, W., Minkwitz, M., Ketter, T. A., Weisler, R. H., et al. (2005). A randomized, double-blind, placebo-controlled trial of quetiapine in the treatment of bipolar I or II depression. *American Journal of Psychiatry, 162*(7), 1351–1360.

Calabrese, J. R., Rapport, D. J., Youngstrom, E. A., Jackson, K., Bilali, S., & Findling, R. L. (2005). New data on the use of lithium, divalproate, and lamotrigine in rapid cycling bipolar disorder. *European Psychiatry, 20*(2), 92–95.

Calabrese, J. R., Shelton, M. D., Rapport, D. J., Youngstrom, E. A., Jackson, K., Bilali, S., et al. (2005). A 20-month, double-blind, maintenance trial of lithium versus divalproex in rapid-cycling bipolar disorder. *American Journal of Psychiatry, 162*(11), 2152–2161.

Calabrese, J. R., Sullivan, J. R., Bowden, C. L., Suppes, T., Goldberg, J. F., Sachs, G. S., et al. (2002). Rash in multicenter trials of lamotrigine in mood disorders: Clinical relevance and management. *Journal of Clinical Psychiatry, 63*(11), 1012–1019.

Calabrese, J. R., Suppes, T., Bowden, C. L., Sachs, G. S., Swann, A. C., McElroy, S. L., et al. (2000). A double-blind, placebo-controlled, prophylaxis study of lamotrigine in rapid-cycling bipolar disorder. Lamictal 614 Study Group. *Journal of Clinical Psychiatry, 61*(11), 841–850.

Callahan, M. (1997). *DHEA: The miracle hormone that can help you boost immunity, increase energy, lighten your mood, improve your sex drive, and lengthen your lifespan.* New York: Signet.

Cameron, L. D., Booth, R. J., Schlatter, M., Ziginskas, D., & Harman, J. E. (2007). Changes in emotion regulation and psychological adjustment following use of a group psychosocial support program for women recently diagnosed with breast cancer. *Psychooncology, 16*(3), 171–180.

Cannell, J. (2004). Treating disease with vitamin D. Retrieved February 2, 2010, from http://www.vitamindcouncil.org/mentalIllness.shtml

Cannell, J. (2010, January 8). Vitamin D and mental illness. Retrieved February 2, 2010, from http://www.vitamindcouncil.org/mentalIllness.shtml

Canter, P. H., & Ernst, E. (2007). Ginkgo biloba is not a smart drug: An updated systematic review of randomised clinical trials testing the nootropic effects of G. biloba extracts in healthy people. *Human Psychopharmacology, 22*(5), 265–278.

Cantoni, G. L., Mudd, S. H., & Andreoli, V. (1989). Affective disorders and S-adenosylmethionine: A new hypothesis. *Trends in Neurosciences, 12*(9), 319–324.

CAP Nutrition Committee. (1990). Megavitamin and megamineral therapy in childhood. Nutrition Committee, Canadian Paediatric Society. *CMAJ, 143*(10), 1009–1013.

Carey, F. A. (2006). *Organic chemistry* (6th ed.). New York: McGraw Hill.

Carhart-Harris, R. L., Mayberg, H. S., Malizia, A. L., & Nutt, D. (2008). Mourning and melancholia revisited: Correspondences between principles of Freudian metapsychology and empirical findings in neuropsychiatry. *Annals of General Psychiatry*, 7, 9.

Carlson, G. A., Dunn, D., Kelsey, D., Ruff, D., Ball, S., Ahrbecker, L., et al. (2007). A pilot study for augmenting atomoxetine with methylphenidate: Safety of concomitant therapy in children with attention-deficit/hyperactivity disorder. *Child and Adolescent Psychiatry and Mental Health*, 1(1), 10.

Carlson, P. J., Merlock, M. C., & Suppes, T. (2004). Adjunctive stimulant use in patients with bipolar disorder: Treatment of residual depression and sedation. *Bipolar Disorders*, 6(5), 416–420.

Carlsten, A., Waern, M., Ekedahl, A., & Ranstam, J. (2001). Antidepressant medication and suicide in Sweden. *Pharmacoepidemiology and Drug Safety*, 10(6), 525–530.

Carney, M. W. (1967). Serum folate values in 423 psychiatric patients. *British Medical Journal*, 4, 512–516.

Carney, M. W., Chary, T. K., Bottiglieri, T., & Reynolds, E. H. (1989). The switch mechanism and the bipolar/unipolar dichotomy. *British Journal of Psychiatry*, 154, 48–51.

Carney, M. W., Chary, T. K., Laundy, M., Bottiglieri, T., Chanarin, I., Reynolds, E. H., et al. (1990). Red cell folate concentrations in psychiatric patients. *Journal of Affective Disorders*, 19(3), 207–213.

Carney, M. W., Toone, B. K., & Reynolds, E. H. (1987). S-adenosylmethionine and affective disorder. *American Journal of Medicine*, 83(5A), 104–106.

Carr, D., Goudas, L., & D, L. (2002). Management of cancer symptoms: Pain, depression, and fatigue. Evidence Report/Technology Assessment No. 61 (Prepared by the New England Medical Center Evidence-Based Practice Center under Contract No 290-97-0019). AHRQ publication No. 02-E032. Rockville, MD: Agency for Healthcare Research and Quality.

Carroll-Ghosh, T., Victor, B., & Bourgeois, J. (2003). Suicide. In R. Hales & S. C. Yudofsky (Eds.), *Textbook of clinical psychiatry* (pp. 1457–1483). Washington, DC: American Psychiatric Publishing.

Carvalho, A. F., Cavalcante, J. L., Castelo, M. S., & Lima, M. C. (2007). Augmentation strategies for treatment-resistant depression: A literature review. *Journal of Clinical Pharmacy and Therapeutics*, 32(5), 415–428.

Carvalho, L. A., Gorenstein, C., Moreno, R., Pariante, C., & Markus, R. P. (2009). Effect of antidepressants on melatonin metabolite in depressed patients. *Journal of Psychopharmacology*, 23(3), 315–321.

Carvalho, L. A., Gorenstein, C., Moreno, R. A., & Markus, R. P. (2006). Melatonin levels in drug-free patients with major depression from the southern hemisphere. *Psychoneuroendocrinology*, 31(6), 761–768.

Casper, R. C., Fleisher, B. E., Lee-Ancajas, J. C., Gilles, A., Gaylor, E., DeBattista, A., et al. (2003). Follow-up of children of depressed mothers exposed or not exposed to antidepressant drugs during pregnancy. *Journal of Pediatrics, 142*(4), 402–408.

Caspi, A., Sugden, K., Moffitt, T. E., Taylor, A., Craig, I. W., Harrington, H., et al. (2003). Influence of life stress on depression: Moderation by a polymorphism in the 5-HTT gene. *Science, 301*(5631), 386–389.

Cassano, P., Lattanzi, L., Fava, M., Navari, S., Battistini, G., Abelli, M., et al. (2005). Ropinirole in treatment-resistant depression: A 16-week pilot study. *Canadian Journal of Psychiatry, 50*(6), 357–360.

Cassano, P., Lattanzi, L., Soldani, F., Navari, S., Battistini, G., Gemignani, A., et al. (2004). Pramipexole in treatment-resistant depression: An extended follow-up. *Depression and Anxiety, 20*(3), 131–138.

Chabrol, H., & Callahan, S. (2007). Prevention and treatment of postnatal depression. *Expert Review of Neurotherapeutics, 7*(5), 557–576.

Chabrol, H., Teissedre, F., Saint-Jean, M., Teisseyre, N., Roge, B., & Mullet, E. (2002). Prevention and treatment of post-partum depression: A controlled randomized study on women at risk. *Psychological Medicine, 32*(6), 1039–1047.

Chamberlain, S. R., Del Campo, N., Dowson, J., Muller, U., Clark, L., Robbins, T. W., et al. (2007). Atomoxetine improved response inhibition in adults with attention deficit/hyperactivity disorder. *Biological Psychiatry, 62*(9), 977–984.

Chambers, C., Moses-Kolko, E., & Wisner, K. L. (2007). Antidepressant use in pregnancy: New concerns, old dilemmas. *Expert Review of Neurotherapeutics, 7*(7), 761–764.

Chambers, C. D., Hernandez-Diaz, S., Van Marter, L. J., Werler, M. M., Louik, C., Jones, K. L., et al. (2006). Selective serotonin-reuptake inhibitors and risk of persistent pulmonary hypertension of the newborn. *New England Journal of Medicine, 354*(6), 579–587.

Chang, K., Saxena, K., & Howe, M. (2006). An open-label study of lamotrigine adjunct or monotherapy for the treatment of adolescents with bipolar depression. *Journal of the American Academy of Child and Adolescent Psychiatry, 45*(3), 298–304.

Chaput, Y., Magnan, A., & Gendron, A. (2008). The co-administration of quetiapine or placebo to cognitive-behavior therapy in treatment refractory depression: A preliminary trial. *BMC Psychiatry, 8*, 73.

Charlton, C. G., & Crowell, B., Jr. (1992). Parkinson's disease-like effects of S-adenosyl-L-methionine: Effects of L-dopa. *Pharmacology, Biochemistry and Behavior, 43*(2), 423–431.

Cheng, J. Y., Chen, R. Y., Ko, J. S., & Ng, E. M. (2007). Efficacy and safety of atomoxetine for attention-deficit/hyperactivity disorder in children and adolescents: Meta-analysis and meta-regression analysis. *Psychopharmacology (Berlin), 194*(2), 197–209.

Chengappa, K. N., Levine, J., Gershon, S., Mallinger, A. G., Hardan, A., Vagnucci, A., et al. (2000). Inositol as an add-on treatment for bipolar depression. *Bipolar Disorders, 2*(1), 47–55.

Cherniske, S. (1998). The DHEA breakthrough. New York: Ballantine.

Chinevere, T. D., Sawyer, R. D., Creer, A. R., Conlee, R. K., & Parcell, A. C. (2002). Effects of L-tyrosine and carbohydrate ingestion on endurance exercise performance. *Journal of Applied Physiology, 93*(5), 1590–1597.

Cho, H. J., Kwon, J. H., & Lee, J. J. (2008). Antenatal cognitive-behavioral therapy for prevention of postpartum depression: A pilot study. *Yonsei Medical Journal, 49*(4), 553–562.

Cipriani, A., Pretty, H., Hawton, K., & Geddes, J. R. (2005). Lithium in the prevention of suicidal behavior and all-cause mortality in patients with mood disorders: A systematic review of randomized trials. *American Journal of Psychiatry, 162*(10), 1805–1819.

Cipriani, A., Smith, K., Burgess, S., Carney, S., Goodwin, G., & Geddes, J. (2006). Lithium versus antidepressants in the long-term treatment of unipolar affective disorder. *Cochrane Database System Reviews,* (4), CD003492.

Claassen, C. A., Trivedi, M. H., Rush, A. J., Husain, M. M., Zisook, S., Young, E., et al. (2007). Clinical differences among depressed patients with and without a history of suicide attempts: Findings from the STAR*D trial. *Journal of Affective Disorders, 97*(1–3), 77–84.

Clayton, A. H., Kornstein, S. G., Rosas, G., Guico-Pabia, C., & Tourian, K. A. (2009). An integrated analysis of the safety and tolerability of desvenlafaxine compared with placebo in the treatment of major depressive disorder. *CNS Spectrums, 14*(4), 183–195.

Clayton, A., Kornstein, S., Prakash, A., Mallinckrodt, C., & Wohlreich, M. (2007). Changes in sexual functioning associated with duloxetine, escitalopram, and placebo in the treatment of patients with major depressive disorder. *Journal of Sexual Medicine, 4*(4 Pt 1), 917–929.

Clayton, A. H. (2007). Extended-release bupropion: An antidepressant with a broad spectrum of therapeutic activity? *Expert Opinion in Pharmacotherapy, 8*(4), 457–466.

Clayton, A. H., Campbell, B. J., Favit, A., Yang, Y., Moonsammy, G., Piontek, C. M., et al. (2007). Symptoms of sexual dysfunction in patients treated for major depressive disorder: A meta-analysis comparing selegiline transdermal system and placebo using a patient-rated scale. *Journal of Clinical Psychiatry, 68*(12), 1860–1866.

Clayton, A. H., Croft, H. A., Horrigan, J. P., Wightman, D. S., Krishen, A., Richard, N. E., et al. (2006). Bupropion extended release compared with escitalopram: Effects on sexual functioning and antidepressant efficacy in 2 randomized, double-blind, placebo-controlled studies. *Journal of Clinical Psychiatry, 67*(5), 736–746.

Clayton, A. H., & Montejo, A. L. (2006). Major depressive disorder, antidepressants, and sexual dysfunction. *Journal of Clinical Psychiatry, 67*(Suppl. 6), 33–37.

Cohen, L. S., Altshuler, L. L., Harlow, B. L., Nonacs, R., Newport, D. J., Viguera, A. C., et al. (2006). Relapse of major depression during pregnancy in women who maintain or discontinue antidepressant treatment. *JAMA, 295*(5), 499–507.

Cohen, L. S., Altshuler, L. L., Stowe, Z. N., & Faraone, S. V. (2004). Reintroduction of antidepressant therapy across pregnancy in women who previously discontinued treatment. A preliminary retrospective study. *Psychotherapy and Psychosomatics, 73*(4), 255–258.

Cohen, L. S., Nonacs, R. M., Bailey, J. W., Viguera, A. C., Reminick, A. M., Altshuler, L. L., et al. (2004). Relapse of depression during pregnancy following antidepressant discontinuation: A preliminary prospective study. *Archives of Women's Mental Health, 7*(4), 217–221.

Cohrs, S., Rodenbeck, A., Guan, Z., Pohlmann, K., Jordan, W., Meier, A., et al. (2004). Sleep-promoting properties of quetiapine in healthy subjects. *Psychopharmacology (Berlin), 174*(3), 421–429.

Collins, J. A., & Rice, V. H. (1997). Effects of relaxation intervention in phase II cardiac rehabilitation: Replication and extension. *Heart and Lung, 26*(1), 31–44.

Connor, K. M., Payne, V., & Davidson, J. R. (2006). Kava in generalized anxiety disorder: Three placebo-controlled trials. *International Clinical Psychopharmacology, 21*(5), 249–253.

Cooper, C., Jakob, F., Chinn, C., Martin-Mola, E., Fardellone, P., Adami, S., et al. (2008). Fracture incidence and changes in quality of life in women with an inadequate clinical outcome from osteoporosis therapy: The Observational Study of Severe Osteoporosis (OSSO). *Osteoporosis International, 19*(4), 493–501.

Coppen, A., & Bailey, J. (2000). Enhancement of the antidepressant action of fluoxetine by folic acid: A randomised, placebo controlled trial. *Journal of Affective Disorders, 60*(2), 121–130.

Coppen, A., & Bolander-Gouaille, C. (2005). Treatment of depression: Time to consider folic acid and vitamin B12. *Journal of Psychopharmacology, 19*(1), 59–65.

Coppen, A., Chaudhry, S., & Swade, C. (1986). Folic acid enhances lithium prophylaxis. *Journal of Affective Disorders, 10*(1), 9–13.

Coppen, A., Whybrow, P. C., Noguera, R., Maggs, R., & Prange, A. J., Jr. (1972). The comparative antidepressant value of L-tryptophan and imipramine with and without attempted potentiation by liothyronine. *Archives of General Psychiatry, 26*(3), 234–241.

Corcoran, C. D., Thomas, P., Phillips, J., & O'Keane, V. (2006). Vagus nerve stimulation in chronic treatment-resistant depression: Preliminary findings of an open-label study. *British Journal of Psychiatry, 189,* 282–283.

Corruble, E., Berlin, I., Lemoine, A., & Hardy, P. (2004). Should major depression with 'high normal' thyroid-stimulating hormone be treated preferentially with tricyclics? *Neuropsychobiology, 50*(2), 144–146.

Costa, J. A., & Silva, E. (2005). World aspects of psychiatry. In B. J. Saddock & V. A. Sadock (Eds.), *Comprehensive textbook of psychiatry* (8th ed., pp. 4047–4060). Philladelphia: Lippincott Williams & Wilkins.

Crossley, N. A., & Bauer, M. (2007). Acceleration and augmentation of antidepressants with lithium for depressive disorders: Two meta-analyses of randomized, placebo-controlled trials. *Journal of Clinical Psychiatry, 68*(6), 935–940.

Curry, J., Rohde, P., Simons, A., Silva, S., Vitiello, B., Kratochvil, C., et al. (2006). Predictors and moderators of acute outcome in the Treatment for Adolescents with Depression Study (TADS). *Journal of the American Academy of Child and Adolescent Psychiatry, 45*(12), 1427–1439.

Czeh, B., & Lucassen, P. J. (2007). What causes the hippocampal volume decrease in depression? Are neurogenesis, glial changes and apoptosis implicated? *European Archives of Psychiatry and Clinical Neuroscience, 257*(5), 250–260.

Daley, A. J., Macarthur, C., & Winter, H. (2007). The role of exercise in treating postpartum depression: A review of the literature. *Journal of Midwifery and Women's Health, 52*(1), 56–62.

Dalton, E. J., Rotondi, D., Levitan, R. D., Kennedy, S. H., & Brown, G. M. (2000). Use of slow-release melatonin in treatment-resistant depression. *Journal of Psychiatry and Neuroscience, 25*(1), 48–52.

Dalton, K. (1985). Pyridoxine overdose in premenstrual syndrome. *Lancet, 1*(8438), 1168–1169.

D'Amico, D. (2007). Antiepileptic drugs in the prophylaxis of migraine, chronic headache forms and cluster headache: A review of their efficacy and tolerability. *Neurological Science, 28*(Suppl. 2), S188–S197.

Danilenko, K. V., & Putilov, A. A. (2005). Melatonin treatment of winter depression following total sleep deprivation: Waking EEG and mood correlates. *Neuropsychopharmacology, 30*(7), 1345–1352.

Danish University Antidepressant Group. (1986). Citalopram: Clinical effect profile in comparison with clomipramine. A controlled multicenter study. *Psychopharmacology (Berlin), 90*(1), 131–138.

Danish University Antidepressant Group. (1990). Paroxetine: A selective serotonin reuptake inhibitor showing better tolerance, but weaker antidepressant effect than clomipramine in a controlled multicenter study. *Journal of Affective Disorders, 18*(4), 289–299.

Darbinyan, V., Aslanyan, G., Amroyan, E., Gabrielyan, E., Malmstrom, C., & Panossian, A. (2007). Clinical trial of Rhodiola rosea L. extract SHR-5 in the treatment of mild to moderate depression. *Nordic Journal of Psychiatry, 61*(5), 343–348.

Davis, E. P., Glynn, L. M., Schetter, C. D., Hobel, C., Chicz-Demet, A., & Sandman, C. A. (2007). Prenatal exposure to maternal depression and cortisol influences infant temperament. *Journal of the American Academy of Child and Adolescent Psychiatry, 46*(6), 737–746.

Davis, L. L., Bartolucci, A., & Petty, F. (2005). Divalproex in the treatment of bipolar depression: A placebo-controlled study. *Journal of Affective Disorders, 85*(3), 259–266.

Davis, L. L., Rush, J. A., Wisniewski, S. R., Rice, K., Cassano, P., Jewell, M. E., et al. (2005). Substance use disorder comorbidity in major depressive disorder: An exploratory analysis of the Sequenced Treatment Alternatives to Relieve Depression cohort. *Comprehensive Psychiatry, 46*(2), 81–89.

Davis, R. L., Rubanowice, D., McPhillips, H., Raebel, M. A., Andrade, S. E., Smith, D., et al. (2007). Risks of congenital malformations and perinatal events among infants exposed to antidepressant medications during pregnancy. *Pharmacoepidemiology and Drug Safety, 16*(10), 1086–1094.

de Abajo, F. J., & Garcia-Rodriguez, L. A. (2008). Risk of upper gastrointestinal tract bleeding associated with selective serotonin reuptake inhibitors and venlafaxine therapy: Interaction with nonsteroidal anti-inflammatory drugs and effect of acid-suppressing agents. *Archives of General Psychiatry, 65*(7), 795–803.

Debonnel, G., Saint-Andre, E., Hebert, C., de Montigny, C., Lavoie, N., & Blier, P. (2007). Differential physiological effects of a low dose and high doses of venlafaxine in major depression. *International Journal of Neuropsychopharmacology, 10*(1), 51–61.

Deckelbaum, R. J., Worgau, T. S., & Seo, T. (2006). N-3 fatty acids and gene expression. *American Journal of Clinical Nutrition, 83*(Suppl. 6), 15205–15255.

DeKosky, S. T., Fitzpatrick, A., Ives, D. G., Saxton, J., Williamson, J., Lopez, O. L., et al. (2006). The Ginkgo Evaluation of Memory (GEM) study: Design and baseline data of a randomized trial of Ginkgo biloba extract in prevention of dementia. *Contemporary Clinical Trials, 27*(3), 238–253.

DeKosky, S. T., Williamson, J. D., Fitzpatrick, A. L., Kronmal, R. A., Ives, D. G., Saxton, J. A., et al. (2008). Ginkgo biloba for prevention of dementia: A randomized controlled trial. *JAMA, 300*(19), 2253–2262.

Delgado, P. L. (2000). Depression: The case for a monoamine deficiency. *Journal of Clinical Psychiatry, 61*(Suppl. 6), 7–11.

Delgado, P. L. (2004). How antidepressants help depression: Mechanisms of action and clinical response. *Journal of Clinical Psychiatry, 65*(Suppl. 4), 25–30.

Delgado, P. L., Brannan, S. K., Mallinckrodt, C. H., Tran, P. V., McNamara, R. K., Wang, F., et al. (2005). Sexual functioning assessed in 4 double-blind placebo- and paroxetine-controlled trials of duloxetine for major depressive disorder. *Journal of Clinical Psychiatry*, 66(6), 686–692.

Delgado, P. L., Charney, D. S., Price, L. H., Aghajanian, G. K., Landis, H., & Heninger, G. R. (1990). Serotonin function and the mechanism of antidepressant action. Reversal of antidepressant-induced remission by rapid depletion of plasma tryptophan. *Archives of General Psychiatry*, 47(5), 411–418.

Delgado, P. L., Miller, H. L., Salomon, R. M., Licinio, J., Heninger, G. R., Gelenberg, A. J., et al. (1993). Monoamines and the mechanism of antidepressant action: Effects of catecholamine depletion on mood of patients treated with antidepressants. *Psychopharmacology Bulletin*, 29(3), 389–396.

Delgado, P. L., Miller, H. L., Salomon, R. M., Licinio, J., Krystal, J. H., Moreno, F. A., et al. (1999). Tryptophan-depletion challenge in depressed patients treated with desipramine or fluoxetine: Implications for the role of serotonin in the mechanism of antidepressant action. *Biological Psychiatry*, 46(2), 212–220.

Delgado, P. L., Moreno, F. A., Onate, L., & Gelenberg, A. J. (2002). Sequential catecholamine and serotonin depletion in mirtazapine-treated depressed patients. *International Journal of Neuropsychopharmacology*, 5(1), 63–66.

Delgado, P. L., Price, L. H., Miller, H. L., Salomon, R. M., Aghajanian, G. K., Heninger, G. R., et al. (1994). Serotonin and the neurobiology of depression. Effects of tryptophan depletion in drug-free depressed patients. *Archives of General Psychiatry*, 51(11), 865–874.

de Montigny, C., Silverstone, P. H., Debonnel, G., Blier, P., & Bakish, D. (1999). Venlafaxine in treatment-resistant major depression: A Canadian multicenter, open-label trial. *Journal of Clinical Psychopharmacology*, 19(5), 401–406.

DerMarderosian, A. (2009). *Medicinal herbs and nutraceuticals The Merck manual of medical information* (2nd home ed.). Whitehouse Station, NJ: Merck.

De Smet, P. (2004). Health risks of herbal remedies: An update. *Clinical Pharmacology and Therapeutics*, 76(1), 1–17.

Diem, S. J., Blackwell, T. L., Stone, K. L., Yaffe, K., Cauley, J. A., Whooley, M. A., et al. (2007). Depressive symptoms and rates of bone loss at the hip in older women. *Journal of the American Geriatric Society*, 55(6), 824–831.

Dincer, S., Babul, A., Erdogan, D., Ozogul, C., & Dincers, L. (1996). Effect of taurine on wound healing. *Amino Acids*, 59-71.

Djaldetti, R., Yust-Katz, S., Kolianov, V., Melamed, E., & Dabby, R. (2007). The effect of duloxetine on primary pain symptoms in Parkinson disease. *Clinical Neuropharmacology*, 30(4), 201–205.

Dolder, C. R., Nelson, M., & Snider, M. (2008). Agomelatine treatment of major depressive disorder. *Annals of Pharmacotherapy*, 42(12), 1822–1831.

Dombrovski, A. Y., Mulsant, B. H., Haskett, R. F., Prudic, J., Begley, A. E., & Sackeim, H. A. (2005). Predictors of remission after electroconvulsive therapy in unipolar major depression. *Journal of Clinical Psychiatry, 66*(8), 1043–1049.

Dopheide, M. M., Morgan, R. E., Rodvelt, K. R., Schachtman, T. R., & Miller, D. K. (2007). Modafinil evokes striatal [(3)H]dopamine release and alters the subjective properties of stimulants. *European Journal of Pharmacology, 568*(1–3), 112–123.

Doree, J. P., Des Rosiers, J., Lew, V., Gendron, A., Elie, R., Stip, E., et al. (2007). Quetiapine augmentation of treatment-resistant depression: A comparison with lithium. *Current Medical Research and Opinion, 23*(2), 333–341.

Druss, B. G., & Rosenheck, R. A. (2000). Use of practitioner-based complementary therapies by persons reporting mental conditions in the United States. *Archives of General Psychiatry, 57*(7), 708–714.

Dukakis, K., & Tye, L. (2006). *Shock: The healing power of electroconvulsive therapy.* New York: Avery.

Dumville, J. C., Miles, J. N., Porthouse, J., Cockayne, S., Saxon, L., & King, C. (2006). Can vitamin D supplementation prevent winter-time blues? A randomised trial among older women. *Journal of Nutrition, Health and Aging, 10*(2), 151–153.

Dunn, A. J., Swiergiel, A. H., & de Beaurepaire, R. (2005). Cytokines as mediators of depression: What can we learn from animal studies? *Neuroscience Biobehavior Review, 29*(4–5), 891–909.

Dunner, D. L., Wilson, M., Fava, M., Kornstein, S., Munoz, R., O'Reardon, J., et al. (2007). Long-term tolerability and effectiveness of duloxetine in the treatment of major depressive disorder. *Depression and Anxiety, 25*(5), E1–E8.

Dwoskin, L. P., Rauhut, A. S., King-Pospisil, K. A., & Bardo, M. T. (2006). Review of the pharmacology and clinical profile of bupropion, an antidepressant and tobacco use cessation agent. *CNS Drug Review, 12*(3–4), 178–207.

Eby, G. A., & Eby, K. L. (2006). Rapid recovery from major depression using magnesium treatment. *Medical Hypotheses, 67*(2), 362–370.

Eby, G. A., 3rd, & Eby, K. L. (2009). Magnesium for treatment-resistant depression: A review and hypothesis. *Medical Hypotheses,* epub.

Edeh, J., & Toone, B. K. (1985). Antiepileptic therapy, folate deficiency, and psychiatric morbidity: A general practice survey. *Epilepsia, 26*(5), 434–440.

Eden Evins, A., Demopulos, C., Yovel, I., Culhane, M., Ogutha, J., Grandin, L. D., et al. (2006). Inositol augmentation of lithium or valproate for bipolar depression. *Bipolar Disorders, 8*(2), 168–174.

Einarson, A. (2005). The safety of psychotropic drug use during pregnancy: A review. *Medscape General Medicine, 7*(4), 3.

Einarson, A., Schachtschneider, A. K., Halil, R., Bollano, E., & Koren, G. (2005). SSRIs and other antidepressant use during pregnancy and potential neonatal adverse effects: Impact of a public health advisory and subsequent reports in the news media. *BMC Pregnancy and Childbirth, 5,* 11.

Einarson, T. R., & Einarson, A. (2005). Newer antidepressants in pregnancy and rates of major malformations: A meta-analysis of prospective comparative studies. *Pharmacoepidemiolog and Drug Safety, 14*(12), 823–827.

Eisenberg, D. M., Davis, R. B., Ettner, S. L., Appel, S., Wilkey, S., Van Rompay, M., et al. (1998). Trends in alternative medicine use in the United States, 1990–1997: Results of a follow-up national survey. *JAMA, 280*(18), 1569–1575.

Eisendrath, S., & McLane, M. (2008). *Mindfulness-based cognitive therapy.* Paper presented at New Frontiers in Depression Research and Treatment, San Francisco.

Elenkov, I. J., Iezzoni, D. G., Daly, A., Harris, A. G., & Chrousos, G. P. (2005). Cytokine dysregulation, inflammation and well-being. *Neuroimmunomodulation, 12*(5), 255–269.

El Idrissi, A., & Trenkner, E. (1999). Growth factors and taurine protect against excitotoxicity by stabilizing calcium homeostasis and energy metabolism. *Journal of Neuroscience, 19*(21), 9459–9468.

Elkashef, A., Fudala, P. J., Gorgon, L., Li, S. H., Kahn, R., Chiang, N., et al. (2006). Double-blind, placebo-controlled trial of selegiline transdermal system (STS) for the treatment of cocaine dependence. *Drug and Alcohol Dependence, 85*(3), 191–197.

Elkin, I., Gibbons, R. D., Shea, M. T., Sotsky, S. M., Watkins, J. T., Pilkonis, P. A., et al. (1995). Initial severity and differential treatment outcome in the National Institute of Mental Health Treatment of Depression Collaborative Research Program. *Journal of Consulting and Clinical Psychology, 63*(5), 841–847.

Elkin, I., Shea, M. T., Watkins, J. T., Imber, S. D., Sotsky, S. M., Collins, J. F., et al. (1989). National Institute of Mental Health Treatment of Depression Collaborative Research Program. General effectiveness of treatments. *Archives of General Psychiatry, 46*(11), 971–982; discussion 983.

Emslie, G., Kratochvil, C., Vitiello, B., Silva, S., Mayes, T., McNulty, S., et al. (2006). Treatment for Adolescents with Depression Study (TADS): Safety results. *Journal of the American Academy of Child and Adolescent Psychiatry, 45*(12), 1440–1455.

Endler, N. S. (1988). The origins of electroconvulsive therapy (ECT). *Convulsive Therapy, 4*(1), 5–23.

Esplen, M. J., & Garfinkel, P. E. (1998). Guided imagery treatment to promote self-soothing in bulimia nervosa. A theoretical rationale. *Journal of Psychotherapy Practice Research, 7*(2), 102–118.

Esplen, M. J., Garfinkel, P. E., Olmsted, M., Gallop, R. M., & Kennedy, S. (1998). A randomized controlled trial of guided imagery in bulimia nervosa. *Psychological Medicine, 28*(6), 1347–1357.

Evans, M. D., Hollon, S. D., DeRubeis, R. J., Piasecki, J. M., Grove, W. M., Garvey, M. J., et al. (1992). Differential relapse following cognitive therapy and pharmacotherapy for depression. *Archives of General Psychiatry, 49*(10), 802–808.

Even, C., Schroder, C. M., Friedman, S., & Rouillon, F. (2008). Efficacy of light therapy in nonseasonal depression: A systematic review. *Journal of Affective Disorders, 108*(1–2), 11–23.

Evins, A. E., Culhane, M. A., Alpert, J. E., Pava, J., Liese, B. S., Farabaugh, A., et al. (2008). A controlled trial of bupropion added to nicotine patch and behavioral therapy for smoking cessation in adults with unipolar depressive disorders. *Journal of Clinical Psychopharmacology, 28*(6), 660–666.

Eyles, D., Brown, J., Mackay-Sim, A., McGrath, J., & Feron, F. (2003). Vitamin D3 and brain development. *Neuroscience, 118*(3), 641–653.

Faraone, S. V., Biederman, J., Spencer, T., Michelson, D., Adler, L., Reimherr, F., et al. (2005). Efficacy of atomoxetine in adult attention-deficit/hyperactivity disorder: A drug-placebo response curve analysis. *Behavior and Brain Function, 1*, 16.

Fava, M. (2007). Augmenting antidepressants with folate: A clinical perspective. *Journal of Clinical Psychiatry, 68*(Suppl. 10), 4–7.

Fava, M., Borus, J. S., Alpert, J. E., Nierenberg, A. A., Rosenbaum, J. F., & Bottiglieri, T. (1997). Folate, vitamin B12, and homocysteine in major depressive disorder. *American Journal of Psychiatry, 154*(3), 426–428.

Fava, M., Farabaugh, A. H., Sickinger, A. H., Wright, E., Alpert, J. E., Sonawalla, S., et al. (2002). Personality disorders and depression. *Psychological Medicine, 32*, 1049–1057.

Fava, M., Mallinckrodt, C. H., Detke, M. J., Watkin, J. G., & Wohlreich, M. M. (2004). The effect of duloxetine on painful physical symptoms in depressed patients: Do improvements in these symptoms result in higher remission rates? *Journal of Clinical Psychiatry, 65*(4), 521–530.

Fava, M., McCall, W. V., Krystal, A., Wessel, T., Rubens, R., Caron, J., et al. (2006). Eszopiclone co-administered with fluoxetine in patients with insomnia coexisting with major depressive disorder. *Biological Psychiatry, 59*(11), 1052–1060.

Fava, M., Papakostas, G. I., Petersen, T., Mahal, Y., Quitkin, F., Stewart, J., et al. (2003). Switching to bupropion in fluoxetine-resistant major depressive disorder. *Annals of Clinical Psychiatry, 15*(1), 17–22.

Fava, M., Rankin, M. A., Wright, E. C., Alpert, J. E., Nierenberg, A. N., Pava, J., et al. (2000). Anxiety disorders in major depression. *Comprehensive Psychiatry, 41*(2), 97–102.

Fava, M., Rush, A. J., Wisniewski, S. R., Nierenberg, A. A., Alpert, J. E., McGrath, P. J., et al. (2006). A comparison of mirtazapine and nortriptyline following two consecutive failed medication treatments for depressed outpatients: A STAR*D report. *American Journal of Psychiatry, 163*(7), 1161–1172.

Fava, M., Thase, M. E., & DeBattista, C. (2005). A multicenter, placebo-controlled study of modafinil augmentation in partial responders to selective serotonin reuptake inhibitors with persistent fatigue and sleepiness. *Journal of Clinical Psychiatry, 66*(1), 85–93.

Fava, M., Thase, M. E., DeBattista, C., Doghramji, K., Arora, S., & Hughes, R. J. (2007). Modafinil augmentation of selective serotonin reuptake inhibitor therapy in MDD partial responders with persistent fatigue and sleepiness. *Annals of Clinical Psychiatry, 19*(3), 153–159.

FDA. (1998). Impurities confirmed in dietary supplement 5-hydroxy-L-tryptophan. Talk Paper. Retrieved from http://vm.cfsan.fda.gov/~lrd/tp5htp.html

FDA. (2001). Information paper on L-tryptophan and 5-hydroxy-L-tryptophan. Office of Nutritional Products, Labeling, Dietary Supplements. Center for Food Safety and Applied Nutrition.

Februhartanty, J., Dillon, D., & Khusun, H. (2002). Will iron supplementation given during menstruation improve iron status better than weekly supplementation? *Asia Pacific Journal of Clinical Nutrition, 11*(1), 36–41.

Feiger, A. D., Rickels, K., Rynn, M. A., Zimbroff, D. L., & Robinson, D. S. (2006). Selegiline transdermal system for the treatment of major depressive disorder: An 8-week, double-blind, placebo-controlled, flexible-dose titration trial. *Journal of Clinical Psychiatry, 67*(9), 1354–1361.

Feinberg, S. S. (2004). Combining stimulants with monoamine oxidase inhibitors: A review of uses and one possible additional indication. *Journal of Clinical Psychiatry, 65*(11), 1520–1524.

Fernandes, P. P., & Petty, F. (2003). Modafinil for remitted bipolar depression with hypersomnia. *Annals of Pharmacotherapy, 37*(12), 1807–1809.

Feske, U., Mulsant, B. H., Pilkonis, P. A., Soloff, P., Dolata, D., Sackeim, H. A., et al. (2004). Clinical outcome of ECT in patients with major depression and comorbid borderline personality disorder. *American Journal of Psychiatry, 161*(11), 2073–2080.

Fieve, R. (1980). *Moodswing.* New York: Bantam.

Fieve, R. (2006). *Bipolar II: Enhance your highs, boost your creativity, and escape the cycles of recurrent depression—the essential guide to recognize and treat the mood swings of this increasingly common disorder.* Emmaus, PA: Rodale.

Findling, R. L., McNamara, N. K., Youngstrom, E. A., Stansbrey, R., Gracious, B. L., Reed, M. D., et al. (2005). Double-blind 18-month trial of lithium versus divalproex maintenance treatment in pediatric bipolar disorder. *Journal of the American Academy of Child and Adolescent Psychiatry, 44*(5), 409–417.

Finger, S., & Franklin, Z. (2006). Benjamin Franklin and shock-induced amnesia. *American Psychologist, 61,* 240–248.

Fink, K. G., Huber, J., Wurnschimmel, E., & Schmeller, N. T. (2008). The use of duloxetine in the treatment of male stress urinary incontinence. *Wiener Medizinische Wochenschrift, 158*(3–4), 116–118.

Firoz, M., & Graber, M. (2001). Bioavailaility of US commercial magnesium preparation. *Magnesium Research, 14*, 257–262.

Fischer, E., Heller, B., Nachon, M., & Spatz, H. (1975). Therapy of depression by phenylalanine. Preliminary note. *Arzneimittel-Forschung, 25*(1), 132.

Fleming, J. E., Boyle, M. H., & Offord, D. R. (1993). The outcome of adolescent depression in the Ontario Child Health Study follow-up. *Journal of the American Academy of Child and Adolescent Psychiatry, 32*(1), 28–33.

Fombonne, E., Wostear, G., Cooper, V., Harrington, R., & Rutter, M. (2001a). The Maudsley long-term follow-up of child and adolescent depression. 1. Psychiatric outcomes in adulthood. *British Journal of Psychiatry, 179*, 210–217.

Fombonne, E., Wostear, G., Cooper, V., Harrington, R., & Rutter, M. (2001b). The Maudsley long-term follow-up of child and adolescent depression. 2. Suicidality, criminality and social dysfunction in adulthood. *British Journal of Psychiatry, 179*, 218–223.

Food and Nutrition Board Institute of Medicine. (2001). Zinc. Dietary reference intakes for vitamin A, vitamin K, boron, chromium, copper, iodine, iron, manganese, molybdenum, nickel, silicon, vanadium, and zinc (pp. 442–501). Washington, DC: National Academy Press.

Food and Nutrition Board, IOM. (1999). The role of protein and amino acids in sustaining and enhancing performance. Retrieved February 2, 2010, from http://www.nap.edu/books/0309063469/html/

Ford, D. E., & Erlinger, T. P. (2004). Depression and C-reactive protein in US adults: Data from the Third National Health and Nutrition Examination Survey. *Archives of Internal Medicine, 164*(9), 1010–1014.

Fors, E. A., Sexton, H., & Gotestam, K. G. (2002). The effect of guided imagery and amitriptyline on daily fibromyalgia pain: A prospective, randomized, controlled trial. *Journal of Psychiatric Research, 36*(3), 179–187.

Fountoulakis, K. N., Kantartzis, S., Siamouli, M., Panagiotidis, P., Kaprinis, S., Iacovides, A., et al. (2006). Peripheral thyroid dysfunction in depression. *The World Journal of Biological Psychiatry, 7*(3), 131–137.

Frampton, J. E., & Plosker, G. L. (2007a). Duloxetine: A review of its use in the treatment of major depressive disorder. *CNS Drugs, 21*(7), 581–609.

Frampton, J. E., & Plosker, G. L. (2007b). Selegiline transdermal system in major depressive disorder: Profile report. *CNS Drugs, 21*(6), 521–524.

Frampton, J. E., & Plosker, G. L. (2007c). Selegiline transdermal system: In the treatment of major depressive disorder. *Drugs, 67*(2), 257–265; discussion 266–257.

Frank, E., Kupfer, D. J., Thase, M. E., Mallinger, A. G., Swartz, H. A., Fagiolini, A. M., et al. (2005). Two-year outcomes for interpersonal and social rhythm therapy in individuals with bipolar I disorder. *Archives of General Psychiatry, 62*(9), 996–1004.

Frank, E., Novick, D., & Masalehdan, A. (2003). Women and depression. National Alliance on Mental Illness. Available from: http://www.nami.org/Content/ContentGroups/Helpline1/Depression_in_Women.htm

Frankle, W. G., Perlis, R. H., Deckersbach, T., Grandin, L. D., Gray, S. M., Sachs, G. S., et al. (2002). Bipolar depression: Relationship between episode length and antidepressant treatment. *Psychological Medicine, 32*(8), 1417–1423.

Franklin, B. (n.d.). *Papers of Benjamin Franklin* (vol. 40). Los Altos, CA: Packard Humanities Institute.

Fraser, L. M., O'Carroll, R. E., & Ebmeier, K. P. (2008). The effect of electroconvulsive therapy on autobiographical memory: A systematic review. *Journal of ECT, 24*(1), 10–17.

Frasure-Smith, N., & Lesperance, F. (2003). Depression and other psychological risks following myocardial infarction. *Archives of General Psychiatry, 60*(6), 627–636.

Frasure-Smith, N., & Lesperance, F. (2006a). Coronary heart disease and depression: The next steps. *Canadian Journal of Psychiatry, 51*(12), 727–729.

Frasure-Smith, N., & Lesperance, F. (2006b). Depression and coronary artery disease. *Herz, 31*(Suppl. 3), 64–68.

Frasure-Smith, N., & Lesperance, F. (2006c). Recent evidence linking coronary heart disease and depression. *Canadian Journal of Psychiatry, 51*(12), 730–737.

Frasure-Smith, N., & Lesperance, F. (2008). Depression and anxiety as predictors of 2-year cardiac events in patients with stable coronary artery disease. *Archives of General Psychiatry, 65*(1), 62–71.

Frasure-Smith, N., Lesperance, F., Gravel, G., Masson, A., Juneau, M., Talajic, M., et al. (2000). Social support, depression, and mortality during the first year after myocardial infarction. *Circulation, 101*(16), 1919–1924.

Frasure-Smith, N., Lesperance, F., Irwin, M. R., Sauve, C., Lesperance, J., & Theroux, P. (2007). Depression, C-reactive protein and two-year major adverse cardiac events in men after acute coronary syndromes. *Biological Psychiatry, 62*(4), 302–308.

Frasure-Smith, N., Lesperance, F., & Julien, P. (2004). Major depression is associated with lower omega-3 fatty acid levels in patients with recent acute coronary syndromes. *Biological Psychiatry, 55*(9), 891–896.

Frasure-Smith, N., Lesperance, F., Juneau, M., Talajic, M., & Bourassa, M. G. (1999). Gender, depression, and one-year prognosis after myocardial infarction. *Psychosomatic Medicine, 61*(1), 26–37.

Freeman, L., Cohen, L., Stewart, M., White, R., Link, J., Palmer, J. L., et al. (2008). Imagery intervention for recovering breast cancer patients: Clinical trial of safety and efficacy. *Journal of the Society for Integrative Oncology, 6*(2), 67–75.

Freeman, M. P. (2009). Omega-3 fatty acids in major depressive disorder. *Journal of Clinical Psychiatry, 70*(Suppl. 5), 7–11.

Freeman, M. P., Hibbeln, J. R., Wisner, K. L., Davis, J. M., Mischoulon, D., Peet, M., et al. (2006). Omega-3 fatty acids: Evidence basis for treatment and future research in psychiatry. *Journal of Clinical Psychiatry, 67*(12), 1954–1967.

Freud, S. (1917). Trauer und Melancholie. *Int. Z. Psychoanal, 4*(6), 288–301.

Friedel, H. A., Goa, K. L., & Benfield, P. (1989). S-adenosyl-L-methionine. A review of its pharmacological properties and therapeutic potential in liver dysfunction and affective disorders in relation to its physiological role in cell metabolism. *Drugs, 38*(3), 389–416.

Frye, M. A., Grunze, H., Suppes, T., McElroy, S. L., Keck, P. E., Jr. , Walden, J., et al. (2007). A placebo-controlled evaluation of adjunctive modafinil in the treatment of bipolar depression. *American Journal of Psychiatry, 164*(8), 1242–1249.

Furlong, R. A., Rubinsztein, J. S., Ho, L., Walsh, C., Coleman, T. A., Muir, W. J., et al. (1999). Analysis and metaanalysis of two polymorphisms within the tyrosine hydroxylase gene in bipolar and unipolar affective disorders. *American Journal of Medical Genetics, 88*(1), 88–94.

Furukawa, T. A., Fujita, A., Harai, H., Yoshimura, R., Kitamura, T., & Takahashi, K. (2008). Definitions of recovery and outcomes of major depression: Results from a 10-year follow-up. *Acta Psychiatrica Scandinavica, 117*(1), 35–40.

Fux, M., Levine, J., & Aviv, A. (1996). Inositol treatment of obsessive-compulsive disorder. *American Journal of Psychiatry, 153*, 1219–1122.

Gadde, K. M., & Xiong, G. L. (2007). Bupropion for weight reduction. *Expert Review of Neurotherapeutics, 7*(1), 17–24.

Gahimer, J., Wernicke, J., Yalcin, I., Ossanna, M. J., Wulster-Radcliffe, M., & Viktrup, L. (2007). A retrospective pooled analysis of duloxetine safety in 23,983 subjects. *Current Medical Research and Opinion, 23*(1), 175–184.

Gaillez, C., Sorbara, F., & Perrin, E. (2007). [Atomoxetine (Strattera), an alternative in the treatment of attention-deficit/hyperactivity disorder (ADHD) in children]. *Encephale, 33*(4 Pt 1), 621–628.

Gallagher, P., Malik, N., Newham, J., Young, A. H., Ferrier, I. N., & Mackin, P. (2008). Antiglucocorticoid treatments for mood disorders. *Cochrane Database Syst Reviews*, (1), CD005168.

Garakani, A., Martinez, J. M., Marcus, S., Weaver, J., Rickels, K., Fava, M., et al. (2008). A randomized, double-blind, and placebo-controlled trial of quetiapine augmentation of fluoxetine in major depressive disorder. *International Clinical Psychopharmacology, 23*(5), 269–275.

Garcion, E., Wion-Barbot, N., Montero-Menei, C. N., Berger, F., & Wion, D. (2002). New clues about vitamin D functions in the nervous system. *Trends in Endocrinology and Metabolism, 13*(3), 100–105.

Gardos, G., Cole, J. O., Matthews, J. D., Nierenberg, A. A., & Dugan, S. J. (1992). The acute effects of a loading dose of phenylalanine in unipolar depressed patients with and without tardive dyskinesia. *Neuropsychopharmacology, 6*(4), 241–247.

Garriock, H. A., Delgado, P., Kling, M. A., Carpenter, L. L., Burke, M., Burke, W. J., et al. (2006). Number of risk genotypes is a risk factor for major depressive disorder: A case control study. *Behavior and Brain Function, 2*, 24.

Gaynes, B. N. (2007). Light therapy and fluoxetine similarly effective for improving seasonal affective disorder. *Evidence Based Mental Health, 10*(1), 26.

Gaynes, B. N., Rush, A. J., Trivedi, M., Wisniewski, S. R., Balasubramani, G. K., Spencer, D. C., et al. (2005). A direct comparison of presenting characteristics of depressed outpatients from primary vs. specialty care settings: Preliminary findings from the STAR*D clinical trial. *General Hospital Psychiatry, 27*(2), 87–96.

Gelber, D., Levine, J., & Belmaker, R. (2001). Effect of inositol on bulimia nervosa and binge eating. *International Journal of Eating Disorders, 29*(3), 345–348.

Gelenberg, A. J., & Gibson, C. J. (1984). Tyrosine for the treatment of depression. *Nutrition and Health, 3*(3), 163–173.

Gelenberg, A. J., & Klerman, G. L. (1978). Antidepressants: Their use in clinical practice. *Rational Drug Therapy, 12*(4), 1–7.

Gelenberg, A. J., Wojcik, J. D., Falk, W. E., Baldessarini, R. J., Zeisel, S. H., Schoenfeld, D., et al. (1990). Tyrosine for depression: A double-blind trial. *Journal of Affective Disorders, 19*(2), 125–132.

Geller, D., Donnelly, C., Lopez, F., Rubin, R., Newcorn, J., Sutton, V., et al. (2007). Atomoxetine treatment for pediatric patients with attention-deficit/hyperactivity disorder with comorbid anxiety disorder. *Journal of the American Academy of Child and Adolescent Psychiatry, 46*(9), 1119–1127.

Gentile, S. (2005a). SSRIs in pregnancy and lactation: Emphasis on neurodevelopmental outcome. *CNS Drugs, 19*(7), 623–633.

Gentile, S. (2005b). The safety of newer antidepressants in pregnancy and breastfeeding. *Drug Safety, 28*(2), 137–152.

Gentile, S. (2006). Escitalopram late in pregnancy and while breast-feeding. *Annals of Pharmacotherapy, 40*(9), 1696–1697.

George, M. S., Nahas, Z., Borckardt, J. J., Anderson, B., Burns, C., Kose, S., et al. (2007). Vagus nerve stimulation for the treatment of depression and other neuropsychiatric disorders. *Expert Reviews in Neurotherapeutics, 7*(1), 63–74.

George, M. S., Rush, A. J., Marangell, L. B., Sackeim, H. A., Brannan, S. K., Davis, S. M., et al. (2005). A one-year comparison of vagus nerve stimulation with treatment as usual for treatment-resistant depression. *Biological Psychiatry, 58*(5), 364–373.

Gershon, A. A., Dannon, P. N., & Grunhaus, L. (2003). Transcranial magnetic stimulation in the treatment of depression. *American Journal of Psychiatry, 160*(5), 835–845.

Ghadirian, A. M., Murphy, B. E., & Gendron, M. J. (1998). Efficacy of light versus tryptophan therapy in seasonal affective disorder. *Journal of Affective Disorders, 50*(1), 23–27.

Ghaemi, S. N., Rosenquist, K. J., Ko, J. Y., Baldassano, C. F., Kontos, N. J., & Baldessarini, R. J. (2004). Antidepressant treatment in bipolar versus unipolar depression. *American Journal of Psychiatry, 161*(1), 163–165.

Ghoniem, G. M., Van Leeuwen, J. S., Elser, D. M., Freeman, R. M., Zhao, Y. D., Yalcin, I., et al. (2005). A randomized controlled trial of duloxetine alone, pelvic floor muscle training alone, combined treatment and no active treatment in women with stress urinary incontinence. *Journal of Urology, 173*(5), 1647–1653.

Gibbons, R. D., Brown, C. H., Hur, K., Marcus, S. M., Bhaumik, D. K., Erkens, J. A., et al. (2007). Early evidence on the effects of regulators' suicidality warnings on SSRI prescriptions and suicide in children and adolescents. *American Journal of Psychiatry, 164*(9), 1356–1363.

Gibbons, R. D., Brown, C. H., Hur, K., Marcus, S. M., Bhaumik, D. K., & Mann, J. J. (2007). Relationship between antidepressants and suicide attempts: An analysis of the Veterans Health Administration data sets. *American Journal of Psychiatry, 164*(7), 1044–1049.

Gibbons, R. D., Hur, K., Bhaumik, D. K., & Mann, J. J. (2005). The relationship between antidepressant medication use and rate of suicide. *Archives of General Psychiatry, 62*(2), 165–172.

Gibbons, R. D., Hur, K., Bhaumik, D. K., & Mann, J. J. (2006). The relationship between antidepressant prescription rates and rate of early adolescent suicide. *American Journal of Psychiatry, 163*(11), 1898–1904.

Gibson, A. P., Bettinger, T. L., Patel, N. C., & Crismon, M. L. (2006). Atomoxetine versus stimulants for treatment of attention deficit/hyperactivity disorder. *Annals of Pharmacotherapy, 40*(6), 1134–1142.

Gijsman, H. J., Geddes, J. R., Rendell, J. M., Nolen, W. A., & Goodwin, G. M. (2004). Antidepressants for bipolar depression: A systematic review of randomized, controlled trials. *American Journal of Psychiatry, 161*(9), 1537–1547.

Gilbody, S., Lewis, S., & Lightfoot, T. (2007). Methylenetetrahydrofolate reductase (MTHFR) genetic polymorphisms and psychiatric disorders: A HuGE review. *American Journal of Epidemiology, 165*(1), 1–13.

Gilbody, S., Lightfoot, T., & Sheldon, T. (2007). Is low folate a risk factor for depression? A meta-analysis and exploration of heterogeneity. *Journal of Epidemiology and Community Health, 61*(7), 631–637.

Gillman, P. K. (2005). Monoamine oxidase inhibitors, opioid analgesics and serotonin toxicity. *British Journal of Anaesthesia, 95*(4), 434–441.

Gilmer, W. S., Gollan, J. K., Wisniewski, S. R., Howland, R. H., Trivedi, M. H., Miyahara, S., et al. (2008). Does the duration of index episode affect the treatment outcome of major depressive disorder? A STAR*D report. *Journal of Clinical Psychiatry, 69*(8), 1246–1256.

Gilmer, W. S., Trivedi, M. H., Rush, A. J., Wisniewski, S. R., Luther, J., Howland, R. H., et al. (2005). Factors associated with chronic depressive episodes: A preliminary report from the STAR-D project. *Acta Psychiatrica Scandinavica, 112*(6), 425–433.

Giovino, G. A. (2004). Tobacco harm reduction involves more than cigarette harm reduction. *American Journal of Public Health, 94*(8), 1294; author reply 1294–1295.

Glassman, A. H., Bigger, J. T., Gaffney, M., Shapiro, P. A., & Swenson, J. R. (2006). Onset of major depression associated with acute coronary syndromes: Relationship of onset, major depressive disorder history, and episode severity to sertraline benefit. *Archives of General Psychiatry, 63*(3), 283–288.

Glassman, A. H., O'Connor, C. M., Califf, R. M., Swedberg, K., Schwartz, P., Bigger, J. T., Jr., et al. (2002). Sertraline treatment of major depression in patients with acute MI or unstable angina. *JAMA, 288*(6), 701–709.

Gloth, F. M., 3rd, Alam, W., & Hollis, B. (1999). Vitamin D vs broad spectrum phototherapy in the treatment of seasonal affective disorder. *Journal of Nutrition, Health and Aging, 3*(1), 5–7.

Gold, P. B., Rubey, R. N., & Harvey, R. T. (2002). Naturalistic, self-assignment comparative trial of bupropion SR, a nicotine patch, or both for smoking cessation treatment in primary care. *American Journal of Addiction, 11*(4), 315–331.

Goldapple, K., Segal, Z., Garson, C., Lau, M., Bieling, P., Kennedy, S., et al. (2004). Modulation of cortical-limbic pathways in major depression: Treatment-specific effects of cognitive behavior therapy. *Archives of General Psychiatry, 61*(1), 34–41.

Goldberg, J. F., Burdick, K. E., & Endick, C. J. (2004). Preliminary randomized, double-blind, placebo-controlled trial of pramipexole added to mood stabilizers for treatment-resistant bipolar depression. *American Journal of Psychiatry, 161*(3), 564–566.

Goldberg, J. F., Perlis, R. H., Ghaemi, S. N., Calabrese, J. R., Bowden, C. L., Wisniewski, S., et al. (2007). Adjunctive antidepressant use and symptomatic recovery among bipolar depressed patients with concomitant manic symptoms: Findings from the STEP-BD. *American Journal of Psychiatry, 164*(9), 1348–1355.

Gonzales, D., Rennard, S. I., Nides, M., Oncken, C., Azoulay, S., Billing, C. B., et al. (2006). Varenicline, an alpha4beta2 nicotinic acetylcholine receptor partial agonist, vs sustained-release bupropion and placebo for smoking cessation: A randomized controlled trial. *JAMA, 296*(1), 47–55.

Goodnick, P. J. (2007). Seligiline transdermal system in depression. *Expert Opinion in Pharmacotherapy, 8*(1), 59–64.

Goodwin, G. M., Bowden, C. L., Calabrese, J. R., Grunze, H., Kasper, S., White, R., et al. (2004). A pooled analysis of 2 placebo-controlled 18-month trials of lamotrigine and lithium maintenance in bipolar I disorder. *Journal of Clinical Psychiatry, 65*(3), 432–441.

Goren, J. L., Stoll, A. L., Damico, K. E., Sarmiento, I. A., & Cohen, B. M. (2004). Bioavailability and lack of toxicity of S-adenosyl-L-methionine (SAMe) in humans. *Pharmacotherapy, 24*(11), 1501–1507.

Grunebaum, M. F., Ellis, S. P., Li, S., Oquendo, M. A., & Mann, J. J. (2004). Antidepressants and suicide risk in the United States, 1985–1999. *Journal of Clinical Psychiatry, 65*(11), 1456–1462.

Grunhaus, L., Hirschman, S., Dolberg, O. T., Schreiber, S., & Dannon, P. N. (2001). Coadministration of melatonin and fluoxetine does not improve the 3-month outcome following ECT. *Journal of ECT, 17*(2), 124–128.

Gruzelier, J. H. (2002). A review of the impact of hypnosis, relaxation, guided imagery and individual differences on aspects of immunity and health. *Stress, 5*(2), 147–163.

Guay, D. R. (2005). Duloxetine for management of stress urinary incontinence. *American Journal of Geriatric Pharmacotherapy, 3*(1), 25–38.

Gupta, M. A. (1986). Is chronic pain a variant of depressive illness? A critical review. *Canadian Journal of Psychiatry, 31*(3), 241–248.

Gupta, P., Singh, S., Goyal, V., Shukla, G., & Behari, M. (2007). Low-dose topiramate versus lamotrigine in migraine prophylaxis (the Lotolamp study). *Headache, 47*(3), 402–412.

Gupta, V. K. (2007). Topiramate for migraine prophylaxis: A reappraisal of the therapeutic premise. *Journal of Child Neurology, 22*(1), 123–124.

Gutierrez, R. L., McKercher, R. M., Galea, J., & Jamison, K. L. (2005). Lamotrigine augmentation strategy for patients with treatment-resistant depression. *CNS Spectrum, 10*(10), 800–805.

Guzzetta, F., Tondo, L., Centorrino, F., & Baldessarini, R. J. (2007). Lithium treatment reduces suicide risk in recurrent major depressive disorder. *Journal of Clinical Psychiatry, 68*(3), 380–383.

Halpin, L. S., Speir, A. M., CapoBianco, P., & Barnett, S. D. (2002). Guided imagery in cardiac surgery. *Outcomes Management, 6*(3), 132–137.

Hammonds, M. D., Shim, S. S., Feng, P., & Calabrese, J. R. (2007). Effects of subchronic lithium treatment on levels of BDNF, Bcl-2 and phospho-CREB in the rat hippocampus. *Basic and Clinical Pharmacology and Toxicology, 100*(5), 356–359.

Haney, E. M., Chan, B. K., Diem, S. J., Ensrud, K. E., Cauley, J. A., Barrett-Connor, E., et al. (2007). Association of low bone mineral density with selective serotonin reuptake inhibitor use by older men. *Archives of Internal Medicine, 167*(12), 1246–1251.

Hänsel, R. (1968). Characterization and physiological activity of some Kawa constituents. *Pacific Science, 22,* 293–313.

Hanusa, B. H., Scholle, S. H., Haskett, R. F., Spadaro, K., & Wisner, K. L. (2008). Screening for depression in the postpartum period: A comparison of three instruments. *Journal of Women's Health (Larchmont), 17*(4), 585–596.

Harmer, C. J., McTavish, S. F., Clark, L., Goodwin, G. M., & Cowen, P. J. (2001). Tyrosine depletion attenuates dopamine function in healthy volunteers. *Psychopharmacology (Berlin), 154*(1), 105–111.

Harrington, R. (2001). Adolescent depression: Same or different? *Archives of General Psychiatry, 58*(1), 21–22.

Harrington, R., Fudge, H., Rutter, M., Pickles, A., & Hill, J. (1990). Adult outcomes of childhood and adolescent depression. I. Psychiatric status. *Archives of General Psychiatry, 47*(5), 465–473.

Harris, S., & Dawson-Hughes, B. (1993). Seasonal mood changes in 250 normal women. *Psychiatry Research, 49*(1), 77–87.

Hartford, J., Kornstein, S., Liebowitz, M., Pigott, T., Russell, J., Detke, M., et al. (2007). Duloxetine as an SNRI treatment for generalized anxiety disorder: Results from a placebo and active-controlled trial. *International Clinical Psychopharmacology, 22*(3), 167–174.

Hartford, J. T., Endicott, J., Kornstein, S. G., Allgulander, C., Wohlreich, M. M., Russell, J. M., et al. (2008). Implications of pain in generalized anxiety disorder: Efficacy of duloxetine. *Primary Care Companion Journal of Clinical Psychiatry, 10*(3), 197–204.

Hartmann, E., & Spinweber, C. L. (1979). Sleep induced by L-tryptophan. Effect of dosages within the normal dietary intake. *Journal of Nervous and Mental Disease, 167*(8), 497–499.

Harwood, A. J. (2005). Lithium and bipolar mood disorder: The inositol-depletion hypothesis revisited. *Molecular Psychiatry, 10*(1), 117–126.

Hasey, G. M., D'Alessandro, E., Cooke, R. G., & Warsh, J. J. (1993). The interface between thyroid activity, magnesium, and depression: A pilot study. *Biological Psychiatry, 33*(2), 133–135.

Hasin, D. S., Goodwin, R. D., Stinson, F. S., & Grant, B. F. (2005). Epidemiology of major depressive disorder: Results from the National Epidemiologic Survey on Alcoholism and Related Conditions. *Archives of General Psychiatry, 62,* 1097–1106.

Hathcock, J. N. (1997). Vitamins and minerals: Efficacy and safety. *American Journal of Clinical Nutrition, 66*(2), 427–437.

Hathcock, J. N., Shao, A., Vieth, R., & Heaney, R. (2007). Risk assessment for vitamin D. *American Journal of Clinical Nutrition, 85*(1), 6–18.

Haykal, R. F., & Akiskal, H. S. (1990). Bupropion as a promising approach to rapid cycling bipolar II patients. *Journal of Clinical Psychiatry, 51*(11), 450–455.

Haynes, L. E., Barber, D., & Mitchell, I. J. (2004). Chronic antidepressant medication attenuates dexamethasone-induced neuronal death and sublethal neuronal damage in the hippocampus and striatum. *Brain Research, 1026*(2), 157–167.

Heaney, R. P., Davies, K. M., Chen, T. C., Holick, M. F., & Barger-Lux, M. J. (2003). Human serum 25-hydroxycholecalciferol response to extended oral dosing with cholecalciferol. *American Journal of Clinical Nutrition, 77*(1), 204–210.

Hegerl, U., Bottner, A. C., Holtschmidt-Taschner, B., Born, C., Seemuller, F., Scheunemann, W., et al. (2008). Onset of depressive episodes is faster in patients with bipolar versus unipolar depressive disorder: Evidence from a retrospective comparative study. *Journal of Clinical Psychiatry, 69*(7), 1075–1080.

Hegerl, U., Plattner, A., & Moller, H. J. (2004). Should combined pharmaco- and psychotherapy be offered to depressed patients? A qualitative review of randomized clinical trials from the 1990s. *European Archives of Psychiatry and Clinical Neuroscience, 254*(2), 99–107.

Hemels, M. E., Einarson, A., Koren, G., Lanctot, K. L., & Einarson, T. R. (2005). Antidepressant use during pregnancy and the rates of spontaneous abortions: A meta-analysis. *Annals of Pharmacotherapy, 39*(5), 803–809.

Hendrick, V., Smith, L. M., Suri, R., Hwang, S., Haynes, D., & Altshuler, L. (2003). Birth outcomes after prenatal exposure to antidepressant medication. *American Journal of Obstetrics and Gynecology, 188*(3), 812–815.

Henkel, V., Mergl, R., Allgaier, A. K., Kohnen, R., Moller, H. J., & Hegerl, U. (2006). Treatment of depression with atypical features: A meta-analytic approach. *Psychiatry Research, 141*(1), 89–101.

Henriksson, S., & Isacsson, G. (2006). Increased antidepressant use and fewer suicides in Jamtland county, Sweden, after a primary care educational programme on the treatment of depression. *Acta Psychiatrica Scandinavica, 114*(3), 159–167.

Herbert, V. (1962). Experimental nutritional folate deficiency in man. *Transactions of the Association of American Physicians, 75*, 307–320.

Herman, K. C., Ostrander, R., Walkup, J. T., Silva, S. G., & March, J. S. (2007). Empirically derived subtypes of adolescent depression: Latent profile analysis of co-occurring symptoms in the Treatment for Adolescents with Depression Study (TADS). *Journal of Consulting and Clinical Psychology, 75*(5), 716–728.

Hernandez, N. E., & Kolb, S. (1998). Effects of relaxation on anxiety in primary caregivers of chronically ill children. *Pediatric Nursing, 24*(1), 51–56.

Hibbeln, J. R. (1998). Fish consumption and major depression. *Lancet, 351*(9110), 1213.

Hibbeln, J. R. (2001). Seafood consumption and homicide mortality. A cross-national ecological analysis. *World Review of Nutrition and Dietetics, 88*, 41–46.

Hibbeln, J. R. (2002). Seafood consumption, the DHA content of mothers' milk and prevalence rates of postpartum depression: A cross-national, ecological analysis. *Journal of Affective Disorders, 69*(1–3), 15 29.

Hibbeln, J. R., Linnoila, M., Umhau, J. C., Rawlings, R., George, D. T., & Salem, N., Jr. (1998). Essential fatty acids predict metabolites of serotonin and dopamine in cerebrospinal fluid among healthy control subjects, and early- and late-onset alcoholics. *Biological Psychiatry, 44*(4), 235–242.

Hibbeln, J. R., Nieminen, L. R., Blasbalg, T. L., Riggs, J. A., & Lands, W. E. (2006). Healthy intakes of n-3 and n-6 fatty acids: Estimations considering worldwide diversity. *American Journal of Clinical Nutrition, 83*(6 Suppl.), 1483S–1493S.

Hicks, J. A., Argyropoulos, S. V., Rich, A. S., Nash, J. R., Bell, C. J., Edwards, C., et al. (2002). Randomised controlled study of sleep after nefazodone or paroxetine treatment in out-patients with depression. *British Journal of Psychiatry, 180*, 528–535.

Hidalgo, R., Hertzberg, M. A., Mellman, T., Petty, F., Tucker, P., Weisler, R., et al. (1999). Nefazodone in post-traumatic stress disorder: Results from six open-label trials. *International Clinical Psychopharmacology, 14*(2), 61–68.

Higdon, J., Drake, V., & DeLuca, H. (2008, November). Micronutrient Information Center: Vitamin D. Linus Pauling Institute. Retrieved February 2, 2010, from http://lpi.oregonstate.edu/infocenter/vitamins/vitaminD/

Hirschfeld, R. M. (2000). Suicide and antidepressant treatment. *Archives of General Psychiatry, 57*(4), 325–326.

Hirschfeld, R. M. (2002). The Mood Disorder Questionnaire: A simple, patient-rated screening instrument for bipolar disorder. *Primary Care Companion Journal of Clinical Psychiatry, 4*(1), 9–11.

Hirschfeld, R. M. (2007). Screening for bipolar disorder. *American Journal of Managed Care, 13*(7 Suppl.), S164–S169.

Hirschfeld, R. M., Calabrese, J. R., Weissman, M. M., Reed, M., Davies, M. A., Frye, M. A., et al. (2003). Screening for bipolar disorder in the community. *Journal of Clinical Psychiatry, 64*(1), 53–59.

Hirschfeld, R. M., Cass, A. R., Holt, D. C., & Carlson, C. A. (2005). Screening for bipolar disorder in patients treated for depression in a family medicine clinic. *Journal of the American Board of Family Practitioners, 18*(4), 233–239.

Hirschfeld, R. M., Holzer, C., Calabrese, J. R., Weissman, M., Reed, M., Davies, M., et al. (2003). Validity of the mood disorder questionnaire: A general population study. *American Journal Psychiatry, 160*(1), 178–180.

Hirschfeld, R. M., Montgomery, S. A., Aguglia, E., Amore, M., Delgado, P. L., Gastpar, M., et al. (2002). Partial response and nonresponse to antidepressant therapy: Current approaches and treatment options. *Journal of Clinical Psychiatry, 63*(9), 826–837.

Hirschfeld, R. M., & Vornik, L. A. (2004). Recognition and diagnosis of bipolar disorder. *Journal of Clinical Psychiatry, 65*(Suppl. 15), 5–9.

Hirschfeld, R. M., Weisler, R. H., Raines, S. R., & Macfadden, W. (2006). Quetiapine in the treatment of anxiety in patients with bipolar I or II depression: A secondary analysis from a randomized, double-blind, placebo-controlled study. *Journal of Clinical Psychiatry, 67*(3), 355–362.

Hirschfeld, R. M., Williams, J. B., Spitzer, R. L., Calabrese, J. R., Flynn, L., Keck, P. E., Jr., et al. (2000). Development and validation of a screening instrument for bipolar spectrum disorder: The Mood Disorder Questionnaire. *American Journal of Psychiatry, 157*(11), 1873–1875.

Holick, M. F. (1995). Environmental factors that influence the cutaneous production of vitamin D. *American Journal of Clinical Nutrition, 61*(3 Suppl.), 638S–645S.

Holick, M. F. (2001). Calciotropic hormones and the skin: A millennium perspective. *Journal of Cosmetic Science, 52*(2), 146–148.

Holick, M. F. (2003). Vitamin D: A millennium perspective. *Journal of Cell Biochemistry, 88*, 296–307.

Hollon, S. D., DeRubeis, R. J., Evans, M. D., Wiemer, M. J., Garvey, M. J., Grove, W. M., et al. (1992). Cognitive therapy and pharmacotherapy for depression. Singly and in combination. *Archives of General Psychiatry, 49*(10), 774–781.

Hollon, S. D., DeRubeis, R. J., Shelton, R. C., Amsterdam, J. D., Salomon, R. M., O'Reardon, J. P., et al. (2005). Prevention of relapse following cognitive therapy vs medications in moderate to severe depression. *Archives of General Psychiatry, 62*(4), 417–422.

Hollon, S. D., Shelton, R. C., Wisniewski, S., Warden, D., Biggs, M. M., Friedman, E. S., et al. (2006). Presenting characteristics of depressed outpatients as a function of recurrence: Preliminary findings from the STAR*D clinical trial. *Journal of Psychiatric Research, 40*(1), 59–69.

Holtzheimer, P., Fawaz, W., Wilson, C., & Avery, D. (2005). Repetitive transcranial magnetic stimulation may induce language switching in bilingual patients. *Brain and Language, 94*(3), 274–277.

Holtzmann, J., Polosan, M., Baro, P., & Bougerol, T. (2007). [ECT: From neuronal plasticity to mechanisms underlying antidepressant medication effect]. *Encephale, 33*(4 Pt 1), 572–578.

Hoogendijk, W. J., Lips, P., Dik, M. G., Deeg, D. J., Beekman, A. T., & Penninx, B. W. (2008). Depression is associated with decreased 25-hydroxyvitamin D and increased parathyroid hormone levels in older adults. *Archives of General Psychiatry, 65*(5), 508–512.

Houtsmuller, E. J., Notes, L. D., Newton, T., van Sluis, N., Chiang, N., Elkashef, A., et al. (2004). Transdermal selegiline and intravenous cocaine: Safety and interactions. *Psychopharmacology, 172*(1), 31–40.

Howard, L. M., Hoffbrand, S., Henshaw, C., Boath, L., & Bradley, E. (2005). Antidepressant prevention of postnatal depression. *Cochrane Database Syst Reviews* (2), CD004363.

Howland, R. H. (1993). Thyroid dysfunction in refractory depression: Implications for pathophysiology and treatment. *Journal of Clinical Psychiatry, 54*(2), 47–54.

Huang, C. C., Wei, I. H., Chou, Y. H., & Su, T. P. (2008). Effect of age, gender, menopausal status, and ovarian hormonal level on rTMS in treatment-resistant depression. *Psychoneuroendocrinology, 33*(6), 821–831.

Hudetz, J. A., Hudetz, A. G., & Klayman, J. (2000). Relationship between relaxation by guided imagery and performance of working memory. *Psychology Reports, 86*(1), 15–20.

Hudetz, J. A., Hudetz, A. G., & Reddy, D. M. (2004). Effect of relaxation on working memory and the Bispectral Index of the EEG. *Psychology Reports, 95*(1), 53–70.

Hurley, D. J., Turner, C. L., Yalcin, I., Viktrup, L., & Baygani, S. K. (2006). Duloxetine for the treatment of stress urinary incontinence in women: An integrated analysis of safety. *European Journal of Obstetric and Gynecological Reproductive Biology, 125*(1), 120–128.

Husain, M. M., Rush, A. J., Sackeim, H. A., Wisniewski, S. R., McClintock, S. M., Craven, N., et al. (2005). Age-related characteristics of depression: A preliminary STAR*D report. *American Journal of Geriatric Psychiatry, 13*(10), 852–860.

Hvas, A. M., Juul, S., Bech, P., & Nexo, E. (2004). Vitamin B6 level is associated with symptoms of depression. *Psychotherapy and Psychosomatics, 73*(6), 340–343.

Hvas, A. M., & Nexo, E. (2006). Diagnosis and treatment of vitamin B12 deficiency—an update. *Haematologica, 91*(11), 1506–1512.

Hypericum Depression Trial Study Group. (2002). Effect of Hypericum perforatum (St John's wort) in major depressive disorder: A randomized controlled trial. *JAMA, 287*(14), 1807–1814.

Ilacqua, G. E. (1994). Migraine headaches: Coping efficacy of guided imagery training. *Headache, 34*(2), 99–102.

Ingram, A., Saling, M. M., & Schweitzer, I. (2008). Cognitive side effects of brief pulse electroconvulsive therapy: A review. *Journal of ECT, 24*(1), 3–9.

Institute of Medicine, & Food and Nutrition Board. (1998). *Dietary reference intakes: Thiamin, riboflavin, niacin, vitamin B6, folate, vitamin B12, pantothenic acid, biotin, and choline.* Washington: National Academy Press.

Iosifescu, D. V., Nierenberg, A. A., Mischoulon, D., Perlis, R. H., Papakostas, G. I., Ryan, J. L., et al. (2005). An open study of triiodothyronine augmentation of selective serotonin reuptake inhibitors in treatment-resistant major depressive disorder. *Journal of Clinical Psychiatry, 66*(8), 1038–1042.

Isacsson, G., Boethius, G., & Bergman, U. (1992). Low level of antidepressant prescription for people who later commit suicide: 15 years of experience from a population-based drug database in Sweden. *Acta Psychiatrica Scandinavica, 85*(6), 444–448.

Isacsson, G., & Rich, C. L. (2005). Antidepressant drug use and suicide prevention. *International Review of Psychiatry, 17*(3), 153–162.

Isbister, G. K., Buckley, N. A., & Whyte, I. M. (2007). Serotonin toxicity: A practical approach to diagnosis and treatment. *Medical Journal of Australia, 187*(6), 361–365.

Izumi, T., Iwamoto, N., Kitaichi, Y., Kato, A., Inoue, T., & Koyama, T. (2006). Effects of co-administration of a selective serotonin reuptake inhibitor and monoamine oxidase inhibitors on 5-HT-related behavior in rats. *European Journal of Pharmacology, 532*(3), 258–264.

Izumi, T., Iwamoto, N., Kitaichi, Y., Kato, A., Inoue, T., & Koyama, T. (2007). Effects of co-administration of antidepressants and monoamine oxidase inhibitors on 5-HT-related behavior in rats. *European Journal of Pharmacology, 565*(1–3), 105–112.

Jacka, F. N., Overland, S., Stewart, R., Tell, G. S., Bjelland, I., & Mykletun, A. (2009). Association between magnesium intake and depression and anxiety in community-dwelling adults: The Hordaland Health Study. *Australia and New Zealand Journal of Psychiatry, 43*(1), 45–52.

Jacka, F. N., Pasco, J. A., Henry, M. J., Kotowicz, M. A., Nicholson, G. C., & Berk, M. (2004). Dietary omega-3 fatty acids and depression in a community sample. *Nutritional Neuroscience, 7*(2), 101–106.

Jallo, N., Bourguignon, C., Taylor, A. G., & Utz, S. W. (2008). Stress management during pregnancy: Designing and evaluating a mind-body intervention. *Family and Community Health, 31*(3), 190–203.

Jamerson, B. D., Krishnan, K. R., Roberts, J., Krishen, A., & Modell, J. G. (2003). Effect of bupropion SR on specific symptom clusters of depression: Analysis of the 31-item Hamilton Rating Scale for depression. *Psychopharmacology Bulletin, 37*(2), 67–78.

Janicak, P. G., Davis J. M., Preskorn S. H., Ayd, F. J., Pavuluri, M. N., & Marder, S. R. (2006). *Principles and practice of psychopharmacotherapy* (4th ed.). Philadelphia: Lippincott Williams & Wilkins.

Janicak, P. G., O'Reardon, J. P., Sampson, S. M., Husain, M. M., Lisanby, S. H., Rado, J. T., et al. (2008). Transcranial magnetic stimulation in the treatment of major depressive disorder: A comprehensive summary of safety experience from acute exposure, extended exposure, and during reintroduction treatment. *Journal of Clinical Psychiatry, 69*(2), 222–232.

Jefferson, J. W., Rush, A. J., Nelson, J. C., VanMeter, S. A., Krishen, A., Hampton, K. D., et al. (2006). Extended-release bupropion for patients with major depressive disorder presenting with symptoms of reduced energy, pleasure, and interest: Findings from a randomized, double-blind, placebo-controlled study. *Journal of Clinical Psychiatry, 67*(6), 865–873.

Jia, F., Yue, M., Chandra, D., Keramidas, A., Goldstein, P. A., Homanics, G. E., et al. (2008). Taurine is a potent activator of extrasynaptic GABA(A) receptors in the thalamus. *Journal of Neuroscience, 28*(1), 106–115.

Joffe, R., Singer, W., & Levitt, A. (1993). A placebo-controlled comparison of lithium and triiodothyronine augmentation of tricyclic antidepressant in unipolar refractory affective depression. *Archives of General Psychiatry, 50,* 387–393.

Joffe, R. T., Levitt, A. J., & Young, L. T. (1996). The thyroid, magnesium and calcium in major depression. *Biological Psychiatry, 40*(5), 428–429.

Joffe, R. T., Singer, W., Levitt, A. J., & MacDonald, C. (1993). A placebo-controlled comparison of lithium and triiodothyronine augmentation of tricyclic antidepressants in unipolar refractory depression. *Archives of General Psychiatry, 50*(5), 387–393.

John, U., Meyer, C., Rumpf, H. J., & Hapke, U. (2004). Depressive disorders are related to nicotine dependence in the population but do not necessarily hamper smoking cessation. *Journal of Clinical Psychiatry, 65*(2), 169–176.

Johns Hopkins Urban Health Institute. (2001). *Special Projects.* Baltimore, MD: Johns Hopkins University.

Johnson, L. (2007). *Vitamin deficiency, dependency and toxicity: The Merck manual of diagnosis and therapy* (Vol. 2010). Whitehouse Station, NJ: Merck.

Jorde, R., Sneve, M., Figenschau, Y., Svartberg, J., & Waterloo, K. (2008). Effects of vitamin D supplementation on symptoms of depression in overweight and obese subjects: Randomized double blind trial. *Journal of Internal Medicine, 264*(6), 599–609.

Jorenby, D. E., Leischow, S. J., Nides, M. A., Rennard, S. I., Johnston, J. A., Hughes, A. R., et al. (1999). A controlled trial of sustained-release bupropion, a nicotine patch, or both for smoking cessation. *New England Journal of Medicine, 340*(9), 685–691.

Jost, W. H., & Marsalek, P. (2005). Duloxetine in the treatment of stress urinary incontinence. *Therapeutics and Clinical Risk Management, 1*(4), 259–264.

Judd, L. L., & Akiskal, H. S. (2000). Delineating the longitudinal structure of depressive illness: Beyond clinical subtypes and duration thresholds. *Pharmacopsychiatry, 33*(1), 3–7.

Judd, L. L., & Akiskal, H. S. (2003). Depressive episodes and symptoms dominate the longitudinal course of bipolar disorder. *Current Psychiatry Reports, 5*(6), 417–418.

Judd, L. L., Akiskal, H. S., Maser, J. D., Zeller, P. J., Endicott, J., Coryell, W., et al. (1998a). A prospective 12-year study of subsyndromal and syndromal depressive symptoms in unipolar major depressive disorders. *Archives of General Psychiatry, 55*(8), 694–700.

Judd, L. L., Akiskal, H. S., Maser, J. D., Zeller, P. J., Endicott, J., Coryell, W., et al. (1998b). Major depressive disorder: A prospective study of residual subthreshold depressive symptoms as predictor of rapid relapse. *Journal of Affective Disorders, 50*(2–3), 97–108.

Judd, L. L., Akiskal, H. S., Schettler, P. J., Coryell, W., Endicott, J., Maser, J. D., et al. (2003). A prospective investigation of the natural history of the long-term weekly symptomatic status of bipolar II disorder. *Archives of General Psychiatry, 60*(3), 261–269.

Judd, L. L., Akiskal, H. S., Schettler, P. J., Coryell, W., Maser, J., Rice, J. A., et al. (2003). The comparative clinical phenotype and long term longitudinal episode course of bipolar I and II: A clinical spectrum or distinct disorders? *Journal of Affective Disorders, 73*(1–2), 19–32.

Judd, L. L., Akiskal, H. S., Schettler, P. J., Endicott, J., Maser, J., Solomon, D. A., et al. (2002). The long-term natural history of the weekly symptomatic status of bipolar I disorder. *Archives of General Psychiatry, 59*(6), 530–537.

Judd, L. L., Schettler, P. J., Akiskal, H. S., Maser, J., Coryell, W., Solomon, D., et al. (2003). Long-term symptomatic status of bipolar I vs. bipolar II disorders. International *Journal of Neuropsychopharmacology, 6*(2), 127–137.

Juri, C., Chana, P., Tapia, J., Kunstmann, C., & Parrao, T. (2005). Quetiapine for insomnia in Parkinson disease: Results from an open-label trial. *Clinical Neuropharmacology, 28*(4), 185–187.

Kagan, B. L., Sultzer, D. L., Rosenlicht, N., & Gerner, R. H. (1990). Oral S-adenosylmethionine in depression: A randomized, double-blind, placebo-controlled trial. *American Journal of Psychiatry, 147*(5), 591–595.

Kamath, J., & Handratta, V. (2008). Desvenlafaxine succinate for major depressive disorder: a critical review of the evidence. *Expert Review of Neurotherapeutics, 8*(12), 1787–1797.

Kang, B. J., Lee, S. J., Kim, M. D., & Cho, M. J. (2002). A placebo-controlled, double-blind trial of Ginkgo biloba for antidepressant-induced sexual dysfunction. *Human Psychopharmacology, 17*(6), 279–284.

Karoum, F., Linnoila, M., Potter, W. Z., Chuang, L. W., Goodwin, F. K., & Wyatt, R. J. (1982). Fluctuating high urinary phenylethylamine excretion rates in some bipolar affective disorder patients. *Psychiatry Research, 6*(2), 215–222.

Karp, J. F., Whyte, E. M., Lenze, E. J., Dew, M. A., Begley, A., Miller, M. D., et al. (2008). Rescue pharmacotherapy with duloxetine for selective serotonin reuptake inhibitor nonresponders in late-life depression: Outcome and tolerability. *Journal of Clinical Psychiatry, 69*(3), 457–463.

Katz, S., & Morales, A. (1998). Dehydroepiandosterone (DHEA) and DHEA-sulfate (DS) as therapeutic options in menopause. *Seminars in Reproductive Endocrinology, 16,* 161–170.

Kaufman, J., Yang, B. Z., Douglas-Palumberi, H., Houshyar, S., Lipschitz, D., Krystal, J. H., et al. (2004). Social supports and serotonin transporter gene moderate depression in maltreated children. *Proceedings of the National Academy of Science, U S A, 101*(49), 17316–17321.

Kelepouris, E., & Agus, Z. S. (1998). Hypomagnesemia: Renal magnesium handling. *Seminars in Nephrology, 18*(1), 58–73.

Keller, M. B., McCullough, J. P., Klein, D. N., Arnow, B., Dunner, D. L., Gelenberg, A. J., et al. (2000). A comparison of nefazodone, the cognitive behavioral-analysis system of psychotherapy, and their combination for the treatment of chronic depression. *New England Journal of Medicine, 342*(20), 1462–1470.

Keller, M. B., Trivedi, M. H., Thase, M. E., Shelton, R. C., Kornstein, S. G., Nemeroff, C. B., et al. (2007). The Prevention of Recurrent Episodes of Depression with Venlafaxine for Two Years (PREVENT) study: Outcomes from the acute and continuation phases. *Biological Psychiatry, 62*(12), 1371–1379.

Kellner, C. H., Knapp, R. G., Petrides, G., Rummans, T. A., Husain, M. M., Rasmussen, K., et al. (2006). Continuation electroconvulsive therapy vs pharmacotherapy for relapse prevention in major depression: A multisite study from the Consortium for Research in Electroconvulsive Therapy (CORE). *Archives of General Psychiatry, 63*(12), 1337–1344.

Kelly, C. B., Ansari, T., Rafferty, T., & Stevenson, M. (2003). Antidepressant prescribing and suicide rate in Northern Ireland. *European Psychiatry, 18*(7), 325–328.

Kelly, C. B., McDonnell, A. P., Johnston, T. G., Mulholland, C., Cooper, S. J., McMaster, D., et al. (2004). The MTHFR C677T polymorphism is associated with depressive episodes in patients from Northern Ireland. *Journal of Psychopharmacology, 18*(4), 567–571.

Kelly, G. S. (2001). Rhodiola rosea: A possible plant adaptogen. *Alternative Medicine Review, 6*(3), 293–302.

Kendler, K. S., Kuhn, J. W., Vittum, J., Prescott, C. A., & Riley, B. (2005). The interaction of stressful life events and a serotonin transporter polymorphism in the prediction of episodes of major depression: A replication. *Archives of General Psychiatry, 62*(5), 529–535.

Kendler, K. S., Myers, J., & Zisook, S. (2008). Does bereavement-related major depression differ from major depression associated with other stressful life events? *American Journal of Psychiatry, 165*(11), 1449–1455.

Kennard, B., Silva, S., Vitiello, B., Curry, J., Kratochvil, C., Simons, A., et al. (2006). Remission and residual symptoms after short-term treatment in the Treatment of Adolescents with Depression Study (TADS). *Journal of the American Academy of Child and Adolescent Psychiatry, 45*(12), 1404–1411.

Kennedy, S. H., Kutcher, S. P., Ralevski, E., & Brown, G. M. (1996). Nocturnal melatonin and 24-hour 6-sulphatoxymelatonin levels in various phases of bipolar affective disorder. *Psychiatry Research, 63*(2–3), 219–222.

Kennedy, S. H., Lam, R. W., Nutt, D. J., & Thase, M. E. (2007). *Treating depression effectively: Applying clinical guidelines* (2nd ed.). London: Martin Dunitz Informa Healthcare.

Kennedy, S. H., Rizvi, S., Fulton, K., & Rasmussen, J. (2008). A double-blind comparison of sexual functioning, antidepressant efficacy, and tolerability between agomelatine and venlafaxine XR. *Journal of Clinical Psychopharmacology, 28*(3), 329–333.

Kessing, L. V., & Andersen, P. K. (2004). Does the risk of developing dementia increase with the number of episodes in patients with depressive disorder and in patients with bipolar disorder? *Journal of Neurology, Neurosurgery, and Psychiatry, 75*(12), 1662–1666.

Kessler, R. C., Soukup, J., Davis, R. B., Foster, D. F., Wilkey, S. A., Van Rompay, M. M., et al. (2001). The use of complementary and alternative therapies to treat anxiety and depression in the United States. *American Journal of Psychiatry, 158*(2), 289–294.

Ketter, T. A., Greist, J. H., Graham, J. A., Roberts, J. N., Thompson, T. R., & Nanry, K. P. (2006). The effect of dermatologic precautions on the incidence of rash with addition of lamotrigine in the treatment of bipolar I disorder: A randomized trial. *Journal of Clinical Psychiatry, 67*(3), 400–406.

Ketter, T. A., Wang, P. W., Chandler, R. A., Alarcon, A. M., Becker, O. V., Nowakowska, C., et al. (2005). Dermatology precautions and slower titration yield low incidence of lamotrigine treatment-emergent rash. *Journal of Clinical Psychiatry, 66*(5), 642–645.

Ketter, T. A., Wang, P. W., Chandler, R. A., Culver, J. L., & Alarcon, A. M. (2006). Adjunctive aripiprazole in treatment-resistant bipolar depression. *Annals of Clinical Psychiatry, 18*(3), 169–172.

Kew, M. C. (2008). Hepatic iron overload and hepatocellular carcinoma. *Cancer Lett, 286*(1), 38-43.

Khan, A., Bose, A., Alexopoulos, G. S., Gommoll, C., Li, D., & Gandhi, C. (2007). Double-blind comparison of escitalopram and duloxetine in the acute treatment of major depressive disorder. *Clinical Drug Investigation, 27*(7), 481–492.

Khan, A., Ginsberg, L. D., Asnis, G. M., Goodwin, F. K., Davis, K. H., Krishnan, A. A., et al. (2004). Effect of lamotrigine on cognitive complaints in patients with bipolar I disorder. *Journal of Clinical Psychiatry, 65*(11), 1483–1490.

Khan, A., Khan, S. R., Leventhal, R. M., & Brown, W. A. (2001). Symptom reduction and suicide risk in patients treated with placebo in antidepressant clinical trials: A replication analysis of the Food and Drug Administration Database. *International Journal of Neuropsychopharmacology, 4*(2), 113–118.

Khan, A., Upton, G. V., Rudolph, R. L., Entsuah, R., & Leventer, S. M. (1998). The use of venlafaxine in the treatment of major depression and major depression associated with anxiety: A dose-response study. Venlafaxine Investigator Study Group. *Journal of Clinical Psychopharmacology, 18*(1), 19–25.

Kidd, P. M. (2007). Omega-3 DHA and EPA for cognition, behavior, and mood: Clinical findings and structural-functional synergies with cell membrane phospholipids. *Alternative Medicine Review, 12*(3), 207–227.

Kilbourne, E. M., Philen, R. M., Kamb, M. L., & Falk, H. (1996). Tryptophan produced by Showa Denko and epidemic eosinophilia-myalgia syndrome. *Journal of Rheumatology, 46* (Suppl.), 81–88; discussion 89–91.

King, J., & Cousins, R. (2006). Zinc. In M. Shils, M. Shike, A. Ross, B. Caballero, & R. Cousins (Eds.), *Modern nutrition in health and disease* (10th ed., pp. 271–285). Baltimore: Lippincott Williams & Wilkins.

Kirmayer, L. J., Robbins, J. M., Dworkind, M., & Yaffe, M. J. (1993). Somatization and the recognition of depression and anxiety in primary care. *American Journal of Psychiatry, 150*(5), 734–741.

Kirsch, I., Deacon, B. J., Huedo-Medina, T. B., Scoboria, A., Moore, T. J., & Johnson, B. T. (2008). Initial severity and antidepressant benefits: A meta-analysis of data submitted to the Food and Drug Administration. *PLoS Medicine, 5*(2), e45.

Klein, D. F. (1990). NIMH collaborative research on treatment of depression. *Archives of General Psychiatry, 47*(7), 682–688.

Klein, D. N., Santiago, N. J., Vivian, D., Blalock, J. A., Kocsis, J. H., Markowitz, J. C., et al. (2004). Cognitive-behavioral analysis system of psychotherapy as a maintenance treatment for chronic depression. *Journal of Consulting and Clinical Psychology, 72*(4), 681–688.

Kocsis, J. H., Rush, A. J., Markowitz, J. C., Borian, F. E., Dunner, D. L., Koran, L. M., et al. (2003). Continuation treatment of chronic depression: A comparison of nefazodone, cognitive behavioral analysis system of psychotherapy, and their combination. *Psychopharmacology Bulletin, 37*(4), 73–87.

Kocsis, J. H., Thase, M. E., Trivedi, M. H., Shelton, R. C., Kornstein, S. G., Nemeroff, C. B., et al. (2007). Prevention of recurrent episodes of depression with venlafaxine ER in a 1-year maintenance phase from the PREVENT Study. *Journal of Clinical Psychiatry, 68*(7), 1014–1023.

Konuk, N., Atasoy, N., Atik, L., & Akay, O. (2006). Open-label study of adjunct modafinil for the treatment of patients with fatigue, sleepiness, and major depression treated with selective serotonin reuptake inhibitors. *Advanced Therapy, 23*(4), 646–654.

Korner, E., Bertha, G., Flooh, E., Reinhart, B., Wolf, R., & Lechner, H. (1986). Sleep-inducing effect of L-tryptophane. *European Neurology, 25*(Suppl. 2), 75–81.

Kornstein, S. G. (2006). Beyond remission: Rationale and design of the Prevention of Recurrent Episodes of Depression with Venlafaxine for Two Years (PREVENT) Study. *CNS Spectrums, 11*(12 Suppl. 15), 28–34.

Kornstein, S. G., Harvey, A. T., Rush, A. J., Wisniewski, S. R., Trivedi, M. H., Svikis, D. S., et al. (2005). Self-reported premenstrual exacerbation of depressive symptoms in patients seeking treatment for major depression. *Psychological Medicine, 35*(5), 683–692.

Kornstein, S. G., & Schneider, R. K. (2001). Clinical features of treatment-resistant depression. *Journal of Clinical Psychiatry, 62*(Suppl. 16), 18–25.

Koury, M. J., & Ponka, P. (2004). New insights into erythropoiesis: The roles of folate, vitamin B12, and iron. *Annual Review of Nutrition, 24*, 105–131.

Kovacs, M., Feinberg, T. L., Crouse-Novak, M., Paulauskas, S. L., Pollock, M., & Finkelstein, R. (1984). Depressive disorders in childhood. II. A longitudinal study of the risk for a subsequent major depression. *Archives of General Psychiatry, 41*(7), 643–649.

Kovacs, M., Rush, A. J., Beck, A. T., & Hollon, S. D. (1981). Depressed outpatients treated with cognitive therapy or pharmacotherapy. A one-year follow-up. *Archives of General Psychiatry, 38*(1), 33–39.

Kozel, F. A., & George, M. S. (2002). Meta-analysis of left prefrontal repetitive transcranial magnetic stimulation (rTMS) to treat depression. *Journal of Psychiatric Practice, 8*(5), 270–275.

Kraguljac, N. V., Montori, V. M., Pavuluri, M., Chai, H. S., Wilson, B. S., & Unal, S. S. (2009). Efficacy of omega-3 fatty acids in mood disorders—a systematic review and metaanalysis. *Psychopharmacology Bulletin, 42*(3), 39–54.

Kratochvil, C., Emslie, G., Silva, S., McNulty, S., Walkup, J., Curry, J., et al. (2006). Acute time to response in the Treatment for Adolescents with Depression Study (TADS). *Journal of the American Academy of Child and Adolescent Psychiatry, 45*(12), 1412–1418.

Kroenke, K., Arrington, M. E., & Mangelsdorff, A. D. (1990). The prevalence of symptoms in medical outpatients and the adequacy of therapy. *Archives of Internal Medicine, 150*(8), 1685–1689.

Kroenke, K., Spitzer, R. L., Williams, J. B., Linzer, M., Hahn, S. R., deGruy, F. V., 3rd, et al. (1994). Physical symptoms in primary care. Predictors of psychiatric disorders and functional impairment. *Archives of Family Medicine, 3*(9), 774–779.

Krystal, A., Fava, M., Rubens, R., Wessel, T., Caron, J., Wilson, P., et al. (2007). Evaluation of eszopiclone discontinuation after cotherapy with fluoxetine for insomnia with coexisting depression. *Journal of Clinical Sleep Medicine, 3*(1), 48–55.

Kupfer, D. J. (1993). Management of recurrent depression. *Journal of Clinical Psychiatry, 54*(Suppl.), 29–33; discussion 34–25.

Kwekkeboom, K. L., Hau, H., Wanta, B., & Bumpus, M. (2008). Patients' perceptions of the effectiveness of guided imagery and progressive muscle relaxation interventions used for cancer pain. *Complementary Therapy and Clinical Practice, 14*(3), 185–194.

Laje, G., Paddock, S., Manji, H., Rush, A. J., Wilson, A. F., Charney, D., et al. (2007). Genetic markers of suicidal ideation emerging during citalopram treatment of major depression. *American Journal of Psychiatry, 164*(10), 1530–1538.

Lam, R. W., Chan, P., Wilkins-Ho, M., & Yatham, L. N. (2008). Repetitive transcranial magnetic stimulation for treatment-resistant depression: A systematic review and metaanalysis. *Canadian Journal of Psychiatry, 53*(9), 621–631.

Lam, R. W., Hossie, H., Solomons, K., & Yatham, L. N. (2004). Citalopram and bupropion-SR: Combining versus switching in patients with treatment-resistant depression. *Journal of Clinical Psychiatry, 65*(3), 337–340.

Lam, R. W., Levitt, A. J., Levitan, R. D., Enns, M. W., Morehouse, R., Michalak, E. E., et al. (2006). The Can-SAD study: A randomized controlled trial of the effectiveness of light therapy and fluoxetine in patients with winter seasonal affective disorder. *American Journal of Psychiatry, 163*(5), 805–812.

Lambert, G., Johansson, M., Agren, H., & Friberg, P. (2000). Reduced brain norepinephrine and dopamine release in treatment-refractory depressive illness: Evidence in support of the catecholamine hypothesis of mood disorders. *Archives of General Psychiatry, 57*(8), 787–793.

Lampl, C., Katsarava, Z., Diener, H. C., & Limmroth, V. (2005). Lamotrigine reduces migraine aura and migraine attacks in patients with migraine with aura. *Journal of Neurology, Neurosurgery, and Psychiatry, 76*(12), 1730–1732.

Lansdowne, A. T., & Provost, S. C. (1998). Vitamin D3 enhances mood in healthy subjects during winter. *Psychopharmacology (Berlin), 135*(4), 319–323.

Lauritzen, L., Odgaard, K., Clemmesen, L., Lunde, M., Ohrstrom, J., Black, C., et al. (1996). Relapse prevention by means of paroxetine in ECT-treated patients with major depression: A comparison with imipramine and placebo in medium-term continuation therapy. *Acta Psychiatrica Scandinavica, 94*(4), 241–251.

Leaf, D. A., & Hatcher, L. (2009). The effect of lean fish consumption on triglyceride levels. *Physical Sportsmedicine, 37*(1), 37–43.

Lecky, C. (1999). Are relaxation techniques effective in relief of chronic pain? *Work, 13*(3), 249–256.

Lee, D. T., & Chung, T. K. (2007). Postnatal depression: An update. *Best Practice Research Clinical Obstetrics and Gynaecology, 21*(2), 183–191.

Leibenluft, E., Feldman-Naim, S., Turner, E. H., Wehr, T. A., & Rosenthal, N. E. (1997). Effects of exogenous melatonin administration and withdrawal in five patients with rapid-cycling bipolar disorder. *Journal of Clinical Psychiatry, 58*(9), 383–388.

Liebowitz, M. R., Manley, A. L., Padmanabhan, S. K., Ganguly, R., Tummala, R., & Tourian, K. A. (2008). Efficacy, safety, and tolerability of desvenlafaxine 50 mg/day and 100 mg/day in outpatients with major depressive disorder. *Current Medical Research and Opinion, 24*(7), 1877–1890.

Leja, A. M. (1989). Using guided imagery to combat postsurgical depression. *Journal of Gerontological Nursing, 15*(4), 7–11.

Leklem, J. (1999). Vitamin B6. In M. Shils, J. Olson, M. Shike, & A. Ross (Eds.), *Modern nutrition in health and disease* (9th ed., pp. 413–421). Baltimore: Williams and Wilkins.

Lekman, M., Laje, G., Charney, D., Rush, A. J., Wilson, A. F., Sorant, A. J., et al. (2008). The FKBP5-gene in depression and treatment response—an association study in the Sequenced Treatment Alternatives to Relieve Depression (STAR*D) cohort. *Biological Psychiatry, 63*(12), 1103–1110.

Lemoine, P., Guilleminault, C., & Alvarez, E. (2007). Improvement in subjective sleep in major depressive disorder with a novel antidepressant, agomelatine: Randomized, double-blind comparison with venlafaxine. *Journal of Clinical Psychiatry, 68*(11), 1723–1732.

Lesser, I. M., Leuchter, A. F., Trivedi, M. H., Davis, L. L., Wisniewski, S. R., Balasubramani, G. K., et al. (2005). Characteristics of insured and noninsured outpatients with depression in STAR(*)D. *Psychiatric Services, 56*(8), 995–1004.

Leverich, G. S., Altshuler, L. L., Frye, M. A., Suppes, T., McElroy, S. L., Keck, P. E., Jr., et al. (2006). Risk of switch in mood polarity to hypomania or mania in patients with bipolar depression during acute and continuation trials of venlafaxine, sertraline, and bupropion as adjuncts to mood stabilizers. *American Journal of Psychiatry, 163*(2), 232–239.

Levine, J. (1997). Controlled trials of inositol in psychiatry. *European Neuropsychopharmacology, 7*(2), 147155.

Levine, J., Barak, Y., Kofman, O., & Belmaker, R. H. (1995). Follow-up and relapse analysis of an inositol study of depression. *Israel Journal of Psychiatry and Related Sciences, 32*(1), 14–21.

Levinson-Castiel, R., Merlob, P., Linder, N., Sirota, L., & Klinger, G. (2006). Neonatal abstinence syndrome after in utero exposure to selective serotonin reuptake inhibitors in term infants. *Archives of Pediatric and Adolescent Medicine, 160*(2), 173–176.

Lewandowski, W., Good, M., & Draucker, C. B. (2005). Changes in the meaning of pain with the use of guided imagery. *Pain Management Nursing, 6*(2), 58–67.

Lewandowski, W. A. (2004). Patterning of pain and power with guided imagery. *Nursing Science Quarterly, 17*(3), 233–241.

Lewinsohn, P. M., Klein, D. N., & Seeley, J. R. (1995). Bipolar disorders in a community sample of older adolescents: Prevalence, phenomenology, comorbidity, and course. *Journal of the American Academy of Child and Adolescent Psychiatry, 34*(4), 454–463.

Lewinsohn, P. M., Rohde, P., & Seeley, J. R. (1998). Treatment of adolescent depression: Frequency of services and impact on functioning in young adulthood. *Depression and Anxiety, 7*(1), 47–52.

Leyton, M., Young, S. N., Pihl, R. O., Etezadi, S., Lauze, C., Blier, P., et al. (2000). Effects on mood of acute phenylalanine/tyrosine depletion in healthy women. *Neuropsychopharmacology, 22*(1), 52–63.

Li, D. (2007). *Practical aspects of suicide assessment*. San Francisco: University of California.

Libby, A. M., Brent, D. A., Morrato, E. H., Orton, H. D., Allen, R., & Valuck, R. J. (2007). Decline in treatment of pediatric depression after FDA advisory on risk of suicidality with SSRIs. *American Journal of Psychiatry, 164*(6), 884–891.

Licht, R. W., & Qvitzau, S. (2002). Treatment strategies in patients with major depression not responding to first-line sertraline treatment. A randomised study of extended duration of treatment, dose increase or mianserin augmentation. *Psychopharmacology (Berlin), 161*(2), 143–151.

Lima, L., Obregon, F., Urbina, M., Carreira, I., Baccichet, E., & Pena, S. (2003). Taurine concentration in human blood peripheral lymphocytes: Major depression and treatment with the antidepressant mirtazapine. *Advances in Experimental Medicine and Biology, 526*, 297–304.

Lin, E. H., Katon, W. J., VonKorff, M., Russo, J. E., Simon, G. E., Bush, T. M., et al. (1998). Relapse of depression in primary care. Rate and clinical predictors. *Archives of Family Medicine, 7*(5), 443–449.

Lin, E. H., Von Korff, M., Katon, W., Bush, T., Simon, G. E., Walker, E., et al. (1995). The role of the primary care physician in patients' adherence to antidepressant therapy. *Medical Care, 33*(1), 67–74.

Linde, K., Ramirez, G., Mulrow, C. D., Pauls, A., Weidenhammer, W., & Melchart, D. (1996). St John's wort for depression—an overview and meta-analysis of randomised clinical trials. *British Medical Journal, 313*, 253–258.

Lipton, M. (1973). *Megavitamin and orthomolecular therapy in psychiatry.* Task force report no. 7, 1–54. Washington, D.C.: American Psychiatric Association.

Lojko, D., & Rybakowski, J. K. (2007). L-thyroxine augmentation of serotonergic antidepressants in female patients with refractory depression. *Journal of Affective Disorders, 103*(1–3), 253–256.

Louzada, P. R., Paula Lima, A. C., Mendonca-Silva, D. L., Noel, F., De Mello, F. G., & Ferreira, S. T. (2004). Taurine prevents the neurotoxicity of beta-amyloid and glutamate receptor agonists: Activation of GABA receptors and possible implications for Alzheimer's disease and other neurological disorders. *FASEB Journal, 18*(3), 511–518.

Macdougall, M. (2000). Poor-quality studies suggest that vitamin B6 use is beneficial in premenstrual syndrome. *Western Journal of Medicine, 172*(4), 245.

Madras, B. K., Xie, Z., Lin, Z., Jassen, A., Panas, H., Lynch, L., et al. (2006). Modafinil occupies dopamine and norepinephrine transporters in vivo and modulates the transporters and trace amine activity in vitro. *Journal of Pharmacology and Experimental Therapy, 319*(2), 561–569.

Maes, M., Vandoolaeghe, E., Neels, H., Demedts, P., Wauters, A., Meltzer, H. Y., et al. (1997). Lower serum zinc in major depression is a sensitive marker of treatment resistance and of the immune/inflammatory response in that illness. *Biological Psychiatry, 42*(5), 349–358.

Maes, M., Verkerk, R., Vandoolaeghe, E., Lin, A., & Scharpe, S. (1998). Serum levels of excitatory amino acids, serine, glycine, histidine, threonine, taurine, alanine and arginine in treatment-resistant depression: Modulation by treatment with antidepressants and prediction of clinical responsivity. *Acta Psychiatrica Scandinavica, 97*(4), 302–308.

Magyar, K., Palfi, M., Tabi, T., Kalasz, H., Szende, B., & Szoko, E. (2004). Pharmacological aspects of (_)-deprenyl. *Current Medicinal Chemistry, 11*(15), 2017–2031.

Magyar, K., & Szende, B. (2004). (_)-Deprenyl, a selective MAO-B inhibitor, with apoptotic and anti-apoptotic properties. *Neurotoxicology, 25*(1–2), 233–242.

Mahmoud, R. A., Pandina, G. J., Turkoz, I., Kosik-Gonzalez, C., Canuso, C. M., Kujawa, M. J., et al. (2007). Risperidone for treatment-refractory major depressive disorder: A randomized trial. *Annals of Internal Medicine, 147*(9), 593–602.

Malcolm, D. E., Yu, P. H., Bowen, R. C., O'Donovan, C., Hawkes, J., & Hussein, M. (1994). Phenelzine reduces plasma vitamin B6. *Journal of Psychiatry and Neuroscience, 19*(5), 332–334.

Mallinckrodt, C. H., Prakash, A., Houston, J. P., Swindle, R., Detke, M. J., & Fava, M. (2007). Differential antidepressant symptom efficacy: Placebo-controlled comparisons of duloxetine and SSRIs (fluoxetine, paroxetine, escitalopram). *Neuropsychobiology, 56*(2–3), 73–85.

Malsch, U., & Kieser, M. (2001). Efficacy of kava-kava in the treatment of non-psychotic anxiety, following pretreatment with benzodiazepines. *Psychopharmacology (Berlin), 157*(3), 277–283.

Manber, R., Rush, A. J., Thase, M. E., Amow, B., Klein, D., Trivedi, M. H., et al. (2003). The effects of psychotherapy, nefazodone, and their combination on subjective assessment of disturbed sleep in chronic depression. *Sleep, 26*(2), 130–136.

Mannix, L. K., Chandurkar, R. S., Rybicki, L. A., Tusek, D. L., & Solomon, G. D. (1999). Effect of guided imagery on quality of life for patients with chronic tension-type headache. *Headache, 39*(5), 326–334.

Marangell, L. B., Martinez, J. M., Ketter, T. A., Bowden, C. L., Goldberg, J. F., Calabrese, J. R., et al. (2004). Lamotrigine treatment of bipolar disorder: Data from the first 500 patients in STEP-BD. *Bipolar Disorders, 6*(2), 139–143.

Marangell, L. B., Rush, A. J., George, M. S., Sackeim, H. A., Johnson, C. R., Husain, M. M., et al. (2002). Vagus nerve stimulation (VNS) for major depressive episodes: One year outcomes. *Biological Psychiatry, 51*(4), 280–287.

March, J., Silva, S., Petrycki, S., Curry, J., Wells, K., Fairbank, J., et al. (2004). Fluoxetine, cognitive-behavioral therapy, and their combination for adolescents with depression: Treatment for Adolescents With Depression Study (TADS) randomized controlled trial. *JAMA, 292*(7), 807–820.

March, J., Silva, S., Petrycki, S., Curry, J., Wells, K., Fairbank, J., et al. (2007). The Treatment for Adolescents With Depression Study (TADS): Long-term effectiveness and safety outcomes. *Archives of General Psychiatry, 64*(10), 1132–1143.

March, J., Silva, S., & Vitiello, B. (2006). The Treatment for Adolescents With Depression Study (TADS): Methods and message at 12 weeks. *Journal of the American Academy of Child and Adolescent Psychiatry, 45*(12), 1393–1403.

Marcus, R. N., McQuade, R. D., Carson, W. H., Hennicken, D., Fava, M., Simon, J. S., et al. (2008). The efficacy and safety of aripiprazole as adjunctive therapy in major depressive disorder: A second multicenter, randomized, double-blind, placebo-controlled study. *Journal of Clinical Psychopharmacology, 28*(2), 156–165.

Marcus, S. M. (2009). Depression during pregnancy: Rates, risks and consequences—Motherisk Update 2008. *Canadian Journal of Clinical Pharmacology, 16*(1), e15–e22.

Marcus, S. M., Young, E. A., Kerber, K. B., Kornstein, S., Farabaugh, A. H., Mitchell, J., et al. (2005). Gender differences in depression: Findings from the STAR*D study. *Journal of Affective Disorders, 87*(2–3), 141–150.

Mariappan, P., Alhasso, A., Ballantyne, Z., Grant, A., & N'Dow, J. (2007). Duloxetine, a serotonin and noradrenaline reuptake inhibitor (SNRI) for the treatment of stress urinary incontinence: A systematic review. *European Urology, 51*(1), 67–74.

Masoliver, E., Menoyo, A., Perez, V., Volpini, V., Rio, E. D., Perez, J., et al. (2006). Serotonin transporter linked promoter (polymorphism) in the serotonin transporter gene may be associated with antidepressant-induced mania in bipolar disorder. *Psychiatric Genetics, 16*(1), 25–29.

Mazza, M., Harnic, D., Catalano, V., Janiri, L., & Bria, P. (2008). Duloxetine for premenstrual dysphoric disorder: A pilot study. *Expert Opinion in Pharmacotherapy, 9*(4), 517–521.

McAfee, T., & France, E. (1998). Sustained-release bupropion for smoking cessation. *New England Journal of Medicine, 338*(9), 619; author reply 620.

McCaffrey, R. (2007). The effect of healing gardens and art therapy on older adults with mild to moderate depression. *Holistic Nursing Practice, 21*(2), 79–84.

McCann, J. C., & Ames, B. N. (2008). Is there convincing biological or behavioral evidence linking vitamin D deficiency to brain dysfunction? *FASEB Journal, 22*(4), 982–1001.

McCann, S. M., Daly, J., & Kelly, C. B. (2008). The impact of long-term lithium treatment on renal function in an outpatient population. *Ulster Medical Journal, 77*(2), 102–105.

McElroy, S. L. (2001). Axis I psychiatric comorbidity and its relationship to historical illness variables in 288 patients with bipolar disorder. *American Journal of Psychiatry, 158*(3), 420–426.

McElroy, S. L., Keck, P. E., Jr. , Pope, H. G., Jr., Hudson, J. I., Faedda, G. L., & Swann, A. C. (1992). Clinical and research implications of the diagnosis of dysphoric or mixed mania or hypomania. *American Journal of Psychiatry, 149*(12), 1633–1644.

McElroy, S. L., Suppes, T., Keck, P. E., Jr. , Black, D., Frye, M. A., Altshuler, L. L., et al. (2005). Open-label adjunctive zonisamide in the treatment of bipolar disorders: A prospective trial. *Journal of Clinical Psychiatry, 66*(5), 617–624.

McGrath, P. J., Stewart, J. W., Fava, M., Trivedi, M. H., Wisniewski, S. R., Nierenberg, A. A., et al. (2006). Tranylcypromine versus venlafaxine plus mirtazapine following three failed antidepressant medication trials for depression: A STAR*D report. *American Journal of Psychiatry, 163*(9), 1531–1541; quiz 1666.

McIntyre, A., Gendron, A., & McIntyre, A. (2007). Quetiapine adjunct to selective serotonin reuptake inhibitors or venlafaxine in patients with major depression, comorbid anxiety, and residual depressive symptoms: A randomized, placebo-controlled pilot study. *Depression and Anxiety, 24*(7), 487–494.

McKinney, C. H., Antoni, M. H., Kumar, M., Tims, F. C., & McCabe, P. M. (1997). Effects of guided imagery and music (GIM) therapy on mood and cortisol in healthy adults. *Health Psychology, 16*(4), 390–400.

McLean, A., Rubinsztein, J. S., Robbins, T. W., & Sahakian, B. J. (2004). The effects of tyrosine depletion in normal healthy volunteers: Implications for unipolar depression. *Psychopharmacology (Berlin), 171*(3), 286–297.

McMahon, F. J., Buervenich, S., Charney, D., Lipsky, R., Rush, A. J., Wilson, A. F., et al. (2006). Variation in the gene encoding the serotonin 2A receptor is associated with outcome of antidepressant treatment. *American Journal of Human Genetics, 78*(5), 804–814.

McQueen, K., Montgomery, P., Lappan-Gracon, S., Evans, M., & Hunter, J. (2008). Evidence-based recommendations for depressive symptoms in postpartum women. *Journal of Obstetric, Gynecological, and Neonatal Nursing, 37*(2), 127–136.

McTavish, S. F., Mannie, Z. N., & Cowen, P. J. (2004). Tyrosine depletion does not cause depressive relapse in antidepressant-treated patients. *Psychopharmacology (Berlin)*, *175*(1), 124–126.

McTavish, S. F., Mannie, Z. N., Harmer, C. J., & Cowen, P. J. (2005). Lack of effect of tyrosine depletion on mood in recovered depressed women. *Neuropsychopharmacology*, *30*(4), 786–791.

MedlinePlus. (2009a). Melatonin. Retrieved February 2, 2010, from http://www.nlm.nih.gov/medlineplus/druginfo/natural/patient-melatonin.html.

MedlinePlus. (2009b). Valerian. Retrieved February 2, 2010, from http://www.nlm.nih.gov/medlineplus/druginfo/natural/patient-valerian.html.

Mendlewicz, J. (1995). Pharmacologic profile and efficacy of venlafaxine. *International Clinical Psychopharmacology*, *10*(Suppl. 2), 5–13.

Menninger, C. (1897). Some reflections relative to the symptomatology and materia medica of typhoid fever. *Transactions of the American Institute of Homeopathy*, *2*, 430.

Menza, M. A., Kaufman, K. R., & Castellanos, A. (2000). Modafinil augmentation of antidepressant treatment in depression. *Journal of Clinical Psychiatry*, *61*(5), 378–381.

Menzies, V., & Kim, S. (2008). Relaxation and guided imagery in Hispanic persons diagnosed with fibromyalgia: A pilot study. *Family and Community Health*, *31*(3), 204–212.

Menzies, V., Taylor, A. G., & Bourguignon, C. (2006). Effects of guided imagery on outcomes of pain, functional status, and self-efficacy in persons diagnosed with fibromyalgia. *Journal of Alternative and Complementary Medicine*, *12*(1), 23–30.

Meyer, J. H., Kruger, S., Wilson, A. A., Christensen, B. K., Goulding, V. S., Schaffer, A., et al. (2001). Lower dopamine transporter binding potential in striatum during depression. *Neuroreport*, *12*(18), 4121–4125.

Miklowitz, D. J., Otto, M. W., Frank, E., Reilly-Harrington, N. A., Kogan, J. N., Sachs, G. S., et al. (2007). Intensive psychosocial intervention enhances functioning in patients with bipolar depression: Results from a 9-month randomized controlled trial. *American Journal of Psychiatry*, *164*(9), 1340–1347.

Miklowitz, D. J., Otto, M. W., Frank, E., Reilly-Harrington, N. A., Wisniewski, S. R., Kogan, J. N., et al. (2007). Psychosocial treatments for bipolar depression: A 1-year randomized trial from the Systematic Treatment Enhancement Program. *Archives of General Psychiatry*, *64*(4), 419–426.

Milane, M. S., Suchard, M. A., Wong, M. L., & Licinio, J. (2006). Modeling of the temporal patterns of fluoxetine prescriptions and suicide rates in the United States. *PLoS Medicine*, *3*(6), e190.

Millan, M. J. (2009). Dual- and triple-acting agents for treating core and co-morbid symptoms of major depression: Novel concepts, new drugs. *Neurotherapeutics*, *6*(1), 53–77.

Millard, R. J., Moore, K., Rencken, R., Yalcin, I., & Bump, R. C. (2004). Duloxetine vs placebo in the treatment of stress urinary incontinence: A four-continent randomized clinical trial. *BJU International, 93*(3), 311–318.

Miller, A. L. (2008). The methylation, neurotransmitter, and antioxidant connections between folate and depression. *Alternative Medicine Review, 13*(3), 216–226.

Miller, C. J., Klugman, J., Berv, D. A., Rosenquist, K. J., & Ghaemi, S. N. (2004). Sensitivity and specificity of the Mood Disorder Questionnaire for detecting bipolar disorder. *Journal of Affective Disorders, 81*(2), 167–171.

Minerals. (2000). *Drug facts and comparisons* (pp. 27–51). St. Louis, MO: Facts and Comparisons.

Miniussi, C., Bonato, C., Bignotti, S., Gazzoli, A., Gennarelli, M., Pasqualetti, P., et al. (2005). Repetitive transcranial magnetic stimulation (rTMS) at high and low frequency: An efficacious therapy for major drug-resistant depression? *Clinical Neurophysiology, 116*(5), 1062–1071.

Miranda, A., & Sood, M. (2006). Treatment options for chronic abdominal pain in children and adolescents. *Current Treatment Options in Gastroenterology, 9*(5), 409–415.

Mischoulon, D., & Rosenbaum, J. (Eds.). (2002). *Natural medications for psychiatric disorders: Considering the alternatives.* Philadelphia: Lippincott Williams & Wilkins.

Mishori, A. (1999). Combination of inositol and serotonin reuptake inhibitors in the treatment of depression. *Biological Psychiatry, 45,* 270–273.

Miyasaka, L. S., Atallah, A. N., & Soares, B. G. (2006). Valerian for anxiety disorders. *Cochrane Database of Systematic Reviews* (Online) (4), CD004515.

Mizushima, S., Nara, Y., Sawamura, M., & Yamori, Y. (1996). Effects of oral taurine supplementation on lipids and sympathetic nerve tone. *Advances in Experimental Medicine and Biology, 403,* 615–622.

Modell, J. G., Rosenthal, N. E., Harriett, A. E., Krishen, A., Asgharian, A., Foster, V. J., et al. (2005). Seasonal affective disorder and its prevention by anticipatory treatment with bupropion XL. *Biological Psychiatry, 58*(8), 658–667.

Moises, H. W., Waldmeier, P., & Beckmann, H. (1986). Urinary phenylethylamine correlates positively with hypomania, and negatively with depression, paranoia, and social introversion on the MMPI. *European Archives of Psychiatry and Neurological Sciences, 236*(2), 83–87.

Mojtabai, R., & Olfson, M. (2008). National patterns in antidepressant treatment by psychiatrists and general medical providers: Results from the national comorbidity survey replication. *Journal of Clinical Psychiatry, 69*(7), 1064–1074.

Monmaney, T. (1998, August 31). Labels' potency claims often inaccurate, analysis finds. *Los Angeles Times.*

Montejo, A. L., Llorca, G., Izquierdo, J. A., & Rico-Villademoros, F. (2001). Incidence of sexual dysfunction associated with antidepressant agents: A prospective multicenter study of 1022 outpatients. Spanish Working Group for the Study of Psychotropic-Related Sexual Dysfunction. *Journal of Clinical Psychiatry, 62*(Suppl. 3), 10–21.

Montgomery, P., & Richardson, A. J. (2008). Omega-3 fatty acids for bipolar disorder. *Cochrane Database of Systematic Reviews* (Online) (2), CD005169.

Montgomery, S. A., Baldwin, D. S., Blier, P., Fineberg, N. A., Kasper, S., Lader, M., et al. (2007). Which antidepressants have demonstrated superior efficacy? A review of the evidence. *International Clinical Psychopharmacology, 22*(6), 323–329.

Montgomery, S. A., & Kasper, S. (2007). Severe depression and antidepressants: Focus on a pooled analysis of placebo-controlled studies on agomelatine. *International Clinical Psychopharmacology, 22*(5), 283–291.

Moody, L. E., Webb, M., Cheung, R., & Lowell, J. (2004). A focus group for caregivers of hospice patients with severe dyspnea. *American Journal of Hospital Palliative Care, 21*(2), 121–130.

Moore, R. J., & Spiegel, D. (2000). Uses of guided imagery for pain control by African-American and white women with metastatic breast cancer. *Integrative Medicine, 2*(2), 115–126.

Morgan, M. L., Cook, I. A., Rapkin, A. J., & Leuchter, A. F. (2005). Estrogen augmentation of antidepressants in perimenopausal depression: A pilot study. *Journal of Clinical Psychiatry, 66*(6), 774–780.

Morgan, O. W., Griffiths, C., & Majeed, A. (2004). Association between mortality from suicide in England and antidepressant prescribing: An ecological study. *BMC Public Health, 4*, 63.

Morone, N. E., & Greco, C. M. (2007). Mind-body interventions for chronic pain in older adults: A structured review. *Pain Medicine, 8*(4), 359–375.

Morris, M. S., Fava, M., Jacques, P. F., Selhub, J., & Rosenberg, I. H. (2003). Depression and folate status in the US population. *Psychotherapy Psychosomatics, 72*(2), 80–87.

Moses-Kolko, E. L., Bogen, D., Perel, J., Bregar, A., Uhl, K., Levin, B., et al. (2005). Neonatal signs after late in utero exposure to serotonin reuptake inhibitors: Literature review and implications for clinical applications. *JAMA, 293*(19), 2372–2383.

Mosnik, D. M., Spring, B., Rogers, K., & Baruah, S. (1997). Tardive dyskinesia exacerbated after ingestion of phenylalanine by schizophrenic patients. *Neuropsychopharmacology, 16*(2), 136–146.

Mossner, R., Mikova, O., Koutsilieri, E., Saoud, M., Ehlis, A. C., Muller, N., et al. (2007). Consensus paper of the WFSBP Task Force on Biological Markers: Biological markers in depression. *World Journal of Biological Psychiatry, 8*(3), 141–174.

Mulleners, W. M., & Chronicle, E. P. (2008). Anticonvulsants in migraine prophylaxis: A Cochrane review. *Cephalalgia, 28*(6), 585–597.

Mulrow, C., Lawrence, V., & Jacobs, B. (2000). *Milk thistle: Effects on liver disease and cirrhosis and clinical adverse effects.* Evidence Report/Technology Assessment No. 21. AHRQ Publication No. 01-E025. Rockville, MD: Agency for Healthcare Research and Quality.

Murphy, F. C., Smith, K. A., Cowen, P. J., Robbins, T. W., & Sahakian, B. J. (2002). The effects of tryptophan depletion on cognitive and affective processing in healthy volunteers. *Psychopharmacology (Berlin), 163*(1), 42–53.

Murray, V., von Arbin, M., Bartfai, A., Berggren, A. L., Landtblom, A. M., Lundmark, J., et al. (2005). Double-blind comparison of sertraline and placebo in stroke patients with minor depression and less severe major depression. *Journal of Clinical Psychiatry, 66*(6), 708–716.

Musazzi, L., Cattaneo, A., Tardito, D., Barbon, A., Gennarelli, M., Barlati, S., et al. (2009). Early raise of BDNF in hippocampus suggests induction of post-transcriptional mechanisms by antidepressants. *BMC Neuroscience, 10,* 48.

Nahas, Z., Marangell, L. B., Husain, M. M., Rush, A. J., Sackeim, H. A., Lisanby, S. H., et al. (2005). Two-year outcome of vagus nerve stimulation (VNS) for treatment of major depressive episodes. *Journal of Clinical Psychiatry, 66*(9), 1097–1104.

Nakagawa, A., Grunebaum, M. F., Ellis, S. P., Oquendo, M. A., Kashima, H., Gibbons, R. D., et al. (2007). Association of suicide and antidepressant prescription rates in Japan, 1999–2003. *Journal of Clinical Psychiatry, 68*(6), 908–916.

Nakagawara, M. (1992). Beta-phenylethylamine and noradrenergic function in depression. *Progress in Neuro-psychopharmacology and Biological Psychiatry, 16*(1), 45–53.

Nakajima, T., Kudo, Y., & Kaneko, Z. (1978). Clinical evaluation of 5-hydroxy-L-tryptophan as an antidepressant drug. *Folia Psychiatrica et Neurologica Japonica, 32*(2), 223–230.

Nardini, M., De Stefano, R., Iannuccelli, M., Borghesi, R., & Battistini, N. (1983). Treatment of depression with L-5-hydroxytryptophan combined with chlorimipramine, a double-blind study. *International Journal of Clinical Pharmacology Research, 3*(4), 239–250.

Narduzzi, K. J., Nolan, R. P., Reesor, K., Jackson, T., Spanos, N. P., Hayward, A. A., et al. (1998). Preliminary investigation of associations of illness schemata and treatment-induced reduction in headaches. *Psychology Report, 82*(1), 299–307.

Nasr, S., Wendt, B., & Steiner, K. (2006). Absence of mood switch with and tolerance to modafinil: A replication study from a large private practice. *Journal of Affective Disorders, 95*(1–3), 111–114.

National Institutes of Health ODS. (2009). Dietary supplement fact sheet: Vitamin D. Retrieved February 2, 2010, from http://ods.od.nih.gov/factsheets/vitamind.asp#about

Natural Standard. (2010a). 5-HTP, monograph. Retrieved February 2, 2010, from Natural Standard Database: http://www.naturalstandard.com/naturalstandard/monographs/monoframeset.asp?monograph=/monographs/herbssupplements/5-htp.asp%3Fprintversion%3Dtrue

Natural Standard. (2010b). Drug depletion database. Retrieved February 2, 2010, from Natural Standard Database: http://www.naturalstandard.com/tools/InteractionHTML/depletions-drugs.asp#

Natural Standard. (2010c). Ginkgo (Ginkgo biloba L.), monograph. Retrieved February 2, 2010, from Natural Standard Database: http://www.naturalstandard.com/monographs/herbssupplements/ginkgo.asp

Natural Standard. (2010d). Kava (Piper methysticum G. Forst), monograph. Retrieved February 2, 2010, from Natural Standard Database: http://www.naturalstandard.com/monographs/herbssupplements/kava.asp?printversion=true

Natural Standard. (2010e). Melatonin, monograph. Retrieved February 2, 2010, from Natural Standard Database: http://www.naturalstandard.com/monographs/herbssupplements/melatonin.asp?printversion=true

Natural Standard. (2010f). Omega-3 fatty acids, fish oil, alpha-linolenic acid; monograph. Retrieved February 2, 2010, from Natural Standard Database: http://www.naturalstandard.com/naturalstandard/monographs/monoframeset.asp?monograph=/monographs/herbssupplements/fishoil.asp&patientVersion=/monographs/herbssupplements/patient-fishoil.asp

Natural Standard. (2010g). Phenylalanine, monograph. Retrieved February 2, 2010, from Natural Standard Database: http://www.naturalstandard.com/naturalstandard/monographs/monoframeset.asp?monograph=/monographs/herbssupplements/phenylalanine.asp

Natural Standard. (2010h). SAM-e, monograph. Retrieved February 2, 2010, from Natural Standard Database: http://www.naturalstandard.com/naturalstandard/monographs/monoframeset.asp?monograph=/monographs/herbssupplements/same.asp&patientVersion=/monographs/herbssupplements/patient-same.asp

Natural Standard. (2010i). Taurine, monograph. Retrieved February 2, 2010, from Natural Standard Database: http://www.naturalstandard.com/naturalstandard/monographs/monoframeset.asp?monograph=/monographs/herbssupplements/taurine.asp&patientVersion=/monographs/herbssupplements/patient-taurine.asp

Natural Standard. (2010j). Vitamin D, monograph. Retrieved February 2, 2010, from Natural Standard Database: http://www.naturalstandard.com/monographs/monoframeset.asp?monograph=/monographs/herbssupplements/patient-vitamind.asp%3Fprintversion%3Dtrue

Naylor, G. J. (1984). Vanadium and manic depressive psychosis. *Nutrition and Health*, 3(1–2), 79–85.

Naylor, G. J., & Smith, A. H. (1981). Vanadium: A possible aetiological factor in manic depressive illness. *Psychological Medicine, 11*(2), 249–256.

Naylor, G. J., Smith, A. H., Bryce-Smith, D., & Ward, N. I. (1984a). Elevated vanadium content of hair and mania. *Biological Psychiatry, 19*(5), 759–764.

Naylor, G. J., Smith, A. H., Bryce-Smith, D., & Ward, N. I. (1984b). Tissue vanadium levels in manic-depressive psychosis. *Psychological Medicine, 14*(4), 767–772.

Nelson, J. C., Lu Pritchett, Y., Martynov, O., Yu, J. Y., Mallinckrodt, C. H., & Detke, M. J. (2006). The safety and tolerability of duloxetine compared with paroxetine and placebo: A pooled analysis of 4 clinical trials. *Primary Care Companion Journal of Clinical Psychiatry, 8*(4), 212–219.

Nelson, J. C., Mazure, C. M., Jatlow, P. I., Bowers, M. B., Jr. , & Price, L. H. (2004). Combining norepinephrine and serotonin reuptake inhibition mechanisms for treatment of depression: A double-blind, randomized study. *Biological Psychiatry, 55*(3), 296–300.

Nelson, J. C., Portera, L., & Leon, A. C. (2006). Assessment of outcome in depression. *Journal of Psychopharmacology, 20*(4 Suppl.), 47–53.

Nemeroff, C. (2004). *Introduction to treatment resistant depression.* Paper presented at the American Psychiatric Association Annual Meeting, New York.

Nemeroff, C. B., Entsuah, R., Benattia, I., Demitrack, M., Sloan, D. M., & Thase, M. E. (2008). Comprehensive analysis of remission (COMPARE) with venlafaxine versus SSRIs. *Biological Psychiatry, 63*(4), 424–434.

Nemeroff, C. B., Heim, C. M., Thase, M. E., Klein, D. N., Rush, A. J., Schatzberg, A. F., et al. (2003). Differential responses to psychotherapy versus pharmacotherapy in patients with chronic forms of major depression and child-hood trauma. *Proceedings of the National Academy of Sciences, U.S. A., 100*(24), 14293–14296.

Neumeister, A. (2003). Tryptophan depletion, serotonin, and depression: Where do we stand? *Psychopharmacology Bulletin, 37*(4), 99–115.

Newcorn, J. H., Kratochvil, C. J., Allen, A. J., Casat, C. D., Ruff, D. D., Moore, R. J., et al. (2008). Atomoxetine and osmotically released methylphenidate for the treatment of attention deficit hyperactivity disorder: Acute comparison and differential response. *American Journal of Psychiatry, 165*(6), 721–730.

Newton, T. F., De La Garza, R., 2nd, Fong, T., Chiang, N., Holmes, T. H., Bloch, D. A., et al. (2005). A comprehensive assessment of the safety of intra-venous methamphetamine administration during treatment with selegiline. *Pharmacology, Biochemistry and Behavior, 82*(4), 704–711.

Newton-Howes, G., Tyrer, P., & Johnson, T. (2006). Personality disorder and the outcome of depression: Meta-analysis of published studies. *British Journal of Psychiatry, 188*, 13–20.

Neylan, T. C., Lenoci, M., Maglione, M. L., Rosenlicht, N. Z., Leykin, Y., Metzler, T. J., et al. (2003). The effect of nefazodone on subjective and objective sleep quality in posttraumatic stress disorder. *Journal of Clinical Psychiatry*, 64(4), 445–450.

Nguyen, M., & Gregan, A. (2002). S-adenosylmethionine and depression. *Australian Family Physician*, 31(4), 339–343.

Nielsen Forman, D., Videbech, P., Hedegaard, M., Dalby Salvig, J., & Secher, N. J. (2000). Postpartum depression: Identification of women at risk. *Bjog*, 107(10), 1210–1217.

Nierenberg, A. A., Farabaugh, A. H., Alpert, J. E., Gordon, J., Worthington, J. J., Rosenbaum, J. F., et al. (2000). Timing of onset of antidepressant response with fluoxetine treatment. *American Journal of Psychiatry*, 157(9), 1423–1428.

Nierenberg, A. A., Fava, M., Trivedi, M. H., Wisniewski, S. R., Thase, M. E., McGrath, P. J., et al. (2006). A comparison of lithium and T(3) augmentation following two failed medication treatments for depression: A STAR*D report. *American Journal of Psychiatry*, 163(9), 1519–1530; quiz 1665.

Nierenberg, A. A., Ostacher, M. J., Calabrese, J. R., Ketter, T. A., Marangell, L. B., Miklowitz, D. J., et al. (2006). Treatment-resistant bipolar depression: A STEP-BD equipoise randomized effectiveness trial of antidepressant augmentation with lamotrigine, inositol, or risperidone. *American Journal of Psychiatry*, 163(2), 210–216.

Nierenberg, A. A., Petersen, T. J., & Alpert, J. E. (2003). Prevention of relapse and recurrence in depression: The role of long-term pharmacotherapy and psychotherapy. *Journal of Clinical Psychiatry*, 64(Suppl. 15), 13–17.

Nierenberg, A. A., Trivedi, M. H., Fava, M., Biggs, M. M., Shores-Wilson, K., Wisniewski, S. R., et al. (2007). Family history of mood disorder and characteristics of major depressive disorder: A STAR*D (Sequenced Treatment Alternatives to Relieve Depression) study. *Journal of Psychiatric Research*, 41(3–4), 214–221.

Nihalani, N. D., & Schwartz, T. L. (2007). Mifepristone, a glucocorticoid antagonist for the potential treatment of psychotic major depression. *Current Opinion in Investigational Drugs*, 8(7), 563–569.

NMCD. (2010a). 5-HTP, monograph. Retrieved February 2010, from Natural Medicines Comprehensive Database: http://naturaldatabase.therapeuticresearch.com/nd/Search.aspx?cs=CE&s=ND&pt=100&id=794&ds=&name=5-Hydroxytryptophan+(5-HTP)&searchid=19177498

NMCD. (2010b). Drug influences on nutrient levels and depletion. Retrieved February 2010, from Natural Medicines Comprehensive Database: http://naturaldatabase.therapeuticresearch.com/ce/ceCourse.aspx?s=ND&cs=CE&pc=08-40&cec=0&pm=5

NMCD. (2010c). Fish oil (omega-3 fatty acids), monograph. Retrieved February 2010, from Natural Medicines Comprehensive Database: http://naturaldatabase.therapeuticresearch.com/nd/Search.aspx?cs=ce&s=ND&pt=100&id=993&ds=&name=Omega+3+Fatty+Acids+(FISH+OIL)&searchid=19263067

NMCD. (2010d). GABA, monograph. Retrieved February 2010, from Natural Medicines Comprehensive Database: http://naturaldatabase.therapeuticresearch.com/nd/Search.aspx?cs=CE&s=ND&pt=100&id=464&ds=&name=GABA+(GABA+(GAMMA-AMINOBUTYRIC+ACID))&searchid=19185627

NMCD. (2010e). Phenylalanine, monograph. Retrieved February 2010, from Natural Medicines Comprehensive Database: http://naturaldatabase.therapeuticresearch.com/nd/Search.aspx?cs=CE&s=ND&pt=100&id=653&ds=&name=PHENYLALANINE&searchid=19177498

NMCD. (2010f). SAM-e, monograph. Retrieved February 2010, from Natural Medicines Comprehensive Database: http://naturaldatabase.therapeuticresearch.com/nd/Search.aspx?cs=CE&s=ND&pt=100&id=786&ds=&name=SAM-e+(SAMe)&searchid=19239646

NMCD. (2010g). Taurine, monograph. Retrieved February 2010, from Natural Medicines Comprehensive Database: http://naturaldatabase.therapeuticresearch.com/nd/Search.aspx?cs=CE&s=ND&pt=100&id=1024&ds=&name=TAURINE&searchid=19177498

NMCD. (2010h). Tryptophan, monograph. Retrieved February 2010, from Natural Medicines Comprehensive Database: http://naturaldatabase.therapeuticresearch.com/nd/Search.aspx?cs=CE&s=ND&pt=100&id=326&ds=&name=Tryptophan+(L-TRYPTOPHAN)&searchid=19177498

NMCD. (2010i). Tyrosine, monograph. Retrieved February 2010, from Natural Medicines Comprehensive Database: http://naturaldatabase.therapeuticresearch.com/nd/Search.aspx?cs=CE&s=ND&pt=100&id=1037&ds=&name=TYROSINE&searchid=19177498

NMHA. (2006). Fast facts on mental health: Mind your health—mental health month. Bethesda: National Mental Health Association. http://www.nmha.org.

Nnadi, C. U., Goldberg, J. F., & Malhotra, A. K. (2005a). Genetics and psychopharmacology: Prospects for individualized treatment. *Essential Psychopharmacology, 6*(4), 193–208.

Nnadi, C. U., Goldberg, J. F., & Malhotra, A. K. (2005b). Pharmacogenetics in mood disorder. *Current Opinion in Psychiatry, 18*(1), 33–39.

Nonacs, R. M. (2004). Looking beyond the symptoms of depression: Considerations for special populations. *Primary Care Companion Journal of Clinical Psychiatry, 6*, 168–175.

Norred, C. L. (2000). Minimizing preoperative anxiety with alternative caring-healing therapies. *AORN Journal, 72*(5), 838–840, 842–843.

Novick, J. S., Stewart, J. W., Wisniewski, S. R., Cook, I. A., Manev, R., Nierenberg, A. A., et al. (2005). Clinical and demographic features of atypical depression in outpatients with major depressive disorder: Preliminary findings from STAR*D. *Journal of Clinical Psychiatry, 66*(8), 1002–1011.

Nowak, G., Siwek, M., Dudek, D., Zieba, A., & Pilc, A. (2003). Effect of zinc supplementation on antidepressant therapy in unipolar depression: A preliminary placebo-controlled study. *Polish Journal of Pharmacology, 55*(6), 1143–1147.

Nowak, G., & Szewczyk, B. (2002). Mechanisms contributing to antidepressant zinc actions. *Polish Journal of Pharmacology, 54*(6), 587–592.

Nowak, G., Szewczyk, B., & Pilc, A. (2005). Zinc and depression. An update. *Pharmacology Reports, 57*(6), 713–718.

Nulman, I., Rovet, J., Stewart, D. E., Wolpin, J., Pace-Asciak, P., Shuhaiber, S., et al. (2002). Child development following exposure to tricyclic antidepressants or fluoxetine throughout fetal life: A prospective, controlled study. *American Journal of Psychiatry, 159*(11), 1889–1895.

Nunes, D. F., Rodriguez, A. L., da Silva Hoffmann, F., Luz, C., Braga Filho, A. P., Muller, M. C., et al. (2007). Relaxation and guided imagery program in patients with breast cancer undergoing radiotherapy is not associated with neuroimmunomodulatory effects. *Journal of Psychosomatic Research, 63*(6), 647–655.

Nurnberger, J. I., Jr., Adkins, S., Lahiri, D. K., Mayeda, A., Hu, K., Lewy, A., et al. (2000). Melatonin suppression by light in euthymic bipolar and unipolar patients. *Archives of General Psychiatry, 57*(6), 572–579.

Nutrition, A. C. o. (1976). American Academy of Pediatrics Commitee on Nutrition: Megavitamin therapy for childhood psychoses and learning disabilities. *Pediatrics, 58*(6), 910–912.

Obayon, M. (2004). Does depression hurt? Epidemiology of physical and depressive symptoms. *Primary Care Companion Journal of Clinical Psychiatry, 6*, 168–175.

Oberlander, T. F., Misri, S., Fitzgerald, C. E., Kostaras, X., Rurak, D., & Riggs, W. (2004). Pharmacologic factors associated with transient neonatal symptoms following prenatal psychotropic medication exposure. *Journal of Clinical Psychiatry, 65*(2), 230–237.

Oberlander, T. F., Warburton, W., Misri, S., Aghajanian, J., & Hertzman, C. (2006). Neonatal outcomes after prenatal exposure to selective serotonin reuptake inhibitor antidepressants and maternal depression using population-based linked health data. *Archives of General Psychiatry, 63*(8), 898–906.

Oberlander, T. F., Warburton, W., Misri, S., Riggs, W., Aghajanian, J., & Hertzman, C. (2008). Major congenital malformations following prenatal exposure to serotonin reuptake inhibitors and benzodiazepines using population-based health data. *Birth Defects Research B: Developmental and Reproductive Toxicology, 83*(1), 68–76.

Oberlander, T. F., Weinberg, J., Papsdorf, M., Grunau, R., Misri, S., & Devlin, A. M. (2008). Prenatal exposure to maternal depression, neonatal methylation of human glucocorticoid receptor gene (NR3C1) and infant cortisol stress responses. *Epigenetics, 3*(2), 97–106.

Oelke, M., Roovers, J. P., & Michel, M. C. (2006). Safety and tolerability of duloxetine in women with stress urinary incontinence. *BJOG, 113*(Suppl. 1), 22–26.

Office of Dietary Supplements. (2006, April 26). Dietary supplement fact sheet: Vitamin B12. Retrieved January 29, 2008, from http://dietary-supplements.info.nih.gov/factsheets/vitaminb12.asp#en1

Office of Dietary Supplements. (2008, January 16). Valerian. Retrieved January 29, 2008, from http://dietary-supplements.info.nih.gov/factsheets/valerian.asp

Ogles, B. M., Lambert, M. J., & Sawyer, J. D. (1995). Clinical significance of the National Institute of Mental Health Treatment of Depression Collaborative Research Program data. *Journal of Consulting and Clinical Psychology, 63*(2), 321–326.

Ohannessian, C. M., Hesselbrock, V. M., Kramer, J., Kuperman, S., Bucholz, K. K., Schuckit, M. A., et al. (2004). The relationship between parental alcoholism and adolescent psychopathology: A systematic examination of parental comorbid psychopathology. *Journal of Abnormal Child Psychology, 32*(5), 519–533.

Olfson, M., Marcus, S. C., Tedeschi, M., & Wan, G. J. (2006). Continuity of antidepressant treatment for adults with depression in the United States. *American Journal of Psychiatry, 163*(1), 101–108.

Olness, K., Hall, H., Rozniecki, J. J., Schmidt, W., & Theoharides, T. C. (1999). Mast cell activation in children with migraine before and after training in self-regulation. *Headache, 39*(2), 101–107.

Olsson, E. M., von Scheele, B., & Panossian, A. G. (2008). A randomised, double-blind, placebo-controlled, parallel-group study of the standardised extract SHR-5 of the roots of Rhodiola rosea in the treatment of subjects with stress-related fatigue. *Planta Medica, 75*(2), 105–112.

Olver, J. S., Ignatiadis, S., Maruff, P., Burrows, G. D., & Norman, T. R. (2008). Quetiapine augmentation in depressed patients with partial response to antidepressants. *Humam Psychopharmacology, 23*, 653–660.

Osher, Y., Belmaker, R. H., & Nemets, B. (2006). Clinical trials of PUFAs in depression: State of the art. *World Journal of Biological Psychiatry, 7*(4), 223–230.

Packer, S., & Berman, S. A. (2007). Serotonin syndrome precipitated by the monoamine oxidase inhibitor linezolid. *American Journal of Psychiatry, 164*(2), 346–347.

Palasciano, G., Portincasa, P., & Palmieri, V. (1994). The effect of silymarin on plasma levels of malon-dialdehyde in patients receiving long-term treatment with psychotropic drugs. *Current Therapeutic Research, 55*(5), 537–545.

Palatnik, A., Frolov, K., & Fux, M. (2001). Double-blind, controlled, crossover trial of inositol versus fluvoxamine for the treatment of panic disorder. *Journal of Clinical Psychopharmacology, 21*, 335–339.

Palhagen, S., Heinonen, E., Hagglund, J., Kaugesaar, T., Maki-Ikola, O., & Palm, R. (2006). Selegiline slows the progression of the symptoms of Parkinson disease. *Neurology, 66*(8), 1200–1206.

Pampallona, S., Bollini, P., Tibaldi, G., Kupelnick, B., & Munizza, C. (2004). Combined pharmacotherapy and psychological treatment for depression: A systematic review. *Archives of General Psychiatry, 61*(7), 714–719.

Papakostas, G. I. (2009). Evidence for S-adenosyl-L-methionine (SAM-e) for the treatment of major depressive disorder. *Journal of Clinical Psychiatry, 70*(Suppl. 5), 18–22.

Papakostas, G. I., Alpert, J. E., & Fava, M. (2003). S-adenosyl-methionine in depression: A comprehensive review of the literature. *Current Psychiatry Reports, 5*(6), 460–466.

Papakostas, G. I., Fava, M., & Thase, M. E. (2007). Treatment of SSRI-resistant depression: A meta-analysis comparing within- versus across-class switches. *Biological Psychiatry, 63*(7), 699–704.

Papakostas, G. I., Kornstein, S. G., Clayton, A. H., Soares, C. N., Hallett, L. A., Krishen, A., et al. (2007). Relative antidepressant efficacy of bupropion and the selective serotonin reuptake inhibitors in major depressive disorder: Gender-age interactions. *International Clinical Psychopharmacology, 22*(4), 226–229.

Papakostas, G. I., Petersen, T., Lebowitz, B. D., Mischoulon, D., Ryan, J. L., Nierenberg, A. A., et al. (2005). The relationship between serum folate, vitamin B12, and homocysteine levels in major depressive disorder and the timing of improvement with fluoxetine. *International Journal of Neuropsychopharmacology, 8*(4), 523–528.

Papakostas, G. I., Petersen, T., Mischoulon, D., Green, C. H., Nierenberg, A. A., Bottiglieri, T., et al. (2004). Serum folate, vitamin B12, and homocysteine in major depressive disorder, Part 2: Predictors of relapse during the continuation phase of pharmacotherapy. *Journal of Clinical Psychiatry, 65*(8), 1096–1098.

Papakostas, G. I., Petersen, T. J., Green, C., Iosifescu, D. V., Yeung, A. S., Nierenberg, A. A., et al. (2005). A description of next-step switching versus augmentation practices for outpatients with treatment-resistant major depressive disorder enrolled in an academic specialty clinic. *Annals of Clinical Psychiatry, 17*(3), 161–165.

Papakostas, G. I., Shelton, R. C., Smith, J., & Fava, M. (2007). Augmentation of antidepressants with atypical antipsychotic medications for treatment-resistant major depressive disorder: A meta-analysis. *Journal of Clinical Psychiatry, 68*(6), 826–831.

Papakostas, G. I., Stahl, S. M., Krishen, A., Seifert, C. A., Tucker, V. L., Goodale, E. P., et al. (2008). Efficacy of bupropion and the selective serotonin reuptake inhibitors in the treatment of major depressive disorder with high levels of anxiety (anxious depression): A pooled analysis of 10 studies. *Journal of Clinical Psychiatry, 69*(8), 1287–1292.

Papakostas, G. I., Worthington, J. J., 3rd, Iosifescu, D. V., Kinrys, G., Burns, A. M., Fisher, L. B., et al. (2006). The combination of duloxetine and bupropion for treatment-resistant major depressive disorder. *Depression and Anxiety, 23*(3), 178–181.

Parfit, K. (Ed.). (1999). *The complete drug reference* (32nd ed.). London: Pharmaceutical Press.

Parkman, C. A. (2002). Another FDA warning: Kava supplements. *Case Manager, 13*(4), 26–28.

Parsey, R. V., Hastings, R. S., Oquendo, M. A., Huang, Y. Y., Simpson, N., Arcement, J., et al. (2006). Lower serotonin transporter binding potential in the human brain during major depressive episodes. *American Journal of Psychiatry, 163*(1), 52–58.

Partonen, T. (1994). Involvement of melatonin and serotonin in winter depression. *Medical Hypotheses, 43*(3), 165–166.

Partonen, T. (1998). Vitamin D and serotonin in winter. *Medical Hypotheses, 51*(3), 267–268.

Pasternak, M. (1998). Sustained-release bupropion for smoking cessation. *New England Journal of Medicine, 338*(9), 619–620.

Patkar, A. A., Masand, P. S., Pae, C. U., Peindl, K., Hooper-Wood, C., Mannelli, P., et al. (2006). A randomized, double-blind, placebo-controlled trial of augmentation with an extended release formulation of methylphenidate in outpatients with treatment-resistant depression. *Journal of Clinical Psychopharmacology, 26*(6), 653–656.

Pauling, L. (1968). Orthomolecular psychiatry. Varying the concentrations of substances normally present in the human body may control mental disease. *Science, 160*, 265–271.

Pawlosky, R. J., Hibbeln, J. R., Novotny, J. A., & Salem, N., Jr. (2001). Physiological compartmental analysis of alpha-linolenic acid metabolism in adult humans. *Journal of Lipid Research, 42*(8), 1257–1265.

Paykel, E. S. (2001). Continuation and maintenance therapy in depression. *British Medical Bulletin, 57*, 145–159.

Pearce, J. M. (2008). Leopold Auenbrugger: Camphor-induced epilepsy—remedy for manic psychosis. *European Neurology, 59*(1–2), 105–107.

Pearson, K. H., Nonacs, R. M., Viguera, A. C., Heller, V. L., Petrillo, L. F., Brandes, M., et al. (2007). Birth outcomes following prenatal exposure to antidepressants. *Journal of Clinical Psychiatry, 68*(8), 1284–1289.

Peet, M., & Horrobin, D. F. (2002). A dose-ranging study of the effects of ethyl-eicosapentaenoate in patients with ongoing depression despite apparently adequate treatment with standard drugs. *Archives of General Psychiatry, 59*(10), 913–919.

Perahia, D. G., Gilaberte, I., Wang, F., Wiltse, C. G., Huckins, S. A., Clemens, J. W., et al. (2006). Duloxetine in the prevention of relapse of major depressive disorder: Double-blind placebo-controlled study. *British Journal of Psychiatry, 188*, 346–353.

Perahia, D. G., Kajdasz, D. K., Desaiah, D., & Haddad, P. M. (2005). Symptoms following abrupt discontinuation of duloxetine treatment in patients with major depressive disorder. *Journal of Affective Disorders, 89*(1–3), 207–212.

Perahia, D. G., Pritchett, Y. L., Desaiah, D., & Raskin, J. (2006). Efficacy of duloxetine in painful symptoms: An analgesic or antidepressant effect? *International Clinical Psychopharmacology, 21*(6), 311–317.

Perahia, D. G., Pritchett, Y. L., Kajdasz, D. K., Bauer, M., Jain, R., Russell, J. M., et al. (2008). A randomized, double-blind comparison of duloxetine and venlafaxine in the treatment of patients with major depressive disorder. *Journal of Psychiatric Research, 42*(1), 22–34.

Perlis, R. H., Brown, E., Baker, R. W., & Nierenberg, A. A. (2006). Clinical features of bipolar depression versus major depressive disorder in large multicenter trials. *American Journal of Psychiatry, 163*(2), 225–231.

Perry, E. B., Berman, R. M., Sanacora, G., Anand, A., Lynch-Colonese, K., & Charney, D. S. (2004). Pindolol augmentation in depressed patients resistant to selective serotonin reuptake inhibitors: A double-blind, randomized, controlled trial. *Journal of Clinical Psychiatry, 65*(2), 238–243.

Perwien, A. R., Kratochvil, C. J., Faries, D. E., Vaughan, B. S., Spencer, T., & Brown, R. T. (2006). Atomoxetine treatment in children and adolescents with attention-deficit hyperactivity disorder: What are the long-term health-related quality-of-life outcomes? *Journal of Child and Adolescent Psychopharmacology, 16*(6), 713–724.

Peters, G., Plohn, S., Buhk, H., & Dahme, B. (2000). [Thought protocols before and after a psychological headache—treatment with imagery]. *Psychotherapie, Psychosomatik, Medizinische Psychologie, 50*(9–10), 391–395.

Petersen, T., Papakostas, G. I., Posternak, M. A., Kant, A., Guyker, W. M., Iosifescu, D. V., et al. (2005). Empirical testing of two models for staging antidepressant treatment resistance. *Journal of Clinical Psychopharmacology, 25*(4), 336–341.

Pilkington, K., Kirkwood, G., Rampes, H., Fisher, P., & Richardson, J. (2005). Homeopathy for depression: A systematic review of the research evidence. *Homeopathy, 94*(3), 153–163.

Pilkington, K., Kirkwood, G., Rampes, H., Fisher, P., & Richardson, J. (2006). Homeopathy for anxiety and anxiety disorders: A systematic review of the research. *Homeopathy, 95*(3), 151–162.

Pilowsky, D. J., Wickramaratne, P. J., Rush, A. J., Hughes, C. W., Garber, J., Malloy, E., et al. (2006). Children of currently depressed mothers: A STAR*D ancillary study. *Journal of Clinical Psychiatry, 67*(1), 126–136.

Pittler, M. H., & Ernst, E. (2003). Kava extract for treating anxiety. *Cochrane Database of Systematic Reviews* (Online) (1), CD003383.

Pjrek, E., Winkler, D., Konstantinidis, A., Willeit, M., Praschak-Rieder, N., & Kasper, S. (2007). Agomelatine in the treatment of seasonal affective disorder. *Psychopharmacology (Berlin), 190*(4), 575–579.

Plante, D. T. (2008). Treatment-emergent hypomania or mania with modafinil. *American Journal of Psychiatry, 165*(1), 134–135; author reply 135.

Poirier, M. F., & Boyer, P. (1999). Venlafaxine and paroxetine in treatment-resistant depression. Double-blind, randomised comparison. *British Journal of Psychiatry, 175*, 12–16.

Poldinger, W., Calanchini, B., & Schwarz, W. (1991). A functional-dimensional approach to depression: Serotonin deficiency as a target syndrome in a comparison of 5-hydroxytryptophan and fluvoxamine. *Psychopathology, 24*(2), 53–81.

Posternak, M. A., & Miller, I. (2001). Untreated short-term course of major depression: A meta-analysis of outcomes from studies using wait-list control groups. *Journal of Affective Disorders, 66*(2–3), 139–146.

Posternak, M. A., & Zimmerman, M. (2005). Dual reuptake inhibitors incur lower rates of tachyphylaxis than selective serotonin reuptake inhibitors: A retrospective study. *Journal of Clinical Psychiatry, 66*(6), 705–707.

Prange, A. (1964). The pharmacology and biochemistry of depression. *Disease of the Nervous System, 25*, 217–221.

Prasad, S., Harpin, V., Poole, L., Zeitlin, H., Jamdar, S., & Puvanendran, K. (2007). A multi-centre, randomised, open-label study of atomoxetine compared with standard current therapy in UK children and adolescents with attention-deficit/hyperactivity disorder (ADHD). *Current Medical Research Opinion, 23*(2), 379–394.

Prasad, S., & Steer, C. (2008). Switching from neurostimulant therapy to atomoxetine in children and adolescents with attention-deficit hyperactivity disorder: Clinical approaches and review of current available evidence. *Paediatric Drugs, 10*(1), 39–47.

Prathikanti, S. (2008). *Complementary and alternative medicine approaches to treatment: What's the evidence?* Paper presented at New Frontiers in Depression Research and Treatment, San Francisco.

Preskorn, S. H. (1996). *Clinical psychopharmacology of selective serotonin reuptake inhibitors*. Caddo, OK: Professional Communications.

Prochaska, J. O., DiClemente, C. C., & Norcross, J. C. (1992). In search of how people change. Applications to addictive behaviors. *American Psychologist*, 47(9), 1102–1114.

Prudic, J., Olfson, M., Marcus, S. C., Fuller, R. B., & Sackeim, H. A. (2004). Effectiveness of electroconvulsive therapy in community settings. *Biological Psychiatry*, 55(3), 301–312.

Przybelski, R. J., & Binkley, N. C. (2007). Is vitamin D important for preserving cognition? A positive correlation of serum 25-hydroxyvitamin D concentration with cognitive function. *Archives of Biochemistry and Biophysics*, 460(2), 202–205.

Puchacz, E., Stumpf, W. E., Stachowiak, E. K., & Stachowiak, M. K. (1996). Vitamin D increases expression of the tyrosine hydroxylase gene in adrenal medullary cells. Brain Research. *Molecular Brain Research*, 36(1), 193–196.

Quitkin, F. M., McGrath, P. J., Stewart, J. W., Deliyannides, D., Taylor, B. P., Davies, C. A., et al. (2005). Remission rates with 3 consecutive antidepressant trials: Effectiveness for depressed outpatients. *Journal of Clinical Psychiatry*, 66(6), 670–676.

Rabe-Jablonska, J., & Szymanska, A. (2001). Diurnal profile of melatonin secretion in the acute phase of major depression and in remission. *Medical Science Monitor*, 7(5), 946–952.

Racagni, G., & Popoli, M. (2008). Cellular and molecular mechanisms in the long-term action of antidepressants. *Dialogues in Clinical Neuroscience*, 10(4), 385–400.

Raison, C. L., Borisov, A. S., Broadwell, S. D., Capuron, L., Woolwine, B. J., Jacobson, I. M., et al. (2005). Depression during pegylated interferon-alpha plus ribavirin therapy: Prevalence and prediction. *Journal of Clinical Psychiatry*, 66(1), 41–48.

Rajkowska, G., & Miguel-Hidalgo, J. J. (2007). Gliogenesis and glial pathology in depression. *CNS and Neurological Disorders Drug Targets*, 6(3), 219–233.

Ramadan, N. M. (2007). Current trends in migraine prophylaxis. *Headache*, 47(Suppl. 1), S52–S57.

Rapaport, M. H., Gharabawi, G. M., Canuso, C. M., Mahmoud, R. A., Keller, M. B., Bossie, C. A., et al. (2006). Effects of risperidone augmentation in patients with treatment-resistant depression: Results of open-label treatment followed by double-blind continuation. *Neuropsychopharmacology*, 31(11), 2505–2513.

Raskin, J., Wiltse, C. G., Siegal, A., Sheikh, J., Xu, J., Dinkel, J. J., et al. (2007). Efficacy of duloxetine on cognition, depression, and pain in elderly patients with major depressive disorder: An 8-week, double-blind, placebo-controlled trial. *American Journal of Psychiatry*, 164(6), 900–909.

Rasmussen, H. H., Mortensen, P. B., & Jensen, I. W. (1989). Depression and magnesium deficiency. *International Journal of Psychiatry Medicine, 19*(1), 57–63.

Rasmussen, N. A., Schroder, P., Olsen, L. R., Brodsgaard, M., Unden, M., & Bech, P. (2005). Modafinil augmentation in depressed patients with partial response to antidepressants: A pilot study on self-reported symptoms covered by the Major Depression Inventory (MDI) and the Symptom Checklist (SCL-92). *Nordic Journal of Psychiatry, 59*(3), 173–178.

Ravindran, A. V., Lam, R. W., Filteau, M. J., Lesperance, F., Kennedy, S. H., Parikh, S. V., et al. (2009). Canadian Network for Mood and Anxiety Treatments (CANMAT) clinical guidelines for the management of major depressive disorder in adults. V. Complementary and alternative medicine treatments. *Journal of Affective Disorders, 117*(Suppl. 1), S54–S64.

Rees, B. L. (1993). An exploratory study of the effectiveness of a relaxation with guided imagery protocol. *Journal of Holistic Nursing, 11*(3), 271–276.

Rees, B. L. (1995). Effect of relaxation with guided imagery on anxiety, depression, and self-esteem in primiparas. *Journal of Holistic Nursing, 13*(3), 255–267.

Rejali, D., Sivakumar, A., & Balaji, N. (2004). Ginkgo biloba does not benefit patients with tinnitus: A randomized placebo-controlled double-blind trial and meta-analysis of randomized trials. *Clinical Otolaryngology and Allied Sciences, 29*(3), 226–231.

Reseland, S., Bray, I., & Gunnell, D. (2006). Relationship between antide-pressant sales and secular trends in suicide rates in the Nordic countries. *British Journal of Psychiatry, 188*, 354–358.

Reynolds, E. H., Preece, J. M., Bailey, J., & Coppen, A. (1970). Folate deficiency in depressive illness. *British Journal of Psychiatry, 117*, 287–292.

Ritter, A., & Cameron, J. (2006). A review of the efficacy and effectiveness of harm reduction strategies for alcohol, tobacco and illicit drugs. *Drug and Alcohol Review, 25*(6), 611–624.

Robert, S., Hamner, M. B., Kose, S., Ulmer, H. G., Deitsch, S. E., & Lorber-baum, J. P. (2005). Quetiapine improves sleep disturbances in combat veterans with PTSD: Sleep data from a prospective, open-label study. *Journal of Clinical Psychopharmacology, 25*(4), 387–388.

Roberts, S. H., Bedson, E., Hughes, D., Lloyd, K., Moat, S., Pirmohamed, M., et al. (2007). Folate augmentation of treatment—evaluation for depression (FolATED): Protocol of a randomised controlled trial. *BMC Psychiatry, 7*, 65.

Robinson, R. G., Schultz, S. K., Castillo, C., Kopel, T., Kosier, J. T., Newman, R. M., et al. (2000). Nortriptyline versus fluoxetine in the treatment of depression and in short-term recovery after stroke: A placebo-controlled, double-blind study. *American Journal of Psychiatry, 157*(3), 351–359.

Roffe, L., Schmidt, K., & Ernst, E. (2005). A systematic review of guided imagery as an adjuvant cancer therapy. *Psychooncology, 14*(8), 607–617.

Rogers, J., & Rogers, S. (2004). *Self-determination for people with psychiatric disabilities: Personal obstacles and facilitators.* Paper presented at the UIC NRTC's National Self-Determination and Psychiatric Disability Invitational Conference.

Rohan, K. J., Roecklein, K. A., Tierney Lindsey, K., Johnson, L. G., Lippy, R. D., Lacy, T. J., et al. (2007). A randomized controlled trial of cognitive-behavioral therapy, light therapy, and their combination for seasonal affective disorder. *Journal of Consulting and Clinical Psychology, 75*(3), 489–500.

Roiser, J. P., McLean, A., Ogilvie, A. D., Blackwell, A. D., Bamber, D. J., Goodyer, I., et al. (2005). The subjective and cognitive effects of acute phenylalanine and tyrosine depletion in patients recovered from depression. *Neuropsychopharmacology, 30*(4), 775–785.

Rosenbaum, J. F., Fava, M., Falk, W. E., Pollack, M. H., Cohen, L. S., Cohen, B. M., et al. (1990). The antidepressant potential of oral S-adenosyl-l-methionine. *Acta Psychiatrica Scandinavica, 81*(5), 432–436.

Ross, J. (2003). *The mood cure: The 4-step program to take charge of your emotions—today.* New York: Penguin.

Rossman, M. L. (2002). Interactive guided imagery as a way to access patient strengths during cancer treatment. *Integrated Cancer Therapy, 1*(2), 162–165.

Roy-Byrne, P. P., Bystritsky, A., Russo, J., Craske, M. G., Sherbourne, C. D., & Stein, M. B. (2005). Use of herbal medicine in primary care patients with mood and anxiety disorders. *Psychosomatics, 46*(2), 117–122.

Rubio, G., San, L., Lopez-Munoz, F., Garcia-Garcia, P., & Alamo, C. (2003). [Combination therapy with reboxetine for major depression patients who are partial or nonresponders to serotonin selective reuptake inhibitors]. *Actas Esp Psiquiatr, 31*(6), 315–324.

Rudisch, B., & Nemeroff, C. B. (2003). Epidemiology of comorbid coronary artery disease and depression. *Biological Psychiatry, 54*, 177–180.

Rudolph, R. L., Fabre, L. F., Feighner, J. P., Rickels, K., Entsuah, R., & Derivan, A. T. (1998). A randomized, placebo-controlled, dose-response trial of venlafaxine hydrochloride in the treatment of major depression. *Journal of Clinical Psychiatry, 59*(3), 116–122.

Ruoff, G. E. (1996). Depression in the patient with chronic pain. *Journal of Family Practice, 43*(6 Suppl.), S25–S34.

Rush, A. J., Kovacs, M., Beck, A. T., Weissenburger, J., & Hollon, S. D. (1981). Differential effects of cognitive therapy and pharmacotherapy on depressive symptoms. *Journal of Affective Disorders, 3*(3), 221–229.

Rush, A. J., Kraemer, H. C., Sackeim, H. A., Fava, M., Trivedi, M. H., Frank, E., et al. (2006). Report by the ACNP Task Force on response and remission in major depressive disorder. *Neuropsychopharmacology, 31*(9), 1841–1853.

Rush, A. J., Marangell, L. B., Sackeim, H. A., George, M. S., Brannan, S. K., Davis, S. M., et al. (2005). Vagus nerve stimulation for treatment-resistant depression: A randomized, controlled acute phase trial. *Biological Psychiatry, 58*(5), 347–354.

Rush, A. J., Sackeim, H. A., Marangell, L. B., George, M. S., Brannan, S. K., Davis, S. M., et al. (2005). Effects of 12 months of vagus nerve stimulation in treatment-resistant depression: A naturalistic study. *Biological Psychiatry, 58*(5), 355–363.

Rush, A. J., Thase, M. E., & Dube, S. (2003). Research issues in the study of difficult-to-treat depression. *Biological Psychiatry, 53*(8), 743–753.

Rush, A. J., Trivedi, M. H., Wisniewski, S. R., Nierenberg, A. A., Stewart, J. W., Warden, D., et al. (2006). Acute and longer-term outcomes in depressed outpatients requiring one or several treatment steps: A STAR*D report. *American Journal of Psychiatry, 163*(11), 1905–1917.

Rush, A. J., Trivedi, M. H., Wisniewski, S. R., Stewart, J. W., Nierenberg, A. A., Thase, M. E., et al. (2006). Bupropion-SR, sertraline, or venlafaxine-XR after failure of SSRIs for depression. *New England Journal of Medicine, 354*(12), 1231–1242.

Rush, A. J., Zimmerman, M., Wisniewski, S. R., Fava, M., Hollon, S. D., Warden, D., et al. (2005). Comorbid psychiatric disorders in depressed outpatients: Demographic and clinical features. *Journal of Affective Disorders, 87*(1), 43–55.

Russell, J. M., Weisberg, R., Fava, M., Hartford, J. T., Erickson, J. S., & D'Souza, D. N. (2008). Efficacy of duloxetine in the treatment of generalized anxiety disorder in patients with clinically significant pain symptoms. *Depression and Anxiety, 25*(7), E1–E11.

Russo, E. (2001). Valerian. *In Handbook of psychotropic herbs: A scientific analysis of herbal remedies in psychiatric conditions* (pp. 95–106). Binghamton, NY: Haworth.

Rusy, L. M., & Weisman, S. J. (2000). Complementary therapies for acute pediatric pain management. *Pediatric Clinics of North America, 47*(3), 589–599.

Sabelli, H. C., Fawcett, J., Gusovsky, F., Javaid, J. I., Wynn, P., Edwards, J., et al. (1986). Clinical studies on the phenylethylamine hypothesis of affective disorder: Urine and blood phenylacetic acid and phenylalanine dietary supplements. *Journal of Clinical Psychiatry, 47*(2), 66–70.

Sachdev, P. S., Parslow, R. A., Lux, O., Salonikas, C., Wen, W., Naidoo, D., et al. (2005). Relationship of homocysteine, folic acid and vitamin B12 with depression in a middle-aged community sample. *Psychological Medicine, 35*(4), 529–538.

Sachs, G. S., Nierenberg, A. A., Calabrese, J. R., Marangell, L. B., Wisniewski, S. R., Gyulai, L., et al. (2007). Effectiveness of adjunctive antidepressant treatment for bipolar depression. *New England Journal of Medicine, 356*(17), 1711–1722.

Sack, R. L., Lewy, A. J., & Hughes, R. J. (1998). Use of melatonin for sleep and circadian rhythm disorders. *Annals of Medicine, 30*(1), 115–121.

Sackeim, H. A., Brannan, S. K., Rush, A. J., George, M. S., Marangell, L. B., & Allen, J. (2007). Durability of antidepressant response to vagus nerve stimulation (VNS). *International Journal of Neuropsychopharmacology, 10*(6), 817–826.

Sackeim, H. A., Rush, A. J., George, M. S., Marangell, L. B., Husain, M. M., Nahas, Z., et al. (2001). Vagus nerve stimulation (VNS) for treatment-resistant depression: Efficacy, side effects, and predictors of outcome. *Neuropsychopharmacology, 25*(5), 713–728.

Sagud, M., Mihaljevic-Peles, A., Muck-Seler, D., Jakovljevic, M., & Pivac, N. (2006). Quetiapine augmentation in treatment-resistant depression: A naturalistic study. *Psychopharmacology (Berlin), 187*(4), 511–514.

Saletu, B., Anderer, P., Di Padova, C., Assandri, A., & Saletu-Zyhlarz, G. M. (2002). Electrophysiological neuroimaging of the central effects of S-adenosyl-L-methionine by mapping of electroencephalograms and event-related potentials and low-resolution brain electromagnetic tomography. *American Journal of Clinical Nutrition, 76*(5), 1162S–1171S.

Salomon, R. M., Miller, H. L., Delgado, P. L., & Charney, D. (1993). The use of tryptophan depletion to evaluate central serotonin function in depression and other neuropsychiatric disorders. *International Clinical Psychopharmacology, 8*(Suppl. 2), 41–46.

San, L., & Arranz, B. (2008). Agomelatine: A novel mechanism of antidepressant action involving the melatonergic and the serotonergic system. *European Psychiatry, 23*(6), 396–402.

Sanacora, G., Kendell, S. F., Levin, Y., Simen, A. A., Fenton, L. R., Coric, V., et al. (2007). Preliminary evidence of riluzole efficacy in antidepressant-treated patients with residual depressive symptoms. *Biological Psychiatry, 61*(6), 822–825.

Santos, M. S., Ferreira, F., Cunha, A. P., Carvalho, A. P., & Macedo, T. (1994). An aqueous extract of valerian influences the transport of GABA in synaptosomes. *Planta Medica, 60*(3), 278–279.

Saransaari, P., & Oja, S. S. (2000). Taurine and neural cell damage. *Amino Acids, 19*(3–4), 509–526.

Saremi, A., & Arora, R. (2009). Vitamin E and cardiovascular disease. *American Journal of Therapeutics*, May 15, epub.

Sarris, J., Kavanagh, D. J., Adams, J., Bone, K., & Byrne, G. (2009). Kava Anxiety Depression Spectrum Study (KADSS): A mixed methods RCT using an aqueous extract of Piper methysticum. *Complementary Therapies in Medicine, 17*(3), 176–178.

Sarris, J., Kavanagh, D. J., & Byrne, G. (2010). Adjuvant use of nutritional and herbal medicines with antidepressants, mood stabilizers and benzodiazepines. *Journal of Psychiatric Research, 44*(1), 32–41.

Sarris, J., Kavanagh, D. J., Byrne, G., Bone, K. M., Adams, J., & Deed, G. (2009). The Kava Anxiety Depression Spectrum Study (KADSS): A randomized, placebo-controlled crossover trial using an aqueous extract of Piper methysticum. *Psychopharmacology (Berlin), 205*(3), 399–407.

Schaefer, M., Schwaiger, M., Garkisch, A. S., Pich, M., Hinzpeter, A., Uebelhack, R., et al. (2005). Prevention of interferon-alpha associated depression in psychiatric risk patients with chronic hepatitis C. *Journal of Hepatology, 42*(6), 793–798.

Schatzberg, A. F., Rush, A. J., Arnow, B. A., Banks, P. L., Blalock, J. A., Borian, F. E., et al. (2005). Chronic depression: Medication (nefazodone) or psychotherapy (CBASP) is effective when the other is not. *Archives of General Psychiatry, 62*(5), 513–520.

Schildkraut, J. (1965). The catecholamine hypothesis of affective disorder: A review of supporting evidence. *American Journal of Psychiatry, 122*, 509–522.

Schlaepfer, T. E., Frick, C., Zobel, A., Maier, W., Heuser, I., Bajbouj, M., et al. (2008). Vagus nerve stimulation for depression: Efficacy and safety in a European study. *Psychological Medicine, 38*(5), 651–661.

Schlager, D., Schwartz, J. E., & Bromet, E. J. (1993). Seasonal variations of current symptoms in a healthy population. *British Journal of Psychiatry, 163*, 322–326.

Schmidt, P. J., Daly, R. C., Bloch, M., Smith, M. J., Danaceau, M. A., St Clair, L. S., et al. (2005). Dehydroepiandrosterone monotherapy in midlife-onset major and minor depression. *Archives of General Psychiatry, 62*(2), 154–162.

Schneider, B., Weber, B., Frensch, A., Stein, J., & Fritz, J. (2000). Vitamin D in schizophrenia, major depression and alcoholism. *Journal of Neural Transmission, 107*(7), 839–842.

Schneider, L. S., Dagerman, K. S., & Insel, P. (2005). Risk of death with atypical antipsychotic drug treatment for dementia: Meta-analysis of randomized placebo-controlled trials. *JAMA, 294*, 1934–1943.

Schramm, E., van Calker, D., Dykierek, P., Lieb, K., Kech, S., Zobel, I., et al. (2007). An intensive treatment program of interpersonal psychotherapy plus pharmacotherapy for depressed inpatients: Acute and long-term results. *American Journal of Psychiatry, 164*(5), 768–777.

Schule, C., Zwanzger, P., Baghai, T., Mikhaiel, P., Thoma, H., Moller, H. J., et al. (2003). Effects of antidepressant pharmacotherapy after repetitive transcranial magnetic stimulation in major depression: An open follow-up study. *Journal of Psychiatric Research, 37*(2), 145–153.

Schweizer, E., Rynn, M., Mandos, L. A., Demartinis, N., Garcia-Espana, F., & Rickels, K. (2001). The antidepressant effect of sertraline is not enhanced by dose titration: Results from an outpatient clinical trial. *International Clinical Psychopharmacology, 16*(3), 137–143.

Seimyr, L., Sjogren, B., Welles-Nystrom, B., & Nissen, E. (2009). Antenatal maternal depressive mood and parental-fetal attachment at the end of pregnancy. *Archives of Women's Mental Health, 12*(5), 269–279.

Selhub, J., Jacques, P. F., Bostom, A. G., D'Agostino, R. B., Wilson, P. W., Belanger, A. J., et al. (1995). Association between plasma homocysteine concentrations and extracranial carotid-artery stenosis. *New England Journal of Medicine, 332*(5), 286–291.

Sempels, C., & Sienaert, P. (2007). [The role of omega-3 fatty acids in the treatment of bipolar disorders: The current situation]. *Tijdschrift voor Psychiatrie, 49*(9), 639–647.

Severus, W. E. (2006). Effects of omega-3 polyunsaturated fatty acids on depression. *Herz, 31*(Suppl. 3), 69–74.

Shamir, E., Barak, Y., Shalman, I., Laudon, M., Zisapel, N., Tarrasch, R., et al. (2001). Melatonin treatment for tardive dyskinesia: A double-blind, placebo-controlled, crossover study. *Archives of General Psychiatry, 58*(11), 1049–1052.

Sharma, R. P., Shapiro, L. E., Kamath, S. K., Soll, E. A., Watanabe, M. D., & Davis, J. M. (1997). Acute dietary tryptophan depletion: Effects on schizophrenic positive and negative symptoms. *Neuropsychobiology, 35*(1), 5–10.

Sharma, V., Khan, M., & Smith, A. (2005). A closer look at treatment resistant depression: Is it due to a bipolar diathesis? *Journal of Affective Disorders, 84*(2–3), 251–257.

Shaw, K., Turner, J., & Del Mar, C. (2001). Tryptophan and 5-hydroxytryptophan for depression. *Cochrane Database of Systematic Reviews* (Online) (3), CD003198.

Sheffrin, M., Driscoll, H. C., Lenze, E. J., Mulsant, B. H., Pollock, B. G., Miller, M. D., et al. (2009). Pilot study of augmentation with aripiprazole for incomplete response in late-life depression: Getting to remission. *J Clin Psychiatry, 70*(2), 208–213.

Sheline, Y. I., Gado, M. H., & Kraemer, H. C. (2003). Untreated depression and hippocampal volume loss. *American Journal of Psychiatry, 160*(8), 1516–1518.

Shelton, R. C. (2002). St John's wort for the treatment of depression. *Lancet Neurology, 1*(5), 275.

Shelton, R. C. (2007). The molecular neurobiology of depression. *Psychiatric Clinics of North America, 30*(1), 1–11.

Shelton, R. C., Williamson, D. J., Corya, S. A., Sanger, T. M., Van Campen, L. E., Case, M., et al. (2005). Olanzapine/fluoxetine combination for treatment-resistant depression: A controlled study of SSRI and nortriptyline resistance. *Journal of Clinical Psychiatry, 66*(10), 1289–1297.

Sher, L. (2006). Combined dexamethasone suppression-corticotropin-releasing hormone stimulation test in studies of depression, alcoholism, and suicidal behavior. *ScientificWorldJournal, 6*, 1398–1404.

Sherman, F. T. (2009). Life-saving treatment for depression in elderly. Always think of electroconvulsive therapy (ECT). *Geriatrics, 64*(4), 8, 12.

Shorvon, S. D., Carney, M. W., Chanarin, I., & Reynolds, E. H. (1980). The neuropsychiatry of megaloblastic anaemia. *British Medical Journal, 281,* 10361038.

Silkaitis, R. P., & Mosnaim, A. D. (1976). Pathways linking L-phenylalanine and 2-phenylethylamine with p-tyramine in rabbit brain. *Brain Research, 114*(1), 105–115.

Silverstone, P. H., McGrath, B. M., & Kim, H. (2005). Bipolar disorder and myo-inositol: A review of the magnetic resonance spectroscopy findings. *Bipolar Disorders, 7*(1), 1–10.

Simon, G. E., & Savarino, J. (2007). Suicide attempts among patients starting depression treatment with medications or psychotherapy. *American Journal of Psychiatry, 164*(7), 1029–1034.

Simon, G. E., Savarino, J., Operskalski, B., & Wang, P. S. (2006). Suicide risk during antidepressant treatment. *American Journal of Psychiatry, 163*(1), 41–47.

Siwek, M., Dudek, D., Paul, I. A., Sowa-Kucma, M., Zieba, A., Popik, P., et al. (2009). Zinc supplementation augments efficacy of imipramine in treatment resistant patients: A double blind, placebo-controlled study. *Journal of Affective Disorders, 118*(1–3), 187–195.

Sloman, R. (1995). Relaxation and the relief of cancer pain. *Nursing Clinics of North America, 30*(4), 697–709.

Smith, K. A., Fairburn, C. G., & Cowen, P. J. (1999). Symptomatic relapse in bulimia nervosa following acute tryptophan depletion. *Archives of General Psychiatry, 56*(2), 171–176.

Smith, T., & Nicholson, R. A. (2007). Review of duloxetine in the management of diabetic peripheral neuropathic pain. *Vascular Health Risk Management, 3*(6), 833–844.

Snitz, B. E., O'Meara, E. S., Carlson, M. C., Arnold, A. M., Ives, D. G., Rapp, S. R., et al. (2009). Ginkgo biloba for preventing cognitive decline in older adults: A randomized trial. *JAMA, 302*(24), 2663–2670.

Sokolski, K. N. (2008). Adjunctive aripiprazole for bupropion-resistant major depression. *Annals of Pharmacotherapy, 42*(7), 1124–1129.

Sokolski, K. N., Conney, J. C., Brown, B. J., & DeMet, E. M. (2004). Once-daily high-dose pindolol for SSRI-refractory depression. *Psychiatry Research, 125*(2), 81–86.

Sola, C. L., Bostwick, J. M., Hart, D. A., & Lineberry, T. W. (2006). Anticipating potential linezolid-SSRI interactions in the general hospital setting: An MAOI in disguise. *Mayo Clinic Proceedings, 81*(3), 330–334.

Solomon, P. R., Adams, F., Silver, A., Zimmer, J., & DeVeaux, R. (2002). Ginkgo for memory enhancement: A randomized controlled trial. *JAMA, 288*(7), 835–840.

Souery, D., Amsterdam, J., de Montigny, C., Lecrubier, Y., Montgomery, S., Lipp, O., et al. (1999). Treatment resistant depression: Methodological overview and operational criteria. *European Neuropsychopharmacology*, 9(1–2), 83–91.

Spalletta, G., & Caltagirone, C. (2003). Sertraline treatment of post-stroke major depression: An open study in patients with moderate to severe symptoms. *Functional Neurology*, 18(4), 227–232.

Spangler, L., Scholes, D., Brunner, R. L., Robbins, J., Reed, S. D., Newton, K. M., et al. (2008). Depressive symptoms, bone loss, and fractures in post-menopausal women. *Journal of General Internal Medicine*, 23(5), 567–574.

Speck, B. J. (1990). The effect of guided imagery upon first semester nursing students performing their first injections. *Journal of Nursing Education*, 29(8), 346–350.

Spencer, T. J., Faraone, S. V., Michelson, D., Adler, L. A., Reimherr, F. W., Glatt, S. J., et al. (2006). Atomoxetine and adult attention-deficit/hyperactivity disorder: The effects of comorbidity. *Journal of Clinical Psychiatry*, 67(3), 415–420.

Spencer, T. J., Kratochvil, C. J., Sangal, R. B., Saylor, K. E., Bailey, C. E., Dunn, D. W., et al. (2007). Effects of atomoxetine on growth in children with attention-deficit/hyperactivity disorder following up to five years of treatment. *Journal of Child and Adolescent Psychopharmacology*, 17(5), 689–700.

Spencer, T. J., Newcorn, J. H., Kratochvil, C. J., Ruff, D., Michelson, D., & Biederman, J. (2005). Effects of atomoxetine on growth after 2-year treatment among pediatric patients with attention-deficit/hyperactivity disorder. *Pediatrics*, 116(1), e74–e80.

Stahl, S. M. (2007). Novel therapeutics for depression: L-methylfolate as a trimonoamine modulator and antidepressant-augmenting agent. *CNS Spectrums*, 12(10), 739–744.

Stahl, S. M. (2008). *Stahl's essential psychopharmacology: Neuroscientific basis and practical applications*. New York: Cambridge University Press.

Starkstein, S. E., Mizrahi, R., & Power, B. D. (2008). Antidepressant therapy in post-stroke depression. *Expert Opinion in Pharmacotherapy*, 9(8), 1291–1298.

Steinberg, S., Annable, L., Young, S. N., & Liyanage, N. (1999). A placebo-controlled study of the effects of L-tryptophan in patients with premenstrual dysphoria. *Advances in Experimental Medicine and Biology*, 467, 85–88.

Stevensen, C. (1995). Non-pharmacological aspects of acute pain management. *Complementary Therapy in Nursing and Midwifery*, 1(3), 77–84.

Stevinson, C., & Ernst, E. (2000). Valerian for insomnia: A systematic review of randomized clinical trials. *Sleep Medicine*, 1(2), 91–99.

Stewart, J. W., Harrison, W., Quitkin, F., & Liebowitz, M. R. (1984). Phenelzine-induced pyridoxine deficiency. *Journal of Clinical Psychopharmacology*, 4(4), 225–226.

Stoll, A. L. (2001). *The omega-3 connection: The groundbreaking omega-3 anti-depression diet and brain program*. New York: Simon & Schuster.

Stoppe, A., Louza, M., Rosa, M., Gil, G., & Rigonatti, S. (2006). Fixed high-dose electroconvulsive therapy in the elderly with depression: A double-blind, randomized comparison of efficacy and tolerability between unilateral and bilateral electrode placement. *Journal of ECT, 22*(2), 92–99.

Suk, M., Oh, W., & Kil, S. (2006). [Guided imagery types on stress and performance of an intramuscular injection of nursing students]. *Taehan Kanho Hakhoe Chi, 36*(6), 976–982.

Sullivan, M. D., Bentley, S., Fan, M. Y., & Gardner, G. (2008). A single-blind, placebo run-in study of duloxetine for activity-limiting osteoarthritis pain. *Journal of Pain, 10*(2), 208–213.

Sullivan, P. F., Neale, M. C., & Kendler, K. S. (2000). Genetic epidemiology of major depression: Review and meta-analysis. *American Journal of Psychiatry, 157*(10), 1552–1562.

Sultan, A., Gaskell, H., Derry, S., & Moore, R. A. (2008). Duloxetine for painful diabetic neuropathy and fibromyalgia pain: Systematic review of randomised trials. *BMC Neurology, 8*, 29.

Suppes, T., Baldessarini, R. J., Faedda, G. L., & Tohen, M. (1991). Risk of recurrence following discontinuation of lithium treatment in bipolar disorder. *Archives of General Psychiatry, 48*(12), 1082–1088.

Suppes, T., Dennehy, E. B., Hirschfeld, R. M., Altshuler, L. L., Bowden, C. L., Calabrese, J. R., et al. (2005). The Texas implementation of medication algorithms: Update to the algorithms for treatment of bipolar I disorder. *Journal of Clinical Psychiatry, 66*(7), 870–886.

Suppes, T., Marangell, L. B., Bernstein, I. H., Kelly, D. I., Fischer, E. G., Zboyan, H. A., et al. (2008). A single blind comparison of lithium and lamotrigine for the treatment of bipolar II depression. *Journal of Affective Disorders, 111*(2–3), 334–343.

Surtees, R., Heales, S., & Bowron, A. (1994). Association of cerebrospinal fluid deficiency of 5-methyltetrahydrofolate, but not S-adenosylmethionine, with reduced concentrations of the acid metabolites of 5-hydroxytryptamine and dopamine. *Clinical Science (London), 86*(6), 697–702.

Szymanska, A., Rabe-Jablonska, J., & Karasek, M. (2001). Diurnal profile of melatonin concentrations in patients with major depression: Relationship to the clinical manifestation and antidepressant treatment. *Neuro Endocrinology Letter, 22*(3), 192–198.

Taibi, D. M., Landis, C. A., Petry, H., & Vitiello, M. V. (2007). A systematic review of valerian as a sleep aid: Safe but not effective. *Sleep Medicine Review, 11*(3), 209–230.

Tanskanen, A., Hibbeln, J. R., Tuomilehto, J., Uutela, A., Haukkala, A., Viinamaki, H., et al. (2001). Fish consumption and depressive symptoms in the general population in Finland. *Psychiatric Services, 52*(4), 529–531.

Tardito, D., Musazzi, L., Tiraboschi, E., Mallei, A., Racagni, G., & Popoli, M. (2009). Early induction of CREB activation and CREB-regulating signalling by antidepressants. *International Journal of Neuropsychopharmacology*, 1–15.

Tatarsky, A. (2003). Harm reduction psychotherapy: Extending the reach of traditional substance use treatment. *Journal of Substance Abuse Treatment*, 25(4), 249–256.

Taylor, J. J., Wilson, J. W., & Estes, L. L. (2006). Linezolid and serotonergic drug interactions: A retrospective survey. *Clinical Infectious Diseases*, 43(2), 180–187.

Taylor, M. J., Carney, S., Geddes, J., & Goodwin, G. (2003). Folate for depressive disorders. *Cochrane Database System Reviews*, (2), CD003390.

Teman, P. T., Perry, C. L., Ryan, D. A., & Rasmussen, K. G. (2006). Nonconvulsive seizures in electroconvulsive therapy: Further evidence of differential neurophysiological aspects of bitemporal versus bifrontal electrode placement. *Journal of ECT*, 22(1), 46–48.

Tew, J. D., Jr. , Mulsant, B. H., Haskett, R. F., Joan, P., Begley, A. E., & Sackeim, H. A. (2007). Relapse during continuation pharmacotherapy after acute response to ECT: A comparison of usual care versus protocolized treatment. *Annals of Clinical Psychiatry*, 19(1), 1–4.

Thase, M. E. (2008). Are SNRIs more effective than SSRIs? A review of the current state of the controversy. *Psychopharmacological Bulletin*, 41(2), 58–85.

Thase, M. E., Corya, S. A., Osuntokun, O., Case, M., Henley, D. B., Sanger, T. M., et al. (2007). A randomized, double-blind comparison of olanzapine/fluoxetine combination, olanzapine, and fluoxetine in treatment-resistant major depressive disorder. *Journal of Clinical Psychiatry*, 68(2), 224–236.

Thase, M. E., Entsuah, A. R., & Rudolph, R. L. (2001). Remission rates during treatment with venlafaxine or selective serotonin reuptake inhibitors. *British Journal of Psychiatry*, 178, 234–241.

Thase, M. E., Entsuah, R., Cantillon, M., & Kornstein, S. G. (2005). Relative antidepressant efficacy of venlafaxine and SSRIs: Sex-age interactions. *Journal of Women's Health*, 14(7), 609–616.

Thase, M. E., Fava, M., DeBattista, C., Arora, S., & Hughes, R. J. (2006). Modafinil augmentation of SSRI therapy in patients with major depressive disorder and excessive sleepiness and fatigue: A 12-week, open-label, extension study. *CNS Spectrums*, 11(2), 93–102.

Thase, M. E., Friedman, E. S., Biggs, M. M., Wisniewski, S. R., Trivedi, M. H., Luther, J. F., et al. (2007). Cognitive therapy versus medication in augmentation and switch strategies as second-step treatments: A STAR*D report. *American Journal of Psychiatry*, 164(5), 739–752.

Thase, M. E., Macfadden, W., Weisler, R. H., Chang, W., Paulsson, B., Khan, A., et al. (2006). Efficacy of quetiapine monotherapy in bipolar I and II depression: A double-blind, placebo-controlled study (the BOLDER II study). _Journal of Clinical Psychopharmacology, 26_(6), 600–609.

Thase, M. E., & Rush, A. J. (1997). When at first you don't succeed: Sequential strategies for antidepressant nonresponders. _Journal of Clinical Psychiatry, 58_(Suppl. 13), 23–29.

Thase, M. E., Rush, A. J., Manber, R., Kornstein, S. G., Klein, D. N., Markowitz, J. C., et al. (2002). Differential effects of nefazodone and cognitive behavioral analysis system of psychotherapy on insomnia associated with chronic forms of major depression. _Journal of Clinical Psychiatry, 63_(6), 493–500.

Thase, M. E., Shelton, R. C., & Khan, A. (2006). Treatment with venlafaxine extended release after SSRI nonresponse or intolerance: A randomized comparison of standard- and higher-dosing strategies. _Journal of Clinical Psychopharmacology, 26_(3), 250–258.

Tiemeier, H., van Tuijl, H. R., Hofman, A., Meijer, J., Kiliaan, A. J., & Breteler, M. M. (2002). Vitamin B12, folate, and homocysteine in depression: The Rotterdam Study. _American Journal of Psychiatry, 159_(12), 2099–2101.

Tomkins, G. E., Jackson, J. L., O'Malley, P. G., Balden, E., & Santoro, J. E. (2001). Treatment of chronic headache with antidepressants: A meta-analysis. _American Journal of Medicine, 111_(1), 54–63.

Tondo, L., & Baldessarini, R. J. (2000). Reduced suicide risk during lithium maintenance treatment. _Journal of Clinical Psychiatry, 61_(Suppl. 9), 97–104.

Tondo, L., Hennen, J., & Baldessarini, R. J. (2001). Lower suicide risk with long-term lithium treatment in major affective illness: A meta-analysis. _Acta Psychiatrica Scandinavica, 104_(3), 163–172.

Tondo, L., Isacsson, G., & Baldessarini, R. (2003). Suicidal behaviour in bipolar disorder: Risk and prevention. _CNS Drugs, 17_(7), 491–511.

Tondo, L., Jamison, K. R., & Baldessarini, R. J. (1997). Effect of lithium maintenance on suicidal behavior in major mood disorders. _Annals of the New York Academy of Sciences, 836_, 339–351.

Tondo, L., Lepri, B., & Baldessarini, R. J. (2007). Suicidal risks among 2826 Sardinian major affective disorder patients. _Acta Psychiatrica Scandinavica, 116_(6), 419–428.

Tong, E. K., Carmody, T. P., & Simon, J. A. (2006). Bupropion for smoking cessation: A review. _Comprehensive Therapy, 32_(1), 26–33.

Toyokuni, S. (2009). Role of iron in carcinogenesis: Cancer as a ferrotoxic disease. _Cancer Science, 100_(1), 9–16.

Trang, H. M., Cole, D. E., Rubin, L. A., Pierratos, A., Siu, S., & Vieth, R. (1998). Evidence that vitamin D3 increases serum 25-hydroxyvitamin D more efficiently than does vitamin D2. _American Journal of Clinical Nutrition, 68_(4), 854–858.

Treatment for Adolescents With Depression Study (TADS) Team. (2005). The Treatment for Adolescents With Depression Study (TADS): Demographic and clinical characteristics. *Journal of the American Academy of Child and Adolescent Psychiatry, 44*(1), 28–40.

Trivedi, M. H., Fava, M., Wisniewski, S. R., Thase, M. E., Quitkin, F., Warden, D., et al. (2006). Medication augmentation after the failure of SSRIs for depression. *New England Journal of Medicine, 354*(12), 1243–1252.

Trivedi, M. H., Rush, A. J., Carmody, T. J., Donahue, R. M., Bolden-Watson, C., Houser, T. L., et al. (2001). Do bupropion SR and sertraline differ in their effects on anxiety in depressed patients? *Journal of Clinical Psychiatry, 62*(10), 776–781.

Trivedi, M. H., Rush, A. J., Wisniewski, S. R., Nierenberg, A. A., Warden, D., Ritz, L., et al. (2006). Evaluation of outcomes with citalopram for depression using measurement-based care in STAR*D: Implications for clinical practice. *American Journal of Psychiatry, 163*(1), 28–40.

Trivedi, M. H., Thase, M. E., Fava, M., Nelson, C. J., Yang, H., Qi, Y., et al. (2008). Adjunctive aripiprazole in major depressive disorder: Analysis of efficacy and safety in patients with anxious and atypical features. *Journal of Clinical Psychiatry, 69*(12), 1928–1936.

Tsapakis, E. M., Soldani, F., Tondo, L., & Baldessarini, R. J. (2008). Efficacy of antidepressants in juvenile depression: meta-analysis. *British Journal of Psychiatry, 193*(1), 10–17.

Tucker, K. L., Rich, S., Rosenberg, I., Jacques, P., Dallal, G., Wilson, P. W., et al. (2000). Plasma vitamin B-12 concentrations relate to intake source in the Framingham Offspring study. *American Journal of Clinical Nutrition, 71*(2), 514–522.

Turecki, G., Rouleau, G. A., Mari, J., Joober, R., & Morgan, K. (1997). Lack of association between bipolar disorder and tyrosine hydroxylase: A meta-analysis. *American Journal of Medical Genetics, 74*(4), 348–352.

Tusek, D. L. (1999). Guided imagery: A powerful tool to decrease length of stay, pain, anxiety, and narcotic consumption. *Journal of Invasive Cardiology, 11*(4), 265–267.

Tusek, D. L., Cwynar, R., & Cosgrove, D. M. (1999). Effect of guided imagery on length of stay, pain and anxiety in cardiac surgery patients. *Journal of Cardiovascular Management, 10*(2), 22–28.

Unutzer, J., Klap, R., Sturm, R., Young, A. S., Marmon, T., Shatkin, J., et al. (2000). Mental disorders and the use of alternative medicine: Results from a national survey. *American Journal of Psychiatry, 157*(11), 1851–1857.

U.S. FDA. (2002a). Kava-containing dietary supplements may be associated with severe liver injury. College Park, MD: Center for Food Safety and Applied Nutrition.

U.S. FDA. (2002b). Letter to health care professionals: FDA issues consumer advisory that kava products may be associated with severe liver injury. College Park, MD: Center for Food Safety and Applied Nutrition.

Vahdat Shariatpanaahi, M., Vahdat Shariatpanaahi, Z., Moshtaaghi, M., Shahbaazi, S. H., & Abadi, A. (2007). The relationship between depression and serum ferritin level. *European Journal of Clinical Nutrition, 61*(4), 532–535.

Vahora, S. A., & Malek-Ahmadi, P. (1988). S-adenosylmethionine in the treatment of depression. *Neuroscience and Biobehavioral Reviews, 12*(2), 139–141.

Valuck, R. J., Libby, A. M., Orton, H. D., Morrato, E. H., Allen, R., & Baldessarini, R. J. (2007). Spillover effects on treatment of adult depression in primary care after FDA advisory on risk of pediatric suicidality with SSRIs. *American Journal of Psychiatry, 164*(8), 1198–1205.

Valuck, R. J., Libby, A. M., Sills, M. R., Giese, A. A., & Allen, R. R. (2004). Antidepressant treatment and risk of suicide attempt by adolescents with major depressive disorder: A propensity-adjusted retrospective cohort study. *CNS Drugs, 18*(15), 1119–1132.

Van Beek, T., Bombardelli, E., Morazzoni, P., & Peterlongo, F. (1998). Ginkgo biloba L. *Fitoterapia, 69*, 195–244.

van den Broek, W. W., Birkenhager, T. K., Mulder, P. G., Bruijn, J. A., & Moleman, P. (2006). Imipramine is effective in preventing relapse in electro-convulsive therapy-responsive depressed inpatients with prior pharmacotherapy treatment failure: A randomized, placebo-controlled trial. *Journal of Clinical Psychiatry, 67*(2), 263–268.

van der Watt, G., Laugharne, J., & Janca, A. (2008). Complementary and alternative medicine in the treatment of anxiety and depression. *Current Opinion in Psychiatry, 21*(1), 37–42.

van Kerrebroeck, P. (2004). Duloxetine: An innovative approach for treating stress urinary incontinence. *BJU International, 94*(Suppl. 1), 31–37.

van Kerrebroeck, P., Abrams, P., Lange, R., Slack, M., Wyndaele, J. J., Yalcin, I., et al. (2004). Duloxetine versus placebo in the treatment of European and Canadian women with stress urinary incontinence. *BJOG, 111*(3), 249–257.

van Praag, H. M. (1981). Management of depression with serotonin precursors. *Biological Psychiatry, 16*(3), 291–310.

van Praag, H. M. (1984). In search of the mode of action of antidepressants: 5-HTP/tyrosine mixtures in depression. *Advances in Biochemical Psychopharmacology, 39*, 301–314.

van Vollenhoven, R. (1997). Dehydroepiandosterone: Uses and abuses. In W. Kelley, E. Harris, Jr., & C. Sledge (Eds.), *Textbook of rheumatology* (vol. 25, pp. 1–25). Philadelphia: WB Saunders.

Varma, A., Kaul, R. K., Varma, P., Kalra, V., & Malhotra, V. (2002). The effect of antidepressants on serum melatonin levels in endogenous depression. *Journal of the Association of Physicians of India, 50*, 1262–1265.

Vasudev, K., Macritchie, K., Geddes, J., Watson, S., & Young, A. (2006). Topiramate for acute affective episodes in bipolar disorder. *Cochrane Database System Reviews,* (1), CD003384.

Vaynman, S., Ying, Z., & Gomez-Pinilla, F. (2003). Interplay between brain-derived neurotrophic factor and signal transduction modulators in the regulation of the effects of exercise on synaptic-plasticity. *Neuroscience, 122*(3), 647–657.

Venkataramanan, R., Ramachandran, V., Komoroski, B. J., Zhang, S., Schiff, P. L., & Strom, S. C. (2000). Milk thistle, a herbal supplement, decreases the activity of CYP3A4 and uridine diphosphoglucuronosyl transferase in human hepatocyte cultures. *Drug Metabolism and Disposition: The Biological Fate of Chemicals, 28*(11), 1270–1273.

Verkerk, G. J., Pop, V. J., Van Son, M. J., & Van Heck, G. L. (2003). Prediction of depression in the postpartum period: A longitudinal follow-up study in high-risk and low-risk women. *Journal of Affective Disorders, 77*(2), 159–166.

Vidal-Alaball, J., Butler, C. C., Cannings-John, R., Goringe, A., Hood, K., McCaddon, A., et al. (2005). Oral vitamin B12 versus intramuscular vitamin B12 for vitamin B12 deficiency. *Cochrane Database System Reviews,* (3), CD004655.

Vieth, R. (1999). Vitamin D supplementation, 25-hydroxyvitamin D concentrations, and safety. *American Journal of Clinical Nutrition, 69*(5), 842–856.

Vieth, R. (2005). The pharmacology of vitamin D, including fortification strategies. In D. Feldman & F. Glorieux (Eds.), *Vitamin D* (2nd ed.). San Diego: Academic Press.

Vieth, R., Chan, P. C., & MacFarlane, G. D. (2001). Efficacy and safety of vitamin D3 intake exceeding the lowest observed adverse effect level. *American Journal of Clinical Nutrition, 73*(2), 288–294.

Vitiello, B., Rohde, P., Silva, S., Wells, K., Casat, C., Waslick, B., et al. (2006). Functioning and quality of life in the Treatment for Adolescents with Depression Study (TADS). *Journal of the American Academy of Child and Adolescent Psychiatry, 45*(12), 1419–1426.

Voderholzer, U., Laakmann, G., Becker, U., Haag, C., Baghai, T., Riemann, D., et al. (1997). Circadian profiles of melatonin in melancholic depressed patients and healthy subjects in relation to cortisol secretion and sleep. *Psychiatry Research, 71*(3), 151–161.

Vorbach, E., & Gortelmeyer, R. (1996). Treatment of insomnia: Effectiveness and tolerance of a valerian extract. *Psychopharmakotherapie, 3*, 109–115.

Wagner, K. D. (2005). Pharmacotherapy for major depression in children and adolescents. *Progress in Neuropsychopharmacology and Biological Psychiatry*, *29*(5), 819–826.

Wagner, K. D., Ambrosini, P., Rynn, M., Wohlberg, C., Yang, R., Greenbaum, M. S., et al. (2003). Efficacy of sertraline in the treatment of children and adolescents with major depressive disorder: Two randomized controlled trials. *JAMA*, *290*(8), 1033–1041.

Wagner, K. D., Jonas, J., Findling, R. L., Ventura, D., & Saikali, K. (2006). A double-blind, randomized, placebo-controlled trial of escitalopram in the treatment of pediatric depression. *Journal of the American Academy of Child and Adolescent Psychiatry*, *45*(3), 280–288.

Wagner, K. D., Robb, A. S., Findling, R. L., Jin, J., Gutierrez, M. M., & Heydorn, W. E. (2004). A randomized, placebo-controlled trial of citalopram for the treatment of major depression in children and adolescents. *American Journal of Psychiatry*, *161*(6), 1079–1083.

Walco, G. A., Varni, J. W., & Ilowite, N. T. (1992). Cognitive-behavioral pain management in children with juvenile rheumatoid arthritis. *Pediatrics*, *89*(6 Pt 1), 1075–1079.

Walinder, J., Skott, A., Carlsson, A., Nagy, A., & Bjorn-Erik, R. (1976). Potentiation of the antidepressant action of clomipramine by tryptophan. *Archives of General Psychiatry*, *33*(11), 1384–1389.

Walker, J. A. (2002). Emotional and psychological preoperative preparation in adults. *British Journal of Nursing*, *11*(8), 567–575.

Walsh, B. T., Seidman, S. N., Sysko, R., & Gould, M. (2002). Placebo response in studies of major depression: Variable, substantial, and growing. *JAMA*, *287*(14), 1840–1847.

Wang, D., Connock, M., Barton, P., Fry-Smith, A., Aveyard, P., & Moore, D. (2008). "Cut down to quit" with nicotine replacement therapies in smoking cessation: A systematic review of effectiveness and economic analysis. *Health Technology Assessment (Winchester, England)*, *12*(2), 1–156.

Wang, H., Qi, H., Wang, B. S., Cui, Y. Y., Zhu, L., Rong, Z. X., et al. (2008). Is acupuncture beneficial in depression: A meta-analysis of 8 randomized controlled trials? *Journal of Affective Disorders*, *111*(2–3), 125–134.

Wang, Y., Zheng, Y., Du, Y., Song, D. H., Shin, Y. J., Cho, S. C., et al. (2007). Atomoxetine versus methylphenidate in paediatric outpatients with attention deficit hyperactivity disorder: A randomized, double-blind comparison trial. *Australia and New Zealand Journal of Psychiatry*, *41*(3), 222–230.

Weinmann, S., Becker, T., & Koesters, M. (2008). Re-evaluation of the efficacy and tolerability of venlafaxine vs SSRI: Meta-analysis. *Psychopharmacology (Berlin)*, *196*(4), 511–520; discussion 521–522.

Weis, M., Mortensen, S. A., Rassing, M. R., Moller-Sonnergaard, J., Poulsen, G., & Rasmussen, S. N. (1994). Bioavailability of four oral coenzyme Q10 formulations in healthy volunteers. *Molecular Aspects of Medicine, 15*(Suppl.), s273–s280.

Weissman, M. M., Pilowsky, D. J., Wickramaratne, P. J., Talati, A., Wisniewski, S. R., Fava, M., et al. (2006). Remissions in maternal depression and child psychopathology: A STAR*D-child report. JAMA, 295(12), 1389–1398.

Weissman, M. M., Wolk, S., Goldstein, R. B., Moreau, D., Adams, P., Greenwald, S., et al. (1999). Depressed adolescents grown up. *JAMA, 281*(18), 1707–1713.

Weissman, M. M., Wolk, S., Wickramaratne, P., Goldstein, R. B., Adams, P., Greenwald, S., et al. (1999). Children with prepubertal-onset major depressive disorder and anxiety grown up. *Archives of General Psychiatry, 56*(9), 794–801.

Wernicke, J. F., Holdridge, K. C., Jin, L., Edison, T., Zhang, S., Bangs, M. E., et al. (2007). Seizure risk in patients with attention-deficit-hyperactivity disorder treated with atomoxetine. *Developmental Medicine and Child Neurology, 49*(7), 498–502.

Wesson, V. A., Levitt, A. J., & Joffe, R. T. (1994). Change in folate status with antidepressant treatment. *Psychiatry Research, 53*(3), 313–322.

West, R., Baker, C. L., Cappelleri, J. C., & Bushmakin, A. G. (2007). Effect of varenicline and bupropion SR on craving, nicotine withdrawal symptoms, and rewarding effects of smoking during a quit attempt. *Psychopharmacology (Berlin), 197*(3), 371–377.

Wester, P. O. (1987). Magnesium. *American Journal of Clinical Nutrition, 45*(5 Suppl.), 1305–1312.

Westrin, A., & Lam, R. W. (2007). Seasonal affective disorder: A clinical update. *Annals of Clinical Psychiatry, 19*(4), 239–246.

Weydert, J. A., Shapiro, D. E., Acra, S. A., Monheim, C. J., Chambers, A. S., & Ball, T. M. (2006). Evaluation of guided imagery as treatment for recurrent abdominal pain in children: A randomized controlled trial. *BMC Pediatrics, 6,* 29.

Wheatley, D. (2004). Triple-blind, placebo-controlled trial of Ginkgo biloba in sexual dysfunction due to antidepressant drugs. *Human Psychopharmacology, 19*(8), 545–548.

Whitehead, W. E., Palsson, O., & Jones, K. R. (2002). Systematic review of the comorbidity of irritable bowel syndrome with other disorders: What are the causes and implications? *Gastroenterology, 122*(4), 1140–1156.

Whyte, E. M., Basinski, J., Farhi, P., Dew, M. A., Begley, A., Mulsant, B. H., et al. (2004). Geriatric depression treatment in nonresponders to selective serotonin reuptake inhibitors. *Journal of Clinical Psychiatry, 65*(12), 1634–1641.

Wigal, S. B., McGough, J. J., McCracken, J. T., Biederman, J., Spencer, T. J., Posner, K. L., et al. (2005). A laboratory school comparison of mixed amphetamine salts extended release (Adderall XR) and atomoxetine (Strattera) in school-aged children with attention deficit/hyperactivity disorder. *Journal of Attention Disorders*, *9*(1), 275–289.

Wijkstra, J., Nolen, W. A., Algra, A., van Vliet, I. M., & Kahn, R. S. (2000). Relapse prevention in major depressive disorder after successful ECT: A literature review and a naturalistic case series. *Acta Psychiatrica Scandinavica*, *102*(6), 454–460.

Wilens, T. E., Haight, B. R., Horrigan, J. P., Hudziak, J. J., Rosenthal, N. E., Connor, D. F., et al. (2005). Bupropion XL in adults with attention-deficit/hyperactivity disorder: A randomized, placebo-controlled study. *Biological Psychiatry*, *57*(7), 793–801.

Wilhelm, K., Mitchell, P. B., Niven, H., Finch, A., Wedgwood, L., Scimone, A., et al. (2006). Life events, first depression onset and the serotonin transporter gene. *British Journal of Psychiatry*, *188*, 210–215.

Wilkes, S. (2006). Bupropion. Drugs Today (Barcelona), 42(10), 671–681.

Wilkins, C. H., Sheline, Y. I., Roe, C. M., Birge, S. J., & Morris, J. C. (2006). Vitamin D deficiency is associated with low mood and worse cognitive performance in older adults. *American Journal of Geriatric Psychiatry*, *14*(12), 1032–1040.

Willems, F. F., Boers, G. H., Blom, H. J., Aengevaeren, W. R., & Verheugt, F. W. (2004). Pharmacokinetic study on the utilisation of 5-methyltetrahydrofolate and folic acid in patients with coronary artery disease. *British Journal of Pharmacology*, *141*(5), 825–830.

Williams, A. L., Girard, C., Jui, D., Sabina, A., & Katz, D. L. (2005). S-adenosylmethionine (SAMe) as treatment for depression: A systematic review. *Medecine Clinique et Experimentale*, *28*(3), 132–139.

Williams, A. L., Katz, D., Ali, A., Girard, C., Goodman, J., & Bell, I. (2006). Do essential fatty acids have a role in the treatment of depression? *Journal of Affective Disorders*, *93*(1–3), 117–123.

Williams, M., Teasdale, J., Segal, Z., & Kabat-Zinn, J. (2007). *The mindful way through depression: Freeing yourself from chronic unhappiness*. New York: Guilford.

Willson, T. M., & Kliewer, S. A. (2002). PXR, CAR and drug metabolism. *Nature Reviews, Drug Discovery*, *1*(4), 259–266.

Winston, J. (1999). *The faces of homeopathy: An illustrated history of the first 200 years*. Tawa, NZ: Great Auk.

Wirz-Justice, A. (2006). Biological rhythm disturbances in mood disorders. *International Clinical Psychopharmacology*, *21*(Suppl. 1), S11–S15.

Wisniewski, S. R., Fava, M., Trivedi, M. H., Thase, M. E., Warden, D., Niederehe, G., et al. (2007). Acceptability of second-step treatments to depressed outpatients: A STAR*D report. *American Journal of Psychiatry, 164*(5), 753–760.

Wolf, J., Fiedler, U., Anghelescu, I., & Schwertfeger, N. (2006). Manic switch in a patient with treatment-resistant bipolar depression treated with modafinil. *Journal of Clinical Psychiatry, 67*(11), 1817.

Wolkowitz, O. (2008). *Strategies in treatment resistant depression.* Paper presented at New Frontiers in Depression Research and Treatment, San Francisco.

Wolkowitz, O., & Reus, V. (2002). Dehydroepiandosterone as a neurohormone in the treatment of depression and dementia. In D. Mischoulon & J. Rosenbaum (Eds.), *Natural medications for psychiatric disorders: Considering the alternatives* (pp. 62–82). Philadelphia: Lippincott Williams & Wilkins.

Wolkowitz, O. M., Reus, V. I., Keebler, A., Nelson, N., Friedland, M., Brizendine, L., et al. (1999). Double-blind treatment of major depression with dehydroepiandrosterone. *American Journal of Psychiatry, 156*(4), 646–649.

Wood, D. R., Reimherr, F. W., & Wender, P. H. (1985a). Amino acid precursors for the treatment of attention deficit disorder, residual type. *Psychopharmacology Bulletin, 21*(1), 146–149.

Wood, D. R., Reimherr, F. W., & Wender, P. H. (1985b). Treatment of attention deficit disorder with DL-phenylalanine. *Psychiatry Research, 16*(1), 21–26.

Wright, C., & Gaull, G. (1988). Role of taurine in the brain development and vision. In G. Huether (Ed.), *Amino acid availability and brain function in health and disease* (pp. 457–468). Berlin: Springer-Verlag, 1988.

Wu, H., Jin, Y., Wei, J., Jin, H., Sha, D., & Wu, J. Y. (2005). Mode of action of taurine as a neuroprotector. *Brain Research, 1038*(2), 123–131.

Wyatt, K. M., Dimmock, P. W., Jones, P. W., & Shaughn O'Brien, P. M. (1999). Efficacy of vitamin B-6 in the treatment of premenstrual syndrome: Systematic review. *British Medical Journal, 318*(7195), 1375–1381.

Wynd, C. A. (1992). Personal power imagery and relaxation techniques used in smoking cessation programs. *American Journal of Health Promotion, 6*(3), 184–189.

Wynd, C. A. (2005). Guided health imagery for smoking cessation and long-term abstinence. *Journal of Nursing Scholarship, 37*(3), 245–250.

Yasuda, S., Liang, M. H., Marinova, Z., Yahyavi, A., & Chuang, D. M. (2009). The mood stabilizers lithium and valproate selectively activate the promoter IV of brain-derived neurotrophic factor in neurons. *Molecular Psychiatry, 14*(1), 51–59.

Yates, W. R., Mitchell, J., Rush, A. J., Trivedi, M. H., Wisniewski, S. R., Warden, D., et al. (2004). Clinical features of depressed outpatients with and without co-occurring general medical conditions in STAR*D. *General Hospital Psychiatry, 26*(6), 421–429.

Yazici, A. E., Bagis, S., Tot, S., Sahin, G., Yazici, K., & Erdogan, C. (2005). Bone mineral density in premenopausal women with major depression. *Joint Bone Spine*, *72*(6), 540–543.

Yip, K. S. (2003). The relief of a caregiver's burden through guided imagery, role-playing, humor, and paradoxical intervention. *American Journal of Psychotherapy*, *57*(1), 109–121.

Yoo, H. J., Ahn, S. H., Kim, S. B., Kim, W. K., & Han, O. S. (2005). Efficacy of progressive muscle relaxation training and guided imagery in reducing chemotherapy side effects in patients with breast cancer and in improving their quality of life. *Support Care Cancer*, *13*(10), 826–833.

Youdim, M. B. (2008). Brain iron deficiency and excess: Cognitive impairment and neurodegeneration with involvement of striatum and hippocampus. *Neurotoxicity Research*, *14*(1), 45–56.

Young, L. T., Joffe, R. T., Robb, J. C., MacQueen, G. M., Marriott, M., & Patelis-Siotis, I. (2000). Double-blind comparison of addition of a second mood stabilizer versus an antidepressant to an initial mood stabilizer for treatment of patients with bipolar depression. *American Journal of Psychiatry*, *157*(1), 124–126.

Youssef, N. N., Rosh, J. R., Loughran, M., Schuckalo, S. G., Cotter, A. N., Verga, B. G., et al. (2004). Treatment of functional abdominal pain in childhood with cognitive behavioral strategies. *Journal of Pediatric Gastroenterology and Nutrition*, *39*(2), 192–196.

Yue, Q. Y., Bergquist, C., & Gerden, B. (2000). Safety of St John's wort (Hypericum perforatum). *Lancet*, *355*, 576–577.

Yukimasa, T., Yoshimura, R., Tamagawa, A., Uozumi, T., Shinkai, K., Ueda, N., et al. (2006). High-frequency repetitive transcranial magnetic stimulation improves refractory depression by influencing catecholamine and brain-derived neurotrophic factors. *Pharmacopsychiatry*, *39*(2), 52–59.

Yurekli, V. A., Akhan, G., Kutluhan, S., Uzar, E., Koyuncuoglu, H. R., & Gultekin, F. (2008). The effect of sodium valproate on chronic daily headache and its subgroups. *Journal of Headache Pain*, *9*(1), 37–41.

Zametkin, A. J., Karoum, F., & Rapoport, J. L. (1987). Treatment of hyperactive children with D-phenylalanine. *American Journal of Psychiatry*, *144*(6), 792–794.

Zarate, C. A., Jr. , Payne, J. L., Quiroz, J., Sporn, J., Denicoff, K. K., Luckenbaugh, D., et al. (2004). An open-label trial of riluzole in patients with treatment-resistant major depression. *American Journal of Psychiatry*, *161*(1), 171–174.

Zarate, C. A., Jr. , Payne, J. L., Singh, J., Quiroz, J. A., Luckenbaugh, D. A., Denicoff, K. D., et al. (2004). Pramipexole for bipolar II depression: A placebo-controlled proof of concept study. *Biological Psychiatry*, *56*(1), 54–60.

Zarate, C. A., Jr. , Singh, J. B., Carlson, P. J., Brutsche, N. E., Ameli, R., Luckenbaugh, D. A., et al. (2006). A randomized trial of an N-methyl-D-aspartate antagonist in treatment-resistant major depression. *Archives of General Psychiatry, 63*(8), 856–864.

Zetin, M., & Hoepner, C. T. (2007). Relevance of exclusion criteria in antidepressant clinical trials: A replication study. *Journal of Clinical Psychopharmacology, 27*(3), 295–301.

Zetin, M., Hoepner, C. T., & Bjornson, L. (2006). Rational antidepressant selection: Applying evidence-based medicine to complex real-world patients. *Psychopharmacology Bulletin, 39*(1), 38–104.

Zieba, A., Kata, R., Dudek, D., Schlegel-Zawadzka, M., & Nowak, G. (2000). Serum trace elements in animal models and human depression: Part III. Magnesium. Relationship with copper. *Human Psychopharmacology, 15*(8), 631–635.

Ziere, G., Dieleman, J. P., van der Cammen, T. J., Hofman, A., Pols, H. A., & Stricker, B. H. (2008). Selective serotonin reuptake inhibiting antidepressants are associated with an increased risk of nonvertebral fractures. *Journal of Clinical Psychopharmacology, 28*(4), 411–417.

Zimmerman, M., Posternak, M. A., Attiullah, N., Friedman, M., Boland, R. J., Baymiller, S., et al. (2005). Why isn't bupropion the most frequently prescribed antidepressant? *Journal of Clinical Psychiatry, 66*(5), 603–610.

Zimmerman, M., Posternak, M. A., & Chelminski, I. (2005). Is the cutoff to define remission on the Hamilton Rating Scale for Depression too high? *Journal of Nervous and Mental Disease, 193*(3), 170–175.

Zisook, S., Rush, A. J., Albala, A., Alpert, J., Balasubramani, G. K., Fava, M., et al. (2004). Factors that differentiate early vs. later onset of major depression disorder. *Psychiatry Research, 129*(2), 127–140.

Zitman, F. G., van Dyck, R., Spinhoven, P., & Linssen, A. C. (1992). Hypnosis and autogenic training in the treatment of tension headaches: A two-phase constructive design study with follow-up. *Journal of Psychosomatic Research, 36*(3), 219–228.

Zittermann, A. (2003). Vitamin D in preventive medicine: Are we ignoring the evidence? *British Journal of Nutrition, 89,* 552–572.

Zittoun, J., & Zittoun, R. (1999). Modern clinical testing strategies in cobalamin and folate deficiency. *Seminars in Hematology, 36*(1), 35–46.

Zupancic, M., & Guilleminault, C. (2006). Agomelatine: A preliminary review of a new antidepressant. *CNS Drugs, 20*(12), 981–992.

Index